THE LIVING GOD

BOOKS BY THOMAS C. ODEN

The Living God

SYSTEMATIC THEOLOGY: VOLUME ONE

Thomas C. Oden

HarperSanFrancisco
A Division of HarperCollinsPublishers

FIRST HARPERCOLLINS PAPERBACK EDITION PUBLISHED IN 1992

Library of Congress Cataloging-in-Publication Data

Oden, Thomas C.
  The living god / Thomas C. Oden. — lst HarperCollins papercover ed.
      p. cm.
  Originally published: San Francisco: Harper & Row, © 1987.
(Systematic theology ; v. 1).
  Includes bibliographical references and indexes.
  ISBN 0–06–066363–4 (pbk.: alk. paper)
    1. God. 2. Revelation. I. Title. II. Series: Oden,
Thomas C. Systematic theology ; v. 1.
  [BT102.032 1992]   91–58395
  231—dc20   CIP

92   93   94   95   96   RRD(H)   10   9   8   7   6   5   4   3   2   1

This edition is printed on acid-free paper that meets the American National Standards Institute Z39.48 Standard.

For my sons,
Clark and Edward

Contents

Preface

Purpose

My basic purpose is to set forth an ordered view of the faith of the Christian community upon which there has generally been substantial agreement between the traditions of East and West, including Catholic, Protestant, and Orthodox. My purpose is not to present the views of a particular branch of modern Christian teaching, such as Roman Catholic or Baptist or Episcopal. Rather it is to listen single-mindedly for the voice of that deeper, ecumenical consensus that has been gratefully celebrated as received teaching by believers of vastly different cultural settings—whether African or European, Eastern or Western, sixth or sixteenth century.

This effort is therefore ecumenical in a larger sense than is usually assumed in the modern ecumenical movement. It wishes nothing more than to identify and follow that ancient ecumenical consensus of Christian teaching of God (cf. credal summaries of Irenaeus, c. 190, Tertullian, c. 200, Hippolytus, c. 215, Council of Caesarea, 325, Council of Nicaea, 325, Marcellus, 340, Cyril of Jerusalem, 350, Council of Constantinople, 381, Rufinus, 404, Council of Chalcedon, 451, CC, pp. 20–37, COC, I, pp. 12–65) that still embraces and empowers not only centrist Protestants and traditional Roman Catholics and Orthodox but also great numbers of evangelicals, liberals, and charismatics.

You are invited to the quiet joy of the study of God—God's being, God's power, God's insurmountable goodness, and God's unfailing care of creation. Over centuries this subject has been the source not only of contemplative happiness but also of unparalleled intellectual fascination, spiritual sustenance, and moral guidance. (On joy in the contemplation of divinity, see Cyril of Jerusalem, *Procatechesis*, FC 61, pp. 69–72; Bonaventure, *Breviloquium*, prologue, pp. 6–22; Tho. Aq., *SCG* II.1, 2, pp. 29–32; Baxter, *PW* XVII, pp. 157 ff.)

Nothing can excuse the audacity of this effort except the urgent need for a study with its premise. My intention may be simply put: I hope to set forth what is most commonly stated in the central Christian tradition concerning God. I am seeking to set forth key constructive arguments of two millennia of ecumenical Christian thinking—*that* God is, *who* God is, and what that *means* for us today. I seek an internally consistent statement of classical Christian thinking about God so as to provide a reliable foundation for the practice of sacred ministry and for the living of Christian life.

No attempt has been made to avoid the classical language of the church. I have not substituted "ground of being" for God, or "redemptive possibility" for Jesus Christ, or "the struggle of liberation" for justification by grace through faith. The study of God does better by letting tested Christian language speak for itself in its own directly powerful way to modern minds and hearts wrestling with the limits and failures of modern consciousness. Modernity presents no tougher set of challenges to Christianity than did the fall of Rome, the collapse of the medieval synthesis, the breakup of the unity of Christendom in the sixteenth century, or the Enlightenment. Modern theology must be written amid the breakup of modernity.

The Audience

This book is especially for those who have become wearied with ever-changing modern theologies and who now hunger for a plausible restatement of classical Christian teaching of God. It is also for those who have quietly despaired of Christian claims about God but wish to see a clearer statement setting forth those claims.

I do not assume that the reader already affirms traditional Christian teaching; I wish only to express in straightforward terms what Christian teaching has always understood about its own grounding and empowerment. I have special respect for those who are frankly skeptical about easy claims concerning God's goodness or power, especially those who through personal integrity either dismiss those claims or are willing to hear them stated more convincingly. I am also reaching out to those who intuitively believe in God as known in Israel's history and in Jesus yet want to see that belief more firmly grounded. (For classical models of the study of God that have intentionally stated and reasonably accomplished these aims in their settings, see Theophilus of Antioch, *To Autolycus*, ANF II, pp. 85–121; Augustine, *On Chr. Doctrine*, preface, bk. I, *LLA*, pp. 3–33; John of Damascus, *Writings, The Fount of Knowledge, Philosophical Chapters*, 1, 2, FC 37, pp. 7–11; *OF* I.1–3, pp. 165–70.)

The center of my target audience is the working pastor. I have wondered whether it is possible to write a systematic study of God that pastors will actually find useful, practical for preaching and pastoral care, and not lacking in a comic sense. I have also wondered whether a single statement of Christian teaching could be usefully read and welcomed by both Protestant and Catholic pastors without awkwardness or offense. I have tried to write such a book. My purpose has not been to avoid giving offense but to look constantly for that way of expressing Christian faith that does indeed embrace and unite the marvelous varieties of Christian traditions. Few pastors study systematic theology, but that is less the fault of pastors than of systematic theologians.

For persons preparing for ordination, this study hopes to review key issues concerning the nature, existence, and work of God that would be assumed to be familiar to anyone seeking to undertake Christian ministry (Gregory Nazianzen, *In Defense of His Flight to Pontus*, or. II.15 ff., *NPNF* 2 VII, pp. 208–12; cf. John Chrysostom, *On the Priesthood* II.2–5, *NPNF* 1 IX, pp. 40–42). For persons inquiring into Christian faith or preparing for baptism or confirmation, it intends to be a basic summary of Christian teaching.

The System of References

Embedded in these sentences are numerous references to classical Christian sources. Their purpose is to reveal the constant need for reference by contemporary theology to classical Christian teachers—a major premise of this study. I do not quote these theologians in order to make intellectual heroes of them or to treat them as geniuses or creative innovators. Oddly enough, most of them, insofar as they were orthodox, were self-consciously *unoriginal* in desiring not to add anything to an already sufficient apostolic faith but only to receive and reappropriate that faith creatively in their particular historical setting and language. They were not seeking to invent new ideas but simply and plainly to understand God's goodness and purpose.

There was indeed creative genius at work in the communities of orthodoxy, but the individual teachers who best served those communities did not think of themselves as creative geniuses; they knew that it was the community itself that was brilliant, and made brilliant by the power of the Spirit. The most powerful writers, such as Gregory Nazianzen and Augustine, were those who most ably and simply gave expression to the faith that was already well understood generally by the community.

Among eccentricities I ask the reader to tolerate is my irregular opinion that the most important thing about this book is its embedded annotations. The text is primarily written as an introduction to the annotations. I feel like a clumsy Little League center fielder introducing all my friends to the 1959 Dodgers. If the text in any way moves or invites readers to search out the original sources that called it forth, the book will have struck its mark.

My concern is not primarily with knocking down beliefs but with upbuilding, not with polemics but with peacemaking, not with differences but with consensus, not with development of doctrine but with the unity of the Christian tradition, which has so astutely and imaginatively addressed so many different cultural environments. Hence I have preferred primary biblical and early Christian sources to secondary sources. My criteria for textual citations need to be candidly stated. I have preferred citing

· biblical texts with clear teaching values, rather than those containing ambiguities or requiring clarification of complex historical conditions and assumptions;
· the most widely received classical teachers rather than ancillary or incidental ones;
· earlier classical writers rather than later teachers where possible; and
· those writings that most clearly, meaningfully, and adequately reflect central apostolic teaching rather than those dealing with special viewpoints and controversial themes (models for this method may be seen in Cyril of Jerusalem, *Catech. Lect.*, *NPNF* 2 VII, pp. 1–157; Vincent of Lerins, *Comm.* I–III, *LCC* IX, pp. 36–39; Gregory the Great, *Epis. XXV*, *NPNF* 2 XII, pp. 80–82; *Pastoral Care* I, *ACW* II, pp. 1 ff.; John of Damascus, *OF*, I.1 ff., *FC* 37, pp. 165 ff.).

Hence I am less prone to quote Origen than Augustine, but I quote Origen on points on which he was generally received by the ancient church and do not quote Augustine on those points on which he was not generally received. On those particular points on which otherwise highly respected patristic writers tended to diverge from the more central ancient ecumenical consensus (e.g., Origenist views that the power of God is limited or that stars have souls, or Novatian's view of the exclusion of the lapsed, or Gregory of Nyssa's universalism, or some of Augustine's views of election and reprobation), I will be less prone to quote them, but I will quote freely from their writings that have been widely received.

Employing these criteria, it is evident that only a few of the most important contemporary contributors will be noted, whereas a much broader spectrum of ancient sources will be cited. The weighting of references may be compared to a pyramid with Scripture and early patristic writers at the base and the most recent references at the narrower apex (cf. Vincent of Lerins, *Comm.* XXIX–XXXIII, *LCC* IX, pp. 82–89). Modern systematic theology has been prone to turn that pyramid of texts upside-down, quoting mostly modern sources and few earlier ones.

Quotations from Scripture are from the New English Bible unless otherwise noted. The biblical texts are not viewed uncritically as "proof-texts," but rather as texts upon which classic Christian exegetes have repeatedly commented. Since the history of Christian teaching is considered here largely as a history of exegesis, it is important that the biblical texts upon which commentary proceeded should be made evident throughout. In some cases, my reference will not constitute a support of the point made but will show some variety of opinion (especially where "cf." is noted) on related points.

Some may think it mildly amusing that the only claim I make is that there is nothing whatever original in these pages. I present no revolutionary new ideas, no easy new way to salvation. The road is still narrow (Matt. 7:14). I do not have the gift of softening the sting of the Christian message, of making it seem light or easily borne or quickly assimilated into prevailing modern ideas (cf. Clement of Alex., *Exhort. to the Heathen,* ANF II, pp. 171–206; Hippolytus, *Refutation of All Her.* IV.47–51, ANF V, pp. 42–46; Origen, *Ag. Celsus* VI.16, ANF IV, pp. 580, 581). I do not wish to make a peace of bad conscience with disreputable "achievements of modernity" or pretend to find a comfortable way of making Christianity tractably acceptable to modern assumptions (Clement of Alex., *Strom.* I.11, ANF II, pp. 311, 312; cf. Kierkegaard, *Judge for Yourselves!*). As Paul found that "the Athenians in general and foreigners there had no time for anything but talking or hearing about the latest novelty" (Acts 17:21), so do we find much that passes today for religion (cf. Mother Theodora, aphorism 2, *SDF,* p. 71). My only aim is to present classical Christian teaching of God on its own terms and not in diluted modern terms.

I have not focused upon answering contrary or odd opinions except when that has served to make the central teaching more clear. I have tried to keep out petty local viewpoints in the interest of clarifying only those teachings upon which the central stream of classical Christian theologians has generally agreed as expressing the mind of the believing church (cf. *Seven Ecumenical Councils* II, Nicaea, *NPNF* 2 XIV, pp. 533–42). At points where that agreement is not fully evident, I either leave the subject for further debate or try to state the principal viewpoints remaining in tension. I hope to constrain my own particular idiosyncratic way of looking at things. My mission is to deliver as clearly as I can that core of consensual belief that has been shared for almost two millennia of Christian teaching. Vincent of Lerins described this core as that which has always, everywhere, and by all Christians been believed about God's self-disclosure (Vincent, *Comm.* II, III, *LCC* VII, pp. 37–39).

During twenty-five years of teaching systematic theology, I seldom imagined that I could or should write a systematic theology. It seemed a task for a mature mind. My writing has focused on less auspicious special topics: the relation of theology to the behavioral sciences, the grounding of ethics, the predicament of pastoral care, interpersonal analysis, the reexamination of classical Christian teaching, and pastoral theology. I am indebted to my astute and patient editor at Harper & Row, John Shopp, for encouraging me to think that I could write a systematic theology.

I have been blessed by many superb theological school and graduate school students of theology at Drew University who have challenged me (often successfully) on virtually every issue broached in this book. I have learned much from them, and I am grateful for their critical energy, friendship, and spirited companionship in the study of God. Especially I am grateful for help in preparing and critiquing this manuscript from my able graduate assistants over several years— David Ford, Daniel Davies, Ruth Richardson, and Donald Thorsen; from Catholic and Protestant pastors Michael Merlucci, Steven van Heest, John Nuessle, Jack Wise, Mark Plummer, and William Pfieffer; and from valued colleagues at Drew University John F. Ollom, James M. O'Kane, Russell E. Richey, Janet F. Fishburn, James Pain, Thomas W. Ogletree, and Bard Thompson.

The Issues

The most intriguing questions of the study of God can be stated in plain, uncomplicated words:

Can God be named?
Is God revealed?
Is God uncreated?
Is God free?

    Is God personal?
    Is God compassionate?
    Does God exist?
    Does Jesus reveal God?
    Does God care about our troubles?
    Why are we born? Why do we die?
    How do we draw closer to God?
    How may we participate in God's life?
    Is Scripture the Word of God?
    Does revelation need reason?

These are among the questions that will occupy us in this volume. Chapters 1, 2, and 3 seek to answer honestly what we mean when we say "God," who we address when we speak God's name, and to whom we pray. Chapter 4 asks upon what reasonable grounds we may conclude that God exists in reality and not in our minds only. Chapter 5 asks whether Christianity's most distinctive and fundamental contribution to the idea of God might be the teaching that God is Father, Son, and Spirit. Chapters 6 and 7 discuss the work of God as creator and whether God provides for the created order as sustainer, as enabler of natural causality, and as guide of history. Chapters 8 and 9 conclude with a discussion of appropriate method in the study of God: whether Scripture is authoritative for Christian teaching and whether Christian tradition, experience, and reason are valued sources in the study of God.

Introduction

Because of piety's penchant for taking itself too seriously, theology—more than literary, humanistic, and scientific studies—does well to nurture a modest, unguarded sense of comedy. Some comic sensibility is required to keep in due proportion the pompous pretensions of the study of divinity.

When the chips pile too high, I invite the kind of laughter that wells up not from cynicism about theology but from lightness about it. This comes from glimpsing the incongruity of humans thinking about God. I have often laughed at myself as these sentences went through their tortuous stages of formation; I ask you to look for the comic dimension of divinity that stalks every page.

The most enjoyable of all subjects has to be God, because God is the source of all joy. God has the first and last laugh. The least articulate of all disciplines deserves something in between.

In tasting the nectar of classical Christian teaching we need not spurn the best achievements of modern scientific, political, and ethical insight (cf. Clement of Alex., *Christ the Educator* I.13, FC 23, pp. 89 ff.; Augustine, *On Chr. Doctrine* II.40, *Whatever Has Been Rightly Said by the Heathen We Must Appropriate to Our Uses, LLA*, pp. 75, 76). Faith is not a sacrifice of intellect. We will take this story step-by-step, avoiding technical phrases and striking for the heart of the matter. For models of the theological clarity, precision, and cohesion we do well to emulate, see Gregory Nazianzen's *Theological Orations* (NPNF 2 VII, pp. 284 ff.) or John of Damascus' *Orthodox Faith* (FC 37, pp. 165–405). Watching them play theology is like watching Willie Mays play center field or Duke Ellington play "Sophisticated Lady."

Classic Christian thinking can be grasped by contemporary critical minds—even those who may resist fiercely at first—especially if they can learn to think historically with a community, rather than individualistically. Only when each one hears his or her own individual experience illuminated by the wisdom of the historical Christian community is it then possible to contribute that illumined personal experience back to the community (cf. Cyril of Jerusalem, *Catech. Lect.*, *Procatechesis*, FC 61, pp. 73–82).

The Subject

The subject matter that we cannot finally evade, if we pursue a reflection on faith's understanding, is our incomparable Subject, the Living God, the insurmountably alive reality whom Moses heard, addressing him as "Yahweh." Yahweh is a name—significantly, a personal noun, not an impersonal noun describing an object. Yahweh is an encountering personal Subject who breaks through and circumscribes all our category systems (Gregory Nazianzen, *First Theol. Or.*, *NPNF* 2 VII, pp. 284–88; Calvin, *Inst.* I.13). The Christian community speaks of a conscious, personal reality who meets us in personal terms as companionable divine Subject, as Thou.

If we must use some pronoun to point to this reality, it can only be (*a*) the solemn personal form of the second person singular, *Thou*, or the more problematic (*b*) *him* or (*c*) *her* (the objective case of *he* or *she*). Note carefully the limited choices: *Thou, you, him, her, he, she*— all fundamentally based on three forms: *Thou, him,* and *her*. The neuter, *it* or *It*, cannot adequately convey personhood. We must say either Thou, Him, or Her because we cannot say *It* if the One with whom we finally must deal is indeed incomparably personal, and if that One's Word comes as a personal address (John 4:1–26; 9:1–12; cf. Tho. Aq., *ST* I Q. 13, I, p. 60).

This makes it difficult to use language in an ordinary way about Yahweh. It would be as if one looked at a list of three courses called physics, political science, and George, for how can you study a person, or make a systematic study of a nameable personal being? The names we have for God (*Gott* in Teutonic languages and, before that, *'Adōnai, 'El, Theos, Deus*) all point to a personal reality that cannot finally be reduced to objective, descriptive sentences or abstract ideas, just as George is always something more than our sentences or ideas about George.

This is why Christian teaching about God is a different sort of study than any empirical science that deals with manipulatable objects. Yet theology is not thereby less organized; nor is it lacking in method or wholly without language (Augustine, *On Chr. Doctrine* I, *LLA*, pp. 7 ff.; Calvin, *Inst.* I.6), any more than our interpersonal relations are without language, for this is where we need language most.

God has left a trail of language behind a stormy path of historical activities. That language is primarily the evidence with which theology has to deal—first with Scripture, then with a long history of interpretation of Scripture called church history and tradition, and finally with the special language that emerges out of each one's own personal experience of meeting the living Christ (Augustine, *On Chr. Doctrine*, *NPNF* 1 II, pp. 519 ff.; cf. John of Damascus, *OF* IV.17, *FC* 37, pp. 373–76; Catherine of Siena, *Prayers*, ch. 6, p. 54; Thirty-nine Articles VI, XX, XXI, XXXIV, *CC*, pp. 267 ff.). This freely, personally revealing God is the unavoidable subject matter of Christian teaching. Thus the object investigated is faith's view of God, but to say that alone may be to neglect the more decisive point: the divine Subject who is constantly confronting us in this study is none other than the holy One present in our midst, the living God who calls forth and enables our responses.

What the Study of God Studies

The object of study in theology must be carefully stated. It is *God as known in the faith of a living community*. This study seeks to know an investigatable reality and thus is not merely speculation. For there actually exists in history a community of persons who hold steadfastly to Christian faith in God. Yet since God is not an object, it is inexact to assert that God is directly, flatly, or empirically viewable as an object of theology. God does not, for our convenience, become a direct object of scientific investigation, since God by definition is not finite and thus not subject to the measurements required by empirical sciences (Gregory of Nyssa, *Answer to Eunomius' Second Book*, *NPNF* 2 V, pp. 250 ff.; cf. Augustine, *CG* X.13, *NPNF* 1 II, p. 189; Tho. Aq., *ST* I Q1, I, pp. 14 ff.; Watson, *TI* I, pp. 5 ff.).

Nonetheless, Christian theology has a definite subject matter to which it devotes disciplined and sustained reflective attention: that knowledge of God as understood in the faith of the community that lives out of Christ's resurrection (Cyril of Jerusalem, *Catech. Lect.* IV.1–17, *NPNF* 2 VII, pp. 19–23). The basis for the study of God becomes confused if theology is presented strictly as a privatized, individual credo, or as a limited confessional statement of a particular communion that views itself as the arbiter of Christian truth for all other communions. Theology is not primarily the repeating of confessional assertions but, rather, the investigation and clarification of the internal consistency of those assertions, their reasoning about their ground, and the way they relate to the problems of daily life. Hence Christian theology has a particular area of research: the worshiping community's understanding of God, viewed consensually from its earliest beginnings and sources.

In this sense the study of God attempts to sustain the greatest possible objectivity insofar as it seeks to understand its object (God as known by faith) as accurately as possible without subjective distortions or idiosyncratic projections (Tho. Aq., *ST* I Q1, I, pp. 4 ff.). God, as viewed by Christian teaching and worship, can and has become the central interest and concern of an academic inquiry, where faith inquires into its own practical and historical self-understanding, as attested by texts of Scripture and tradition. The very idea of a university was spawned in the medieval period by the seriousness and extent of this inquiry (Bonaventure, *Breviloquium*; cf. J. H. Newman, *The Idea of a University*; H. Rashdall, *UEMA* I, pp. 38 ff.). Faith's inquiry is not merely into itself but also into its ground and enabler— God, the source, subject, and end of faith's understanding of itself— and into all things as they relate to God (Augustine, *Enchiridion*, *NPNF* 1 III, pp. 237 ff.; Calvin, *Inst.* I.1.1).

K·L·C.   Only God can reveal God (Hilary, *On Trin.* I.18, *NPNF* 2 IX, p. 45), just as a person can only become known when that person decides to reveal his or her inner feelings, spirit, will, or intention to another. For who among us knows the thoughts of another, Paul asked, except as that person chooses to reveal him or herself? "In the same way no one knows the thoughts of God except the Spirit of God. We have not received the spirit of the world but the Spirit who is from God, that we may understand what God has freely given us. This is what we speak, not in words taught us by human wisdom but in words taught by the Spirit" (1 Cor. 2:10–13, NIV). Yet even prior to hearing the gospel of God in Jesus, "what may be known about God" through human reasoning and moral awareness was plain to everyone because "God has made it plain" (Rom. 1:19, NIV).

Paul was convinced that "the wisdom of this age," which "comes to nothing," must be sharply distinguishable from the "message of wisdom among the mature," who know of "God's secret wisdom" (1 Cor. 2:6, 7, NIV), that is, divine revelation in Christ. He implied that a profound inquiry was proceeding among the faithful in Corinth concerning the "deep things of God" (*ta tou theou*, 1 Cor. 2:11; the "thoughts of God," RSV; "what God is," NEB) as understood by faith (1 Cor. 2:9–11; cf. Tertullian, *Ag. Marcion* II.2, *ANF* III, pp. 297–98).

In these passages (1 Cor. 2 and Rom. 1, 2), Paul suggests and anticipates the complex relationship that would later develop between these two tendencies in theology: *revealed* theology, which speaks of God's revelation in history, and *natural* theology, which is given by divine grace as a longing for divinity that develops out of human natural reasoning and moral awareness (Clement of Alex., *Strom.* II.1–4, ANF II, pp. 347–51; Origen, *Ag. Celsus* VI, ANF IV, pp. 573–610; Augustine, CG X.32, NPNF 1 II, pp. 202–4). Following the classical Christian consensus, we will be primarily concerned in this study with revealed theology.

Defining the Study of God

The study of God is an attempt at orderly, consistent, and reasoned discussion of the Source and End of all things (John of Damascus, OF I ff., NPNF 2 IX, pp. 1 ff.). The term *theology* is itself a rudimentary definition, indicating discourse about God.

Theology (from the Latin *theologia*, which comes from two crucial Greek root words: *theos*, God, and *logos*, discourse, language, study), is reasoned discourse about God gained either by rational reflection or by response to God's self-disclosure in history (Conf. of Saxony IX, HPC, p. 12; Hollaz, ETA, pp. 1 ff.; Jackson, *Works* V.9; Watson, TI I, pp. 5 ff.). *Christian theology* is the orderly exposition of Christian teaching. It sets forth that understanding of God that is made known in Jesus Christ (Augustine, *On Faith and the Creed*, NPNF 1 III, pp. 321–33; *Concerning Faith of Things Not Seen* V, NPNF 1 III, pp. 339, 340). It seeks to provide a coherent reflection on the living God as understood in the community whose life is "in Christ."

Theology presupposes the study of Scripture and of the history of the community's reflection upon Scripture. It seeks to provide a fit ordering of scriptural teachings and of central themes of the history of Scriptural interpretation (Jerome, *Ag. Rufinus* XII–XVI, FC 53, pp. 75–80; Calvin, *Inst.* I.13). Systematic theology provides resources for apologetics, Christian ethics, pastoral theology, and the study of comparative religion (Irenaeus, *Ag. Her.* III.24, IV. 20, ANF I, pp. 458, 459, 487–92), but in no case may it be reduced to these disciplines. Subsequently when we use the term *theology* we will refer to Christian theology.

The essential purpose of theology is to study and bring into a fitting, consistent expression the Christian faith. The primary task is neither logical demonstration nor normative proclamation of established truth, nor the refining of rigorous proofs for faith, but rather

clarification of faith's understanding of itself and its ground (cf. Anselm, *Monologium, BW*; Belgic Conf., *COC* III, pp. 383–436). This
clarification asks for fair-minded analysis, critical reasoning, tolerance,
and logical coherence, as well as active listening to Scripture and
tradition (Tho. Aq., *ST* I Q1, I, pp. 48 ff.).

If we begin by assuming the existence of God and the authority of
Scripture, we are open to the charge that we have not credibly established those assumptions. Hence the first chapter will take only those
necessary preliminary steps that are required in order to begin naming God. We will reserve until the last two chapters the task of
working more carefully through specific problems and dilemmas of
the knowledge of God: why Scripture is authoritative; whether tradition is a source of revelation and whether the study of God requires
internalization through personal experience amid a community of faith;
and how faith reasons, having reasons that reason does not know. For
classical treatments that provide models for the sequence of topics that
we will follow, see Cyril of Jerusalem (*Catecheses*, IV.15, V.12, *FC* 61,
pp. 127, 128, 146 f.), John of Damascus (*OF* I.1 ff., *FC* 37, pp. 165 ff.),
Thomas Aquinas (*ST* I Q1, I, pp. 11 ff.), and Calvin (*Inst.* I.1 ff.;
Catechism of the Church of Geneva, SW, pp. 245–66).

Natural and Revealed Theology

Revealed theology focuses on God's search for humanity; natural
theology focuses on the human search for God. Though we will follow
a central ecumenical stream (represented by Irenaeus, Gregory Nazianzen, John Chrysostom, Ambrose, Augustine, John of Damascus,
Melanchthon, Calvin, and Wesley) in not ruling out all possibility of
natural reasoning concerning God, our primary aim is to reason out
of Scripture's revelation.

Classical Christian teachers have repeatedly argued that by grace
God has provided a natural inclination in human consciousness to
seek God (Lactantius, *Div. Inst.* IV.1–4, *ANF* VII, pp. 101–4; John of
Damascus, *OF* II.30, *FC* 37, pp. 264–66). Humanity has a natural
hunger for God and a tendency to religious awareness (Minucius Felix,
Octavius 17–19, *ACW* 39, pp. 76–85; Tertullian, *Apol.* XVII, *ANF* III,
pp. 31, 32; Fulgence, *Letters, To Theodore, FEF* III, p. 886).

A limited reasoning toward and about God (or *logos* about *theos*)
can proceed, without direct reference to Scripture or the history of
revelation, on the basis of natural human intuition, moral insight, and
reasoning, whether it is called natural theology or the philosophy or

psychology of religion. That the term *theology* had been in use prior to its being adopted by Christian teaching is clear from many ancient writings (cf. Aristotle, *Metaphysics* I.3, *BWA*; Josephus, *Ag. Apion*, I.2, EL, p. 169; Cicero, *De Natura Deorum* III.212; cf. Augustine, *City of God* VI.5; Calovius, *Isagoge* I.8; Buddeus, *Inst.* 48 ff.).

Such natural reasoning about God is distinguishable from that knowledge of God that exists as a faithful, trusting, celebrative response to God's own self-disclosure, God's self-manifestation in the history of Israel and Jesus (Irenaeus, *Ag. Her.* I, II, *ANF* I, pp. 315–413; cf. Clementina, *Hom.* XVII.17, *ANF* VIII, p. 323; Calvin, *Inst.* I.14 ff.; Quenstedt, *TDP* I, pp. 253–55; Chemnitz, *LT* I.20–22; Belgic Conf. IX, *HPC*, pp. 33 ff.; Heppe, *RD*, pp. 1–12).

Both Jewish and Christian forms of theology ordinarily proceed as a reflection upon God's own self-disclosure as God becomes known through historical events. Such an inquiry in the Christian tradition has usually been called *revealed theology* (because it has to do with the way God becomes self-revealed), or *symbolic* or confessional theology (because it grounds itself in the symbols and confessional statements of the community of faith), or, in some traditions, *dogmatics* (because it states the *dogmata*, the irreducible tenets of Christian religion; cf. *COC* III, pp. 193 ff.).

The truth, wherever it is to be found, is God's truth (Justin Martyr, *Hortatory Address to the Greeks* VII, IX, *ANF* I, pp. 276, 277; Clement of Alex., *Christ the Educator* X, *FC* 23, p. 83; *Strom.* I.19, *ANF* II, p. 321; Augustine, *On Chr. Doctrine* II.40, *NPNF* 1 II, p. 554). The early Christian teachers argued that God is revealed in history in a way that corresponds to the fundamental hungers of the human soul (Cyril of Jerusalem, *Catechesis* VI.6, *NPNF* 2 VII, p. 34; Gregory Nazianzen, or. XXVIII.17, 31, *NPNF* 2 VII, pp. 294, 300; John Chrysostom, *Letter to Fallen Theodore* I.11, *NPNF* 1 IX, p. 100; Augustine, *CG* XI.29, *NPNF* 1 II, p. 222). Hence, rightly understood, divine grace has already bridged the chasm we perceive between natural and revealed theology.

The Fairness Issue

There is one sensitive issue in current Christian theology that merits special preliminary attention. This concerns the frequent use by traditional Christian teaching of masculine names and pronouns in referring to God. It is my intention in this study to treat that question deliberately at numerous points along the way (especially on the question of naming God, on analogy, on the Holy Spirit, and on human existence). I intend to hold as closely as possible to the classical Christian affirmation that neither of the sexual types, "He" or "She," adequately reflects the fullness of the divine being (cf. Gregory Nazianzen, *First Theol. Or.*, or. XXVII, *NPNF* 2 VII, pp. 284–88; John of Damascus, *OF* I.4–8, *FC* 37, pp. 170–85).

Yet it is not possible to speak in a wholly sexless way of God, giving up all personal pronouns. There are times when the tradition has thought it more fitting to transcend personalization with terms like *the Holy One of Israel* or *the Eternal*. I am grateful that this pattern is available, but it must not be followed at the price of forgoing all personal pronouns, since God is frequently viewed through personal metaphors in Scripture (Cyril of Jerusalem, *Catech. Lect.* VI.8, IX.1, *NPNF* 2 VII, pp. 35, 51). Since naming conveys power, the naming of God normatively or exclusively as "he" tends to limit the idea of God by human sexual categories. Even when its intent may have been universalist or generic, the tradition's language has sounded exclusionary to many, who regrettably may then too readily dismiss the tradition on the grounds of language alone before allowing it a reasonable hearing. I can only ask that the reader not prejudge the fairness of classical Christian language without seeking to understand it. These are not problems that can or should be addressed in detail in an introduction, but I appeal to the reader to withhold predisposing judgment, letting each of the language issues develop organically. Meanwhile I remain indebted to colleagues who have carefully combed this text both for imbalanced language and fidelity to ancient ecumenical Christian teaching.

One way I have sought to redress the balance practically is by not neglecting to quote, where pertinent, those important women contributors to the classic Christian theological tradition. There are many: Melania the Elder and Melania the Younger (in Palladius, *Lausic History, ACW*), Amma Theodora, Amma Sarah (among the Desert Ascetics, *SDF*), Macrina (sister of Basil, whom Gregory of Nyssa called "the Teacher," *NPNF* 2 V, pp. 430–68), Paula (in Jerome, *MPL*, sec. 320), Clare of Assisi, Hildegard of Bingen, and especially Catherine of Genoa, Julian of Norwich, Catherine of Siena, and Teresa of Avila. By this means I hope to some degree to show that the voices and writings of astute, learned, and faithful women have been important in the life and witness of classic Christianity. They will speak as theologians in their own right, as the way was led by Amma Sarah, who pointedly said to detractors who criticized her teaching: "According to nature I am a woman, but not according to my thoughts" (Sarah 4, *SCD*, p. 193).

The crux of the language fairness issue hinges on whether Father-Son language, with the reference to God as "he," is primarily the result of male-dominated social structures, and is therefore degrading to the dignity of women and men, or whether such language is a part of the scandal of particularity that accompanies all claims of historical revelation—that is, that God is made known through a particular history, and that the Word of God is spoken through the life of a man born of woman, which remains an intrinsic part of God's historical self-disclosure, hence actually seeks to promote the dignity and healthy self-identity of women and men when rightly understood. In view of our central purpose and method (allowing the classical Christian tradition to speak for itself), we will maintain faithfulness to the historic language of the church but, in doing so, seek fairness and balance in our contemporary use of language.

The same point applies to the inestimable African tradition of Christian theology. Anyone who reads these pages will quickly see how deeply indebted I am to the early tradition of African Christianity—few authors will be referred to more often than Athanasius, Augustine, Origen, Clement of Alexandria, Tertullian, and Cyprian. I am especially troubled when Christianity is portrayed as an essentially European religion, since it has its roots in cultures that are far distant from Europe and preceded the development of modern European identity, and some of its greatest minds have been African.

Knowing from the Heart

The study of God and delight in knowing God requires a mode of understanding that transcends simply empirical data gathering, logical deduction, or the dutiful organization of scriptural or traditional texts into a coherent sequence. The Christian study of God intrinsically involves a mode of knowing from the heart that hopes to make the knower "wise unto salvation" (2 Tim. 3:15, KJV, i.e., a knowing grounded in the "sacred writings which have power to make you wise and lead you to salvation," NEB), to save the soul, to teach the sinner all that is needed to attain saving knowledge of God (Clement of Alex., *Who Is the Rich Man That Shall Be Saved?* pp. 591–604; Catherine of Siena, *Prayers* 7, pp. 58–61; Baxter, *PW* II, pp. 23–25; Wesley, *WJW* VIII, pp. 20 ff., 290 ff.).

Faith's knowing is distinguishable from objective, testable, scientific knowledge, although not necessarily inimical to it. It is a form of knowing that embraces the practical question of how we choose to live in the presence of this Source and End of all (Clement of Alex., *Exhort.*

to the Heathen IX, *ANF* II, pp. 195–97; Teresa of Avila, *CWST*, III, pp. 219–22; Calvin, *Inst.* I.11–13).

It need not embarrass theology that it is a *logos*, a way of speaking and reasoning through words—"just talk," in a sense, about God. These are our human words—limited, fragile, inadequate—pointing beyond themselves to nothing less than *Theos*, the Source and End of all things. Christian teaching lives out of a conversation that is found in a living Christian community about this One. It is our reasoning about the mystery Whence we come and to Whom we return (Augustine, *On the Profit of Believing, NPNF* 1 III, p. 363; cf. H. R. Niebuhr, *RMWC*, pp. 122 ff.).

Credo: A Prologue to the Series *Systematic Theology*

The Living God is the first volume of *Systematic Theology*. Succeeding portions will deal with *The Word of Life* and *Life in the Spirit*.

Christians who first said *credo* did not do so lightly, but at the risk of their lives under severe persecution. We listen carefully to those who are prepared to sacrifice their lives for their belief. To say *credo* (I believe) genuinely is to speak of oneself from the heart, to reveal who one is by confessing one's essential belief, the faith that makes life worth living. One who says *credo* without willingness to suffer, and if necessary die, for the faith has not genuinely said *credo*.

Christians have a right and a responsibility to know the meaning of their baptism. This is the purpose of Christian theology and of this study: to clarify the ancient ecumenical faith into which Christians of all times and places are baptized. It is expected of all who are baptized that they will understand what it means to believe in God the Father Almighty, in God the Son, and in God the Spirit (Gregory of Nyssa, *The Great Catech.*, prologue, *NPNF* 2 VII, p. 474; Luther, *Sermons on the Catech.*, *ML*, p. 208).

The Apostles' Creed is the most common confession of Christians. This ancient confession will serve as a framework for this series of volumes. Like other ancient baptismal confessions, it is divided into three parts, corresponding with the three Persons of the one God (Luther, *Small Catech.* II.44, p. 42; cf. *Brief Expl.*, *WML* II, p. 368). The first part confesses trust in God the Father Almighty, maker of heaven and earth. This is the subject of this first volume of the series *Systematic Theology*.

Other early ecumenical confessions, such as the Nicene Creed (325), the Constantinopolitan Creed (351), and the Athanasian Creed (c. 500) were organized in the same three-part way, to teach inquirers and the faithful the significance of baptism in the name of the Father,

Son, and Spirit. Earlier creedal prototypes, such as the Letter of the Apostles (c. 150; CC, p. 17), the confession reported by Justin Martyr (c. 165; CC, p. 18), the Balyzeh Papyrus (c. 200 or later; CC, p. 19), the Interrogatory Creed of Hippolytus (c. 214; CC, p. 23), the Oriental Creed (CC, p. 27), and the Creed of Caesarea (Eusebius 325; CC, pp. 27, 28) all follow this threefold pattern. As early as about 190, Irenaeus of Lyons (fl. c. 175–c. 195) summarized the faith of Christians in this concise way, which plots the trajectory of this series:

The Church, though dispersed throughout the whole world, even to the ends of the earth, has received from the apostles, and their disciples, this faith:
• [She believes] in one God, the Father Almighty, Maker of heaven, and earth, and the sea, and all things that are in them;
• and in one Christ Jesus, the Son of God, who became incarnate for our salvation;
• and in the Holy Spirit, who proclaimed through the prophets the dispensations of God. (*Ag. Her.* I.10.1, *ANF* I, p. 330)

Scripture itself provides the structural basis for the organization of the baptismal teaching, and of this study. The same sequence for summarizing Christian teaching appeared in Matthew 28:19, the climactic point of Matthew's Gospel, in the formula for baptism. There the resurrected Lord concluded His earthly teaching with this summary charge: "Therefore go and make disciples of all nations, baptizing them in the name of the Father and of the Son and of the Holy Spirit, and teaching them to obey everything I have commanded you. And surely I will be with you always, to the very end of the age" (Matt. 29:19, 20, NIV).

In this way, Jesus forever linked two crucial actions: baptizing and teaching. In subsequent periods of Christian history they have remained intimately interwoven. Implicitly included in the instructions for baptism is the charge to teach its significance. This is why the Christian study of God has been so often organized into these three divisions. For Christian teaching is baptismal teaching, and Christian baptism has required some clarification of itself as faith in God the Father, Son, and Spirit. Christian theology came into being to explain Christian baptism (Cyril of Jerusalem, *Catech. Lect.* XX.4, *NPNF* 2 VII, pp. 146, 147).

Topics of Christian teaching are not taken up in a miscellaneous, nonsequential way: "The teaching of all doctrine has a certain order, and there are some things which must be delivered first, others in the second place, and others in the third, and so all in their order; and if these things be delivered in their order, they become plain," so that "he who enters rightly upon the road, will observe the second place in due order, and from the second will more easily find the third" (Clementina, *Recognitions* III.34, *ANF* VIII, p. 123). The best way to "enter the road" is by dealing first with "God Almighty, Maker of heaven and earth," the first volume of this series.

The earliest summaries of Christian teaching were lectures to prepare people for baptism. Our organization of key themes of Christian teaching will depend heavily upon the thought-sequence of those most influential early summaries by Cyril of Jerusalem (*Catechetical Lectures*), Gregory of Nyssa (*The Great Catechism*), John Chrysostom (*Baptismal Instructions*), and Augustine (*Catechising of the Uninstructed* and *On Faith and the Creed*).

Teachers as varied as Augustine, Thomas Aquinas, and Luther have held that the Apostles' Creed remains the best condensed statement of Christian faith and the most reliable way to learn the heart of faith. In professing the Creed, Cyril explained, the believer is helped to keep closely to the center of faith as delivered by the apostles, "which has been built up strongly out of all the Scriptures":

For since all cannot read the Scriptures, some being hindered from the knowledge of them by lack of learning, and others because they lack leisure to study, in order that the soul should not be starved in ignorance, the church has condensed the whole teaching of the Faith in a few lines. This summary I wish you both to commit to memory when I recite it, and to rehearse it with all diligence among yourselves, not writing it out on paper, but engraving it by the memory upon your heart, taking care while you rehearse it that no catechumen may happen to overhear the things which have been delivered to you. I wish you also to keep this as a provision through the whole course of your life, and beside this to receive no alternative teaching, even if we ourselves should change and contradict our present teaching. (*Catech. Lect.* V.12, *NPNF* 2 VII, p. 32, is here slightly amended)

Key scriptural teachings are grouped by classical Christian exegetes under these three headings: The first article teaches of God, creation, and providence. The second deals with Christ and redemption. The third teaches of the Spirit that enlivens the church (Cyril of Jerusalem, *Catech. Lect.* VI–IX, X–XV, XVI–XVIII, *NPNF* 2 VII, pp. 33 ff.; cf. Hilary, *On Trin.*, *NPNF* 2 IX, pp. 40 ff.; Luther, *Sermons on the Catech.*, *ML*, p. 208; Anglican Thirty-nine Articles of Religion; Council of Trent; Helvetic Conf. I and II, Conf. of Wirttemburg, Conf. of Scotland, in *CC*, *COC*, and *HPM*).

The Creed is a "short word" summarizing biblical faith, approved by the apostles as "standard teaching to converts," "a badge for distinguishing" those who preach Christ according to apostolic rule (Rufinus, *Comm. on Apostles' Creed*, intro., *ACW* 20, p. 29), constructed "out of living stones and pearls supplied by the Lord" (p. 31). Rufinus (345–410), who was among the earliest of many commentators on the Creed, thought that the Holy Spirit has superintended its transmission in order that it "contain nothing ambiguous, obscure, or inconsistent" (p. 29). Poignantly, he explained: "The reason why the creed is not written down on paper or parchment, but is retained in the believers' hearts, is to ensure that it has been learned from the tradition handed down from the Apostles, and not from written texts, which occasionally fall into the hands of unbelievers" (p. 30). Rufinus based his commentary on the personally remembered "text to which I pledged myself when I was baptized in the church of Aquileia" (p. 32).

The ancient creeds all begin with "I believe" (*credo*). What does it mean to believe? "And what is faith?" the Letter to Hebrews asked. "Faith gives substance to our hopes, and makes us certain of realities we do not see" (Heb. 11:1). "Without faith it is impossible to please God, because anyone who comes to him must believe that he exists and that he rewards those who earnestly seek him" (Heb. 11:6, NIV). Just as no farmer sweats to plant a field without some faith that the seeds will grow, and no one sets out to sea without some confidence of being able to survive, so: "In fact, there is nothing in life that can be transacted without a preliminary readiness to believe" (Rufinus, *Comm.*, *ACW* 20, p. 32). In entering the doorway of religious belief, the inquirer must first listen empathetically to what the worshiping community says about the ground of its faith.

Part I

THE LIVING GOD

CHAPTER 1

The Naming of God

Every inquiry has its postulates. No scientific inquiry proceeds altogether without assumptions. Nothing can be studied scientifically, for example, without postulating the intelligibility of the universe, something that itself is, strictly speaking, not subject to empirical verification.

Like every other inquiry, theology proceeds with postulates, out of which its data gathering and induction of facts proceeds (Origen, *De Princip.* I, *ANF* IV, pp. 239–69). Chief among the postulates of Christian teaching is the assumption that God has taken initiative to make God's purpose known, to become self-disclosed, to address humanity through human history (Origen, *Ag. Celsus* I.11, *ANF* IV, p. 401).

The shorthand term for this primary postulate is *revelation*. Revelation may be viewed in a general or a specific sense.

Whether God Is Revealed

What Is Meant by Revelation in the General Sense?

The word *revelation* unites the two biblical ideas of an unveiling (*apokalypsis*, disclosure, appearing, coming) of God and a making known (*phanerōsis*, exhibition, manifestation, expression) of divine mysteries previously concealed (Eph. 3:3; cf. Job 12:22; Dan. 2:22–29). Revelation is the unveiling and making known of God's redemptive purpose toward humanity (Augustine, *CG* XI.2, *NPNF* 1 II, p. 206). The revelation of God has its central locus in a single personal history, of Jesus the Christ. Yet the shock waves from that center resound in the farthest reaches of the cosmos (Rom. 8:18–30; 11:15; Calvin, *Inst.* 1.1–6; Quenstedt, *TDP*, I, p. 32).

Revelation may occur in fragmented ways in dreams, in visions, in theophanies, and in the divine illumination of the intellect (Tho. Aq., *ST* I Q57, I, pp. 283 ff.). Revelation includes every manifestation of God to human consciousness, reason, conscience, and historical awareness. The term *general revelation* (sometimes called common revelation) encompasses all forms of divine disclosure (Origen, *De Princip.* I.1–9, *ANF* IV, pp. 242–45; Augustine, *Conf.* VII.10, *LCC* VII; *CG* V.11, *NPNF* 1 II, p. 93).

In the maturing religion of the Hebrew covenant, revelation gradually focused more upon the divine requirement, human destiny, and the divine-human covenant. The law set forth the divine command; the prophets interpreted the meaning of history; and the priestly tradition provided a ritual order of atoning for sin. In the consummation of revelation, God the Revealer appeared in person—the central datum of Christian experience to which the apostolic witness bears testimony (Tho. Aq., *ST* I Q57, I, pp. 287 ff.; Kierkegaard, *Training in Christianity*, pp. 40–78).

By revelation is meant not primarily the imparting of information but rather the disclosure, appearance, self-giving, self-evidencing of God. It is God who allows God to become recognized. Rightly known, God illumines all reality, all human experience, all revelation, and all religion (Julian of Norwich, *Showings*, pp. 229, 230, 312 ff.).

In its broadest sense, revelation consists of those events through which humanity becomes aware of God. In this general sense, revelation is present in the history of all religions and, indeed, is a familiar theme in the study of religions. Judaism and Christianity participate in that history of religions, yet in a special way in that they have understood themselves to be fulfilling the quest and promise of that history (Justin Martyr, *Dialogue with Trypho*, *ANF* I, pp. 194–270; see chap. 9).

General revelation should be carefully distinguished from the slow, laborious process of scientific inquiry. In science secrets are gradually unveiled about physics, space, time, atomic structures, DNA, biological processes, and so on. But we do not call these divine revelation or the disclosure of the mysteries of God. This is because we ourselves find them out by looking ever more intently. The very character of revelation, on the other hand, implies the self-offering of God on God's own initiative to allow the divine One to become known (Gal. 1:12; 2:2).

At one level, the reception of revelation is a highly inward matter of intuitively confirming that God has spoken or has become self-revealed in a way that makes its own sense and that corresponds with one's own experience (1 Cor. 14). In such a crucial arena, no one person can answer for another. One must finally decide for oneself whether revelation has occurred, although one cannot imagine such a decision apart from a community of faith (Eph. 3:3; cf. Lev. 4:13–27; Num. 16).

At another level, the reception of revelation is a highly social process that occurs through communities of prayer and teaching; the memory of God's way of becoming known is transgenerationally stored and presented and represented through families, tribes, archetypal memories, and vast modes of institutional influence (Exod. 16; Basil, *On the Spirit* XXVII.65–68, *NPNF* 2 VIII, pp. 40–43; Anglican Thirty-nine Articles XX, *CC*, p. 273).

General Revelation in Scripture

Scripture teaches of a general revelation of God to all humanity. The covenant with Noah signals the intention of God to care for all humanity (Gen. 9:8–11), for the covenant was with all the descendants of Noah, that is, all humanity (2 Pet. 2:5 viewed Noah as a "herald of righteousness" prior to Abraham, and inclusive of all humanity). God has not left himself without witness in any corner of human affairs (1 Kings 19:18; Acts 14:17; *Apost. Const.* VIII.1, p. 480).

The Lord is a "revealer of mysteries" (Dan. 2:47; 2:22, NIV), who "reveals the deep things of darkness, and brings deep shadows into the light" (Job 12:22). God "reveals his thoughts" to humanity (Amos 4:13, NIV). "Surely the Sovereign Lord does nothing without revealing his plan" (Amos 3:7, NIV). Revelation may be known by some, yet be awaiting the appointed time to be revealed to others (Hab. 2:2).

The New Testament witnesses to a general revelation of God in creation and providence, discernible through conscience, prior to the coming of Jesus and outside the covenant with Israel (Rom. 1:13–2:16; 1 Cor. 10:18–11:1; John 1:9; 2 Tim. 1:3). God can make himself known in creation at any time, anywhere, at any point in history. The revelation in Christ does not hamper or limit these broader disclosures, but completes and culminates them and makes them more understandable. God has spoken "at sundry times and in divers manners" (not merely in one time in one manner) in a way that prepares humanity for the coming of the Son, the Revealer, God himself (Heb. 1:1, KJV).

At the least, this general revelation performs the negative function of leaving humanity without excuse if they should ever claim that they never knew God existed. "When Gentiles who do not possess the law carry out its precepts by the light of nature, then, although they have no law, they are their own law, for they display the effect of the law inscribed on their hearts. Their conscience is called as a witness, and their own thoughts argue the case on either side, against them or even for them, on the day when God judges the secrets of human hearts through Christ Jesus" (Rom. 2:14–16).

The light that in due time appeared in Jesus was a light "which enlightens every man" that "was even then coming into the world" prior to the coming of Jesus (John 1:9). So impressed was Justin Martyr with the general revelation of God that he argued that "those who live according to reason are Christians, even though they are accounted atheists. Such were Socrates and Heraclitus among the Greeks, and those like them" (First Apol. XLVI.4, DCC, p. 6; cf. ANF I, p. 178). "Whatever has been uttered aright by any men in any place belongs to Christians" (Justin, Second Apol. II.13, DCC, p. 7; cf. Second Apol. X, ANF I, p. 191). Even Tertullian could praise the "noble testimony of the soul by nature Christian" (Apol. XVII, ANF II, p. 32). Even though at times exaggerated, these statements show how far some early Christian writers were willing to affirm the general revelation of God accessible to good conscience and reason.

Special Revelation in the History of Israel

Although God is generally knowable throughout all nature and history, God has become specially known through a particular history, the history of a people set aside, a holy place, and a salvation history (Esther 3:8; Ps. 122; Matt. 20:17; Augustine, First Catech. Instr. VI, ACW, p. 26; Calovius, SLT I, pp. 268 f.). The Bible tells of a holy land, a special place in which God has disclosed himself gradually through the developing history of a special people, Israel. It was Yahweh who chose a special city, Jerusalem, in which the worship of this people would be centered (Deut. 12). Even after the predicted destruction of the holy city, the New Testament looked toward the restoration of a new Jerusalem as the city of God (Rev. 3:12; Justin Martyr, Dialogue with Trypho LIII, ANF I, pp. 221 f.). Jerusalem was the city in which the final events of the life of the Revealer occurred as promised, and to which his return was promised (Rev. 21:10; Divine Liturgy of James, ANF VII, pp. 537 ff.).

There remains a "scandal of particularity" in all historical revelation. If God is to become known in history, then that must occur at some time and some place. It cannot occur at every time and in every place. The history of salvation is about those particular times and places and events (Deut. 6:20–25; First Helvetic Conf. V, HPC, p. 5; New Hampshire Conf. VI, CC, p. 336). The Scripture tells the story of this people of Israel, a set-apart kingdom of priests, a holy nation (Exod. 19:6). It is Holy Writ because it records the story of these times and places (Ps. 145:1–12; Edwardian Hom., *CC*, pp. 239 ff.; Wesley, *Scripture Way of Salvation, CC*, pp. 360 ff.).

Although God is revealed to both women and men alike, God became fully self-revealed in the life of a particular man born of a particular woman (Matt. 1:16; Luke 1:5–2:40). This particularity is a scandal or offense in the sense that God condescends to become human not generally in all but particularly in one (Athanasius, *Four Discourses Ag. Arians* III.27, 28, *NPNF* 2 IV, pp. 413–22; Kierkegaard, *Training in Christianity*, pp. 86 ff.). That the Messiah is born male, according to Jewish expectation, is a less crucial point than that the Messiah was *born* at all, and was born as a single *individual* (hence not male *and* female), and was born as a *Jew* (among whom the Expected One was a male heir of the Davidic line; Matt. 1:1–20; Luke 2:4; Rom. 1:3; Rev. 22:16; Augustine, *CG* XVII.8 ff., *NPNF* 1 II, pp. 348 ff.).

If one takes it as a premise that God makes himself known in history, consequences abound everywhere for the study of God. For then the primary witnesses to those events in which God becomes known must be thereafter accorded primary importance in assessing the events of revelation (Acts 10:42; 26:16; Lactantius, *Div. Inst.* III.27, *ANF* VII, pp. 96 ff.; Calvin, *Inst.* 1.6; 1.16). In revelation God does not merely speak to himself but to human beings—particular human beings, persons with names like Abraham, Isaac, Miriam, Amos, Naomi, Jeremiah, Paul, John, and Mary. In prayer humans speak and God listens; in revelation God speaks to human hearers, thus allowing a dialogue between humanity and God (Augustine, *Sermons, NPNF* 1 VI, p. 482; Catherine of Siena, *Prayers*, pp. 158 ff.).

The Revealer

Christian revelation refers to the disclosure of God in the person and work of Christ. Christ himself is God's own revelation, God's Word. Through Christ all the other moments of divine disclosure become more understandable. All of God's other manifestations, past and future, become better received, remembered, and clarified. In the light of Christ, all previous revelation through the history of Israel and the nations becomes increasingly meaningful. Christ is the One whom the angels have longed to see, "the desire of all nations," the goal toward which all the history of revelation prior to Christ had been tending (Hag. 2:7; John 1; Eph. 1). In Christ the eternal purpose of God, the mystery hidden for ages, the one secret of God, is revealed

(1 Cor. 2:7; 4:1; Eph. 3:1–5). Christ is a single truth, plural in meaning. Christ is the sum and hidden interior meaning of all other genuine revelations of God (John Chrysostom, *Hom*. 82, *NPNF* 1 X, p. 495).

In Christ all who behold attentively are able to "grasp God's secret. That secret is Christ himself; in him lie hidden all God's treasures of wisdom and knowledge" (Col. 2:2, 3). "Great beyond all question is the mystery of our religion: 'He who was manifested in the body, vindicated in the spirit, seen by angels; who was proclaimed among the nations, believed in throughout the world, glorified in high heaven' " (1 Tim. 3:16). Even as Christ became for Christians the inner meaning of the Old Testament history, so does the Old Testament history bestow otherwise hidden meaning upon Christ. Jesus did not come to destroy, but to fulfill, the law (Matt. 5:7). "Our knowledge and our prophecy alike are partial, and the partial vanishes when wholeness comes" (1 Cor. 13:9).

There is in the Christian revelation both an embrace of universal history and attention to a particular history. The Word spoken in Jesus is relevant for all humanity (Rom. 5; Col. 1). The particular history remembers gratefully that this Word was spoken in a particular time and place and through a particular person who taught, did good, died and was raised (Matt. 1:18; Luke 1:1–4; Luther, *Brief Expl.*, *WML* II, pp. 370 ff.). The New Testament does not assert the universal against the particular or the particular against the universal. Christianity refuses to acknowledge any other Source and End than the One who makes himself known in Jesus (Basil, *Letters* CCXXXIII, *NPNF* 2 VIII, p. 273; Gregory of Nyssa, *Ag. Eunomius* II, *NPNF* 2 V, pp. 101 ff.). Yet those who believe in Jesus cannot set boundaries upon the Spirit of God who came through him.

Human beings do not set the conditions for what God can do or how God can become self-revealed. But Christian faith has gained confidence that God will not reveal himself in a way contrary to the way he has revealed himself in Jesus Christ (Calvin, *Inst*. 2.10; 3.1; Watson, *TI* I, pp. 62 ff.). Christianity does not limit revelation to Christ, but through Christ sees God's revelation as occurring elsewhere and finally, echoing everywhere.

The clearer God is seen in Christ, the clearer God is seen everywhere. This does not result in a syncretism that then quickly forgets that God was made known in Christ and looks for God independently elsewhere (Basil, *Letters* CCXXXIV, *NPNF* 2 VIII, p. 274). For the general revelation of God everywhere is now all the more knowable through the Revealer. The revelation given in Christ is not therefore best understood as complementary to other revelations so that by a process of synthesis and syncretism all these revelations could be brought together in a completed way. Rather, Christ is precisely the unparalleled and unrepeatable Revealer through whom other revelations are best to be understood (Justin, *Hortatory Address*, ANF I, pp. 273–89; cf. Calvin, *Inst.* 1.14–17; 3.20 ff.).

Christianity stands in a unique relation to the Hebrew Bible and Judaism, however. Judaism is not viewed by Christianity as one among other religions that emerge out of human striving for God. Rather, the God and Father of Jesus Christ is made known in the history of Israel. The Holy Writ of Israel is also the church's Holy Writ. The salvation history of the people of Israel is also salvation history for Christians. The two covenants need each other; one to promise, the other to fulfill (Acts 7:17; cf. Luke 4:21; Matt. 26:54–56; John 19:24–37; cf. Clementina, *Hom.* XVIII.17–20, ANF III, p. 329, Will Herberg, FEH).

The Recipient of Revelation

Even though God is the center of interest in faith's understanding of itself, humanity is deeply implicated in the subject matter of theology. Since God cares for humanity, the study of God studies God's care for humanity (Lactantius, *On the Workmanship of God*, ANF VII, pp. 281–300).

Rightly used, the word *theology* therefore embraces all that pertains to the study of humanity, insofar as understanding of humanity is pertinent to understanding why and how God cares for it (Gregory of Nyssa, *On the Making of Man* V, NPNF 2 V, p. 391). There is nothing in humanity or the cosmic setting of human history that is not related to God. Theology therefore seeks an integral understanding and comprehensive picture of the human situation before God (Augustine, *CG* V.11, NPNF 1 II, p. 93). This is why historically the university sprang directly and organically out of the study of God (H. Rashdall, *UEMA*, I, pp. 40 ff.).

Humanity is God's constant concern throughout the biblical witness. The Christian study of God cannot neglect God's own prevailing interest, the redemption of humanity. No Christian theology can speak only of God and never of human beings; there is no part of Christian teaching that does not touch upon their salvation. In the Genesis narrative, the creation of human beings is the decisive act of divine creation, in which they are provided with a capacity for communion with God exceeding that of all other earthly creatures. Christ the Redeemer is completely human while not ceasing to be truly God. The Holy Spirit speaks to human hearts. From beginning to end, the biblical story is the story of the creation of humanity, the fall of humanity, and the redemption of humanity. Revelation is *for* human salvation, the mending of human brokenness (Athanasius, *On the Incarnation of the Word* III–XIX, *NPNF* 2 IV, pp. 37–46; Gregory of Nyssa, *On the Making of Man*, *NPNF* 2 VII, pp. 387–427).

If God becomes self-revealed to human beings, that implies that they have some grace-bestowed capacity to receive revelation. Why would God bother to speak to one who could not hear? Humanity is—more than trees or animals—uniquely the *recipient* of revelation. Human reasoning is created by God with a capacity for reaching toward God by thinking, choosing, and speaking. Human freedom is created by God with a capacity for responsiveness to God. Human personality is created with the restless yearning for communion with the unseen but present personal God (Augustine, *Conf.* I.1, *LCC* VII, p. 7). Human *eros* is created with some capacity, however distorted, to love God and to love creatures through God. If any creature exists that is relatively more than others prepared for the divine self-disclosure, it surely must be the human creature (Lactantius, *Div. Inst.* II.9, *ANF* VII, pp. 52–56). God comes as incomparably personal Visitor, as Father, Son, and Spirit, into interpersonal meeting with men and women.

Faith's Reasoning from Revelation

Faith is that response to God's revelation which beholds and trusts that God speaks truly through the written Word. In faith revelation becomes a matter of inner certitude and assurance. That same faith also presents evidences to reason, both one's own reasoning and the shared reasoning of a community, so that faith may have a chance to become consensually received and its joy known corporately and socially (Heb. 11:1; Clement of Alex., *Strom.* II, *ANF* II, pp. 347–80).

Revelation bears testimony to God's action, and faith receives and believes and thereby transforms the knowing process. Faith then shapes reasoning (Origen, *Ag. Celsus* I.9, *ANF* IV, p. 400). "By faith we perceive that the universe was fashioned by the word of God, so that the visible came forth from the invisible" (Heb. 11:3). Reason judges according to what it can see and know by sense experience. Faith nurtures reason's seeing (Clementina, *Recognitions* II.69, *ANF* VIII, p. 116).

Faith is to the invisible world what the senses are to the visible (Wesley, *WJW* VII, pp. 334 ff.). We may indeed refuse these testimonies: "A man who is unspiritual refuses what belongs to the Spirit of God; it is folly to him; he cannot grasp it, because it needs to be judged in the light of the Spirit" (1 Cor. 2:14). The Spirit is at work in the believing process, convincing, testing, probing, and helping people to understand revelation (Rom. 8:14–39; Luther, *Magnificat*, WML III, p. 127).

Faith Seeking Intelligibility

Christian theology seeks to understand in a reflective and orderly way what God has revealed (Cyril of Jerusalem, *Catech. Lect.* V, *NPNF* 2 VII, pp. 29–32). It is not merely reading the Bible as such, although it presupposes having read the Bible. It seeks to put the many sentences, episodes, and maxims of the Bible into a whole, orderly, consistent statement about the overarching meaning of the message revealed in Holy Writ (Cyril of Jerusalem, *Catech. Lect.* IV.33–36, *NPNF* 2 VII, pp. 26–28). There is no Christian theology without the Bible, yet there is no Bible without an inspirited community to write, remember and translate it, to guard it and pass it on, to study it, live by it, and invite others to live by it. The Bible provides means by which the Christian message can be received into the minds and hearts of each new generation (Augustine, *CG*, FC 8, pp. 222 ff.). It is from the Bible that Christianity learns how God is revealed.

The Christian study of God is a faith seeking understanding (*fides quaerens intellectum*; cf. Anselm, *Proslog.* I, *BW*, pp. 1 ff.), a branch of learning in which the faith of the Christian community is seeking intelligibility. Faith trusts that God's self-disclosure in history as attested by Scripture is true, reliable, and worthy of experiential trust. Faith reasons as far as it may in seeking to understand the mysteries of God revealed in history and in Christ (Eph. 1:9). Although these mysteries are greater than human intellect, if reason illumined by faith studies the history of God's self-disclosures in a thoroughgoing and receptive way, it may grow toward understanding, for understanding is susceptible to growth (Augustine, *Answer to Skeptics*, FC 1, pp. 134 ff.).

It is this sort of emergent, maturing understanding that the study of God seeks to attain and articulate. It is a knowledge that is not to be equated with faith, but that emerges out of faith. It is not a form of knowing that is simply infused or given directly to the recipient by God, but acquired only with human effort enabled by grace. It is a knowledge that differs from philosophical inquiry about God because it exists as a response to revelation (Hab. 2:2, 3). Its reasoning is not self-sufficient, but lives out of its being enlightened by faith (Augustine, *Enchiridion* XXX, XXXI, *NPNF* 1 III, pp. 247, 248; Calvin, *Inst.* 3.2; 4.8).

Method of Inquiring into Revelation

The *method* of studying revelation (to be more fully explored in Part IV) may be summarized: *Christian teaching has its external source in God's self-disclosure, whose record is Scripture as preserved, studied, and remembered by the living tradition, and its internal source in faith personally experienced and reasonably ordered.*

Modern theology has often required that a discussion of method precede any discussion of the Christian proclamation or of theological content. In early Christian theology the attention to method did not develop until long after the major lines of theological content were well formed. Hence Augustine's *theory* of hermeneutics depended upon Irenaeus' *practice* of that hermeneutic long before. Even the most embryonic, fragmentary accounts of theological method (by writers such as Origen, Clement of Alexandria, and Tertullian) followed by several generations the primary task of proclamation, baptism, and early Christian catechetics (as seen in Clement of Rome, Ignatius, Polycarp, Athenagoras, and the Didache). We will maintain this classic sequence, discussing first faith's substantive reasoning about revelation of the living God and asking later how such a One can rightly be studied.

Accordingly, we will reserve until the end of this book a deliberate reflection upon whether the study of God can be viewed as an academic discipline and, if so, how it proceeds; how the study of God grounds itself in Scripture, tradition, experience, and reasoning; how and why Scripture is the fundamental norm and source of Christian teaching; how the experience of other Christians and our own experience are assumed to be important; and how tradition has employed reason and experience to interpret Scripture in ever-new historical situations. (For classical treatments that provide models for proceeding along these lines, see John of Damascus, *OF* I.1 ff., *FC* 37, pp. 165 ff.; Tho. Aq., *ST* I Q1, I, pp. 11 ff.; Calvin, *Inst*. I.1 ff.). These are issues that become significant, however, only in the context of the astonishing claims made by Christian teaching concerning the living God.

Whether God Can Be Defined

A simple organization is fitting to the study of One celebrated as the most simple of all realities. This chapter focuses upon a question so plain that it cries out for a plain answer: What do we mean when we say "God"? Is any language fitting to God? We begin with the underlying issue:

Can God Be Defined?

Classical Christianity argues that God cannot be objectively defined (in the sense of being circumscribed) by human language, yet this has not prevented Christians from speaking of God altogether or from developing a preliminary description of God's way of acting as known in Scripture. There are two ways of asking whether God can be defined. In one sense God cannot be defined; in another sense it is possible modestly to say what Christians mean when they speak the word *God*. How can this be?

At one level the question Can God be defined? must be answered no. If definition means clarifying the boundaries of a thing so that it is placed in a known category and compared to other species, then God cannot be defined. For God is not an object that can fit into our categories of objects (John of Damascus, *OF* I.1, *NPNF* 2 IX, p. 1; Tho. Aq., *ST* I Q1.7 ff., I, pp. 4 ff.; *ST* I Q17, I, pp. 95 ff.). Our minds and language cannot specify accurately the limits of that reality which transcends measurement in space and time (Augustine, *On Chr. Doctrine* II.2 ff., *LLA*, pp. 8 ff.). God "surpasses human wit and speech. He knows God best who owns that whatever he thinks and says falls short of what God really is" (Tho. Aq., *Opuscula* X, *Exposition, de Causis* VI, *TAPT*, p. 89).

Suppose your best friend is named George. Suppose I ask you to define George. What makes it especially difficult to define a person? A thing can be defined more easily than a person because a thing can be fitted into objective categories (Hilary, *Trin.* IV.36 ff., *NPNF* 2 IX, pp. 148 ff.). As it is hard to define a human person, so it is harder to define the divine person.

Hence Gregory the Theologian cautioned: "It is difficult to conceive God, but to define Him in words is an impossibility" (Gregory Nazianzen, *Second Theological Or.* XXVIII, *NPNF* 2 VII, p. 289). "It is impossible to express Him, yet even more impossible to conceive Him. For that which may be conceived may perhaps be made clear by language, if not fairly well, at any rate imperfectly, to any one who is not quite deprived of hearing or slothful of understanding. But to comprehend the whole of so great a Subject as this is quite impossible and impracticable, not merely to the utterly careless and ignorant, but even to those who are highly exalted, and who love God" (pp. 289–90).

Classic Christian teaching has often acknowledged that the being of God is ultimately indefinable because God overreaches our comprehension. This point is explicitly stated in the Scripture that speaks of God as "dwelling in unapproachable light" (1 Tim. 6:16a), as "the one

whom no mortal eye has ever seen or ever can see" (1 Tim. 6:16b,
Phi.). Only the infinite God can fully comprehend the infinite (Au-
gustine, *On Chr. Doctrine* I.6 ff., *LLA*, pp. 10 ff.; Hilary, *Trin.* I.6,
NPNF 2 IX, p. 41).

Must God then remain completely undefined? If so, this book must
end here, for it is about God, and one cannot write a book about a
Subject that is in every sense unknowable.

Can God be defined? While acknowledging the divine ineffability,
it *is* nonetheless possible to say more, as did Paul: "For (in the words
of Scripture) 'who knows the mind of the Lord? Who can advise him?'
We, however, possess the mind of Christ" (1 Cor. 2:16). Happily, there
is a limited, constrained way to answer cautiously and unpretentiously
yes. For there is another, more modest definition of definition that
does allow us a definition of God. For if to define means to state the
meaning of something, to describe and explain what a term means by
its attributes and distinctive properties in such a way as to distinguish
that one from all others, then God can be defined. It is possible to
distinguish God from everything else (Clement of Alex., *Strom.* VIII.2,
ANF II, pp. 558, 559; Augustine, *On Chr. Doctrine* I.6 ff., *LLA*, pp. 11
ff.). In this sense it is not only possible but surprisingly easy to define
God, for God is *not* finite, *not* time-bound, *not* many divisible things,
not partial, *not* dependent, and so on. This approach is sometimes
called apophatic theology (meaning that it proceeds by negation, from
apophasis, denial).

It is on this basis that short definitions such as that of the Augsburg
Confession are formed, largely showing what God is not, and distinguishing God from all created things. There God is defined as "*without*
body, *without* parts, of *in*finite power, wisdom and goodness" (Augsburg Conf., italics added, *CC*, p. 68). At least we hear that God is not
a material body, not divided, not limited in power, not partial in
wisdom or goodness.

Definitions such as this are primarily composed of a listing of the
qualities or attributes of God. They delineate a series of terms that are
properly ascribed in their full dimension only to God.

Hence the preliminary definition of God in Christian teaching hinges
primarily upon the intensive clarification of a series of terms, called
the attributes of God. They show what God is *not* in the slightest
degree and *is* to the largest possible degree (Maimonides, *Guide for the
Perplexed* I.58; Tho. Aq., *ST* I Q13.2, I, pp. 60 ff.). One of the most
influential of classical Protestant attempts at such a definition is the
Westminster Larger Catechism, whose prefatory definition of God

brings together many of the terms that we will discuss in Chapters 2 and 3: "God is a Spirit in and of Himself infinite in being, glory, blessedness and perfection; all-sufficient, eternal, unchangeable, incomprehensible, everywhere present, almighty, knowing all things, most wise, most holy, most just, most merciful and gracious, long-suffering, and abundant in goodness and truth" (Westminster Larger Catechism; for similar short definitions one may examine the Creed of Dositheus, art. I, *CC*, p. 486; Abstract of Principles, art. II, *CC*, p. 340; New Hampshire Conf., art. II, *CC*, p. 335; Batak Conf., art. I, *CC*, p. 556; and the World Council of Churches Statement of Faith of 1959, *CC*, pp. 590 f.). These terms are all viewed as attributes of God, defining who God is.

In pursuing "what we mean when we say 'God,' " a simple form of language about God serves better than technical terms. Some special words have been so much overused during centuries of controversy that they have collected conflicting meanings, and sometimes comic associations, so as to render them less serviceable. Note the ambiguous history of such terms as *immutability* (does it imply complete unresponsiveness in God, or constancy of covenant intent?), *substance* (is it the material of which a thing is made, or the unchanging essence underlying a thing?), *perfection* (is it a completely excellent quality, or a process of becoming excellent in the highest degree?), *myth* (is it a deception, or a profound means of conveying truth?), and *dogma* (is it stubborn rigidity, or valid ecumenical teaching?). Is an oblate a flattened spheroid, or an offering of a sacrifice to God, or a title in a religious order? Most of the issues of the study of God can be dealt with in simple, straightforward language. One can just as easily say "appearance" as "theophany" or "conciliate" as "propitiate."

A Classical Approach Toward Defining God

The classical exegetes thought that we understand God best by looking at Jesus. "Anyone who has seen me has seen the Father" (John 1:9b). If God is made known in Jesus, then we do well to define God in relation to what we know of Jesus. Classic exegesis has sought to define God's character by beholding the character, teaching, life, ministry, death and resurrection of Jesus the Christ (Athanasius, *Letter LX to Adelphius*, NPNF 2 IV, pp. 575–78).

Christian teaching approaches the problem of the definition of the term *God* from the standpoint of Christian memory and celebration of God's revelation in history. This standpoint does not reject the resources of logic and scientific method, or of reason and experience, but neither does it view them as completely or independently adequate to the subject matter—God (Theophilus of Antioch, *To Autolycus* I.7, *ANF* II, p. 91; Augustine, *Answer to Skeptics*, FC 1, pp. 134 ff.).

Although the term *god* (meaning idol, an object worshiped) may be rightly used as a noun to speak of a class of projected or assumed divinities, the word *God* as used in Christian worship is the *name* of the One worthy of true worship. We make our first mistake if we think of *God* as a common noun rather than a personal noun. *God* is a *name*, the way of addressing a person (Hilary, *On Trin.* I.5, FC 25, p. 5). A personal noun is distinguished from a common noun, which indicates what an individual object has in common with other objects of its class. *God* cannot be a common noun because there is nothing else in God's class (Justin Martyr, *Second Apol.* VI, *ANF* I, p. 190; Luther, *Bondage of the Will*, ML, pp. 173–74; Calvin, *Inst.* 1.10; 3.20). *God* is a personal noun, just like *David* or *Mary*, because *God* names an incomparably personal being having consciousness and freedom (John Chrysostom, *Hom. on Philippians* VII, *NPNF* 1 XIII, pp. 212–18; Bonaventure, *Soul's Journey into God* VI, CWS, pp. 102–9).

Christian teaching does not view God as one among the class of objects called gods, for there is "none like him" (Isa. 46:9). Of this reality there can only be one (Tho. Aq., *ST* I Q45–48, I, pp. 232–53). Nothing else that we can conceive or know in the world has the insurmountably good qualities that are uniquely ascribed to God.

When we speak of God as the Source and End of all things, we are already indicating that God is different from everything else. To express that difference in a careful way is the subject matter classically discussed under the heading of "God's names and attributes" (John of Damascus, *OF* I.2 ff., *NPNF* 2 IX, pp. 2 ff.; cf. Calvin, *Inst.* I.10.3; I.13–16).

We will clarify what we mean when we say God (Chapters 2–4) before we ask whether God exists (Chapter 5). Our intention is first to set forth that understanding of God that arises in Christian worship and then inquire whether we can provide plausible reasons for believing that this incomparable reality exists. Note that this classical sequence is reversed in modern discussions. Here we will follow the classical order by setting forth the characteristics of God as understood by the worshiping community, and only then seeing if it is reasonable to believe that such a God does indeed exist as claimed (Theophilus, *To Autolycus*, Book I on the nature and attributes of God, e.g., precedes Books II and III on the unreality of the gods, philosophical reasoning concerning God, creation, and various views of the existence of God,

ANF II, pp. 89–121; cf. Augustine's *First Catech. Instr.*, *ACW*, *On the Trin.*, *NPNF* 1 II; *On Faith in Things Unseen*, *FC* 16; *On the Spirit and the Letter*, *LCC* VIII).

A Christian definition of God means a clarification of what is meant by the term *God* in Christian prayer and proclamation, a conception of God that emerges out of the shared memory of historical Christian experience. It is a true definition of God only if Christ's revelation of God is true, and truly remembered (Augustine, *On Chr. Doctrine* I.6, *LLA*, pp. 10 ff.). If ten believers got together and wrote a definition of God and then approved it, for instance, by a seven-to-three vote, this would not make it normative for Christian teaching. It becomes true for Christian teaching not by changing styles of popular consensus but by resonance with the consensus of apostolic teaching and ancient ecumenical clarification (Irenaeus, *Ag. Her.* III.1–4, pp. 414–17; Vincent of Lerins, *Comm.* II, *NPNF* 2 XI, pp. 132 ff.).

A Preliminary Definition

If it is possible to provide some plausible clarification of the primary meanings associated with the name God, then the study of God can begin. A short, preliminary definition (to be further unpacked step-by-step in Chapters 2–4) is as follows:

God is the uncreated source and end of all things; one; incomparably alive; insurmountable in presence, knowledge, and power; personal, eternal spirit, who in holy love freely creates, sustains, and governs all things.

Many alternative forms of language are possible, but these terms and their cognates are among the most widely used in the classic Christian tradition. The following essential features are embraced in this spare sentence, pointing toward a deepening sequence of four levels or layers or dimensions of the right naming of God:

The Transcendent Nature of God—God alone is One, eternal, infinite, necessary, sufficient, independent, uncreated, Source of all.
The Outreaching Majesty of God—God in relation to creatures is almighty, all-knowing, and everywhere present.
The Free Personal Spirit of God—God is incomparably free and irreducibly Spirit, while remaining personally addressable.
The Moral Character of God—is holy love.

Only a fuller clarification of these four levels or sets of qualities will constitute a meaningful and functional preliminary clarification of the meanings associated with the name God, insofar as the Holy One allows the divine life to be defined by us. If such a clarification is possible, then Christian teaching will not be forever appealing to sheer mystery in its speech about God, or always need to resort to obscurantism, vague claims, or mere subjective feelings when asked what it is that Christianity means in speaking of and to God.

Naming God

God in Scripture does not deal with humanity anonymously (without a name). God is willing to let the recipients of divine mercy know the divine name, Yahweh (He who is, Gen. 2:4–9; Exod. 4:1 ff.; Ps. 23:1).

Indeed, many names have emerged in the history of salvation to speak of this incomparable reality. Among Scripture's names for God are *Yahweh* (Lord, Isa. 6:3), *Yah* (a contraction of *Yahweh*, Exod. 15:2); *'El* (Mighty One, Gen. 14:18 ff.; Ps. 90:2), *'Elōhīm* (Gen. 1:1), *'Elōah* (Job 33:12), *'Adōnaī* (Lord, Ps. 38:22), *'Ādōn* (Lord, Ps. 8:1, 9), *'El Shaddaī* (God Almighty, All-sufficient, Gen. 28:3), *Theos* (God, Mark 1:24), *Kyrios* (Lord, Mark 1:3). Though different, these names point to a single reality, God. God is the teutonic languages' way (cf. also *Gott*, *Gud* from the Gothic *gheu*, to invoke or to sacrifice) of calling the name of the One who in Scripture is called Yahweh, 'El, and Theos (*TDOT* I, pp. 242–61; cf. Luther, *Bondage of the Will*, *ML*, pp. 190–92; Calvin, *Inst.* 1.10.3; cf. *TDNT* on "*theos*," and *OED* on "God"; Max Mueller, *Science of Language*, pp. 449 ff.).

Characteristically in Hebraic Scripture, God's being is revealed to us through sublime names that designate who God is. The revelation of God's personal character is closely connected with these names that reveal God's nature. The discussion of divine *attributes* is best viewed as a fuller development and clarification of scriptural *names* for God. They assist Christian teaching in ordering, limiting, and regulating Christian language about God (Origen, *Ag. Celsus* I.24 ff., *ANF* IV, pp. 406 ff.; Gregory of Nyssa, *On the Holy Trin.*, *NPNF* 2 V, pp. 328–30; Calvin, *Inst.* 1.5).

In no case do these scriptural names imply that God can be fully comprehended in essence (as God is to himself) merely by being named (Gregory Nazianzen, *First Theol. Orat.*, or. XXVII, *NPNF* 2 VII, pp. 284–88; Hilary, *On Trin.* IV.2, *NPNF* 2 IX, p. 71). For God is the "King of kings and Lord of lords" (Rev. 19:16) who lives in unapproachable light (1 Tim. 6:16). But this does not mean that God is wholly unnameable. When Moses prayed that God would reveal his glory, "The Lord answered, 'I will make all my goodness pass before you, and I will pronounce in your hearing the name Jehovah. . . . '

But he added, 'My face you cannot see, for no mortal man may see me and live' " (Exod. 33:18–20). Thus, though invisible, God is not nameless or in all ways unknowable (Tertullian, *Ag. Praxeas* XIV ff., *ANF* III, pp. 609–11).

Two of these names in particular—Yahweh (Lord) and 'Elōhīm (God)—point succinctly to the divine reality. They are especially powerful and laden with meaning when combined in the condensed ascription: Lord God (Yahweh 'Elōhīm, Gen. 2:4).

The name Yahweh (Jahweh or Jehovah or YHWH) is closely connected with the intensification of the Hebrew verb *to be*. "Then Moses said to God: 'If I go to the Israelites and tell them that the God of their forefathers has sent me to them, and they ask me his name, what shall I say?' God answered, 'I AM, that is who I am. Tell them I AM has sent you to them' " (Exod. 3:13–14). Yahweh (I AM) suggests the awesome meaning: "HE WHO IS" or "HE WHO IS WHAT HE IS" (RSV alternatively translates: "I WILL BE WHAT I WILL BE"). Yahweh incomparably IS.

One named "I am because I am," suggests that there is no external cause for God's existence outside himself. The name Yahweh appears to unite the notion of One who purely is with the notion of One who is in the process of continually becoming and becoming disclosed through historical revelation (Justin Martyr, *First Apol.* LXIII, *ANF* I, pp. 184 f.; Gregory of Nyssa, *FGG*, pp. 81 ff.). Later, in a remarkable passage, John's Gospel would recall that Jesus said of himself: "In very truth I tell you, before Abraham was born, I am" (John 8:58), in a way that suggests that in Jesus we meet nothing less than the personal self-disclosure of YHWH, "I am" (Irenaeus, *Ag. Her.* IV.13 ff., *ANF* I, pp. 477 ff.; Athanasius, *Incarnation of the Word* XI, *NPNF* 2 IV, p. 42).

'El, the most frequent name by which God is called in Scripture and by the Semites in general, has the root meaning of "Strong and Mighty One," the One whose incomparable power elicits reverent fear or awe (Ignatius, *Ephesians* XI, *ANF* I, p. 54; cf. John Cassian, *Conferences*, 2d pt., XI.11–13, *NPNF* 2 XI, pp. 419–21; Tho. Aq., *ST* I–IIae Q41–44, I, pp. 759 ff.; Calvin, *Inst.* 3.1; 3.4.31 ff.; 3.12.1). 'Elōah and 'Elōhīm are related terms referring to this unspeakably powerful One whose awesome presence instantly inspires reverential awe. 'Elōhīm, plural in form, is an intensive suggesting the fullness or glory of all the powers of the divine nature. When Yahweh and 'El are united, as in Lord God, 'Elōhīm is the generic name for God and Yahweh is the personal or proper name.

Among other names are 'El Shaddaī, "God Almighty" (NT: pantocratōr); 'El 'Elyōn, "God Most High" (Greek Septuagint: Hypsistos); 'El
'Ōlām, "the Everlasting God" (Aiōnios, Rom. 16:26); Yahweh Sābāōth,
"Lord of Hosts" (Ps. 46:7). These primitive, personalized names of
God suggest attributes (such as almighty power, omnipresence, infinite
wisdom, etc.) and have in time become the nucleus of the tradition's
more deliberate reflection on the divine attributes (Justin Martyr, Second Apol. VI, ANF I, p. 190; Dialogue with Trypho, chap. 126, ANF I,
pp. 262 f.; Irenaeus, Ag. Her. II.30, ANF I, p. 406). These names
correlate closely with the attributes we will be discussing: majesty,
eternity, omnipotence and holiness.

The special name 'Adōnaī, "my Lord," arose about 300 B.C. out of
the reluctance of pious Jews to pronounce the divine name, later
translated into Greek as Kyrios. The testimony of Thomas to the lordship of Christ, "my Lord and my God" (John 20:28), brings together
in the New Testament the two earlier traditions of naming God as
'Adōnaī (for Yahweh) and 'Elōhīm (God). The single New Testament
text that best draws together in Greek these most important Hebraic
names for God ('Elōhīm, Yahweh, 'Adōnaī, and Shaddaī) is the remarkable ascription in Revelation 1:8, where the divine Word declares:
" 'I am the Alpha and the Omega,' says the Lord [Kyrios, i.e., 'Adōnaī]
God [Theos, i.e., 'El], who is and who was and who is to come, the
sovereign Lord [Pantokratōr, i.e., 'El Shaddaī] of all." It is through the
historical activity of the One thus named that God's character has been
made known to the remembering community (Tertullian, Ag. Praxeas
XXII, ANF III, pp. 617 ff.; Ag. Marcion, I.6 ff., ANF III, pp. 275 ff.).

Father (patēr, 'āb) suggests a caring, nurturing, parental relationship. In intention the term may apply to analogies of both mothering
and fathering. Scripture views God as the parent of all things by
creation (Gen. 2:4; James 1:17), especially of human beings, as their
personal guide and protector (Isa. 63:16; Acts 23:28), but even more
so of those who have through baptism become God's children by
adoption and grace (Luke 11:2; John 3:3–10; Rom. 8:15 ff.; John 2:23
ff.). That God is Father is most fully beheld and understood in the
light of the Son (John 10:15 ff.). So decisive is this parental metaphor
that it becomes the leading contribution of Christianity to the Hebraic
understanding of God.

Whether God's Character Can Be Ascertained

Five Methods of Knowing God's Character

In classical Christian teaching five methods of knowing God's character interweave. (1) It is essentially from God's own self-disclosure that God's character has become known. Thus the *revelation* set forth in Scripture and fulfilled in Jesus is crucial to all Christian speech about God's qualities (Irenaeus, *Ag. Her.* III, *ANF* I, pp. 414 ff.). These characteristics are not to be abstracted, as if separable, from the events of the history of covenant. (2) Nonetheless, some attributes can be partially inferred through reasoning about causality, that is, from effect to cause (the way of causality, *via causalitatis*), by attributing to God the cause (original, virtual, or permissive) of every effect (Tho. Aq., *ST* I Q44, I, pp. 230–32). (3) Other attributes may be derived through reasoning by way of negation (*via negativa*), denying as applicable to God the limits and defects we find in creaturely things (Novatian, *On Trin.* IV ff., *ANF* V, pp. 614 ff.), and (4) by way of heightening, or eminence (*via eminentiae*), ascribing to God in the highest degree all the best that we behold in creaturely life (Tho. Aq., *ST* I Q5, I, pp. 23 ff.). (5) Finally, there are qualities of the divine character that can be inferred *a priori* or deductively by means of thinking consistently about the consequences of the very idea of God—for whatever is essential to the idea of perfect being we may reliably know to be characteristic of God alone (Anselm, *Proslog.* II–V, pp. 7–11; for alternative views of these varied approaches, see Dionysius, *Div. Names* I.5; Bonaventure, *Soul's Journey into God*, CWS, pp. 59 ff.; Tho. Aq., *ST* I Q12.12; *ST* I Q13.1; Calvin, *Inst.* 1.1 ff.; 1.14–16; Tho. Jackson, *Works* V, p. 36; Schmid, *DT* I.1, pp. 103 ff.).

In due course all of these five methods will be examined. In the last section of this chapter we will deal primarily with the ways of negation and heightening. In Chapter 5 we will detail the arguments from causality and the idea of perfect being. We proceed now with the first of the methods of knowing God's character—through revelation as declared in Scripture—which was the primary mode known to the classic Christian writers.

What Are Attributes?

Attributes of God are qualities that belong to God's essential nature and that are found wherever God becomes self-revealed. They are those reliable character patterns that belong to God as God. We find

ourselves attributing these to God based upon what we know of God's
self-disclosure in history. Only God has these qualities (John of Damascus, *OF* I.14, *NPNF* 2 IX, p. 17; Calvin, *Inst.* 1.5). If God is rightly
understood as the Source and End of all things, full of goodness and
truth, then God may be said to have a definable character, and may
be counted upon to act in ways consistent with that incomparably
merciful, just, loving, almighty, good character.

Accordingly, knowing is not a divine attribute, but that mode of
knowing which knows all is a quality attributable only to God. Merely
having will is not an attribute of God, for creatures have wills, but
having a will that is perfect in holy love and able to perform all that it
desires is an attribute of God. Having life is not an attribute of God,
because all living things have life, but having life in such an incomparable way that all things live through that life is an attribute of God
(Tertullian, *Ag. Praxeas* XXV, XXVII, *ANF* III, pp. 622–25; Quenstedt,
TDP I, p. 300; Chemnitz, *LT* I, p. 43).

Attributes are distinguishable from actions of God. George's act is
not in the fullest sense George. So God's character is more fully
definitive of God than is a single action of God. It is out of God's
essential nature and qualities that God's actions come (Hilary, *On Trin.*
VII.21, *NPNF* 2 IX, pp. 126 ff.; Calvin, *Inst.* 1.13; 2.3.10). It is best
not to call the attributes by the special name *properties*, since this is a
technical term that has been used to speak of the characteristics of
the interior relations of the persons of the Godhead. Attributes are
intrinsic to God, posited as essential to the divine nature, hence are
not subject to being gained or lost by God.

The root meaning of the verb *to attribute* is to ascertain or designate
the distinguishing qualities or character of something. To attribute to
God such qualities as infinity or mercy is to concede them as belonging
rightfully to God as an essential and permanent feature of God's
character. The essence of something is understandable from its abiding
attributes and qualities. This applies to all objects of knowledge; they
are revealed and knowable not in themselves but only in and through
their attributes. Similarly, the nature of God is made understandable
to us by our looking at the qualities that are intrinsic to God's being
and therefore always present in God's activity. God would be completely unknowable if he had no operations, energies, or qualities
attributable to him, but solely an essence known only to himself. God
could not become a matter for our reflection if God's being were never
manifested through any definable attributes or qualities (Novatian,

Trin. I, *ANF* V, pp. 611 ff.; Clementine, *Hom.* II.42 ff., *ANF* VIII, p. 237; X.19, *ANF* VIII, p. 283).

Why Attributes Are Possible and Necessary in Speaking of God

It would be absurd and impossible to try to worship God without implicitly thinking of some divine attributes, such as attentiveness, presence, power, mercy, holiness, or love. Every thought of God or prayer to God, properly understood, assumes something about God's attributes. There is no way to speak to, of, or about God without speaking in some way of God's abiding attributes or qualities. Only by clarifying these can one arrive at an adequate statement of what is meant in Christian teaching by the proper name *God* (John of Damascus, *OF* I.1 ff., *NPNF* 2, IX, pp. 1 ff.).

The purpose of Christian teaching of the divine attributes is not to show *whether* God exists but *who* God is, and what God's distinctive *character* is, in order that faith may have some idea of what to expect from God. Christian teaching has a duty to say as straightforwardly as possible just what is meant by the word *God*, in order to provide a preliminary definition for the major subject of theology: God as understood by the faith of the Christian community. Christian teaching builds upon the modest awareness that God is truly and sufficiently revealed to us, and that the qualities of God's being are made known to us through a history. God has not misrepresented himself through revealing to us these names and characteristics (Calvin, *Inst.* 1.10; Chemnitz, *LT* I, p. 43; Quenstedt, I, pp. 300, 320; Hollaz, *ETA*, pp. 235 ff.).

It is fitting first to consider the question of *who* God is (God's being), and then to ask *whether* God is (God's existence), for it seems relatively meaningless to ask whether something exists until one has first tried to define, envision, or imagine it. This is why some of Christianity's earliest teachers tended to defer the question of the reality or existence of God until the being of God had been sufficiently clarified (Novatian, *Trin.* I–IX, *ANF* V, pp. 611–18; Cyril of Jerusalem, *Catech. Lect.* IV.4, V.1 ff., *NPNF* 2 VII, pp. 20, 29 ff.). They began their discussion of God with a clarification of the divine attributes (Irenaeus, *Ag. Her.* II.1–2, *ANF* I, pp. 359–62; Gregory Nazianzen, *Second Theol. Or.* I–IV, *NPNF* 2 VII, pp. 288–90) and subsequently spoke of reasons for proclaiming that such an incomparable One truly exists (Theophilus, *To Autolycus*, Bks. I.3–6, II.3 ff., *ANF* II, pp. 89, 90, 94 ff.; cf. Irenaeus, *Ag. Her.* IV.15, pp. 479 ff.; Gregory Nazianzen, *Second*

Theol. Or. V–VII, pp. 290, 291). Though it is relatively unfamiliar in modern theology, this procedure will be followed here.

The Unity of Diverse Attributes

The qualities intrinsic to God are one in God yet many in our perception. In their unity they reveal God's singular character and personality. In their variety they allow us to behold and praise various aspects of the divine activity, and to name the one God by different names and through varied metaphors. "The diverse names we give to God are not synonyms, for they convey diverse meanings, though everything is one in his reality" (Tho. Aq., *Compend.* 25, *TAPT*, p. 94). The beauty of God's holiness blends all attributes into a single unified effulgence of the divine glory (Gregory of Nyssa, *On the Holy Spirit*, *NPNF* 2 V, pp. 324, 325; *FGG*, pp. 231–34).

Classic Christian teachers warned against emphasizing one attribute at the expense of another. Just as a good person will manifest good but varied behavior in situations where different responses are called for (and in so doing does not become "different persons"), so God is an infinitely good One with many varied qualities that are unified in the divine character (Hilary, *On Trin.* IV.15, *NPNF* 2 IX, pp. 71–75; Anselm, *Monologium* XVII, *BW*, pp. 66 ff.; Wesley, "The Unity of the Divine Being," *WJW* VII, pp. 263–73). God's perfectly integrated character is precisely the appropriate balance of these excellences or insurmountably good qualities (sometimes rendered "perfections"; cf. Tho. Aq., *ST* I, Q19 ff., I, pp. 103 ff.; Oden, *TAG*, Epilogue on Divine Attributes, pp. 125 f.). As history unfolds there may be one occasion when one of the attributes (such as justice or holiness) may seem to the believer to be relatively more recognizable or dominant; at another time another attribute (eternality or mercy) may come more clearly into view. But regardless of which attribute may be recognizable at any given moment, all attributes are unified in an appropriate integration in the being of God. "Perfections manifold and divided in other things are simple and united in God" (Hilary, *Trin.* VII.1–3, *NPNF* 2 IX, pp. 118, 119; Tho. Aq., *ST* I Q13.4, *TAPT*, p. 95; cf. Calvin, *Inst.* 1.13; Chemnitz, *LT* I.43).

The history of theism is plagued by errors caused by overemphasizing a single one or set of attributes while neglecting others. Aristotle stressed God's absolute essence, aseity (underived existence), self-contemplation, transcendence, and immutability, yet failed to grasp God's relationality, closeness, and covenant love toward humanity. Kant rightly grasped God's justice as it impinges upon human reason and conscience but did not fully acknowledge God's mercy, grace, and power. Wieman understood God's temporality but did not sufficiently affirm God's consciousness, freedom, and infinity (Aristotle, *Metaphy.*, *BWA*, pp. 689 ff.; Kant, *Fundamental Principles of the Metaphy. of Morals*, pp. 63 ff.; H. N. Wieman, *Source of the Human Good*, pp. 54 ff.; cf. Hartshorne and Reese, *PSG*, passim).

A healthy equilibrium in the Christian teaching of God grows as one becomes firmly grounded in the interpenetrating qualities of the divine attributes so as to not overemphasize one to the neglect of others (Tho. Aq., *ST* I Q12, I, pp. 48 ff.; Pearson, *Apostles' Creed*, pp. 40 ff.). Each attribute complements the others so that taken together the glory of God embraces and manifests all attributes in perfect tension, correspondence, and complementarity (Cyril of Jerusalem, *Catech. Lect.* VI, *NPNF* 2 VII, pp. 33–43; Tho. Aq., *ST* I Q15, Q31, I, pp. 16 ff., 164 ff.; cf. Oden, *TAG*, pp. 52–69, 125, 126).

Hence all the attributes are united and inseparable in God's being. It is not as if one could separate God's being from God's acting, or God's essence from God's energies, or God's activity from God's character. Rather, Scripture shows that God's name (hence character) is known precisely through events in which God's activity has been recognized and received by the community of faith. It is not an abstract, nonrelational, or rationalistic speculation that God is incomparably just, good, powerful, and present. For God has revealed himself as such through historical activity, through the divine-human encounter, through meeting with sinners (*Letter to Diognetus*, 6–12, *ANF* I, pp. 27–30; Athanasius, *Ag. Heathen* 38–40, *NPNF* 2 IV, pp. 24, 25).

It is nonetheless possible to distinguish these attributes, even though in God's unitary being they remain inseparable. For God's presence, for example, is not the same as God's knowing. Though distinguishable in language, they are united in God. God's integral, self-congruent being fully expresses each of these distinguishable attributes.

In God, to be is to be incomparably strong. To be God is to be unfailingly merciful. God's way of being is loving. God is all wisdom, all spirit, all light, all intelligence, and wholly just. God *is* merciful, just, and holy. God is the Way, Truth, and Life, without ceasing to be simply God (Wesley, "The Unity of the Divine Being," *WJW* VII, pp. 264 ff.; Heppe, *RD*, pp. 57 ff.). No single characteristic can be viewed independently, as if separable from the rest.

God is not at one moment unmercifully strong and at another moment unwisely omnipotent. God is always mercifully strong and wisely omnipotent, and omnipotently wise and strongly merciful. Nor is God at one time just, at another time loving, and at another time all-knowing. God's whole being, inclusive of all attributes, is present in each of the discrete attributes that faith recognizes and celebrates. God is fully and simultaneously all these attributes, and more than any language could attribute (Novatian, *On Trin*. II, *ANF* V, pp. 612, 613). This notion is interwoven with faith's affirmation of God's simplicity. God is not divided up into our petty conceptions of God's attributes. In all attributes, God is, and remains, simply and completely God (John of Damascus, *OF* I.9, *NPNF* 2 IX, pp. 12 ff.; Hilary, *On Trin*. IX.1 ff., *NPNF* 2 IX, pp. 155 ff.; Tho. Aq., *ST* I Q3, I, pp. 14 ff.; Calvin, *Inst*. 1.10.3).

The Biblical Revelation of the Character of God

In Hebraic religion, God is known by what God does. What God does is remembered and recollected as history—the history of God's encounter with humanity. In these encounters, God is remembered as having a definable, discernible character by those whom God has met: "He made known his ways to Moses and his acts to the people of Israel" (Ps. 103:7; cf. Irenaeus, *Ag. Her*. IV.9, *ANF* I, pp. 472, 473). It is through that story of God's actions that we come to say something in language about God's character, reliability, and personhood (Julian of Norwich, *SGL* VI, pp. 15–18; Calvin, *Inst*. I.8 ff.).

The ways of this One are disclosed for our enjoyment, celebration, salvation, and instruction (Pss. 25:4; 119:3). The Jewish-Christian study of God inquires into a history (the history of Israel and universal history) to find out how God has become known (Deut. 5:6). Yet history is a highly complex, enormous cacophony of extended multigenerational human experience. It seems virtually impossible to condense all that experience into a single, central, revealing insight or meaning. Yet in the events surrounding the ministry of Jesus, Christianity understands and proclaims that God has become self-disclosed so as to reveal the inner meaning, direction, and end of universal history (Augustine, *CG* XVI–XVIII, *NPNF* 1 II, pp. 309 ff.).

There remains a tension between the Bible and systematization that at times has comic-pathetic overtones (Kierkegaard, *Concl. Unsci. Post*., pp. 250 ff., 347 ff., 430 ff.). The vitality of the biblical history of God's acts does not easily boil down to the clear, consistent formulations about God attempted by systematic theology. Try as we may, the biblical history resists systematization. Yet since the Bible wishes to address each hearer as a whole person, it invites and to some degree requires that each believer seek to bring its loose ends together, to

listen for its unity, and to try to see it integrally. In that sense the
Bible invites systematic, cohesive thinking about its varied events and
messages. Christian teaching does well not to pretend finally to resolve that tension.

God is made known in history. That remains a constant frustration
to our systematic attempts to get God safely boxed into our changing
linguistic packages. History does not readily lend itself to systematic
statement or definition, yet Christian teaching rightly persists in modestly seeking internal consistency and clear definition concerning God's
self-disclosure in history (Justin Martyr, *Dialogue with Trypho* VI ff.,
ANF I, pp. 198 ff.; cf. Kierkegaard, *Concl. Unsci. Post.*, pp. 49 ff.;
Authority and Revelation, pp. 98 ff.).

It has never been a central worry of biblical writers that reasonable
arguments be established that God exists. Whether or in what sense
God "exists" must indeed remain a major concern of Christian apologetics, which seeks to make God plausible to those who do not
participate in the community of faith. But biblical writers were far
more concerned with polytheism than with atheism, and with idolatry
than with theism. Their central problem was not *whether* God is, but
rather *who* God is (Gen. 28:10–22; Ps. 20:1 ff.; Isa. 9:6), that is, What
is the character of God? If God has come to us, what is reliably known
of God? To Whom do we address our prayers? What sort of language
can one ascribe to this mysterious, wholly exceptional, transcendent
reality? Who is this Holy One, which is to say, by what name shall we
call Him? (Exod. 3:13–16). If God has become self-revealed in history,
just as human beings make themselves known by disclosure to other
human beings, what kind of character can we say God has? (Gen.
22:1–18; Gen. 37–50). This is the core biblical issue underlying classical Christian discussions of the attributes of God, which we are approaching step-by-step.

There is still room for *doubt* in biblical faith. The exodus wanderers
were subjected to despair and anxiety that God might not fulfill his
promises ("Is the Lord in our midst or not?" Exod. 17:7). Jeremiah
complained that God was like a deceitful *wadi*, as if God occasionally
came in like rain on the desert and swept everything away, and then
did not appear for a long while (Jer. 15:16). Job was tormented by
questions about the fairness of God and the remoteness of God (Job
9, 10).

Some say, "God has forgotten; he has hidden his face and has seen
nothing" (Ps. 10:11; cf. Jer. 5:12). Doubts of this type are intensely
present in Scripture, but they have emerged precisely out of a radical

sense of the sovereignty of God and the providential presence of the almighty God—precisely because God *has* appeared at some points in history. Worshipers who today experience profound doubts about God can at least know that they belong to a community whose greatest minds have from time to time experienced such doubts (Job 3:1 ff.; Jer. 2:4–37; cf. Augustine, *Conf.* II.9, *LCC* VII, p. 60).

Whether God Can Be Known by Negation or Analogy

The metaphors of limiting and heightening are among the most important of classic attempts rightly to name God. We will speak first of the uses and abuses of analogies, then of the way of negation (*via negativa*) and the way of heightening or intensifying (*via eminentiae*).

The Usefulness of Analogy

Classical discussions of the qualities or characteristics of God make cautious but important use of analogies. The self-constrained use of analogy has helped Christian teaching speak in a disciplined way about the qualities characteristic of God.

Analogy is distinguished from (*a*) rigid, *univocal* language, which allows only a single meaning to a word, and (*b*) evasive, ambiguous, uncertain *equivocal* language, which inordinately allows words to have multiple meanings and thereby makes definite statements impossible.

Every language has the word *good* or its equivalent in its vocabulary. All users of the word *good* know in their own way what goodness is and that there are degrees of goodness. When Christian teachers have cautiously applied that ordinary human word *good* to God, they have applied it analogically, that is, by some proportional comparison to what we know to be *like* human goodness, remaining aware that God's goodness is also vastly *unlike* human goodness (Gregory of Nyssa, *Ag. Eunomius* XI.1, 2, *NPNF* 2 V, pp. 230, 231; Bonaventure, *Soul's Journey into God*, *CWS*, VI, pp. 102 ff.). Although God is insurmountably good, we know that even our best conceptions of goodness do not do full justice to the infinitely wise, eternal goodness of God.

We do well to avoid using the word *good* univocally, as if the word had only one strict meaning that applied in exactly the same way to our goodness and God's goodness (Novatian, *On Trin.* II, *ANF* V, 612). Yet in avoiding this extreme we must not bend so far as to apply language too ambiguously or equivocally, which would suppose that human goodness is wholly different from God's goodness. In this case we would equivocate on two completely different meanings of the

word *good*. Rather, we rely upon a constrained *analogy* (which is neither univocal nor equivocal) that says that God's goodness is in some
ways akin to and in other ways distinct from what we know of human
goodness (Tho. Aq., *Compend.* secs. 24–27, pp. 26–27; *ST* I Q13, I,
pp. 59 ff.; Calvin, *Inst.* 4.17.21, 32). This is one example of how limited
analogies have been particularly useful in the classical Christian study
of God.

Thomas Aquinas, with good comic imagination, summed it up:

A term may be predicated of various subjects in three ways, univocally,
equivocally, and analogically. Univocally, if the same term and meaning is
used in exactly the same sense, as when *animal* is predicated of a man and a
donkey, for to both the definition of animal applies, namely sensitive animate
substance. Equivocally, if the term is the same but the meaning and definition
different, as when *dog* is used of an animal and a star. Analogically, if various
objects, though diverse by meaning and definition, bear on some one common
meaning, as when health is ascribed to organic body and urine and drink,
but not with the same force, for in the first case the subject is given, in the
second the symptom, in the third a cause. (Tho. Aq., *De Principiis Naturae ad
fratrem Silvestrum, TAPT*, p. 93)

Analogy proportionally compares God's insurmountable goodness
with our limited but real goodness, so that what we know of human
goodness is in some sense really correlated, though modestly and self-
critically, with what we know about God. Thus we can say with some
confidence, in recollecting the history of language about the divine
human encounter, that *God is good*, although God's goodness is not to
be finally constricted (univocally) in terms of our limited, culturally
shaped, class-oriented conceptions of goodness (Origen, *De Princip.*
II.5, *ANF* IV, pp. 278 ff.; Tho. Aq., *ST* I Q6, I, pp. 28 ff.). Analogy is
a most important intellectual tool in Christian teaching, yet is best
used modestly and self-critically.

This is how the best Christian teaching has carefully used language
about God—aware of the exceptional mystery of the subject matter
with which we are engaged, yet not willing prematurely to concede
the complete unknowability of that mystery, because we are talking
about a mystery that has become self-revealed. God has allowed the
divine activity to become known to humanity, freely permitting our
understanding, welcoming our reflection, investigation, and praise.
The Eastern Christian tradition has spoken of God as unknowable in
essence, but knowable in energies, that is, in the activities through
which God has become self-revealed (Gregory of Nyssa, *Ag. Eunomius*
I.19, 20, II.1 ff., III.3, 4, XI.1 ff., *NPNF* 2 V, pp. 57 ff., 101 ff., 143 ff.,

230 ff.). All attempts at discussion of God are dubious if God is completely unrevealed mystery and absolutely unknowable. Rather than taking that extreme position, Christian teaching has argued that God is reliably and sufficiently knowable, even if incomprehensible. God can be known at the points at which God has made the divine activity accessible to belief (John Chrysostom, *Concerning the Statues*, hom. XII.8 ff., *NPNF* 1 IX, pp. 421 ff.). God is *app*rehensible, not *com*prehensible.

Classic Christian theism has found it easier to say what God is not than what God is. Hence the way of negation, next to be discussed, is an easier way than the way of analogy. Neither of these ways reveals how God is perceived by God. That is impossible to state or articulate, since the only perceiver is God (Novatian, *Trin.* II, *ANF* V, p. 612). God transcends every definition of God. Though God is sufficiently revealed to the apostles in Christ, much remains as yet unrevealed: "No eye has seen, no ear has heard, no mind has conceived what God has prepared for those who love him" (1 Cor. 2:9, NIV; cf. Isa. 64:4). With all these caveats stated clearly, the Christian community proceeds nonetheless on the confident assumption that this Source and End of our being wishes to become known by us, has become intentionally revealed to us, and in fact is to some degree knowable by us by constrained analogies (Julian of Norwich, *Showings, CWS*, p. 175, 311 ff.; cf. Clement of Rome, *Corinthians* 39, *ANF* I, p. 15). "We know in part" (1 Cor. 13), that is, within the frail limitations of human perception, listening, intelligence, intuition, language, and egocentric willing. We see through a glass, even if darkly, and live in hope that a fuller disclosure awaits the end of history (Gregory Nyssa, *On Infants' Early Deaths*, *NPNF* 2 V, pp. 375 f.; cf. Origen, *De Princip.* I.6, *ANF* IV, pp. 260 ff.).

Clarifying What God Is Not: The Negative Way

Having cautioned of the limited uses of analogy, we are prepared now to set forth the two major, complementary ways that classical theism has found to attribute human, descriptive language to God: The first is by constantly saying no. "God is *not* . . . " Fill in the blank within anything finite, limited, dependent, caused, or created. This is the negative way (*via negativa*). This way seeks to form an appropriate idea of the greatness of God by removing from thought and language everything that would make God small or limited, or less just or wise than we know God to be. We know with certainty that there are some things that God clearly is *not*, such as air, earth, fire, and water, fireflies, comets, and buzzards (although God may at some time be metaphorically described as something like any of these). The negative way tries to trim from our language about God all those words that imply limitation and imperfection (Dionysius the Areopagite, *Myst. Theol.* II, III, pp. 194 ff.). "What manner of being God is not may be known by eliminating characteristics that cannot apply to him, such as composition, change, and so forth" (Tho. Aq., *ST* I Q3, *TAPT*, p. 67).

The second way, classically called the way of heightening or eminence (*via eminentiae*), proceeds positively by comparing God with that which is already known to be to some degree good or great, noble or just, and worthy of admiration. We learn to compare God with observed excellence and with whatever powers and virtues we regard as most valuable and great. The positive way of heightening of temporal excellence puts back into our language references to God that show that God is like the best we can envision, the eminent (highest) degree of the most perfect things we know (Dionysius the Areopagite, *Myst. Theol.* III, pp. 196, 197; Hollaz, *ETA*, pp. 190 ff.; Gerhard, *LT* III, p. 86).

The more simple, and probably more ancient, of these two ways is the negative way. Rooted in a long tradition influenced by Greek, Talmudic, and Islamic thought, the negative way patiently teaches what God is not. Philo, Dionysius, and Maimonides have been among the most influential exponents of the negative way, which has doggedly argued: "God is not like that." "God is more than that." "No, God is not this." In fact, God is not *anything* to which one can point objectively, for God is no object. In this way one *can* derive some reliable knowledge of God (if only by negation), in the sense that one can know what God is not (Dionysius, *Myst. Theol.* II, III, pp. 194–99).

Even on this narrow basis it is surprising the extent to which classic writers could speak of God. For if it is apparent that God is *not* anything finite, then one may speak rightly of God's *in*finity, ruling out from the reference to God anything that is limited, countable, and measurable. If one can know that God is not visible, then we can speak of God's *in*visibility, ruling out from the being of God anything capable of being seen or objectified. Insofar as God is not circumscribed by any particular space or restricted to the changing temporal order, it is possible to speak of God as *im*measurable and *im*mutable. These prefixes beginning with *in* or *im* or *un* (implying negation) therefore may help clarify many characteristics of the divine life: incomprehensible, incorporeal, immeasurable, immortal, immutable, infinite. All belong to the negative way, wherein we sing: "Immortal,

invisible, God only wise, in light inaccessible hid from our eyes"
(W. C. Smith, *Christian Worship: A Hymnal*, p. 159).

Though philosophies of God have spoken cautiously and impersonally by negation, the language of Scripture has dealt with these
same themes in a most intimate, personal way. Psalm 139 fittingly
declared the personally present transcendence of God exceeding all
our categories of understanding:

> O Lord, you have searched me, and you know me. You know when I sit
> and when I rise; you perceive my thoughts from afar. You discern my going
> out and my lying down; you are familiar with all my ways. Before a word is
> on my tongue you know it completely, O Lord. You hem me in behind and
> before; you have laid your hand upon me. Such knowledge is too wonderful
> for me, too lofty for me to attain. Where can I go from your Spirit? Where can
> I flee from your presence? (Ps. 139:1–7)

Here, as in the negative way, there is in God no finitude, no
temporal restriction, no limited locality. There are no limits to God's
knowledge of the world and humanity. There is no way to escape the
presence of the living God. God knows our human downsittings and
uprisings, actions and movements. God is acquainted with our habits,
ways, plans, despairs. If at times we may deceive our fellow creatures,
we cannot deceive this One. To speak rightly of God, we must first
rule out all conceptions that imply unself-imposed limitation. The
negative way attempts to do this in a disciplined and deliberate way.
It is a way of knowing what God is not, which becomes an important
avenue toward reliable knowledge of what God is (Novatian, *On Trin.*
IV–VIII, *ANF* V, pp. 614–17; Tho. Aq., *ST* I Q12, I, pp. 48 ff.).

The Way of Heightening: Attributions from Proximate Creaturely Perfections

Distinguished from the negative way of knowing God is a positive
way that posits (*poser*, to place, to postulate) divine excellence on the
basis of observation of human excellences. This way of thinking about
God, the way of heightening or eminence (*via eminentiae*), proceeds by
intensifying or raising human excellences to their absolute degree and
positing them of God. Note that we are not now referring to immanence (to indwell, from *in manere*), but to eminence as the height of
perceivable goodness.

The way of eminence beholds something knowably good and attributes it in fullest dimension or proportion to God (Tho. Aq., *ST* I Q5,
6, I, pp. 23 ff.). The argument begins by looking at limited creaturely

things, interpersonal relationships, ourselves and our societies. There we behold striking evidences of justice, goodness, beauty, and other recognizable excellences. By this means we come to speak of God as the fullest measure of the best that we know, even if known in an imperfect way. Whatever we find in this world of greatest excellence, even though not perfect, we take hold of and say God is like that except in the highest degree, to the dimension of perfection (Cyril of Jerusalem, *Catech. Lect.* VI.4–9, *NPNF* 2 VII, pp. 34, 35).

If one knows what it means to be treated unjustly, then implicitly one knows something about justice. Since it is better to be treated fairly than unfairly, justice is a desired excellence. The eminent way of reasoning would take the relative excellence of justice and posit its fullest expression in God, so that God becomes conceived as that One who is fair in the highest degree imaginable, that is, perfectly just (Anselm, *Monologium*, *BW*, XVI, pp. 64 ff.; Tho. Aq., *ST* II–IIae Q58, pp. 1434 ff.). One who speaks of God as completely just is at that moment thinking eminently, that is, positing the highest degree of perfection from that which is found less than perfect in this temporal sphere (Margery Kempe, *On Contemplation as Taught by Our Lord*, *CSK*, pp. 41–43, "On Perfect Love").

The Supremely Good Being: From Degrees of Being and Excellence

This positive way of reasoning by height (eminence) can be illustrated in the term *Supreme Good*, by picturing a scale of degrees of excellence:

DEGREES OF EXCELLENCE

> Better than the best we know
> The best we know
> Good
> Not so good
> Lacking good altogether

Degrees of excellence or goodness are recognizable in most human experience. All know that some things are not so good, some are fairly good, some are a little better, some are really and invariably good, and some are indescribably good, even beyond our imagination. If so, is it not possible (even necessary) to hypothesize that there is something better than the best we know? This is what the tradition has meant by the way of eminence, the attribution to God of the height of goods and perfections, analogous to what is in part known, but

beyond complete knowing (Tho. Aq., *ST* I Q12, I, pp. 48 ff.). Traditionally the term *perfections of God* has been reserved to those qualities
that intrinsically belong to the divine essence. Divine attributes are
qualities that our language attributes to God that seek to do proximate
justice to the divine perfections (Tho. Aq., *ST* I Q4, I, pp. 20 ff.).

Similarly, the point can be illustrated by the concept of "Supreme
Being." For one can imagine a scale of degrees of conscious participation in being:

DEGREES OF CONSCIOUS PARTICIPATION IN BEING

That which most completely *is* and is aware that it is, transcending
our capacity to understand how fully such a being could be
Human life, consciousness and freedom
Animal life, limited consciousness and movement
Plant life, vegetative growth and reproductive life
Lifeless, inorganic matter
That which never has been
That which never has been or can be

We begin at the bottom of the scale. Some things can be imagined
that never can be, and have never been. Others could have been but
were not. Some things participate in being at a very low level of
participative awareness. The capacity for plants to participate interac-
tively in being is greater than the capacity for rocks to participate in
being. Yet rocks are participants in being in an important sense,
inasmuch as they last much longer than plants, even though without
life. Human intelligence is far more capable of self-consciously participating in being than is instinctual animal consciousness.

By analogy one may posit another reality at the apex of the scale:
One who insurmountably *is* more than anything else thinkable and
more fully shares in being, grounds being, embraces all being; hence
One who more fully *is*, and is conscious of fully being, than any other
conceivable being. To posit that One who supremely *is*, by the way of
heightening or eminent thinking, is to reliably know, learn, and affirm
something about God, namely, that God supremely *is* (i.e., Supremely
Being, or the Supreme Being). For how is it reasonable to have a scale
of degrees of perfection without also positing the apex of that scale?
Leaving it blank does not solve this dilemma. The scale itself requires
that it be completed, with null at one end and infinity at the other
end, with nonbeing at one end and supreme being at another end;
otherwise the scale itself is defective and incomplete (Tho. Aq., *ST* I
Q4, 5, 12, I, pp. 20 ff., 48 ff.).

This is an appropriate point at which to note that, rightly under-stood, the word *being* (cognate with the direct name "I AM") is a more intensive word than the flatter word *existence* (even in English, but more so in its Latin and Greek roots). Existence, as its root meaning (*existere*) suggests, includes an *ex*, a standing-out, a coming out of being into definite manifestations. Existence requires a "stand-ing" (*sistere*) "out from" (*ex*) being. The English language has to stretch in order to say that being in this sense may be thought of as the ground of existing, but the Greek and Latin terms that were familiar to the early church teachers made this point more transparent. For one cannot exist (stand out) without something to stand upon (being), just as one cannot subsist (stand firm, from *sub* + *sistere*) without having something (being, *esse*) to support one's subsistence.

This is a technical point that some will find tedious, but it lies quietly embedded in our daily use of the words *be* and *exist*. Even in modern nuances, *existing* seems a less full term than *being*, and "merely to exist" less weighty than "to be." One would never render Shake-speare's "To be or not to be" by saying, "To exist or not to exist." In English we freely use both terms (*being* and *existence*) interchangeably of God, for it is no less fitting to say that God exists than that God has being or simply is. God indeed participates in natural and histor-ical existence, but God *is* more fully, completely, awarely, and amply than any creature could be. Thus the term *existence* does not pertain to God in precisely the same way that it pertains to creatures. For God *is*—immeasurably, necessarily, and eternally—whereas creatures exist measurably, contingently, and temporally (Tho. Aq., *ST* I Q2, I, pp. 11 ff.; *SCG* I.13, pp. 85 ff.). Hebrew Scriptures did not use Greco-Latin terms like God's *essence* or *substance*, but they did speak often of God as Yahweh (the incomparable "I AM"), the One who insurmount-ably *is*.

In this chapter we have asked whether God can be defined, whether scriptural names for God are ways of talking about God's attributes, whether God's character can be ascertained and by what means, whether the character of God is known through God's own revelation of that character in the events to which Scripture witnesses, and whether analogy, negation, and heightening are reliable and self-constrained ways of knowing God. We have now come to an important turn in our discussion from *preparing* the way to speak to *speaking* of God's attributes.

The Sequence of Attributes

How shall the characteristics of the divine life be properly ordered into a whole mosaic that brings them fittingly together, or into a sequential argument that moves easily from one point or level to another?

The most satisfactory classification distinguishes *primary, relational, interpersonal,* and *moral* attributes—namely (*a*) those attributes that belong to God's essence apart from God's creative work; (*b*) those that arise necessarily out of the relation of God with the created order; (*c*) those that arise out of personal and interpersonal analogies, inasmuch as the revelation of God is personal, and human beings, the recipients of revelation, are persons; and (*d*) those that arise necessarily out of the relation of personal beings capable of goodness and moral activity.

These four levels may be distinguished as follows:

a. The primary or essential attributes (sometimes called absolute, incommunicable, quiescent, or prerelational) are intrinsic to God prior to any possible connection or relation with creatures.
b. The relational attributes (sometimes called relative, communicable, operative, or postrelational) are also intrinsic to God, but can only be conceived in relation with time and space and creation.
c. The interpersonal and personal attributes are also intrinsic to God, but can be conceived only by analogies from personal existence and from interpersonal excellences.
d. The moral attributes (sometimes technically called axiological, areteological, or teleological), like all attributes, are intrinsic to God, but these may be conceived only in the moral sphere of a relationship between responsible and free beings.

These four levels will be set forth in the next two chapters (primary and relational in Chapter 2, and personal and moral in Chapter 3).

Some arrangement or organization is required. It is not aesthetically, psychologically, or logically satisfactory merely to list the attributes alphabetically or arbitrarily. Scripture itself does not provide a specific or definitive order, although it does provide terms that tend to fall into a certain sequence that reason can reflect upon, aesthetically arrange, and logically place in order symmetrically. The sequence that will follow is derived not from any single classic Christian exegete but from many in combination, which we seek to harmonize. Most important are the discussions of divine attributes by Novatian, Cyril of Jerusalem, Hilary of Poitiers, Gregory Nazianzen, Augustine, and John of Damascus. Their exegesis helps provide a way of looking synoptically at the characteristics of the divine life.

This organization of terms provides key building blocks for a preliminary clarification of the meaning of the biblical name Yahweh 'Elōhīm, or the Lord God, to whom Christian worship is addressed. This classification seeks to be consistent with scriptural priorities and church tradition, rational in its conception and sequence, meaningful to experience, and aesthetically appropriate to a sense of rational design:

ATTRIBUTES OF GOD

I: THE NATURE OF GOD (Chapter 2):

THE DIVINE SUFFICIENCY: Primary and Essential Attributes Inapplicable to Creatures and Not Communicable to Creatures
> The Uncreated One (Aseity, Independence, Necessity)
> The Unity of God (Oneness and Simplicity)
> The Infinity of God (in relation to space, Immensity; in relation to time, Eternality)
> The Living God (Incomparable Aliveness, "I Am-ness")

THE DIVINE MAJESTY: Relational Attributes Displaying God's Way of Being Present, Knowing and Influencing the World
> God's Way of Being Present (Omnipresence)
> God's Way of Knowing (Omniscience, Prescience, Foreknowledge, Wisdom)
> God's Way of Influencing (Almighty Omnipotence, All-Powerful and All-Empowering)

II: THE CHARACTER OF GOD (Chapter 3):

THE DIVINE THOU: Active and Interpersonal Attributes Belonging to the Divine-Human Relationship and Analogous to Personal Experience
> God as Incomparably Personal (the Divine Selfhood; Personal Agency; All-Experiencing One; Congruent in Feeling, Sensibility, Emotivity, Affection)
> The Spiritual Nature of God (Spirituality, Invisibility)
> The Freedom of God (Radically Free, Choosing, Electing Will; Interpersonally Interactive, All-Encountering One)

THE DIVINE GOODNESS: Moral Qualities Intrinsic to the Divine
Character

> The Holiness of God (Moral Purity: Holiness, Righteousness, Justice)
> The Goodness of God (Benevolence and Integrity: Congruence,
>   Veracity, Faithfulness, Persistence)
> The Compassion of God (Love: Grace, Mercy, Forbearance)
> Conclusion: *The Blessedness of God*

Other ways of organizing the sequence of attributes have been
proposed and are available, but most ancient ecumenical Christian
teachers have reasoned in a way that is generally consistent with this
arrangement. Some have preferred to organize all divine attributes
into two categories: quiescent and operative (i.e., prior to divine action
and through divine action); or essence and energies; or incommunicable attributes (unique qualities for which no counterpart can be
found in humans, thus qualities unable to be communicated to creatures, or without analogies in creatures) as distinguished from communicable attributes (qualities of God for which at least a partial
counterpart can be found in human experience, divine qualities that
are in some limited ways similar to the qualities of creatures). Some
schemes propose to divide the divine attributes into attributes of God
as God is *in se* (in Himself), as distinguished from God as God is in
relation to the world. Yet these distinctions correspond to a large
degree with our proposed organization.

No conceptualization, however careful, can be adequate to its Subject. For even if God is revealed, yet God may have characteristics that
remain unknown to us. But though our knowledge of God's attributes
is admittedly incomplete, that does not dislodge the confidence of
Christian teaching that the revelation of God in Scripture is sufficient
for salvation. Furthermore, if we accept the hypothesis that perfect
Being must be internally congruent and self-consistent, then the worshiping community can affirm that whatever characteristics God has
that remain *unknown* nevertheless must be in harmony with what God
has made *known* and accessible through the history of revelation, the
historical experience of the believing community, and rational reflection.

CHAPTER 2

The Nature of God

The groundwork has now been laid for setting forth and amplifying the first of four parts on the characteristics of the divine life: God is uncreated, necessary, one, infinite, immense, eternal being, the life of all that lives.

These terms are called primary or essential attributes. Later we will speak of how God brings the world into being and enters into a relation with the world. It is this independent One who deals intimately with creation, this infinite One who sponsors and nurtures finitude at every level, this immense One who cares about the whole cosmos and the smallest sparrow, this eternal One who gives and sustains time and temporal flow.

At this stage, however, we are reflecting at a more basic level upon what might be knowable about the primordial nature of God that preconditions any activity in or relationship with the world. If God minus the world is still God, then we must ask, with the aid of the classical Christian exegetes, what God might conceivably be, or what characteristics might God be said to have primordially, presumptively antecedent to the positing of the world and time.

Hypothetically speaking, God does not need a world to be God, at least not a particular world. But, as the ancient ecumenical exegetes well knew, to imagine God as prior to creation is exceptionally difficult for minds that are themselves the products of creation (Novatian, *On Trin.* III, *ANF* V, pp. 613, 614; Augustine, *Conf.* VII.17, *LCC* VII, pp. 151, 152). To think of God as logically antecedent to time is mind-boggling to us who think only within the confines of time and space (Augustine, *Conf.* XI.11–13, *LCC* VII, pp. 252 ff.). The attributes or qualities that inhere in such a hypothesized pre-relational, pre-time, pre-space, pre-world being are sometimes called attributes of absolute essence, or primary attributes of God inapplicable to creatures. They have sometimes been called incommunicable attributes, in the sense that they cannot be ascribed to creatures or bestowed upon or shared with creatures, for no creature is or can become uncreated or utterly self-sufficient (Gregory Nazianzen, *First Theol. Or.*, *NPNF* 2 VII, pp. 284 ff.; cf. Calvin, *Inst.* 1.10 ff., 1.13 ff.; Anglican Thirty-nine Articles, *CC*, pp. 266 ff.; Hollaz, *ETA*, p. 237; Watson, *TI* I, pp. 342 ff.). Accordingly, Christian Scriptures and tradition view God as independent of all other existences, that is, as uncreated, underived, one, infinite, eternal, self-sufficient, necessary being. We will take these points one at a time to show precisely how they are attested in Scripture, interpreted by tradition, organized by reason, and existentially related to the hungers of human experiencing.

THE DIVINE SUFFICIENCY

The Uncreated One

God Is Self-sufficient, Independent, Necessary, Underived Being

Scripture attests that God is the Uncreated One, the underived Source and End of all things (Ps. 90; Isa. 40:28; 1 Cor. 1:30). "Before me there was no god fashioned nor ever shall be after me. I am the LORD, I myself" (Isa. 43:10; cf. Calvin, *Inst.* 1.7). God is by definition self-sufficient, in the sense that this One cannot be dependent upon any other being, since all things have their beginning and end in this One (Augustine, *Conf.* II.5, XI.2, *LCC* VII, pp. 55 f., 245 ff.; *Trin.* I.6, *NPNF* 1 III, pp. 21 ff.; Anselm, *Monologium* V, VI, *BW*, pp. 45–47).

The most penetrating Hebraic name for God, "I AM" (Yahweh), suggests that God simply and incomparably *is*. If one should try to speak of some "cause of God," that would imply discarding God and ascribing deity to that prior cause (Novatian, *Trin.* III, *ANF* V, pp. 613, 614). Job is asked by Yahweh: "Where were you when I laid the earth's foundations?" (Job 38:4). This uncreated cause of all things is addressed personally, unlike the "other gods": "O Lord our God, other lords than thou have been our masters, but thee alone do we invoke by name" (Isa. 26:12, 13). To this independent, self-sufficient being "everything is possible" (Mark 10:27). Later, when theologians would speak of God as underived existence or as uncaused, they would reflect the intent of the prophetic affirmation "I am the first and I am the last, and there is no god but me" (Isa. 44:6; cf. Theophilus, *To Autolycus* I.1–5, *ANF* II, pp. 89 ff.; Tho. Aq., *ST* I Q5, I, pp. 25 ff.).

To affirm that God is independent or necessary means that God depends on no cause external to God. God's life is contingent upon nothing else. This is sometimes called aseity (from *a se*, of or from itself) or self-existence, or underived existence. To say that God is uncreated or self-existent (or self-subsistent) means simply that God is without origin, that God is the only ground of God's being, and that there is no cause prior to God (Tho. Aq., *ST* I Q7, 8, I, pp. 30 ff.). This insight arises necessarily out of the awareness that if any effects exist at all, then there must be causes, and consequently some reality must ultimately be uncaused, or have the cause in itself (i.e., such a being must exist in itself, requiring no antecedent cause).

This supreme being has not at some point in time *become* the Supreme Being, but simply *is*, and has never been otherwise. This underived being whose nature is to be, the Hebrews called Yahweh ("I am Who I am," Exod. 3:14) and Teutonic languages have called God. God has no cause external to God, and this is precisely what makes God God, and not something else (Hilary, *On Trin.* I.5, *NPNF* 2 IX, pp. 41 f.). Since God is uncaused, it is better not to speak of God as self-caused, which, ironically, might seem to imply that before God "willed" it, God did not exist. God does not come into being because God wills it. Rather, being is eternally necessary and essential to God's nature and essence, and God's willing is an expression of God's being (John of Damascus, *OF* I.9, *NPNF* 2 IX, p. 12; Tho. Aq., *ST* I Q19, I, pp. 103 ff.; Calvin, *Inst.* 3.20 ff.).

Some may object that this attribute by its very language shuts out creatures and points to a being who needs no one to "complete himself," and "nothing but himself" in order to be. In a subsequent discussion of creation we will seek to correct the impression left by some natural theology that God could have been happy and better blessed without creation, but here our intention is to establish the primordial independence of God that preconditions God's engagement with the world (Gregory Nazianzen, or. 30, *NPNF* 2 VII, pp. 310 ff.; Hilary, *On Trin.* II.2, II.6, *FC* 25, pp. 39 ff., 41 ff.). Essential attributes are those that are intrinsic to God apart from and, hypothetically, prior to any expression of God's energies in the created order (Gregory Nyssa, *To Eunomius* III.5 ff., *NPNF* 2 V, pp. 147 ff.). "Prior to" is used hypothetically, because time begins with creation; so *chronologically* there is no time prior to creation, but *logically* God is prior to and the ground of creation (Augustine, *Conf.* XIII.34 ff., *LCC*, VII, pp. 330 ff.).

The relations that God creates and enables are not necessary to God's being, for God alone created them. No relation in which the necessary being freely engages can place a final limit on God's own primordial being. The *blessedness* of the divine being, as celebrated by the psalmists, John, Paul, Augustine, and Bonaventure, both transcends and embraces all entanglements of history. God's freely chosen relationships do not fundamentally displace or frustrate this divine blessedness (Deut. 28:3 ff.; Ps. 119:12; Rom. 4:6, 9; 9:5; cf. Calvin, *Inst.* 2.8).

God's independence has no limit except whatever limit God chooses freely to permit, such as God's gracious choice to create and share being with other beings. God's underived existence is not conditioned by anything except that which God elects to provide and permit through a world in which other beings temporarily are empowered through God's unlimited power (Job 21:15; Ps. 91:1; Heb. 6:3; Rev. 21:22; Calvin, *Inst.* 1.17–18).

The Unity of God

One God

The Source and End of all things is One. "Hear, O Israel, the Lord is our God, one Lord" (Deut. 6:4). This reality—God, Yahweh, 'Elō-hīm, Theos—the central subject of all Jewish-Christian Scripture, is one, not sixteen (Catherine of Siena, *Prayers* 1 and 2, pp. 28–32). Any polytheistic conception is by definition inadequate (Arnobius, *Ag. the Heathen* III ff., *ANF* IV, pp. 464 ff.; cf. Tertullian, *Ag. Hermogenes* III, *ANF* III, p. 478). "Is there any God beside me?" (Isa. 44:8).

There is no pantheon. "I am God, there is no other" (Isa. 45:22). There are no gradations of divinity. God is the one and only incomparable divine being. Jesus affirmed the ancient way of Israel that maintained: "The Lord our God is the only Lord" (Mark 12:29). "Among the gods not one is like thee, O Lord, no deeds are like thine. . . . Thou alone art God" (Ps. 86:8, 10). "Among the gods" is not a tacit affirmation of polytheism, but a way of exposing the futility of faith in pagan deities. Similarly, Paul: "For us there is one God, the Father, from whom all being comes, towards whom we move" (1 Cor. 8:6). There is no other "god" to which God can be compared (Origen, *De Princip.* I.1, *ANF* IV, p. 243). There is nothing simpler than God, because God unifies all things (Augustine, *CG* XI.10, *NPNF* 1 II, p. 210; Anselm, *Monologium* XVII, pp. 66 ff.; Julian of Norwich, *SGL*, pp. 229 f., 264 f.; Wesley, "Unity of the Divine Being," *WJW* VII, pp. 264–73).

A statue, photograph, or graven image of God cannot rightly be made because God's being cannot be reduced to creaturely matter, even though God's being shows through creaturely beings (Second Council of Nicaea, session I, *NPNF*, 2 XIV, pp. 533–35). In the Old Testament there is a symbolic visualization of seraphim and cherubim in the holy of holies; however, they are not worshiped as God but only as pointing beyond themselves, an expression of the aura of God's presence, a reflection of the manifold glory of the one God (Basil, *Letters* 8, *NPNF* 2 VIII, p. 116; Calvin, *Inst.* 1.10.3; Quenstedt, *TDP* I, p. 286; John Pearson, *Expos. of the Creed* I).

With his usual precision, John of Damascus summarized the point: "If there are many Gods, how can one maintain that God is uncircumscribed? For where the one would be, the other could not be" (John of Damascus, *OF* I.5, *NPNF* 2 IX, p. 4; cf. Tho. Aq., *ST* I Q15, I, pp. 16 ff.). The reason there can only be one God was argued rightly by Irenaeus, who in his rejection of Marcion's view of two gods stated:

> For how can there be any other Fulness, or Principle, or Power, or God, above Him, since it is matter of necessity that God, the Plērōma (Fulness) of all these, should contain all things in His immensity, and should be contained by no one? But if there *is* anything beyond Him, He is not then the Plērōma of all, nor does He contain all. . . . Thus, by that very process of reasoning on which they depend for teaching that there is a certain Plērōma or God above the Creator of heaven and earth, anyone who chooses to employ it may maintain that there is another Plērōma above the Plērōma, above that again another, and above Bythus another ocean of Deity, while in like matter the same successions hold with respect to the sides; and thus, their doctrine flowing on into immensity, there will always be a necessity to conceive of other Plērōmata, and other Bythi, so as never at any time to stop, but always to continue seeking for others besides those already mentioned. (*Ag. Her.* II.1, *ANF* I, pp. 359, 360)

Indivisibly Simple

To assert that God is absolutely simple is to stand against the proposition that God could be divisible into parts (Ambrose, *On Chr. Faith* I.16, *NPNF* 2 X, p. 218; Augustine, *Trin.* V.5, *NPNF* 1 III, p. 20; Basil, *Letters* 234, *NPNF* 2 VIII, p. 274). Simplicity is the opposite of composition. Since God is one, not composed of parts, God is completely, not partially, present in all of God's activities (Clement of Alex., *Strom.* V.12, *ANF* II, p. 464; Hilary, *On Trin.* I.6, *NPNF* 2 IX, pp. 41 ff.; Tho. Aq., *ST* I Q3, I, pp. 14 ff.). The triune teaching, to be discussed later, strongly affirms the unity of God, for God is "not three gods," but Three-in-*One* (Gregory of Nyssa, *On "Not Three Gods," NPNF* 2 V, pp. 331–36), and indivisible, hence simple.

By analogy, the whole person is integrally present in any particular human action, although not so simply as God is present in any particular divine act. All attributes of this incomparable One are interfused and joined together in the one indivisible divine essence in a way that transcends partial human perception (Novatian, *On Trin.* I–III, *ANF* V, pp. 611–14).

The essence of anything is that which makes a thing what it is, that to which its definition points. The essence of God is simply to exist in the way that only God can exist (Athanasius, *Defense of Nicaea*, chaps. 22 f., *NPNF* 2 IV, pp. 164 ff.; Tho. Aq., *ST* I Q3, I, pp. 14 f.). In a sense, nothing is less complicated than this One, who simply *is*. There is no "has been" or "will be" for God, for whom all temporal events are simultaneously experienced. Whatever God has been, God is eternally. Whatever God can be, God is eternally (Augustine, *Conf.* VII.10 ff., *LCC* VII, pp. 146 ff.; *CG* VIII.6, XI.10, *NPNF* 1 II, pp. 148 f., 210 f.). And in whatever distinctions human imagination might apply to God, God remains *one* through and beyond such distinctions (Athanasius, *Ag. the Heathen* 38, 39, *NPNF* 2 IV, pp. 24, 25).

The Infinity of God

The infinite is that which has no end, no limit, no finite boundary, and thus cannot be measured or timed by any finite standard (Catherine of Siena, *Prayers* 12, pp. 99–105). The infinite cannot be reached by successive addition or exhausted by successive subtraction of finite numbers, parts, or qualities. It might seem correct to say that the infinite is unsurpassable in spatial extension (immensity) and temporal duration (eternity). That way of putting it, however, tends inadvertently to make infinity captive to time and space rather than that which transcends time and space (Gregory Nazianzen, *On Theophany* VII, *NPNF* 2 VII, p. 347).

All of God's excellences are said to be without end or limit (Hilary, *On Trin.* II.6, *NPNF* 2 IX, pp. 53 f.). Hence infinity is a quality that applies to every divine attribute, for God is infinitely merciful, infinitely holy, infinitely just (Calvin, *Inst.* 1.13).

Although *infinite* at first appears to be a negative word, merely negating the finite, it carries positive religious meaning for supplicants. Whereas true worshipers acknowledge their human, natural, and historical limitations in time and space, their petitions implicitly point beyond all times and spaces toward that unsurpassable One who transcends and embraces all times and spaces (Gregory Nazianzen, or. XLV.3, *NPNF* 2 VII, pp. 423, 424; Anselm, *Monologium* XV ff., pp. 61 ff.; Teresa of Avila, *Life* XXXIX, *CWST* I, pp. 179–290).

Infinity, rightly conceived, belongs only to God. By definition it cannot be applied to any finite creature, even though creatures may participate in and refract the infinity of God. The notions of "infinite space" and "infinite time," however, tend to be self-contradictory and confusing, because space and time, being finite, cannot be extended infinitely. It is only when infinity is attributed to God that the concept has precise, plausible, and consistent meaning (John of Damascus, *OF* I.13, *NPNF* 2 IX, p. 15). Yet if God is infinitely beyond our thoughts, how can the believer think about God? Hilary said that one who reverently pursues the infinite, even though he or she may never attain it, will yet advance by pressing on (Hilary, *On Trin.* II.10, *NPNF* 2 IX, p. 55; cf. Tho. Aq., *On Trin.* II.1.7, *TAPT*, p. 267).

Immeasurability

The divine immensity is the divine infinity regarded from the point of view of space. "Great is the Lord, and greatly to be praised; and of His greatness there is no end" (Ps. 145:3; Tho. Aq., *SCG* I.43, I, p. 169). The medieval Scholastics said that "God's center is everywhere, God's circumference nowhere" (cf. Bonaventure, *Soul's Journey into God* II, *CWS*, pp. 69 ff.). The attribute of the divine immensity suggests that God transcends all spatial relations, while remaining their cause and ground (Hermas, *The Pastor* II.1; Irenaeus, *Ag. Her.* IV.20; Tertullian, *Ag. Praxeas* XVI, *ANF* III, pp. 611, 612). Thus the thought of the divine immensity incorporates both the transcendence and immanence of God. Having built the temple, Solomon rightly prayed: "But can God indeed dwell on earth? Heaven itself, the highest heaven, cannot contain thee; how much less this house that I have built" (1 Kings 8:27).

This attribute is not attested by reason alone, but by Scripture. How is human imagination and reason to measure God? After Job had inquired of God, being unable to fathom the divine purpose, God then inquired of Job: "Have you comprehended the vast expanse of the world? Come, tell me all this, if you know" (Job 38:18). "Can you bind the cluster of the Pleiades or loose Orion's belt?" (Job 38:31). "Tell me, if you know and understand" how the earth's foundations were laid. "Who settled its dimensions? Surely you should know. Who stretched his measuring-line over it?" (Job 38:4, 5). Human imagination stands in numbed silence in the presence of the Measurer of all our measurements (Julian of Norwich, *Showings, CWS*, pp. 232–35).

Space is transcended by the infinite God, making terms like *beyond* or *transcended* inexact and usable only in a metaphorical sense. God is both infinitely near and infinitely far, yet in speaking in this way we do not imply that God is finitely localized, but rather the cause and ground of all locales (Hilary, *On Trin.* I.1, *NPNF* 2 IX, pp. 40 ff.) "For where can any of us flee to, from His mighty hand; or what sort of world will receive one who is a fugitive from him. . . . Where then is there for a man to go, or where can he elude One whose grasp is all-encompassing?" (Clement of Rome, Letter to the Corinthians, *ECW*, p. 38).

The objection is sometimes lodged that if there were an infinite being, then no other being could exist, since that being would take up all available space. The logical deficit in that argument is that the feature of impenetrability is inadvertently substituted for infinity, whereas the infinity of God does not imply impenetrability. For only God can, while transcending space and time, enter spatial and temporal creatures without dislodging them, while still being omnipresent invisibly and spiritually in every place and time (John 19:20–31; cf. John Chrysostom, *Hom. on John* LXXXVII, *NPNF* 1 XIV, pp. 327–31).

As time cannot encompass eternity, so the totality of space cannot encompass the divine immensity. God is not containable or measurable by even our most extensive or intensive categories of measurement (John of Damascus, *OF* I.13, *NPNF* 2 IX, p. 15). As an autobiographical note, the specific moment when I remember being stunned by the paradox of the infinite in relation to space was while sleeping out under the stars one summer night as a twelve-year-old. I was struck by this dilemma, which I clearly grasped even if I could not articulate it well at that age: I saw all that space above. "But what is beyond that space?" I asked myself. Suppose space ends somewhere. If so, what could be "beyond" it? Or suppose space does not end. How could that be?—it seemed even less plausible. It was not until decades later in reflecting upon the immensity of God that the answer became clear in an equally stunning way: Space does not go on endlessly. However great, space is finite. Space is transcended by the infinite, not finite, immensity. It is merely a fragile linguistic metaphor to speak of God as "beyond" space or "outlasting" time. For in each case one is using either a spatial metaphor to speak of that which undergirds and therefore transcends space, or a temporal metaphor to speak of that which creates and transcends time (cf. Tho. Aq., *The Infinity of God, ST* I Q7, I, pp. 30 ff.).

Immense in its Latin root is "unmeasured" (*im-mensus*, not to measure), suggesting to classic Christian teachers boundlessness or unfathomability, beyond bounding or fathoming. God is so boundless that our very word *immensity* remains a weak and inexact way of pointing to the relation of God and space. It is only of God that one can rightly speak of infinite immensity (Tho. Aq., *ST* I Q7, I, pp. 30, 31), for only God is neither measured nor measurable by spatial measures, nor enclosed by space.

By this means we are walking on a negative path (*via negativa*) toward knowledge of God, where limitations and imperfections are, one by one, removed from the character of God by affirming that God is clearly *not* any of those things that can be measured. Every creaturely being can be measured—even galaxies, if we had a big enough measuring device (Ambrose, *Of the Chr. Faith* II.8 (59–73), *NPNF* 2 X, pp. 231, 232; Wesley, *WJW* VI, pp. 316 ff.).

The attributes of infinity, immensity, eternity, and omnipresence are closely intertwined. For *immensity* is infinity regarded from the viewpoint of space, whereas *eternity* is infinity regarded from the viewpoint of time. God's infinity is eternal in relation to time and immeasurable in relation to space. *Omnipresence* is God's mode of being present to all ranges of both space and time. Although God is present in all time and space, God is not locally limited to any particular time or space. God is everywhere and in every now (Calvin, *Inst.* 1.13.1, 21; Quenstedt, *TDP* I, p. 288).

At first glance it may seem that talk of the divine immensity is far removed from Christian worship and the practice of prayer, yet rightly viewed this divine perfection powerfully lifts human thoughts toward a necessary being above all creaturely measurement (Teresa of Avila, *Way of Perfection* XIX, *CWST*, I, pp. 76 ff.). Its complementary attribute, omnipresence, speaks reassuringly of the presence of this exalted being throughout all space as intimately available to every supplicant. The thought of a being who is everywhere present is awesome, but even more awesome is the thought that this exalted One above all space and time has condescended to become human—a man born of woman—share our time and space, and reach out in redemptive love to the world (Novatian, *Trin.* II, *ANF* V, pp. 612 ff.).

Eternity

That which is eternal is without beginning, without ending, and with respect to divine purpose, without change. According to Clement of Alexandria, God who is without beginning, produces beginning (*Strom.* V.14, *ANF* II, p. 476). Boethius provided the key definition of the divine eternity for medieval Scholasticism: "simultaneous and perfect possession of interminable life" (*Consolation of Phil.*, V, 6; cf. Augustine, *True Religion*, chap. 40). The cause of time is the eternal God. For God, all time is now (Tho. Aq., *ST* I Q10, I, pp. 40 ff.; Watson, *TI* I, pp. 353 ff.; Kierkegaard, *Phil. Frag.* II). "With the Lord one day is like a thousand years and a thousand years like one day" (2 Pet. 3:8; cf. Ps. 90:4).

Only God does not grow older with time (Julian of Norwich, *Showings*, *CWS*, chaps. 54–58, pp. 282–95). For us who are time-bound, it is difficult to imagine that all time is present to this divine consciousness. God is the indefatigable one who outlasts every time. "Thou art the same and thy years have no end" (Ps. 102:27; cf. Isa. 40:28, Rev. 1:4). "The guardian of Israel never slumbers, never sleeps" (Ps. 121:4). " 'I am the Alpha and the Omega' says the Lord God, who is and who was and who is to come, the sovereign Lord of all" (Rev. 1:8N; cf. Rev. 4:8). The eternity of God is a recurrent theme of the Pentateuch: "The eternal God is thy refuge, and underneath are the everlasting arms" (Deut. 33:27, KVJ; cf. Athenagoras, *A Plea for Chr.*, chap. 31, *ANF* II, p. 146).

God had no beginning, for who would be there to begin God? "From age to age everlasting thou art God" (Ps. 90:2). If God were a temporal being, God would have to have had a beginning. God utterly transcends time. Abraham at Beersheba "invoked the Lord, the everlasting God, by name" (Gen. 21:33). "The Lord, the everlasting God, creator of the wide world, grows neither weary nor faint" (Isa. 40:28). Later, the moving benediction of Jude would reaffirm this view that God is before all time: "Now to the One who can keep you from falling and set you in the presence of his glory, jubilant and above reproach, to the only God our Saviour, be glory and majesty, might and authority, through Jesus Christ our Lord, before all time, now, and for evermore. Amen" (Jude 25).

The faithful share eternal life, but not in the same unbeginning sense that God lives eternally, for they were not always sharing in eternal life, but only when they believed and entered into life "in Christ." The eternal I AM is before and after every space and time (Catherine of Siena, *Prayers*, 15, pp. 127–36). God is the incomparable One present in every time, yet the eternity of God is not an indefinite extension of temporal duration. Eternity is an attribute intrinsic to God and to God alone.

Time is the valued gift of the eternal one who "made the ages" (Heb. 1:2, KJV). All moments of time's succession unfold in eternal simultaneity in the presence of the maker of time. God enjoys two relations to time: (1) as giver of time, the divine essence is in itself absolutely independent of time permitting time as wholly contingent upon the divine will; yet (2) this same eternal One chooses also to create the temporal world and to enter into relationships with creatures, freely wills to participate in time, and orders and guides the temporal process, not as if it were necessary to God's essential being, but as contingent upon the divine giving (Cyril of Jerusalem, *Catech. Lect.* IV.5, *NPNF* 2 VII, p. 20; Gregory of Nyssa, *Ag. Eunomius* VIII.1, *NPNF* 2 V, pp. 200–2; Wesley, *On Eternity, WJW* VI, pp. 189 ff.).

Strictly speaking, there can be no time prior to time. Those who are time-bound in every moment of consciousness may tend understandably to think of eternity as infinite duration or infinite time, an inexact and confusing idea. Since human reason and experience are so saturated with the assumption of time, it is difficult for us to fathom this mystery. We search to understand the eternal God by fragile analogies: Eternity is like a circle that continues endlessly in the same line, yet its circumference can be divided and measured. It is as if God were on a mountain watching a river. Humans see the flow of this river only from a particular point on the bank, but God, as if from high above, sees the river in its whole extent, at every point, simultaneously (Hilary, *On Trin.* XII.39 ff., *NPNF* 2 IX, pp. 227 ff.; Calvin, *Inst.* 2.8.13; 2.10.15–18).

The decisive Christian analogy concerning time is that between the eternal indwelling in time and the incarnation. Brilliantly, the classical exegetes taught that the creation of time is analogous to the incarnation in this way: The Father inhabits time, just as the Son inhabits human flesh (Hilary, *On Trin.* III, *NPNF* 2 IX, pp. 62 ff.; Nemesius, *On Nature of Man* III, *LCC*). As in creation God is manifested in time, so in the incarnation God is manifested bodily in the flesh. Just as the Son does not cease to be God while becoming and being human— feeling, experiencing, and acting as a human being—so does the Father not cease to be God while entering time—while feeling, experiencing, and acting as God in and through the conditions of time (Augustine, *On Trin.* XIV, *NPNF* 1 III, pp. 182–98; cf. *Letters* 143.7; Tho. Aq., *ST* I Q10, I, pp. 40 ff.).

If, as we shall later seek to establish, the eternal One is also infinitely blessed and wise, then we may also add one remarkable observation to the celebration of God's eternality: There can be no desire to cease to be in One who is insurmountably blessed and wise. God could never end his own life, because that would be inconsistent with God's blessed enjoyment of life. To God, merely to be is a source of infinite enjoyment. God would not do less than *be* in full plenitude. That being is eternal, and the joy that comes from being is eternal joy. Thus it is said that God is infinitely happy simply and eternally to *be* (Tho. Aq., *ST* I Q26, I, pp. 142 ff.).

God has set eternity in the heart of humanity, yet within bounds, for there is "no comprehension of God's work from beginning to end" (Eccles. 3:1). To every person belongs a sense of time, with hints and indications of eternity written into one's human constitution, yet the time-bound intellect and imagination is incapable of fully grasping the will of the eternal One (Maria de Agreda, *The Myst. City of God, SSM,* p. 170). We glimpse the eternal only in part and await the end of history in which the purposes of the eternal One will be made fully clear: "Now we see only puzzling reflections in a mirror, but then"—that is, when the divine purpose is finally revealed at the end of history—"we shall see face to face. My knowledge now is partial; then it will be whole, like God's knowledge of me" (1 Cor. 13:12, 13).

The Living God

The living God (*chai 'elōhīm, theo zōntos*) is the Subject of holy Scripture (1 Sam. 17:26; Ps. 42:2; Matt. 16:16; 1 Thess. 1:9; Heb. 12:22; Rev. 7:2). God's unutterable aliveness is contrasted sarcastically by the prophets with the immobility and impotence of "the gods." Jeremiah spoke of God (*'Elōhīm*), in contrast to humanly fashioned idols, as "God in truth, a living [*chai*] God" (Jer. 10:10). Idols do not live, except in the imagination of death-bound mortals (Ps. 115:3–9). "The gods who did not make heaven and earth shall perish from the earth" (Jer. 10:11). In response to the incomparable aliveness of God, the psalmist exclaimed: "My whole being cries out with joy to the living God" (Ps. 84:2). Hence classical Christian exegetes sought to clarify the incomparable sense in which it is said that God is alive and that God lives (Irenaeus, *Ag. Her.* III.6, *ANF* I, pp. 418–20; Clementina, hom. XVI, *ANF* VIII, pp. 312 ff.; Cyril of Jerusalem, *Catech. Lect.* XVIII.29, *NPNF* 2 VII, p. 141).

The life of God is the eternal, underived energy of his being, ever-active within God himself, enabling movement and change in creation. Life is that which differentiates a plant, animal, or human being from something that is dead—inorganic, nonliving matter (Tho. Aq., *ST* I Q18, I, pp. 99 ff.). God's being is intrinsically characterized by life, by being alive (Gregory of Nyssa, *Ag. Eunomius* VIII.5, *NPNF* 2 V, p. 210; Tho. Aq., *ST* I Q18, I, pp. 100 ff.). It cannot be properly conceived that God could die, because life is intrinsic to God, an attribute of the divine essence. Even when we despair of life (Job 9:21; 2 Cor. 1:8), God continues to give us life (Kierkegaard, *Sickness unto Death*).

It is God's very nature to be alive, so much so that God is properly known as the life of all that lives (John Chrysostom, *Hom. on John* XLVII, *NPNF* 1 XIV, pp. 248–50; Calvin, *Inst.* 2.3.20; Quenstedt, *TDP* I, 289; Watson, *TI* I, p. 350). John's Gospel proclaimed that God the Father "has life-giving power in himself" (John 5:26; Novatian, *Treatise Concerning the Trin.* XIV, *ANF* V, p. 623). God's way of living is dissimilar, yet not completely dissimilar, to that of other forms of life. Plants, animals, and humans enjoy life at different scales of consciousness, movement, and self-determination. But in all plants, animals, and humans, bodily life ends in death. From the moment of conception, the processes of decay and death are at work in our bodies. Not so in God's life. God's life is eternal life. God's life is not only without end but without beginning. For before anything was alive, God was alive (Gen. 1:1 ff.). When this world is gone, God remains alive (Luke 1:33; Heb. 7:3; John Chrysostom, *Hom. on Hebrews* XII, *NPNF* 1 XIV, pp. 324–426).

The lives of plants, animals, and humans depend radically upon God, but the life of God does not depend upon something external to God's life. "It is not because he lacks anything that he accepts service at man's hands," Paul preached, "for he is himself the universal giver of life and breath and all else" (Acts 17:25, 26; cf. Wesley, *WJW* VII, pp. 320 ff.). That which is alive has soul, or aliveness, animation. Insofar as creatures are alive, they share in the life of God (Augustine, *Conf.* X.5 ff., *LCC* VII, pp. 205 ff.; cf. Tertullian, *On the Soul*, *ANF* III, pp. 181 ff.; Wesley, *WJW* V, p. 232).

The faithful know themselves to be alive, but God is known to be more alive than any imaginable living being. God has no trace of decay or death at work in himself. It is to the living God that faith prays, present amid the people in radical, unceasing spontaneity and limitless energy. The language of Exodus at Mount Horeb at the moment that God's name is revealed as Yahweh suggests the sense of dynamism and intensity surrounding this reality: "I am that which I am," or "I am that I am." This tetragrammaton (YHWH) points awesomely to God's incomparable aliveness (Origen, *De Princip.* I.3, p. 253). Not only is God living, but also the source of our life—active and tireless (Isa. 40:28; Ps. 121:4). God is unfailingly alert and aware, as distinguished from "the gods," who, without life, are without consciousness or power (Hilary, *On Trin.* VIII.43 ff., *NPNF* 2 IX, pp. 150 ff.).

The Living God Is Eternally Active

God's way of being alive is activity (*melā'kāh, energeia,* through energies, operations, workings). History, according to the Hebraic view, is the story of the acts of God (Deut. 11:7; 1 Sam. 12:7; Ps. 150:2). God is active from the beginning to the end of time, from every here to every there of space, from every now to every then, in every person and society. It is an active, engaged God that is portrayed in Scripture, not quiescent, not merely letting creation be or leaving men and women to their own devices (Irenaeus, *Ag. Her.* III.5 ff., *ANF* I, pp. 418 ff.; Augustine, *CG* V.11, *NPNF* 1 II, p. 93; Calvin, *Inst.* 2.3.10; Quenstedt, *TDP* I, p. 289; Watson, *TI* I, p. 350). The essence of God is known only through God's energies and activities (Gregory of Nyssa, *Ag. Eunomius* I.18, *NPNF* 2 V, pp. 55 ff.).

God's way of acting remains consistent with everything else we know of God. God acts justly, wisely, benevolently, with full knowledge of all creation, throughout all levels of natural causality, with full power to do the divine will, yet unafraid of empowering others and quite willing to allow companionate willing creatures. The multiplicity, variety, and prodigious variability of God's actions suggest that God is *purus actus,* pure actuality, which means that the God who most *is* is eternally active, that God's willing is eternally operative, and that God's power is never static or latent but always completely present and active. Contrary to Aristotle's passive God, Yahweh is always working, ever doing, eternally in motion, never immobilized, never stalemated, never depressed (Isa. 40:1 ff.; Jer. 27:1 ff.; cf. Tho. Aq., *ST* I Q3.1, 2, I, pp. 14 ff.; *SCG* I.13, pp. 96 ff.; Luther, *Comm. on Galatians, ML,* pp. 126–31; cf. Hartshorne and Reese, *PSG,* pp. 335–410).

THE DIVINE MAJESTY

Relational Attributes Displaying God's Presence, Knowledge, and Power in the World

Thus far we have been considering only those aspects of the divine life that exist without reference to creatures, namely, that God is uncreated, necessary, independent, sufficient, One, infinite, immeasurable, eternal, and alive—all qualities that are logically prior to acts of creating and sustaining. They are ordinarily grouped together as primary or essential attributes.

Now we turn to those qualities intrinsic to God that display God's way of being present to, knowing, and influencing the world of creatures. Since these characteristics all presuppose a creation and a world of creatures, they are called relational attributes, inasmuch as they cannot be conceived apart from God's relation to creation. For how could God be conceived to be omnipresent without a world to which to be present, or omnipotent without a world through which the divine influence is everywhere felt?

Note the difference, for it is useful in understanding how classical Christian exegetes distinguished and organized language referring to God: The primary or *essential* qualities of the divine being are intrinsic to God alone, without reference to creatures. The *relational* qualities of the divine outreaching are intrinsic to God's distinctive way of relating to the world of creaturely beings.

No being relates to the world as God does. The unique ways God relates to the world are called relational attributes (Quenstedt, *LT* I.289; Watson, *TI* I, pp. 365 ff.), wherein God is accommodating to creatures' limits and capacities (Hilary, *On Trin.* IV.17 ff., VI.16 ff., VIII.43 ff., *NPNF* 2 IX, pp. 76 ff., 103 ff., 150 ff.; Heppe, *RD*, pp. 57 ff.; Schmid, *DT*, pp. 177 ff.). Under "relational attributes" we will consider three that are closely interrelated: God's ubiquitous presence in the world (omnipresence); God's complete knowledge of the world and time (omniscience); and God's almighty power (omnipotence).

God's Way of Being Near: Omnipresence

Paul preached that God is "not far from each one of us, for in him we live and move, in him we exist" (Acts 17:28). That the holy God is present in all things is repeatedly affirmed in Scripture. " 'Am I a God nearby,' declares the Lord, 'and not a God far away? Can anyone hide in secret places so that I cannot see him?' declares the Lord. 'Do I not fill heaven and earth?' declares the Lord" (Jer. 23:24, NIV).

No atomic particle is so small that God is not fully present to it, and no galaxy so vast that God does not circumscribe it. No space is without the divine presence. God is in touch with every part of creation. God cannot be excluded from any location or object in creation (Augustine, *Greatness of the Soul* XXXIV, *ACW* 9, pp. 106, 107; *Second Helvetic Conf.* III, *HPC*, pp. 18, 19; Wesley, *The Omnipresence of God*, *WJW* VII, pp. 238 ff.).

The only alternative to affirming the divine omnipresence is to exclude God from some part of creation. To affirm that God is infinite in relation to space requires the notion of omnipresence. Every finite object exists in some place. Only God is able to *be* without being in some specific location to the exclusion of all others. We measure the size of finite things by how much space they occupy, but God does not fit into our categories of location. God's presence is not simply in one location, as is ours, but all locations (Cyril of Jerusalem, *Catech. Lect.* IV.5, *NPNF* 2 VII, p. 20). In the church we receive the memory of One who is the intimate companion of our existence but, at the same time, the intimate companion of all other existences, while transcending each and all (Athanasius, *Incarnation of the Word* I.8–10, *NPNF* 2 IV, pp. 40–41; Watson, *TI* I, pp. 365 ff.).

The Christian teaching of God's ever-present companionship is more than a cold, abstract idea without personal significance to worshipers. It is an intimate comfort to supplicants to know of and experience the divine availability (Teresa of Avila, *Interior Castle* I, *CWST* II, pp. 201–7). God is a very present help in time of need (Ps. 46:1; cf. Rom. 8:39). To affirm that God is high and lifted up above creaturely reality does not imply that God is distant or absent from creatures (Gregory Nazianzen, *Second Theol. Or.* XI–XXI, *NPNF* 2 VII, pp. 292–96; Calvin, *Inst.* 1.11.3). The holy One is precisely the One who is personally nearest: "Thus speaks the high and exalted one, whose name is holy, who lives for ever: I dwell in a high and holy place with him who is broken and humble in spirit, to revive the spirit of the humble, to revive the courage of the broken" (Isa. 57:15). But being near does not imply that God is absent from other locations (Jer. 23:23). "The Lord looks out from heaven, he sees the whole race of men; he surveys from his dwelling-place all the inhabitants of the earth. It is he who fashions the hearts of all men alike, who discerns all that they do" (Ps. 33:13, 14; cf. Tho. Aq., *ST* I Q8, I, pp. 34 ff.).

The *presence* of God was thought by classical exegetes to encompass the widest possible range of creaturely activity:

God is *naturally* present in every aspect of the natural order, every level of causality, every fleeting moment and momentous event of natural history (Ps. 8:3; Isa. 40:12; Nah. 1:3 ff.; Origen, *Ag. Celsus* VII.34, *ANF* IV, p. 624; Cyril of Jerusalem, *Catech. Lect.* IV.5, *NPNF* 2 VII, p. 20).

God is *actively* present in a different way in every event of history, as provident guide of human affairs (Ps. 48:7 f.; cf. Augustine, *CG* VII.30 ff., *NPNF* 1 II, pp. 140 ff.).

God is in a special way *attentively* present to those who call upon his name, intercede for others, who adore God, who petition, who pray earnestly for forgiveness (Matt. 18:19 f.; Acts 17:27; Cyprian, *Epistles* VII, *ANF* V, pp. 285, 286).

God is *judicially* present in moral awareness, through conscience (Ps. 48:1, 2; cf. Athanasius, *Ag. Heathen* XLI ff., *NPNF* 2 IV, pp. 26 ff.).

God is *bodily* present in the incarnation of his Son, Jesus Christ (John 1:14; Col. 2:9; cf. Hilary, *On Trin.* VIII.24 ff., *NPNF* 2 IX, pp. 144 ff.).

God is *mystically* present in the Eucharist, and through the means of grace in the church, the body of Christ (Eph. 2:12 ff.; John 6:56; cf. Ambrose, *On the Mysteries* V ff., *NPNF* 2 X, pp. 320 ff.).

God is *sacredly* present and becomes known in special places where God chooses to meet us, places that become set apart by the faithful, remembering community (1 Cor. 11:23–29), where it may be said: "Truly the Lord is in this place" (Gen. 28:16; cf. Gen. 23:18; Matt. 18:20; cf. Augustine, *CG* XXII.29, *NPNF* 1 II, pp. 507 ff.).

In all these ways God is present to the world, in both general and special ways that make this divine intimacy far more than an abstract speculation (Augustine, *Letters* 137.2, *NPNF* 1 I, pp. 473 ff.). Even though God is uniformly present in all creation, God's presence is not everywhere experienced in the same way. At times God is quietly present, at other times actively; at times hiddenly, at other times revealed.

God's Way of Knowing: Omniscience

Only God knows creation omnisciently, without limitation or qualification. The psalmist praised God's wisdom as "beyond all telling" (Ps. 147:5; cf. Ps. 94:9–11; Ps. 139) and God's understanding as immeasurable (Ps. 147:4 f.; Augustine, *On Psalms* CXLVII.1–10, *NPNF* 1 VIII, pp. 665–67). God's incomparable way of knowing knows the end of things even from the beginning: "I reveal the end from the beginning, from ancient times I reveal what is to be; I say, 'My purpose shall take effect, I will accomplish all that I please.' " (Isa. 46:9, 10; cf. Clement of Alex., *Strom.* VI.17, *ANF* II, p. 517).

Jesus taught his disciples: "Your Father knows what your needs are before you ask him" (Matt. 6:8). Paul exclaimed: "O depth of wealth, wisdom, and knowledge in God! How unsearchable his judgments, how untraceable his ways! Who knows the mind of the Lord? Who has been his counsellor?" (Rom. 11:33, 34). The New Testament constantly echoed the theme of the fully aware God found in the psalms and prophets: "There is nothing in creation that can hide from him; everything lies naked and exposed to the eyes of the One with whom we have to reckon" (Heb. 4:13; cf. Catherine of Genoa, *Spiritual Dialogue* II, *CWS*, pp. 115–17). God, who is greater than our self-condemning conscience, "knows all" (1 John 3:20; Augustine, *CG* V.9, *NPNF* 1 II, pp. 90 ff.; *Enchiridion* 104, *NPNF* 1 III, p. 271).

How can we get our sluggish intellects in touch with the awesome conception that God knows all? The divine omniscience is best viewed as the infinite consciousness of God in relation to all possible objects of knowledge. God knows past, present, and future (John of Damascus, *OF* II.10, *NPNF* 2 IX, p. 28). God knows external events and inward motivations (Hilary, *On Trin.* IX.29, 61 ff., *NPNF* 2 IX, pp. 164 ff., 176 ff.). God does not perceive fragmentarily as humans perceive, as if from a particular nexus of time, but knows exhaustively, in eternal simultaneity (Catherine of Siena, *Prayers* 7, pp. 58–61; cf. Irenaeus, *Ag. Her.* II.26 ff., *ANF* I, pp. 397 ff.). God's understanding is spoken of as an infinite understanding. God looks to the ends of the earth, sees the whole of the heavens (Isa. 46; Job 28), knows the secrets of the heart (Ps. 44:21). "Thou hast traced my journey and my resting places, and art familiar with all my paths. For there is not a word on my tongue but thou, Lord, knowest them all" (Ps. 139:3, 4). "Such knowledge is beyond my understanding, so high that I cannot reach it" (v. 6). "Darkness is no darkness for thee and night is luminous as day; to thee both dark and light are one" (v. 12).

Jesus' metaphor that the very hairs of our heads are numbered by the Father (Matt. 10:30) suggests that every discrete aspect of personal existence is known to God (cf. Justin Martyr, *First Apol.* chap. 12, *ANF* I, p. 166). No sparrow falls without God's recognition (Matt. 10:29; Kierkegaard, *Gospel of Suffering*). God searches the hearts of all (Rom. 8:27). We know some things, but God knows incomparably more, greater, and better (Ambrose, *To Gratian on Chr. Faith* V.6, *NPNF* 2 X, p. 294; Augustine, *On Trin.* XV.22, *LCC* VIII, pp. 151 ff.; *CG* XII.18 ff., *NPNF* 1 II, pp. 238 ff.; Tho. Aq., *ST* I Q14.13, I, pp. 74 ff.). "The eyes of the Lord are everywhere, surveying evil and good men alike" (Prov. 15:3), implying that God sees all simultaneously by looking in every direction at the same time. God knows objects as distanced from one another, but not from God, for there can be no distance of any object from God (Augustine, *CG* V.11, *NPNF* 1 II, p. 93).

The divine person does not merely have will, but a knowing will. The divine presence is not merely a dumb, flat, unknowing presence, but an incomparably intelligent presence. God's knowing is said to be (*a*) eternally actual, not merely possible; (*b*) eternally perfect, as distinguished from a knowledge that begins, increases, decreases, or ends; (*c*) complete instead of partial; and (*d*) both direct and immediate, instead of indirectly reflected or mediated (Tho. Aq., *SCG* I.63–71, pp. 209–38).

Pantheism claims the opposite, that the only awareness God has is that which creatures have. Pantheism has argued that God, being all things, is conscious only in and through the consciousness of finite creatures. Such knowing cannot be infinite knowing. This is why pantheism has been so often rejected by Christian teaching (Hippolytus, *Refutation of All Her.* I.21, *ANF* V, pp. 21, 22; Augustine, *Concerning Faith of Things Not Seen*, *NPNF* 1 III, pp. 337–43). For in seeking to affirm that God is in all things, it forgets or ignores that God is prior to, above, and beyond all things.

This incomparable mode of knowing is always being complemented and balanced by other divine qualities. For God does not know unmercifully, or as lacking in power, or unjustly (Novatian, *Trin.* II, III, *ANF* V, pp. 612–14; R. Owen, *Dogm. Theol.* IV.11; Wesley, *WJW* VII, pp. 265 ff.). The wisdom of God is God's incomparable ability to order all things in the light of good, to adjust causes to effects, and means to ends, so that the divine purposes are ensured and never finally thwarted. Divine knowledge grasps things as they are. Divine wisdom grasps fitting means to good ends (Prov. 2:2; Isa. 10:13; 1 Cor. 1:21; Calvin, *Inst.* 1.16 ff.).

Divine Foreknowledge

A special perplexity of the divine omniscience is the relation between human freedom of the will and divine foreknowing. God foreknows the use of free will, yet this foreknowledge does not determine events. Rather, what God foreknows is determined by what happens, part of which is affected by free will. God knows what will happen, but does not unilaterally determine each and every event immediately, so as not to respect human freedom and the reliability of secondary causes. God fully understands and knows all these specific secondary determining causes that are at work in the natural order, but that does not imply that merely by fiat God constantly acts so as to overrule or circumvent these causes. God's merely foreknowing these causes does not negate or damage their causal reality (Athanasius, *Incarnation of the Word* 1–6, *NPNF* 2 IV, pp. 36–39; Hilary, *Trin.* IX.61–75, *NPNF* 2 IX, pp. 176–81).

Foreknowledge does not imply direct influence or omnicausality or absolute determination, but merely knowing what other wills are by the divine permission doing (Justin Martyr, *First Apol.* XLV–LIII, *ANF* I, pp. 178–80). God's knowledge is precisely of free choice, of human and creaturely willing (Athanasius, *Four Discourses Ag. Arians* III.30, *NPNF* 2 IV, pp. 425–31; cf. Augustine, *CG* V.9, *NPNF* 1 II, pp. 90 ff.; Luis de Molina, *Scientia Media, RPR*, pp. 424 ff.).

A fine point must be sharpened in this connection: God not only grasps and understands what actually will happen, but also what could happen under varied possible contingencies. If God's knowing is infinite, God knows even the potential effects of hypothetical but unactualized possibilities, just as well as God knows what has or will become actualized. Put differently, God knows what would have been had things been otherwise and had different historical decisions been made (Augustine, *On Spirit and Letter* 58, *NPNF* 1 V, p. 109; *Ag. Two Letters of Pelagians* III.25–IV.4, *NPNF* 1 V, pp. 414–18; cf. Watson, *TI* I, pp. 371 ff.; Calvin, *Inst.* 3.21, 22).

This assumes that God knows, easily and without effort, an infinite number of alternative universes that could have been but as yet are not. This affirmation is encompassed in the affirmation of omniscience. God knows not only what is, but what possibly might be, yet is not, and what can be but will never be, and what might eventually be chosen but as yet remains undecided and subject to creaturely freedom. This has been called "God's knowledge of the hypothetical" or *scientia media* (God's knowledge of the middle or hypothetical ground between freedom and necessity, which is neither the necessary knowledge that God has of himself, *scientia necessaria*, nor the knowledge that God has of the freedom of his creatures, *scientia libera*; cf. Tho. Aq., *ST* I Q14, pp. 82 ff.; Watson, *TI* I, pp. 375 ff.). Hence it is said that "God's necessary knowledge precedes every free act of the divine will; free knowledge follows the act of will" (Alsted, *Theologia Scholastica* 98, *RD* p. 79; cf. Augustine, *On Spirit and Letter* 58, *NPNF* 1 V, p. 109).

Suppose the opposite were true, that God's knowing were almost infinite but not quite; and that God knew only what has happened and will happen, but not what might have happened; and that God knew what free agents have chosen and will choose, but not what they will consider choosing but reject. This alternative blocks God from awareness of the inward depths of the free subject self, seeking to decide between possibilities. Such an alternative has generally been rejected, because of its failure to grasp the biblical vision of the One who "knowest all, whether I sit down or rise up; thou hast discerned my thoughts from afar. Thou hast traced my journey and my resting places, and art familiar with all my paths. For there is not a word on my tongue but thou, Lord, knowest them all" (Ps. 139:1–4).

The more difficult question on omniscience has to do with carefully correlating it with the affirmation of the future and contingent freedom of creatures. If God knows what I later will do, does that take away my freedom? Although it may at first seem so, the consensus of classical Christian teaching is to answer no. Human freedom remains freedom, significantly self-determining, even if divinely foreknown (John of Damascus, *OF* IV.21, *NPNF* 2 IX, p. 94; cf. Augustine, *CG* V.9, pp. 90–92). God's foreknowledge of events does not destroy the reality of other influences than the divine influence. God knows whether a marigold seed will bear a flower, but that knowledge does not take the place of natural forces and levels of causality other than God's own direct and immediate action. God knew that Napoleon would be defeated, but no one imagines that simply that foreknowledge in itself directly, unilaterally caused the defeat without any other historical, human, or natural forces or influences at work. The central biblical principle underlying such distinctions is "God makes all His works good, but each becomes of its own choice good or evil" (John of Damascus, *OF* IV.21, *NPNF* 2 IX, p. 94; cf. Gen. 1–3).

If it were asserted that God's knowledge of future events completely destroys the efficacy of the self-determining influences God foresees, that would constitute a fatalistic negation of human freedom. For that would be tantamount to asserting that there is only one will in the universe, the will of God, and no other wills exist. That is an extreme view, contrary to Christian teaching about creation, human freedom, self-determination, and human dignity (Luis de Molina, *Scientia Media, RPR*, pp. 424–30).

Origen's debate with Celsus was the prototype of all these arguments. It grew out of an exegetical issue: Did Judas freely commit his traitorous deed, or since it was prophesied in Scripture (Ps. 108), must God be held responsible, since God foreknew it? Celsus argued the latter. Origen argued both that Judas willed it and that God foreknew it. "Celsus imagines that an event, predicted through foreknowledge, comes to pass because it was predicted; but we do not grant this, maintaining that he who foretold it was not the cause of its happening" (*Ag. Celsus* II.20, *ANF* VI, p. 440). In this way Origen deftly demolished Celsus' oversimplified scheme of divine foreknowledge, which held that " 'being a God He predicted these things, and the predictions must *by all means* come to pass.' Now, if by *'by all means'* he means *'necessarily,'* we cannot admit this. For it was quite possible, also, that they might *not* come to pass. But if he uses *'by all means'* in the sense of *'simple futurity,'* which nothing hinders from being true (although it was possible that they might not happen), then the argument is rightly stated" (*Ag. Celsus* II.20, *ANF* II, pp. 440, 441, italics added).

Those who imagine that classic theology is without humor may share the delight that Origen took in quoting, in this connection, an "idle argument" by a Sophist on advice to a sick person: "If it is decreed that you should recover from your disease, you will recover whether you call in a physician or not; but if it is decreed that you should not recover, you will not recover whether you call in a physician or not. But it is certainly decreed either that you should recover, or that you should not recover; and therefore it is in vain that you call in a physician" (p. 440). Such was the foolishness of saying that in whatever God foreknows there is no freedom, thought Origen, for it is precisely the acts of free will that God foreknows.

A related problem: If God is immutable, how can God know duration or succession? If God is infinite in knowing the world, God must be aware of duration and succession, even though not bound by them. If God did not understand duration and succession, God would understand even less about time than we do. God does not cease being eternal in the process of knowing time. God as independent, necessary being views all times as eternal now, but God as relationally creative and redemptive amid the world beholds and understands the process of temporal succession. We do not know next year until next year, but God knows next year already. We learn only successively through experiencing, but God does not have to learn something God already knows. We know things in part and by pieces, but God knows things fully, all at once, yet without being unaware of how temporal things slowly come to be or evolve. What we consider to be future events are to God not future but present events, so what we call divine foreknowledge is to God simply present knowledge (Tho. Aq., *SCG* I.70, 71, pp. 231–38; cf. Calvin, *Inst.* 3.22; Quenstedt, *TDP* I, 289). Hence God is said to *conceive* all things simultaneously but to *perceive* all things in terms of their duration and succession (Watson, *TI* I, pp. 371 ff.; Pope, *Compend.*, p. 83).

God's Way of Influencing: Omnipotence

All-Powerful and All-Empowering

God's influence upon the world is unlike any other mode of influence—unlimited in capacity. Omnipotence may be defined as the perfect ability of God to do all things that are consistent with the divine character (Athanasius, *Ag. Heathen* 28–47, *NPNF* 2 IV, pp. 18–30; Augustine, *CG* V.10, *NPNF* 1 II, pp. 92 ff.). God can do all that God wills to do. Omnipotence points to the necessary form of power pertinent to the infinite eternal One, that power required for God to be God (Hilary, *On Trin.* III.6 ff., IX.72, *NPNF* 2 IX, pp. 63 ff., 180 ff.; Quenstedt, *LT* I, p. 289; Pearson, *On the Creed*, passim; Watson, *TI* I, pp. 371 ff.). God is not limited in any of his attributes by anything external to himself. No power has any other source than God (Ps. 59:11–16; Rom. 13:1; Heb. 6:5; Calvin, *Inst.* 1.5).

When it was announced to Abraham that Sarah at ninety would have a son and become "the mother of nations," Abraham laughed, and Sarah laughed too (Gen. 17:15–17; 18:12), but Yahweh said: "Is anything too hard for the Lord?" (Gen. 18:14, NIV). After the fall of Jerusalem in the sixth century B.C. and its subsequent captivity, everyone thought it utterly impossible that the course of history would reverse and their land would be returned to them. Under these oppressive conditions, Jeremiah affirmed his confidence that "There is nothing too hard for thee" (Jer. 32:17, KJV). Having spoken of how hard it is for the rich to enter the kingdom of God, Jesus, when asked who could be saved, similarly affirmed the boundless power of God: "For men this is impossible; but everything is possible for God" (Matt. 19:26). Nothing that God conceives and wills to do is beyond God's ability or power to accomplish (Augustine, *On the Creed*, *Shorter Treatises*, *LF*, pp. 563 ff.; Calvin, *Inst.* 2.7.5).

"Almighty" refers to God's way of expressing His will. It is how God alone exercises influence: everywhere and over all. This extent of the influence of God is called omnipotence, that is, over all things, yet over all things in such a way as to empower and enable the freedom of other things besides God. This does not imply that God wills in every instance everything that God can possibly will, for that would suggest that God is capable only of willing but not also capable of not willing (Clement of Alex., *Exhort. to the Heathen* IV, *ANF* II, pp. 185 f.; Tho. Aq., *ST* I Q25, I, pp. 136 ff.; *ST* I Q19, I, pp. 103 ff.).

The Scriptures abound in expressions of the almighty power of God. God "does whatever pleases him" (Ps. 115:3). "The Lord God omnipotent reigneth" (Rev. 19:6, KJV). Underscoring this scriptural theme, the Nicene and Apostles' creeds began by affirming: "I believe in God the Father *Almighty*" (cf. *Der Balyzeh Papyrus, CC*, 19; Athanasius, *Defense of the Nicene Definition* III, *NPNF* 2 IV, pp. 153 ff.; Cyril of Jerusalem, *Catech. Lect.* VI, *NPNF* 2 VII, pp. 33 ff.).

God's strength is contrasted with flimsy human and historical powers. God's power is everywhere—in Mesopotamia, in Egypt, in Babylon, in Russia, in the Americas, in Campuchia, in the heavens, under the earth—in every conceivable world and in galaxies other than those known to us. God's power is not just over Israel, but over all history (Amos 1:1–2:16). For this One is the giver and ground of all natural and historical powers. God's power employs natural, historical, and human means for its accomplishment, but the use of means does not imply that God is limited by means that God alone created and freely sustains (Clementina, *Recognitions* VIII.1–30, *ANF* VIII, pp. 165–73, *Hom.* III.33, p. 244; Gregory of Nyssa, *On "Not Three Gods,"* *NPNF* 2 V, pp. 331 ff.).

God's power is not always coercive, but may—honoring the freedom of creatures—exercise itself as persuasive (Augustine, *CG* V.10, 11, *NPNF* 1 II, pp. 92, 93). It is a power whose depth is most fully known through self-giving love, as made known on the cross (Col. 2:14, 15). It is a power that also works through limited, but real, finite historical processes. God does not exert the kind of coercive power that directly determines all historical processes unilaterally. Such power God could exercise, if need be. But God's power is so great that it is nondefensively able even to allow other freedoms to challenge it without being anxious about its own security or identity (Gen. 11:1–9). God is at ease with human competencies, free to laugh about desperate human powers (Ps. 2:4).

Israel remembers the power of God through their own deliverance from Egypt, the wilderness experience, the conquest of Canaan, and the return from exile. These are widely shared memories of the ways and means by which that almighty power has been made known. That story forms a crucial part of early Hebraic awareness that God can do whatever God wills. From this premise unfolds the story attested in Scripture. It is a story of God's willing and acting, creating and ordering all things, providing for human life. It is from beginning to end the story of the one and only uncomparably powerful God (Theophilus of Antioch, *To Autolycus* I.4, *ANF* II, p. 90; Augustine, *CG* XI.1 ff., *NPNF* 1 II, pp. 205 ff.). Creation itself required no effort. God spoke and it was done (Gen. 1:1–2:4). The nations are, in the presence of God, less than nothing, like a drop in the bucket (Isa. 40:15).

In order to accomplish an act of human willing it is necessary that one (a) know what is to be done; (b) decide or will to do it; and (c) have the power to do what is willed. One may fail to accomplish an act of willing by either (a) failing to know how something is to be done; or (b) knowing what should be done but not willing it; or (c) knowing and willing that it should be done, but still lacking the power to do what is willed. God lacks none of these since: (a) God enjoys untrammeled awareness of what can be done; (b) God wills that the good be done, even if beyond the range of our finite perceptions; and (c) God has the power to accomplish what God wills (cf. Irenaeus, *Ag. Her.* I.22, *ANF* I, p. 347; Tertullian, *Ag. Hermogenes*, chaps. 8, 17, *ANF* III, pp. 481, 486 ff.; Tho. Aq., *SCG* I.72–88, pp. 239–70).

Is Anything Too Hard for the Lord?

Omnipotence is sometimes asserted in undisciplined, inexact ways. The case is sometimes put in pastoral care as to whether God can do that which is logically self-contradictory, or by definition impossible. Can God abolish the past? Can God make a square into a triangle? Can God make a stone larger than God can lift? (Origen, *Ag. Celsus* V.23, *ANF* IV, p. 553; cf. Charles Hartshorne, *A Natural Theology for Our Time*, pp. 116 ff.). Each of these questions hinges on a comic premise that must not be accepted at face value. To answer either yes or no without inquiring into the absurdity or contradiction presumed in the question is to fall into an unnecessary trap that can easily be avoided.

There is only one way of speaking properly of any restriction upon God's power that does not detract from God's almighty power: God "cannot deny himself" (2 Tim. 2:13; Tho. Aq., *ST* I–IIae Q100, I, p. 1045; Calvin, *Inst.* 3.15.2). This key biblical principle of the divine self-constraint can be stated in several ways:

• God would not do that which is inconsistent with God's intelligence or repugnant to God's goodness, or not in accord with other qualities of God's character (John Chrysostom, *Hom. on Timothy* V, *NPNF* 1 XIII, pp. 492, 493).
• God "cannot lie," for this would be inconsistent with God's goodness (Tho. Aq., *ST* Q25, I, pp. 137 ff.). God cannot deceive himself, for this would be counter to God's integrity, congruity, omniscience, and constancy.

• God cannot cease being, or even desire to cease being, because that would be inconsistent with God's very being as eternal and blessed, eternally happy in the divine enjoyment of being (Augustine, *CG* V.10, *NPNF* 1 II, pp. 92, 93).

Scripture clearly affirms that it is "impossible for God to lie" (Heb. 6:18, KJV; Calvin, *Inst.* 1.17). If God is incomparably merciful, God will not do anything that lacks mercy. God "cannot" be not good. God "cannot" be unjust (Tho. Aq., *SCG* II.25). "Cannot" is expressed in hypothetical quotation marks, for aside from that which is inconsistent with God's being, there is nothing that God cannot do, hence it is a kind of comic playing with language to say "cannot."

It is God's nature to be self-consistent, and thus to act in a way that is congruent with God's essential being and character. God's power is expressed in harmony with God's wisdom, justice, and love, not as if God's power were completely detachable from these attributes. Only that being is omnipotent who is able to effect all things that are consistent with the divine character and with the divine perfections (Gregory of Nyssa, *Great Catech.*, prologue, *NPNF* 2 V, pp. 473, 474; Pearson, *Apostles' Creed* I; Petavius, *De Deo* V.5–11; Suarez, *Summa*, pt. I, V.1; Wesley, *WJW* VII, pp. 265 ff.).

Thus, the premise of "omnipotence" is improperly (yet comically) asserted insofar as it implies that God is able to do that which is intrinsically inconsistent with the divine being or irrationally self-contradictory or unworthy of God. Omnipotence does not include the power of God to act in ungodly ways (Tho. Aq., *ST* I Q25, I, pp. 137–41). It is only a lack of imagination that might prematurely call this a limitation on the power of God.

The essential idea of omnipotence is that God has adequate ability to do whatever being God requires. God has sufficient power to *do* the divine will. It belongs to the nature of God's power to work in perfect correspondence with God's character and in orderly conjunction with other attributes. To say that God "cannot" act unjustly is not a reduction of God's power, but rather an expression of the adequacy of God's power to do what being God requires, namely, act justly. Thus one might say that there are some things that God either could not do without denying himself, or would not do being who God is (Tho. Aq., *ST* I Q25, I, p. 141; Calvin, *Inst.* 1.4.2; 1.14.3).

It is no diminution of the divine majesty to acknowledge that God "cannot" do that which by definition intrinsically cannot be done. If one asserts that God can do that which is intrinsically contradictory, that does not increase the power of God, but, rather, inadvertently traps the idea of God in a comic premise. Contradictions are by definition unable to be actualized (such as that *A* may be both *A* and not *A*), so what good does it do to elevate them to some presumed dignity by the spurious assertion that God can actualize them? (Tho. Aq., *SCG* II.25). It is not an offense against the divine integrity to insist that God does not know what is intrinsically unintelligible (Alvin Plantinga, *God, Freedom, and Evil*, pp. 39 ff.). Likewise it does not diminish the most perfect doer that God does not do what is intrinsically undoable.

Yet what may seem to finite minds to be contradictory may in God's wisdom be at a different level entirely possible, whether within or transcending the multilayered spheres of natural causality. One of the most moving New Testament ascriptions to God celebrates God's capacity to do *more* than we can conceive: "Now to him who is able to do immeasurably more than all we can ask or conceive" (Eph. 3:2). The ancient ecumenical theologians rigorously fought the notion of a limited God in their rejection of certain propositions of Origenists in the fifth ecumenical synod: "If anyone says or thinks that the power of God is limited, and that he created as much as he was able to compass," this opinion is to be rejected (Ecumenical Council of Constantinople II, *NPNF* 2 XIV, p. 320).

It is useful to consider the issue of the so-called limits of divine power in conjunction with divine knowledge and presence. It is no disparagement to the divine omniscience or constancy that God knows changing contingencies as changing contingencies. It is no depreciation of the divine omnipresence or infinity that God is present to particular locations in creation or that God is present in finitude. Rather it would be a diminution of God's knowledge to assert that God could not know contingencies, or to God's presence to assert that God could not be present in finite localities. Similarly, it is no disparagement to divine omnipotence that God cannot do what by definition cannot be done, or to the divine will that God is free to adapt freely and responsively to the conditions of changing events (Anselm, *Proslog.* VII, pp. 12 ff.).

God's Power and Other Powers

Another pastorally relevant question is the relationship of God's power to other powers that God has created. Human freedom is grounded in, permitted by, and derived from the power of God. Human freedom can assert itself against God's power, but only in limited and fragmentary ways that can never finally alter or challenge the power of God (Augustine, *CG* XI.12 ff., *NPNF* 1 II, pp. 212 ff.; Calvin, *Inst.* 1.18.1, 2).

God does not always necessarily exercise every conceivable form of power in every situation, for God has also the power to withhold influence, and to allow other powers to influence and other wills to have their own effect (Tho. Aq., *ST* I Q25, I, pp. 137 ff.). With unsearchable wisdom, God even allows wills contrary to the divine will to act and express influence within fleeting temporal limits. Wills that are able to stand but liable to fall are permitted to fall (Wesley, *On Divine Prov.*, *WJW* VI, pp. 313–25; *The Deceitfulness of the Human Heart*, *WJW* VII, pp. 335–44; *Original Sin*, *WJW* IX, pp. 191 ff.).

It is nothing short of astonishing to many biblical writers that the all-powerful God paradoxically sustains in being those creatures that oppose God's authority and goodness! (Westminster Conf. V–VI, *CC*, pp. 200–2). That constitutes a deep mystery of faith, but an even deeper one is the awareness that when fallible wills fall, God continues to act to nurture, support, encourage, and redeem these wills, and finally to consummate his purpose by bringing good out of evil and by bringing fallen creation to a redeemed consummation (Justin Martyr, *On the Sole Government of God*, *ANF* I, pp. 290 ff.; Westminster Conf. VII–XV, *CC*, pp. 202–10; Wesley, *Thoughts upon God's Sovereignty*, *WJW* X, pp. 361 ff.; *On Working Out Our Own Salvation*, *WJW* VI, pp. 506–13).

God's Ordinate Power Through Secondary Causes

Classical pastoral care has wisely distinguished God's absolute power from God's ordinate power, that is, God's power as expressed through the orderly conditions of nature. God's absolute power, in classical theology, is without limit and can be exercised without mediating causes in the creation, as in miracle or direct agency. God's ordinate power works through the order of nature by means of secondary causes and influences (Origen, *De Princip.* II.9, *ANF* IV, pp. 289–93; Quenstedt, *TDP* I, pp. 290 ff.; Watson, *TI*, I, pp. 355 ff.). That both can be asserted, each without the denial of the other, is commonly held by ancient Christian teachers.

The effective power of God is exercised uniformly through the orderly operation of secondary causes in a reliable, intelligible, natural causal order (Lactantius, *On the Workmanship of God*, *ANF* VII, pp. 281 ff.; Tho. Aq., *SCG* I.70, I, pp. 232 ff.). Absolute, unmediated divine power is not the usual way we experience the power of God. Rather, it is usually expressed through mediated powers in nature and history. If one drops a book, it will fall; one can count on that every day, no matter what the subjective state of one's mind. At that level, the world is intelligible. God works through nature without denying God's absolute power. Yet it is also within God's power to transcend the very nature that God has freely provided. Although eighteenth-century rationalism wanted to rule out miracle, classical Christianity affirmed that God is capable of transcending the very order God creates (Augustine, *CG* XII.2 ff., *NPNF* 1 II, pp. 227 ff.; cf. C. S. Lewis, *Miracles*).

To summarize: God's way of being with the world is omnipresence. God's way of knowing the world is omniscience. God's way of influencing the world is omnipotence. In speaking of God's presence, knowledge, and power in creation, we are identifying *relational* divine attributes, those that emerge out of God's relation to the creation, distinguishable from divine qualities characteristic of the independent existence of God apart from creatures.

The Holy One Present in Our Midst

The unlimited presence, knowledge, and influence of God has often been summarized in a single idea: *transcendence.* Yet transcendence has sometimes been inordinately asserted of God so as to neglect the divine immanence. Characteristically the Holy One (*gadosh*) of Israel is understood to be "among you" (Isa. 12:6), constantly addressed as intimate partner in dialogue, "my refuge and defense" (Isa. 12:2).

God is the utterly transcendent One (Gregory Nazianzen, *Second Theol. Or.*, *NPNF* 2 VII, pp. 288 ff.) who is nonetheless incomparably present in our midst (*Third Theol. Or.*, pp. 301 ff.; Calvin, *Inst.* 1.5.5; Wesley, *Thoughts upon God's Sovereignty, WJW* X, pp. 361–63). Transcendence and immanence are not separable in the Hebraic faith. The very One who is beyond the finite and human is intimately manifested and warmly knowable within the human sphere. It is a common misjudgment to take only one side of the transcendence/immanence dialectic, which is to miss the chief interfacing point: it is precisely the holy God who is *with* us, the transcendent God who is immanent, indwelling in the world (Athanasius, *Incarnation of the Word*, *NPNF* 2 V, pp. 36 ff.; Tho. Aq., *That God Knows Lowly Things*, *SCG* I.70, I, pp. 231 ff.).

Through Hosea's eyes, we behold in God the compassion of the eternal One who is in love with a beloved partner who tragically does not return that love. Yet God's way of loving does not cease, as if contingent on its being received. Such metaphors express the intimacy, constancy, and faithfulness of God's covenant love (Augustine, *On Chr. Doctrine* I.25 ff., pp. 22 ff.; Kierkegaard, *Phil. Frag.*, chap. 2). How better could Scripture express the closeness of God to humanity than in analogies from human intimacy? Can one express through human language anything that is more passionately intertwined than human intimacy?

These images of closeness are assumed to be completely consistent with the affirmation that God is the transcendent, radically other, holy One. If the study of God loses that tension, it ceases to speak of the God of Scripture. Charles Hartshorne and other process thinkers who have criticized traditional Christian theism for overemphasizing the transcendence of God (*PSG*, pp. 76 ff.) have sometimes neglected the persistent concern of Christian theism for the close engagement of God in the historical process (Augustine, *CG*, X.29 ff., pp. 199 ff., XII.15 ff., pp. 235 ff.).

Human existence remains fragile, perishable, ever dying away—"like the grass," as Isaiah says (40:6). The divine life is that completely different reality that defies all comparison. " 'To whom then will you liken me, whom set up as my equal?' asks the Holy One" (Isa. 40:25). Yet, this One remains everywhere at home, every moment engaged, ceaselessly involved in the world. No one is a stranger to this One. God shows toward Israel (and through Israel all peoples) the affection that the vine keeper shows toward the vineyard (Isa. 5:4).

The biblical tension between transcendence and immanence remains taut: The source of all things has the tenderness of a father (Hos. 11:1), or a mother (Isa. 49:15). This holy God above all has chosen to be radically accommodating to human capacities (John 1; Hilary, *On Trin*. IV.17 ff., *NPNF* 2 IX, pp. 76 ff.; Tho. Aq., *ST* I Q25, I, p. 137; Kierkegaard, *Training in Christianity*).

CHAPTER 3

The Character of God

Each step in the clarification of divine attributes leads to greater personalization, complexity, and mystery, as we are led ever closer to the divine-human interaction. *To this point* we have been considering only those characteristics of the divine life that are attested by Scripture *(a)* as intrinsic to God without reference to creatures (in that God is necessary, infinite, eternal, one, and alive), that is, primary or *essential* attributes, and *(b)* as displaying God's way of being present to, knowing, and influencing the world of creatures generally (omnipresence, omniscience, and omnipotence), that is, *relational* attributes, conceivable primarily in relation to creaturely beings.

Now we speak of those attributes of God attested by Scripture that manifest qualities of personality, freedom, and will. It may seem that these qualities are formed primarily by analogies to human personality, freedom, and willing, but the classical Christian exegetes instead have argued that human personality itself is best understood in light of the divine personality, and human willing in light of the divine will. These divine qualities are called personal (or interpersonal) attributes because they have personal analogies, or analogies toward or from human willing, feeling, and knowing, yet in such a way as to mark sharp differences between divine and human freedom. The personal attributes are divine qualities, such as life, spirit, will, and freedom, that God as eternal spirit enjoys perfectly, and that God communicates to human beings in finite measure (Hilary, *On Trin.* I.19, IV.2, VI.9, VII.29 ff., *NPNF* 2 IX, pp. 45, 70 f., 100, 131 ff.; Augustine, *Trin.* XV. 42, *LCC* VIII, pp. 169 ff.; Tho. Aq., *ST* I Q29, I, pp. 155 ff.; Watson *TI* I, pp. 336 ff.).

God is free, living, active, spiritual, and personal, while not ceasing to be what we have already described God to be—incomparably present, knowing, and influential. We are searching for a definition of God that is adequate to the divine reality insofar as possible. The personalizing terms of that definition are the special interest of this chapter. The adequacy of a definition hinges on the clarity of discrete terms that go into it. What follow are scripturally attested attributes of God that emerge primarily out of the divine relation to persons, or the person-to-Person, human-divine relationship (Tho. Aq., *ST* I Q6, I, pp. 28 ff.; Quenstedt, *TDP* I, p. 288; Heppe, *RD*, pp. 68 ff.).

THE DIVINE THOU

God as Incomparably Personal

A personal relationship involves and requires an interactive speaking and listening relationship of free beings. Even though God's way of being a person far transcends human ways of being persons, nonetheless the divine-human encounter is portrayed by Scripture as a personal relationship of meeting, speaking, listening, getting acquainted, becoming mutually committed and involved, experiencing frustrations and failures, splitting up, and becoming reconciled (Exod. 28:43; Num. 11:33; 1 Sam. 10:1–5; Pss. 4:1; 17:1; 74:1; Hos. 14:1; cf. Irenaeus, *Ag. Her.* II.1, *ANF* I, pp. 359 ff.).

Scripture speaks constantly of God by means of these personal and interpersonal analogies: God is viewed as a self-determining, conscious, feeling, and willing Self who has relationships with other personal beings (Matt. 7:21; 26:39; Augustine, *Trin.* XV.42, *LCC* VIII, pp. 169 ff.). God is known and celebrated in the life of prayer as personal, and understood by means of metaphors of human personal responsiveness (Matt. 6:10; John 6:38–40).

Persons by definition have feelings. Each one has an identifiable self, intellect, and capacity for response. God is represented in Scripture as having much of the psychological makeup of what we know as personhood. God has intellect and emotion; God speaks (Gen. 1:3), sees (Gen. 11:5), and hears (Ps. 94:9). Metaphorically it is said that God repents (Gen. 6:6) and can be angry (Deut. 1:37), jealous (Exod. 20:5), and compassionate (Ps. 111:4). Only personal beings can feel such emotions (Tho. Aq., *ST* I Q29, pp. 155 ff.). No stone or abstract idea or amoeba can speak words, listen, care for others, get angry, respond to hurts—only persons do these things.

Although God is far more than what we can signify by our term *personal*, God is certainly not less than personal being. But what do we mean when we speak of God as "person"? Two correlated points help with the answer: God speaks as "I," and God has a *name*.

God Speaks as "I"

God can say "I." Whatever being can say "I" is a person. For knowing oneself or another as capable of saying "I" requires self-consciousness, intentionality, the will to communicate, and self-determination. Rocks and plants, however beautiful, cannot call themselves "I" because they lack awareness; they lack words to say it, and they lack the freedom to conceive it. This is why rocks and plants are so different from human beings and superpersonal intelligences (*angeloi*, angels) and God. All share being, but all do not share personhood.

One central aspect of personal identity, of that which can say "I," is a unity that is sustained over varied experiences (Augustine, *Conf.* I–III, *LCC* VII, pp. 1–75). Even with a vastly varied history of experience, the person remains an "I" throughout all those stages of development. I am different in experience from what I was as a child, but I still remain the same person. I may choose this in one moment, that in another. Memory helps me grasp the continuity in my choosing, and to identify what it means when I say "I." I could not have a sense of personal unity that is implied in the term *I* unless I had memory. Memory binds together my awareness of my self as a history of choosing (Kierkegaard, *Either/Or* II.2). God is spoken of in Scripture as one who chooses, has memory, lives through a history of choosing, and whose character is known as One who has made certain choices. Only a person can do this.

The notion of a "memory of God" is a useful but limited metaphor whose meaning must be placed in the context of the all-present One who experiences all times in eternal simultaneity. But in relation to time and the concrete events of history, God holds in unified integrity the awareness of all events. Hence God's memory is in some ways like, but in more ways unlike, human memory. There are times when God *seems* to have forgotten the faithful (Pss. 13:1; 44:24) and when God is earnestly asked to remember the people in their affliction (Lam. 3:19). Yet Scripture marveled that God would always remember the covenant, remaining ever faithful to it, even when the people had forgotten it (Gen. 9:15, 16; Lev. 26:42; Jer. 44:21).

God Has a Name

God has a name. This points to a key difference between persons and things. God is not a nameless energy or abstract idea. God is not an "it." God is inadequately described by impersonal terms such as *ground of being* or *the Unconditioned* (Tillich, *Syst. Theol.* I), *external infinity* (S. Alexander, *Space, Time, and Deity*, II, pp. 353 ff.), *Reality Idealized* (E. S. Ames, *Religion*, pp. 153–55), *the Absolute* (Hegel, *Phenomenology of Mind*), or *the Creative Event* (H. N. Wieman, *Source of the Common Good*, pp. 6 ff.). For to none of these abstract descriptions is a personal name attached.

Different from these is the God of Scripture, whose name is constantly being revealed through events to persons in history. God's name is revealed specifically and variously (as Yahweh, 'El, 'Elōhīm, 'El Shaddaī, see Chapter 1) to others who had specific and various names (Abraham, Moses, Mary, Paul). The history of revelation is the history of the meeting of named beings, not unnameable abstractions or distilled propositions. The Pentateuch reports that as early as Cain and Abel, persons "began to invoke the Lord by name" (Gen. 4:26). Calling Yahweh *by name* is something quite different than speaking abstractly of an "unmoved Mover," or trying to pray to "Reality Idealized," or petitioning to an undifferentiated "ground of being" (Aristotle, *Metaphy.*; Ames, *Religion*; Tillich, *Syst. Theol.* I), all of which circumvent a personal name for God.

Ordinarily one does not name a machine or a stone or a material object. The only exceptions, significantly, are those machines or objects that have special personlike characteristics, such as a car named "Betsy," or a baseball bat "Bubba," or a battleship "Calamity Jane," or a pet rock "Harvey." In these cases the objects remind us of persons, so we give them the honor of elevating them to surrogate personhood by calling them a name. This reveals the importance of naming in human cultures and its unique relationship to the qualities of personhood. This makes it all the more significant that scriptural accounts constantly call God by name, and therefore assume from the outset a divine-human interpersonal relationship, a meeting between personal beings (Irenaeus, *Ag. Her.* III.1 ff., *ANF* I, pp. 414 ff.; cf. Tertullian, *Ag. Praxeas* XVII ff., *ANF* III, pp. 613 ff.).

Pronouncing the divine name of the incomparably holy One (Yahweh, 'El, 'Adōnaī) was thought to be in itself a most serious matter. "You shall not make wrong use of the name of the Lord your God; the Lord will not leave unpunished the man who misuses his name" (Exod. 20:7). Names in the Hebrew tradition were thought to reveal something decisive of the character of the person named and to convey something of the one named. It was no small or accidental matter that God revealed the divine name as Yahweh or 'El or 'Elōhīm or 'El

Shaddai, for these names provided clues to what sort of person God is (Exod. 20:24; 23:21; Ezek. 43:7–8; Calvin, *Inst.* 1.10.3; 1.13.3–4).

Why Impersonal Terms Are Inadequate for God

If one wrote a definition of God and thoughtlessly left out the fact that God is personal, something decisive would be missing. If one omitted personhood from the divine attributes, the conclusion might be drawn that personhood is not intrinsic to the divine character, but merely an ascription accidentally applied to God or projected upon God out of our human needs. Far more than this is meant by the attribute of divine personality. It means that God *is* a person and cannot properly be thought of other than in personal terms (Hilary, *On Trin.* III.23 ff., *NPNF* 1 IX, pp. 68 ff.; Augustine, *Conf.* V, *LCC* VII, pp. 95 ff.).

Why was this point so vigorously pursued by early Christian exegetes? It became an important part of the careful regulation of Christian language about God. It helped to defend Christian teaching

• from pantheism, the view that God is the world (which cannot see any difference between God and the world, or between creator and creature)

• from polytheism (which abuses the analogy between human personality and divine personality by unilaterally attributing to God human limitations and faults)

• from agnosticism (which denies that anyone can know the divine person even if such a person existed)

• from atheism (which denies that any eternal personal being exists)

Is divine personhood known and knowable from human personhood, or vice versa? It is more theologically precise to say that the fullness of personhood exists in God alone, and that our limited understandings of personality and personalization are inadequate reflections of the genuine freedom and responsible self-determination that we find incomparably in God and only inadequately in ourselves (Augustine, *Trin.* XV.42, pp. 169 ff.; cf. Barth, *CD* I/1, pp. 279 ff., III/4, p. 245; Oden, *KC* IV, pp. 114 ff.). Yet this is not to deny that human beings, too, have personhood, which is not wholly dissimilar from God's personhood (Tho. Aq., *ST* I Q29, I, p. 157).

God Is Spirit

"God is Spirit" is the only direct definition of God Jesus ever gave (John 4:24). Jesus was speaking to a woman of Samaria, teaching that "those who worship him must worship in spirit and in truth." He was correcting the idea that the worship of God is confined to particular places such as Mount Gerizim of Jerusalem (John Chrysostom, *Hom. on St. John* XXXIII, XXXIV, *NPNF* 1 XIV, pp. 115–22).

God as Spirit cannot be objectified in the same way that bodily and physical matter may be viewed as objects (Origen, *De Princip.* I.1, *ANF* IV, pp. 242 ff.). *Pneuma* (spirit), like the wind, is known only by its effects (Tertullian, *On the Soul* XI, XII, *ANF* III, pp. 190–92). God is invisible, for "No one has seen God at any time" (John 1:18; Gregory Nazianzen, *Second Theol. Or.*, *NPNF* 2 VII, pp. 288–91; Calvin, *Inst.* 1.13.14; 2.2.20).

God is pure Spirit, and "the Father of our spirits" (Heb. 12:9, NIV), who creates other self-determining, responsible beings, and enters into interpersonal interaction and communion with them (Augustine, *Trin.* VIII.3, *LCC* VIII, pp. 40, 41). At best, the ascription of spirituality to God implies a celebration of the human spirit, a humble acknowledgment that the human spirit is akin to God the Spirit (Clement of Alex., *Strom.* IV.3, *ANF* II, p. 410). It is also a guard against the demeaning of humanity and the physical-temporal localization of God (Athenagoras, *A Plea for the Chr.* XV, *ANF* II, pp. 135 f.).

When we speak metaphorically of God as incomparably spiritual and personal, we are referring to One who thinks, feels, and wills, yet not as creatures think, feel, and will from only one temporal locus. Intellect, affect, and volition are essential powers of personal spirit. We know this because we possess in lesser degree these competencies that God possesses in completeness (Tertullian, *On the Resurrection of the Flesh* VII, VIII, *ANF* III, pp. 550 ff.; Augustine, *CG* XIII.24, *NPNF* 1 II, p. 259).

It is from our thinking that we are able to think about God thinking. It is due in part to our own individuated experience of feeling that we can feel that God also feels. It is from our own acts of willing that we can understand in some small measure that God has infinitely self-determining freedom.

Christian teaching does not conclude, however, that the human ability to think, feel, and will is capable of providing a fully adequate understanding of God's mind, experience, and will. Rather, our natural analogies stand constantly under the guidance and critique of Scripture, of tradition's exegesis of Scripture (Tho. Aq., *ST* I Q13, I, pp. 63 ff.; Calvin, *Inst.* 1.13.20). Moreover, it is on the basis of God's knowing, feeling, and willing that it is possible rightly to behold human knowing, feeling, and willing (Augustine, *Enchiridion* XXVI, *LCC* VII, p. 399; cf. Barth, *CD* III/4; cf. Oden, *KC* II).

When Scripture directly ascribes to God the distinctive attribute of spirituality (John 4:24), this signifies that God is invisible and incorporeal, that is, not a body however vast, not reducible to matter, not an object of empirical investigation, not visible to our eyes even through electronic telescopes and electron microscopes (cf. Tho. Aq., *ST* I Q3, I, p. 19). "The God who created the world and everything in it, and who is Lord of heaven and earth, does not live in shrines made by men. It is not because he lacks anything that he accepts service at man's hands, for he is himself the universal giver of life and breath and all else" (Acts 17:24; cf. Irenaeus, *Ag. Her.* III.12.9–14, *ANF* I, pp. 434, 435). Although Scripture does speak of God as present within localities, that does not localize God's essence. For God is spirit, and being spirit, God is no object (John of Damascus, *OF* IX–XII, *NPNF* 1 IX, pp. 12 f.; Watson, *TI* I, pp. 343 ff.).

In Hebraic religion it was forbidden to reduce God to a visible image or idol or object of the senses. This moral requirement corresponds with the divine attribute of spirituality. For "On the day when the Lord spoke to you out of the fire on Horeb, you saw no figure of any kind; so take good care not to fall into the degrading practice of making figures carved in relief, in the form of a man or a woman, or of any animal on the earth or bird that flies in the air, or of any reptile on the ground or fish in the waters under the earth" (Deut. 4:15–17). Similarly the New Testament declared that "we ought not to suppose that the deity is like an image in gold or silver or stone, shaped by human craftsmanship and design" (Acts 17:29). For God is intrinsically nonobjectifiable, uninvestigable as a laboratory object, unseeable as phenomenon.

Pantheism, in saying that the finite world is God, and that God is therefore finite, essentially regards God as a body and the world as God's body, indistinguishably. In doing so it has met consistent resistance from classic Christian exegesis, whether pantheism appears in ancient or modern form. Although Scripture speaks metaphorically of God's hands, feet, eyes, hearing, and so on, these are metaphors intended to be read imaginatively (Athenagoras, *A Plea for the Christians* XVI, *ANF* II, p. 136; Cyril of Jerusalem, *Catech. Lect.* VI.6–9, *NPNF* 2 VII, pp. 34, 35).

The Freedom of God

How Is God Understood to Be Free?

Pivotal among scripturally attested personal qualities attributed to God is *will*. What is God's distinctive way of being *free*? How is divine freedom like and unlike human freedom? When we speak of divine freedom are we merely ascribing to God in infinite degree an analogy from the experience of something we know quite well: personal freedom?

Indeed, as we move into the subject of willing, we are suddenly thrust into an arena in which we already have knowledge—intimate, personal knowledge—of ourselves as free (Josh. 24:15; Phil. 2:13; Origen, *De Princip.* III.1.1–12, *ANF* IV, pp. 301–13; cf. Augustine, *CG* V.10, *NPNF* 1 II, pp. 92, 93; Calvin, *Inst.* 2.3). For every person capable of thinking about these questions is already aware that he or she possesses a certain capacity to will, or power of self-determination (Cyril of Jerusalem, *Catech. Lect.* IV.18–21, *NPNF* 2 VII, pp. 23, 24; cf. Augustine, *On Free Choice of the Will* II.28, pp. 77 ff.; Anselm, *On Freedom of Choice* III, *TFE*, pp. 125 ff.). No sentence could be read without assuming the power to read or not read it. Yet the divine will is not merely an extension or projection of human willing (Gregory Nazianzen, *Second Theol. Or.*, *NPNF* 2 VII, p. 293; anticipating Feuerbach, *Essence of Christianity*, pp. 12 ff.; and Freud, *The Future of an Illusion*, *CPWSF* 21, pp. 25 ff.). It is rather the premise and ground of human willing.

The power of God's will is the effective energy inherent in God by which God is able to do all things consistent with the divine nature. The divine will is the infinite power of God to determine God's own intentions, execute actions, and use means adequate to the ends intended (Tho. Aq., *ST* I Q19, I, pp. 103 ff.; Calvin, *Inst.* 1.18.1 ff.). The will of God is utterly free, ever self-determined toward the good; hence it is a will that lives in complete felicity (Augustine, *CG* XXII.30, *NPNF* 1 II, pp. 509–11).

The freedom of God is the sufficient reason why anything exists at all (John of Damascus, *OF* III.14, *NPNF* 2 IX, pp. 57–60; cf. Calvin, *Inst.* 2.3.10). "Whatever the Lord pleases, that he does" (Ps. 135:6). The will of God is present in all things and known by the divine intellect, and thus intrinsically connected with the divine attributes of omnipresence and omniscience. Since it is God who is willing, that will must be independent, unified, and eternal (Hilary, *Trin.* IX.26 ff., *NPNF* 1 IX, pp. 164 ff.; Anselm, *Monologium* VII ff., *BW*, pp. 49 ff.; Tho. Jackson, *Works*, V, pp. 292 ff.).

It is fitting to ascribe willing or volition to God for several reasons: First, we ourselves experience self-determination as incalculably good, and anything that is good to such an extraordinary degree we may properly ascribe in infinite proportion to God (an argument by way of heightening, the way of eminence; Tho. Aq., *ST* I Q96; cf. Augustine, *Trin.* X.13, *LCC* VIII, pp. 85 ff.; Hollaz, *ETA,* p. 190). Second, we know that God wills because we see the effects of willing in the causal order, for if there is any movement or change at all in the causal order, it must be caused, and to avoid the embarrassment of an infinite regress, we reasonably hypothesize a primal source of all causes (Gregory Nazianzen, *Second Theol. Or.* VIII, *NPNF* 2 VII, p. 291; Tho. Aq., *ST* I Q19, I, pp. 103 ff.). Thus we ascribe will to God based on the argument from causality (to be further elaborated in the next chapter). Third, we ascribe willing to God because we experience our willing as radically dependent upon some Whence (or source of all possibilities), without which our willing would remain absurd and unexplainable (Hilary, *Trin.* VIII.12 ff., *NPNF* 1 IX, pp. 140 ff.; Schleiermacher, *Chr. Faith*). Fourth, most significantly, Christian teaching ascribes willing to God because such attributions are constantly found in Scripture. Scriptural texts continually use personal and volitional images, analogies, and metaphors to speak of God as a free, deciding, choosing, self-determining being, yet without ceasing to point toward that same One whose will from the beginning must be antecedent to creation, eternally present, and knowing of all (John of Damascus, *OF* II.24–30, *NPNF* 1 IX, pp. 38 ff.; Heppe, *RD,* pp. 85 ff.).

The Divine Will and Other Wills

It might seem that power and self-determination are so closely linked as to be virtually identical. Since we have already discussed God's power, it might seem superfluous to speak further of God's freedom. Although intricately enmeshed and formally inseparable, they may be functionally distinguished. For may not one have power without willing to exercise it? (Tho. Aq., *ST* I Q25, I, pp. 135 ff.).

In inquiring into the will of God, we encounter an aspect of the study of God into which we have not previously entered—studying God's qualities of personhood in close conjunction with our own self-examination, with personal self-knowledge (Catherine of Genoa, *Purgation, CWS,* pp. 74 ff.; cf. Calvin, *Inst.* 1.1.1, 3.2–4). For what we mean by being a person is to some large extent precisely this: the capacity to will.

Choice is definitive of personal existence. What makes us persons is that we know ourselves to be able to act in this rather than that way. Human freedom shares in divine freedom, yet within the limits of finitude. Both kinds of freedom are assumed in Scripture: "Freely you have received, freely give" (Matt. 10:8; cf. John 8:32–36; 1 Pet. 2:16). "Grant me a willing spirit" (Ps. 51:12). Scripture frequently attests to the derived character of human freedom, derived, that is, from God's own freedom (Irenaeus, *Ag. Her.* III.17.1–2, *ANF* I, pp. 444, 445). "In Christ indeed we have been given our share in the heritage, as was decreed in his design whose purpose is everywhere at work. For it was his will that we, who were the first to set our hope on Christ, should cause his glory to be praised" (Eph. 1:11).

God wills to empower other wills. Thomas Aquinas astutely reasoned that God wills in different ways, for God "wills himself and things other than himself; himself as the end, other things as ordered to that end. It befits the divine goodness that other things should be partakers therein" (Tho. Aq., *ST* I Q19.2, *TAPT*, p. 113). Human freedom is ordered in relation to divine freedom. We are persons because God is a person. It is from divine freedom that human freedom is derived and made understandable.

The Primordial and Consequent Will of God

Classical Christian exegesis holds that God's will may be viewed in two ways, first, primordially, God wills what God wills eternally, that is, before creation, and second, consequentially, God wills what God wills in consequence of creation and in the light of the specific contingencies of creaturely beings (Ps. 143:10; Eph. 1:1–9; John of Damascus, *OF* IV.19–21, *NPNF* 2 IX, pp. 92–94; cf. Andreae Hyperius, *Methodi theologiae*, pp. 138 ff.; Heppe, *RD*, pp. 90 ff.; Hodge, *Syst. Theol.*, I, pp. 404 ff.). As the divine intellect knows all things eternally, and thus antecedently to the world and time, so the divine volition wills all things antecedently from the viewpoint of eternity, yet as history subsequently develops, God is and remains free to express the divine will within history (Ps. 40:8; Matt. 6:10; John 7:17; cf. Origen, *De Princip.* III.1.6–22, *ANF* IV, pp. 305–28).

First, God is said to will primordially or antecedently when God wills something independently of creatures, without regard to other wills or any subsequently developing contingent or conditional circumstances. For example, it is said that God antecedently wills the good (Rom. 12:2). This general will predates later developing historical circumstances in which the divine good will is willed particularly in and through contingent circumstances, such as those following the fall (Tho. Aq., *ST* I Q19, I, pp. 103 ff.; T. Jackson, *Works* V, pp. 331–36).

In this primordial sense it is said that God's antecedent (sometimes called secretive or absolute or decreeing) will is single, simple, independent, eternal, efficacious, and inseparable from God's very being (Rom. 9:18, 19; Heppe, *RD*, pp. 90 ff.).

Secondly, within the conditions of history, however, God is said to will consequent to various changing historical circumstances. As a consequence of particular contingencies occurring in the history that God creates and permits, God *consequently wills* with particularity under special and contingent conditions (cf. 1 John 5:14). Even after human wills have done all the damage and good they can do through the divine permission, God still rules and overrules, commands and countermands, prewills, wills, and postwills through and beyond all human willing. God remains free to respond to what is humanly willed. The consequent will of God responsively follows after human willing (Rom. 1:10; 1 Cor. 16:12; cf. Amandus Polanus, *STC* II, p. 19). It is the will of God in response to human willing (1 John 2:17; John 7:17). "It is possible to will a thing to be done now, and its contrary afterwards; and yet for the will to remain permanently the same" (Tho. Aq., *ST* I Q19, I, p. 109).

Thus the divine will exists in itself, prior to the complications of fallen human history, yet the divine will also operates and functions in response to human fallenness. God can express the divine good will amid changing historical circumstances and contingencies, but it must be remembered that God's will remains the same, eternal covenant love, even amid intensive responsiveness to whatever human or historical misery (Cyril of Jerusalem, *Catech. Lect.* IV.4, 5, *NPNF* 1 VII, p. 20; Hooker, *Eccl. Polity* I.5.1; T. Jackson, *Works* V, pp. 105 ff.).

Although God can will changes, God does not change the eternal divine purpose. Though God can respond to contingencies, God does not make the divine eternal will finally contingent upon the contingencies God has permitted (Tho. Aq., *ST* I Q86, I, pp. 442 ff.; Molina, *Scientia Media*, *RPR*, pp. 425 ff.). This is why classical Christian exegetes have often distinguished between God's single, unified "necessary will" antecedent to creation, and God's "free will," freely utilizing variable means of response to the freedom of creatures (Eph. 1:1–11; Matt. 21:28–32; cf. John of Damascus, *OF* XIX ff., *NPNF* 2 IX, pp. 92 ff.).

The terms *primordial* and *consequent will of God* may be prematurely assumed by some modern readers to be the product of the recent tradition of process philosophy and theology (Whitehead, Hartshorne, Cobb, Ogden), but it is evident that Whitehead himself borrowed these concepts from classical Christian teaching (Clement of Alex., *Instr.* I.9, *ANF* II, pp. 228 ff.; Tertullian, *Ag. Marcion* II.4–17, *ANF* III, pp. 299–310; John of Damascus, *OF* XIX ff., *NPNF* 2 IX, pp. 92 ff.; Tho. Aq., *ST* I Q19, I, pp. 107 ff.; Heppe, *RD*, pp. 85 ff.). The irony is that Whitehead's followers, apparently unaware of how the classical tradition employed deliberate distinctions between the necessary and the free will of God, between the antecedent and the consequent will of God, and between the absolute and the ordinate will of God, have used the distinction between primordial and consequent willing in God as the basis of a sustained polemic against the very tradition of classical theism upon which their reasoning depends. Once again ancient Christian teaching has been borrowed, diminished, and fashioned into a tool by which its borrowers have then "transcended" classical Christian theism.

The Interfacing of Divine and Human Will

We have previously discussed God's knowledge as foreknowledge (that God foreknows free human acts without destroying their freedom). Similarly, instead of foreknowing we are now speaking of God's primordial willing, or foreordaining. God's primordial willing is in a sense before all time, since God is the causal source of the entire range of temporal events. God's will, like God's being, is immutable, when viewed as God's eternal will that is the ground and source of time. Yet God allows and invites the personal freedom and self-determination of other wills within the history that God has enabled and created, and to which God is responsive within the framework of time (1 Pet. 4:2, 3, 19; Clementina, *Hom.* III.43 ff., *ANF* VIII, pp. 246 ff.).

Human volition is and remains, however deeply corrupted, always the gift of the divine volition. God's fundamental or primordial (antecedent) will is that humanity be saved, but on the way to the last day, many contingencies emerge. This paradoxical aspect of the divine will is seen in Jesus' poignant exclamation: "O Jerusalem, Jerusalem, the city that murders the prophets and stones the messengers sent to her! How often have I longed to gather your children, as a hen gathers her brood under her wings; but you would not let me. Look, look! there is your temple, forsaken by God. And I tell you, you shall never see me until the time when you say, 'Blessings on him who comes in the name of the Lord'" (Matt. 23:37–39). That means: God antecedently wills to save Jerusalem—and all humanity by extension of the metaphor—but Jerusalem has the power of will, divinely granted, momentarily to delay, or temporarily to "not let God complete" the antecedent divine intention except at the high cost of God's having to destroy or override the gift of human freedom. Thus human willing at that point of historical development is able to resist the will of God temporarily, though never ultimately (John Chrysostom, *Concerning the Statues* XVII, *NPNF* 1 IX, p. 457; cf. Calvin, *Inst.* 2.3).

God does not deal with human beings as sticks. God does not throw them, like stones, into excellent responses; otherwise they would not be free personal responses. Rather, God deals with human beings not coercively but persuasively, on the basis of human freedom and its ever-present correlate, human responsibility. God's moral instruction is revealed through the law, through conscience and moral self-awareness. As the good parent does not allow the child in the street though there is nothing intrinsically wrong with the street, so does God command and require humanity not to sin, to make no false gods, and not to treat creaturely goods as God. Yet when we do so God is still able to take our idolatry and sin and make it work toward a greater good, and all to God's glory. All such contingencies may be viewed as the consequent will of God, that is, consequent to historical challenges, failures, and fallenness (Heb. 10:5–10).

The Divine Will Hidden and Revealed

At times the divine will seems completely hidden to finite searching, while at other times it seems clear and revealed. The distinction between the hidden and revealed will of God is found in Deuteronomy: "There are things hidden, and they belong to the Lord our God, but what is revealed belongs to us and our children for ever; it is for us to observe all that is prescribed in this law" (Deut. 29:29). Paul warned against claiming prematurely that one could discern the will of God, for we "know in part and prophesy in part" (1 Cor. 13:9 NIV). Irenaeus, speaking of the mystery of the divine will, wrote: "It becomes us, therefore, to leave the knowledge of this matter to God, even as the Lord does of the day and hour [of judgment], and not to rush to such an extreme of danger that we leave nothing in the hands of God" (*Ag. Her.*, ANF I, p. 401).

This does not imply, however, that nothing is ever in due course revealed. God's revealed will is made known to the remembering community in at least five different ways, according to Thomas Aquinas, by means of five marks or "signs," through

- operations—when God works to effect something
- permissions—when God allows something

•   precepts—when God positively commands an action
•   prohibitions—when God negates or negatively requires something not to be enacted
•   counsels—when God teaches or advises but does not coerce an action (cf. Tho. Aq., *ST* I Q19, I, pp. 103 ff.; Schouppe, *Elem. Theol. Dog.*, V, p. 158).

Thomas Aquinas commented upon these five levels or modes through which will is expressed:

> By these signs we name the expression of will by which we are accustomed to show that we will something. A man may show that he wills something either by himself or by means of another. He may show it by himself, by doing something either directly, or indirectly and accidentally. He shows it directly when he works in his own person; in that way the expression of his will is *his own working*. He shows it indirectly, by not hindering the doing of a thing; for what removes an impediment is called an accidental mover. In this respect the expression is called *permission*. He declares his will by means of another when he orders another to perform a work, either by insisting upon it as necessary by *precept*, and by *prohibiting* its contrary; or by persuasion, which is a part of *counsel*. Since in these ways the will of man makes itself known, the same five are sometimes denominated with regard to the divine will, as the expression of that will. (*ST* I Q19, I, p. 112, italics added)

God continues to reveal his will amid history's contingencies and defects, which themselves impose upon God's will (Tho. Aq., *ST* I Q19, I, pp. 103 ff.; Calvin, *Inst.* 1.4; 3.20–24).

> Since the divine will is supremely effective, it follows not only that those things are done which God wills to be done, but also that they are done in the way that he wills. He wills some to come about necessarily and others contingently, so that there may be a pattern of things for the complement of the universe. And therefore he prepares necessary causes for some effects, unfailing causes when effects derive of necessity, and contingent and defective causes for other effects, causes from which events derive contingently. (Tho. Aq., *ST* I Q19.8, *TAPT*, p. 115)

Having spoken earlier of God as necessary being, it may seem curious that Christian teaching now proposes to speak of God's freedom. How is it possible that God could be both necessary and free? Classical Christian thought has argued that *that which is most free must be most necessary*, for God is the most necessary of all beings and the most free. Freedom and necessity are naively placed in uncomplicated opposition by some interpreters, as if the more causes one could identify the less freedom the agent must have (Voltaire, *Of Miracles*,

TGS, pp. 231 f.; B. F. Skinner, *Beyond Freedom and Dignity;* cf. Bonhoeffer, *Letters and Papers from Prison*). Yet the eternal and independent One who is the ground of all causes cannot be other than that One who is most free (Calvin, *Inst.* 3.20–24).

Here we draw near to the paradox that we find so deeply in the consciousness of the worshiping community, that "In his service is perfect freedom," (*BCP*). This is deeply correlated with the juxtaposition of two divine attributes: Only if God is uncontingently necessary is God also perfectly free. "Since then God necessarily wills His own goodness, but other things not necessarily," concluded Thomas, "He has free will with respect to what He does not necessarily will" (Tho. Aq., *ST* I Q19, I, p. 111). How could such a sentence be written without echoing the laughter that comes from God?

THE DIVINE GOODNESS

We have now discussed three of four sets of attributes of the divine life:

· the divine being (primary and essential attributes of God: sufficiency, underived existence, unity, infinity, immeasurability, eternity, life)
· the divine majesty (the relational attributes of God: all-present, all-knowing, almighty)
· and the divine Person (free, congruent, interactive Spirit)
We are now poised for the fourth and last series of qualities that clarify the One named as Yahweh in Scriptures:
· the divine goodness

Moral Qualities Intrinsic to the Divine Character

Among chief moral characteristics attributed by Scripture to God are holiness, perfection, justice, righteousness, constancy, veracity, goodness, and love. Moral attributes are divine qualities beheld primarily in God's meeting with, fidelity to, and guidance of finitely free creatures who are morally accountable within human history. These are the features intrinsic to the divine character as made known by Scripture in the history of salvation. Classical Christian exegetes were constrained by Scripture to acknowledge that God is incomparably holy (Ps. 105:3; Isa. 43:14, 15), good (Pss. 25:8; 86:5), merciful (Ps. 130:7; Jer. 33:11), and just (Isa. 45:21; Zeph. 3:5).

But are not plants, animals, and even inorganic matter also the recipients of God's faithfulness, constancy, justice, and love? Indeed it is true that plants, animals, and earth are recipients of divine mercy, justice, and love, but they are not held morally accountable for appropriate responses as are human beings, who are endowed with accountable freedom. Higher capacities for reason, language, and responsiveness are lacking in these creatures, in comparison with human beings (Gregory of Nyssa, *On the Making of Man* XXVII–XXX, *NPNF* 2 V, pp. 418–27). This is why these attributes are best seen in relation to human moral consciousness, where the potential for moral accountability greatly exceeds that in other forms of earthly life.

Honesty, justice, and love are required in the maintenance of human society, for child raising, for human happiness. These moral qualities are viewed in Scripture as intrinsic to the divine being itself and most fully beheld in God alone (Hilary, *On Trin.* VI.19 ff., IX.61, *NPNF* 2 VII, pp. 77 ff., 176 f.; Basil, *Hex.* IX, *Letters* II–VII, *NPNF* 2 VIII, pp. 104 ff., 110–15).

The great variety of moral qualities attributed to God by Scripture hinges particularly upon two—*holiness* and *love*. These may be said in summary form to compose the moral character of God (Ps. 93:5; Hos. 11:1–9; John 17:11–26).

Holiness (*godesh*) is the essential perfection of God that necessarily stands opposed to all idolatry and sin (Amos 4:1–3). Among attributes that adhere closely to holiness are righteousness, justice, moral purity, veracity, and faithfulness.

The love of God is that by which God communicates himself to creatures capable in varying degrees of reflecting the divine goodness. Among attributes that Scripture most closely associates with divine love are goodness, grace, mercy, and compassion.

God's holiness is not an unloving holiness, and God's love is not an unholy love (Calvin, *Inst.* 2.8–16). It is only by keeping these two primary moral qualities of the divine being closely related that we may rightly behold the character of God (Pss. 31:21–24; 146:8; John 3:16; 1 John 2:15; 4:7–21; Rev. 15:4).

We have already sought to show that God's goodness interpenetrates the eternal power of God (Ps. 90; Tho. Aq., *ST* I Q25, I, p. 141), God's mercy accompanies the omnipresence of God (Ps. 51), God's compassion pervades the judgment of God (Ps. 103). But such connections seem hollow and unconvincing apart from an actual history of God's merciful and compassionate activity. Now we must clearly indicate how the moral characteristics of God shape, qualify, and interface the divine omnipresence, omniscience, and will.

Classical Christianity sought to penetrate the intuited connection between the moral conscience of human beings and the moral character of God. Many Christian teachers argued that the moral requirements that responsible persons feel impinging upon them through conscience and legitimate law correspond in some degree to qualities that are ascribed in their unlimited degree to God (Tertullian, *An Answer to the Jews* I, II, *ANF* III, pp. 151–53; *Ag. Marcion* II.12–16, pp. 307–10; Cyril of Jerusalem, *Catech. Lect.* IV.15–21, *NPNF* 2 VII, pp. 22–24; Ambrose, *Duties of Clergy* I.24 ff., *NPNF* 2 X, pp. 18 ff.).

The Holiness of God

God Is Holy

The moral quality that best points to God's incomparably good character, as one incomparable in power, is holiness, for holiness (*godesh*) implies that every excellence fitting to the Supreme Being is found in God without blemish or limit. It also implies that all other divine moral excellences (goodness, justice, mercy, truth, and grace) are unified and made mutually harmonious in infinite degree in God (Isa. 6:1–10; 43:10–17; 1 Pet. 1:12–16; Rev. 4:8; John of Damascus, *OF* I.14, *NPNF* 2 IX, p. 17).

In saying such things we are struggling with frail human language to express an insight that emerges deeply from the interior life of Christian worship, a radical awareness of the difference that lies between God's goodness and our own. So deeply is this experienced that it seems impossible for fragmentary human languages to conceptualize anything at all about God's perfect goodness, because of the blemishes we feel in our moral awareness and earth-bound finitude. Indeed no propositions of Christian teaching are able to give adequate expression to God's holiness. Often we do best finally to stand in awe of God and silently celebrate God's holy presence (Gregory Nazianzen, *Second Theol. Or.*, *NPNF* 2 VII, pp. 288–301). But because we must say something rather than nothing, and because this quality of God is so central to worship and so prevalent in Scripture—and regarded as so decisive in accounting for the character of God—it is necessary to make some attempt to express it with language.

It is best not to draw too firm or absolute a distinction between God's holiness and God's perfection. It is more fitting to view God's perfection precisely as God's holiness. For to say that God is holy is nothing other than to say that God is perfect in goodness, both in essential nature and in every energy, operation, or activity that proceeds out of that nature (Gregory of Nyssa, *Answer to Eunomius' Second Book*, NPNF 2 VII, pp. 287 ff., 309 ff.). If holiness is perfect goodness, it includes within it already the idea of perfect being, which Anselm defined as "that than which nothing greater can be conceived" (*Proslog.* III, IV, BW, pp. 8–10). It is that limitless goodness to which Jesus called his disciples to respond: "There must be no limit to your goodness, as your heavenly Father's goodness knows no bounds" (Matt. 5:48; cf. 1 Pet. 1:15, 16; cf. Clement of Alex., *Strom.* VI.12, ANF II, p. 502). Jesus taught his disciples to pray, "Hallowed be thy name," and thereby attributed holiness to God the Father (Matt. 6:9, KJV).

God's holiness consummates and harmonizes all the other divine characteristics (Athanasius, *Ag. Heathen* 38–40, NPNF 2 IV, pp. 24, 25; Catherine of Genoa, *Spiritual Dialogue*, CWS, pp. 118 ff.; Watson, *TI* I, pp. 436 ff.; Pope, *Compend.* I, 304). Holiness points especially to the undivided glory of God in all of God's diversely good qualities (Tho. Aq., *ST* II–IIae Q81, II, pp. 1528 ff.). All attributes of God are indivisible, due to the unity of God, for God's being is fully present in each attribute. Hence holiness is not to be conceived as one trait among many other divine traits in such a way that these other traits may or may not include holiness. Rather, holiness summarizes, unifies, and integrates all the other incomparably good characteristics of the divine life.

This is partially analogous in human life to the way in which one may speak of the general excellence of a particular human being, meaning the overarching, integrated virtue of that person as combining and consummating so many other excellences in a fitting balance. Of such a person one might say that he is a holy man, or she a woman who is holy throughout her diverse behavior, whose holy life is to a high degree manifested in each specific action. God's incomparable holiness in this way may become refracted in and through human experience, as in Ezekiel: "When they see that I reveal my holiness through you, the nations will know that I am the Lord, says the Lord God" (Ezek. 36:23; cf. Tertullian, *Of Idolatry* XIV, ANF III, p. 69; Wesley, *WJW* VI, pp. 414 ff., 526 ff., XIII, pp. 349 ff.).

The Holiness of God's Character, Activity, and Requirement

Holiness is the fullness of God's moral excellence intrinsic to the divine character, and as such it is the criterion of God's own activity and of the action of creatures (Calvin, *Inst.* 2.8.14 ff.; 3.12.1 ff.; cf. Heppe, *RD*, pp. 92 ff.). Three distinguishable aspects are embedded in this statement—the holiness of God's character, God's activity, and God's requirement:

1. Holiness implies the perfect goodness of God's character, that God is good without defect. "Who is like thee, O Lord, among the gods? Who is like thee, majestic in holiness, worthy of awe and praise, who workest wonders?" (Exod. 15:11; cf. H. R. Niebuhr, *RMWC*, pp. 125 ff.). "Thou alone art holy" (Rev. 15:4). "God is untouched by evil" (James 1:13).

   To affirm the freedom of God is to celebrate God's freedom from sin. "By day and by night without a pause," the end time celebrants of the Book of Revelation sing: "'Holy, holy, holy is God the sovereign Lord of all, who was, and is, and is to come!'" (Rev. 4:8). Previously we have shown that Scripture attests to God's infinite greatness or majesty; now we explicitly point to the incomparably good way in which God's majesty confronts others as it manifests itself in the moral sphere. All divine acts are rooted in the divine moral character.

   It is impossible to stand in the presence of this holy One without profoundly feeling the moral inadequacy of human life. In being called of God, Isaiah was grasped by this overwhelming sense of awe as he felt his own radical moral limitation and the moral taint pervading human culture: "Holy, holy, holy is the Lord of Hosts; the whole earth is full of his glory. . . . Woe is me! I am lost, for I am a man of unclean lips and I dwell among a people of unclean lips" (Isa. 6:3–5; cf. Jer. 51:17, 18; Calvin, *Inst.* 1.1.3, R. Otto, *The Idea of the Holy*). Yet the same prophet called for holiness of life among God's people (Isa. 35:8; cf. Theophilus, *To Autolycus* II.34, *ANF* II, pp. 107 f.). Amidst this humbling awareness of human moral limitation there is nonetheless a corollary sense of radical joy that comes from the awareness that God is better, holier, purer than we can imagine (Ps. 71:22, 23), whose goodness creatures can mirror within finitude (Catherine of Siena, *Prayers* 3, pp. 35 ff.).

2. The divine holiness does not, however, apply only to God's essential or inner being, but also to God's works—everything God does, the entirety of God's activity (Gregory of Nyssa, *Ag. Eunomius* I.17–24, *NPNF* 2 V, pp. 54–67; Calvin, *Inst.* 2.12). All God's actions are holy, for there is no inconsistency between God's being and God's activity. God acts so as to express God's character, which summarizes and unifies all other divine excellences. The perfection of God's action expresses the perfection of God's being (Tho. Aq., *SCG* I.40, 41, pp. 156 ff.).

   Even when God does temporarily allow the flourishing of evil, there is an awareness in Scripture that it occurs with some purpose consistent with God's holiness (Hab. 1:13). God does not forever countenance wrongdoing, and will in time overrule it and bring it to a better purpose (Augustine, *Enchiridion* III ff., *LCC* VII, pp. 341 ff.). God's ultimate redemptive activity can be counted upon because of God's character—replete with infinite goodness.

3. God's holiness is finally the criterion for human moral activity, even though our finitude is such that we can reflect perfect goodness only inadequately. "I am the Lord your God; you shall make yourselves holy and keep yourselves holy, because I am holy" (Lev. 11:44). This is not to say that God requires what is impossible. For it is not impossible for creatures to reflect proportionally the goodness of God as their gifts and capacities allow it (Origen, *De Princip.* I.3.5–7, *ANF* IV, pp. 253–55). It is in this sense that God calls men and women to be holy and provides them with the means of grace (prayer, Scripture, sacraments) in order to reflect God's holiness in partial, yet real, vital, and individual ways (Gregory of Nyssa, *Comm. on the Canticle*, sermon 5, *FGG*, pp. 183–203; Wesley, *WJW* V, pp. 187 ff.; VI, p. 510; VIII, pp. 322 ff.). This requirement is to be understood in the light of the end of history being already anticipatively made known in Jesus' resurrection:

You must therefore be mentally stripped for action, perfectly self-controlled. Fix your hopes on the gift of grace which is to be yours when Jesus Christ is revealed. As obedient children, do not let your characters be shaped any longer by the desires you cherished in your days of ignorance. The One who called you is holy; like him, be holy in all your behaviour, because Scripture says, "You shall be holy, for I am holy." (1 Pet. 1:13–16)

Refracting the Divine Holiness

God creates beings who are capable of creaturely goodness and thereby are also capable of reflecting the incomparable divine goodness. God does not coerce creatures into doing good. That would deny one of the most fundamental goods of human creatures, freedom (Irenaeus, *Ag. Her.* IV.37, *ANF* I, pp. 518 ff.). Would it not take away from human freedom all the ancillary achievable goods of discipline, education, and the habituation of will that adhere closely to the very notion of moral good, if God were to coerce good or make creatures unable to do evil? Only those who despair of freedom think that God would have done better by making it such that freedom would necessarily, inevitably, and unerringly will and do the good (Origen, *De*

Princip. II.1, 2, *ANF* IV, pp. 302–34; cf. Augustine, *CG* XIV.11, *NPNF* 1 II, pp. 271 ff.).

Insofar as idolatry and sin infest human life, God actively opposes them, and this opposition is another expression of God's holiness. Sin impedes the moral goodness for which God created the world. God permits sin to come into human life, but only on behalf of a greater good—namely, freedom—and God overrules sin wherever it appears to threaten God's longer-range purpose (Augustine, *Enchiridion* IV–IX, *LCC* VII, pp. 342–59). It is in this light that Scripture speaks metaphorically of God as angry at our sins and jealous of our gods, for God's love in this way resists idolatry and sin. God the Spirit supports and encourages our efforts to recover the capacity to better reflect God's holiness. In this sense God's anger is an unremitting expression of God's own holiness. Hebrew Scriptures frequently portray God as standing in controversy with his people (Isa. 5:25; 9:12 ff.; Jer. 32:29–31; Zeph. 3:8). The New Testament understood that the divine-human conflict had been reconciled in Jesus' life, death, and resurrection, which anticipatively revealed the meaning, and therefore the end, of history (Rom. 5:10, 11; 2 Cor. 5:18, 19).

God's holiness includes the idea of set-apartness or *separation* from all that is sinful, unworthy of God, or unprepared for God's righteousness. Seen in this way, the holiness to which we are called in response to God's holiness is consecration, or separation from anything that would separate one from God (Gregory Nazianzen, *In Defense of His Flight to Pontus, NPNF* 2 VII, pp. 204 ff.; cf. Teresa of Avila, *Life CWST*, I, pp. 288 ff.). There is profound ethical and political import in the doctrine of God's holiness. God is free from every moral evil; therefore those who are called to holiness of heart and life (Mother Syncletica, 19, *SDF*, p. 196; cf. Wollebius, *CTC* XIII, XIV, *RD*, pp. 75–84; cf. Baxter, *PW* XV, pp. 539–44; Wesley, *WJW* VII, pp. 266 ff.) are thereby called to consecrate themselves to a life of radical responsiveness to God's love and accountability to God's own justice.

The attribute of holiness sharply distinguishes God from all that is profane, or subject to corruption, worldly, temporal. God's holiness demands, according to the Hebraic priestly tradition, that everything that comes into God's temple be purified, made sacramentally holy or ritually clean (Catherine of Genoa, *Purgation, CWS*, pp. 71 ff.; cf. Calvin, *Inst.* 2.8; 4.17; Schmid, *DT*, pp. 466, 469). This became a major concern of the cultus of the Old Testament, namely, the requirement that one who is to come into God's presence must be prepared for God's undiminished holiness, that is, ready for genuine worship. Thus priests were expected to be without physical blemish, and worshipers were not to present blemished sacrifices in response to the flawlessness of God (Lev. 1:3; 4:3; 11:42 ff.; R. Hooker, *Laws of Eccl. Polity* V.75.2–3, *Works* II, pp. 471 ff.).

Nor is this call to holiness absent in the New Testament. For Paul instructs the church at Corinth to "not unite yourselves with unbelievers; they are no fit mates for you. What has righteousness to do with wickedness? . . . The temple of God is what we are" (2 Cor. 6:14–16). He exhorted them: "Separate yourselves." "Touch nothing unclean" (v. 17). "Let us therefore cleanse ourselves from all that can defile flesh or spirit, and in the fear of God complete our consecration" (2 Cor. 7:1; cf. Calvin, *Inst.* 14.14.21). Sinners need the cleansing of repentance and faith, to come into God's presence (John Chrysostom, *Baptismal Instructions* IX.21, *ACW* 31, pp. 138 ff.; Luther, *Ninety-five Theses* I, *ML*, p. 490). God is so purified from corruption that even to enter into the presence of this One—to go properly into the sanctuary where this One is recalled, remembered, and celebrated—one rightly goes through a period of penitence, centering, mortification, purification, and discipline (*askesis;* cf. Teresa of Avila, *Way of Perfection* X, *CWST*, II, pp. 42–46).

God is not to be treated like any worldly reality. We are called in faith to be partakers of God's holiness (Heb. 12), restored to our primordial capacity to reflect, like a mirror, the radical holiness and purity of God, even though our mirroring is inadequate (Irenaeus, *Ag. Her.* V.16, *ANF* I, p. 544).

Is God Accountable Only to Himself?

Interlude: Some have wrongly argued that since all moral beings are accountable to something, therefore God must be accountable to something external to himself. This question hinges on a potentially comedic category mistake that includes God in the same category of moral beings as human moral beings. No doubt God indeed is an incomparably moral being, since God is utterly good, but God's moral awareness is unutterably better than the best achieved by finite creatures. Therefore it is said only of God that God is responsible only to himself in the particular sense that God is not responsible to some external moral being or claim or will that allegedly "transcends God" (John of Damascus, *OF* I.5, 14, *NPNF* 2 IX, pp. 4, 17). This does not imply that God lacks responsiveness to humanity.

Only God may be said to be accountable to himself alone, to trust himself alone, to follow his own truth. God is the ground of the claim that human creatures experience in conscience and law; God alone embodies eternally all the requirements of those moral claims (Origen, *De Princip.* II.5, *ANF* IV, pp. 278 ff.). Creatures are good by participating in God's goodness—not the reverse (Tho. Aq., *ST* I Q6, I, p. 30).

Since God is the ground of righteousness, God does not require a principle of moral action external to himself. So there is an ironic sense in which the best thing God can do is assert his own will, whereas our best acts consist in following God's will rather than asserting our own egocentric will. God's perfection requires only that God follow his own will, something that would be a mark of imperfection in human activity. God's perfections consist simply in being God and doing what God does. By contrast, our perfection does not consist primarily in asserting our own wills or feeling our own feelings, but, insofar as possible, in following God's way, truth, and life so as to appropriate the divine perfection that God offers in the law and the gospel (1 Pet. 1:16; Tertullian, *On Monogamy, ANF* III, pp. 59 ff.; Calvin, *Inst.* 2.12; 3.17 ff.; 4.13).

God's holiness expresses itself in the form of holy love. To affirm that the holy God is the God of love suggests that God is not centered in himself but reaches out toward others with ease and pleasure. So it would be a mistake to stress inordinately that aspect of God's holiness by which the standard of God's moral action is simply God alone (as if apart from others), if thereby we should miss the point that God's love reaches out to those in despair and in sin, to the lost and the demoralized (Eph. 3:17–19; 1 John 2:5 ff.).

God's Justice and Righteousness

The biblical ground for insisting upon fair dealings between people is that God, being righteous, requires righteousness (Amos 5:24; Mic. 6:8; Ps. 15:1–2). God, as One wholly just, requires justice in human relationships. Especially those who are called and authorized to exercise public justice and mete out judgment in human affairs are to be placed beside the plumb-line of divine justice (Amos 7:7, 8).

Justice is most often defined as the perpetual and constant will to render to each his or her due or right. This God does faithfully to creatures (Tho. Aq., *ST* I Q58.1, I, p. 1435). The one God is none other than the source of human justice: "These are the words of the Lord: Maintain justice, do the right; for my deliverance is close at hand, and my righteousness will show itself victorious. Happy is the man who follows these precepts" (Isa. 56:1, 2; Clement of Alex.,

Strom. VI.12, *ANF* II, pp. 502–4; Augustine, *CG* XX.28, *NPNF* 1 II, pp. 447 f.).

That God will judge justly in the final judgment is a source of comfort to believers and a call to penitence to those who pervert justice. But there is a sober awareness in the New Testament that all human righteousness falls short of divine righteousness, for "All have swerved aside, all alike have become debased" (Rom. 3:12). The good news is that God has provided the gift of Christ's righteousness to clothe us in God's own uprightness in the time of final judgment (Rom. 5:17; John Chrysostom, *Hom. on Timothy* IV, *NPNF* 1 XIII, pp. 419–23).

The righteousness of God implies that God's will is unfailingly determined by God's goodness (Justin Martyr, *On the Sole Government of God, ANF* I, pp. 290 ff.; Tho. Aq., *ST* I Q19, I, pp. 110 ff.). The righteousness of God, therefore, consists simply in the fulfillment of God's own will as invariably shaped by God's incomparable goodness, so that God works always in accord with his own good purpose. It is impossible for God to lack righteousness, for righteousness itself is understandable only in relation to God (Theophilus, *To Autolycus* III.9–12, *ANF* I, pp. 113 f.). It is impossible for sinners to act aright except by God's assistance (Justin Martyr, *Dialogue with Trypho* XCII, *ANF* I, p. 245; Tho. Aq., *ST* I–IIae Q56, I, pp. 822 f.).

Divine righteousness may be viewed in four distinguishable modes: Since righteousness is *essential* to God's moral nature, it is viewed as a moral attribute of God. Divine righteousness is *legislative* righteousness insofar as God is viewed as the author and ground of moral law and human responsibility. Divine righteousness is viewed as *administrative* (or dispensational) righteousness insofar as God administers and executes the divine law and requirement in human conscience and history. Finally, divine righteousness is viewed as *judicial* righteousness insofar as God becomes the end-time judge of all human and historical activities.

First, what we call righteous in its most complete form exists *essentially* in God alone. Since righteousness (*tsedeqāh*) is essential to God's moral character, it is viewed as a moral attribute of God: "All his ways are just" (Deut. 32:4). God "does no wrong, righteous and true is He!" (Deut. 32:4). "Righteousness and justice are the foundation of his throne" (Ps. 97:1, 2; cf. Ps. 89:14). The righteousness of God is revealed in God's covenant love and faithfulness: "Thy unfailing love, O Lord, reaches to heaven, thy faithfulness to the skies. Thy righteousness is like the lofty mountains, thy judgements are like the great abyss" (Ps. 36:5, 6; cf. Novatian, *Trin.* IV, *ANF* V, pp. 614, 615; Calvin, *Inst.* 1.17; 3.11–13).

Divine righteousness differs from the kind of justice that operates in business affairs, which is based upon equal partner exchange, for in dealing with God we are not dealing with an equal partner, as Paul noted: "Who has ever made a gift to him, to receive a gift in return?" (Rom. 11:35). Rather, the justice ascribed to God hinges on the more fundamental awareness that God "gives to all things what is right, defining proportion, beauty, order, arrangement, and all dispositions of place and rank for each, in accordance with that place which is most truly right" (Dionysius, *Div. Names* VIII.7, p. 158). Thus, we strive against God's justice when we despairingly complain that "Immortality should belong to mortal things and perfection to the imperfect . . . and immutability to those which change, and the power of accomplishment to the weak, and that temporal things should be eternal, and that things which naturally move should be unchangeable, and that pleasures which are but for a season should last for ever" (p. 159). When we despair over our inevitable human condition we lay an implicit charge against the justice of God.

Christian teaching seeks to speak rightly of God's justice (*theos-dike*, theodicy) under conditions in which it is assailed. Theodicy seeks meaningfully to set forth God's goodness and justice as seen in creation and redemption, despite apparent contradictions of them in history (Justin Martyr, *Dialogue with Trypho*, chaps. 92 ff., *ANF* I, pp. 245 ff.; Augustine, *Enchiridion* III–VI, *LCC* VII, pp. 342 ff.). God has not left humanity without conscience, reason, and moral law. Seemingly unfair distribution of rewards and punishments must be viewed from the anticipated resurrection of the just and unjust, and the last judgment. This will be the culminating end-time vindication of God's justice, beyond history's injustices. What each deserves this side of the resurrection is in part assessed in relation to our created nature, made in God's image for participation in God's blessing, and by the habitual moral behaviors that we acquire through which we become more or less fit recipients of God's blessing, (Origen, *Ag. Celsus* IV.6 ff., *ANF* IV, pp. 499 ff.; Tertullian, *Resurrection of the Flesh*, *ANF* III, pp. 545 ff.).

The best that human choosing can do is to follow God's requirement insofar as conscience, law, and grace make it known, and while lacking completeness, affirm God's own righteousness as completing what is humanly incomplete: "The Lord is our Righteousness" (Jer. 23:6; Luther, *Treatise on Good Works* XI, *WML* I, pp. 196 ff.). It is folly for humans to "ignore God's way of righteousness, and try to set up their own" (Rom. 10:3).

Second, the *legislative* aspect of the righteousness of God is that which provides the law, and enables it to be heard in the human heart. God's righteousness stamps the law with God's own completeness (Clementina, *Hom.* VIII.10, *ANF* VIII, p. 272; Gregory Nazianzen, *Second Or. on Easter* XI ff., *NPNF* 2 VII, pp. 426 ff.). "The law of the Lord is perfect and revives the soul. The Lord's instruction never fails, and makes the simple wise. The precepts of the Lord are right and rejoice the heart. The commandment of the Lord shines clear and gives light to the eyes" (Ps. 19:7, 8; Wesley, *WJW* V, pp. 439 ff.).

Even Paul, who was so keenly aware that human sin could pervert the best of laws and the law in turn could intensify sin, nonetheless affirmed, "The law is in itself holy, the commandment is holy and just and good. Are we to say then that this good thing was the death of me? By no means" (Rom. 7:12, 13). The deepest moral requirement, whether of conscience or law, has its source and ground in none other than "the Lord our judge, the Lord our law-giver" (Isa. 33:22; Origen, *De Princip.* II.6, *ANF* IV, p. 280; Calvin, *Inst.* 2.7).

God's own actions exceed in the performance of the same law required of humanity. God does not follow a lesser code or law than God gives to others (Clement of Alex., *Strom.* I.26–29, *ANF* II, pp. 338 ff.). God's actions best express what God requires. "The Lord in her midst is just; he does no wrong; morning by morning he gives judgement, without fail at daybreak" (Zeph. 3:5).

Nor does God lay upon creatures the burden of having to follow infinitely expanding requirements to do the impossible. For with the law is provided mercy and forgiveness. "The Lord is righteous in all his ways . . . very near is the Lord to those who call to him, who call to him in singleness of heart" (Ps. 145:17, 18). The law is God's way of adapting the divine requirement to the limitations of human existence (Rev. 17:7; Origen, *De Princip.* II.5, *ANF* II, pp. 278–81).

Third, the *administrative* expression of God's righteousness is seen in the history of providence. God's guiding and overruling governance in history is grasped only by examining universal history. God's righteousness patiently and surely pervades the historical process, assuring its rightful outcome, yet honoring human freedom by allowing it to actualize itself under both sin and grace (Rom. 1:18–25; 3:21–28; 5:1 ff.).

Central to the account of God's righteousness made known in history is the gospel, that God's righteousness is made known in

Jesus Christ and is available to all who believe (Rom. 3:22). Paul preached that the same righteousness of God that was known by Abraham and the prophets was made known in the history of Jesus (Rom. 1:17; 3:21; 4:3–6). Righteousness has God as its source (Phil. 3:9). It is most fully revealed in Christ's death and resurrection. Through his perfect obedience to God's will in life and death, Christ bore the curse of our alienation from God (Gal. 3:13; John Chrysostom, *Comm. on Galatians* IV, *NPNF* 1 XIII, pp. 30–35; Tho. Aq., *ST* I Q21, I, pp. 117 ff.; Wesley, *WJW* V, pp. 313 ff.). The sinner receives Christ's righteousness by grace through faith (2 Cor. 5:21; Eph. 2).

Fourth, God's *judicial* righteousness is expressed by divine justice and judgment, both within and beyond history (Athenagoras, *Resurrection of the Dead* XVII, XVIII, *ANF* II, pp. 158, 159). It would hardly be just if God provided the instruction of the law and then entirely ignored whether creatures followed the law or not. The One who grounds and offers the law also justly judges when we fulfill or negate it. We feel God's judging righteousness very immediately and personally in the serenity of a good conscience or the pain of an offended conscience (Justin Martyr, *The Sole Government of God*, *ANF* I, pp. 290–93; Calvin, *Inst.* 3.2; 3.10; 3.19 f.; Wesley, *WJW* VI, pp. 186 ff.).

"Remember where you stand," warned the Epistle to the Hebrews, which viewed all current ethical judgments within the context of final divine judgment: "You stand before Mount Zion and the city of the living God, heavenly Jerusalem, before myriads of angels, the full concourse and assembly of the first-born citizens of heaven, and God the judge of all, and the spirits of good men made perfect, and Jesus the mediator of a new covenant" (Heb. 12:18–24). Similarly Paul envisioned a final judgment: "God's just judgement will be revealed, and he will pay every man for what he has done. To those who pursue glory, honour, and immortality by steady persistence in well-doing, he will give eternal life; but for those who are governed by selfish ambition, who refuse obedience to the truth and take the wrong for their guide, there will be the fury of retribution" (Rom. 2:6–8; Clement of Alex., *Strom.* IV.24, *ANF* II, pp. 437, 438).

God's anger toward sin (Exod. 22:24; Deut. 32:21 f.; Jer. 42:18; Rom. 1:18), however, does not imply any diminution of the love of God toward morally straying creatures (Augustine, *Trin.* XV.25, *LCC* VIII, pp. 155 ff.; Tho. Aq., *ST* I Q3.2, I, pp. 15 ff.). Unrepented and unexpiated sin will not be rewarded by a just God. God's dispensational justice is an aspect of the righteousness of God. At the end, God with perfect justice will dispense happiness to creatures according to the responsiveness of each to the law of God, which itself becomes rightly fulfilled in Christ. Made in the image of God, humanity is intended to participate in the blessed life. As persons who acquire habits, personality traits, and, in the long run, moral or immoral characters, we habitually come to act in ways that make us more or less fit to receive divine blessings. As moral decision makers we act concretely in good or evil works that either please or displease the holy, just, and good God (Prov. 29:26; Luke 11:48; Clementina, *Recognitions* IX.13, *ANF* VIII, p. 186).

God is just in punishing sin, yet in Jesus God has taken our sin upon himself: "We come to you therefore as Christ's ambassadors. It is as if God were appealing to you through us: in Christ's name, we implore you, be reconciled to God! Christ was innocent of sin, and yet for our sake God made him one with the sinfulness of men, so that in him we might be made one with the goodness of God himself" (2 Cor. 5:20, 21). In Christ, "God's justice has been brought to light. The Law and the prophets both bear witness to it: it is God's way of righting wrong, effective through faith in Christ for all who have such faith—all, without distinction" (Rom. 3:21). It is God's own righteousness, therefore, that has become "the remedy for the defilement of our sins, not our sins only but the sins of all the world" (1 John 2:2; cf. Origen, *Ag. Celsus* VIII.13, *ANF* IV, p. 644; Teresa of Avila, *Interior Castle* VII, *CWST* III, pp. 302–9).

Is the law good because God wills it, or has God willed it because it is good? Medieval nominalists argued that it is God's choice that makes an action right, whereas realists argued that God chooses the right because it is right. The question comes down to whether the will of God or God's nature or essence is the standard of right and wrong. The questions is best solved by recalling that there is harmony between the willing and being of God. The standard that God offers and to which God alone conforms is not external to God but is God's own essence: perfect justice. The moral law is rooted in God's own nature (John Chrysostom, *Concerning the Statues*, hom. XII, XIII, *NPNF* 1 IX, pp. 418 ff.). The final standard of the law is the very nature of God.

The Constant Goodness of God

The Divine Reliability—Constant, Unchanging Love (Immutability)

Scripture stresses the divine reliability, the constancy of God's purpose, the trustworthiness of the divine nature. Other things "shall pass away, but thou endurest; like clothes they shall all grow old; thou shalt cast them off like a cloak, and they shall vanish; but thou art the same" (Ps. 102:26–27). Even though the people change their minds about the covenant, the Lord does not alter commitment to the covenant: "I am the Lord, unchanging" (Mal. 3:6; Anon., *Twelve Topics on the Faith*, ANF VI, p. 51). The psalmist marveled at the reliability of the Lord whose "plans shall stand for ever, and his counsel endure for all generations" (Ps. 33:11; Origen, *Ag. Celsus* I.21, ANF IV, p. 405).

The celebration of divine constancy is reflected also in the New Testament, for whom God is the source of every good gift, "the Father of the lights of heaven. With him there is no variation, no play of passing shadows" (James 1:17). God remains always consistent with his own nature as insurmountably good (Gregory of Nyssa, *Great Catech.* I, NPNF 2 V, pp. 474–76; Catherine of Siena, *Prayers* 10, pp. 78–83). God's essential nature does not change from better to worse, but remains always only the best (Julian of Norwich, *Showings*, CWS, pp. 197–99). God as known in Christ is "the same yesterday, today and for-ever" (Heb. 13:8). Classical Christianity's deepest objection to Arianism was its notion that "the Son of God is variable or changeable" and therefore less than God (Nicene Creed, NPNF 2 XIV, p. 3).

The theme of divine reliability is caricatured when stated without reference to other divine qualities, such as mercy, love, and justice. If pressed in isolation from God's character as responsive, empathic, and compassionate, then the assertion of the divine reliability turns easily into an abstract, speculative assertion of divine rigidity and unresponsiveness (Hartshorne and Reese, "The Standpoint of Panentheism," *PSG*, pp. 1–25). The divine constancy does not imply immobility or lack of empathy. The celebration of divine reliability is a religious affirmation that no change can or will take place in the divine nature— that God will never cease being God, incomparably good and powerful. But that does not imply that God cannot relate to changing human circumstances. And that God is capable of responsive interaction in the divine-human encounter does not imply changes in the essential nature or intention or will of God. "For, continuing unchangeable in His essence, He condescends to human affairs by the economy of His Providence" (Origen, *Ag. Celsus* IV.14, ANF IV, p. 502).

God can will a change, but this does not imply that God changes in essential nature as good (John Chrysostom, *Exhort. to Theodore* I.6, NPNF 1 IX, p. 95). Augustine showed that God changes works without changing plans, for God is "unchangeable, yet changing all things, never new, never old, making all things new, yet bringing old age upon the proud, and they know it not; always working, ever at rest; gathering, yet needing nothing" (*Conf.* I.4, *LCC* VII, p. 33; cf. *CG* XIV.10 ff., *NPNF* 1 II, pp. 271 ff.).

It is precisely because God is unchanging in the eternal purpose of self-giving love that God is so attentively answerable, so free in responding to changing historical circumstances, and so versatile in personal response. "The unchangeable God holds an unchangeable purpose, but steadiness of purpose requires variety in execution" (Hall, *DTh* III, p. 89; cf. Whitehead, *Process and Reality*, pp. 521 ff.). Early Christian exegesis held tautly together the unchanging love of God with the responsiveness required by that unchanging love: "For abiding the same, He administers mutable things according to their nature, and His Word elects to undertake their administration" (Origen, *Ag. Celsus* VI.42, *ANF* IV, p. 602; cf. *PSG*, pp. 1–164, 499 ff.; an example of how process theology has depended upon classic Christian theism against which it has constantly polemicized).

Thomas Aquinas brilliantly argued that everything temporal tends to change toward better and worse qualities; hence God's will, justice, and holiness do not change toward better and worse, because they are always already insurmountably good (Tho. Aq., *ST* I Q9, I, pp. 38 ff.). Although God's wisdom is capable of addressing itself to changing modes and conditions of history now in one way, and later in another, God's wisdom itself does not change (Job 12; Jer. 10:12). It is God's wisdom precisely because it is capable of relating itself to different historical situations with incomparable divine understanding (1 Cor. 1:17–30). God can never be more wise, more holy, more merciful than God is, and eternally will be (John of Damascus, *OF* I.9, *NPNF* 2 IX, p. 12; cf. Hilary, *Trin.* IX.72 ff., *NPNF* 2 IX, pp. 180, 181).

The biblical witness views God not as immobile or static, but as consistent with his own nature, congruent with the depths of his own personal being, stable, not woodenly predictable. If God promises forgiveness, "he is just, and may be trusted to forgive our sins" (1 John 1:9), because the character of God is dependable.

In this connection the classical exegetes rigorously probed those Scriptures that speak of God "repenting" (*nacham*, Gen. 6:6, 7; Exod. 32:14; 1 Sam. 15:35; Jer. 26:3, 13, 19; Amos 7:3; Jon. 3:10; Clementina, *Hom.*, III.39, *ANF* VIII, p. 245). Do they imply a fundamental change in the divine being or essence, or in the divine plan? No. The Scriptures employ anthropomorphic metaphors and analogies to speak of God's free responsiveness to human needs amid changing historical circumstances. They represent God in human terms as responsively dealing with new human contingencies by taking ever-new initiatives and thereby relinquishing older ones to which there had been inadequate human response (Tertullian, *Ag. Marcion* II.24, *ANF* III, p. 315; John of Damascus, *OF* I.11, 12, *NPNF* 2 IX, pp. 13, 14). But such passages never imply that something has changed in the essential being of God or that any divine attributes have mutated.

What may appear to be a change of God's mind may upon closer inspection be a different phase of the unfolding of the divine plan. God's sovereign freedom is able to will changes within the contingencies of history. This is not a contradiction of the divine reliability. Rather, the execution of the divine purpose is firm precisely because it is responsive to temporal contingencies (Augustine, *CG* XXII.2, *NPNF* 1 II, p. 480; cf. Julian of Norwich, *Showings*, *CWS*, pp. 231–33).

The divine constancy is often referred to in the Psalms: "From age to age everlasting thou art God" (Ps. 90:2). Creaturely purposes, actions, and intentions have a beginning and an end, but God's character does not change. The truth of God does not change. In dealing flexibly with the changing scenes of history, God remains faithful to his own unchanging will to sustain, love, and redeem creation (Lactantius, *Div. Inst.* IV.12, *ANF* VII, pp. 110, 111; Calvin, *Inst.* 2.8–10; 3.2; 3.8).

Immutability is sometimes stated in wooden, Aristotelian terms that wholly lack these vital energies of the biblical witness to God's constancy. One of the most persistent criticisms of classical Christian theism by the process theologians is what they regard as an inordinate exaggeration of this immutability, making it appear that God is unresponsive to human need (Hartshorne, *Natural Theology for Our Times*). Overestimating the stranglehold of Aristotle upon the ancient ecumenical Christian tradition, recent theologians may have *under*estimated the perduring counter-Aristotelian influences of the tradition of exegesis of the psalms, Isaiah, Paul, and John. The divine immutability of purpose and essence does not mean that God is unresponsive or incapable of interaction, but that the deeper intentionality of the will of God—*chesed*, God's unfailing holy love—is sure and unchanging (Hos. 3:1; 11:1–4). That Christ is the same yesterday, today, and forever (Heb. 13:8) does not imply divine unresponsiveness or that the living Christ whom we meet in the sacrament is incapable of relating to us. Rather, it celebrates that the same one whom we met at the Lord's table last epiphany, or last Easter, will be there the next time we break bread. God's compassions do not fail (James 1:17). They are new every morning (Lam. 3:23). Scripture marvels at the constant newness of God (Ps. 96:1; Heb. 8:8–13; Rev. 21:1–5). It is ever new precisely because the steadfast love of God does not change (Catherine of Siena, *Prayers* 15, pp. 127–36).

That time changes is a familiar notion to us. Times change, but does God change times? The idea of time changing was surprisingly reversed in the God of Daniel, who was said to be constantly "changing the times," yet according to a changeless divine purpose: "Blessed be God's name from age to age, for all wisdom and power are his. He changes seasons and times; he deposes kings and sets them up; he gives wisdom to the wise" (Dan. 2:20–21). Yahweh was disclosed to Moses as "compassionate and gracious, long-suffering, ever constant and true, maintaining constancy to thousands, forgiving iniquity" (Exod. 34:6, 7).

The covenant God is One who remains loyal to the covenant partner Israel, as Hosea unfailingly loved Gomer. For some unfathomable reason, God loves Israel, and through Israel wishes to make known the divine love toward all humanity. God chose Israel as covenant partner, a people "set apart" (Ps. 4:3; Isa. 14:1). That covenant does not change: God does not forget. Israel forgets. Israel ignores and fails to understand the covenant, but God chooses to sustain the covenant despite all negations from the covenant partner. The covenant remains, though Israel has dismissed and ignored it. That is what is meant by *chesed*—the steadfast, unfailing, holy love of God (Irenaeus, *Ag. Her.* IV.9, 10, *ANF* I, pp. 472, 473; Westminster Conf., *CC*, pp. 202, 203; Watson, *TI* I, pp. 398 ff.).

The Divine Veracity, Faithfulness, and Congruence

Closely related to constancy is the scriptural attestation to God's *truthfulness* (veracity), which implies God's faithfulness to the divine truth that God alone is and knows. God is not torn apart within. There is a steady congruence between who God is and what God does. God's actions and disclosures are in no way inconsistent with God's essential goodness (John Chrysostom, *Hom. on John* LXXIII, *NPNF* 1 XIV, p. 269; Augustine, *Of True Religion* 94–113, *LCC* VI, pp. 273–83; Calvin, *Inst.* 2.8).

By veracity we mean simply that God is true, and being true, tells the truth, and becomes revealed as truth through history. That God not only makes known the truth but *is* the truth, is a constant theme of Scripture (John 3:33; 8:13–26; 1 Cor. 11:10; Augustine, *On Profit of Believing* XXXIV, *NPNF* 1 III, pp. 363 f.). It is "impossible for God to lie" (Heb. 6:18, KJV). Yahweh is the "God of truth" (Ps. 31:5). "Thy word is founded in truth" (Ps. 119:160). Jesus said: "I am the way; I am the truth and I am life" (John 14:6). In Jesus "the true God" is revealed (1 John 5:20).

In Jesus' prayer for his disciples recorded in John 17, he prays to the "only true God" (John 17:3) that the disciples would be consecrated "by the truth" amid the evils of a false and darkened world (John 17:17). John's Gospel sets forth the teaching in detail that God is truth, that truth is essential to the nature of God, that the truth is revealed in Jesus, the Christ ("thy word is truth," v. 17b), and that the believer is sustained by the truthfulness of God even amid historical false-hoods, as branch is sustained by vine (John 15:1 ff.; John Chrysostom, *Hom. on John*, hom. XXXI, *NPNF* 1 XIV, pp. 106–11; Tho. Aq., *ST* Q16 I, pp. 89 ff.; Calvin, *Inst.* 1.10.2; 3.20.41; Watson, *TI* I, pp. 444 ff.).

The faithfulness of God means that God proves true to his prom-ises by keeping them. God's faithfulness is a steady, reliable applica-tion of divine truth to changing, developing historical circumstances. Trusting God's fidelity, the faithful are kept by him "sound in spirit, soul, and body, without fault when our Lord Jesus Christ comes. He who calls you is to be trusted; he will do it" (1 Thess. 5:23, 24). For "the Lord is faithful" (2 Thess. 3:3, KJV), the incomparably "true one" (Rev. 3:7) upon whom supplicants can rely as trustworthy (Irenaeus, *Ag. Her.* IV.20 ff., *ANF* I, pp. 487 ff.; cf. Luther, *Preface to the Psalms*, *ML*, pp. 37–40).

God does not cease being truthful while sharing in human es-trangement. For precisely amid God's condescension to share our hu-manity, God's righteousness and integrity as sovereignly free Lord are maintained and manifested. God's participation in human estrange-ment without becoming estranged is analogous to the congruence of the empathic therapeutic agent in psychotherapy. The church fathers were aware, long before modern psychotherapy, that one of the pri-mary conditions of constructive psychological change is congruence, the capacity to feel one's feelings fully, to remain in touch with one's experiencing process, and to share in another estrangement without losing one's self-identity (Ambrose, *Letters to Priests*, *FC* 26, pp. 336, 361; Catherine of Siena, *Treatise on Prayer*, p. 253). When one senses the inner congruence of another, and knows one is in the presence of another who is in touch with him- or herself, that is when it becomes possible to enter more fully into one's own estrangement, and become more congruent within oneself (Carl Rogers defined congruence as the state in which "self-experiences are accurately symbolized, and are included in the self-concept in this accurately symbolized form," "A

Theory of Therapy, Personality and Interpersonal Relationships," in *Psychology: A Study of a Science*, p. 206; cf. Oden, *KC*, chap. 2). Scripture portrays God similarly as true to himself, knowing himself fully and without self-deception, as being the true God he appears to be (Irenaeus, *Ag. Her.* III.11 ff., *ANF* I, pp. 426 ff.; Tho. Aq., *ST* I Q16, 17, I, pp. 93–97); hence One in whose presence our deceptions are healed.

The Divine Benevolence: God as Incomparably Good

The psalmists delighted in meditating on the goodness of God (Pss. 1:2; 77:12). For "The goodness of God endureth continually" (Ps. 52:1). "Thou, O God, in thy goodness, providest for the poor" (Ps. 68:10). "How great is thy goodness" (Ps. 31:19). The same divine goodness is celebrated in the New Testament as leading to repentance (Rom. 2:4) and providing the gifts and fruits of the Spirit (Gal. 5:22; Eph. 5:9).

The divine goodness is that attribute through which God wills the happiness of creatures and desires to impart to creatures all the goodness they are capable of receiving (Tertullian, *Ag. Marcion* II, *ANF* III, pp. 297 ff.; Augustine, *Trin.* VIII.4, 5, *NPNF* 1 III, pp. 118, 119; Anselm, *Proslog.*, XXIII–XXV, pp. 145–51). The first of these goods is life itself, so that creatures may share in life with the living God. Thus the created order is not boringly limited merely to inanimate, lifeless objects (Gen. 1:20; 2:7). Suppose there were a world full of Grand Canyons; if no living, perceiving, sapient being were there to behold them, the aesthetic benefits would be unreceivable and unreceived.

Having given the primary value of life, God then allows life to be sustained and perpetuated, to propagate and defend itself, to further define itself adaptively, and in so doing to enable innumerable secondary values (Neh. 9:20, 21; Song of Sol. 1:15–2:6; Tho. Aq., *SCG* I.38 ff., pp. 152 ff.; N. Hartmann, *Ethics* II). God displays the goodness intrinsic to the divine character by bestowing upon living creatures prolific capacities for enjoying creation, for receiving the goods God has created, and for creating secondary goods that both God and creatures can enjoy. There is no bound to the goodness of God, which without ceasing to be good is at the same time eternally just, holy, and lacking in nothing (Gregory of Nyssa, *Great Catech.* I, *NPNF* 2 V, pp. 474–76; Tho. Aq., *ST* I Q6, I, pp. 28 ff.).

God is not only good in himself, but wills to communicate this goodness to creatures. Not merely possessing goodness, but communicating it to others, is characteristic of Scripture's attestation of God.

This may be viewed in the light of triune teaching. For within the Godhead, there is an eternal communication of the Father's benevolent self-existence and life to the Son by eternal generation, even as Father and Son eternally communicate their goodness to the Spirit, and the three communicate the effulgence of divine glory to each other and to creation (Hilary, *On Trin.* XI.42–49, *NPNF* 2 IX, pp. 215–17). God's goodness is wholly voluntary—not imposed upon God by something else (Cyril of Jerusalem, *Catech. Lect.* VI.7, *NPNF* 2 VII, p. 35).

Divine goodness profoundly qualifies all other divine attributes, for there is no divine power apart from its being benevolent. There is no divine justice that could ignore what is good. There is no truth of God that is not good for creatures. The being of God encompasses every excellence that can properly belong to the One eternal, personal Spirit who is incomparably good, undiminished by defects, uncorrupted by evil motives, and unsurpassable in holiness (Catherine of Siena, *Prayers* 9, pp. 69–74). In human history we experience many temporal goods, but they are all corruptible, prone to defect, mixed with tainted intentions. Only God can be said to be that one good that is good without qualification. "No one is good except God alone" (Luke 18:19; Tertullian, *Ag. Marcion* IV.36, *ANF* III, pp. 409–11).

God's goodness corresponds with, yet transcends, the best conceptions of moral good of which we are capable (John of Damascus, *OF* I.4, 9, 12 ff., *NPNF* 2 IX, pp. 3, 12, 13 ff.). "Make no mistake, my friends. All good giving, every perfect gift, comes from above, from the Father of the lights of heaven" (James 1:17). "What do you possess that was not given to you?" Paul asked (1 Cor. 4:7).

The *patience* of God's power in the face of creatures' persistent idolatry is evidence of God's unhurried goodness, which itself has a profound instructional intent: "Do you think lightly of his wealth of kindness, of tolerance, and of patience, without recognizing that God's kindness is meant to lead you to a change of heart?" (Rom. 2:4; Tertullian, *On Patience, ANF* III, pp. 707 ff.; Origen, *Hom. XXVII on Numbers, CWS*, pp. 251 ff.).

In this section on the constant goodness of God, the varied themes of the divine reliability, veracity, and benevolence have been constantly and necessarily interwoven with the theme of the love of God. As divine goodness is the bridge between God's holiness and God's love, so does divine love constitute the aim, end, and zenith of all divine attributes. We have indicated that holiness and love are summative moral qualities of God. Aware of how intricately these themes intermesh, we now deal more specifically with the attribute of divine love.

The Compassion of God

God Is Love

Nowhere is God defined more concisely than in the First Epistle of John: "God is love" (1 John 4:16; cf. Hilary, *Trin.* IX.61, *NPNF* 2 IX, p. 176). That God is love implies that benevolent affection, good will, and empathic understanding are the characteristic qualities in God through which God relates compassionately to creatures (Clement of Alex., *Strom.* IV.16–18, *ANF* II, pp. 427–30). If God is love, then in order to grasp what love is we can do no better than to look at the outpouring of God's energies at work in the redemption of sin: "This is love: not that we loved God, but that he loved us and sent his Son as an atoning sacrifice for our sins" (1 John 4:10; cf. Augustine, *On Patience* 15, *NPNF* 1 III, p. 532). Consequently *love* is of all terms the one most directly attributable to God as essential to God's being.

To speak only of God's holiness without speaking of God's love might seem to imply that God cares only about his own life and not the lives of others. God's holiness does not remain trapped within itself, but reaches out for others. When Scripture tells the story of how God reaches out, it does not merely use objective, descriptive, or scientific language, but rather the warmest, most intimate, most involving, engaging, and powerfully moving metaphor in human experience: love (Clement of Rome, *First Epis.* 48–56, *ANF* I, pp. 18–20; cf. the terms *amor, dilectio, caritas,* in Augustine, *CG* XIV.7, *NPNF* 1 II, p. 266). It is impossible to speak of Christian teaching without speaking of God's love. To make clear what God's love means is the central task of Christian preaching (Tertullian, *Ag. Marcion* IV.16, *ANF* III, pp. 370–72; Calvin, *Inst.* 2.16.1–4). The music God makes in creation is not a dirge but a love song to, for, and through creatures (Origen, *Song of Songs, Prologue,* CWS, pp. 219 f., 226–29).

God's love reveals the divine determination to hold in personal communion all creatures capable of enjoying this communion (Catherine of Genoa, *Purgation and Purgatory, CWS,* pp. 77–81; *The Spiritual Dialogue,* pp. 108–12). Love is God's desire to communicate the depth of divine goodness to each and every creature and to impart appropriate goods to all creatures proportional to their capacity to receive the good (Tho. Aq., *SCG* I.91, pp. 277–82). All things are loved by God, but all things are not loved in the same way by God, since there are degrees of capacity, receptivity, and willingness among varied creatures to receive God's love (Tho. Aq., *ST* I Q20, I, pp. 113 ff.).

To say that God is love does not imply that God is love according to a partial, mean, weak, distorted, or halfhearted definition of love. The primary purpose of creation is that God wishes to bestow love and teach love, so that creatures can share in the blessedness of divine life, of loving and being loved (Teresa of Avila, *Way of Perfection* VI, VII, *CWST,* pp. 26–37). No other purpose of creation transcends this one (Basil, *Hex.* VII.5, *NPNF* 2 VIII, p. 93; Calvin, *Inst.* 1.15–16).

We are not without some knowledge of love as human beings, for no person can grow to maturity without it. Love is a confluence of two seemingly paradoxical impulses: the hunger for the desired object and the desire to do good for the beloved. One impulse takes and the other gives (Ambrose, *Duties* II.7, *NPNF* X, pp. 48–50; Luther, *Heidelberg Disputation* 28, *LW* 31, p. 57). In Greek, the passion to possess another is called *eros,* whereas self-giving love is called *agapē.* They are in tension in all human love.

Agape **and** Eros

Although *agapē* and *eros* seem to be opposites, they may come together and flow in balanced simultaneity and support each other's impulses. Both are expressions of the inestimably high value the heart sets upon that which is loved (Gregory of Nyssa, *On the Soul and the Resurrection, NPNF* 2 V, p. 450). Both involve a prizing: love prizes the beloved so earnestly that it cannot rest without its possession (*eros*), without experiencing the completion of itself in the other; love prizes the beloved so highly that it cannot withhold any available, feasible gift or service (*agapē*). Both involve a yearning: love as *eros* yearns for the self's fulfillment through another; love as *agapē* yearns for the other's fulfillment even at a cost to oneself (Catherine of Genoa, *Purgation and Purgatory,* pp. 71, 72; C. S. Lewis, *The Four Loves*).

To separate *eros* and *agapē* or to oppose them or set them absolutely off against each other as alternatives (cf. Nygren, *Agapē and Eros*) is to view love incompletely and to fail to understand how one dimension may strengthen the other. *Agapē* may give itself unstintingly for the other, while it yet longs for answering love from the beloved. John's epistle deftly captured the heart of this reciprocity: "We love because he loved us first" (1 John 4:19, RSV; cf. Wesley, *WJW* XI, pp. 421 ff.).

One who loves may love wrongly or unworthily. Augustine thought that the heart of the problem of sin was misguided love, which loves the lesser rather than the greater good (Augustine, *Chr. Doctrine* I.23–33, *NPNF* 1 II, pp. 528–32; cf. *On Patience* 14 ff., *NPNF* 1 III, pp. 532 ff.). But even when love loves poorly or wrongly or tragically, it still contains some dimension of these two intertwining aspects of yearning for the other's good and one's own good through the other, both prizing and desiring the other. Those who recognize only the selfish side of love expressing itself constantly may ignore the fact that it is healthy to deem oneself worthy and needful of being loved. Admittedly the egocentric aspect of love often dominates the self-giving aspect. But the deeper that love becomes rooted in reality (i.e., the reality of divine love), the more fully is the passion for the other complemented by the self-giving impulse (Clement of Alex., *Strom.* IV.15 ff., *ANF* II, pp. 426 ff.). The one who best understands that it is more blessed to give than receive (Acts 20:35) is the one who learns truly to love in response to the One most lovable (John Chrysostom, *Homilies on John* LXXVIII, LXXIX, *NPNF* 1 XIV, pp. 286–95).

Love may remain completely unreturned without ceasing to be love. Love for one's beloved is not finally dependent upon its being reciprocated. Love that promises to be returned yet remains for a long time unreturned, or love that confronts enormous obstacles while seeking to be returned, is the subject of the greatest literature and drama (Abelard, *The Story of My Misfortunes*; Kierkegaard, "Quidam's Diary" in *Stages Along Life's Way, The Works of Love*). "Even its shadows are beautiful" (Clarke, *CDG*, p. 85). But love that becomes fulfilled is that which finds some balance of giving and receiving, of self-fulfillment and fulfillment of the other, of *eros* and *agapē*, of love received and love poured out (Ambrose, *Duties* II.7.37, *NPNF* 2 X, p. 49). A perfect love would be that which receives to the limit whatever goods can be received from a relationship and gives without bounds whatever goods can be given (Tho. Aq., *SCG* I.91, pp. 277–82; Teresa of Avila, *Way of Perfection* VI, pp. 67 ff.).

God's way of loving is not wholly discontinuous with what we know of loving. If it seems shocking to think that we could reason about God's love from human love, then we do well to listen carefully to Jesus: "Is there a man among you who will offer his son a stone when he asks for bread, or a snake when he asks for fish? If you, then, bad as you are, know how to give your children what is good for them, how much more will your heavenly Father give good things to those who ask him!" (Matt. 7:9–11). Although Jesus is realistic about the inadequacies of human love, he nonetheless invites us to think of God's care in comparison with good parental care (Tho. Aq., *ST* I Q20, I, pp. 113–16; Wesley, *WJW* V, p. 333).

Self-love means that the self is both the lover and the one loved. Ironically it is self-love that best proves that love requires two, a lover and beloved, even if the self is counted twice. It is not a heresy in Christian teaching to say that God loves himself, for what more worthy and beautiful object of love could be conceived? (Gregory of Nyssa, *On the Soul and the Resurrection*, NPNF 2 V, p. 450). We are called to love God "as ourselves" (Luke 10:27), thus assuming that we will be loving ourselves, prizing ourselves, acknowledging our own worth, and putting a high value upon our own lives (Ignatius, *Ephesians* XIV, ANF I, p. 55; Augustine, *On Chr. Doctrine* I.23–26, NPNF 1 II, pp. 528, 529; Luther, *WA* 2, p. 578, in *WLS* II, p. 830). But to organize our lives primarily around the love of ourselves is wretched and dehumanizing, because we were intended to love a more encompassing object of love than ourselves alone (Augustine, *Of True Religion* 87 ff., LCC VII, pp. 270 ff.).

God's love for humanity, like all love, is reciprocal. God prizes the world, and values especially human creatures, who have the freedom and imagination to respond to God and to share with God consciousness and compassion. God holds creatures dear and desires their fellowship, and grieves that human history should mire in sin (Catherine of Siena, *Prayers* 12, pp. 99–105). God, however, does not love creatures out of need or out of a lack of something in himself but rather because God beholds in them the good he created and preserved, even if it has become distorted (Augustine, *On Chr. Doctrine* I.12 ff., NPNF 1 II, pp. 525 ff.).

God loves humanity, but humanity is a world of particular persons. When it is said that God loves humanity, what is meant is that God loves each person individually, as well as in aggregate. God prizes each soul, and does not wish that anyone should perish (1 Tim. 2:4). The reciprocity of this divine-human relationship is viewed metaphorically in Hosea, who portrayed God's steadfast love for Israel as a yearning for Israel's return and continuing to love even when rejected by Israel—longing for reciprocation in the answering love of Israel (Hos. 1:3 ff.; Irenaeus, *Ag. Her.* IV.20.12, ANF I, p. 492).

God loves all creatures in the twofold sense that God unapologetically enjoys them for their own sake and desires their answering, enjoying love in response to eternally patient, self-sacrificial love (Augustine, *On Chr. Doctrine* I.22, NPNF 1 II, pp. 527, 528). God *is* love in these two senses—enjoyment of the beloved, and self-giving for the beloved's good—in perfect fullness, balance, harmony, and completeness. God *feels the worth of creatures* and *longs to do them good*. Because God loves in both of these ways in full and fitting balance, we say that God *is* love. God loves creatures in the first form (*eros*) of desiring and loving to hold them, in possessing and enjoying them, as parents enjoy children. In perfect desire God desires creatures to be what they can be. But this perfect enjoyment melds with the second dimension of love, *agapē*, the will to be radically for creatures even when creatures are stubbornly against themselves.

Sacrificial Love

Ultimately the cost is God's only beloved Son, Jesus Christ, the most crucial reversal in the drama of God's love. "God loved the world so much that he gave his only Son, that everyone who has faith in him may not die but have eternal life" (John 3:16). As God loves in this way, by self-sacrificial giving and serving the needy neighbor, so do we learn how to love, by loving as God loved, in whatever measure is possible for us as enabled by grace (Augustine, *Hom. on the First Epis. of John* VI–VII, *NPNF* 1 VII, pp. 493–505; Tho. Aq., *ST* I Q20, I, pp. 113 ff.; Calvin, *Inst.* 2.7).

God's love is directed toward both the godly and the ungodly, to those who more and less fully reflect God's own goodness, but in different ways. Those are particularly objects of God's love who refract God's holy love through their hearts and lives, who follow God's way of caring for the poor and rejected. God also loves sinners, because he sees in them something they may not see in themselves, namely, lovability, or at least potential lovability, and the possibility of restoration to the fullness of the divine fellowship (Augustine, *Treatise Concerning Man's Perfection in Righteousness*, *NPNF* 1 V, pp. 159–76). Paul wrote:

> For at the very time when we were still powerless, then Christ died for the wicked. Even for a just man one of us would hardly die, though perhaps for a good man one might actually brave death; but Christ died for us while we were yet sinners, and that is God's own proof of his love towards us. (Rom. 5:6–8)

Consummate Love

God's perfect love is viewed in the Johannine letters in the context of history's end. The end of history is understood in the light of Jesus' resurrection, which anticipates the end and through which believers can share in the end and therefore the meaning of history.

> He who dwells in love is dwelling in God, and God in him. This is for us the perfection of love, to have confidence on the day of judgement; and this we can have, because even in this world we are as he is. There is no room for fear in love; perfect love banishes fear. (1 John 4:16, 18)

Despite all the distortions of human loving, the faithful are enabled by grace to experience perfect love in the form of hope, viewed in relation to the end time. Perfection in love is precisely to have confidence in the work that God is working in Christ. That means, for Christians, that perfect love lives out of a deep affinity with faith. For perfect love is none other than "to have confidence" in God's redemptive work. This perfect love we can have. For it is within our reach, enabled by grace, to trust in God's love (Gregory of Nyssa, *On the Soul and the Resurrection*, NPNF 2 V, pp. 450–54; *On Perfection, FGG*, pp. 83, 84; Teresa of Avila, *The Way of Perfection* VI, *CWST*, II, pp. 26 ff.).

God is holy love. Holiness and love point directly to the center of the character of God. In God's holiness all of God's moral excellences are summed up and united. In God's love, God's holiness is manifested in relation to creatures (Augustine, *On Nature and Grace*, 84, *NPNF* 1 V, p. 151). God loves by desiring to impart holiness to creatures. The circle of this love is complete only with the answering love of the beloved, when the creature's heart and life joyfully reflect the beauty of God's holiness (Pss. 29:2; 96:9; Augustine, *On Psalms* XCVI, *NPNF* 1 VIII, pp. 472–74).

Holiness and Love Brought Together in Atonement

We must anticipate, at this pivotal juncture in the discussion of divine attributes, the issues of atonement to be thoroughly treated later in discussing salvation. But they pertain necessarily to this discussion, for where are we better able to recognize the coalescence of holiness and love than in the atoning work of God the Son? Atonement is the act of reconciliation (making "at-one") that Jesus as mediator effected by his death for the redemption of humanity, satisfactorily repairing the breach between God and humanity caused by sin.

Keep in mind that the holiness and love made known in Jesus Christ is nothing other than God's own holiness and love (Athanasius, *Incarnation of the Word* IV.6–16, *NPNF* 2 V, pp. 39–45). Christ is the once-and-for-all manifestation of the holy love of God that belongs to the essential definition of God, which is so crucial to God's character that it is rightly called the pivot of the moral attributes of God.

Holy love is most radically beheld in God's treatment of sin, especially in the cross of Christ, but this does not imply that prior to human fallenness these qualities were not melded in the divine character. Holy love is attested by Scripture of God from the beginning. The "Lamb that was slain" fulfills a promise set forth "since the world was made" (Rev. 13:8), even "before the foundation of the world" (1 Pet. 1:20).

Expressing the eternal purpose of God, the atonement in Jesus

Christ occurred as a historical event, as a sentence of execution, a death, and a risen life. It is especially through beholding and responding to this salvation event, Jesus Christ, that Christians have come to understand the holy love of God and the relation between God's holiness and God's love. As it was the *love* of God that sent the only Son (John 3:16), it was the *holiness* of God that required the satisfaction of divine justice through the sacrifice of the Son. These two themes are brought together powerfully in the first Johannine letter: "The love I speak of is not our love for God, but the love he showed to us in sending his Son as the remedy for the defilement of our sins" (1 John 4:10; John Chrysostom, *Hom. on John* XXVII, XXVIII, *NPNF* 1 XIV, pp. 93–99; Augustine, *Hom. on the First Epis. of John* VII, *NPNF* 1 VII, pp. 501–5; *Enchiridion* XXXII, *LCC* VII, pp. 411, 412).

Similarly in Paul's letters, it is precisely in God's act of *love* that God's *righteousness* and holy justice "has been brought to light" (Rom. 3:21). "It is God's way of righting wrong, effective through faith in Christ for all who have such faith—all without distinction" (v. 22; Luther, *Comm. on Galatians, ML,* pp. 109–15). Although holiness and love are not one and the same attribute, since there is a real difference between them, nonetheless they are unified in the cross of Christ, where love is the way holiness communicates itself under the conditions of sin and holiness loves with an unsullied, undefiled love (Clement of Alex., *Instr.* I.9, *ANF* II, pp. 228–32).

Wherever holiness is spoken of in Scripture, love is nearby; wherever God's love is manifested, it does not cease to be holy. Neither holiness nor love alone could have sufficed for the salvation of sinners (Anselm, *Cur Deus Homo* I, *BW,* pp. 178 ff.). For love without holiness would not be just in ignoring the offensiveness of sin, and holiness without love would not be able to effect the reconciliation.

But God's holy love bridges the gulf. "It is precisely in this that God proves his love for us; that while we were yet sinners, Christ died for us" (Rom. 5:8, NAB). At times God's holiness seems to take the leading role in reconciliation, such as when Paul wrote that "God designed him to be the means of expiating sin by his sacrificial death, effective through faith" (Rom. 3:25), yet that very faith immediately speaks of "the love of God shed abroad in our hearts" by the Holy Spirit (Rom. 5:5, KJV).

It is God's holiness that elicits divine anger at sin. For "men preferred darkness to light because their deeds were evil" (John 3:19). Yet this is preceded by the proclamation that "God so loved the world that he gave his only Son" (John 3:16, RSV). The most profound New

Testament moral injunctions hold together God's holiness and love precisely as they had become manifested in Christ: "Live in love as Christ loved you, and gave himself up on your behalf as an offering and sacrifice whose fragrance is pleasing to God" (Eph. 5:2; cf. Ignatius, *Letter to Ephesians* I, *ANF* I, pp. 49 ff.). The mystery and power of this fragrance is to be found precisely in the delicately balanced dialectic of holiness and love.

Although God's holiness detests sin, the motive of reconciliation is God's love for the sinner, which is so great that it is willing to pay the costliest price to set it aright. That God loves sinners does not imply that God any less resists sin. Yet in Christ, finally "Mercy triumphs over judgment" (James 2:13; Tho. Aq., *ST* I Q21, I, pp. 117 ff.). Holy love is manifested by the Father, through the intercession of the Son, by the power of the Holy Spirit (Augustine, *On Trin.* VIII.7, *NPNF* 1 III, pp. 122, 123; cf. Pope, *Compend.* I, p. 352).

The Court, the Temple, and the Family

Three powerful atonement metaphors clearly convey this unique constellation of meanings centering on the holiness of God's love. They are diverse scenes: the court of final justice, the temple of holiness, and the family of God.

In the courtroom metaphor, God the Son is pictured as the Judge judged in our place (Rom. 5:16–18; 1 John 2:1; Barth, *CD* IV/1). There is in this court not the slightest relaxation of the requirement of law or the necessity of justice. The sinner is convicted, yet the Advocate of sinners, the Son of God, takes the penalty of the sinner upon himself. In this saving event, the sinner is accepted and received by the divine judge because clothed in the righteousness of Christ, so that through faith in Christ's righteousness one is justified (Rom. 3:21–31; 5:1–18; 1 Cor. 6:11; 1 John 2:1, 2; 3:5; 5:9, 10).

In the family metaphor, God is pictured as the caring parent who loves all in the household, and whose love is great enough to discipline the children and to suffer on their behalf. The atonement, which was viewed as justification in the courtroom image, now becomes in the family metaphor a reconciliation of the parent with the prodigal child (Luke 15:11–32). "But while he was still a long way off his father saw him, and his heart went out to him. He ran to meet him, flung his arms round him, and kissed him" (Luke 15:20).

In the temple metaphor, God is pictured as the Holy One who is present in the holy place where propitiatory sacrifices are being made to satisfy the radical requirement of divine righteousness. The Son is here pictured as the high priest, who, as sinners approach the altar, cleanses, purifies, and readies them for meeting with the Holy One. At the altar of this high priest, the faithful are consecrated and sanctified to the service of God through the mediation of the Son, by the power of the Holy Spirit (Heb. 2:17; 3:1; 7:1 ff.).

In all three metaphors, God's holiness and God's love are held together in the closest way (Pope, *Compend.* I, p. 352; cf. Minear, *Images of the Church in the New Testament;* Bultmann, *TNT* I). They provide the most concise glimpse in the history of revelation of the character of God's love as holy love.

Grace and Mercy: The Forbearance and Kindness of God

Three other terms are necessary to complete our review of the characteristics of the divine life: *grace, mercy,* and *forbearance.* Closely intertwined, they are nonetheless distinguishable. The reckoning of divine attributes rings hollow without them.

Grace means unmerited favor. To affirm that God is gracious is to affirm that God does not deal with creatures on the basis of their works, merit, or deserving but rather out of upwelling, abundant divine compassion (Ignatius, *Magnesians* IX–X, *ANF* I, pp. 62, 63; Luther, *Comm. on Galatians, ML,* pp. 103 ff.). Through God's grace, mercy is freely given precisely to sinners (Matt. 9:36). Grace is inseparable from the *kindness* of God. In Christ God has shown "how immense are the resources of his grace, and how great his kindness to us in Christ Jesus" (Eph. 2:7; John Chrysostom, *Hom. on Ephesians* I, *NPNF* 1 XIII, pp. 50–55).

Divine *mercy* is the disposition of God to relieve the miserable, salve the wounds of the hurt, and receive sinners, quite apart from any works or merit (John Chrysostom, *Hom. Philippians* IV, *NPNF* 1 XIII, pp. 198–202; Luther, *The Freedom of a Chr., LW* 31, pp. 352 ff.; Calvin, *Inst.* 3.2.7; 3.12.4–8). Yet this gift does not imply that recipients have no responsibilities in response to it: "For it is by grace you are saved, through trusting him; it is not your own doing. It is God's gift, not a reward for work done. There is nothing for anyone to boast of. For we are God's handiwork, created in Christ Jesus to devote ourselves to the good deeds for which God has designed us" (Eph. 2:8–10; cf. Augustine, *On Grace and Free Will, NPNF* 1 V, pp. 443–67).

The *forbearance* of God is seen when divine love and mercy delay or lessen retribution, making one aware that "God's kindness is meant to lead you to a change of heart" (Rom. 2:4; Calvin, *Inst.* 2.8). The psalmist prayed for the kindness of God to be revealed: "But you, O

Lord, are a compassionate and gracious God, slow to anger, abounding in love and faithfulness. Turn to me and have mercy on me; grant your strength to your servant" (Ps. 86:15, 16, NIV).

The long-suffering love of God was made known to Moses in "Jehovah, the Lord," who is "compassionate and gracious, long-suffering, ever constant and true, maintaining constancy to thousands, forgiving iniquity, rebellion, and sin, and not sweeping the guilty clean away" (Exod. 34:6, 7). God is slow to anger, withholding righteous indignation (Rom. 9:22, 23), continuing patiently to offer a way of return for the prodigal (Luke 15). The mercy of God is patient: "With the Lord one day is like a thousand years, and a thousand years like one day. It is not that the Lord is slow in fulfilling his promise, as some suppose, but that he is very patient with you, because it is not his will for any to be lost, but for all to come to repentance" (2 Pet. 3:8, 9; cf. 1 Pet. 3:20).

God's *mercy* to sinners is the decisive expression of God's great compassion for lost and alienated creatures. God's mercy is not cheap, and never dissociated from God's holiness or justice (Anselm, *Cur Deus Homo* I.19–II.4, *BW*, pp. 222–44; Tho. Aq., *ST* I Q21, I, pp. 119 ff.). Where sin gains power over the human will, God offers mercy, seeking to restore the will to the obedience of faith. The restoration comes only through the suffering of the Son who willingly dies for sinners. The Spirit works in our hearts to awaken in us the awareness of God's incomparable merciful deed, reconciling the world to himself (Rom. 8:1 ff.; 1 Cor. 5:11–21). Mercy is the form taken by divine love when sin has blocked off other avenues. Nowhere is God's almighty power manifested more clearly than in showing mercy to sinners (*BCP*, "Collect for 11th Sunday After Trin."; cf. Watson, *TI* I, pp. 433 ff.). No power is greater than that beheld on the cross, reaching out to redeem sin.

Consequently, grace, mercy, forbearance, and kindness are characteristics of God's holy love. They temper God's power and manifest God's goodness.

Having now dealt with the primary attributes of God (uncreated, sufficient, necessary being, eternity, life), the relational attributes (insurmountable influence, presence, and knowing), the personal attributes of the divine life (spirit, will, freedom, self-determination), and the moral attributes (holy love, grace, mercy, and forbearance), we are now able to bring these all together in the extraordinary notion of divine happiness, or blessedness. Only God can be happy in the way that God is happy.

Conclusion: The Blessedness of God

To say that God is eternally blessed means that God rejoices eternally in the outpouring of goodness, mercy, and love upon creatures, each in accordance with their ability to participate in God's being. The blessedness of God, or divine beatitude, means that God's life is full of joy, both within the Godhead and in relation to creatures. God's enjoyment of redeemed creation is compared to the joy of a bridegroom who rejoices over the bride (Isa. 62:5). God's joy is eternal joy (Calvin, *Inst.* 3.25.10–12), causing the rivers to "clap their hands"; "let the mountains sing together for joy; let them sing before the Lord" (Ps. 98:8, 9; cf. Catherine of Genoa, *Spiritual Dialogue*, CWS, 91–103).

The blessedness of God is enjoyed and shared by the angelic hosts and by the faithful, and for that reason they are called, by way of refraction, blessed (Augustine, *CG* XI.11, 12, *NPNF* 1 II, pp. 211 f.; Valerian, *Hom.* XV, XVI, *FC* 17, pp. 399 ff.). The Lord takes delight in the celebration of the faithful (Prov. 15:8). The fitting response of the faithful to the joy of God is the life of praise. There is no end to the life of praise, for the blessed, sharing in the eternal life of God, thereby participate in eternal life, in ceaseless divine blessedness (Catherine of Siena, *Prayers* 17, pp. 147–53). "Now this is eternal life: that they may know you, the only true God, and Jesus Christ, whom you have sent" (John 17:3, NIV). The faithful "share in a common life, that life which we share with the Father and his Son Jesus Christ" (1 John 1:3). "As the abounding grace of God is shared by more and more, the greater may be the chorus of thanksgiving that ascends to the glory of God" (2 Cor. 4:15).

It is this divine beatitude that the psalmist celebrated: "May the glory of the Lord stand for ever and may he rejoice in his works!" (Ps. 104:31). Hence, "Bless the Lord, all his angels, creatures of might who do his bidding. Bless the Lord, all his hosts, his ministers who serve his will. Bless the Lord, all created things, in every place where he has dominion. Bless the Lord, my soul" (Ps. 103:20–22).

One is blessed who "has whatever he wills and who wills nothing evil" (Tho. Aq., *SCG* I.100, p. 300, referring to Augustine, *Trin.* XIII.5, *NPNF* 1 III, p. 171). God has what he wills and wills nothing evil, and is therefore incomparably blessed. "Through blessedness every desire is given rest, because, when blessedness is possessed, nothing else remains to be desired, since it is the ultimate end. He must, therefore, be blessed who is perfect in relation to all the things that He can desire" (Tho. Aq., *SCG* I.100, p. 299). In this way beatitude belongs in full measure only to God, and to creatures in proportion to their nearness to God (Tho. Aq., *ST* I Q26, I, p. 142; Teresa of Avila, *Exclamations of the Soul to God, CWST* II, pp. 402–20).

It is also said that God is angry and grieved over idolatry and sin. Does this constitute an interruption of the divine happiness? Terms such as "God's anger" are based on analogies that point to God's rejection of sin. These analogies are best used with constraint. Since the foreknowledge of God always already envisions the triumph of grace over sin, and since God is eternally aware of both fallenness and its being overcome, and since the fall only provides for God a new contingency in which God's mercy and grace can once again be powerfully manifested, God rejoices also at the overcoming of sin, even while sin is amid history gradually being judged and overruled (Julian of Norwich, *Showings, CWS*, pp. 263–65, 320 f.; Calvin, *Inst.* 2.10 ff.). "Where sin was thus multiplied, grace immeasurably exceeded it, in order that, as sin established its reign by way of death, so God's grace might establish its reign in righteousness, and issue in eternal life through Jesus Christ our Lord" (Rom. 5:21; Tertullian, *Ag. Marcion* V.13, 14, *ANF* III, pp. 456–61).

The gamut of divine attributes is therefore brought to a joyful culmination in Scripture's witness to the beauty of God's holiness. The grandeur and beauty of creation is ample evidence that God calls forth beauty and immanentally works within all natural creation to manifest that beauty. The awareness that God has redeemed what has fallen into distortion makes the beauty of God ever more wonderful. That God's holiness is beautiful is recurrently celebrated by the faithful: "One thing I ask of the Lord, one thing I seek: that I may be constant in the house of the Lord all the days of my life, to gaze upon the beauty of the Lord and to seek him in his temple" (Ps. 27:4). "Might and beauty are in his sanctuary" (Ps. 96:6). The presence of God is described by Ezekiel as an "encircling radiance," "like a rainbow in the clouds" (Ezek. 1:28).

The most stunning glimpse of the beauty of God is, ironically, in the Expected One who was despised and rejected, from whom beholders shrank at the sight of him, as something of "no account, a thing from which men turn away their eyes" because in his suffering his beauty had been disfigured (Isa. 53:2, 3), yet it is this very one who became recognized as "the Lily of the Valley," "the fairest of ten thousand to my soul" (hymn adapted from Song of Songs 5:10).

Conclusion

It is fitting that we have given detailed attention to the divine attributes, even though the way may have seemed arduous. For among all themes of Christian teaching, none is more capable of eliciting aesthetic theological pleasure than the study of the divine perfections. It is a joyful act to study eternal joy. It is merciful that God has allowed us to study God's mercy. It is the delight of theological reflection to see in their proper light the unity, harmony, balance, and proportion of the characteristics of the divine life. A right understanding of this proportionality goes far to prevent persistent misunderstandings of God and distortions of Christian teaching. This is why the divine attributes have so often been considered an essential part of catechetical instruction (cf. Cyril of Jerusalem, *Catech. Lect.*; John Chrysostom, *Two Instr. to Candidates for Baptism*; Augustine, *Instr. of the Uninstructed*; Luther, *Smaller Catech.*; Westminster Conf.).

We have sought to show how various terms attributable to God have been viewed as essential to God's being. Each of these terms rightly belongs to the preliminary definition of God—preliminary, that is, to subsequent Christian instruction, and a definition insofar as the reality of God yields to human language and definition. Each term of the next paragraph provides a small part of a mosaic pattern of characteristics of the divine life that seek to be beheld and celebrated in their wholeness. Now, in a single sentence, we embrace those terms attributable to God as essential to the divine life, which rightly belong to the attempt to distinguish God from creatures according to Christian Scripture and tradition:

God is the source and end of all things, that than which nothing greater can be conceived; uncreated, sufficient, necessary being; infinite, unmeasurable, eternal One, Father, Son, and Spirit; all-present, all-knowing, all-powerful, and all-empowering creator, redeemer, and consummator of all things; immanent without ceasing to be transcendent, Holy One present in our midst; whose way of personal being is incomparably free, self-determining, spiritual, responsive, and self-congruent; whose activity is incomparably good, holy, righteous, just, benevolent, loving, gracious, merciful, forbearing, kind; hence eternally blessed, eternally rejoicing, whose holiness is incomparable in beauty.

No one of these characteristics is adequately knowable exclusively through reason, but only through the history of revelation culminating in Jesus as declared in Scripture. Tradition, reason, and experience serve to clarify the unity, internal consistency, balance, and congruent interrelationship of perfections essential to God's being attested in Scripture. The remainder of this study will seek to clarify whether such a reality exists, and whether and in what sense this One is triune creator, provider, and source and end of all things.

Part II

THE REALITY OF GOD

CHAPTER 4

Whether God Is

It is evident already that God exists as a conception in our minds, for we have already formed this conception. The larger question remains for Christian teaching and pastoral care as to whether that One who exists in our minds also exists in reality.

In asking whether God exists, we are asking whether we can affirm that any being exists worthy to be called God. Does any being exist that indeed is eternally caringly present, whose counsel is infinitely wise and just, whose actions and motives are holy, whose goodness is such that it is worthy of being called infinitely good, whose power is such that it is worthy of being called infinitely powerful? (Anselm, *Monologium; Proslog.*; Calvin, *Inst.* 1.1.3; Descartes, *Method* IV, *Meditations* III; Witsius, *ESS* IV, pp. 33 ff.).

The name God refers to that necessary eternal, personal, spiritual being whose presence, knowing, and influencing are infinite, encompass all things, are the source and end of all things, incomparably good, just, holy, and loving. The question of the *existence of God* hinges on whether that necessary, eternal being remains merely a conceptual idea in our heads that we imaginatively *project* toward reality (as Feuerbach and Freud thought, cf. Feuerbach, *The Essence of Christianity*, pp. 12 ff., Freud, *The Future of an Illusion*, *CPWSF* XXI, pp. 10 ff.; whose arguments were anticipated by Gregory Nazianzen, *Second Theol. Or.* XXVIII.15, *NPNF* 2 VII, pp. 293, 294) or whether our *idea of God's being is derived from God's actual being* (pp. 294 ff.; cf. or. XXX, *NPNF* 2 VII, pp. 316 ff.; Anselm, *Proslog.* II ff., pp. 117 ff.; Descartes, *Meditations* V, *Phil. Works* II, p. 186).

Whether the Existence of God Can Be Reasonably Argued

Concerning the Question "Does God Exist?"

Modern theology has not generally proceeded in this way, by first establishing a clear conceptual idea of God, then asking whether that One exists. Rather, modern theology has more often sought *first* to establish that "God" in some sense (with spare definition) exists, then *secondly* to tack on to that bare definition of God the most vital attributes of the Scripture's understanding of God—will, spirit, freedom, personhood, justice, wisdom, and so on. Classic Christian exegetes have proceeded in the opposite way. They have been more likely to begin with the divine attributes attested in Scripture and only subsequently to deal with arguments for God's existence.

It has long been recognized that a natural theology that barely argues for the existence of God has more modest aims than pastoral caring requires. Often such attempts only aim at establishing that there is a First Cause or unmoved Mover or cosmic Orderer, without reference to the characteristics attributed to God in Scripture. It is more difficult but more meaningful to establish that God as defined in Christian teaching exists, rather than that "a Supreme Being" or "that which is necessary" exists (Augustine, *On Trin.* V.3, *NPNF* 1 III, pp. 88 f.; Kierkegaard, *Phil. Frag.*, pp. 51 ff.; Barth, *CD* II/1).

It invites ambiguity and confusion to try first to prove God's bare existence and then wait until later to state more specifically what Christian teaching really means by "God." For so long as what one means by "God" remains wholly ambiguous, it is hardly an exercise of great meaning to prove God's existence. It is less pivotal to biblical faith that an unmoved Mover exists than that the caring God of Abraham, Isaac, and Jesus lives indeed and acts as attested in Scripture (Hilary, *Trin.* V.3–25, *NPNF* 2 IX, pp. 86–92; Calvin, *Inst.* 1.14.1–3). The most urgent and demanding question for Christian teaching is not whether "a God of some kind" exists, but rather whether this incomparably good and powerful and caring source and end of all things, who meets us in Israel and in Jesus Christ, truly *is* as revealed in Scripture (Augustine, *Expos. on Psalms*, Ps. 135:5, *NPNF* 1 VIII, pp. 625 ff.; *On the Profit of Believing*, *NPNF* 1 III, pp. 147 ff.).

Thus it is more meaningful to proceed, as did the history of Christian proclamation and exegesis, to state first candidly what Christians *mean* by the caring God and only then to ask whether that One *is* as characterized and whether that set of meanings is true to the facts we can gather. Hence we have proceeded in a way that is unconventional in modern times but traditionally familiar, by defining God as caring, holy love. Now we are ready to introduce classic reasoning concerning the existence of God.

Detailed and rigorous theistic reasoning did not develop early in the Christian tradition. In the second century, there was minimal effort given to arguing *that* God exists. The earliest writers, such as Clement of Rome, Ignatius of Antioch, and Polycarp of Smyrna, were concerned primarily with the proclamation of the love, power, and justice of God the Father through the Son. The generation of writings represented by the Epistle to Diognetus, the Epistle of Barnabas, and the Didache contained only the slenderest forms of specific theistic arguments for the existence of God. They preceded the primitive theistic reasoning of Christian writers such as Justin Martyr, Irenaeus, Theophilus, and Clement of Alexandria, who did begin in due time to set forth in a preliminary way reasons for the existence of God.

There is already some implicit argumentation for God's existence quietly embedded in previous arguments on the divine attributes, for how could something necessary to existence not exist? (Anselm, *Monologium* I.1 ff., pp. 35 ff.; Tho. Aq., *ST* I Q12 ff.). The forthright statement of the very concept of God indeed has genuine self-evidencing power. But that latent or implicit reasoning must now be laid bare.

A Decisive Pastoral Question

It may seem at first glance that it is futile even to attempt to argue that this Christianly understood God exists. To some it seems so obvious that it hardly even can claim to be the subject of serious inquiry or doubt. Yet God's existence has in fact been doubted (Tho. Aq., *ST* I Q1, I, pp. 11 ff.). Also, some who believe in the existence of God have doubted that it can be demonstrated or that any argument could be edifying (Augustine, *Soliloquies* I.6–12, *LCC* VI, pp. 26–31; John of Damascus, *OF* I.4, 5, *NPNF* 2 IX, pp. 3, 4; cf. Kierkegaard, *Concl. Unsci. Post.* I.2, pp. 49–57).

Whether God exists is, at one level, a question of fact, not merely of theory. For the question is, quite simply: Is this so? A fact (from *facere*, to do or make) is a thing done, that which has actual existence, as distinguished from a fancy. Whether God exists cannot be reduced to a matter of empirical fact, since God does not yield to measurability, but the question "whether God exists" does ask stubbornly whether God *is*, whether the assertion is based on fact, whether it is factual, whether God is only an idea in our minds, or a reliable, plausible, credible reality. It is too late to ask whether we have adequately conceptualized God; that was the subject of the previous chapters. Now we must ask whether these scripturally attested attributes of the divine reality indeed correspond with One who truly exists. It is a decisive, practical, pastoral question (Irenaeus, *Ag. Her.* II.6, *ANF* II, p. 365; Augustine, *Conf.* VII.10 ff., *LCC* VII, pp. 146 ff.).

Whether God exists is a question to be assessed as other questions are assessed, on the basis of such knowledge of ourselves, our history, our human condition, and social experience that we can bring together into a larger pattern of internally corresponding meaningfulness. Whether God exists is a question that must be tested, as other profound questions are rigorously tested, on the basis of all the other facts we can reasonably ascertain (Tho. Aq., *SCG* I.3, pp. 63–66). It appeals, as do other inquiries, to clear perception, sound judgment based upon wide observation, the broadest possible data base (i.e., history), and upon one's inward moral, aesthetic and/or intuitive sense of appropriateness of argument (Clement of Alex., *Strom.* II.2, *ANF* II, p. 348; Tho. Aq., *SCG* I.3–8, pp. 63–76; *ST* I Q1, I, pp. 12 ff.). No one can decide this question for another. Every person must judge for him- or herself whether this One is as allegedly self-declared in Scripture (Luther, *Letters of Spiritual Counsel*, *LCC* XVIII, pp. 109 ff.; Kierkegaard, *Concl. Unsci. Post.*, pp. 23–169).

Yet to decide that this One exists is not quite like deciding that anything else exists. For this decision assumes a wider implication that the decider shall order his or her life around the existence of this One, if this One exists at all. It is not merely a casual or theoretical decision that makes no necessary difference to the way one lives the rest of one's life (Luther, *Letters of Spiritual Counsel*, *LCC* XVIII, pp. 14 ff.). For if this One exists, then everything else about life must be ordered in terms of this datum. Rightly understood, it is an all-embracing, intrusive question, and for this reason many prefer to dodge it or to proceed as if it were an abstract, theoretical question.

If God exists in the way that Christianity proclaims, God's existence implies far more than intellectual consent (Kierkegaard, *Either/ Or* II, "Ultimatum," pp. 343–56). It invites enjoyment of all life in the light of the joy this One takes in life (Augustine, *Conf.* XIII.18, *LCC* VII, pp. 311–13; Kierkegaard, "Joyful Notes in the Strife of Suffering," in *Christian Discourses*). It implies befitting adoration, ceaseless praise of this incomparable being, and active love of the most lovable of all beings through loving all other beings (Augustine, *Conf.* VII.1 ff.; H. R. Niebuhr, *RMWC*, pp. 123 ff.). There is an urgent, practical,

consequential dimension that attaches itself to the seemingly harmless
and simple question, Does God exist?

Religious leaders who think they can proceed in their activities
without having to face this question are in for a rude awakening. Even
though the question is thought by some intellectuals to be passé, and
by some mystics to be unanswerable, it continues to come up in
unexpected quarters and to require urgent attention.

We seek to make practical and pastoral use of classic arguments
for the existence of God. Yet doubts have arisen about whether one
can even use argument at all to establish or point to the existence of
God. Hence our first steps are to speak about the modest, corrobora-
tive function of argument in relation to belief. Then we will clarify
biblical assumptions concerning the existence of God; pursue the reasons why the question cannot be evaded; and, finally, distinguish
between different types of arguments.

Can Faith Be Established by Argument?

Scripture speaks of God as "dwelling in unapproachable light,"
whom "no man has ever seen or ever can see" (1 Tim. 6:16). All talk
of God's existence must begin with self-critical acknowledgment that
our terms cannot grasp or encapsulate the divine reality, even though
they can point to God. The classical formula is: God can be known,
but not comprehended (*Deus cognosci potest, comprehendi non potest*,
Lombard, *Sent.* I.3; cf. Tho. Aq., *SCG* I.5 ff.; Heppe, *RD*, pp. 52 ff.).
Only the infinite can adequately know the infinite (Gregory of Nyssa,
Ag. Eunomius I.25 ff., *NPNF* 2 V, pp. 69 ff.). The only understanding
of God we have is "on the way" (*theologia viatorum*) toward the end,
amid the pilgrimage of ambiguous human choices. We do not have in
hand an absolute or final theology of the perfected of the beatified
(*theologia beatorum*, Calvin, *Inst.* 1.2.2; 1.5; Heppe, *RD*, pp. 5 ff.; Schmid,
DT, p. 17; cf. Clement of Alex., *Strom.* I.20, *ANF* II, p. 322; *Instr.* I.6,
ANF II, p. 218). Yet within the frame of this time and this world,
something must be said about whether this infinite One exists. Otherwise the misleading impression may be left that Christian teaching
appeals merely to mystery or obscurantism and not in any sense to
the truth of good sense and the history of revelation (Basil, *Letters*
235, *NPNF* 2 VIII, pp. 274 ff.; Augustine, *On Trin.* VIII.1 ff., *LCC* VIII,
pp. 38 ff.; Tho. Aq., *SCG* I.10–12, pp. 79–85).

The faith of the Christian community assumes the reality of God
who creates the world, governs creation providentially, and redeems
it from fallenness (Justin Martyr, *Dialogue with Trypho* 61, 62, *ANF* I,

pp. 227, 228; Luther, *Small Catech.* II, pp. 12–14). Indeed God's existence is a *presupposition* of Christian teaching rather than a doctrine that is derived *after* one goes through a series of precise rational exercises. The worshiping community confesses and intercedes on the basis of, not the theory of God's existence, but the assumption of God's existence. God does not come into being on the basis of the success or failure of our rational arguments. "The heart has its reasons which reason does not know" (Pascal, *Pensées*, EL, p. 277). Nonetheless, rational arguments are not meaningless (Origen, *Ag. Celsus* VII.37, *ANF* IV, p. 625; Tho. Aq., *SCG* I.7, pp. 74 ff.).

Christianity shares with Judaism, Islam, and other theistic religions a belief in God's existence (John of Damascus, *OF* I.1 ff.; Qur'an 3:3 ff.; Maimonides, *Guide to the Perplexed*; Tho. Aq., *SCG* I.4 ff.). From its beginnings, wherever Christianity was preached among those who did not have a monotheistic faith in a personal God, it was necessary to explain why the existence of such a God is an assumption of Christian teaching (e.g., Acts 17:22–31). Even in the New Testament, when the gospel was proclaimed to the Gentiles (where Jewish belief in God was not assumed), this question had to be answered: In what way might the God of the Jews, of Abraham, Isaac, and Jacob, the God of Jesus, correspond to Greek and Roman assumptions about whether gods exist or God exists? (1 Cor. 3:3 ff.; Rom. 9–11; Col. 1:9 ff.; Acts 24:3 ff.).

In developing evidences for theism, the classical Christian teachers were not referring to a complete, personal trust in God's mercy or a wider knowledge of God's love, power, or justice, but only narrowly considering whether God exists, and if so, what arguments may support that assertion (Hilary, *On Trin.* I.5, FC 25, 5; Tho. Aq., *SCG* I.5–7; Calvin, *Inst.* 1.3–5).

Classical Christian teaching has held that these rational arguments are confirmatory to faith. They corroborate what faith knows, rather than produce or establish faith (Anselm, *Proslog.*, preface, I, pp. 103–15). These are not independent, airtight, unchallengeable "proofs," but taken together, they tend to confirm and rationally to validate what faith already knows of God's existence and to corroborate faith's persistently intuited conviction that God exists (Augustine, *Conf.* III ff., *LCC* VII, pp. 61 ff.). They are a form of loving God with our minds (Tho. Aq., *SCG* I.91, pp. 277 ff.; *ST* I Q11).

These arguments are not just aesthetically interesting or fascinating to personal or pastoral imagination, although they do have a certain beauty (Tho. Aq., *ST* I Q25). Rather, they are intrinsically profound and deserve modern interest and pastoral study. Yet the church has never taken these arguments with absolute seriousness, as if everything hinged upon the success of our arguments about God. God does not depend upon our thoughts about God (Gregory Nazianzen, *On the Great Athanasius, NPNF* 2 V, pp. 269, 272–74; Augustine, *CG* XI.2–6, *NPNF* 1 II, pp. 205–8; Calvin, *Inst.* 1.5, 6).

We do well to expect enough but not too much of these arguments. Since God is infinite spirit, not a finite object, we cannot expect the same kinds of objective proof or results of hard laboratory clinical testing that we find available in the finite sphere and that we rightfully expect and require with scientific method. Those who present evidence for the existence of God do not present it in the same way that one would present evidence in a zoology class or an experimental psychology class, because one is not dealing with a manipulatable, quantifiable object or datum or with a single variable to be observed (Origen, *Ag. Celsus* VII.46, *ANF* IV, pp. 630 ff.; John of Damascus, *OF* I.1–3, *NPNF* 2 IX, pp. 1–3).

Despite limits, the classical theistic arguments for God's existence have a cumulative effect when taken seriously (Gregory Nazianzen, or. XXVIII.6, *Second Theol. Or., NPNF* 2 VII, p. 290; cf. F. R. Tennant, *Philosophical Theol.* II, chap. IV, pp. 79 ff.). No one argument can be sufficient for so great a reality. Any single argument may be found lacking in this or that way, but taken together they have been held by the tradition to be sufficient to bind the inquiring, rational, self critical mind to the sure knowledge that this caring God exists (Tho. Aq., *SCG* I.5 ff., pp. 69 ff.; Watson, *TI* I, pp. 263 ff.).

Whether God in fact has the character attested by Scripture can only be established on the basis of a wide correspondence of insights from widely different spheres of knowing—natural, moral, intuitive, logical, scientific, and religious. The conclusion that God exists as revealed is seldom firmly reached on the basis of a single syllogism of reasoning, but rather on the basis of subtly diverse insights carved out of one's own personal history, yet brought together intuitively in an inward yes that has rich plausibility if not certitude (Augustine, *Conf.* VIII, *LCC* VII, pp. 157 ff.). Although this plausibility may grow slowly, in time it may come to have the character of a life-shaping conviction (pp. 178 ff.; cf. Kierkegaard, *Concl. Unsci. Post.*, pp. 312 ff.).

Consequently, not every argument that follows will be, or should be expected to be, sufficient to any particular human situation or existential question. Doubt creatively accompanies each of these arguments. Doubting the arguments is an appropriate way of seeking to ascertain how firmly they are indeed rooted in reality. A critical, probing faith is a necessary and useful stage toward an assured and confirmed faith (Job 3:1–26; Clement of Alex., *Strom.* VIII.9, *ANF* II, p. 564; Luther, *Letters of Spiritual Counsel, LCC* XVIII, pp. 109–38).

The Biblical Assumption That God Exists

It does not seem to have occurred to any of the writers of the Old or New Testament formally to prove or even argue in detail for the existence of God. God's existence was so widely assumed that it was thought that "only a fool would say in his heart 'there is no God '" (Ps. 14.1).

Hilary argued that there is nothing so proper to God as to be (*On Trin.* I.5, *FC* 25, p. 5; Watson, *TI* I, p. 356). Augustine thought that God's existence was more certain than our own (*Conf.* VII.10 ff., *LCC* VII, pp. 147 ff.).

Scripture's first phrase, "In the beginning, God" (Gen. 1:1), unmistakably expresses this prevailing biblical assumption, not that we arrive at a well-argued conclusion that God is, but from the beginning God *is*, and only later may we perhaps debate, think, and argue about it (Tho. Aq., *SCG* I.4, pp. 66 ff.). It does not say, "In the beginning we have a rational capacity that enables us to generate the idea of God's existence, which in due time is able to conclude that God exists." Rather, before any human rationality or argument, there is God.

The theistic tradition has often argued that belief in God's existence is so widely known and generally intuited in human history that it hardly requires elaborate argument. When Paul spoke of the Gentile world in Romans 1 and 2, he assumed they already had a prior elementary knowledge of God written on their hearts (Rom. 1:18 ff.): "They display the effect of the law inscribed on their hearts. Their conscience is called as a witness" (Rom. 2:15). Christian theistic argumentation came after, not before, Christian proclamation, the conversion of believers, and the writing of Scripture.

Nonetheless, rational and experiential argument has a modest but important function in the care of souls. Personal faith may not be established by argument, but it may be supported and confirmed by argument (Lactantius, *Div. Inst.* VII.9, *ANF* VII, p. 205; Anselm, *Proslog.* I, *BW* I, pp. 3 ff.). Faith in God existed before any arguments were articulated. Faith in God will be around after all the skeptical arguments have mounted their most determined challenges. The reason faith persists in looking for rational clarity and confirmation of its premises is that its premises are felt to be so valuable that they deserve the best intellectual reflection possible to confirm argumentatively what faith already knows inwardly (cf. Augustine, *Letters* 102, 103, *NPNF* 1 I, pp. 414 ff.; Tho. Aq., *SCG* I.10, pp. 79 ff.).

Why Ask?

When we fail to use our best intelligence around such pivotal questions as the existence of God, we may debase or diminish the power of faith by the dullness of our minds. We are being called to love God with our minds. We are called to apply our best intellectual resources to test the validity of every argument concerning God (Augustine, *Soliloquies* I.3 ff., *LCC* VI, pp. 24 ff.; Tho. Aq., *ST* I Q2, I, pp. 11 ff.).

In the first question of *Summa Theologica*, Thomas Aquinas set forth two erroneous views that oppose all theistic argumentation. It is said to be worthless to argue for the existence of God because: (1) There can be no argument about a self-evident truth or about an undemonstrable mystery, since the contrary is self-evidently impossible. Why waste mental energy trying to think about whether God exists, some say, if God necessarily exists? (2) It is said by others that if we already have a solid, sincere faith, we surely would not want to detract from piety or faith by substituting argument for it, or to amplify faith by attempted proofs. Thomas noted that both these assertions tend to be a lazy embarrassment to a reasoned faith, which could, if it utilized its intellectual abilities, provide plausible reasons for its faith (Tho. Aq., *ST* I Q2, pp. 11 ff.; cf. *SCG* I.5 ff., pp. 69 ff.).

Further, when we examine the main alternatives to theistic reasoning, we find the critics of theism just as heavily laden with difficulties (Garrigou-Lagrange, *God*, vol. I; Tillich, *Syst. Theol.*, vol. I; Mascall, *He Who Is*, pp. 41 ff.; Hick, *The Existence of God*, pp. 6 ff.). It provides mild comic relief to realize that radical skepticism argues not only that we cannot know anything about God, but that we cannot reliably know anything about anything (Hume, *Dialogues Concerning Natural Religion*, pp. 57 ff.). The opposite of skepticism is simple-minded, antiintellectual, blind belief that decries any need for reasoning. Whereas skepticism underrates our mental ability to reason concerning God, oversimplified faith-claims overrate zeal or emotional fervor as an adequate substitute for faith's duty to reason about itself (Tho. Aq., *SCG* I.5, pp. 69 ff.; cf. Wesley, *WJW* VI, pp. 351 ff.).

Healthy theism, as argued by Athanasius, Augustine, Anselm, and Thomas, takes a median view between these two extremes (that reason can know nothing or that faith can thoughtlessly know everything without reason) by arguing that we can use some modest and self-constricting modes of inference to speak of God's existence (Augustine, *On the Profit of Believing*, NPNF 1 III, pp. 347–66; Anselm, *Proslog.*, BW, pp. 1–11; Tho. Aq., *ST* I Q2 ff., I, pp. 12 ff.).

Five types of argument have been predominant in classical Christian theistic reasoning:

1. Arguments from Order and Design (Teleological Arguments)
2. Arguments from Humanity: Mind, Human Nature, and General Consent (Innate and Anthropological Arguments)
3. Arguments from Change, Causality, Contingency, and Degrees of Being (Cosmological Arguments)
4. Arguments from Conscience, Beauty, Pragmatic Results, and Congruity (Moral, Aesthetic, and Pragmatic Arguments)
5. Argument from the Idea of Perfect Being (Ontological Argument)

We will set forth selected forms of these arguments that have appeared repeatedly in the classical Christian tradition:

Arguments from Order or Design

The argument from order or design, the most ancient, simplest, and clearest of all theistic arguments, has close relevance to the practice of pastoral care. Aristotle thought that it was known by Hermotimus of Clazomenae (*Metaphy.* I 13, 984b, BWA, p. 696). An ancient fragment of Anaxagoras stated the essential argument: "All things that were to be, all things that were but are not now, all things that are now or that shall be, Mind arranged them all" (Anaxagoras frag. B 12, in *The Presocratic Philosophers*, sec. 503, p. 373). Argued by Augustine (*Conf.* XI.5, LCC VII, p. 248; cf. *Letters* 137, NPNF 1 I, pp. 473–81), it became the fifth of Thomas's five ways, called the teleological argument because it argues to God from purposes and ends (i.e., final causes, Tho. Aq., *ST* I Q2.3; *SCG* I.13). It has two principal forms: order and design.

The Argument from Order

The premise: Order is everywhere observable. Even the doubtful or despairing can see that there is order, a useful arrangement of things in a system of nature that implies intelligence and purpose in the world. The universe is characterized by extraordinarily complex layers and modes of order. It is implausible that these could have occurred by chance (Athanasius, *Ag. Heathen* 38, NPNF 2 IV, p. 24). It remains a premise of scientific inquiry that the world is characterized by intelligibility, which itself is often called the "natural order." Even when physicists discover an odd principle of indeterminacy, such as the Heisenberg principle, when nature at times appears unpredictable, those who have pursued that principle have found that there is, even in the principle of random indeterminacy of atomic interaction, a meaning and order. Careful observation of plant and animal life, physical elements, centrifugal forces, stellar movements yields that overwhelming conviction of orderliness (Gen. 1; Ps. 8; Lactantius, *Div. Inst.* I.2 ff., *ANF* VII, pp. 11 ff.; cf. *Testaments of the Twelve Patriarchs* VIII.2, *ANF* VIII, p. 27; Gregory of Nyssa, *On Infants' Early Deaths*, *NPNF* 2 IX, pp. 375–81).

The argument: If there is any order at all in the world, it is necessary to hypothesize an orderer, not necessarily a divine orderer, but an orderer of some kind (Augustine, *Conf.* XI.5, *LCC* VII, pp. 248 f.). There cannot be orderliness or purposiveness without a ground of order or a mind that shapes the order of a thing. Governance in the world implies some kind of governor (Plato, *Laws* X.904, *Dialogues* II, p. 646; Cicero, "On the Nature of the Gods" II, V; cf. Hume, *An Enquiry Concerning Human Understanding*, sec. XI; Hume, *Dialogues*, pt. V; Kant, *Critique of Pure Reason*, p. 520).

Formally the argument may be summarized in this way: (*a*) The visible world is a cosmos, an orderly unity whose order is constant, uniform, complex, and intrinsic to the universe itself. (*b*) Such an order cannot be explained unless it be admitted that the universe has a cause that displays remarkable intelligence, able to understand and produce this order, and a will capable of bringing it into being. (*c*) Therefore, such a cause of the universe exists, which is to say, God exists as the intelligent cause of the universe (Tho. Aq., *ST* I Q2.3, I, p. 14).

John of Damascus reasoned that discordant elements cannot work harmoniously together unless by some intelligent direction (*OF* I.3, *NPNF* 2 IX, pp. 10 ff.). Thomas Aquinas argued that "in the world we find that things of diverse natures come together under one order, and this is not rarely or by chance, but always or for the most part. There must therefore be some being by whose providence the world is governed. This we call God" (*SCG* I.13, p. 96).

The argument is found in Scripture: "Does he that planted the ear not hear, he that moulded the eye not see? Shall not he that instructs the nations correct them? The teacher of mankind, has he no knowledge?" (Ps. 94:9–10). The argument from order cannot be adequately pursued or held without suggesting or implying two of the divine attributes we have previously discussed: the omniscience by which God is able fully to know the created order so as to order it, and the omnipotent power by which God is able to bring such an order into being. Thus this theistic argument offers a reason to believe that the all-wise and almighty God to whom Scripture witnesses, exists in reality and not merely as a conception in our minds (Gregory Nazianzen, *Orat.* 28.2, *NPNF* 2 VII, p. 289; Calvin, *Inst.* 1.5.5; 1.14.20; Watson, *TI* I, pp. 286 ff.).

The power of this argument is best seen by taking seriously its opposite hypothesis, that there is no cause of order. For then one is attributing the order to chance, which in the long run still would leave the order unexplained. To say the order occurred by chance means either that we are unable to ascertain what the cause is while nonetheless affirming that some cause must exist, or that there is no cause and events occur without any reason or possible explanation (Tho. Aq., *ST* I Q105, I, pp. 515–21; Calvin, *Inst.* 1.5.11; 1.16.5 ff.; Garrigou-Lagrange, *God* I). Both of these ways of viewing chance fail to account for the primary evidence—order in the world—which demands some sufficient explanation. This argument is on some occasions found useful in caring for persons trapped in syndromes of doubt or despair, to remind them that their doubt or despair exists within an intelligible order (Eccles. 2:20 ff.; 1 Cor. 1:8; cf. Clement of Alex., *Strom.* VII.7, *ANF* II, p. 564; Luther, *Letters of Spiritual Counsel, LCC* XVIII, pp. 131–36).

The Argument from Design

The most concise statement of the argument from design came from Thomas Aquinas: "We observe that things without consciousness, such as physical bodies, operate with a purpose, as appears from their co-operating invariably, or almost so, in the same way in order to obtain the best result. Clearly then they reach this end by intention and not by chance. Things lacking knowledge move toward an end only when directed by someone who knows and understands, as an arrow by an archer. There is consequently an intelligent being who directs all natural things to their ends; and this being we call God" (*ST* I Q2.3, *TAPT*, p. 63). An arrow moving through the air is a metaphor of a guided, orderly trajectory of an inanimate object moving toward a predetermined end, since the arrow is guided by intelligible forces that determine its path. To have guidance, one must hypothesize a guide. The conceiving of ends, and the choosing of means appropriate for the attainment of ends, can be done only by a personal mind—an intelligent being. If purposiveness is experienced in the world, then one must hypothesize a purposing being (Methodius, *On Free Will*, chap. 2, *ANF* VI, p. 357). If one found a watch, one could assume that some intelligent mind had worked on it and produced it. This conclusion would be even more plausible if one discovered that its complex structure is adapted to the measurement of time (Paley, *Natural Theol.* I, pp. 37 ff.; cf. critique by D. Hume, *Dialogues Concerning Natural Religion*, V, IX).

The instinct of animals serves as an illustration of an activity toward an intelligible purpose that the animal itself has not understood or foreseen. A chickadee or a hoot owl builds a nest in spring without having been taught. Under the guidance of instinct it fulfills a purpose that it has not grasped: the perpetuation of the species. Although the owl does not understand its own mating and nesting, these are not meaningless or merely shaped by chance, but filled with purpose, with complicated means that tend toward ends unknown but meaningful. If these ends are present, but unknown to the owl, they must be in some sense known by some mind or the intelligence of some other being. For it seems implausible to have any meaning in the universe that is not ever perceived by anyone as meaningful.

Some may object that the principle of natural selection explains nest building, and this, it seems, would eliminate the need for a principle of design or a purpose presupposed in the activity (cf. Huxley, *Essays of a Biologist*, VI). According to this naturalistic explanation, nothing in nature aims at anything, nothing has or requires purpose; the only explanation required is adaptation to environment for survival. Accordingly, it is said, through millions of years the present order that we find in the universe has been slowly developing, not as a result of any original or subsequent design or organizing intelligence, but by mere chance.

The problem with such an oversimplified view of evolution is that it settles the intellectual quest too cheaply and unscientifically by substituting the hypothesis of chance for a causal explanation. Naturalistic reductionism in its evolutionary form cannot squelch the question of meaning merely by an assertion, namely, that no ordering principle is required in a complex process of natural selection. Rather, the opposite is required: The very language regularly used in much evolutionary theory, such as "fitness," "adaptivity," "selectivity," "survival," and "law," constantly implies ends (i.e., purposes) of instinctual animal behavior. Suppose there is no larger intelligence under or beyond or prior to animal instinct to understand and order this complex history of behavioral change. The question still remains as to how such a complex order could emerge without an orderer (Origen, *Ag.*

Celsus I.23, *ANF* IV, p. 405). To what purpose is something fitted or adapted? If evolutionary theory is to speak profoundly of adaptation and fitness, it must think more thoroughly about that to which the evolution of animal behavior is adapted or fitted. It hardly helps to appeal to a "law" of natural selectivity if one has undercut the possibility of law by ascribing behavior to chance, spontaneity, or blind necessity or fate (Tatian, *Or. Ag. the Greeks*, chap. 4, *ANF* II, p. 66; Calvin, *Inst.* 1.2.1; 1.16.8–9; cf. H. Bergson, *Creative Evolution*, pp. 57 ff.).

Strictly speaking, the argument from design does not establish the existence of infinite intelligence, but only of that remarkable degree of intelligence required to produce this orderly cosmos. The infinity of the divine intelligence must be argued on other grounds than the argument from design (Hume, *Dialogues Concerning Natural Religion* V, pp. 37 ff.).

It may be further objected that nature fails more often than it succeeds, as in the case of many seeds going ungerminated, and so the amount of failure in the world would accordingly be attributed to a lack of intelligence in the cosmos, or to a dull or poor cosmic intelligence. To answer this it is necessary only to fantasize the disastrous consequences of everything in the world being "successful," for example, if every human sperm became a baby. Thus there is purpose in that which from a narrower point of view is regarded as the "failure" of seed or sperm. The many forms of plant and animal life that are adaptive to and includable within the natural order must develop together, in ecological interaction, on the planet as a whole life system, with no absolute dominance by any species (cf. Gregory of Nyssa, *On the Making of Man* XXX, *NPNF* 2 V, pp. 422–27; Arnobius, *Ag. the Heathen*, *ANF* VI, pp. 440 ff.; F. R. Tennant, *Philosophical Theol.* II, chap. IV, pp. 79 ff.).

To those who have more cynically argued that the cosmic design itself is flawed and the whole admittedly orderly mechanism tends toward the diminution of the good, classic Christian writers have responded fully, but these arguments will be taken up later when discussing creation, providence, and theodicy (Augustine, *Enchiridion* IV, *LCC* VII, pp. 343 ff.; Calvin, *Inst.* 1.15.1; 2.1 ff.).

ARGUMENTS FROM HUMANITY:
MIND, HUMAN NATURE, AND GENERAL CONSENT

The second group of closely associated theistic arguments hinges on the analysis of human consciousness, human nature, or human social experience as the basis for the necessary conclusion that God exists. They form a bridge between the argument from design and the moral arguments to be discussed later. That all theistic arguments tend to converge in mutual complementarity is one of their most important features (Tho. Aq., *ST* I–II Q109, I, pp. 1123 ff.).

Accounting for the Appearance of Mind in Nature

The emergence of mind in evolutionary history requires the hypothesis that God exists. The pervasive presence of intelligibility in the evolving world and in our minds requires the premise of God. There cannot be a universe without a Universal Mind that in some ways corresponds with our own finite minds (cf. C. S. Pierce, *Collected Papers* VI, pp. 345 ff.; F. R. Tennant, *Philosophical Theol.* II, chap. IV, pp. 79 ff.; H. Bergson, *Creative Evolution*, pp. 60 ff.; Calvin, *Inst.* 1.5; 1.14 ff.). The argument from mind differs from the arguments from order or design in that they use largely inanimate or animal metaphors (arrows, clocks, animal adaptation), whereas the argument from mind proceeds from the empirical observation of emerging intelligence in history and natural-historical development, especially human mind.

This argument begins with the remarkable fact that intelligent consciousness undeniably exists in the world. Not only is the world itself intelligible, but also our minds are capable of grasping that intelligibility. That we live in an intelligible world is a fact that is absolutely necessary to any language or discourse whatever. The premise of intelligibility is a necessary precondition of our minds' even thinking about this question or any other (cf. Clement of Alex., *Strom.* V.13, *ANF* II, pp. 465 ff.; Calvin, *Inst.* 1.3). That intelligence exists to apprehend that intelligibility is itself the most astonishing fact of natural history's development.

Human reasoning begins with a fundamental trust in its own power of reasoning. Although at times the senses may deceive, the only way we can grasp those deceptions is on the basis of the larger assumption of the intelligibility of things and the trustworthiness of the inquiring mind in ferreting out deceptions. Descartes rightly reasoned that the one thing he could not possibly doubt was that he had the capacity to doubt (Descartes, *Principles of Philosophy* I.7, *Works* I, pp. 211 ff.; cf. Hollaz, *ETA*, pp. 187 ff.). If I can doubt my own thoughts, I must be able to think, to inquire, to examine, and to criticize, and these are functions that could not work without both an intelligible world and a perceiving intelligence.

Human consciousness grows slowly, through evolutionary adaptation, acculturation, socialization, and education, to understand, explore, question, and grasp the structure, order, and intelligibility of reality. Through the study of chemistry, astronomy, physics, botany, biology, and psychology, we look for reliable knowledge of ourselves and our world. We formulate reliable laws of causation based upon these observations, and then we subject these laws to reexamination, constant scrutiny, and revision. No such examination could occur without the dual premise of the intelligibility of these things and perceiving intelligence (Bonaventure, *Breviloquium*; Tho. Aq., *The Division and Method of the Sciences*, QV, VI, of *Comm. on Boethius*; Watson, *TI* I, pp. 271 ff.). The scientific enterprise assumes that there is a fundamental correspondence between our minds and the intelligibility of what we know (Kant, *Critique of Pure Reason*). The world is understandable, at least in part, and if in any part, then in principle it is understandable as a whole, even if beyond our present finite understanding. Scientific inquiry appeals to commonly duplicatable experimentation as the basis of validating that an experience has been accurately observed (Tho. Aq., *SCG* I.7, pp. 74, 75; *ST* I Q1, I, pp. 1 ff; Nicolas de Cusa, "Concerning Experiments in Weight," *U&R*, pp. 241 ff.). Logical inquiry appeals to reliable laws and rules of rational deduction and inferences in making conclusions, and we assume that these laws and rules must apply to all cultures, otherwise they are considered deficient in some way and subject to further investigation and revision (Augustine, *Conf.* IV.10, *LCC* VII, pp. 85 ff.; *CG* XII, *NPNF* 1 II, pp. 226 ff.; cf. Hume, *Dialogues Concerning Natural Religion, Phil. Works*, vol. II, pp. 457 ff.).

Let us suppose that our minds were intelligent but the world was not intelligible. In such circumstances, we could think about nothing, because intelligence can think about only what is intelligible (Tho. Aq., *ST* I Q14.1, I, pp. 72 ff.). This conclusion has wide-ranging relevance for Christian teaching about God. There is only one universe. That is what uni-verse means: there is only one (*uni*) turn (*vertere*), one circle of being (Gregory of Nyssa, *Ag. Eunomius* I.22, *NPNF* 2 V, pp. 61 ff.). If there were two universes, then it would be necessary to hypothesize some relation between these universes, which itself would then be an embracing universe, of which there could be only one. It is precisely this *universe* in its totality that displays an order or intelligibility that corresponds with the order and intelligibility that we experience in our own minds (Tertullian, *Ag. Praxeas* V.6, *ANF* III, p. 601; Tho. Aq., *SCG* I.55 ff., pp. 192 ff.; Watson, *TI* I, pp. 271 ff.).

If such a *universe* exists, and if our minds are able to grasp anything about it, both it and we must display intelligibility. If intelligibility exists at all, it must have some ground and source. It is implausible to hypothesize a spontaneous emergence of intelligibility for such a massive order of intelligible events and beings as the observed universe, natural evolving history, and human history (Wm. Temple, *Nature, Man, and God*; Paley, *Natural Theol.*, passim; cf. S. Alexander, *Space, Time and Deity* II, pp. 353 ff.).

The point: The intelligibility or mind that we find everywhere in the universe could only be the result of an unsurpassably intelligent being. Reason suggests what Scripture attests: that the One revealed as all-wise reaches out to illumine the human spirit (Tho. Aq., *ST* I Q12, I, pp. 45 ff.). As the law of gravity exists prior to our discovering it, as the laws of motion are there prior to our moving anything, so must the larger intelligibility of the world exist prior to any intelligent awareness that we might have of it (cf. Tho. Aq., *ST* I Q19, I, pp. 103 ff.).

It is true that we cannot see the world as a crab or eagle or termite or elephant sees it. But the world is experienced as intelligible by crabs in a crablike way and termites in a termitelike way, since these creatures respond elaborately through instinct and adaptation to the world, not miscellaneously or by chance or without plan. Their perceptions of the world, however foreign to our own, do not and must not lack the essential premise that to them the world is ordered, and through instinct and adaptation they experience that order very concretely, adaptively, and practically. Still, the principle holds for real amoebas and fantasized Martians as well as humans, that if intelligibility exists at all, it must reflect the intelligence of something, and that something must, on the basis of our experience of it, be vastly greater than any intelligence we know in the animal or human sphere. The complexity of the known world suggests, in fact, that it must be infinitely great (Tho. Aq., *SCG* I.54 ff., pp. 189 ff.).

One can hypothesize an ordered world without a particular finite mind—the world can get along without your mind or my mind—but it cannot do without some mind. There is no perceived "orderly world" without some mind to enable it and some mind to perceive it (cf. Tertullian, *Ag. Marcion* I.10, *ANF* III, pp. 278 ff.; Tho. Aq., *ST* I Q44 ff., I, pp. 229 ff.).

It is useful here to note the difference between things and minds. It is misleading to think simplistically of minds as things. Whereas things are inert, minds are alive, conscious and capable of perceptions, feelings, and willing. Finite minds, of course, exist within finite bodies. The body is a thing, but as death shows, the thing a body is without mind is radically different from the thing a body is with mind. Bodies are perceived by minds, never without minds. Here reason intuits what Scripture proclaims clearly: As there cannot be any ordered body or thing without some sort of mind to order it, so there cannot be a human mind or universal history without positing a greater source, ground, and end of human intelligence. This we call God (cf. Lactantius, *Div. Inst.* I.2, *ANF* VII, pp. 11 ff.; Watson, *TI* I, pp. 285 ff.).

The Clementine Homilies contain a concise, fourth-century Christian statement of this essential argument:

> There is an unbegotten artificer who brought the elements together, if they were separate; or, if they were together, artistically blended them so as to generate life, and perfected from all one work. For it cannot be that a work which is completely wise can be made without a mind which is greater than it. (Clementina, *Hom.* VI.25, *ANF* VIII, p. 267)

Inspirer of the Personal Good

A related argument proposes that since we are persons and as such experience a constant struggle for values that we regard as expressive of our being, then we must hypothesize One who engenders in us the desire to actualize value. The human person is more complex and rich than any mechanical analogy can describe.

The assumption is that personhood is history's highest achievement and most precious value. Accordingly, a divine person must be posited as the premise of human personhood. One cannot reasonably have human personality drop out of the blue in evolving history without hypothesizing a divine person that elicits and awakens human personality (cf. Justin Martyr, *Second Apol.* VI, *ANF* I, p. 190; John of Damascus, *OF* I.1, *NPNF* 2 IX, pp. 1 ff.; Whitehead, *Religion in the Making*, pp. 154 ff.; Hartshorne, *PSG*, pp. 233 ff.).

Idealism from Plato to Hegel has viewed matter as inspirited. According to Hegel, Spirit is unfolding itself reasonably in time, and Absolute Spirit is embodying itself inexorably in history (Hegel, *Phenomenology of Mind; Reason in History*, passim; cf. Augustine, *CG*, XII ff.). Accordingly, everything that happens in the material world is Spirit coming into ever-new actualizations. Every time (*Zeit*) is an expression of Spirit (*Geist*). The highest form of Spirit thus far manifested in history is human personality. This idealist notion is a secularized way of speaking obliquely about God as necessary for human personality (Baron Freidrich von Huegel, *Essays and Addresses on Phil. of Relig.*, 2d ser., pp. 197 ff.). Humans are not just out there alone in an autonomous struggle for the good. It does not make any sense for existence to be enmeshed in the struggle for good without being in some sense supported by an ultimate person or transcendent mind who also struggles for the good (for extreme expressions of this argument, see H. N. Wieman, *The Source of Human Good*, pp. 53–81; and E. S. Brightman, *The Problem of God*, pp. 87 ff.).

The Argument from the Constitution of Human Nature

This argument leads us to another variation, which, though seeming to be slight, represents a deeper turn: the very thought of God in the human mind assumes and requires that God is. Stated differently, God must exist because the idea and understanding of God is an element of human nature itself. Thus the very constitution of human nature points beyond itself to its Creator (Origen, *De Princip.* I.1.7, *ANF* IV, pp. 244 f.; Tho. Aq., *SCG* II.4).

This brings us to the doorstep of the ontological argument (that the idea of perfect being requires the existence of perfect being—to be discussed later), but it does not enter that door because it does not rely primarily upon deductive logic as the ontological argument does. Rather, this is an induction from the observation of human experience: everywhere there is human consciousness, the idea of God seems again and again to reappear, almost as if it is a necessary premise of ordinary human thought and experience.

Scripture to some degree attests to this insight: At the Areopagus, Paul seems to argue that God who created the world and all in it created humanity so that every culture and period of history are destined in their own way "to seek God, and, it might be, touch and find him; though indeed he is not far from each one of us, for in him we live and move, in him we exist; as some of your own poets have said, 'We are his offspring'" (Acts 17:27, 28; cf. Calvin, *Inst.* 1.5). The assumption that human beings cannot be defined apart from God was integral to biblical anthropology: "On the day when God created man he made him in the likeness of God" (Gen. 5:1).

Despite sin, the image of God has not been completely obliterated, and still is by grace restorable in its capacity to reflect the goodness

of God. This capacity to know God is capable of becoming intellec-
tually twisted, morally stunted, and developmentally skewed. It is
distortable into polytheisms, idolatries, animisms, superstitions, and
pantheisms of various sorts, as the history of the idea of God shows
(Tho. Aq., *ST* I Q74, I, pp. 919 ff.; Calvin, *Inst.* 2.1 ff.). Paul showed
in Romans 1 and 2 how the truth of God implanted in the human
heart has become corrupted and obscured by sin in human history.
Through sin the will deceives itself by adoring creaturely goods as
greater than the Creator (Rom. 1:26, 27; Tertullian, *Chaplet* VI, *ANF*
III, p. 96; Calvin, *Inst.* 1.18; 2.1). Yet repeatedly in Scripture the
assumption is made that in the nature and constitution of humanity
there is an awareness of One upon whom everything else depends,
One to whom all are finally responsible (Gen. 1:26, 27; Pss. 8, 19, 51;
Rom. 1, 2; Heb. 2:6; John 1:9; cf. Augustine, *Conf.* XIII.10, *LCC* VII,
pp. 305 ff.).

It is on this basis that some classic exegetes came to argue that the
awareness of the existence of God is innate and connate, that is,
existing in a person from birth (*in-nasci*) and coming with birth (*con-
nasci*), and therefore belonging to the essential or original constitution
of humanity (Tho. Aq., *ST* I Q75 ff., I, pp. 363 ff.; Calvin, *Inst.*
1.15.1–4; Gerhard, *LT* I, pp. 250 ff.; Watson, *TI* I, pp. 271 ff.). This is
not to say that the diffuse awareness of the existence of God that
accompanies all human existence is itself fully formed or well developed from the beginning without any need for moral development or
rational reflection or spiritual education. Nor does it suggest that the
idea of God is fully and adequately imprinted on the mind in such a
way that it develops instinctively, as insect behavior might, apart from
the self-determining growth of moral reasoning. Rather, it means that
the constitution of human nature is such that it is intrinsically capable
of developing an awareness of God as self-consciousness emerges,
accompanied in due time by language, moral development, socialization, memory, reason, and will (Augustine, *Conf.* X.15 ff., *LCC* VII,
pp. 215 ff.; cf. Tho. Aq., *SCG* I.8, pp. 75 ff.).

The point: If humanity has the idea of God implanted in its very
nature, then some sufficient reason must be hypothesized. Of many
possible hypotheses, the most evident and plausible one is that God
implanted it. Although such an argument lacks the force of a demonstration or proof, it must be dislodged by some better hypothesis.

Argument from the General Consent of Human Cultures

Another notion, once frequently employed, then generally ignored,
but now recovering some of its lost credibility, hinges on the "general

consent of human cultures to the premise that God is" (*consensus gentium*, the consensus of peoples). This is another corroboratory argument that, lacking the force of a fully adequate demonstration, is best used only to support and amplify other arguments, yet it cannot be altogether ignored.

The argument is strengthened by making a firm disclaimer at the outset: the claim for consensus is not the same as the claim for unanimity. No major teacher of the Christian tradition has been so careless as to suggest that every single human being in fact consciously knows or believes that God exists, even though the argument is sometimes caricatured in this way.

Rather, it is argued that belief in God is so widespread both in primitive cultures and throughout history, and atheism so theoretical, limited, and sporadic, that it is demonstrably a human consensus, despite occasional disclaimers, that God exists (Theophilus, *To Autolycus*, ANF II, pp. 85 ff.; Lactantius, *Div. Inst.* I.5 ff., ANF IV, pp. 13 ff.). To argue the contrary—that God does not exist—is to ignore and dismiss the historical weight of human experience. If humankind at virtually all known times and places has assumed belief in a divine order that transcends human and historical disorders, then that is a fact that cannot be completely ignored by serious investigators (Justin Martyr, *First Apol.* II.6, ANF I, p. 164; Origen, *Ag. Celsus* VII.32, ANF II, pp. 625 ff.).

Admittedly the argument from consensus should not be used in isolation from other arguments, but neither should it be completely set aside. Arbitrarily or capriciously to adopt a conviction contrary to that which is most widely prevailing in human history can hardly be called scientific (Clement of Alex., *Strom.* V.12–14, ANF II, pp. 462 ff.). General consent is not a formally complete argument, although it should not be viewed either as lacking plausibility altogether, since it relies upon the weight of so much human experience and reasoning. General consent implies wide human experiencing and reflection out of many different cultural assumptions in all historical periods—far more varied cultures, for example, than have affirmed modern empirical method in the last century. Whether these reasons and experiences are valid or not must not be decided in advance by arbitrarily rejecting the hypothesis (Justin Martyr, *First Apol.* XVIII–XXIV, ANF I, pp. 169–71).

The prevalence of varied forms of belief in God is an astonishing fact of human history. Even when one looks at societies in which brutal, systematic attempts have been made to eradicate belief in God (such as the Soviet Union, and China during the period of the Cultural

Revolution), the belief continues to persist, and even to show through with special poignancy and power amidst persecution (Justin Martyr, *Dialogue with Trypho*, chap. 93, *ANF* I, p. 246; Tertullian, *The Soul's Testimony*, *ANF* III, pp. 181 ff.; A. Solzhenitsyn, *The Cancer Ward; The Gulag Archipelago*). Atheistic systems also have profound practical analogies to belief systems, so much so that atheistic belief itself may be argued as essentially an inverted form of theistic belief (R. Niebuhr, *NDM* I.1–5; Herberg, "The Christian Mythology of Socialism," *FEH*, pp. 180–90).

That there is general consent of humanity to the belief that God exists was an idea widely held among early Christian teachers (Clement of Alex., *Strom.* V.12–14, *ANF* II, pp. 462 ff.; Theophilus, *To Autolycus*, *ANF* II, pp. 85 ff.; Minucius Felix, *Octavius*, chaps. 32 ff., *ANF* IV, pp. 193 ff.; Tertullian, *The Soul's Testimony*, *ANF* III, pp. 181 ff.). This fact of consent is usually connected with the intuited notion that the idea of God is naturally implanted or inborn or innate in human consciousness (Justin Martyr, *First Apol.* chap. 2 ff., *ANF* I, pp. 163 ff.; *Dialogue with Trypho*, chap. 93, *ANF* I, p. 246; Clement of Alex., *Strom.* V.12 ff., *ANF* II, pp. 462 ff.; Tertullian, *The Soul's Testimony* II, *ANF* III, pp. 182 ff.; Origen, *Ag. Celsus* VII.37, *ANF* IV, pp. 625 ff.; *De Princip.* IV, *ANF* IV, pp. 349 ff.; Lactantius, *Div. Inst.* I.2.5; Augustine, *Conf.* X.23 ff., *LCC* VII, pp. 221 ff.).

It is not the view of classical theism that every person always explicitly acknowledges or knows God adequately. Medieval Christian teachers appealed to the Aristotelian principle that the real nature of a thing is whatever it becomes when the process of its development is complete (Aristotle, *Categories, Metaphy.*, *BWA*, pp. 7 ff., 689 ff.). Accordingly, religion is best assessed not by its primitive forms of development but its higher and more advanced forms, especially monotheistic religion, which according to Christian teaching is best fulfilled in the teachings and history of Jesus. Atheists indeed exist, but are on the whole exceptional, if all cultures and universal history be surveyed (Origen, *Ag. Celsus* VII.37, *ANF* IV, pp. 625 ff.; cf. Calvin, *Inst.* 1.3–5), and there is no evidence whatever that their ranks are increasing.

The consensual argument does not claim that the voice of the people is the voice of God in an unqualified sense. Nonetheless its power lies in the tenacity with which this belief has been held by so many in so many times and places. It has persisted in spite of persecution and in the face of vigorous attacks by the minority of empowered skeptics who may aggressively disbelieve it (Herberg, *FEH*, pp. 242 ff.; Solzhenitsyn, *The Gulag Archipelago*).

No theory of consent is complete, however, until it is linked firmly with the previously stated argument on the innate awareness of divinity implanted intrinsically in human consciousness. These then become even more plausible when linked with other theistic arguments, particularly arguments from conscience and from design. Human reasoning, moral awareness, and consciousness are inveterately theistic in intuition. An antitheistic premise must somehow account for the weight of that historical experience. Whether they wish to or not, atheistic systems must struggle to make themselves plausible over against this powerful *consensus gentium*, as in the case of Soviet society, where after sixty painful years of official government attempts to stamp out belief in God with highly repressive measures, it continues apace (note the correlation of persecution and faith in Cyprian, *Treatise V, Address to Demetrianus* 12–25, *ANF* V, pp. 461–65; cf. Eusebius, *CH*, chap. VI, *NPNF* 2 I, pp. 239 ff.).

The force of this argument is less theoretical or logical than historical, social, and empirical. It is, in fact, less an argument in the formal sense than a description of the actual milieu in which the question of God is raised. The question of whether God exists cannot be raised in such a way as to evade completely such an obviously wide range of historical experiences (John of Damascus, *OF* I.4.1, *NPNF* 2 IX, pp. 4 ff.).

Thus, Christian study of God does not proceed as if the theologian must suddenly invent belief in God, or bring God into being through a reasoned argument (Gregory Nazianzen, *Orat.* XXXIV.3–21, *NPNF* 2 VII, pp. 335–38). For believing in God apparently has been a part of human experiencing as far back as history can be traced. Countless human beings have regarded this belief as so crucial to their existence that they have been willing to die, and have in fact died, rather than be forced to deny it. It is possible to die for false beliefs, but it is difficult to think of any other idea in human history for which so many caring and intelligent persons have been willing to offer their very lives (Augustine, *CG* XVIII.51, 52, *NPNF* 1 II, pp. 392 ff.).

The burden of proof, then, must lie with those who wish to dismiss this evidence. It is unscientific and unreasonable to reject a hypothesis so widely affirmed simply on the basis that it refers to something thought to be beyond scientific validation or empirical observation. Rather, belief in God might as well be regarded as presumptively true, on the basis of this general consent, until decisively *dis*proved. Even if disproved, the problem would still remain of why the idea has achieved and continues to maintain such tenacity in human consciousness (Justin Martyr, *First Apol.* II.6, *ANF* I, p. 164).

Arguments from Change, Causality, Contingency, and Degrees of Being

Does God exists? The only kind of answer some will consider plausible is made by providing reasons based upon observation of evidence gathered in the world of experience. Arguments that deliberately proceed in this way are called cosmological arguments, since they are based on knowledge of the world. The four principal forms of cosmological arguments are from motion, change, contingency, and degrees of being.

Types of Argument

The formal arguments for the existence of God have often been divided into two types: *a posteriori* arguments, which reason inductively from effects to causes, from experience, not from axioms; and *a priori* arguments, which reason deductively from assumed axioms, or from causes to effects, logically from postulates to their consequences.

In this first section we are rehearsing common arguments for the existence of God that come *after* experience, or following sensory evidence, hence *a posteriori*, meaning "after the fact of"; that is, as a result of experience or following our knowledge of the experienced world, we can say certain things about God. (In the last section of this chapter, we will discuss the *a priori* arguments, which stand necessarily prior to experience and thus are not dependent upon sensory data. They are viewed as purely deductive rational arguments, which are essentially an analysis of our ideas prior to any gathering of empirical data from the world of experience; hence they are purely acts of cognitive reflection, not involving any presentation of sensory evidence but only logical reasoning.)

The experience-based arguments we now consider begin with sensory evidence—with observation of effects—reasoning back from observed effects to their causes (Augustine, *Conf.* VII.3–5, 12–16; *Enchiridion* chaps. 3–5; *CG* XI.1–9; Tho. Aq., *SCG* I 13, pp. 85 ff.). Scripture suggests this type of argument when it speaks of beholding the invisible God through visible reality (Rom. 1:20; Heb. 11:17–27).

Chief among classical exponents of these arguments is Thomas Aquinas, whose "five ways" of reasoning toward God from the world constitute the principal historical statement of the cosmological arguments. (One of these "five ways," the argument from design, we have already considered.) Although Thomas did not invent these arguments, he brilliantly synthesized them and organized them for future use, relying heavily upon Aristotle, John of Damascus, Augustine, Dionysius, and Maimonides. Each start from a solid base in the world of experience and posit God as the source of that world as we experience it. We begin here with the most elementary of these, the argument from motion.

Any Motion Requires an Original Mover: The Argument from Change

The first cosmological argument begins with a simple, testable observation: our constant awareness of change or motion. Look around you, Thomas asks: Do you see anything moving? Motion, he thought, is the most obvious thing about the world. Things are in motion. Things change. Something must have moved the motions that we see moving. Observed motion Z is moved by some motion Y, which is moved by X, which is moved by a long series of previous motions. Is it reasonable to assume that there was never any original motion that started such movement? Wherever you see a process of movement, it is more reasonable to hypothesize that movement is moved by some thing, for it cannot in every respect cause its own movement. Whatever is moving is moved by something. Everything that changes is changed by something influencing it (cf. the Athenian stranger in Plato, *Laws* X.894 ff., in *Dialogues* IV, pp. 463–69; *Phaedrus*, p. 245; Aristotle, *Metaphy.* BWA II, XII; cf. David Hume, *Dialogues Concerning Natural Relig.*, parts II–IV, IX; Kant, *Critique of Pure Reason*).

"All mutables bring us back to a first immutable" (Tho. Aq., *On Truth* II, *TAPT,* p. 51). If you wish to provide an explanation of change, you have only two alternatives: either you must hypothesize (*a*) an infinite regression of change with no explanation of an original mover, which is an intellectual embarrassment, an offense to reason (Gregory Nazianzen, *Second Theol. Or.* VI, *NPNF* 2 VII, p. 290), or (*b*) you must hypothesize some unchanging ground that lies prior to all the multiple changes we experience in ordinary life (Tho. Aq., *Compend. Theol.*, pp. 9 ff.). Christian teaching has generally assented to the rational conclusion that if change exists anywhere in the world, there must be some Source of change, or some Originative Change Agent (Tho. Aq., *ST* I Q2, I, pp. 11 ff.; *SCG* I.44, pp. 170 ff.; *SCG* III.66 ff., pp. 218 ff.). That agent cannot be other than the same reality Christian worship celebrates and Scripture attests as God (Tho. Aq., *SCG* I.13, pp. 86–89).

This argument is anticipated in Scripture: "Every house is built by someone, but he that built all things is God" (Heb. 3:4). That which

Aristotle and Thomas Aquinas called the unmoved Mover, or Prime Mover, or unchanging source of change, points through reason beyond reason toward the incomparable One celebrated in Christian worship as God the Creator (Aristotle, *Physics*, *BWA* VIII, pp. 354 ff.; Tho. Aq., *Compend. Theol.*, chap. 3, p. 9; *SCG* I.13, pp. 85 ff.; *Comm. on Aristotle's Physics*, chap. VIII).

Effects Point to an Original Cause: The Argument from Causality

The second argument appears to be much like the first one, but it is as different as cause is from change. The argument from cause begins similarly by looking at the effects and thinking backward to causes. Efficient causes are causes that have been effected by something other than themselves. The natural world is full of efficient causes, and the scientist's task is to ferret them out. Each cause itself has been effected by previous causes, which themselves are rooted in prior causes, for no effect can exist without some cause. Reasoning demands a sufficient cause for every effect. One cannot, without fundamental offense to the human intellect, assert that those causes go on and on without ending and without any sufficient causal explanation. If every event has a cause, and the universe is a system of causes and effects, it stands to reason that there must be an underived causal agent and necessary being that underlies and enables all these causes and effects (Tho. Aq., *ST* I Q2, I, pp. 11 ff.; *SCG* I.14 ff., pp. 96 ff.; *SCG* I.50 f., pp. 180 ff.; *SCG* II.31 ff.). "If there were an infinite regress among efficient causes, no cause would be first" (Tho. Aq., *SCG* I.13, p. 95). "We must, therefore, posit that there exists a first efficient cause. This is God" (*SCG* I.13, p. 95).

Every discrete effect must have a reason for its occurrence. What we say of every discrete event, we must also say of the universe, which as a whole is not exempt from the law of causation. If so, we must judge what sort of cause would be adequate to this immense effect: the cosmos. The only cause conceivable to such a vast and incalculable effect must be an independent, sufficient mind and infinite will capable of conceiving and initiating the universe. Such a mind must be capable of knowing the entire universe that becomes effected by it, and must have the will and power adequate to bringing such a vast outlay of causes into effect. These are precisely the qualities previously described as intrinsic to the God attested by Scripture: free, personal, eternal Spirit capable of infinite power and knowledge (Gen. 17:1; Exod. 6:3; Athanasius, *Ag. Heathen*, 34, 35, *NPNF* 2 IV, pp. 22 ff.). That infinitely capable mind is what Christian confession calls

God. The infinitely powerful and knowing Mind, however, has a direct kinship and correspondence with our minds, and with the underlying intelligibility of the universe (Calvin, *Inst.* 1.16–18; Watson, *TI* I, pp. 275 ff.). For mind has in fact appeared in the natural and evolutionary history of the universe.

Scripture implicitly sets forth this basic argument in the form of metaphor: "Long ago thou didst lay the foundations of the earth, and the heavens were thy handiwork. They shall pass away, but thou endurest; like clothes they shall all grow old; thou shalt cast them off like a cloak, and they shall vanish; but thou art the same and thy years shall have no end" (Ps. 102:26, 27; Origen, *De Princip.* I.6, *ANF* IV, pp. 260–62; cf. Calvin, *Inst.* 1.13.23).

Objections to this argument are more difficult to maintain than they at first might seem. "An infinite series of efficient causes in essential subordination is impossible. Causes essentially required for the production of a determinate effect cannot consequently be infinitely multiplied, as if a block could be shifted by a crowbar, which in turn is levered by a hand, and so on to infinity" (Tho. Aq., *ST* I Q46.2, *TAPT*, p. 54, cf. *ST* I Q46, p. 244). It is very difficult even to imagine the notion of any temporal event that is without cause or totally disconnected from a causal nexus. The reason it is so difficult is quite simple: Causality is an idea that is necessary to all finite thought. It is impossible to think without positing causality (Tho. Aq., *Compend. Theol.*, chaps. 68 ff., pp. 63 ff.). Thus the string of suppositions that attempt to go contrary to this theistic argument get us into even greater logical difficulties.

Suppose, as some forms of absolute idealism suppose, that everything we observe could be an illusion (Berkeley, *Principles*, 1–5; *Three Dialogues, First Dialogue*, pp. 174 ff.). Even if existence were an illusion, that illusion would still require a causal explanation. So enormous would be the illusion that it would require some ingenious account of such a vast pretense of existence.

Or, take an alternative view and suppose that no original cause of all universal effects ever existed. Suppose nothing caused the universe. That is an even less plausible hypothesis than that an intelligent Mind created these vast complexities of matter and spirit. For if nothing caused the universe, how could it exist as an effect? How could such an assertion remain consistent with everything else we know of causality and reality?

Suppose one objects that the appearance of mind in history is merely a natural development of an essentially material evolutionary process. This does not by any means do away with the embarrassment of an unexplained cause. For there must be some plausible cause to initiate and sustain this evolving natural process. Merely to stretch the development out over a long period of time does not lessen the problem. For is it not well known in physics that, according to the law of atrophy, the second law of thermodynamics, motion tends to grow less and less in time, that is, proceed from higher to lower forms, from greater to lesser energy? Yet most evolutionary hypotheses suppose that natural and evolutionary history moves from lower to higher forms, from lesser to greater manifestations of intelligence and adaptation, without offering any systematic explanation. Evolution, which is sometimes argued as if it were eliminating the idea of an intelligent source of natural and material development, actually demands the supposition of such a ground of emerging intelligence (W. Temple, *Nature, Man and God,* VIII, pp. 198–203; cf. Calvin, *Inst.* 1.16; Tennant, *Phil. Theol.* II, pp. 79 ff.).

Suppose that matter never had a beginning, but always existed. Still that requires a causal explanation. For that assertion does not exempt the universe from causal inquiry. If eternal matter, whence came the matter? How did it become so elaborately organized? Even more, how can we make sense out of the astonishing fact that mind emerged within the matter? To assert that matter can spontaneously produce mind is to assert an effect greater than the cause (W. Temple, *Nature, Man and God* VIII, pp. 198 ff.). The causal argument has been widely received by theistic philosophers, but some have objected to it (Kant, *Critique of Pure Reason, Transcendental Dialectic* II.4). Hume, for example, challenged its premise on the grounds that causality itself cannot be rationally proven but rather has merely become a habit of mind. Hume attributed the idea of causation to the observation of invariable sequence in nature. This makes the idea of causation a product of human experience, not a necessary truth or premise of rational intelligence. But Hume's argument, however influential in an earlier period, has minimal plausibility. For how could the observation of invariable sequence even take place without first presupposing the intelligibility of sequence, and therefore presupposing the idea of causation as a necessary idea? Before and after Hume's critique there has remained the persistent hunger of intelligence to look for causes in any given effect. If every event must have a cause, then a cause of the universe must necessarily be posited, short of the intellectual embarrassment of an infinite regression of causes (Tho. Aq., *SCG* I.13; *ST* I Q46; cf. Calvin, *Inst.* 1.16, 17; A. Plantinga, *Faith and Philosophy*; for an alternative view, see David Hume, *A Treatise of Human Nature*).

Schiller objected that it is not possible for this argument to establish the existence of an infinite cause from a finite world. "No evidence can prove an infinite cause of the world, for no evidence can prove anything but a cause adequate to the production of the world, but not infinite" (Schiller, *Riddles of the Sphinx*, p. 304). Strictly speaking, however, the argument from causation does not attempt to establish that the first cause is infinite, but only that it exists. Infinity is established by other arguments of Christian teaching, not by causality.

Argument from Contingency

The third cosmological argument is drawn from the fact of contingency. A contingent being is one that depends upon something else (Calvin, *Inst.* 1.16.8, 9). Contingency is the opposite of necessity and is only understandable in relation to necessity.

Look about you, said Thomas Aquinas, and you will see a world full of things that are dependent on other things. These things, if they are dependent, have the character of not being necessary, in the sense that they can either be or not be. They do not exist by some absolute necessity. They come and they go. To explain the existence of a contingent being, one must refer to something else upon which it depends (Tho. Aq., *SCG* I.15, pp. 98 ff.), for existence does not belong to its essence. On the other hand, a necessary being would be a being that *must exist*. Existing would belong to that being's very essence. The completely sufficient reason for its existence would be in itself. It would not depend upon some other being for its existence (Tho. Aq., *ST* I Q2.3, I, p. 13).

The heart of the argument is that the existence of contingent beings requires that we admit the existence of some necessary being. If any contingent being whatsover exists, then there must be some necessary being. Contingent beings evidently exist. Therefore, the unconditionally necessary being must exist as the sufficient explanation of any contingent being (Tho. Aq., *ST* I Q3.7, I, p. 19; *SCG* II.30).

The hinge point is that everything cannot be contingent. "Were this true, nothing would ever have begun, for what is does not begin to be except because of something which is, and so there would be nothing even now. This is clearly hollow. Therefore all things cannot be might-not-have-beens; among them must be a being whose existence is necessary" (Tho. Aq., *ST* I Q2.3, *TAPT*, p. 56). For if everything is contingent and unnecessary, then there was once nothing, and it is impossible that there was once nothing, since a nonexistent contingency can only be brought into existence by something upon which it is contingent, upon something that already exists. Hence reason suggests what Scripture attests, that such a necessary being exists, which the worshiping community has called God.

Degrees of Being or Grades of Perfection

The fourth of Thomas's five ways is the argument from the degrees or grades of perfection. Thomas says if you look about you in the world, you will see different grades in being. We frequently use the words *more* and *less*. Without such comparative terms we would be hard put to say what we often have to say. This is evidence that some perception of grades of being and goodness is built into the structure of human language, regardless of what language we speak.

For example, it is evident that everything does not participate equally in *life*. Some things are not alive, others potentially alive, others actually alive; some live longer lives, others shorter. There are gradations of aliveness. Some acts are less noble, some more noble. There are gradations of truth, wisdom, and perception; one does not need faith in order to see that. If one has a more and a less, that necessarily implies an idea of the perfection of that category of being, for how could one have a more or a less without a most?

Everyone knows how it feels to be treated unjustly. The difference between more just and less just implies a gradient, a standard of judgment concerning degrees of fairness. If you have degrees of justice, that indirectly points toward what is absolutely or incomparably just, that reality that is to the highest possible degree just. One who recognizes relative justice at all must posit that absolutely just being in relation to which rough modes of justice are to be measured. One cannot talk about a scale of gradation and leave open the maximum of that scale. If one were to hypothesize that there is nothing there at the maximal level, then the scale itself would be incomplete and deficient (Tho. Aq., *SCG* II.15; *ST* I Q2.3, I, p. 14; *ST* I Q44.1, I, p. 229).

This is clearly seen in common language about the *good*. At one point we see something with minimal good in it, another with some good in it, and another with very great good in it. If there exist any such degrees of goodness, then there must exist that which is good without qualification, without which there would be no way of measuring the relative degree of goodness of things. If one can conceive at all the notion of something that is less good or slightly better, then one must hypothesize that by which "better and worse" is measurable. This is a persistent assumption of moral language. One cannot posit a good and a better without a best. Thomas argued that we define any degree of a genus in relation to the maximum of that genus, just "as fire, which is the maximum of heat, is the cause of all hot things. Therefore there must also be something which is to all beings the cause of their being, goodness, and every other perfection; and this we call God" (Tho. Aq., *ST* I Q2.3, I, p. 14).

Similarly with *being*: If anything at all exists, then there must be to all beings something that most completely *is*, that most fully expresses being. If there are degrees of being, there must be that reality that absolutely exists, without any possible diminution of being. If there are degrees of truth, we must posit that absolute truth in relation to which those gradients of relative truth are to be measured. Any assessment of relativity of being or goodness implies a standard in terms of which that relative good is seen as good. If there are goods, more and less, there must be that which is insurmountably good (Augustine, *CG* XIX, *NPNF* 1 II, pp. 397 ff.; *Letters* 162, *FC* 20, p. 375; cf. John of Damascus, *OF* I.9, *NPNF* 2 IX, p. 12). That reality corresponds to what Scripture attests as God. Any conceivable relative good, for example in architecture, points to the source of good: "One piece of architecture is more sham than another, one more genuine; throughout a comparison is implied with what is true without qualification and most of all. We can go farther and conclude that there is something most real, and this we call God" (Tho. Aq., *SCG* I.13, *TAPT*, p. 58).

Thomas found the same basic argument in Plato, Aristotle, Augustine, and Avicenna: Aristotle, for example, argued that "what is most true is also most a being" (Tho. Aq., *SCG* I.13, p. 95; cf. Aristotle, *Metaphy.* II.1.993b, *BWA*, pp. 712 f.). Thomas concluded:

> Whatever is good yet not identified with its goodness is said to be good by sharing. A previous good must then be presupposed, from which is received the real form of derivative goodness. To go back to infinity is not possible especially as regards final causes, for indefiniteness is repugnant to the nature of purpose and the good has the force of a purpose or end. We must therefore reach some first good thing, which is not a derivative good by sharing, nor a good by reference to something else, but which is good essentially of itself. And this is God. (Tho. Aq., *SCG* I.38, *TAPT*, p. 61)

Arguments from Conscience, Beauty, Pragmatic Results, and Congruity

The Argument from Moral Awareness

In addition to the arguments for the existence of God based on sensory experience of the world (externally based), there are also

arguments based upon moral awareness, or arguments from conscience (subjectively based).

The heart of this classical argument is that the existence of moral
obligation establishes the existence of God as the cause of the moral
order. It begins by observing the presence of a keen sense of obligation
or moral requirement found generally in human consciousness. Just
as relative moral necessity cannot be required of the will except by
that which is relatively good, so absolute moral necessity cannot be
caused by any good less than the insurmountable good. A sense of
absolute obligation can only come from One to whom absolute moral
authority is fittingly and legitimately ascribed. It is to this transcendent ground of obligation that conscience witnesses. For conscience
does not pretend to make the laws that it dictates (Clement of Alex.,
Christ the Educator III.1, *FC* 23, p. 199; cf. Augustine, *Answer to Letters
of Petilian* II.85, *NPNF* 1 IV, pp. 572–75).

Conscience would not be able to bind our wills so radically and
unconditionally if it were merely that we were binding ourselves. Just
as order in the world suggests an intelligent orderer as its cause, so
does moral awareness in human decision making suggest and require
a sufficient source of moral consciousness and ground of moral authority in the universe (Augustine, *On the Profit of Believing* XVI.34,
NPNF 1 III, pp. 363 f.; Kant, *Crit. Pract. Reason*; J. H. Newman,
Grammar of Assent).

The moral argument emerges out of an irrepressible internal dialogue. There are some ways in which my freedom actualizes itself that
are not adequately in touch with who I really am. I tell myself, "That
is not me, or not the best me." That is conscience. There emerges a
sense of serenity when I follow that conscience. I feel at one with
myself. There is a sense of guilt, subjective brokenness, and self-
alienation when I actualize my freedom in a way that I know is not
really consistent with what I ought to be or do (Luther, *Comm. on
Galatians*, *ML*, pp. 100–9; Calvin, *Inst.* 3.19.15; Wesley, *WJW* V, pp.
135 ff.).

The root word for conscience (*conscientia* or *syneidēsis*) implies
knowledge of oneself, a knowledge one has with one's self, a knowledge accompanying one's own choosing and intrinsic to the process of
choosing. I go about choosing; I make these choices and then I have
to live with my choices. Conscience is the knowledge I have of my
own choosing and the way in which I compare my decisions with my
truer, deeper self and with that silent measurer of my true self within
myself that transcends myself (Rom. 2:15; 1 Cor. 8:7–12; 1 Tim. 1:5,

19; 4:2; Heb. 9:9 ff.; 1 Pet. 3:16 ff.; Acts 23:1). Every conscious and rational human being has that self-knowing capacity (Calvin, *Inst.* 3.2–3; Kant, *Fundamental Principles of the Metaphys. of Morals, LLA,* pp. 11 ff.). Most of the Western intellectual tradition, including Christian theism, has argued that everyone has some form of conscience.

The Ground of Practical Reason's Moral Claim

Although Immanuel Kant's views are notoriously difficult to understand, his importance in modern theistic reasoning (especially liberal Protestant) is so great that he cannot be omitted. Though Kant viewed the cosmological arguments as wholly unsatisfactory, he thought they could be replaced by the reframing of the moral argument that had long been a part of classic Christian theistic reasoning. Kant sought to demolish most of the arguments that we have previously discussed. In his view no empirical or speculative reasoning could be sufficient to establish reliable proofs of God's existence. All reason could do was correct the misunderstandings of various dubious or ambiguous arguments for God's existence (Kant, *Critique of Pure Reason,* "On the Impossibility of the Physico-Theological Proof"; cf. his *Religion Within the Limits of Reason Alone*).

Instead, Kant sought to employ practical reason, a form of reason that emerges out of moral consciousness, as the sole basis for arguing the existence of God (*Critique of Practical Reason* II.2.5, pp. 128 ff.). Eternity must ultimately right temporality's wrongs, conscience, moral freedom, responsibility, and law would be absurd if there were no moral law or lawgiver. Such a lawgiver every rational being has in the impingement of conscience. Any reasonable person by self-examination can come to hear and be aware of the absolutely rational claim of the categorical imperative, which is, "Act as if the maxim of thy action were to become by thy will a universal law of nature" (Kant, *Fundamental Principles of Metaphy. of Morals, LLA,* p. 38). This moral consciousness does not accrue as a matter of gathering experience in the world, but rather is something given to consciousness prior to data gathering. Thus the idea of God, he argued, is a necessary postulate universally and practically required by moral reasoning (*Crit. Pract. Reason* II.2.5, pp. 130 ff.).

Consequently we have a modern form of argument for the existence of God that is based exclusively upon a certain kind of reasoning, namely, *a priori* moral reasoning. God becomes the necessary hypothesis of the moral conscience. God (Kant hypothesized) is needed to bring virtue and happiness into fitting conjunction, for in this world they do not correspond. Since injustice prevails from time to time in history, there must be a transhistorical way of rectifying wrongs. One cannot have a moral order without a divinely fair mind that undergirds the rights and transcends the wrongs of history. Kant's argument is based not on revelation but, in his view, upon reason alone, and in fact a particular type of reason—moral reasoning (Kant, *Crit. Pract. Reason* II.2.1 ff., pp. 111 ff.).

Kant's dilemma centered on the sad fact that in this world "the wicked prosper"—some who are morally evil gain greater temporal happiness. For Kant that stubborn fact stood as a fundamental obstacle to making moral sense. To overcome this obstacle, reason must hypothesize three postulates: freedom, immortality, and God. We must have *freedom* if we are to sustain any idea of moral responsibility. Only if one can freely respond to a moral claim can one reasonably be addressed with, or address oneself with, a moral claim. *Immortality* is necessary because in this world happiness and virtue are not conjoined perfectly, so the reasonable person must hypothesize another world beyond this sphere that somehow will make right what is temporarily wrong in this world. *God* is a necessary hypothesis of the moral consciousness because God alone can, in some final way beyond our present experience, rightly bring into harmony the disjunctive relation of virtue and happiness (*Crit. Pract. Reason* II.2.4–6, pp. 124 ff.). It is an ethical justification for religion that has come to dominate some modern Protestant traditions, particularly Protestant liberalism, which may be in large part defined as a Kantian ethic melded with selected strands of Protestant theology (cf. A. Ritschl, *Justification and Reconciliation*; A. Harnack, *What Is Christianity?*; W. Herrmann, *Syst. Theol.*).

The Message of Conscience

In his *Grammar of Assent*, John Henry Newman presented the moral argument to the modern mind more subtly and with a deeper acquaintance with the varied strands of ancient Christian theism. He too began with conscience: All feel responsibility. No human consciousness can fully succeed in escaping some awareness of guilt and shame. We have an inner sense of sin or moral revulsion when we do something wrong and a sense of moral justification and serenity when we do something right. This cannot be simply explained sociologically or in terms of finite parenting. The depth, extent, and power of these moral feelings require the explanation of a moral Requirer (Newman, *A Grammar of Assent*, pp. 104–15; cf. Hastings Rashdall, *The Theory of*

Good and Evil, vol. II, bk. III, chap. I, pp. 206 ff.; W. D. Ross, *The Right and the Good,* pp. 34 ff.).

"The wicked man runs away with no one in pursuit" (Prov. 28:1), the proverb knew, but from whom is one running away? What is one afraid of? To say merely "oneself" may not fully account for the fact that this voice within oneself, conscience, points to that which is beyond oneself. Newman did not argue that conscience is a direct or immediate revelation of God in specific detail. Yet conscience is not something we merely give (and therefore could fail to give) ourselves, but is latently God-bestowed within every self, and constitutive of the self (Newman, *Grammar of Assent,* pp. 112 ff.).

It may be objected that it is merely I who give myself moral require-ments, and that does not imply any transcendent source. Yet if persons experience in themselves such a moral imperative or sense of moral necessity that it seems to be speaking, as it were, from above them-selves, then what could the sufficient reason for this imperative be? It is not enough to say I give it to myself. Far more pertinently, I often wish I could get rid of it. I wish it would not continue to bother me. Conscience is not self-imposed, but rather is unavoidable, as if a transcendent witness within (Newman, *Grammar of Assent,* pp. 395 ff.; *Certain Difficulties Felt by Anglicans in Catholic Teaching* II, pp. 248 ff.; cf. W. Temple, *Nature, Man and God* VII, pp. 166 ff.; Wesley, *WJW* VIII, pp. 132 ff., IX, pp. 218 ff.).

Such a sense of moral responsibility cannot be explained except by supposing the existence of a superior lawgiver, a Holy One who is present and impinging upon our responsibility with the claim that we do the good we know and avoid the evil we know. Some Requirer must be implied in the subtle, inward, unavoidable requirement of conscience (Origen, *Ag. Celsus* I.4, *ANF* IV, p. 398; Schmid, *DT,* p. 105). In this way the will of the Creator is hypothesized as the neces-sary and sufficient reason for the existence of moral obligation. Con-science is both immanent within us and transcendent beyond us. For this is the way God expresses the divine claim, at least indirectly, in the form of potential guilt, hiddenly meeting one at the closest possible quarters—the inner precincts of each individual person's moral self-awareness (Newman, *Grammar of Assent,* pp. 121 ff.; cf. Kierkegaard, *Concl. Unsci. Post.,* p. 138; *Works of Love,* pp. 136 ff.). The arguments of Kant, Newman, and Kierkegaard preceded the intensive study of cultural moral relativism and cross-cultural pluralism in the late nine-teenth century and since then. Yet the most exacting comparative anthropologist would be hard put to cite a society that has no moral awareness whatever, no imperatives, no guilt, and no evidence of any pangs of conscience (cf. Claude Levi-Strauss, *Structural Anthropology*, III, pp. 167 ff.).

Moral awareness, in its more profound forms, is painfully conscious that it exists in relation to that which transcends it. It desires and longs for communion and reconciliation with the One who gives moral order. It knows that it cannot be sufficiently explained in terms of environmental influences or education, although conscience is subject to further education and refinement, but rather is an element essential to human consciousness, preconditioning education and socialization. Conscience is immediately grasped and universally known in all human cultures (Lactantius, *Div. Inst.* VI.8–10, *ANF* VII, pp. 170–73; Ambrose, *Duties* I.8–14, *NPNF* 2 X, pp. 4–10; Luther, *Comm. on Galatians, ML*, pp. 118–21).

Nor can the presence of evil fundamentally undermine the moral argument, as if to say, "God could not exist in a world as bad as that one to which conscience attests." Rather, theistic exponents of the moral argument view the painful awareness of persistent evil as a powerful validation rather than a rejection of the argument, implying that "God does exist, because we are awakened to the persistence of evil through conscience in a way that points beyond the law to the Lawgiver and leads to repentance, redemption, and reconciliation." As viewed by classical Christianity, no evil to which conscience attests is so far distanced from the divine will that it cannot become subsequently a greater good, or through its evil reflect the good. Evil willing belongs to creatures, not the Creator. God permits evil to emerge out of freedom in the interest of the greater good of enhancing self-determination and personhood, and with the longer-range intent and hope of discipline and correction—all of which tends ultimately toward a more complete actualization of the divine good purpose (Augustine, *Enchiridion, LCC* VII, pp. 353 ff.; Calvin, *Inst.* 3.19.7 ff.).

The Argument from Beauty

Beauty is that quality or combination of qualities within a thing that gives pleasure to the senses or pleasurably exalts the mind or spirit. So universal is the capacity for admiration of beauty that this capacity is regarded as a normal competence of human existence, so much so that the absence of any sense of beauty would be regarded as abnormal and a diminution of human dignity (cf. Pss. 50:2; 96:6; Isa. 52:7; Methodius, *Or. on the Psalms, ANF* VI, pp. 394–99). Beauty is that by reason of which we behold things in admiration or behold things as objects of disinterested satisfaction. Something beautiful is intrinsically pleasing, is capable of pleasing anyone who looks at it, and ought to please all (Tho. Aq., *ST* I–IIae Q34.2 ff., I, pp. 736 ff.; cf. Kant, *Critique of Practical Judgment*).

Beauty cannot be reduced to utility, for often we admire things whose usefulness cannot be established unless one appeals back to the primary value of beauty itself. Augustine sharply distinguished between those things to be used and those to be enjoyed. "To enjoy something is to cling to it with love for its own sake. To use something, however, is to employ it in obtaining that which you love, provided that it is worthy of love. For an illicit use should be called rather a waste or an abuse" (*On Chr. Doctrine* I.4, *LLA*, p. 9). We may try to make "use" of God, as if God were a thing. Things are to be used, but God is to be enjoyed (p. 10). "No one rightly uses God, for he is to be enjoyed. The last end is not a utility" (Tho. Aq., *ST* I–IIae Q16.3, *TAPT*, p. 77).

Nor can beauty be reduced to pure subjectivity or petty preference or quirks of autobiographical history. For beauty to some degree can be shared, leading beholders to the conviction that there is something objective about beauty, that it is admirable in itself, as a sunset would not be made less beautiful if no one were there to behold it (cf. Clement of Alex., *Instr.* III.1, *ANF* II, pp. 271, 272; Francis Hutcheson, *Inquiry into the Original of Our Ideas of Beauty and Virtue;* Edmund Burke, *The Sublime and the Beautiful*) Were this not true, there could be no history of art.

Some reductive naturalism has sought to account for beauty in terms of its evolutionary survival value. This view makes some sense in relation to sexual selection, but it seems far less plausible in explaining the beauty of inorganic life, the sky, the ocean, the grandeur of mountains, the twilight tinting of great canyons. It seems as though there may be a profound intention at work in and through inorganic nature that it be intrinsically beautiful and be perceived by any rational being as beautiful. For what other purpose or sufficient reason can one hypothesize that the Grand Canyon has been so beautiful for so many millions of years before human beings came, belatedly, to behold it?

The aesthetic argument for the existence of God is the unadorned observation that if beauty exists at all in this extraordinary universe, then it must be accounted for by some sufficient cause. In view of the abundance and power of the forms of beauty in this world, no cause is sufficient short of hypothesizing a Creator who cares about creation enough to make it beautiful and recognizable as such. Where beauty is found, one must hypothesize a ground and giver of the beautiful, a source of beauty that transcends naturalistic accounts of its origin (Tho. Aq., *ST* I Q5, I, pp. 25 ff.).

This insight is known in Scripture and tradition: "The heavens tell out the glory of God, the vault of heaven reveals his handiwork. One day speaks to another, night with night shares its knowledge, and this without speech or language or sound of any voice. Their music goes out through all the earth, their words reach to the end of the world" (Ps. 19:1–4). Hence the faithful are repeatedly called to beautify (*paar*) the house of the Lord (Ezra 7:27; Isa. 60:13) as a fitting response to the beauty of the Lord (Ps. 27:4; cf. Song of Songs, 6:4).

The theistic argument from beauty was inimitably formulated by Augustine as follows:

> The world itself, by its well-ordered changes and movements, and by the fair appearance of all visible things, bears a testimony of its own, both that it has been created, and also that it could not have been created save by God, whose greatness and beauty are unutterable and invisible. (Augustine, *CG* XI.4, *NPNF* 1 II, p. 207)

Since Thomas Aquinas viewed beauty in the closest proximity to divine goodness, the argument from beauty becomes for him an alternate version of the argument from degrees of goodness: "The beautiful is the same as the good, but with a difference of accent. Good is what all desire; therefore it is of the essence of beauty that at the knowledge and sight of it the desire is stilled. . . . The good is that which simply pleases desire, the beautiful that which pleases on being perceived" (Tho. Aq., *ST* I–IIae Q27.1.3, *TAPT*, p. 79). Hence if degrees of beauty exist, as our common language constantly assumes, then that which is unsurpassably beautiful, or filled with the glory of beauty, must be posited, and that we call God. It is in this sense that the psalmist sought all the days of his life to "behold the beauty of the Lord" (Ps. 27:4, KJV) and to "worship the Lord in the beauty of holiness" (Ps. 96:9, KJV), for "strength and beauty are in his sanctuary" (Ps. 96:6, KJV). "Things are beautiful," noted Thomas, "by the indwelling of God" (Tho. Aq., *Expos. of Psalms* XXV.5, *TAPT*, p. 79).

Gregory of Nyssa more directly argued that the soul that recognizes its own beauty rightly sees that beauty as a reflection of God's own beauty: "The Deity is in very substance Beautiful; and to the Deity the soul will in its state of purity have affinity" and will embrace God as like the beauty of the soul herself (*On the Soul and the Resurrection, NPNF* 2 V, p. 449). Hence "the soul copies the life that is above," and "the Beautiful is necessarily lovable to those who recognize it" (p. 450). Although this recognition was expected finally in the resurrection, Gregory thought, it may be anticipatively experienced in the soul's ascent to God here and now. When this happens "enjoyment takes the place of desire, and the power to enjoy renders desire useless and out of date." Then the soul will "know herself accurately, what her actual nature is, and should behold the Original Beauty reflected in the mirror" (p. 449).

The Pragmatic Argument

The modern pragmatic argument for the existence of God was primarily formulated by the psychologist William James, who came to the conclusion that the reality of God is practically validated by the fact that believing in God makes people function better and feel better and makes lives more productive. If one acts on the assumption that God exists, life works better. Those who believe in God are going to be better able to take risks, and will have better emotional health, because they trust that some intelligible power grounds the universe and their behavior. The premise that God exists is both psychologically healthier and sociologically more productive. This is an argument from results, and therefore pragmatic (W. James, *Essays on Faith and Morals*, pp. 115 ff., 212 ff., 256 ff.; cf. C. S. Pierce, *Collected Papers*, vol. VI, par. 467, cf. Hartshorne and Reese, *PSG*, pp. 262 ff.). Modern audiences are less familiar with James's teaching than with popular transformations of it by media preachers such as Norman Vincent Peale, Reverend Ike, Robert Schuller, and others (cf. W. James, "The Gospel of Relaxation," *Essays on Faith and Morals*, pp. 238 ff.).

The argument, as formulated by James, is closely intertwined with previously stated classical arguments from consent and degrees of being and with the argument from comprehensive complementarity, to be discussed later:

A God, whether existent or not, is at all events the kind of being which, if he did exist, would form *the most adequate possible object* for minds framed like our own to conceive as lying at the root of the universe. My thesis, in other words, is this: that *some* outward reality of a nature defined as God's nature must be defined, is the only ultimate object that is at the same time rational and possible for the human mind's contemplation. *Anything short of God is not rational, anything more than God is not possible.* . . . Our gain will thus in the first instance be psychological. We shall merely have investigated a chapter in the natural history of mind, and found that, as a matter of such natural history, God may be called the normal object of the mind's belief. Whether over and above this he be really the living truth is another question. . . . [that belongs] to the province of personal faith to decide. (James, *Essays on Faith and Morals*, pp. 115 ff.)

The argument is quintessentially modern, in that it is psychological at its center, metaphysically skeptical, and avoids dealing with the truth question—attending only to results. Yet its spirit is to some degree anticipated by numerous Christian writers who have appealed to "doing" the truth as a basis for understanding it (notably Baxter, Wesley, Phoebe Palmer, and Kierkegaard), stressing the importance of praxis in the knowing of God's greatness and goodness (esp. John Cassian, Ignatius Loyola, and Teresa of Avila).

Amma Theodora, one of the fourth-century ascetic Desert Mothers, recognized the principle that when "one believes one is ill" the soul tends toward illness. She told the amusing story of the "monk who was seized by cold and fever every time he began to pray, and he suffered from headaches, too. In this condition, he said to himself, 'I am ill, and near to death; so now I will get up before I die and pray,'" yet simply by getting up, his fever abated (*SDF*, p. 71). Merely by doing something positive—just getting up—he was taking a step of faith that tended toward his health. Hence there is a pragmatic test that can be applied to any argument concerning God: Does the premise of God improve the human condition?

Causal Law Prior to Thought

Another corroboratory argument hinges on the basic insight that causal law exists before its discovery. In the scientific world we sometimes hear the spurious assertion that the more science advances, the further theology must retreat. Hence the more that is known about the causal order, the less needs to be known about the hypothesis of the existence of God (Bonhoeffer, *Prisoner for God*). If that should be true then there would be an irreversible decline of the study of God as scientific inquiry proceeds. In this view, belief in God has been temporarily used to explain phenomena that are not as yet accounted for by scientific or causal law; as soon as scientific inquiry extends the network of causality to cover all phenomena of nature, then belief in God will have been whittled away (Feuerbach, Essence of Christianity, pp. 12–67, 92–100; Marx, *Humanitarianism and Liberalism, Writings of Young Marx*, pp. 64–66, 94–96; Nietzsche, *The Will to Power*, pp. 164–72, 200–2).

The following argument tries to answer that assumption. The question is raised: "What are causal laws?" They are formulas that are defended by scientific inquiry. They are stated by people who are seeking to discover the way insects feed, the way the physical universe works, the structure of the atom. But all these causal laws were true and in operation before they were discovered. What existence did these causal laws have before they were formulated by us? They existed as adequately as now, but without recognition by us (Augustine, *Of True Religion* 21, LCC VI, pp. 244 f.). The ideas are prior to our discovery (Augustine, *On Free Choice of the Will LLA*, II.9, pp. 57 ff., *On the Trin.* XIV.21, LCC VI; Sir James Jeans, *Physics and Philosophy*, pp. 215 ff.; E. S. Brightman, *Moral Laws*, pp. 1 ff.; *A Phil. of Relig.*, pp. 43 ff.; L. H. DeWolfe, *Theol. of Living Church*, pp. 48 ff.).

If laws of causality exist before they are formulated by human minds, then one must posit either a divine Mind or chance. That these laws of causality have occurred by chance or random events is far less plausible than that they correspond to a Mind that underlies all things. Such a Mind corresponds with what the worshiping community calls God (Augustine, *On Free Choice of the Will* II.6, *LLA*, pp. 48 ff.).

The Argument from Congruity: Comprehensive Complementarity

One of the most powerful of theistic arguments cannot be stated until all the above arguments have been clarified. It is the argument from congruity or comprehensive complementarity. It does not depend upon any single one of the arguments just described, but builds upon the accumulation of all of them.

The center of this argument is: *that postulate which best explains the most distantly related facts is more probably true.* It is a probability hypothesis. Any postulate that gathers together a great number of disparate facts and accounts for them intelligibly and integrally is more likely true than one that accounts for fewer facts. It is argued that the hypothesis of the existence of God provides the most congruent available basis for explaining otherwise absurdities, moral and intellectual, and gives an integral, purposeful clarification of otherwise disparate facts of our mental, spiritual, and physical existence.

If God in fact exists, then the virtually universal belief in divine reality is accounted for. If God exists, then the intellectual hunger to ask for a first cause of causes is satisfied without the embarrassment of an infinite regress of causes or unaccounted-for motions. If God exists, then our inveterate religious nature has an object. If God exists, then the uniformity of natural law finds adequate explanation. If God exists, then human moral awareness is vindicated from the charge of being an immense absurdity. There is a kind of cumulative effect from the various arguments in which one hypothesis— that God exists—solves recalcitrant problems that are far harder to solve without it (Tho. Aq., *ST* I Q3, I, pp. 14–19; cf. W. James, *Essays on Faith and Morals*, pp. 115 ff.; cf. E. L. Long, *A Survey of Christian Ethics*, pp. 310–14 for clarification of the concept of "comprehensive complementarity).

Argument from the Idea of Perfect Being

The Idea of Perfect Being Requires Its Existence

The argument for the existence of God that is the most aesthetically beautiful is the simplest, yet hardest to grasp at first. After the argument has been stated, unless it is studied carefully, the casual reader is not likely to be even slightly impressed by it. It is so simple that its profundity escapes our notice. I have been through this argument so many times with so little effect on so many audiences that I do not expect the beholder joyfully to leap to receive it immediately, partly because of its intrinsic simplicity. But because of its exceeding importance, I will set it forth as clearly as possible. It is an argument that requires some quiet meditation in order that in due time it may grasp one's soul.

This argument for the existence of God is not based on sensory experience, but is prior to experience (thus called *a priori*, i.e., discoverable through rational reflection alone without the help of sensory input). We are at this point relying exclusively upon a rational analysis of ideas, not the support of facts or the data of experience.

The ontological argument finds in the very idea of God the proof of God's existence. If that does not strike you as meaningful, let us express it differently: If properly thought, the very idea of God requires that the referent of that idea, God, exists. God is the only idea that refers to a reality that must exist if properly conceived.

Once more: We have an idea of an absolutely perfect being. It is possible to have that idea. The heart of the argument is this: Existence is a necessary characteristic of that particular idea, the idea of perfect being. For the idea of perfection would not be perfect if that to which it refers did not exist. *An absolutely perfect being must exist if it is to be absolutely perfect.* The reality to which that idea refers must exist, otherwise that idea is not a perfect idea. That is it. If it went by too fast, we will take it step-by-step in its classic formulation.

That Than Which Nothing Greater Can Be Conceived Must Exist

Anselm's formulation has hardly been improved upon in eight hundred years. Anselm was asking in the *Proslogion* whether it is possible to reach the notion of the existence of God through reasoning, although he himself acknowledged the living presence of God through faith. Anselm defined God in a particular way: God is *that than which nothing greater can be conceived* (Anselm, *Proslog.* II, *BW*, p. 8). Anyone who is going to speak with another about this argument does well to learn the phrase "that than which nothing greater can be conceived"— try three times out loud if all else fails. Augustine had anticipated Anselm in arguing that the thought of God "takes the form of an endeavour to reach the conception of a nature than which nothing more excellent or more exalted exists" (*On Chr. Doctrine* I.6, *NPNF* 1 II, p. 524).

According to Anselm, there is no difficulty in conceiving of the *idea* of that than which nothing greater can be conceived (*Proslog.* II, *BW*, p. 8). The phrase means that we are speaking of perfect being, that being who is greater (in goodness, being, and power) than any other being we can conceive. Yet there are two possible ways of thinking that idea:

That Than Which Nothing Greater Can Be Conceived
as an

A   or   B
Idea in Mind Only	**Idea as Existing**
The idea refers to that which exists in our minds, but not in reality itself.	The idea refers to that which exists in reality, and not in our minds only.
Which idea is greater?

Ask yourself, Which idea is greater: the idea as existing in the mind only, an idea of "that than which nothing greater can be conceived" but that exists in our minds only and not in reality, *or*, the second idea, an idea of "that than which nothing greater can be conceived" that exists in reality and not just in the understanding alone?

If you say the second idea is greater, you have made an important decision, and have accepted the ontological argument. For if so, you attribute existence to that idea. You have decided that if that idea *(B)* exists in reality, it is greater than that idea *(A)* that exists only conceptually, in our minds. The lesser is lacking in only one small way: its referent does not exist.

That is the crux of the argument. Most people answer with Anselm that such an idea—if in our minds only—cannot be "that than which nothing greater can be conceived" because its referent does not exist in reality; that is, it lacks something, making it something less than "that than which nothing greater can be conceived." So the referent of the second idea must exist if that idea is to be the greater. If the second is the greater idea, as Anselm thought it must be, then the referent of that idea is implied in the idea itself.

Thus God's existence is implied in the very idea of God, properly conceived. It is necessary that God exist, because the very idea of God, properly conceived, requires God's existence. For if you opt for the first idea (conceiving of God merely as an idea in our minds, without existing), then Anselm thought that you still have not arrived at the proper conception of that than which nothing greater can be conceived. Since the first idea is a foolish idea of God, it invites fools to say, "There is no God" (Ps. 14:1), which is the biblical text for Anselm's *Proslogium* (*Proslog.* II ff., *BW*, pp. 8 ff.).

In his second, somewhat refined, statement of the argument, Anselm further argued that God

cannot be conceived not to exist. For, it is possible to conceive of a being which cannot be conceived not to exist; and this is greater than one which can be conceived not to exist. Hence, if that, than which nothing greater can be conceived, can be conceived not to exist, it is not that, than which nothing greater can be conceived. (Anselm, *Proslog.* III, *BW*, p. 8)

"Therefore, he who understands that God so exists, cannot conceive that he does not exist" (*Proslog.* IV, *BW*, p. 10). The same crucial passage in the translation by Charlesworth reads:

And certainly this being so truly exists that it cannot be even thought not to exist. For something can be thought to exist that cannot be thought not to exist, and this is greater than that which can be thought not to exist. Hence, if that-than-which-a-greater-cannot-be-thought can be thought not to exist, then that-than-which-a-greater-cannot-be-thought is not the same as that-than-which-a-greater-cannot-be-thought, which is absurd.

Something-than-which-a-greater-cannot-be-thought exists so truly then, that it cannot be even thought not to exist. (*Proslog.* III, p. 119)

Another striking way of stating the argument begins with a different question: Does God minus the world equal God? If one answers yes, then it must be conceded that the very idea of God is greater than the idea of the world or anything in or of the world. If that idea of such a greater-than-world being is rightly conceived, it cannot fail to have included or assumed in its definition that it exists in reality and not in our minds only. For what is greater than the world could not exist merely as an idea in our minds. The obvious evidence is that the world exists.

Gaunilo, a monk of Marmoutiers, countered that the idea of a perfect being does not imply its existence. We can easily form the idea of purely imaginary beings, he said, but that does not bring them into being. We can imagine an island, or money in our pockets, but that does not mean they exist (Gaunilo, *A Reply on Behalf of the Fool, BW,* pp. 143 ff.; *Proslog.,* pp. 157–67). Gaunilo's argument has been taken to be a standard, and I think inaccurate, refutation of the ontological argument.

Anselm's response to Gaunilo was far more profound: An island and money in my pocket are finite things. This argument does not apply to anything that is finite. The reason is that "that than which nothing greater can be conceived" is not and cannot be finite, since the infinite can be conceived to be greater than the finite. The only object to which this argument can be applied is "that than which nothing greater can be conceived, when conceived as existing in reality and not in our mind only." Gaunilo's objection is valid with respect to any imperfect, finite being, because in its case actual existence is not necessary to the content of the idea. But it is a flawed argument in relation to the idea of perfect being. For in this case the actual existence of the being conceived must be included in the necessary content of the idea (Anselm, *Reply to Gaunilo, BW,* pp. 153 ff.; *Proslog., A Reply to the Foregoing by the Author of the Book in Question,* pp. 169–91).

The more subtle (Kantian) objection to the argument is that existence is not an attribute or predicate. An idea is an idea whether it is thought to be in our heads or in reality, Kant argued. For example, if God did not exist in reality, that would not change our idea of him existing in reality (*Critique of Pure Reason* II.3.4, trans. Smith, pp. 502 ff.). This perplexity had been anticipated by Descartes, who reformulated the argument so as to say that the existence of God must be affirmed in order to account for the origin of the idea of God in our minds:

We possess the idea of an infinitely perfect Being. As we are finite, this idea could not have originated with us. As we are conversant only with the finite, it could not have originated from anything around us. It must, therefore, have come from God, whose existence is thus a necessary assumption. (*Meditations* V, *Philosophical Works* II, p. 186)

In arguing that the idea of God is innate to the mind, Descartes used the word *innate* in the special sense that the ordinary constitution of the mind causes the idea to arise inevitably and spontaneously under normal conditions of experience and reflection. Once suggested, the idea of God is seen to be a necessary accompaniment of thought and is recognized as pointing to that which necessarily exists. The idea of a perfect being, Descartes thought, must have come from such a being, whose actual existence is a necessary assumption of that being's perfection. (For additional statements of the ontological argument, see Leibniz, *New Essays Concerning Human Understanding* IV, chap. 10; *Monadology* 44, 45; Spinoza, *Ethics*, pt. I, prop. 7–11; W. Stillingfleet, *Origines Sacrae* III.1; Charles Hartshorne, *Man's Vision of God*, chap. X; for objections, see Tho. Aq. *ST* I Q2.1; Locke, *Essays Concerning Human Understanding* IV.10; Kant, *Critique of Pure Reason*, pp. 379 f.; cf. Edwards, *Freedom of Will*, pt. II.3; G. W. F. Hegel, *Lectures on the Phil. of Relig.* III, pp. 347 ff.; and *Lectures on the Hist. of Phil.* III, pp. 62–67.)

One objection is formally unanswerable, namely, that the necessity of conceiving God as really existing does not prove that God really exists except on the supposition that rational ideas must correspond with reality. Although this indeed is a supposition beyond demonstration, it nonetheless is presupposed in all demonstration, otherwise there would be no necessary correlation between reason and reality.

This is at one level merely an argument, yet an argument that has remarkable power. The seminal idea of the argument is found in a remark by Augustine: "God is more truly thought than He is described, and exists more truly than He is thought" (my translation, *On Trin.* VII.4, cf. *NPNF* 1 II, p. 109; cf. VIII.3). Even more subtly was the argument anticipated by Hilary, in a profound reflection written during his exile in Phyrgia (356–59), commenting on the divine name, "I AM WHO I AM" (Exod. 2:14):

For no property of God which the mind can grasp is more characteristic than existence, since existence, in the absolute sense, cannot be predicated of that which shall come to an end, or of that which has had a beginning, and He who now joins continuity of being with the possession of perfect felicity could not in the past, nor can in the future, be non-existent; for whatsoever is

Divine can neither be originated nor destroyed. Wherefore, since God's eternity is inseparable from Himself, it was worthy of Him to reveal this one thing, that He is, as the assurance of His absolute eternity. (Hilary, *Trin.* I.5, *NPNF* 2 IX, p. 41)

Hence with remarkable prescience, long before Anselm, Hilary had pointedly concluded *(a)* that existence is intrinsic to the idea of God; *(b)* that since those things that exist normally have a beginning and end, the notion of existence is not adequate to indicate fully the eternal way in which God *is; (c)* that God cannot be thought not to exist; and *(d)* that the eternal way in which God exists is revealed by God already in the disclosure of God's name, "I AM WHO I AM."

After many years of teaching the ontological argument in systematic theology classes, I still can seldom state it without being profoundly moved by it. All the arguments stated so far have been inductive arguments from experience; this argument is essentially deductive and analytical in relation to a particular idea, that of perfect being. That Thomas (*ST* I Q2.1; cf. also *SCG* I.10, 11) and Kant (*Critique of Pure Reason*, II.3.4, pp. 509 ff.) rejected it without fully understanding it is regrettable. That Hegel (*Phenomenology of Mind*), Leibniz (*New Essays Concerning Human Understanding* IV, chap. 10, p. 504), and Hartshorne (*Anselm's Discovery* and *The Divine Perfections*) have affirmed and elaborated it is to their credit. Carelessly stated, the ontological argument seems simply to beg the question by making sure that one's conclusions are already embedded in the premises. Yet when properly formulated, it is hard to counter.

Conclusion

We began this chapter with the question of whether the previously described idea of God is indeed true—whether this God exists. Not only reason, but Scripture, tradition, and experience have assisted in answering the question insofar as it is answerable. We have necessarily relied on rational argumentation and natural theology more than in any other part of this study, since the question is intrinsically apologetic: Upon what reasonable grounds can God be said to exist, or even be thought not to exist? Therefore we have listened to, refashioned, and restated the classical and other arguments through which Scripture and tradition have reasoned that God exists.

Although the results of such an inquiry will always seem inadequate to some and remain always open to further refinement, they are not meaningless. These modest arguments need to be further complemented with doctrinal teachings to be developed later, including creation, providence, and humanity under sin and grace. Nonetheless, we come away from these arguments with a cumulative pattern of reasoning that in its totality is sufficient to support the claim that God exists, and exists in the way that Christian teaching has said God exists.

In summary:

If purpose exists there must be a Purposer, if order, an Orderer. If we see design in the world, we must hypothesize a Designer of sufficient intelligence to produce an intelligible world. If mind exists in evolving history, some incomparable Mind must have enabled and created the possibility of our minds. If it is so difficult to be a human being without knowing something of God, then there must be a sufficient reason for this awareness being so persistent in human cultures and societies, even when suppressed. If such wide consent exists in history to the existence of God, that fact must be accounted for with a sufficient reason. If the idea of God is intrinsic to human consciousness, then God must exist. From the fact of change we must hypothesize a change agent. If anything moves, something must have first moved everything. There must be a being that causes all causes and that moves all movement. If contingent beings exist, there must be a necessary being. If we experience moral obligation as relentlessly as we do, even against parents, against society, against superego constraints, then we must hypothesize a ground of moral obligation calling us to the highest good and possessed of weightiest moral authority. In addition to all this, it appears to be the case that the very idea of perfect being requires the existence of perfect being, otherwise that idea is less than the idea of perfect being.

From this we conclude that God, to whose existence these arguments point, exists more fully than we who are reasoning and arguing exist (Augustine, *Conf.* VII.10, *LCC* VI, p. 147) and that there is nothing so proper to God as to be (Hilary, *On Trin.* I.5, *NPNF* 2 IX, p. 41). We have ample grounds upon which to say: God exists. In this way reason begins to confirm that to which Scripture attests, that God incomparably *is*.

CHAPTER 5

Whether God Is Triune

The idea that the one God meets us in three persons is thought to be among the most opaque and least accessible of all Christian teachings. Yet we must speak of Trinity, as Augustine knew, not because we are able to fathom it with overweening confidence, but because we cannot keep silence on a matter so central to faith (Augustine, *On Trin.* I.2, 3, *NPNF* 1 III, p. 18).

In now discussing the mystery of God the Father, God the Son, and God the Spirit, we are now belatedly introducing a new theme into our discussion, for we have already referred frequently to the triune God by speaking of (*a*) God as Father Almighty, who is the source of life, who makes Himself known in (*b*) Jesus Christ by the power of (*c*) the Spirit of God who is present throughout the historical process, working to transform it according to God's purpose. Thus we are not veering away from previous subjects in dealing now with the triune God, but only seeking to provide increased clarity on how the living God may and must be triune.

In all Christian traditions, baptism occurs in the name of the Father, Son, and Holy Spirit. Christian theology, best thought of largely as a commentary on baptism, has the happy and awesome task of trying to explain to the one baptized what baptism in the triune name means and implies. This is no elective, nonobligatory task or minor, subordinate duty that Christian theology can either choose or refuse. For God appears in the New Testament as Father, Son, and Spirit. "When I say God," remarked Gregory Nazianzen, "I mean Father, Son, and Holy Ghost" (or. XXXIII.8, *NPNF* 2 VII, p. 347).

The Anglican Catechism states this threefold understanding concisely: "First, I learn to believe in God the Father who hath made me, and all the world. Secondly, in God the Son who redeemeth me, and all mankind. Thirdly, in God the Holy Ghost, who sanctifieth me, and all the elect people of God" (Catech., *BCP*).

This triune affirmation seeks to summarize the essential Christian teaching of God. For almost two millennia the Christian community has been using this language as a means of bringing together in summary form its most irreducible affirmations concerning God. Modern readers are urged not to reject prematurely trinitarian thinking on the assumption that it amounts to flat and implausible tritheism, a view consistently rejected by the classical Christian writers (Gregory of Nyssa, *On "Not Three Gods," NPNF* 2 V, pp. 331–36).

The triune understanding of God gives us a way of looking at the meaning of the whole of history, which, as the arena of God's revelation, is the subject of theology. Trinity rehearses and embraces the entire story of salvation, attesting to the church's attempt to view history synoptically, to try to grasp a unified picture of God in creation, redemption, and consummation. Classical Christian exegetes have viewed the history of salvation as an inclusive threefold movement from beginning to end: It begins with an originally good creation, which includes a primordially unfallen condition of human existence that plunged into radical alienation of human freedom, into sin, guilt, and death. The pivot of history is the incarnation, ministry, death, and resurrection of Jesus Christ, God's own personal engagement in the human condition, where the Son of God speaks the Father's Word of forgiving love to human history. God's own Spirit is sent in order to enable faith, hope, and love in those who are willing to hear and to engender response to the divine Word, enabling faith to grow toward reflecting the divine goodness within human limits (Gregory of Nyssa, *On the Holy Trin., NPNF* 2 V, pp. 326–30).

Universal history is therefore a history of the activity of the triune God: Given all by the Father of all, the fall of humanity from its original uprightness is redeemed through God's justifying activity in the Son, and our faithful response is elicited through the power of the Spirit. To say that creation as given is good, that the fall of freedom is uprighted by justification and consummated by sanctification, is therefore another way of saying that God meets us in history as Father, Son, and Spirit (Hilary, *On Trin.* VII, *NPNF* 2 IX, pp. 118–36). Sanctification is the process by which our own spirits are awakened and renewed by God's Spirit and faith is enabled to be embodied in a life of responsible love, so that God's justifying activity then becomes manifested in our personal and social existence. In this way God's saving activity leads to a recovery of what was lost. This triune history of salvation brings together all the basic issues of Christian theology: creation, redemption, and consummation in and beyond history.

This view of history is intimately interwoven with the triune understanding of God: God the Father is understood as the giver and ground of all things; God the Son is God Himself entering into this sphere to declare the primordial love of God and make known God's Word to us; God the Spirit empowers the fulfillment of the divine purpose in redemption (Gregory of Nyssa, *On the Baptism of Christ*, *NPNF* 2 V, pp. 518–24). We now exist in an ongoing historical process in which, through the gifts of the Spirit, this love is appropriated through church, sacraments, and ministry in the hope of sanctification, through which God perfects what God has created and redeemed. The Holy Spirit has been eternally present throughout the whole historical process, but is now powerfully present in the mission of assisting in enabling faith in the Son and guiding the church "into all truth" (John 16:13; Augustine, *Hom. on John*, tractates XCVI–C, *NPNF* 1 VII, pp. 371–87; cf. John Chrysostom, *Hom. on John* LXXIX, *NPNF* 1 XIV, pp. 291–95).

Experiential Roots of Trinitarian Reasoning

Deciding About Jesus

This summary way of thinking began very early, even while Scripture was being written, when people began to try to make up their minds about what was happening in their encounter with Jesus of Nazareth. For they recognized that in Jesus they had come to know God the Father through his Son. Jesus himself often spoke of God as Father (*patēr*, Mark 11:10, 25 f.; 13:32; 14:36; Matt. 6:1–32; 10:20–37; 18:10–35; 26:39–42) or familiarly as *Abba* ("papa," Mark 14:36). The familiar *Abba* echoes through Pauline letters (Rom. 8:14; Gal. 4:6). At Pentecost, the disciples received the promise of the Father (Acts 1:4; 2:32).

It was not merely that Jesus was teaching about God, the Father. Rather, the church believed that God the Father was intimately and personally present in Jesus' ministry, and that Jesus himself was personally present in the life of the community as resurrected Lord. They felt the real presence of the Father with them. If, as they concluded, Jesus' presence was truly nothing less than God's own living, personal presence, God's own Word, then that seemed to present a dilemma in their affirmation that there can be only one God.

The Johannine epistle reasoned in a way that would influence all triune teaching: "We know also that the Son of God has come and has given us understanding, so that we may know him who is true. And we are in him who is true—even in his Son Jesus Christ. He is the true God and eternal life" (1 John 5:20, NIV). It is not merely that in Jesus God was made known, but that "God was in Christ reconciling the world to himself" (2 Cor. 5:19). "God's only Son, he who is nearest to the Father's heart, has made him known" (John 1:18; cf. Irenaeus, *Ag. Her.* IV.22.7, *ANF* I, pp. 489, 490). Christ not only made God known, but was God; not only revealed the truth, but was the truth; and the worshiping community understood its life to be hid "in Christ." It was this Word of God who was "with God in the beginning" and who "was God," who "came from the Father," who had "become flesh and lived for a while among us" (John 1:1–14, NIV; cf. Irenaeus, *Ag. Her.* III.11, *ANF* I, pp. 426–29). In these passages, we are listening in on the primitive Christian community seeking to articulate accurately its actual experience as it compellingly felt the real presence of God in Jesus.

This implied no diminution of the oneness of God. The earliest Christians were steeped in monotheistic faith, but they had to make sense out of this inescapable revelatory event—this living, resurrected presence of the Lord in their midst. They understood Jesus to be not a demi-God, not part God, not proximately similar to God, but in the fullest sense "true God" (John 17:3; 1 John 5:20; Rev. 3:7; cf. Irenaeus, *Ag. Her.* III.9, *ANF* III, pp. 422 f.). This is the reason we have triune thinking. If the disciples had not had that fundamental experience, we would not be talking about the Trinity today.

The disciples not only experienced the presence of Father and Son but further experienced a powerful impetus of some radically motivating divine Spirit that brought the Son to them and enlivened their awareness of the Father. They understood that this Spirit was working within their community to awaken and teach them the significance of the Christ event: counseling them, helping them to understand, praying with them, accompanying them. This gave them incredible courage. The Holy Spirit was that living and present reality in the life of the community, distinguishable from, but not separable from, the same one God who was self-disclosed and present in Jesus. Gradually, as the Christian community moved from Jerusalem into Hellenistic and Roman environments, and especially during the period of martyrdom, they struggled to articulate this experience in varied language and symbol structures (Irenaeus, *Ag. Her.* III.17, *ANF* I, pp. 444 f.; Tertullian, *Ag. Praxeas* I–XV, *ANF* III, pp. 597–610; cf. Tatian, *To the Greeks* XV, *ANF* II, pp. 71 ff.).

Christians today continue to be encountered by the same loving Father, the living Lord, and empowering Spirit. Christians today have learned to address God as Father of our Lord Jesus Christ through the guidance of the Spirit. Christians today live out of a remembered history of the saving deeds of God as Father, Son, and Spirit. We have at hand a history of experience, the salvation history of Israel—so varied, yet nonetheless having a center in Christ, engendered by the love of the Father, and an anticipated completion in the Spirit.

This is not to suggest three chronologically separable modes in God (as in modalism), as if God meets us in disjunctive, successive modes in a progressive sequence, one outdating another. That was firmly rejected precisely because it tended to lose sight of God's eternal unity. The purpose of triune teaching has been to affirm the equality and unity, and yet the distinguishability, of Father, Son, and Spirit.

Analogies

In many areas of experience we note an implicit three-in-oneness. Objects have three dimensions—length, breadth, and height—that are distinguishable, but inseparable, unified in a single object, yet three-dimensional. Our experience of the physical world always has three dimensions—space, time, and matter—unified in the being of any physical object, yet distinguishable. The seeming paradox of three in one is familiar to the human experience of physical reality (Augustine, *Trin.* VIII.10, *NPNF* 1 III, p. 124; IX, pp. 125 ff.; cf. Tho. Aq., *ST* I Q12, 13, I, pp. 48–71).

In similar ways, Augustine saw trinitarian vestiges abundantly in creation. For God, he thought, had left triune footprints everywhere in the created order. For instance, there are in perception (a) external objects encountering (b) the mind that is capable of (c) perceiving external objects. Thus in a common human function (perception), there is a threefold unity—the unified act of perception itself, which requires the mind, objects, and perceiving (Augustine, *On Trin.* IX.1–12, *LCC* VIII, pp. 57–65).

Even more meaningfully, the unity of selfhood is made up of memory, understanding, and willing, showing how a single subject-self may remain one while being three (Augustine, *On Trin.* X.17–19, *LCC* VIII, pp. 87–90). "Whatever else can be predicated of each singly in itself, is predicated of them all together in the singular and not in the plural. . . . I remember that I possess memory and understanding and will: I understand that I understand and will and remember: I will my own willing and remembering and understanding. And I remember at

the same time the whole of my memory and understanding and will"
(p. 88).

Similarly, love requires a lover, one who is loved, and the love that
unites them, in a kind of three-in-oneness, for in speaking of these
three, we are speaking only of one thing, love (Augustine, *On Trin.*
VIII.4–10, IX.9–12, *NPNF* 1 III, pp. 118–24, 131–33). In these examples are the conceptual requisites of tri-unity: all have unity, equality,
and distinguishability (Tho. Aq., *ST* I Q42, I, pp. 214 ff.).

Tri-unity

The English word *trinity* from the Latin *trinitas (tres,* three, *unus,*
one) signifies that God is three-in-one, or triune, that is, one God—
Father, Son, and Holy Spirit. That God is triune is a teaching peculiar
to Christianity. It is hardly found at all in philosophical theisms, and
only rarely in the history of non-Christian religious consciousness. Its
key assumptions are indirectly suggested, but not expressly taught,
in the Old Testament, yet it is already to be found in the oral tradition
antecedent to many New Testament writings (Pauline, Johannine, Mat-
thean, Lukan).

Some will resist the notion of trinity because it is thought to be
not found expressly in Scripture. We will show that the Scriptures not
only contain the fundamental idea to which trinity refers, but require
some teaching of one God—Father, Son, and Spirit. Many technical
terms familiar to Christian teaching, like *eschatology, anthropology, pneu-
matology, hamartiology,* and *cosmology,* are not found expressly in Scripture but derive explicitly from scriptural teaching. So it is with trinity.
Even critics of trinitarian thought acknowledge that the idea of a triune
God is necessary to explain some particular texts of Scripture (Joseph
Priestly, *History of the Corruptions of Christianity*). We will show that
these texts embrace a wide range of scriptural sources and are found
throughout, and especially in crucial summative points of biblical
teaching (Augustine, *On Trin.* I.6 ff., *NPNF* 1 III, pp. 20 ff.; Calvin,
Inst. 2.14, 15; Heppe, *RD,* pp. 105–33; Watson, *TI* I, pp. 447 ff.).

Tri-unity is a shorthand term used to express in a single word what
Scripture teaches in many discrete passages, but which took the proclaiming church some time to think through and organize into a clear
and distinct teaching. From the time of the apostolic fathers, triunity
has been considered definitive of the Christian teaching of God, accepted alike by Protestants, Catholics, and Eastern church communions (Council of Nicaea, *NPNF* 2 XIV, pp. 1 ff.; cf. Gregory Nazianzen,
or. XXXVIII.8, *NPNF* 2 VII, p. 347, *CC,* passim). It is not merely a
speculative or theoretical or incidental or optional teaching, but is

regarded by consensus as essential to the Christian understanding of God (Gregory Thaumaturgus, *COC* II, p. 24; Athanasius, Athanasian Creed, *COC* II, pp. 66–71; Augsburg Conf. I, *COC* II, pp. 3 ff.; Thirty-nine Articles, *COC* III, pp. 486 ff.).

If Arianism had been correct, baptism would have been adminis-tered in the name of one God and two creatures (Athanasius, *Four Discourses Ag. Arians* II.41 ff., *NPNF* 2 IV, pp. 370 ff.; Gregory Nazian-zen, *On the Great Athanasius* 13, *NPNF* 2 VII, pp. 272, 273). Scripture insists, however, that the Son and Holy Spirit are not creatures, but God himself. Scripture constrains Christian teaching to speak of Jesus as God's own Son, not a creature, and not less than God; and the Holy Spirit as God's own Spirit, not less than God, and not a creature. To say less would be to ignore insistent masses of scriptural teaching (Hilary, *Trin.* I.6 ff., *NPNF* 2 IX, p. 41; Calvin, *Inst.* 2.14.3–8).

At first glance the triune teaching may seem to assert a contradic-tion: that God is three, and that God is one. One early incomplete teaching (modalism) attempted to "resolve" this contradiction by stat-ing that God has three distinct modes that are not simultaneous: only one of these modes is manifested at any given time. The early church vigorously opposed this premature solution on the grounds that it did not make sufficiently clear that God always *is* the Son and always *is* the Holy Spirit, and that God does not cease being the Father when God is the Son (Dionysius, *Ag. the Sabellians,* ANF VII, pp. 365, 366).

The classical ecumenical resolution of the dilemma was agreed upon at the First Ecumenical Council at Nicaea in A.D. 325, and was widely affirmed (after fifty years of turmoil) as valid teaching wherever Christians worship. The post-Nicene fathers understood the triune God as one *ousia* (essence or substance) and three *hypostases* (persons; Gregory Nazianzen, or. XXXIX, *On the Holy Lights* XI, *NPNF* 2 VII, p. 355; cf. Athanasius, *To the Bishops of Africa* 4, *NPNF* 2 IV, pp. 490, 491; *COC* II, pp. 60 ff.). But when particular nuances and meanings at-tached to these terms no longer had vital power, it became a continu-ing problem of Christian teaching to clarify in the languages of various cultures and historical periods in what sense God is Father, Son, and Spirit while still remaining one God. In subsequent centuries, when the triune teaching sought expression in post-Hellenistic settings, it nonetheless typically relied gratefully upon the achievement of the Nicene and post-Nicene fathers (Second Helvetic Conf. III, *COC*, pp. 240 ff.; cf. Batak Conf. II, III, *CC*, pp. 556 ff.).

The triune teaching includes two crucial aspects: unity and distinc-tion. God is one in three distinct persons. To affirm these two aspects does not require a sacrifice of intellect to blatant contradiction, for they refer to the Godhead in different ways, one to the nature of God (as one) and the other to the persons (as three; cf. Belgic Confession, *COC* III, pp. 390 ff.).

To affirm that God *is* Son and *is* Spirit implies that Son and Spirit are eternal. Even though the Son who is with the Father from the beginning has a particular mission within world history, the Son (Jesus) is nothing less than eternal God (Hilary, *Trin.* IX.39, *NPNF* 2 IX, p. 168). To recollect with John's Gospel the obedience of the Son to the Father (John 15:10) does not imply that the Son is inferior to the Father. The Son did not become less than the Father by becoming eternally obedient to the Father's will (Phil. 2:5–11). Enabling the Son's ministry to the world, the Spirit, who was with the Father from the beginning, became willingly responsive to carry out the ministry of the Son, but again that does not imply that the Spirit is inferior to the Son (Tho. Aq., *STae* I Q31, VI, pp. 83 ff.). The Spirit serves the mission of the Son on behalf of the Father: "When he comes who is the Spirit of truth, he will guide you into all the truth; for he will not speak on his own authority, but will tell you only what he hears; and he will make known to you the things that are coming. He will glorify me" (John 16:13, 14).

Whether Scripture Teaches Triunity

Old Testament Preparation for the Triune Teaching

A primordial, implicit triune teaching appears in generalized form in the Old Testament, as if a mystery were being prepared for subsequent fuller disclosure: God the creator addresses humanity by his Word, in which God himself is actively present, and through the Spirit that enlivens hearts to understand his word. The triune teaching is intimated in the Old Testament in the same degree as are many other truths of Christian teaching: not with unambiguous specificity or refinement, but with preliminary intuition and prophetic imagination (Athanasius, *Ag. Arians* IV.24 ff., *NPNF* 2 IV, pp. 442 ff.; Aphraates, *Demonstrations, NPNF* 2 XIII, p. 352).

Anyone familiar with modern Old Testament exegesis may balk at this idea. The intention of classical exegetes deserves to be taken seriously, and doing so does not require giving up the achievements of modern OT scholarship. We have been cautioned repeatedly not to read the NT thoughtlessly into the OT. In many ways the OT stands on its own self-authenticating ground as a witness to revelation. We do well to be cautious about inordinately allowing NT images to dominate our reading of the OT, but the debate continues as to what is inordinate. At least we cannot deny that the classical Christian exegetes virtually without exception began with a radical assumption: that the NT has made more clear the meaning of the OT. They could not read about the promise of God to Abraham, Moses, and Isaiah without noticing that these promises had been fulfilled in Jesus Christ. Hence I ask for forbearance from those in whom modern OT exegesis has been deeply ingrained, that they bear with me patiently and at least give a fair hearing to classic exegetes. For on this question of the triune teaching, their voice is strongly in favor of the hypothesis that it is anticipated in the OT. If the following section seems a bit detailed, it is because modern theology has not heard these arguments for a long time. What follows is an attempt to set forth major consensual views of influential classical exegetes like Cyril of Alexandria, Hilary of Poitiers, Athanasius, Augustine, and others on how the God revealed to Israel is none other than the same triune God revealed in Jesus Christ.

Our thesis: The triune teaching has been subjected necessarily to a steady, unfolding development through successive stages: preindications in the Old Testament; the central disclosure of God as Father, Son, and Spirit in the New Testament; and the full development of church teaching in the Nicene definition and its subsequent interpretations.

Principal Old Testament References

Even in the first two verses of the Bible, God and the Spirit of God appear to be distinguished; for it is said that "God created," and "the Spirit of God was moving over the face of the waters" (Gen. 1:1, 2, RSV; cf. Hilary, *Trin.* II.13–16, *NPNF* 2 IX, pp. 56, 57). God and God's Spirit appear distinguishable, yet God is one (cf. Ambrose, *Of the Holy Spirit* II.1, *NPNF* 2 X, p. 115).

The Spirit of God is often referred to throughout the Old Testament (Exod. 31:3; 35:31; Num. 11:17–29; 1 Sam. 16:13–23; Ps. 51:10, 11; Isa. 11:2; cf. Gregory Nazianzen, *On Pentecost* IX, *NPNF* 2 VII, p. 382). The Spirit of God is giver of life: "For the spirit of God made me, and the breath of the Almighty gave me life" (Job 33:4; cf. Ps. 33:6). The same Spirit inspired Moses and the prophets: "Then the Lord came down in the cloud and spoke with him, and he took of the Spirit that was on him and put the Spirit on the seventy elders. When the Spirit rested on them, they prophesied" (Num. 11:24, 25, NIV). The Spirit is omnipresent: "Where can I go from your Spirit? Where can I flee from your presence?" (Ps. 139:7, NIV). Yet the Spirit often appears to be distinguished in prophetic Scripture from Yahweh and from the messianic Servant (Isa. 48:16; 61:1; 63:9, 10).

Isaiah 48:16 is a principal prophetic text from which classical exegetes have argued an implicit triune intimation. The speaker is the Lord's Servant, the promised Messiah: "'Come near to me and listen to this: From the first announcement I have not spoken in secret; from the time it happens I am there.' And now the sovereign Lord has sent *me*, with his *Spirit*" (Isa. 48:16, NIV, italics added). The first person *me* has been widely thought by classical exegetes to be anticipatory of the Son (viewed by analogy of faith from the New Testament), who speaks of the Lord God by whom he is sent and the Spirit with whom he is sent, thus keeping all the primary elements of triunity in place: unity, distinction, and complementary mission (Origen, *Ag. Celsus* I.46, *ANF* IV, p. 416; Augustine, *On Trin.* II.5, *NPNF* 1 III, pp. 40 ff.; Tho. Aq., *ST* I Q31, I, pp. 164 ff.).

Another crucial Old Testament text that has repeatedly suggested to classical exegetes three persons in one deity is from the prophet Haggai, who spoke in this unusual way of the restoration of the temple: "These words came from the Lord through the prophet Haggai: . . . Begin the work, for *I* am with you, says the Lord of hosts, and my *spirit* is present among you. Have no fear. For these are the words of the Lord of Hosts" (Hag. 2:1–5, italics added; cf. exegesis by Cyril of Jerusalem, *Catech. Lect.* XVI.25–28, *NPNF* 2 VII, pp. 121, 122). The passage first distinguishes between God as Lord of hosts and God as Spirit and then points to the promise of the coming redeemer: "This is what the Lord Almighty says: . . . 'I will shake all nations, and the *desired of all nations* will come, and I will fill this house with glory' says the Lord Almighty" (Hag. 2:6–7, NIV, italics added to indicate messianic reference). In such passages the patristic exegetes saw spiritually adumbrated the Father, Son, and Holy Spirit of the New Testament, three distinct voices in unity and distinguishability (cf. Tertullian, *An Answer to the Jews* XIV, *ANF* III, p. 173).

In the appearance of Yahweh to Abraham (Gen. 18:1–19) and to Lot (Gen. 19:1 ff.) the angel is both addressed as "Lord" and sent by Yahweh. In the narrative of Hagar, God both sends and is sent; is both "the Lord" and sent "of the Lord" (Gen. 16:7–16; Hilary, *Trin.* IV.23, *NPNF* 2 IX, pp. 78 ff.; cf. Augustine, *On Trin.* II.18.34, *NPNF* 1 III, p. 53; III.9.25, *NPNF* 1 III, p. 66). The One who brings the people out of Egypt and accomplishes mighty acts in history is one God, but spoken of as *God* and the *angel of God* (a messianic reference as classically interpreted—Exod. 3:2–4; 14:19; 23:20; 32:34) and as the *Spirit of God* (Isa. 63:7–14). The One who says "I am who I am" also says "I am He" (Exod. 3:14; Deut. 32:39), suggesting to the classical exegetes an interpersonal dialogue within the Godhead. In the psalmist's exclamation, "By the *Word* of the *Lord* were the heavens made, their starry host by the *breath* of this mouth" (Ps. 33:6, NIV, italics added), the classical exegetes heard the quiet echo of Lord, Word, and Spirit (breath; Irenaeus, *Ag. Her.* I.22, III.8, *ANF* I, pp. 347, 421; Tertullian, *Ag. Praxeas* VII, XIX, *ANF* III, pp. 602, 614).

The occurrence in prophetic literature of a threefold repetition of the divine name has been viewed by classical exegetes as an intimation of triunity. Isaiah saw the Lord "high and exalted" in the year of King Uzziah's death. The attendant seraphim were "calling ceaselessly to one another, 'Holy, holy, holy is the Lord of Hosts: the whole earth is full of his glory'" (Isa. 6:2, 3; Origen, *De Princip.* I.3, *ANF* IV, p. 252; Ambrose, *Of the Holy Spirit* III.16, 109–11, *NPNF* 2 X, pp. 150–51). This threefold repetition of the divine name, again viewed as an anticipatory reference to the Trinity, is rehearsed once more in Revelation: "Holy, holy, holy is God the sovereign Lord of all, who *was*, and *is*, and *is to come!*" (Rev. 4:8, italics added; Athanasius, *On Luke 10:22*, sec. 6, *NPNF* 2 IV, p. 90).

In the early Hebraic tradition, the name of God is often repeated three times, as in Numbers 6:23–26 (the Aaronic blessing, where the Levitical priests were commanded to pronounce the name of God over Israel and bless them). Classical exegetes found no other number so frequently associated with the divine name. When the Lord appeared to Abraham by the oaks of Mamre, he appeared in the guise of "three men standing in front of him" (Gen. 18:2), yet it is clearly the one Lord who is revealed. In announcing the coming birth of a child to the aged Sarah, they spoke as one. Abraham "saw three and worshipped One," commented Ambrose (*Of the Holy Spirit* II.Intro.4, *NPNF* 2 X, p. 115).

There are intimations in the Old Testament of dialogue between God and God's Son, as in Psalms 2:7, where the Son of God is mentioned in reference to the Davidic kingdom, which classical exegetes have viewed as a type of the coming messianic kingdom: "Why are the nations in turmoil?" "The Lord who sits enthroned in heaven laughs them to scorn." "Of me he says, 'I have enthroned my king on Zion my holy mountain.' I will repeat the Lord's decree: 'You are my *son*,' he said; 'this day I become your *father*. Ask of me what you will'"

(Ps. 2:1–8, italics added; cf. Tertullian, *Ag. Praxeas* VII, XI, *ANF* III, pp. 601, 605; Athanasius, *Four Discourses Ag. Arians* II.23, 24, *NPNF* 2 IV, pp. 360–61; Ambrose, *Of the Chr. Faith* V.10.122, *NPNF* 2 X, p. 300).

Almost all classical Christian exegetes have argued that broadly scattered throughout the Old Testament are prophetic anticipations of triune teaching, as if the teaching was being prepared to be revealed at the proper time, yet was still awaiting that "fullness of time" (Gal. 4:4; Eph. 1:10; cf. 1 Pet. 1:5 ff.). It may seem odd that such a pivotal and summative teaching is not more explicitly presented by the Old Testament writers. According to some patristic writers, it was necessary that it be held in reserve while the oneness of God was being firmly implanted in historical consciousness, and because the revelation of the Son had to await the fulfillment of time—the conditions that prevailed at the coming of the Christ (Irenaeus, *Ag. Her.* IV.32, *ANF* I, pp. 511 ff.).

No single text of the Old Testament has been viewed as standing alone, yet many references to Fatherhood, Sonship, Word, Wisdom, and Spirit have been viewed in correlation with each other and with the New Testament texts as triune adumbrations. This exegesis has proceeded under the principle of the analogy of faith, by which one passage of Scripture is seen and understood in relation to what is known of other passages (Calvin, *Inst.* 1.6–9, 1.13.3; Baxter, *PW* XII, pp. 141–47, XV, pp. 59–63). In this way the truth of Scripture is revealed not as separable parts, but as a whole, to be grasped integrally and intuitively by the discerning reader as a single, reliable revelation of truth.

If indeed the triune teaching is never explicitly set forth in the Old Testament, then at least it must be admitted that certain passages require awkward explanations without it and are amenable to clarification with the hypothesis of triunity, as seen from the viewpoint of revelation in Christ (Novatian, *Trin.* XVII–XXII, *ANF* V, pp. 626–34). It is consistent with historical revelation that some aspects of the divine self-disclosure remain unclear until later occurrences; otherwise it might be un-Hebraically supposed that the history itself is incidental or unnecessary.

Augustine argued that humanity was made in the image of the triune God so as to reflect, in memory, understanding, and will, the imprint of the triune interpersonal dialogue. He found in numerous Old Testament passages that assume a divine plurality the veiled speech of the triune God (*CG* XVI.6, *NPNF* 1 II, p. 313; *Conf.* XIII.5).

Similarly, many classical Christian teachers argued that the one Yah-weh who is so frequently designated by plural forms of speech (*'Elō-hīm*) is thereby implicitly attested as triune (Athanasius, *Four Discourses Ag. Arians* II.31, *NPNF* 2 IV, pp. 364, 365; Ambrose, *Of the Holy Spirit* II.Intro.2, *NPNF* 2 X, p. 115). Though this suggestion might at first seem to be wholly spurious and farfetched, its durability for over a millennium of Christian teaching leads us not to dismiss it thought-lessly. It is sometimes argued that the plural forms of speech for God are merely linguistic intensives, emphasizing the effulgence of the divine majesty, the glory of the Lord of hosts. Yet it should not miss our notice that when "God said, 'Let us make man in our image and likeness'" (Gen. 1:26), a startling implication emerges: The one God is speaking in the first person in plural form. The same dilemma is embedded in Genesis 1:1: "In the beginning of creation, when God made heaven and earth," where the *'Elōhīm* (God) spoken of is a plural noun, oddly enough linked with a singular verb.

The plural is at times preferred even when the intent is to assert the unity of God, as in the Shema': "Hear, O Israel, the Lord is our God"—literally, "our Gods," *'Elōhēnū*—"one Lord" (Deut. 6:4). "Re-member your Creator in the days of your youth" (Eccles. 12.1) is literally "Remember your Creators" (*Eth–Bōr'ekā*). However one may seek to explain this unusual use of language, it cannot establish an Old Testament triune teaching, but can point indirectly to some mys-terious plurality in the intrasubjectivity of God. Even if this linguistic point does not carry the strength of an adequate argument, it has been viewed as a corroboratory point for the pious reading of Scripture that has become subsequently informed by fuller triune teaching (Athanasius, *Four Discourses Ag. Arians* II.23 ff., *NPNF* 2 IV, pp. 360 ff.; Hilary, *Trin.* VII.10, *NPNF* 2 IX, pp. 121 ff., XII.37 ff., pp. 229 ff.; Watson, *TI* I, pp. 467 ff.).

Although it is not likely that the pentateuchal writers had in mind the Christian triune teaching, at least one New Testament writer ar-gued that Old Testament inspiration was implicitly a trinitarian inspiration:

This salvation was the theme which the prophets pondered and explored, those who prophesied about the grace of *God* awaiting you. They tried to find out what was the time and what the circumstances, to which the spirit of *Christ* in them pointed, foretelling the sufferings in store for Christ and the splendours to follow; and it was disclosed to them that the matter they treated of was not for their time but for yours. And now it has been openly announced to you through preachers who brought you the Gospel in the power of the

Holy Spirit sent from heaven. These are things that angels long to see into. (1 Pet. 1:10–12, italics added)

Christ is viewed as being already alive in the prophets, and the Holy Spirit, who brings to the hearts of hearers the Word "sent from heaven," is nothing less than God. The Holy One is being revealed in distinguishable voices or persons, as Father, Son, and Spirit (Irenaeus, *Ag. Her.* IV.IX–XIII, *ANF* I, pp. 472–78). This passage has triune nuances that it projects reflectively back upon the prophets of the Old Testament, as if the Christ the apostles had come to know was the very spirit of Christ in the prophets that made them already aware of the coming revelation of God at the end (Irenaeus, *Ag. Her.* IV.32, *ANF* I, p. 511; cf. Cyril of Jerusalem, *Catech. Lect.* X.6–9, *NPNF* 2 VII, pp. 58, 59).

Some classical Christian exegetes tended to exaggerate the triune teaching in the Old Testament, not only neglecting the historical development of God's revelation, but also exposing the later triune teaching to premature dismissal by antitrinitarian critics who easily were able to counter their bloated trinitarian exegesis. The Old Testament does not provide Christian teaching with a full disclosure of the triune teaching, but it does contain important preindications of it. This is what we might reasonably expect if we affirm consistently that God's will is revealed through his Word speaking through history, so that subsequent historical events are illumined by and illuminate God's self-presentation in prior events. Scripture does not treat the triune teaching as an abstract proposition of speculation, but rather reveals the unity of the diversely active God in creation, providence, redemption, and consummation.

The New Testament Unfolding of the Triune Teaching

In order to counter the premature generalization that the triune teaching is not found in the New Testament, we will follow the exegesis of Tertullian, Novatian, Cyril of Jerusalem, the Cappadocians, and Hilary by examining those texts that require and assume that God is Father, Son, and Spirit. This exploration will make clear that Trinity is not merely a belated Hellenistic invention of the post-Nicene fathers; rather, it is from the New Testament that ancient ecumenical teaching derived its primary conclusions that the Father is God, that the Son is God, that the Spirit is God, and that God is One.

Whether the Father Is God

Jesus insistently taught his disciples to call God by the name "Father." This is clear in the Fourth Gospel's recollection of Jesus' response to Mary: "I am now ascending to my Father and your Father, my God and your God" (John 20:17). It is this Father who sends "his only Son, that everyone who has faith in him may not die but have eternal life" (John 3:16). The affirmation of God as Father was precisely what caused the Jews to become "still more determined to kill" Jesus, "because he was not only breaking the Sabbath, but *by calling God his own Father, he claimed equality with God*" (John 5:18, italics added; cf. Novatian, *Trin.* XXI–XXVII, *ANF* V, pp. 632–36).

The clearest way to establish that the Father is God, the Son is God, and the Spirit is God is by a classical fourfold exegetical procedure that shows how in Scripture *(a)* each Person (Father, Son, Spirit) is distinguishably addressed by divine *names; (b)* each is assumed to have divine *attributes; (c)* each engages in *actions* that only God can accomplish; and *(d)* each is thought worthy of divine *worship* (Cyril of Jerusalem, *Catech. Lect.* VII ff., *NPNF* 2 VII, pp. 44 ff.; cf. Tho. Aq., *ST* I Q33, I, pp. 173 ff.; Quenstedt, *TDP* I, p. 329; Watson, *TI* I, pp. 475 ff.; Bavinck, *DG*, IV).

The first conclusion drawn by classical exegetes was that God is Father. The primary textual evidence for this conclusion is as follows:

Jesus characteristically called God "Father" (*patēr, abba,* Matt. 5:45; 6:6–15; Mark 14:36). Paul began his letter to the Galatians by a salutation: "Grace and peace to you from God the Father and our Lord Jesus Christ" (Gal. 1:3). The Fourth Gospel repeatedly calls God by the *name* "Father": "The Father loves the Son" (John 5:20); "the Father raises the dead and gives them life" (5:21); the Son "does only what he sees the Father doing" (5:19). From these texts the classical exegetes had no hesitation in concluding that the Father is God (Cyril of Jerusalem, *Catech. Lect.* XI, *NPNF* 2 VII, pp. 66–70; Hilary, *Trin.* IX.61, *NPNF* 2 IX, p. 176).

To the Father *attributes* are ascribed that could only belong to God. Among them are holiness, "Holy Father" (John 17:11); sovereignty, "Father, Lord of heaven and earth" (Matt. 11:23); eternity, "Eternal God" (Gen. 21:33; Jer. 10:10); all-powerfulness, "'Abba, Father,' he said, 'all things are possible to thee'" (Mark 14:34). One who is holy, almighty, and eternal must be nothing less than God (Cyril of Jerusalem, *Catech. Lect.* VII.1 ff., *NPNF* 2 VII, pp. 44 ff.; Hilary, *Trin.* XI.16, *NPNF* 2 V, pp. 207, 208; Tho. Aq., *ST* I Q33, I, pp. 173 ff.).

To the Father are ascribed *works* done by God alone: "For us there is one God, the Father, from whom all being comes, towards whom we move" (1 Cor. 8:6). "Praise be to the God and Father of our Lord Jesus Christ, who in his great mercy gave us new birth into a living hope by the resurrection" (1 Pet. 1:3). The Father sends the Son (John 5:37). One who does the works of God must be none other than God (Athanasius, *Four Discourses Ag. Arians* III.25, *NPNF* 2 IV, pp. 339–407; cf. Hollaz, *ETA*, pp. 301, 305; Watson, *TI* I, pp. 447 ff.).

All these conditions make it appropriate that God be *worshiped* as Father: "The time approaches, indeed it is already here, when those who are real worshippers will worship the Father in spirit and in truth. Such are the worshippers whom the Father wants" (John 4:23). "If you ask the Father for anything in my name, he will give it you" (John 16:23). One to whom worship is due must be worthy of the name God (Novatian, *Trin.* VII, *ANF* V, pp. 616 f.; Hilary, *Trin.* VI.30, *NPNF* 2 IX, pp. 108, 109).

Whether the Son Is God

Classical exegetes have sought by the same procedure to establish that the Son is God by pointing to Scriptures of four classes: in which the Son is called by divine names, is ascribed divine attributes, does divine works, and therefore is worthy of divine worship. Although few modern sources have followed this structure of interpretation, it remains a most economical and plausible way of establishing our point.

The lordship and divinity of the Son are established and set forth in the New Testament constantly by the *titles* given him. Christ is the *Word of God*, who was from the beginning with God, and *was God* (John 1:1). Jesus Christ, the Son, is repeatedly and unhesitatingly called *God* (Matt. 1:23; John 20:28; Rom. 9:5; Titus 1:3; 2:13; Heb. 1:8; cf. anon., *Epis. to Diognetus* chap. 7, *ECW*, pp. 177 ff.). Christ is frequently called *Lord* (Matt. 12:8; Mark 2:28; Luke 6:46; John 13:13, 14; Acts 10:36; Rom. 14:9; 1 Cor. 2:8; Gal. 1:3; 2 Thess. 2:16) or with intensives such as *Lord from heaven* (1 Cor. 15:47), *Lord of heaven and earth* (Matt. 11:25), *Lord of all* (Acts 10:36), or *Lord of lords and King of kings* (Rev. 17:14; 19:16).

Thomas, upon touching the resurrected Lord, exclaimed: "My *Lord* and my *God!*" (John 20:28; italics added). "We know that the *Son of God* has come," wrote John, and "This is the *true God*" (1 John 5:21, italics added). Of the Son it was said in the Letter to the Hebrews: "Thy throne, O God, is for ever and ever" (Heb. 1:8), and "therefore

O God, thy God has set thee above thy fellows, by anointing with the oil of exultation" (Heb. 1:9). It would be difficult to find a monotheistic interpretation of this otherwise strong, idiosyncratic phrase ("O God, thy God") if we did not have access to a trinitarian premise. This Son is explicitly described as equal to God the Father (John 15:17 ff.; cf. Gregory Nazianzen, *Orat.* XXXVIII.8, *NPNF* 2 VII, p. 347; Ambrose, *Of the Chr. Faith* III.3, *NPNF* 2 X, pp. 244–46).

Christ is remembered not merely as Son but as *"only Son"* of the Father (John 1:14), "God's only Son" who is "nearest to the Father's heart" (John 1:18). The frequency and intensity of these ascriptions of lordship and unique divine sonship to Christ make this one of the most distinctive and unavoidable themes of the New Testament (Gregory Nazianzen, *Fourth Theol. Or., On the Son* XX, *NPNF* 2 X, pp. 244–46). Those who try to interpret the New Testament without the triune premise have great difficulty making sense of many New Testament texts.

These names point to the mysterious depth and intimacy of the Father-Son relationship. In the synoptic Gospels, Jesus is called "my Son, my Beloved" at his baptism (Matt. 3:17; Mark 1:11; cf. Matt. 17:5; Luke 3:22). The Johannine language is more likely to speak of Jesus as the "only begotten Son" or "only Son" of the Father (John 1:14, 18; 3:16, 18; 1 John 4:9). Paul speaks also of Jesus as God's "own Son" (Rom. 8:32). His name is "above every name" (Phil. 2:9 ff., KJV, cf. Athanasius, *Defence of the Nicene Definition* III, *NPNF* 2 IV, pp. 153 ff.; Tho. Aq., *SCG* IV.11, IV, pp. 79 ff.; Watson, *TI* I, pp. 478 ff.).

Christ is celebrated in Scripture as having *attributes* that could be intrinsic qualities of God alone: The Son of God is eternal (Matt. 28:20; Heb. 1:8; 13:8; John 1:1, 14; 1 John 1:2)—only God can be eternal. The Son is uncreated, underived, self-existent, for the Son "has life-giving power in himself" and this "by the Father's gift" (John 5:26); the Son "exists before everything" (Col. 1:17; Calvin, *Inst.* 1.13.8). Only God can be uncreated (Athanasius, *Four Discourses Ag. Arians* I.4, *NPNF* 2 IV, pp. 312–27).

The Son is remembered as being all-knowing: "He knew men so well, all of them, that he needed no evidence from others about a man, for he himself could tell what was in a man" (John 2:25). Peter said to Christ: Lord, "you know everything" (John 21:17). The Son is remembered as foreknowing, "I saw you under the fig-tree before Philip spoke to you" (John 1:48); as infinitely capable of presence, "For where two or three have met together in my name, I am there among them" (Matt. 18:20); and as unchanging in constant love, for of the

Son it was said, "Thou art the same, and thy years shall have no end" (Heb. 1:12), "Jesus Christ is the same yesterday, today, and for ever" (Heb. 13:8). Only God is all-knowing, everywhere present, and unchanging in constant love (Novatian, *Trin.* III–X, *ANF* V, pp. 612–20; Hilary, *On Trin.* V.34–39, *NPNF* 2 IX, pp. 95–97).

Christ is called by Paul the "power of God and the wisdom of God" (1 Cor. 1:24). To the Son is ascribed power above all human and historical powers, "He put everything in subjection beneath his feet" (Eph. 1:22); in the end Christ will transfigure our bodies "by the very power which enables him to make all things subject to himself" (Phil. 3:21). "Full authority in heaven and on earth has been committed to me" (Matt. 28:18). Only God has such power. Thus the classical exegetes concluded that, if Christ has God's attributes, then Christ is God, and the Son has been properly named as the Son of God (Athanasius, *De Synodis, Councils of Ariminum and Seleucia* III.49–52, *NPNF* 2 IV, pp. 476–78; Cyril of Jerusalem, *Catech. Lect.* XI, *NPNF* 2 VII, pp. 64 ff.; Confession of Wittenberg II, *HPC*, pp. 43 f.).

If this were not enough to establish Christ's divine sonship, they argued further that Christ, the Son of God, does *works* that are peculiar to God, and thus must be God. For who but God could create (John 1:3; Col. 1:16; Heb. 1:10); preserve and govern all things in being (John 5:17; 1 Cor. 8:6; Col. 1:17; Heb. 1:3); or oversee the expected consummation? (2 Cor. 1:2; John 5:22). Who but God can forgive sins? (Mark 2:7). Who but God can save from sin? He was given "the name Jesus (Saviour), for he will save his people from their sins" (Matt. 1:21). Who but God can raise the dead? (John 6:39 f.; 11:25). Jesus did all these things (Gregory Nazianzen, *Orat.* III, *On the Son, NPNF* 2 VII, pp. 301 ff.). It was the New Testament first (and only later the ecumenical exegetes) that described Jesus as greater than Moses, greater than David, greater than Solomon, greater than John or the prophets, and greater than the superpersonal intelligences that inhabit the higher regions (Matt. 3:11; 12:41 f.; Mark 12:37; Luke 11:31, 32; John 1:17; Eph. 1:21; Heb. 1:4 f.; cf. Cyril of Jerusalem, *Catech. Lect.* XII.15, *LCF*, p. 36).

Only God is *worthy of worship*, for that is what it means to be God. If the Son is called God, if the Son is like God in every personal attribute or quality intrinsic to God, and if the Son of God does what God does, then the Son is worthy of worship as the only true God. This is why "the men in the boat fell at his feet, exclaiming, 'Truly you are the Son of God'" (Matt. 14:33). It was a response so radical that Jesus would certainly have rejected it immediately if it were not true. This is why baptism is administered also in the name of the Son, and not of the Father or Spirit alone (Matt. 29:19). For "Worthy is the Lamb, the Lamb that was slain, to receive all power and wealth, wisdom and might, honour and glory and praise!" (Rev. 3:13). The Fourth Gospel affirmed it as the Father's will "that all should pay the same honour to the Son as to the Father. To deny honour to the Son is to deny it to the Father who sent him" (John 5:23). When Stephen was stoned, he prayed "Lord Jesus, receive my spirit" (Acts 7:59). When Jesus urged his disciples to "Trust in God always; trust also in me" (John 14:1), he was not pointing to two different sources of trust (John Chrysostom, *Hom. on John* LXXII–LXXIV, *NPNF* 1 XIV, pp. 263–74; cf. Augustine, *On Trin.* I.10–31, *NPNF* 1 III, pp. 28–36).

These Scriptures jointly teach the essential unity and equality of the Son and the Father. The Son is to be equally honored with the Father (John 5:22; cf. Athanasius, *Four Discourses Ag. Arians* II.24, *ECF*, p. 282; *Defence of the Nicene Definition* XXVII, *NPNF* 2 IV, p. 168; Watson *TI* I, p. 476). The relation to the Father is consistently described in the New Testament as one of identity and unity, yet assuming distinguishability (John 1:18; 5:17–19; 14:7–11; Heb. 1:3; Col. 1:15, 19; 1 John 2:23, 24). The Son is *equal* in knowledge (Luke 10:22), equal in nature (Phil. 2:6; Col. 2:9), and equal in mighty works (John 5:17–23; Luke 7:47–49). This equality was the Son's by right, yet it was not the Son's purpose or mission to try to snatch at or protect this equality, but rather to empty himself in self-giving love (Augustine, *On Trin.* IV.20, *NPNF* 1 III, pp. 83–85; Second Helvetic Conf. 4, 5, *HPC*, pp. 20 ff.).

Yet Father and Son remain clearly *distinguishable*. One is said to send, the other to be sent. One gives, the other is given. One bestows power, the other receives it (John 12:44–49; 17:18–25; John of Damascus, *OF* III.45, *NPNF* 2 IX, pp. 45 ff.). Thus we cannot come away from these New Testament texts saying that God is at one time Father and at another time Son (as modalism asserts), but eternally both— distinguishable, yet equal (Hilary, *Trin.* IV, V, *NPNF* 2 IX, pp. 71–97). It is the New Testament itself and not just subsequent exegesis that insists upon a distinction between equal persons in the triune God. A personal relation eternally exists between Father and Son. This is why the New Testament teaching of God is so irrevocably triune.

Whether the Spirit Is God

That the Holy Spirit is a personal, encountering, interacting Thou distinguishable from the Father and Son is clearly a recurrent teaching of Scripture. The Spirit speaks in the first person as "I": "It was I who sent them" (Acts 10:20), the Spirit said to the perplexed Peter. It was the Holy Spirit who said, "I have called them" (Acts 13:2). None but a person can say "I." The Spirit acts in the self-determined ways that persons act. Who but a person could teach (John 14:26), stand as witness (Rom. 8:16), send (Acts 13:2), and give gifts? (1 Cor. 12:4–11).

The Spirit of God does what only personal agents can do: the Spirit grieves (Eph. 4:3), struggles with other persons (Gen. 6:3; Isa. 63:10), provides leadership (Rom. 8:14), witnesses to believers that they are God's own (1 Cor. 1:22; 5:5; Eph. 1:13, 14), and bestows gifts on others (Eph. 6). Scripture teaches that God's own Spirit is personal and as such is distinguishable from Father and Son, yet at the same time sent by them (Athanasius, *Four Discourses Ag. Arians* I.12, 13, *NPNF* 2 IV, pp. 333–43, III.25, pp. 399–407; cf. Gregory Nazianzen, *Orat.* V, *On the Spirit*, *NPNF* 2 VII, pp. 318 ff.).

Following classical exegesis, we will ask whether the names ascribed to the Spirit are names that could be ascribed only to God; whether the attributes of the Spirit are God's own attributes; whether the works done by the Spirit are God's own works; and whether the worship due the Spirit is a worship due only to God.

Scripture views the Spirit as nothing less than God because the *names* ascribed to the Spirit are names that could only be ascribed to God. God the Spirit is called "the Spirit of God," "the Holy Spirit," "the Spirit of Christ," "the Spirit of grace," "the Holy Spirit of promise," "the Spirit of wisdom," "the Spirit of truth," and the Counselor or Comforter (Acts 1:8; John 4:24; 14:21; 15:26; Rom. 8:14; Cyril of Jerusalem, *Catech. Lect.* XVI, *NPNF* 2 VII, pp. 115 ff.; cf. Tho. Aq., *ST* I Q36, I, pp. 188–91). Scriptures report God as addressing hearers through "My Spirit" (Gen. 6:3; Prov. 1:23; Isa. 44:3; Ezek. 36:27; 39:29; Joel 2:28; Matt. 12:18; Acts 2:17, 18). The "Spirit of God" and "Spirit of the Lord" are frequently used in both Testaments. The prophets, according to the First Letter of Peter, were trying to "find out what was the time, and what the circumstances, to which the spirit of Christ in them pointed" (1 Pet. 1:11). "It was not through any human whim that men prophesied of old; men they were, impelled by the Holy Spirit, they spoke the words of God" (2 Pet. 1:20, 21).

The Spirit is divine Counselor (Advocate, Comforter, Paraclete), according to John, who counsels in a way incomparable to any human counseling (14:16; 15:26; 16:7). "The Counselor, the Holy Spirit, whom the Father will send in my name, he will teach you all things, and bring to your remembrance all that I have said to you" (John 14:26,

RSV). "It is to your advantage that I go away, for if I do not go away, the Counselor will not come to you; but if I go, I will send him to you. And when he comes, he will convince the world of sin and of righteousness and of judgment." "When the Spirit of truth comes, he will guide you into all the truth" (John 16:7–13, RSV; cf. Hilary, *Trin.* VIII.19 ff., *NPNF* 2 IX, pp. 142 f.; Calvin, *Inst.* 1.13.15). Only God could guide the believer to all truth.

Scriptures view the Spirit as God because the *attributes* of the Spirit are God's own attributes. The Spirit is eternal (Heb. 9:14), omniscient (1 Cor. 2:10–12), all-powerful (Luke 11:20; Rom. 15:18, 19). Only the Spirit of God is able to "explore everything, even the depths of God's own nature" (1 Cor. 2:10; cf. Cyril of Jerusalem, *Catech. Lect.* XVI.1–11, *NPNF* 2 VII, pp. 115–17; Gregory Nazianzen, *Fifth Theol. Or. NPNF* 2 VII, pp. 318–28; Ambrose, *On the Holy Spirit* I.5 ff., *NPNF* 2 X, pp. 100 ff.; Calvin, *Inst.* 1.13; Watson, *TI* I, pp. 628 ff.).

The *works* done by the Spirit are God's own work. It is through the Spirit that "God has revealed to us" "things beyond our imagining" (1 Cor. 2:10). Paul argued that it was the Holy Spirit who "spoke to your fathers through the prophets" (Acts 28:25). It is this same Spirit of God who bears witness to the truth in Jesus Christ (Acts 5:30–32); who gives new life to believers (Titus 3:5); who strengthens the faithful (1 Cor. 6:19); who gives the gifts of ministry (1 Cor. 12; Eph. 6). The same Spirit is the Advocate who "confutes the world," showing "where wrong and right and judgement lie," able to "convince them of divine judgement" (John 16:8–11). Only God can remit sin (John 3:5), give life (John 6:63), sanctify (2 Thess. 2:13; 1 Pet. 1:2), perform miraculous works (Matt. 12:28; Luke 1:35), govern the church rightly (Acts 13:2; 15:28), and bring life out of death (Rom. 8:11; cf. Augustine, *Trin.* V.8–16, *NPNF* 1 III, pp. 91–96; Calvin, *Inst.* 1.13.14; Wesley, *On the Holy Spirit*, *WJW* VII, pp. 508 ff.).

The Spirit is God because the *worship* due the Spirit is a worship due to God alone (Gregory Nazianzen, *Orat.* V.1–12, *NPNF* 2 VII, pp. 318–21; Basil, *On the Holy Spirit* XVIII, *NPNF* 2 VIII, p. 29; John of Damascus, *OF* I.7, *NPNF* 2 IX, p. 5). For "God is spirit, and those who worship him must worship in spirit and in truth" (John 4:24). Paul's benediction to Corinth joined together the presence of the Spirit with the love of God and the grace of Christ (2 Cor. 13:13). Wherever persons are baptized, they are baptized in the name not only of the Father and the Son but also of the Spirit, one God (Matt. 28:19).

A Summative New Testament Teaching

The preceding effort has sought to establish that there can be no triune teaching without Scripture, and there can be no adequate clarification of Scripture without the triune hypothesis. The Scriptures intend to make it unavoidably clear that the Father is God, the Son is God, the Spirit is God, and that God is one (John Chrysostom, *Hom. VII on 2nd Corinthians NPNF* 1 XII, p. 319; John of Damascus, *OF* I.8, *NPNF* 2 IX, pp. 6–11). Although the triune teaching is not set forth in Scripture with all the intricate post-Nicene nuances with which we associate the word *trinity*, nonetheless the Scriptures conspicuously affirm the deity and unity of Father, Son, and Spirit so thoroughly that we must conclude that the Nicene exegetes were right to develop the triune teaching in the way they did in their historical context.

It only remains now for us to speak of those passages of Scripture in which Father, Son, and Spirit are coordinately presented, so as to make clear that even in New Testament times the rudiments of the triune teaching were already being formed. There are twelve *locus classicus* texts that reveal the triune teaching in this cohesive sense. They come from reliable texts of major writers of the New Testament: Paul, Matthew, John, and others. If we had nothing but these twelve passages, it could be reliably established that the triune teaching was already powerfully present in the oral and written traditions of the New Testament period.

THE BAPTISMAL FORMULA

The apostles were commissioned by Christ to "Go forth therefore and make all nations my disciples; baptize men everywhere in the name of the Father and the Son and the Holy Spirit" (Matt. 28:19; for classical exegesis, see Hilary, *Trin.* II.15, *NPNF* 2 IX, pp. 52, 53; Basil, *Epis.* 159.2, *NPNF* 2 VIII, p. 212; John Chrysostom, *Hom. on John*, *NPNF* 1 XIV, pp. 288–89). If there is no distinction between Father, Son, and Spirit, why the necessity of the three distinct names? If there is no equality of these persons, why are they linked together at such a crucial moment in the early church? If they are not one, then would not the entire premise of monotheism be destroyed or bypassed?

Christian baptism is administered "in the name of" not three Gods, not two creatures plus one God, not three parts of God, and not three stages of God, but one God who is eternally Father, Son, and Spirit (Gregory of Nyssa, *On "Not Three Gods," NPNF* 2 V, pp. 331–37). The history of Christian theology is best understood as an extended commentary on the baptismal formula (Gregory Nazianzen,

Ag. Eunomius II.1, 2, *NPNF* 2 V, pp. 100 f.; Ambrose, *On Sacr.* I.18, II.14–24, *LCF,* pp. 182, 183). Its liturgical importance, its strategic location in the Gospel of Matthew as the final command of the Lord, and the fact that it has been so frequently referred to by early Christian writers make this text the centerpiece of triune teaching. It implicitly affirms the divinity, the distinctness, the equality, and the unity of the Father, Son, and Spirit. It assumes and calls for an act of adoration and profession of faith in the triune God (Cyril of Jerusalem, *Catech. Lect.* XVI.4, *NPNF* 2 VII, p. 116).

JESUS' BAPTISM

The Father, with the Spirit, blesses the Son at Jesus' baptism, according to Matthew's Gospel. When Jesus was baptized, the Holy Spirit descended upon the Son, and the Father spoke from above: "After baptism Jesus came up out of the water at once, and at that moment heaven opened; he saw the Spirit of God descending like a dove to alight upon him; and a voice from heaven was heard saying, 'This is my Son, my Beloved, on whom my favour rests'" (Matt. 3:16, 17). In this passage, Father, Son, and Spirit are all present in an explicit triune inauguration of the messianic ministry (cf. Didache 7:3; Irenaeus, *Ag. Her.* III.9, *ANF* I, p. 423; John of Damascus, *OF* III, *NPNF* 2 IX, pp. 60 ff.).

PAUL'S APOSTOLIC BENEDICTION

The Pauline tradition carries many indications that the triune formulas were available in oral tradition prior to Paul's writing. Notably, Paul closed his second letter to Corinth with a threefold benediction that joined together equally and distinctly the Spirit with God and Christ: "The grace of the Lord Jesus Christ, and the love of God, and the fellowship in the Holy Spirit, be with you all" (2 Cor. 13:13). It must be remembered that this is a solemn benediction offered up in supplication to God at a critical moment of the Epistle—its conclusion. In specifying the three names, Paul assumed their equal worthiness to receive divine praise and reverence, and their distinguishability (Gregory of Nyssa, *Ag. Eunomius* I.16, *NPNF* 2 V, pp. 53, 54; cf. Ambrose, *Of the Holy Spirit* I.12.131, *NPNF* 2 X, p. 110). If Christ and the Spirit were not thought to be fully God, then how could Paul ever again admonish the Corinthians against idolatry? The benediction appears to have a distinctly triune form, even though its usual order is changed. It suggests that the prototrinitarian assumption was already so familiar to Paul's audience that he not only appropriated it but revised its order.

THE VARIETIES OF GIFTS

Paul wrote: "No one can say 'Jesus is Lord!' except under the influence of the Holy Spirit. There are varieties of gifts, but the same spirit. There are varieties of service, but the same Lord. There are many forms of work, but all of them, in all men, are the work of the same God" (1 Cor. 1:4–6). The classical exegetes recognized in this passage the variety of the Spirit's gifts and the oneness of God through the work of the Spirit attesting the Son (Athanasius, *Four Discourses Ag. Arians* III.13, *NPNF* 2 IV, p. 401; John Chrysostom, *Hom. XXIX on 1st Corinthians*, *NPNF* 1 XII, pp. 168–75). It is the Spirit of God who enables the faithful to believe in the Son of God. Yet he who works through the Son and Spirit is the One and only God, "the same God."

THE EPHESIAN FORMULA

"Through him"—Christ Jesus—"we both alike have access to the Father in the one Spirit" (Eph. 2:18). This language suggests that there existed an oral tradition prior to the writing of this letter in which Father, Son, and Spirit, as in the baptismal formula, were frequently linked. Thus in the same letter there is an appeal to believers to live "in the unity which the Spirit gives." They are further instructed: "There is one body and one Spirit, as there is also one hope held out in God's call to you; one Lord, one faith, one baptism, one God and Father of all, who is over all and through all and in all" (Eph. 4:3–6). The letter to Ephesus provides a clear affirmation of the oneness of God who is "Father of all," of the Lord Jesus Christ, and of the "one Spirit" that unifies the church and provides spiritual gifts (Hilary, *Trin.* VIII.13, XI.1, *NPNF* 2 IX, pp. 147 f., 203; cf. Wesley, *WJW* VI, pp. 392 ff.).

JUDE'S SUMMARY INSTRUCTION

"Continue to pray in the power of the Holy Spirit. Keep yourselves in the love of God, and look forward to the day when our Lord Jesus Christ in his mercy will give eternal life" (Jude 20, 21). Once again, this pivotal instruction, encompassing the love of God, the hope of Christ, and the power of the Spirit, occurs at the climactic moment of the Epistle, when the writer is seeking to provide a summative statement of its instruction. Its conspicuous position at the end of the Epistle reinforces the importance of the teaching to the hearers, as if the triune teaching were already so well known to them that the confirmation of it increased the credibility and plausibility of the instruction.

THE JOHANNINE PROLOGUE AND FAREWELL DISCOURSES

Nowhere is the triune teaching stated more profoundly than in John's report of Jesus' last discourse to his disciples, in which the Son promises the "Advocate, the Holy Spirit whom the Father will send in my name" (John 14:26). Here are the roots of much later trinitarian language: The Son sends, the Spirit is sent, and the Spirit proceeds from the Father. "When your Advocate has come, whom I will send you from the Father—the Spirit of truth that issues from the Father— he will bear witness to me" (John 15:26; cf. Tertullian, *Prescript. Ag. Her.* XXVIII, *ANF* III, p. 256; Augustine, *On Trin.* IV.20, *NPNF* 1 III, pp. 83–85).

The most highly developed teaching of God as Father, Son, and Spirit is in the Fourth Gospel, where all key elements come into more explicit expression. The prominence of the theme of preexistence of the Son is evident from the fact that John takes up the issue at the very outset in the prologue to his Gospel. The Son is prior to all things. "When all things began, the Word already was. The Word dwelt with God, and what God was, the Word was. The Word, then, was with God in the beginning, and through him all things came to be; no single thing was created without him. All that came to be was alive with his life, and that life was the light of men" (John 1:1–4; cf. Tertullian, *Ag. Praxeas* XV, *ANF* III, pp. 610 f.). The Word is God, not less than God, not other than God, but God undiminished. The Word is God's speech to the world, God's way of letting the divine presence become known to the world. "So the Word became flesh; he came to dwell among us, and we saw his glory, such glory as befits the Father's only Son, full of grace and truth" (John 1:14; Irenaeus, *Ag. Her.* III.10, *ANF* I, pp. 423–26).

The triune distinction is richly embedded in the Johannine pro- logue: The Word (Jesus) *is* God and is *with* God. One can be God and be with God only by being God in one sense and being with God in another sense. If Christ is God, then Christ is not less than God. If Christ is with God, then there is a distinction in the Godhead or in God's own personal being that does not change or limit the unity of God but allows for an intrapersonal dialogue within the eternal being of God (Hilary, *Trin.* II.23–35, *NPNF* 2 IX, pp. 58–61; cf. Novatian, *Trin.* XIII ff., *ANF* V, pp. 622 ff.).

THE JOHANNINE LETTERS

The language of the Johannine letters is even more explicit. No one who reads 1 John: 3–5 can reasonably conclude that there are no prototrinitarian conceptions in the New Testament. "And this is his commandment, that we should believe in the name of his Son Jesus Christ and love one another. . . . And by this we know that he abides in us, by the Spirit which he has given us. . . . By this you know the Spirit of God: every spirit which confesses that Jesus Christ has come in the flesh is of God, and every spirit which does not confess Jesus is not of God" (1 John 3:23–4:3, RSV). "This is the victory that overcomes the world, our faith. Who is it that overcomes the world but he who believes that Jesus is the Son of God? This is he who came by water and blood, Jesus Christ, not with the water only but with the water and the blood. And the Spirit is the witness, because the Spirit is the truth. There are three witnesses, the Spirit, the water, and the blood; and these three agree. If we receive the testimony of men, the testimony of God is greater; for this is the testimony of God that he has borne witness to his Son. He who believes in the Son of God has the testimony in himself" (1 John 5:4–10, RSV; Cyprian, *Treatises* I.6, *ANF* V, p. 423). Some exegetes have mistakenly interpreted the "three witnesses" as the three persons of the Trinity—inconsistent with the text. Nonetheless all essential assumptions of triune teaching appear in the passage: Jesus is the Son of God, who abides in us by the Spirit whom the Father has given us, who together constitute the revelation of the One God.

THE APOCALYPSE SALUTATION

The salutation to the churches in the Revelation of John was also a rich mine in which classical exegetes recognized a triune form: "Grace be to you and peace, from him who is and who was and who is to come," namely, the one God, Father Almighty, "from the seven spirits before his throne," that is, the seven gifts of the Holy Spirit, and "from Jesus Christ," the Son, who is "the first born from the dead and ruler of the kings of the earth. To him who loves us and freed us from our sins with his life's blood, who made of us a royal house, to serve as the priests of his God and Father—to him be glory and dominion for ever and ever! Amen" (Rev. 1:4–6; Tho. Aq., *ST* I Q39, I, pp. 199–203).

KENOSIS IN PHILIPPIANS 2:5–11

In this passage, Jesus Christ is proclaimed as eternal God: "The divine nature was his from the first." Christ's engagement in human history was an act of humility and obedience to His Father. Though he had the divine nature from the outset,

yet he did not think to snatch at equality with God, but made himself nothing, assuming the nature of a slave. Bearing the human likeness, revealed in human shape, he humbled himself, and in obedience accepted even death— death on a cross. Therefore God raised him to the heights and bestowed on him the name above all names, that at the name of Jesus every knee should bow—in 'heaven, on earth, and in the depths—and every tongue confess, "Jesus Christ is Lord," to the glory of God the Father. (Phil. 2:6–11)

This early Christian text, usually thought to predate Paul, assumed that Jesus Christ is God, and with God from the beginning. This paradoxical distinction (that Jesus Christ is God and is with God from the beginning) is the invariable premise of trinitarian belief (Athanasius, *Four Discourses Ag. Arians* I.11, *NPNF* 2 IV, pp. 327–33). God is one, and within God there is a distinction not of parts (not as if God were separable into composite parts) but of persons. It is as if God is capable of internal dialogue or trialogue within the Godhead, even as human consciousness is capable of internal dialogue or trialogue. Yet this internal trialogue is eternally present to God, whereas our internal trialogue of memory, understanding, and will is temporally present to us only under the constricted conditions of finitude (Novatian, *Trin.* XXII, *ANF* V, pp. 633, 634; cf. Augustine, *On Trin.* IX, *NPNF* 1 III, pp. 125 ff.).

INTRODUCTORY ARGUMENT OF COLOSSIANS

Similarly, in Colossians, chapter 1, the Pauline tradition spoke comprehensively of the ways in which God as Father and Son acts to save the world: "He rescued us from the domain of darkness and brought us away into the kingdom of his dear Son, in whom our release is secured and our sins forgiven. He is the image of the invisible God; his is the primacy over all created things. In him everything in heaven and on earth was created" (Col. 1:13–16). It is through the Son that the Father acted to redeem the world. This is the same one who "exists before everything, and all things are held together in him," that is, in Christ. Christ is not therefore separable from God, but God himself, yet with God from the beginning in dialogue and interactive love and eternal communion. The communities who receive this word are called to manifest "love in the Spirit" (Col. 1:8, NIV; cf. Athanasius, *Four Discourses Ag. Arians* II.19, *NPNF* 2 IV, pp. 372–76).

LETTER TO THE HEBREWS' SUMMARY OF SALVATION HISTORY

The final prototriune text is the opening passage of the letter to Hebrews:

When in former times God spoke to our forefathers, he spoke in fragmentary and varied fashion through the prophets. But in this the final age he has
spoken to us in the Son whom he has made heir to the whole universe, and
through whom he created all orders of existence: the Son who is the effulgence
of God's splendour and the stamp of God's very being, and sustains the
universe by his word of power. When he had brought about the purgation of
sins, he took his seat at the right hand of Majesty on high, raised as far above
the angels as the title he has inherited is superior to theirs. (Heb. 1:1–4)

Note the triune assumptions of the text: Christ is preexistent, one
with God, the stamp of God's very being, not less than God, higher
than the angels and all creaturely powers, yet distinguishable from the
Father, whose coming is attested by the Holy Spirit (Heb. 9:8; 10:15;
Athanasius, *Four Discourses Ag. Arians* I.13, *NPNF* 2 IV, pp. 337, 338;
cf. Origen, *De Princip.* I.2.6, *ANF* IV, pp. 247, 248).

Triune Teaching a Necessary Hypothesis of New Testament Proclamation

The teaching of God as Father, Son, and Spirit emerged in relation
to the church's reflection upon the meaning of the ministry of Jesus.
Although the teaching was well formed in the oral tradition that led
to the writing of the New Testament, it was not formally developed as
dogma until after a lengthy process of reflection, spurred by the
necessity of addressing heresies. It was well into the fourth century
before it was classically formulated, and even now it is still being
reflected upon.

The triune God is not an extracanonical teaching, even though it
did not become fully explicit and distinctly explicated until some time
after the New Testament writings. Yet it was inevitable that some
cohesive teaching concerning God as Father, Son, and Spirit would
need to be developed out of the New Testament, for the language of
Philippians 2, Colossians 1, the Fourth Gospel, and Hebrews 1 could
not remain permanently unexamined. These passages invited intense
exegetical reflection as the Christian community moved toward increasing contact with the Hellenized world.

Hence when we speak of triune teaching in the New Testament,
we are not speaking of a few isolated texts. We are speaking of the
fundament of the Gospel of John, the Johannine Epistles, and Revelation, and crucial passages in the Pauline tradition, the pastoral letters,
and numerous texts of the synoptic Gospels. Antitrinitarian or non-
trinitarian exegesis is hard put to show that these recurrent formulations are accidental, or textually spurious, or minor additions, or quirks

of a single author. The conclusion of classical exegetes is: New Testament teaching of God is inevitably and necessarily a triune teaching of God.

Our hypothesis is that the teaching of the triune God occurred in these primary phases: the implicit preparation for the teaching in the Old Testament, the primary explicit unfolding of the teaching of the New Testament, and the secondary explicit unfolding in the clarification of that teaching in the first four centuries of ecumenical, consensual doctrinal formulation, and in the post-Nicene reflection that has followed from it.

Historical Triune Teaching and Its Alternatives

The historical unfolding of the scriptural teaching of the triune God was a refinement of teachings implicit in Scripture and required by consistent reflection upon them. Essentially present in the earliest baptismal formulas, the embryonic triune teaching was present in the pre-Pauline oral tradition, was received and developed by Paul and the synoptic writers, and emerged in its fullest New Testament expression in the Johannine Gospel and letters; but it awaited the ante-Nicene, Nicene, and post-Nicene periods for its formal and explicit definition and development.

Why was the triune doctrine not delivered fully and completely in Scripture, if Scripture is sufficient for Christian teaching? Classical exegetes observed that it took some time for the proclaiming church to grasp the range of implications of what had happened to it in Jesus Christ under the power of the Spirit (Eusebius, *CH* VI–X, *NPNF* 2 I, pp. 249–387; Theodoret, *EH* IV, *NPNF* 2 III, pp. 107–31). These implications were strongly intuited in the New Testament, but not fully developed as rigorous doctrine that could answer questions that surfaced more sharply amid the Hellenizing environment. It was only as the church moved further into the Greco-Roman world that it was required to answer highly specialized queries (Athenagoras, *A Plea for Christians* X, *ANF* I, p. 133; Tertullian, *Ag. Praxeas* II, *ANF* III, p. 598). Only after having worked through considerable reflection, accompanied by tragic discord and political strife, did it come finally to the precision of the formulations of the general councils of Nicaea and Constantinople, which by that time had critically and consensually digested the New Testament triune teaching. To require of the New Testament writers that they should have fully answered questions that would not be posed until over a century later is unreasonable.

If asked whether the process of interpreting the triune teaching has been absolutely concluded with Nicaea, we must acknowledge that it has not ended and will continue as the Spirit continues to unfold its meanings in ever-new historical and cultural configurations (John Chrysostom, *Hom. on John* LXXVIII, LXXIX, *NPNF* 1 XIV, pp. 286–95; Newman, *Development of Doctrine*). The Spirit is still guiding the church "into all truth" (John 16:13), and thus the church's reflection upon the triune God is subject to ever-new rediscovery, eliciting ever-richer modes of awareness of God's triune being (Tertullian, *Ag. Praxeas* XXX, XXXI, *ANF* III, pp. 626, 627; Gregory of Nyssa, *On the Holy Spirit*, *NPNF* 2 V, pp. 315–25).

It is useful to distinguish between the scriptural teaching itself and the dogmatic formulation of that teaching under conditions of controversy. For dogmatic definition sought to refine and make explicit the nuances of scriptural doctrine in response to serious intellectual and moral challenges. The first major dogma to be worked through thoroughly in this way was the triune teaching, which awaited the fourth century to receive full dogmatic definition and has since remained the standard summary of the ancient ecumenical Christian teaching of God (*Trent*, Canons, Third Session, *COC* II, p. 77–79; Orthodox Conf. of 1643, *COC* II, p. 275, Augsburg Conf., *COC* III, pp. 7–9).

But how is it known that the triune teaching was sustained between the New Testament texts and the Nicene definition? The evidence is abundant: For example, the triune teaching is clearly found embedded in Polycarp's prayer before his martyrdom (ca. 156) as remembered by the church of Smyrna: "I glorify thee, through the eternal and heavenly High Priest, Jesus Christ, thy beloved Servant, through whom be glory to thee with him and the Holy Spirit both now and unto the ages to come" (*The Martyrdom of Polycarp*, *LCC* I, p. 154).

When Ignatius of Antioch (d. ca. 110) appealed to the Magnesians to "Study, therefore, to be established in the doctrines of the Lord and the apostles," he prayed that they proceed "in faith and love; in the Son, and in the Father, and in the Spirit," and that they be subject to the bishop "as Jesus Christ to the Father, according to the flesh, and the apostles to Christ, and to the Father, and to the Spirit" (Ignatius, *Magnesians* XIII, *ANF* I, pp. 64 f.; cf. Eph. 9:1; Clement of Rome, *First Epis.* XVIII, *ANF* I, p. 21).

Athenagoras (d. ca. 180) must have relied upon a well-defined tradition of triune thinking when in the second century he sought to

answer the charge of atheism with one of the earliest summaries of
Christian teaching of God:

That we are not atheists, therefore, seeing that we acknowledge one God,
uncreated, eternal, invisible, impassible, incomprehensible, illimitable, who is
apprehended by the understanding only and the reason, who is encompassed
by light, and beauty, and spirit and power ineffable, by whom the universe
has been created through His Logos, and set in order. . . . the Son of God is
the Logos of the Father, in idea and in operation; for after the pattern of Him
and by Him were all things made, the Father and the Son being one. And the
Son being in the Father and the Father in the Son, in oneness and power of
spirit, the understanding and reason of the Father is the Son of God. . . . Who,
then, would not be astonished to hear men who speak of God the Father, and
of God the Son, and of the Holy Spirit, and who declare both their power in
union and their distinction in order, called atheists? (*A Plea for Christians* X,
ANF I, p. 133)

Explicit use of the term *trias* (trinity) prior to Tertullian is also
found in Theophilus of Antioch (d. ca. 185/191), who spoke of the
first three days of creation as suggesting "*types* of the trinity: of God,
and His Word, and His wisdom" (*To Autolycus*, II.15, *ANF* II, p. 101,
italics added).

Tertullian wrote a detailed reply to Praxeas (post–A.D. 213) in
which he answered intricate questions on the interpretation of the
triune God that were under vigorous debate. One must assume that
there was at this time an available ecumenical oral tradition of extraordinary familiarity with triune teaching in order for Tertullian to write
to his audience in such sophisticated terms as the following: "Thus
the connection of the Father in the Son, and of the Son in the Paraclete,
produces three coherent Persons, who are yet distinct One from Another. These Three are one essence, not one Person, as it is said, 'I
and my Father are One'" (*Ag. Praxeas* XXV, *ANF* III, p. 621; cf. *On
Modesty* XXI, *ANF* IV, pp. 99, 100). That Tertullian himself did not
invent but rather passed on this language is evident from his own
testimony that "this rule of faith has come down to us from the
beginning of the gospel, even before any of the heretics, much more
before Praxeas" (*Ag. Praxeas* II, *ANF* III, p. 598).

According to Origen (writing about A.D. 215): "For it is one and
the same thing to receive participation in the Holy Spirit as to receive
it in the Father and the Son, since, of course, the nature of the Trinity
is one and incorporeal" (Origen, *De Princip.*, CWS, p. 210). One
cannot say "when" or "never" of the Trinity, because these words
imply the notion of time; "but what is said about the Father, the Son,

and the Holy Spirit must be understood above all time, above all ages" (p. 206). It would have been impossible for Origen to address his audience in this way if there had not been an available oral tradition in which such language was understood and under sophisticated debate. Hence the triune teaching was, long before Nicaea, widely received and understood in an explicit and detailed way. It was only on the basis of complexity of the pre-Nicene discussion that the debate that led to Nicaea may be understood.

The First Major Challenge to Triune Teaching: Must the Son Be Eternally God?

There is evidence that many challenges to the triune teaching were mounted and debated during the first two centuries (cf. Irenaeus, *Ag. Her.* I, *ANF* I, pp. 315 ff., Hippolytus, *Refutation of All Her.* V–X, *ANF* V, pp. 47–153). One of the earliest major challenges to the triune teaching came from Theodotus, who around A.D. 190 argued that prior to Jesus' baptism Jesus was not the Son of God, but that only upon Jesus' baptism did he become adopted as the Son of God. "(Theodotus maintains) that Jesus was a (mere) man, born of a virgin, according to the counsel of the Father, and that after he had lived promiscuously with all men, and had become pre-eminently religious, he subsequently at his baptism in Jordan received Christ, who came from above and descended (upon him) in form of a dove" (Hippolytus, *Refutation of All Her.*, VII.23, *ANF* V, pp. 114, 115). This was quickly rejected by consensual Christian teaching and never developed a widespread following because it so obviously failed to give due account to John's Gospel, which spoke of the eternality of the Son—that the Son was with the Father from the beginning and was God (John 1; Ignatius, *Trallians* XI, *ANF* I, p. 71).

Another early challenge came from Paul of Samosata, who developed the idea, later rejected at the Council of Antioch in 268, that the Word of God is essentially the command of God, not necessarily with reference to Jesus, and that the Word is therefore not known essentially through the Son (Malchion, *Synod of Antioch Ag. Paul of Samosata, ANF* VI, pp. 169–71). Although the Samosatans named Father, Son, and Holy Spirit in administering baptism, they gave a false meaning to the baptismal formula and did not use the words *Son* and *Spirit* in the sense of the uncreated God (Athanasius, *Four Discourses Ag. Arians* IV.30–36, *NPNF* 2 IV, pp. 445–47).

The Second Challenge: Are Father and Son Distinguishable?

The next major challenge came from Noetus of Smyrna, from Praxeas (remembered largely for Tertullian's response to him), and more
importantly, from Sabellius of Ptolemais. These controversialists tried
to circumvent the distinction between the Father who sends and the
Son who is sent. The three persons were thought to be merely different aspects of God: God in himself, God revealed, and God active in
us, but these differences are merely subjective differences in our perceptions and terms concerning God, not distinctions in God. It was
argued that there could be no real distinction in the Godhead between
persons, but only a superficial distinction in name only. This resulted
in a Trinity not of persons but of names only. God only *appears* to be
a distinguishable person in the Son. Father, Son, and Spirit are merely
linguistic pointers to the one God who comes to us in nominally
different modes. This is why this view was called modalism: Father,
Son, and Spirit are identical, yet only appear to come in a series of
revelations of one single person, God. God is not three persons of one
substance, but rather one person with three differently named roles
or manifestations, or modes (Tertullian, *Ag. Praxeas, ANF* III, pp. 597
ff.; Athanasius, *Four Discourses Ag. Arians* IV.1–5, *NPNF* 2 IV, pp.
433–35). Some forms of modalism argued that God appeared first as
Yahweh, then more fully as the Son, and ever more fully as the Spirit,
thus placing a valuational priority upon the Spirit. This form of modalism wrongly viewed the Trinity as a succession of stages (Tho. Aq.,
SCG IV.5, IV, pp. 43–48).

Modalism was rejected because it did not distinguish between
Father and Son as sharply as the Scriptures do. In the Fourth Gospel
the Father speaks of and to the Son; the Son speaks of and to the
Father, and prays to the Father; and the Spirit is clearly distinguished
from both Father and Son (John 14–16). Modalism failed to hold
together the essential eternal unity of the three persons (by making
them successive stages), the distinction between the three persons (by
making them nominal), and the equality of the three persons (by
losing the distinctiveness of Son and Spirit).

The Most Fundamental Challenge: Is the Son Less Than God?

The most formidable challenge came from a presbyter named Arius
(A.D. 256–336) of Alexandria, who envisioned Christ as above creation, yet not fully God. The Son is before cosmic creation, yet still a
creature, and different from the Father in essence. The Son is not

therefore God, but only like God. Both Son and Spirit are creatures. Arianism had a long struggle of spectacular wins and losses in the imperial court, and among the churches especially of the East. It took the extremely astute and subtle mind of Athanasius to challenge and expose it as a highly consequential distortion of scriptural teaching (*Four Discourses Ag. Arians*, passim, *NPNF* 2 IV, pp. 306 ff.; Tho. Aq., *SCG* I.6, 7, I, pp. 51–61).

This issue came to a climax at the Council of Nicaea in A.D. 325. It had been very difficult to pin down a decisive test to sort out Arian from orthodox views. For the Arians were willing to ascribe to the Son the divine name and attributes, yet only in an indirect and secondary sense. Finally the test for orthodoxy was devised and given sharp form: It was necessary to ask (a) whether one believed that "there was once a time when the Son was not"—Arians answered yes—and (b) Is the Son of the same substance with the Father (*homoousion*), or merely of similar substance (*homoiousion*) to the Father? The formula of the Creed of Nicaea contained both these tests when it confessed the Son as "begotten [*gennēthenta*], not made, of the same substance [*homoousion*] as the Father" (Creed of Nicaea, *FEF*, p. 281). Although Arianism has reappeared again and again in church history since the Nicene definition, it has never been able to make a sustained challenge to ecumenical Christian teaching, and its ideas have never since become incorporated into the creed or confession of any major church body.

The church of the fourth century, therefore, deemed it necessary to add highly specific, technical language to the New Testament teaching in order to define it precisely and protect it from distortion. Why was this postcanonical, technical language necessary, beyond a simple reliance upon Scripture itself? Classical exegetes thought that they had a duty to defend the faith against distortion; it could not be done unambiguously by using only the terms of Scripture, because of the tendency of challengers to circumvent and redefine those terms (Athanasius, *Four Discourses Ag. Arians* I.1 ff., *NPNF* 2 IV, pp. 306 ff.). It became necessary to develop language that expresses scriptural truth in such a way that it is not distortable—so it could not be covertly twisted and circumvented. The two crucial terms, *gennēthenta* and *homoousion*, were, after careful debate, included in the formulation, as if footnotes to the scriptural texts, so that God would not be taught as if created or divided in essence or the three persons confused or conflated (Council of Nicaea, *NPNF* 2 XIV, pp. 1–57).

This definition was not thought to be a new invention of the Nicene fathers but in full continuity with the apostolic teaching as delivered by New Testament writers and as held consensually by the church from its very beginnings, even though an extended historical process was required before its full and explicit definition was unfolded (cf. Second Council of Constantinople I ff., *CC*, p. 46; Fourth Lateran Council, *CC*, p. 57). For Christ himself, according to John's Gospel, taught that the Father is distinguishable from the Son (John 5:32, 37) and the Spirit is distinguishable from the Son and the Father (John 14:16); that the Father begets and the Son is begotten (John 1:14, 18; 3:16); that the Son was sent and the Father sends (John 16:36; Gal. 4:4); and that the Spirit proceeds from the Father (John 15:26) and is sent by the Father and the Son (John 14:26; 15:26). These phrases were not the innovations of the fourth century but, rather, were intrinsic to the Johannine understanding of the relation of Father, Son, and Spirit and deeply interwoven in the earliest traditions of Christian preaching.

The Unity of God as Father, Son, and Spirit

The central affirmations of the triune teaching are that God is one; that the Son is God and the Spirit is God, even as the Father is God; and that the distinction between the three is not merely of mode or manifestation but is real and personal (Athanasius, *Four Discourses Ag. Arians* I.13.58; III.1–6, *NPNF* 2 IV, pp. 340, 393 ff.).

If God is one indivisible unity, any distinction referred to must not divide God into two, three, or more separable parts. "God is one," proclaimed the New Testament, echoing ten centuries of Hebraic monotheism (1 Tim. 3:20). "For there is one God, and also one mediator between God and men, Christ Jesus, himself man, who sacrificed himself to win freedom for all mankind" (1 Tim. 2:5, 6). Jesus himself clearly affirmed the Hebraic teaching of the unity of God when asked which is the first commandment: "Hear, O Israel: the Lord our God is the only Lord" (Mark 12:29). Unity is implied in the very idea of God, properly conceived (Tho. Aq., *ST* I Q39, I, pp. 193–203). There cannot be more than one necessary being (John of Damascus, *OF* I.5, *NPNF* 2 IX, p. 5).

Hence it is not a contradiction, but consistent with Christian experience, Scripture, and tradition, to say that there are three who are God yet one God. For Christian teaching does not say that they are three in the same sense that they are one, which might cause us to say foolishly, "He are one" or "they is three." God is one. Father, Son, and Spirit are three. God's unity is not a unity of separable parts but of distinguishable persons.

Three as One

Christian Scripture and early teaching assumed that Jesus Christ is true God and truly human. The problem faced by early Christian teaching was not whether Christ was God but how, within the bounds of monotheistic faith, the unity of God could be maintained while holding equally to the deity of One who is distinct from God the Father.

To speak of God revealed in Christ through the power of the Spirit, one must speak of trinity. But trinity is not merely a concept. One does not first define trinity conceptually and then begin worshiping the triune God. Rather it is the triune God who is approached from the outset in Christian worship. Gregory Nazianzen's poem on the Trinity revealed how central was the triune understanding of God in early Christian worship:

From the day whereon I renounced the things of the world to consecrate my soul to luminous and heavenly contemplation, when the supreme intelligence carried me hence to set me down far from all that pertains to the flesh, to hide me in the secret places of the heavenly tabernacle; from that day my eyes have been blinded by the light of the Trinity, whose brightness surpasses all that the mind can conceive; for from a throne high exalted the Trinity pours upon all, the ineffable radiance common to the Three. (*Poemata de seipso* I, *MPG* XXXVII, p. 984, in *MTEC*, p. 44)

The contemplation of the triune mystery leads beyond language, logical categories, or concepts proper to human thought, beyond dialectic and beyond dialogue, to the Three in One, into whom the faithful are baptized,

the One Godhead and Power, found in the Three in Unity, and comprising the Three separately, not unequal, in substances or natures, neither increased nor diminished by superiorities or inferiorities . . . the infinite conjunction of Three Infinite Ones, Each God when considered in Himself; as the Father so the Son, as the Son so the Holy Ghost; the Three One God when contemplated together; Each God because Consubstantial; One God because of the Monarchia. No sooner do I conceive of the One than I am illumined by the Splendor of the Three; no sooner do I distinguish Them than I am carried back to the One. When I think of any One of the Three I think of Him as the Whole, and my eyes are filled, and the greater part of what I am thinking of escapes me. I cannot grasp the greatness of That One so as to attribute a greater greatness to the Rest. When I contemplate the Three together, I see but one torch, and cannot divide or measure out the Undivided Light. (Gregory Nazianzen, or. XL.41, *On Holy Baptism*, *NPNF* 2 VII, p. 375)

Our thought races relentlessly between ephemeral dialectical poles when we seek to get a conceptual grasp of the triune mystery. But worship in ancient Christianity was apophatic, in that it did not desire to lay hold of the Trinity but only to behold God as triune.

God is neither one nor three without being three in one, yet always one and always three. God transcends Hellenistic polytheistic multiplicity. God transcends monotheistic unity unrevealed. God transcends dualism that divides. Two is the number that divides; three is the number that transcends division (Gregory Nazianzen, or. XXIII.10, *MPG* XXXV.1161C, in *MTEC*, p. 47).

Oneness and multiplicity are united and embraced by Trinity, "for Godhead is neither diffused beyond These [Three], so as to introduce a mob of gods, nor yet bounded by a smaller compass than These, so as to condemn us for a poverty-stricken conception of Deity, either Judaizing to save the Monarchia, or falling into heathenism by the multitude of our gods" (Gregory Nazianzen, or. XLV.4, *Second Or. on Easter*, *NPNF* 2 VII, p. 424).

Any number other than three in one is inadequate. Yet when criticized that they were submitting God to an external criterion, namely, the idea of number, Basil replied: "For we do not count by way of addition, gradually making increase from unity to multitude, and saying one, two, and three,—nor yet first, second, and third. For 'I,' God, 'am the first, and I am the last.' And hitherto we have never, even at the present time, heard of a second God. Worshipping as we do God of God, we both confess the distinction of the persons, and at the same time abide by the Monarchy" (Basil, *On the Spirit* XVIII.45, *NPNF* 2 VIII, p. 28). The number three, when applied to the deity, does not serve as a calculation or quantity but as a referent to the divine unity, so in this case $3 = 1$.

One enters the triune mystery only through that ignorance that passes by all concepts, philosophical constructs, and categories. Having glimpsed that divine light, that holy ignorance then returns again to seek language to express itself. Such a language was that of the fourth century, which spoke of the consubstantiality of the Three, the unity of the one nature, and the distinction of the three hypostases. They availed themselves of the terms *ousia* (substance) and *hypostasis* (*persona*, or person) to bespeak the mystery of the identity of monad and triad.

The West was more likely to express the triune mystery by beginning from one essence to arrive at three persons; the East tended to begin concretely with the three hypostases and behold in them one nature. Gregory Nazianzen sought to bring the two approaches together:

When I speak of God you must be illumined at once by one flash of light and by three. Three in Individualities or Hypostases, if any prefer so to call them, or persons, for we will not quarrel about names so long as the syllables amount to the same meaning; but One in respect of the Substance—that is, the Godhead. For they are divided without division, if I may so say; and they are united in division. For the Godhead is one in three, and the three are one, in whom the Godhead is, or to speak more accurately, Who are the Godhead. Excesses and defects we will omit, neither making the Unity a confusion, nor the division a separation. We would keep equally far from the confusion of Sabellius and from the division of Arius. (Gregory Nazianzen, or. XXXIX.11, *On the Holy Lights, NPNF* 2 VII, pp. 355, 356)

The very idea of person comes from early Christian theology. The essence of personality is that it is not reducible to concepts, it cannot finally be defined or put into categories, because any person is *sui generis*. The personality of something can only be grasped by direct meeting and intuition. It cannot be derived conceptually by definition or objective description. So with the Three Divine Persons: As three suns hold together in perfect equality without separating, they give light that is mingled and joined together as one (John of Damascus, *OF* I.8, *FC* 37, pp. 182 ff.).

Father, Son, and Spirit are one in every way except that of being unbegotten, of filiation and of procession.

For the Father is without cause and unborn; for He is derived from nothing, but derives from Himself His being, nor does He derive a single quality from another. Rather He is Himself the beginning and cause of the existence of all things in a definite and natural manner. But the Son is derived from the Father after the manner of generation, and the Holy Spirit likewise is derived from the Father, yet not after the manner of generation, but after that of procession. And we have learned that there is a difference between generation and procession, but the nature of that difference we in no wise understand. (John of Damascus, *OF* I.8, *NPNF* 2 IX, p. 9)

If asked further to define the modes of generation and procession, Gregory the Theologian answered: "What is the procession of the Holy Spirit? Do you tell me first what is the Unbegottenness of the Father, and I will explain to you the physiology of the generation of the Son, and the procession of the Spirit, and we shall both of us be frenzy-stricken for prying into the mystery of God" (Gregory Nazianzen, or. XXXI.8, *On the Holy Spirit, NPNF* 2 VII, p. 320). It is sufficient to distinguish that the Son is begotten and the Spirit proceeds from the Father, following John's Gospel, and leave speculation to others.

The Triune Structure of Christian Teaching

In whatever cultural setting Christian teaching has found itself, it has recurrently organized itself around the threefold structure of the baptismal formula (Cyril of Jerusalem, *Catech. Lect.* VII–XVI, esp. XVI.4, *NPNF* 2 VII, p. 116). Whether in patristic, medieval, or Reformation periods, Christian teaching has found itself using and requiring triune language, and for good reason. If God is personally revealed, and if God wills to speak to human history in person without ceasing to be the transcendent God, then we must hypothesize a personal distinction in God between the Sender and Sent (Augustine, *On Trin.* I.11–13, *NPNF* 1 III, pp. 29–36). The incarnation requires that one hypothesize two persons: the Father who wishes to make himself known in the Son.

But if there are only Father and Son, and no Spirit, that is, nothing after the revelatory event, then the divine Word lacks divine follow-up and remains a past event without reappropriation. Suppose Jesus came and nothing else happened. Then there would be only two persons in the divine mission, and we would have a binity, not a trinity. But Jesus' mission was in fact followed by an empowering of the Spirit, acting to fulfill and consummate this mission (Ambrose, *Of the Holy Spirit* I.7–16, *NPNF* 2 X, pp. 104–16). This was not just an odd order into which Christian teaching accidentally fell. Rather, this triune hypothesis belongs intrinsically to the very idea of God's personal self-disclosure that seeks reappropriation and consummation in history.

The *Epistula Apostolorum* (c. 150), one of the earliest creedal summaries, confessed its faith

> In the Father, the Ruler of the Universe,
> And in Jesus Christ, our Redeemer,
> In the Holy Spirit, the Paraclete, in the Holy Church and the Forgiveness of Sins. (CC 17)

It is not some historical fluke or accident that the Apostles' Creed has three articles: God the Father Almighty, God revealed in the Son, and God the Spirit currently present in the church manifesting the power of the resurrection (cf. Interrogatory Creed of Hippolytus, CC, p. 23). Early Christian theology developed in order to explain concisely to the believer the meaning of his or her baptism. From the beginning the apostolic tradition has been baptizing in the name of the Father, the Son, and the Holy Spirit. Christian theology has always been essentially a reasoning toward, from, about, and for baptism, a summary explanation of the meaning of the baptismal celebration of entry into this community (*Seven Ecumenical Councils*, *NPNF* 2 XIV, pp. 3, 163 ff., 225, 262 ff.).

In both covenants of the Bible, God is made known through his word. In the prophets, this word is speech. In the New Testament, this word becomes flesh in a person, and therefore is personalized as Son of the Father. God's Spirit accompanies this revelation at every step in both Old and New Testaments (Ambrose, *On the Holy Spirit* II.5–13, *NPNF* 2 X, pp. 118–35). God the Father, made known in Jesus Christ his Son, is present to us in the fullness of the Spirit (John 17; Luke 4:18). Nothing less than God's own forgiveness is implied in Jesus' acts of forgiveness (Mark 2:1 ff.), an assertion that elicited intense opposition from Pharisees (Tertullian, *On Baptism* X, *ANF* III, p. 674; *On Modesty* XXI, *ANF* IV, p. 98). The Son is born into the world, suffers, and is crucified, buried, and raised. The Spirit continues and shares that same ministry, God's own ministry to the human condition (Hilary, *Trin.* II.29–35, *NPNF* 2, IX, pp. 60, 61).

Note carefully the coherent logic of a traditional diagram (see figure below) found in medieval symbolism.

This diagram is taken from W. J. and G. Audsley, *Handbook of Christian Symbolism* (London: Day and Son, 1865), plate III, p. 50.

This "shield of the Holy Trinity" teaches that the Father (P = *Pater*) is not (*non est*) the Son (F = *Filius*), the Son is not the Holy Spirit (SS = *Spiritus Sanctus*), and the Holy Spirit is not the Father. The Father is distinguishable from the Son, the Son is distinguishable from the Holy Spirit; and the Holy Spirit is distinguishable from the Father. However the Father is God (*est Deus*), nothing less, and the Son is God, nothing less, and the Holy Spirit is God, nothing less, and God is essentially one (*una substantia, ousia*; W. J. and G. Audsley, *Handbook of Christian Symbolism*, p. 50; cf. Tho. Aq., *ST* I Q31, I, pp. 164 ff.; M. D. Wyatt, *Geometrical Mosaics of the Middle Ages*; J. Strozygowski, *Origins of Chr. Church Art*).

This picture grasps the essential logic of triune teaching that avoids tri-theism, the heterodox view that Christians worship three Gods. God's unity is affirmed in three persons. God is *una substantia*, one substance, which means that God remains essentially one while becoming known in *tres persona*, three persons (Augustine, *On Trin.* VII.4–6, *NPNF* 1 III, pp. 109–14). The Father is God, the Son is God, the Spirit is God.

The Struggle for Clearer Definition

Some thought that Jesus was not God; others, that Jesus, being God, was not fully human. The Ebionitic view inordinately stressed the humanity of Jesus divinely adopted at his baptism; the Docetic view mistakenly thought of Jesus as not fully human but as too divine ever to become flesh. Thus the ecumenical consensus had to attempt to correct both of those mistaken alternatives by speaking of Jesus as truly God, truly human, *vere Deus, vere homo* (Council of Chalcedon, *NPNF* 2 XIV, p. 262), following Johannine and Pauline understandings of Christ (to be discussed fully later). Those who said that Jesus is either not truly God or not truly human did not have in mind the Jesus remembered in the New Testament.

Jesus did not elevate himself from ordinary humanity to divinity by obedience and devotion. Rather, the early church remembered Jesus as God's own Word from the beginning of all things, the divine Son beloved of the divine Father who so loved the world that he gave his Son—that which to the Father was most valued, his only begotten Son (John 3). God by his own volition was willing to enter the world and live in our midst. God's own Spirit, with God from the beginning, was to accompany Jesus' ministry and ensure its fulfillment (Council of Nicaea, *NPNF* 2 XIV, pp. 3 ff.).

To pray to Father, Son, and Spirit is quite different that to philosophize, which is about ideas. That God is willing to experience concretely our human alienations, sorrows, suffering, and death is quite different from philosophical concepts of transcendence and immanence. Hence philosophical idealisms from Plotinus to Hegel have stood somewhat aghast or dumbstruck by the triune mystery, even though often intrigued by it, while at times attempting to include it within their "systems" (Hegel, *Phenomenology of Mind*; cf. Kierkegaard, *Concl. Unsci. Post.*).

The philosopher's ideas may interest us, but faith in the triune God requires response to the One who enters our human sphere of finitude and suffering. Rational morality and natural theology may speak of the human capacity to know and do the good, but Christian proclamation trusts and prays to the eternal One who knows what it means to be betrayed and unjustly condemned, to suffer, to be crucified, and to die.

The fundament of the Trinity has to do with this enlivening experience of God's fully personal presence in the midst of the worshiping community. The faithful are living in Christ, sharing in his resurrection, praying to the Father through the Son. The Spirit is eliciting and sustaining their understanding of what happened in Jesus' resurrection (Heb. 1–3; 1 Pet. 1; 1 John 4, 5; Council of Ephesus, *NPNF* 2 XIV, pp. 202 f.).

By analogy, these pages are made up only of words, not life blood. There is a sense in which these words cannot be separated from me, the author—who I am, my experience, my struggle, my own attempt to understand. If the reader could have seen me while these pages were in preparation, what would have been visible? Picture me at my desk as I write. You would have seen these ideas only in a hidden form as I struggled with them, trying to probe the texts and sort out my own understanding. All you would have seen outwardly was me in my study, sweating, wiping my brow, writing, sighing. That preparation led up to this moment when you are reading these pages long in preparation. The lengthy period of reflection was required to lead up to the printed page, which you read quickly, in order that my language should become better formed and so that I could try to communicate the sense in which God as three is one. But my word to you in this paragraph only became manifested to you at the instant you started reading this paragraph. Ten minutes ago this paragraph did not exist for you. Before I reached you through this book, my word to you was at best latent or hidden, or more probably, so far as you were concerned, nonexistent. Only through this book that you now hold in your hands did my word to you become hearably spoken.

By analogy, God's Word spoken in history is something like a word spoken in a book, although obviously different. Both are spoken quickly in a moment, even though long in preparation (cf. Eusebius, *Preparation for the Gospel* I.1–7, I, pp. 1–19; Stephen Niell, *WCB* I, pp. 16 ff.). Any heard word is to some degree like revelation, like the Son, revealed at one time but long awaiting the fulfilled time. I am, in a sense, father to the book; the book is my word, and my spirit reaches out to the reader for understanding. God's own communication of himself to us in Jesus through the Spirit is something like that. The communication process itself implies a rudimentary triune structure: the idea in preparation, the word addressed concretely in a moment, and the appropriation of that word in the life and mind of the hearer.

The purpose of these pages is to bring you within range of hearing what classical triune teaching says of God. My intention is that you hear this word and bring it into some kind of living understanding that makes sense to you, so that you can integrate it into your existence. There is a spirit at work in the communication process in which one seeks to share an idea with another. What was hidden becomes revealed, and what is revealed is for the purpose of active embodiment. Yet the communication has a single purpose, and the threefold process is one (Augustine, *Trin.* IV.preface, 1, 2, *NPNF* 1 III, pp. 69–71).

The obvious limit of the analogy is that I am not on a cross dying for you. In these pages, I am not risking my life—only some sweat. God's Word is spoken through a cross, lived through a death.

The Triune Mystery and the Limits of Language

Intransigent problems remain in referring to the triune mystery with ordinary personal pronouns. In an era in which the worshiping community is struggling toward greater fairness, many wish that orthodox Christian faith had not become locked into speaking only in masculine terms of God, the Father, the Son, and the Holy Spirit. I have tried to speak at times of the Trinity as God the Parent, God the Child, and God the Spirit of love, but this tends to ignore the Father-Son relationship so deeply embedded in the New Testament. Yet it is a sincere, even if inadequate, attempt to break through to a more inclusive view of the triune God. More intriguing is the fact that the Hebrew root of *Spirit* is feminine. In neither Hebrew nor Greek is *spirit* masculine. In the Hebrew (*rûach*) Spirit is feminine, and in Greek (*pneuma*) it is neuter. That gives some linguistic warrant, at least, to speak of the third person in the Holy Trinity using feminine pronouns.

I do not necessarily promote this specific path, but more generally a use of language that does not imply unfairness in God.

Regardless of the pronouns or symbols we employ, the church in speaking of the triune God has always known itself to be pointing to an enigma—the mystery of God's presence, God hidden and God revealed, the way in which God works in our midst. We cannot fully articulate the presence we know; we cannot fully comprehend, although we can apprehend.

Imagine a scale with at the bottom, no life, then, ascending on the scale, organic life moving from plants toward lower animals, invertebrates, then vertebrates, and, finally, human existence. It is a scale of increasing complexity of intelligence, from life without motion to life with motion, then life with motion and intelligence, and then finally, in human beings, life, motion, intelligence, and spirit. At each of those levels of consciousness, one can talk about some form of communication with the other levels, for there are many points of contact.

In the communication between vastly different spheres of being, the higher form is always more encompassing than the lower form. We know more about our goldfish that they do about us. The family dog or cat knows more about how a family member feels than does the tomato plant. But how explicitly or accurately does that animal grasp or understand how one really thinks or what one specifically wishes to say? There is knowledge, but it is radically limited. So is ours of the triune God. There is a sense in which the dog cannot ever truly grasp the complexities of human language and consciousness, although the dog certainly can be directly and meaningfully in touch with human language and consciousness and can respond meaningfully to what it knows. It cannot comprehend, but it can apprehend many meanings in human speech (S. Neill, *WCB* I).

There is a crucial principle at work in the process of communication between these spheres. The higher form always remains in some ways *mysterious* to the lower form. By analogy, the triune One who creates us, who works in our midst, who reveals himself to us and who calls us to respond—that One is very much present in our consciousness, and yet we cannot fully explain how. Triune language is our frail, but necessary, way of pointing to that One (Ambrose, *Of Chr. Faith* IV.X.92, *NPNF* 2 X, p. 274). Augustine concluded that the reason we talk about trinity at all is not because we *can* say something adequately about it, but rather because, in the absence of adequate speech, we *must* say something.

Part III

THE WORK OF GOD

CHAPTER 6

God the Creator and Creation

It is inevitable that the truth about ultimate origins, which lies beyond direct human experience, will remain a mystery (Basil, *Hex.* I, *NPNF* 2 VIII, pp. 52 ff.; Calvin, *Inst.* 1.14). What is known of creation is only partially understood through reason, but known more fully through the Creator's self-disclosure through the revealed Word (Justin Martyr, *First Apol.* XIII, *FEF* I, p. 52; Athanasius, *On the Incarnation of the Word* II, *NPNF* 2 IV, pp. 37 ff.). Christian faith in God the Creator relies primarily on Scripture's attestation of divine revelation, but partial witness to the truth of revelation may occur through scientific investigation and rational inquiry (Augustine, *On Catech. of Uninstructed* XVIII, *NPNF* 1 III, pp. 302 f.).

The universal church has always believed that the one true God made all things (Irenaeus, *Ag. Her.* II.9.1, 2, *ANF* I, p. 369). God is the ungenerate, original cause of the coming to be, continuance, and destiny of all creatures (*Letter to Diognetus* 7.2; Tho. Aq., *ST* I Q44, I, pp. 229–32; Westminster Conf. IV, *CC*, pp. 199 ff.). The making of the world by God is an article of Christian faith (Tho. Aq., *ST* I Q46, I, p. 242).

The created order was made out of nothing (*ex nihilo*), without preexisting materials (Irenaeus, *Ag. Her.* II.10, 11, *ANF* I, pp. 369 ff.; Augustine, *Conf.* XII.7; Dordrecht Conf. I, *CC*, pp. 292 ff.). This counteracts the pantheistic implication that matter is eternal, as well as the dualistic implication that another kind of power stands eternally over against God. Yet humanity is not made "out of nothing" but out of "the dust of the ground" (Gen. 2:19), as wild animals and birds were "formed out of the ground" by God (Gen. 2:19). There is no other source of creation than the will of God (Heb. 11:3; Calvin, *Inst.* 2.2.20).

The world was not created coeternal with God (Augustine, *CG* XI.4, 5, *NPNF* 1 II, pp. 206 ff.; *Conf.* XI.14). The world was not put together out of pieces of God (Augustine, *Conf.* XI.5, XII.7). The creation is only of God, and only God could create the world (Shepherd of Hermas, *Mandate* I.1, *FEF* I, p. 34). Cosmic creation is a work peculiar to God (Athanasius, *Four Discourses Ag. Arians* II.16, *NPNF* 2 IV, pp. 357–61).

Time did not always exist. The world was created *with* time (Augustine, *CG* XI.6, *NPNF* 1 II, pp. 208 ff.). Space and time came into being only with creation, not prior to it. Although contemplation of the creation of time and space is filled with enigma, the created order is thought to be intrinsically intelligible (Theophilus, *To Autolycus* I.4–5, *ANF* II, p. 90; John of Damascus, *OF* II.3, *NPNF* 2 IX, p. 19).

The Energy of Divine Activity

Creation and providence are pivotal teachings of Christianity (Basel Conf. I, *HPC*, pp. 53 f.) profoundly shared with Judaism and, to some degree, with other monotheistic faiths. Providence, the care of God over all things, will be discussed in the next chapter.

Clarity about creation must be sought prior to entering into some of the thornier issues of the study of God (Chemnitz, *LT*, I, pp. 112 ff.; Heppe, *RD*, pp. 190 ff.). Subsequently we will ask: Does God's providence deny human freedom? Does evil negate divine goodness? If sin is socially caused, how is the individual responsible? To prepare correctly for these vexing questions, we must seek greater clarity about the context in which they are raised: the created order. To omit this theme would be like building a house without a foundation or starting a symphony without a first note.

The activity of God (sometimes called *opera dei*, the work, energy, or workings of God), as distinguished from the being of God, is now of central interest. For Christian teaching asks not only about who God *is*, but what God *does*—how God's power, mercy, and patience are manifested in creative, preservative, redemptive, and completing activities (Gregory of Nyssa, *Great Catech.* XII, *NPNF* 2 V, p. 486; Calvin, *Inst.* 2.3–5).

Hence Christian teaching does not deal merely with "God in himself" as if God could be viewed abstractly apart from God's works or historical activity. God is known through what God does. God's essence is beheld only indirectly through the outworking of God's energies, the working (*energeia*) of God in and through creatures (John Chrysostom, *Concerning the Statues*, hom. X.8, 9, *NPNF* 1 IX, pp. 410, 411;

Gregory of Nyssa, *On the Holy Trin. NPNF* 2 V, pp. 326–30, *Answer to Eunomius*, sec. bk., *NPNF* 2 V, pp. 287 ff.; cf. Irenaeus, *Ag. Her.* IV.20, *ANF* I, pp. 487–92).

These works of God are stated in summary form under three great headings: *creation, redemption,* and *sanctification* (Luther, *Small Catech.*; Anglican Catech., *COC* III). These three terms intend to summarize the whole range of activities of the triune God. These three activities of God correspond generally to the three persons of the Trinity, and find their unity in the one triune God. The existential effects of creation, redemption, and sanctification are subjectively experienced by the faithful as gracious in three ways: (1) finite creatures are radically dependent for their existence upon Another (i.e., One who wholly transcends all things, God the Father); (2) when human creation falls into sin it is lifted up by Another (i.e., help comes from afar, from a distant Other who comes close, to Son born of woman); and (3) when human freedom seeks to respond to the mercy and love of God it is assisted by Another (God's own Spirit). Accordingly, the one God— Creator, Redeemer, and Sanctifier—is none other than the One God— the Father, Son, and Spirit.

In Part Two we sought to establish *that* God *is*, and is triune. In Part Three we now seek greater clarity about *what* the triune God *does* (Lactantius, *Div. Inst.* I.2, *ANF* VII, p. 11; cf. John Chrysostom, *Concerning the Statues*, hom. V–VII, *NPNF* 1 IX, pp. 371–95; cf. Calvin, *Inst.* 2.3, 4; Chemnitz, *LT* I, pp. 112 ff.).

The first of all God's good acts is the creation of the world. How could it be otherwise, for how can anything be good unless it first had existence? Chronologically and logically, creation is the proper starting point of any talk of the historical activity of God, for history begins with creation.

If theology is to speak of the God of history, there must be a stage on which history is played out. There is a redemptive intent from the beginning in creation, so there is a subtle sense in which God's redemptive purpose is prior to God's creative purpose (1 Cor. 2:7; 2 Tim. 1:9; Titus 1:2; Rev. 13:8; John 1:1–20; Eph. 1:5–11; Barth, *CD* 2/ 2). But there is a less subtle sense in which creation is prior to redemption, for how could one have something to redeem if that something did not exist?

Hence Theophilus of Antioch, having spoken of the nature and existence of God (*To Autolycus* I, *ANF* II, pp. 88–93), then turned immediately to discuss the works of God in creation and providence (II.1–21, *ANF* II, pp. 94–102). Similarly, having discussed the triune

God in his Catechetical lecture (*On Creation*, lect. IX, *NPNF* 2 VII, pp. 51–56), Cyril then proceeded to detailed lectures on Christ (pp. 57 ff.), following the order of the Creed yet never assuming that creation and Christ are separable themes. Thus also Thomas's treatise on creation (*ST* I Q44 ff., I, pp. 229–319) precedes his treatises on divine governance (*ST* I Q103–19, I, pp. 505–82), and incarnation (*ST* II–III Q1 ff., II, pp. 2025 ff.). Calvin's doctrines of creation (*Inst.* 1.13–15) and providence (*Inst.* 1.16–18) precede his full exploration of Christology (*Inst.* 2.1 ff.), never imagining, however, that it would be right or possible to discuss creation or providence without Jesus Christ. Thus, in considering creation prior to our full discussion of Christology (in the next volume), we do not imply that creation is separable from Christ, for as we will show, creation is the work of the triune God—Christ and the Holy Spirit, as well as the Father, all working in perfect union.

The Living God and the Gift of Life

One cannot speak of the Creator without also mentioning the next most important aspect of the subject—the creatures (inanimate and animate, material and spiritual) whom God thought it important enough to create (Gregory of Nyssa, *Great Catech.* V, VI, *NPNF* 2 V, pp. 478–80). Accordingly, Christian teaching about creation includes our interpersonal and personal responses to the creaturely gifts we are given, none of which is more fundamental or stunning than the extraordinary gift of simply being given anything at all, the unpurchasable gift of living.

Some complain it is unfair that living creatures were never once consulted first about whether they wanted to be alive. Consider the structural inconsistency underlying the complaint. For one to have been consulted first about whether one wanted to live, one would have had already to *be*, that is, to have life of some kind. That would still leave unattended the question of how the one being consulted got there. The conclusion holds: Life is radically *given* to us prior to any choice of our own. No creature who has ever lived has earned it. According to Heidegger's somewhat harsh and thankless image, we are "thrown" into existence (*Being and Time* V.32 ff., VI.41, pp. 188 ff., 235 ff.). What we call human freedom can only be conceived after life is given and a slow process of development has occurred.

The gift of *life* preconditions all other gifts. Nothing can experience, receive, or elicit a good without first having life. Even if something "good" were to happen to a stone, it could not recognize or receive it

because it is not alive (at least in any recognizable sense). The inexorable rule is this: Nothing lives without having first being *given* life
unmerited. No creature got here by choosing to be alive (Basil, *Hex.*
IX, *NPNF* 2 VIII, pp. 101–7; Calvin, *Inst.* 3.9.3). The inanimate cannot
choose to be animate. The nonexistent cannot choose existence Any
creature that is sufficiently alive to be aware of life has already received
creation's most extraordinary gift—life itself (Tho. Aq., *ST* I Q18, I,
pp. 100, 101; Luther, *Smaller Catech.* I, *CC*, pp. 115 f.; cf. Kazantzakis,
Saviors of God). An invaluable gift calls for an unreserved, grateful,
active response (Catherine of Genoa, *Spiritual Dialogue, CWS*, pp. 132,
133).

Christians who follow current physics may feel some gratification
in hearing of the probable validation of the "big bang" theory over
against the "steady state" theory, which appears to provide some
scientific validation of creation out of nothing (*ex nihilo*), as opposed
to views of the eternality of matter. However, this "bang" could be one
of many, perhaps an infinite series, according to big bang advocates.
In any event, the Christian doctrine of creation is not focused primarily upon scientific description of what happened perhaps thirty thousands of millions of years ago. Christian faith in creation is compatible
with accurate scientific description, but not identical. For the bang
echoes through time to the eventful now. Creation also has to do with
the here-and-now responses of created beings, the answering of creatures to the daily, nightly speech of their Creator (Ps. 19:1–4)—and
the way we accept or despair over this gift (Kierkegaard, *Sickness unto
Death* I.1.C, pp. 150 ff.; *The Gospel of Suffering, The Glory of Our Common
Humanity*, pp. 199 ff.).

Biblical Views of God the Creator

Scripture speaks often of God's creation, not only "in the beginning," but throughout the story of salvation. Creation theology is not
just found in Genesis then quickly forgotten through the rest of the
Bible. The creation teaching is widely diffused throughout the Scripture in the psalms, the Prophets, the synoptic Gospels and letters
(Tertullian, *Ag. Hermogenes* XXIII–XXXVI, *ANF* III, pp. 495–97; Basil,
Hex. II–VI, *NPNF* 2 VIII, pp. 58 ff.). Although Genesis is the most
quoted and prototypical reference, the classical exegetes have often
turned for wisdom about creation to other powerful scriptural affirmations of God's creating will, such as Isaiah 40, Amos 4:13, Psalms
90 and 104, Jeremiah 10, John 1, Acts 17, and Colossians 1 (cf. also

Job 26:7–14; 38:4–11; Pss. 33:6–9; 102:25; Isa. 45:5 ff.; 45:18; Neh. 9:6; Rom. 1:20 ff.; 9:20; Heb. 1:2; 11:3; Rev. 4:11; 10:6). Our proper starting point, however, is where the Bible begins: Genesis 1 and 2.

Genesis

According to many scholars, the earlier of the two creation narratives in Genesis is the second, usually referred to as the Yahwist account since the author's preferred name for God is Yahweh (Gen. 2:4 ff.). It is more concerned with the creation of human beings, man and woman, and their dominion and destiny from the beginning, including the account of the fall and the alienation of human freedom (Tertullian, *Ag. Marcion* II.1–17, *ANF* III, pp. 297–311; Augustine, *CG* XIII.12 ff., *NPNF* 1 II, pp. 250 ff.).

In the Yahwist account there is from the beginning an acknowledgment of human freedom as a gift accountable to God and of human sexual differentiation as a divine gift, assuming that however different female and male may be, they are equally given life, freedom, and sexual generation because God wills to bless them through these (Gen. 1:27). Always easily distortable, human freedom and sexuality are a crucial part of God's good creation and intention, intended for generativity, productivity, dominion, and stewardship of the earth (John Chrysostom, *Hom. on Ephesians* XX, *NPNF* 1 XIII, pp. 143–52).

The Genesis narratives, taken together, express much of the heart of the Jewish and Christian teaching on creation: that we are given life by one who is wise and free, who creates us for our good and whose goodness is displayed throughout the creation. They constitute a decisive rejection of all dualisms, pantheisms, and polytheisms. There are never assumed to be two or more gods at work in creation. Under the category of true God there can be only one (Irenaeus, *Ag. Her.* II.2.1–5, *ANF* I, pp. 361, 362; Cyril of Jerusalem, *Catech. Lect.* VI, *NPNF* 2 VII, pp. 33–43). The Yahwist themes will be treated more fully later under the Christian teaching about human existence. Our present concern is more with the priestly account of the orderly creation of the world, light, life, and nature (Gen. 1:1–2:4a).

The priestly prologue, Genesis 1:1–2:4, serves as a kind of all-embracing introduction to the history of salvation. It is the Bible's way of beginning the best of all stories. It begins by constructing the stage on which covenant history is to be played. Even though that covenant is broken, God in due time heals that brokenness and calls humanity back to covenant relationship, redeeming creation after it falls. The creation narrative sets the scene and provides the context in which

God's purpose is to be worked out in history (Origen, *Ag. Celsus* VI.50–70, *ANF* IV, pp. 596–605).

Creation is not, according to the Hebraic tradition, primarily objective, descriptive scientific talk of how nature evolves or emerges, as if this were merely a matter of accurate observation, or as if the fate-laden historical choices of previous humans did not make much real difference to the destiny of the beholder (John Chrysostom, *Concerning the Statues*, hom. VII, *NPNF* 1 IX, pp. 390–95). Rather, the scriptural witness to creation is from the first line more like a drama, the beginning of the acts of God, the first of many mighty deeds, upon which hinges both life's current meaning and the eternal destinies of participants.

The drama is all about a relationship. It is the thorny, conflicted, seductive, unpredictable unfolding epic of a covenant relationship between Yahweh and Adam, Yahweh and Abraham, Yahweh and Israel, Yahweh and humanity. The real story concerning creation is about the creature/Creator relationship, not about creatures as such as if creation were to be considered an autonomous, independent, underived value in itself (Irenaeus, *Ag. Her.* II.10.1–4, *ANF* I, pp. 369, 370).

The Bible does not rule out scientific cosmologies and other ways of understanding the primitive history of the world. The natural emergence of the cosmic, geological, vegetative, and animal spheres can remain a matter of scientific investigation. The creation narratives do not pretend to describe in empirical detail, objectively, descriptively, or unmetaphorically, the way in which the world came into being; rather, they declare the awesome primordial fact that the world is radically dependent on the generosity, wisdom, and help of God, the insurmountably good and powerful One (Dionysius, *Div. Names* VIII.7–9, pp. 158–61; Tho. Aq., *ST* I Q44–46, I, pp. 229 ff.).

The world is not God. Being finite, the creation itself is not eternal. It lies within the cosmic parenthesis between the beginning and end of all things. The whole world and everything in the world owes its being to the free, sovereign act of God (Tho. Aq., *Compend.*, p. 96). God created the world by a word. God speaks—as simple as that—and there it is.

The world is not a divine emanation. Emanation would mean that the world gradually seeps or leaks out (*e*, out, *manare*, flow) of the edges of the being of God, according to the analogy of fragrance emanating from flowers. Theories of emanation have been consistently rejected by Jewish and Christian teachers because they fail to make a sharp distinction between God and the world. God is not the world (Hippolytus, *Refutation of All Her.* X, *ANF* V, pp. 140–53).

God minus the world is still God. If God should turn out to be indistinguishably merged with the world, Christian teaching would become another pantheism, which reduces God to the world, collapses God and the world into one continuous amalgam. Only when God is unmistakably distinguishable from the world, the Uncreated from the created, can we have theism in its Jewish and Christian sense (Tertullian, *Ag. Hermogenes* XVII–XXXI, *ANF* III, pp. 486–94; cf. Tho. Aq., *ST* I Q45, I, pp. 232 ff.; Calovius, *SLT* III, p. 899).

The Days of Creation: Hexaemeron

The word *day* (*yōm*) has several levels of meaning. It is used in biblical Hebrew to mean not only a twenty-four-hour day but also a time of divine visitation or judgment, or an indefinite period of time, as in Psalms 110:5, Isaiah 2:11, 12, and Jeremiah 11:4–7; 17:16 ff. To insist on a twenty-four-hour day as the word's only meaning is to intrude upon the text and to disallow the poetic, metaphorical, and symbolic speech of Scripture (Pss. 2:7; 18:18; Isa. 4:1, 2; Jer. 44:1–23).

Classical exegesis of Genesis 1 focused upon the threefold divine act of (1) creating, (2) ordering (distinguishing), and (3) adorning the world. Numerous classical exegetes have written detailed treatises on the making, distinctions, and adornments done by God in the six days (*hexaemeron*) of divine creativity (Theophilus of Antioch, *To Autolycus* II.11–18, *ANF* II, pp. 98–101; cf. Basil, *Hex.*; John Chrysostom, *Hom. on Genesis*; Ambrose, *Hex.*; Augustine, *Literal Interp. of Gen.*; Dionysius, *Div. Names*; John of Damascus, *OF*; Bede, *Hex.*; and Tho. Aq., *ST* I Q66–74).

The creative activity of God is viewed in a pattern of six "days," or periods, each introduced by the words "And God said" (Augustine, *Literal Interp. of Gen.* I.8). The first chapter of Genesis has often been the basis of extended theological meditations on the acts of God the creator, orderer, and beautifier, following this pattern:

FIRST DAY

(v. 3): Light, with night following day is created (Theophilus, *To Autolycus* II.11–13, *ANF* II, pp. 98–100; Basil, *Hex.* I, II, *NPNF* 2 VIII, pp. 52–65). This is the first of three days of the work of distinction or divine differentiation of creatures (Tho. Aq., *ST* I Q67, I, pp. 334–37). It is fitting and necessary that the production of light occur on the first day, since "that without which there could not be day, must have been made on the first day" (Tho. Aq., *ST* I Q67, I, p. 336).

SECOND DAY

(Gen. 1:6): The vault of heaven, waters below to form the sea and waters above to form the rain, and the firmament are created (Theophilus, *To Autolycus* II.14, *ANF* II, p. 100; Basil, *Hex.* III, pp. 65–71; Tho. Aq., *ST* I Q68, I, pp. 338–42). Although heaven is spoken of in the singular, as in "Praise the Lord out of heaven" (Ps. 148:1), it is also spoken of in the plural, "praise him, heaven of heavens" (v. 4). A multitude of refined distinctions arose among classical Christian writers seeking to understand the witness of Scripture concerning the creation of many heavens. This summary of Thomas Aquinas brings together concisely the essence of many such speculations:

Scripture speaks of heaven in a threefold sense. Sometimes it uses the word in its proper and natural meaning, when it denotes that body on high which is luminous actually or potentially, and incorruptible by nature. In this body there are three heavens; the first is the empyrean, which is wholly luminous; the second is the aqueous or crystalline, wholly transparent, and the third is called the starry heaven, in part transparent, and in part actually luminous, and divided into eight spheres. One of these is the sphere of the fixed stars; the other seven, which may be called the seven heavens, are the spheres of the planets. (Tho. Aq., *ST* I Q69, I, p. 342)

THIRD DAY

(vv. 9–10; v. 11 ff.): Seas, the lands, and plant life, yielding fresh growth and bearing seed, are all created (Basil, *Hex.* IV, *NPNF* 2 VIII, pp. 72–76; Tho. Aq., *ST* I Q69, I, pp. 342–45). The classical writers intuited with remarkable acuity the order of emergent life later to be known more clearly from scientific observation. The precious gift of life first appeared in plants, but remained "hidden, since they lack sense and local movement," and therefore "their production is treated as a part of the earth's formation" (Tho. Aq., *ST* I Q70, I, p. 345).

FOURTH DAY

(Gen. 1:14): Luminaries, sun, moon, stars, giving light, governing night and day (Theophilus, *To Autolycus* II.15, 16, *ANF* II, pp. 100, 101; Basil, *Hex.* VI, *NPNF* 2 VIII, pp. 81–89)—the first of three days of the work of the adornment of creation (Tho. Aq., *ST* I Q70, I, pp. 345–49). "The sun, the moon and the stars—all the heaven array" are not to be worshiped, but they have been "apportioned to all the nations under heaven" (Deut. 4:19). They render a threefold service to all humanity: for *light* to see by; for the changes of the *seasons*, "which prevent weariness, preserve health, and provide for the necessities of food"; and for *weather*, fair or foul, "as favorable to various occupations" (Tho. Aq., *ST* I Q70, I, p. 347). It is for these varied purposes that the lights are said to "serve as signs both for festivals and for seasons and years" (Gen. 1:14; Tertullian, *Ag. Marcion* V.6, *ANF* III, p. 440).

FIFTH DAY

(v. 29): Countless living creatures of the water (fish) and air (birds) (cf. Theophilus, *To Autolycus* II.16, *ANF* II, p. 101; Basil, *Hex.* VII, *NPNF* 2 VIII, pp. 89–101; Tho. Aq., *ST* I Q71, I, pp. 350 f.). Water is adorned with fish, and air adorned with birds. In the Genesis account we behold the creation of "different grades of life" from the life of plants, which vegetate, to the life of great and small "living creatures that live and move in the waters," to "every kind of bird" (Gen. 1:21), to the life of land animals that are more complex, having "living souls with bodies subject to them," so that by this means "the more perfect is reached through the less perfect," in a food chain by which higher life forms feed off the lower (Tho. Aq., *ST* I Q73, I, pp. 351, 352) in an amazingly intricate and beautiful creation that is well fitted for many evidences of providential care.

SIXTH DAY

(vv. 24 ff.): More complexly sensate living creatures appear, each "according to their kind: cattle, reptiles, and wild animals," and finally humanity, male and female (Theophilus, *To Autolycus* II.17, 18, *ANF* II, pp. 101 f.; Basil, *Hex.* IX, *NPNF* 2 VIII, pp. 101–7; Tho. Aq., *ST* I Q72, I pp. 351–52). Humanity, as finitely free, is both very like and very unlike the animals, since grounded in nature yet capable of freedom, self-transcendence, and consciousness, as in the divine image. Humanity is *unlike* plants and animals, which "may be said to be produced according to their kinds, to signify their remoteness from the Divine image and likeness, whereas man is said to be made 'to the image and likeness of God.'" Yet humanity is *like* the various animals in that all receive the blessing God gives by "the power to multiply by generation." The same blessing of sexual generativity given to animal life is distinctly repeated in the case of humanity "to prevent anyone from saying that there was any sin whatever in the act of begetting children" (Tho. Aq., *ST* I, Q73, I, p. 352). Hence human life is viewed as a paradoxical, potentially disjunctive, interfacing of nature and transcendence, of finitude and freedom, of animal-like passions and likeness to God, of sexuality and fidelity. Adam and Eve are misunderstood if the tension is lost in this complex interfacing that the ancient Christian writers called *compositum*.

SEVENTH DAY

Divine rest. God "blessed the seventh day and made it holy, because on that day he ceased from all the work he had set himself to do" (Gen. 2:2, 3). "Nothing entirely new was afterwards made by God" (Tho. Aq., *ST* I Q74, I, p. 353). The seventh day is said to be sanctified "because something is added to creatures by their multiplying and by their resting in God" (p. 355).

Let us review the sequence: The first three periods prepare the world for the next three periods, in which living inhabitants are set in a well-prepared place and provided a rhythm of life. There are living beings for each of the four elemental regions of *air* (birds), *earth* (plants, animals, humanity), *water* (fish), and *fire*(the sun is needed for the warmth and illumination of all). The seventh day is for rejoicing over the goodness of the former six, providing a pattern for human life: working six days and resting on the seventh.

In this way the work of God the Creator is beheld in its intrinsic moral and spiritual intelligibility as a complete act of *creation* in which heaven and earth were produced, yet without form; a work of *distinction*, in which heaven and earth were given order and beauty; and a work of *adornment* in which, just as our bodies are adorned with clothing, so God adorns the world with the production of things that move in heaven and on earth. All the elements for life—air, earth, fire, and water—receive their form through the work of distinction (Tho. Aq., *ST* I Q70, I, p. 346). The classical exegetes marveled at the beautiful symmetry and completeness of this biblical account: of the six days, the first three are for the work of distinction, the second three for the work of adornment, and the last for divine Sabbath. The work of distinction is divided into heaven, water, and earth.

The first part, then, is distinguished on the first day, and adorned on the fourth, the middle part distinguished on the middle day, and adorned on the fifth, and the third part distinguished on the third day, and adorned on the sixth. . . . Thus, then the perfection of the Divine works corresponds to the perfection of the number six, which is the sum of its aliquot parts, one, two, three; since one day is assigned to the forming of spiritual creatures, two to that of corporeal creatures, and three to the work of adornment. (Tho. Aq., *ST* I Q74, I, p. 355)

It is fitting that such a perfectly wrought order should be duly celebrated on the seventh day.

Let It Be

The Genesis narrative is written in a recurrent permissive form: "Let there be" (vv. 3, 6, 14, 15, 20, 24). The created order springs directly from the word of God, the simple divine address: "God said" (vv. 3, 6, 9, 11, 14, 20, 24, 26). It is produced, ordered and approved— all by God's speech. The command is: "Let it be." And it is. God said, in effect, "I permit creation" (or nonwords to that effect), and it was there. One gets the impression that it was easy for almighty God to create the world. "There is nothing too hard for thee," declared Jeremiah (32:17, KJV). God does not have to strain to create the world. God does not have to go through any particular difficulties. It is simply there because God spoke.

Creation is viewed as a divine language that only God can speak (Tho. Aq., *GC*, p. 260). It is ordered at once by the divine will and just as quickly received and approved. The permission, command, production, ordering, receiving, and approval are all set forth in the first chapter of Genesis (Tertullian, *Ag. Praxeas* XII, *ANF* III, p. 607). God's approbation of the goodness of creation builds majestically from good, to more good, to "very good" (Gen. 1:4, 10, 14, 21, 31; cf. Wesley, *WJW* VI, pp. 206–15).

God brings forth out of nothing, according to his sovereign will, the visible universe and the invisible or spiritual sphere. Creation is entirely an act of divine freedom (Augustine, *CG* XI.24, *NPNF* 1 II, pp. 219 ff.). Angels too are creatures, not coeternal with God. There is no eternal body of uncreated matter that existed before God.

If the world is created simply by God's permitting a big bang, merely speaking the explosive divine Word, then does that make it impossible to speak of any natural cause of the universe? Rather than rule out natural causality, classical writers have wished to distinguish various levels of causality operative in the world (after Thomas Aquinas often depending to some degree on Aristotelian categories: original, final, formal, and efficient levels of causality; cf. Tho. Aq., *ST* I Q104, I, pp. 511 ff.). Accordingly, God can be first and final cause and still allow other causes to be present in the universe. "Creation is the proper act of God alone" (Tho. Aq., *ST* I Q45, I, p. 235; cf.

Athanasius, *Four Discourses Ag. Arians* II, XVI.20, 21, *NPNF* 2 IV, p. 359), yet that does not imply that God is powerless to communicate the power of creating to others. For "God can communicate to a creature the power of creating, so that the latter can create minister-ially, not by its own power" (Tho. Aq., *ST* I Q45, I, p. 235; cf. P. Lombard, *Sentences*, IV.5). Hence, "nothing can be, unless it is from God" (Tho. Aq., *ST* I Q45, I, p. 233).

Creator of Heaven and Earth

Modernity no less than antiquity remains fascinated with the heav-ens. Scripture speaks of heaven as the abode of God. Moses prayed that God would "look down from heaven, thy holy dwelling-place" (Deut. 26:15). Jesus prayed to "Our Father in heaven" (Matt. 6:9). It is a key mark of Christian confession that God created not only the earth but also the full extent of the heavens (Gen. 1:1; Tertullian, *Ag. Hermogenes* XVII–XXXIV, *ANF* III, pp. 486–96).

The heavens embrace all cosmic creation transcending the earth. John of Damascus stated concisely the ancient ecumenical consensus on this subject: "The heaven is the circumference of things created, both visible and invisible. For within its boundary are included and marked off both the mental faculties of the angels and all the world of sense. But the Deity alone is uncircumscribed, filling all things, and surrounding all things, and bounding all things, for He is above all things, and has created all things" (John of Damascus, *OF* II.6, *NPNF* 2 IX, p. 21). Some things, however, had to be created before other things. "The first things created were these four," Thomas speculated, "the angelic nature, the empyrean heaven, formless corporeal matter, and time" (Tho. Aq., *ST* I Q66, I, p. 333), all this on the first day ("when God made heaven and earth," Gen. 1:1).

There is also an eschatological use of the term *heaven*, in the sense that the present world is not eternal, but will vanish away, and there will be "a new heaven and a new earth" (Isa. 65:17; 66:22). Without a sense of terror or anxiety the psalmist expected that ultimately all things, including the heavens, would pass away, yet life with God would not end: "Long ago thou didst lay the foundations of the earth, and the heavens were thy handiwork. They shall pass away, but thou endurest; like clothes they shall all grow old; thou shalt cast them off like a cloak, and they shall vanish; but thou art the same and thy years shall have no end; thy servants' children shall continue, and their posterity shall be established in thy presence" (Ps. 102:25–28; cf. 2 Pet. 3:10–12; Tertullian, *Ag. Hermogenes* XXXIV, *ANF* III, p. 496). The

Revelation of John envisioned "a new heaven and a new earth, for the first heaven and the first earth had vanished, and there was no longer any sea. I saw the holy city, a new Jerusalem, coming down out of heaven from God, made ready like a bride adorned for her husband" (Rev. 21:1, 2). There remain many theories of history (between Beginning and End) that have been advanced by classical exegetes. "Seven ages of this world are spoken of," summarized John of Damascus, "that is, from the creation of the heaven and earth till the general consummation and resurrection of man. For there is a partial consummation, viz., the death of each man, but there is also a general and complete consummation, when the general resurrection of men will come to pass. And the eighth age is the age to come" (OF II.1, NPNF 2 IX, p. 18). Other visions of the end time will be reserved for discussion in a subsequent volume.

The Angelic Hosts

An angel (angelos) is a messenger of God, a spiritual creature endowed with free will and capable of divine praise, yet unencumbered with bodily existence (Irenaeus, Ag. Her. III.8, ANF I, p. 421; John of Damascus, II.3 ff., NPNF 2 IX, p. 18; Quenstedt, TDP I, p. 444; Heppe, RD, pp. 201 ff.; Wesley, WJW VI, pp. 361 ff.).

Angels are incorporeal, lacking bodies (Athanasius, Four Discourses Ag. Arians II.19, NPNF 2 IV, p. 358; cf. Tho. Aq., ST I Q51, I, pp. 264 ff.). They are not limited to the here and now (Gregory Nazianzen, Second Or. on Easter, or. 45.5, NPNF 2 VII, p. 424; cf. Tho. Aq., ST I Q51, I, p. 259). Since endowed with free will, angels may be tempted. "An angel, then, is an intelligent essence, in perpetual motion, with free-will, incorporeal, ministering to God, having obtained by grace an immortal nature" (John of Damascus, OF II.3, NPNF 2 IX, p. 19). Fallen angels who have disavowed their uncorrupted essence and have conspired in disobedience (Tertullian, On the Flesh of Christ XIV, ANF III, p. 533; Augustine, CG XII.6, NPNF 1 II, p. 229; Chemnitz, LT I, p. 122; Quenstedt, TDP I, pp. 443 ff.; Wesley, Of Evil Angels, WJW VI, pp. 380–81) are to be discussed later.

God is said to communicate to humanity through the appearance of angels, according to Scripture: the divine messenger Gabriel instructed Daniel (Dan. 8:16 ff.); Zacharias had a divine visitor (Luke 1:11–20); similarly Mary was visited (Luke 1:26–38). Jesus himself was a recipient of the ministry of angels (Matt. 4:11; Luke 22:43). A countless number of angels are said to surround the throne of God (Heb. 12:22; Rev. 5:11).

Little may be said descriptively of the trans-empirical appearance of angels except the brightness of their countenance, a luminosity unlike any of this world (Matt. 28:2–4; Luke 2:9; Acts 1:10). "They have no need of tongue or hearing but without uttering words they communicate to each other their own thoughts and counsels. . . . It is not as they really are that they reveal themselves to the worthy men to whom God wishes them to appear, but in a changed form which the beholders are capable of seeing. . . . They behold God according to their capacity, and this is their food" (John of Damascus, *OF* II.3, *NPNF* 2 IX, p. 19).

So what? Why do we discuss angels in the modern world, a world whose naturalistic assumptions seem largely to have undercut even the hypothesis of angels? Because our purpose is to represent accountably the classical Christian understanding of God the Creator, which virtually without exception has held an understanding of the spiritual world, created by God, that hypothesizes superpersonal intelligences—angelic hosts. Liturgy, Scripture, and hymnody are filled with such images. Without this hypothesis, even if implausible to modernity, the view of the world in most premodern times would have seemed to them implausible, lacking something essential to creation, namely, spiritual beings. The Creed affirms faith in One who created, not just earth and physical matter, but also the heavens, the world of spirit that transcends empirical vision.

Although Christianity does not require belief in a particular worldview, at least it requires some empathic effort to enter into the worldviews of those who make known to us the revelation of God that both transcends and penetrates all particular worldviews. Even within the frame of contemporary scientific worldviews (and there are many, even as there are many premodern worldviews) it is hardly reasonable to rule out superpersonal intelligences in this vast cosmos that we know so minimally.

Prophetic Views of Creation

Several themes pervade the Hebrew prophets' witness to the Creator:

ISRAEL WITHOUT YAHWEH IS NOTHING

The prophets of the eighth, seventh, and sixth centuries B.C. grasped and developed this surprising analogy: God created the people of Israel out of nothing, just as God creates everything else. As God creates Israel as a nation "from nothing" (as later Latin writers would speak of creation *ex nihilo*, out of nothing), so does God create all things (Augustine, *Conf.* XII.7, *LCC* VII, p. 274). The people of Israel were nobody. God created them from dust. As Israel was not a people except for Yahweh, so the prophet declared that the world would be nothing except for Yahweh (Isa. 43:16–21; Jer. 31:17–25).

Hence, the creative power of God is to be found not only in the beginning but in the process of history, in currently unfolding history (Augustine, *CG* III.17–31, *NPNF* 1 II, pp. 53–63). God not only creates Israel, but comes back when Israel is down to nothing and then wonderfully re-creates Israel (Isa. 40:1 ff.; Jer. 30:12 ff.; Dan. 3:1 ff.). Out of the awareness that Israel had been created by the divine mercy and covenant, the prophets then reflected back on the creation of all things by analogy to Israel's special creation (Augustine, *CG* XVI.36–43, *NPNF* 1 II, pp. 331–36; cf. Calvin, *Inst.* 2.8.29; 2.10.1).

Even when Israel abandoned or forgot its origin, destiny, and covenant responsibility, God remembered, sustained, and re-created the covenant. Thus a "new covenant," a "New Jerusalem" is attested by Jeremiah and others (Jer. 31:31; Isa. 65; cf. Irenaeus, *Ag. Her.* IV.9, *ANF* I, p. 472). The cosmogony emerges by analogy from Israel's historical experience. God is always doing something new in history, always creating or re-creating a new people, ever restoring that which has fallen to nothing (Athanasius, *On the Incarnation* 4–15, *NPNF* 2 IV, pp. 38–44). Through the unexpected turns of history, Yahweh is making known unchanging divine covenant love (*chesed*, cf. Ezek. 16; Isa. 54:5; Mark 2:19 ff.; Calvin, *Inst.* 1.5.1–12; 1.17.2). The prophetic expectation of God as creator of a new people is directly grounded in Israel's actual historical experience, from being no people to becoming a people, and having lost their national identity rediscovering it as secured by Yahweh (Hos. 1:8–11).

THE RELIABILITY OF NATURE POINTS TOWARD THE DIVINE RELIABILITY

The constancy of the laws established by God for the universe was viewed by the prophets as a sign that the covenant would endure forever. The analogy is between the natural order, which is reliable, and divine creation, which depends upon the divine faithfulness (Isa. 45; cf. Lactantius, *Div. Inst.* III.28, *ANF* VII, pp. 97 f.; Tho. Aq., *GC*, pp. 82 ff.).

CREATION LOOKS TOWARD CONSUMMATION

Some Hebrew prophets envisioned that the whole universe would eventually share in the renewal of all things. History awaits "a new heaven and a new earth" (Isa. 65:17; 66:22, cf. 2 Pet. 3:13; Rev. 21:1). The new heaven and the new earth are not alien to the old heaven and the old earth but a fulfillment of it, a continuation and fulfillment of God's original purpose in creation. When the primordial design of God has been distorted by human sin, God continues to re-create and restore covenant companionship. Hence God's creative action is not something that exists only at the beginning of time but remains and persists here and now, to be beheld in personal and national life (Isa. 40:26–28; Mal. 2:10; R. Niebuhr, *NDM* I).

In this way the prophetic vision of beginnings is linked with an eschatological vision of endings. The prophets beheld both the beginning of history and the end of history as God's active work. They hoped for a culmination of distorted history in a way that would be consistent with the divine purpose from the beginning (Augustine, *CG* XII.21–25, *NPNF* 1 II, pp. 499–504).

THE RELATIVITY OF TEMPORAL POWERS

The Hebrew prophets were keenly aware of the radical difference between God and world, eternal and temporal power, Giver and gift. Before Yahweh the nations are counted as nothing (Pss. 113–4; Isa. 30:28). The most massive and durable physical creations—mountains and seas—are nothing in God's hands. "Who has measured the waters in the hollow of his hand, or with the breadth of his hand marked off the heavens? Who has held the dust of the earth in a basket, or weighed the mountains on the scales and the hills in a balance?" (Isa. 40:12). This same incomparably powerful One who enabled all things to be, now and ever again enables Israel to be. The Creator is the Redeemer of Israel. It is one God, not many, who creates the world, permits its freedom to fall, acts to redeem what has fallen, and brings the whole story to fitting consummation (Athanasius, *Incarnation of the Word* 20–32, *NPNF* 2 IV, pp. 47–53; Second Helvetic Conf. VI ff., *HPC*, pp. 51 ff.). Those who viewed "matter as God's equal" were to be resisted firmly (Tertullian, *Ag. Hermogenes* III, *ANF* III, p. 479).

THE CREATOR-CREATURE RELATIONSHIP, BROKEN AND RENEWED

The Scriptures give wrenching account of a long-term, rocky relationship between God and the people of God. The relation of God and Israel mirrors more fundamentally the entire human relation to God. Creation itself is seen as evidence of covenant from the beginning, but the meaning of the covenant is only gradually revealed through historical events (Augustine, *CG* XI.21 ff., *NPNF* 1 II, pp. 216 ff.; Gallic Conf., art. VII ff., *COC* III, pp. 356 ff.; Westminster Conf. IV ff., *CC*, pp. 199 ff.). The covenant intention of God is present from the beginning, but it becomes clarified and appears more palpable only slowly through a meandering history in which the covenant relationship is declared, established, tested, thought about, sweated over, struggled through, worried about, redeemed, and consummated. It is a relationship between God and the people of God. God creates the world in order to enter into a covenant relationship with the world, the human scene—particularly through Israel, by whom God's covenant love is mediated to the rest of the world.

Covenant is not merely an idea, but a history; it takes time—centuries, in fact—gradually to manifest itself and become experientially embraced. It is something like a friendship—it does not just momentarily happen. Can you imagine a personal relationship that appears suddenly, totally, with no possibility or need for further disclosure? Friendships are more often experienced through a history of disclosure; we discover, through knowing and dealing with some other person, whether that person is reliable or not, is caring or not. Covenant history is something like such a gradually developing relationship. Such human relationships have to be fought for and won, defended, reworked, and tested. This is the kind of relationship that comes to exist between God and Israel, something like a rocky marriage or an important but embattled friendship. Many events are remembered and recollected to establish an awareness of God's dependability. The relationship does not simply or flatly exist, but must be hammered out through a series of hazardous and wonderful experiences (Hos. 1:1 ff., cf. Irenaeus, *Ag. Her.* IV.20–25, *ANF* I, pp. 492–96).

Throughout all these experiences, God is creative, continuing to create, re-create, and sustain this covenant relationship. It is through this kind of history that the people of Israel understood themselves to be recipients of the covenant love of God, yet they understood the whole of that history to be already present in the preknowing, eternal mind of God and saturated with the intentional will of God from the very beginning (Augustine, *CG* V.9, *NPNF* 1 II, pp. 90, 91; Tho. Aq., *GC*, p. 87). Nehemiah grasped the correspondence of God's activity as Creator and Redeemer in these terms: "Thou alone art the Lord; thou hast made heaven, the highest heaven with all its host, the earth and all that is on it, the seas and all that is in them. Thou preservest all of them, and the host of heaven worships thee. Thou art the Lord, the God who chose Abram and brought him out of Ur" (Neh. 9:6, 7).

The analogy: Abram (hence Israel) is called to being and faith by the One who calls all into being.

Wisdom in Creation

The postexilic wisdom literature (Job, Proverbs, Ecclesiastes, and certain Psalms) provided new variations on these themes. Whereas the priestly account focused on the six days of creation followed by the Sabbath, the Yahwist on the creation of humanity and the divine-human relationship, and the prophetic accounts more on God's creative activity in history, the psalms and wisdom literature shift the focus somewhat more toward God's creative activity in nature, while sustaining all of these previous themes. In this genre, the world becomes a spectacular object of human research, observation, and enjoyment (Ps. 104; cf. Eccles. 1:5 ff.). The world evokes astonishment (Ps. 19), humility (Job 38:1–42:6), and hymns of praise (Pss. 48:10; 68:32–35). Its order and beauty are testimonies to the presence of God: "When I consider your heavens, the work of your fingers, the moon and the stars, which you have set in place, what is man that you are mindful of him?" (Ps. 8:3, 4; cf. Augustine, *On the Psalms* VIII, *NPNF* 1 VIII, pp. 27–32). "The heavens show forth the glory of God," while this firmament, this creaturely sphere, shows endless evidences of God's handiwork (Ps. 19; Augustine, *On the Psalms* XIX, *NPNF* 1 VIII, pp. 54–56). There are creation hymns in the Psalms that speak of the whole world as filled with the wisdom of God (Pss. 104; 136:1–9; cf. Origen, *De Princip.* II.9, *ANF* IV, p. 291; Gregory Thaumaturgus, *Four Hom.*, *Hom. One*, *ANF* VI, p. 59). Creation mirrors the incalculable wisdom, power, and glory of God (Theophilus of Antioch, *To Autolycus* II.10, 11, *ANF* II, pp. 97, 98; Origen, *De Princip.* I.2.9–12, *ANF* IV, pp. 249–51; Lactantius, *Div. Inst.* VII.5–6, *ANF* VII, pp. 199–203).

Wisdom is present with God from "the beginning of his works, before all else that he made, long ago. Alone, I was fashioned in times long past, at the beginning, long before earth itself. When there was yet no ocean I was born, no springs brimming with water. Before the mountains were settled in their place, long before the hills I was born" (Prov. 8:22–25). All creation is good as given because it is imprinted with the providential image of Wisdom (Athanasius, *Four Discourses Ag. Arians* II.78, 79, *NPNF* 2 IV, pp. 390, 391; Basil, *Hex.*, hom. IX.3–6, *NPNF* 2 VIII, pp. 102–7).

This corresponds with another theme in the wisdom literature: the beauty of God, and of God's world, rightly leading to praise (Gregory

Nazianzen, *On the Theophany, or Birthday of Christ* or. XXXVIII.10, *NPNF* 2 VII, pp. 347, 348). The earth is an appropriate object of celebration, provided we avoid idolatry (Tertullian, *On Idolatry, ANF* III, pp. 61 ff.; Calvin, *Inst.* 1.11.12; Wesley, *WJW* VII, pp. 268 ff.). The divine majesty appears in these works (Ps. 139:14–17; Eccles. 3:11). God is a master craftsman who pours out his creative activity upon the world. The world reflects this artistry and is made radiant by a glory that points back to its Creator, mirroring the divine generosity (Basil, *Hex.*, hom. VI.1 ff., *NPNF* 2 VIII, pp. 81 f.; John Chrysostom, *Concerning the Statues*, hom. X.5, 6, *NPNF* 1 IX, pp. 408, 409).

To summarize: God freely creates everything. God is the cause of all things. The Maker transcends all that is made. Creation is a wise and good act. All things depend radically upon God. God is good in creation, and creation, well designed and beautiful, is to be praised (Irenaeus, *Ag. Her.* IV.18, *ANF* I, p. 486; John of Damascus, *OF* II.3, *NPNF* 2 IX, p. 19).

The Triune Creator

The apostolic witnesses did not quarrel with Torah, the Prophets, or the wisdom literature in their views of creation, idolatry, covenant, and the divine handiwork. Yet the earlier teachings on creation became transmuted in the light of the apostles' experience of Jesus of Nazareth (Irenaeus, *Ag. Her.* IV.20, *ANF* I, pp. 487, 488; Athanasius, *Four Discourses Ag. Arians* II.19–24, *NPNF* 2 IV, pp. 358–61). The Jewish tradition of creation was reappropriated, yet reconceived through the lens of their relation with the Son, the unique Revealer of the Father's purpose in creation (Tertullian, *Ag. Marcion* V.5, *ANF* III, pp. 438–40; Cyril of Alex., *Treasury of Holy Trin.*, *FEF*, p. 212).

The early Christians prayed in much the same language as did Jews before them "to the sovereign Lord, maker of the heaven and earth and sea and everything in them" (Acts 4:24). God created the world by direct address (2 Cor. 4:6). God called into being what did not exist (Irenaeus, *Ag. Her.* II.10.1–4, III.8, *ANF* I, pp. 369, 370, 421, 422). These were all typical phrases found in Jewish celebrations of divine creation. But the New Testament view of creation developed this major difference: In John's prologue, the world is created by the Word of God. The Word of God in Jesus is coeternal with the Father. The Word was the God from the beginning, and the Word was God (John 1:1–17; cf. Basil, *On the Holy Spirit* VIII.21, *NPNF* 2 VIII, pp. 14 ff.; Gregory of Nyssa, *Ag. Eunomius* II.8–11, *NPNF* 2 V, pp. 112–22).

The Word of God is God himself, Creator of the universe. The Creator, made flesh in Jesus, comes into our history to present himself clearly to our view.

John's Gospel begins in a conscious parallel to Genesis 1: "In the beginning was the Word" (John 1:1, RSV). The evangelist could not make any more dramatic affirmation than to identify Christ with the Word present in creation, by whom the world was made. There was no better place to start in making contact with Jewish belief than to identify the Word spoken in Jesus as the same Word who is from the beginning (Col. 1; cf. Tatian, Or. Ag. Greeks 7, ANF II, p. 67). "The Word, then, was with God at the beginning, and through him all things came to be; no single thing was created without him" (John 1:2, 3; 1:14; cf. Irenaeus, Ag. Her. III.11, ANF I, pp. 426–29; Athanasius, Four Discourses Ag. Arians I.11–21, NPNF 2 IV, pp. 312–19; Ambrose, Of the Holy Spirit II.1–4, NPNF 2 X, p. 115; Of the Chr. Faith, I.54–57, NPNF 2 X, pp. 209, 210).

Paul took a similar beginning point in the letter to the Romans: God's divinity and eternity are known through creatures. Look at the creation carefully, and you will see some stamp, some distinct impression of the Creator's purpose. God's invisible nature is known through that which is visible (Rom. 1:20). This is the One made known in Jesus: "Source, Guide, and Goal of all that is—to him be glory for ever! Amen" (Rom. 11:36; cf. Origen, Ag. Celsus VI.65, ANF IV, p. 603; Gregory of Nyssa, Ag. Eunomius II.7, NPNF 2 V, pp. 109–12). Paul proclaimed "the God who makes the dead live and summons things that are not yet in existence as if they already were" (Rom. 4:17). Acts reports that Paul spoke to the Athenians of "The God who created the world and everything in it, and who is Lord of heaven and earth," who is "himself the universal giver of life and breath and all else. He created every race of men of one stock, to inhabit the whole earth's surface" (Acts 17:24–26).

The letter to the Colossians began by speaking of "the Son, in whom our release is secured," who is "the image of the invisible God; his is the primacy over all created things. In him everything in heaven and on earth was created, not only things visible but also the invisible orders of thrones, sovereignties, authorities, and powers: the whole universe has been created through him and for him" (Col. 1:15–17; cf. Origen, De Princip. II.6, ANF IV, p. 281; Basil, Hex., hom I.6, NPNF 2 VIII, p. 55; On the Holy Spirit XVI, NPNF 2 VIII, pp. 23, 24). In Christ all things were created and now subsist. It is he who sustains the universe by his word of power. He is the word of God, existing with God from the beginning, yet becoming flesh in the fullness of time (Athanasius, *Defence of the Nicene Definition* III.7 ff., *NPNF* 2 IV, pp. 154 ff.). In Hebrews it was written, "By faith we perceive that the universe was fashioned by the word of God, so that the visible came forth from the invisible" (Heb. 11:3; Gregory Nazianzen, *Second Theol. Or.* VI, *NPNF* 2 VII, p. 290; *On Pentecost*, or. XLI.14, *NPNF* 2 VII, p. 384; Cyril of Jerusalem, *Catech. Lect.* IX.1, 2, *NPNF* 2 VII, p. 51).

In this way the New Testament church affirmed the received Jewish tradition's celebration of God's goodness in creation and of the radical dependence of all things upon God, yet added a decisive point of interpretation: creation is seen through the light of Jesus Christ. The purpose of the Father is fully revealed in the Son, to whom fitting response is enabled through the Spirit (Augustine, *On Trin.* III.4, *NPNF* 1 III, pp. 58, 59; cf. V.13–15, pp. 94, 95).

The work of creation is "always applied in Scripture not partially but to the whole, entire, full, complete Godhead" (Dionysius, *Div. Names* II, p. 65). "For in the [Nicene] Creed, to the Father is attributed that 'He is the Creator of all things visible and invisible'; to the Son is attributed that by Him 'all things were made'; and to the Holy Ghost is attributed that He is 'Lord and Life-Giver'"—hence, "to create is not proper to any one Person, but is common to the whole Trinity. . . . God the Father made the creature through His Word, which is His Son; and through His Love, which is the Holy Ghost," who "quickens what is created by the Father through the Son" (Tho. Aq., *ST* I Q45, I, pp. 237, 238). Both Augustine and Thomas argued that in all creatures there is found the trace of the Trinity (p. 238; cf. Augustine, *CG* XI.24 ff., *NPNF* 1 II, pp. 218 f.; *On Trin.* VI.10, *NPNF* 1 III, pp. 102, 103). It is as if the mystery of creation had been waiting for generations to be revealed. The prophets, priests, and apocalypticists had waited for the disclosure that the New Testament understood as having just occurred: the revelation of the same one who creates and renews and gives all things, Jesus Christ, the wisdom of God (1 Cor. 1), who, being God Himself, is Creator just as much as is God the Father and God the Spirit (Augustine, *Literal Interp. of Gen.* IX.15.26, *FEF* III, p. 86).

The same motif is rehearsed in Hebrews 1, which proclaimed the coming of a Son whom God has appointed to inherit all things, for it was through this Son that God created this world of time. All creation depends for its support upon this Word. A similar idea is found in Revelation 22: "I am the alpha and the omega; the beginning and the end." The Christian community affirmed a thoroughly Hebraic notion of the creation of the world, while viewing it from the premise of the eternal Word spoken in Jesus (Fulgence, *Rule of Faith* 25, *FEF* III, p. 295).

The New Creation

Not only does Christ reveal the purpose of creation, the Spirit also works to create anew a resurrected fellowship, a new community of the resurrection. The New Testament doctrine of creation is not just about the first thing that happens in time but also about the new creation occurring in the community of faith, and to us in our hearts, by analogy to the first creation, where there was nothing (Clement of Alex., *Who Is the Rich Man That Shall Be Saved?* XII ff., *ANF* II, pp. 594 ff.). Christ "re-formed the human race" (Irenaeus, *Ag. Her.* IV.24.1, *ANF* I, p. 495). "When anyone is united to Christ, there is a new world; the old order has gone, and a new order has already begun" (2 Cor. 5:17; cf. Epistle of Barnabas V, *ANF* I, pp. 139, 140). The focus is not on an objective description of primal events, but on a report of the renewal of existing individuals and societies here and now. The analogies are spiritual gestation, embryonic formation, and the joy of birth (Clementina, *Recognitions* IX.7, *ANF* VIII, p. 184; Wesley, *WJW* V, pp. 212 ff., 224 ff.).

New creation is a motif that had already appeared powerfully in the Prophets (Isa. 65:17; 66:22; Jer. 31; Lam. 3:23). It took on deepened meaning in the New Testament view that the new creation had already begun in Jesus Christ by the power of the Spirit. Where two or three are gathered together (Matt. 18:20), there the living Christ is in their midst and the new age begun. "Circumcision is nothing; uncircumcision is nothing; the only thing that counts is new creation!" (Gal. 6:15; Calvin, *Inst.* 2.11.11; Wesley, *WJW* I, p. 161).

This new creation is already begun, not only in the life of the faithful, but also extending into the life of the world. Paul's vision of the new creation has relevance not only for human history, but for the whole cosmos:

> The creation waits in eager expectation for the sons of God to be revealed. For the creation was subjected to frustration, not by its own choice, but by the will of the one who subjected it, in hope that the creation itself will be liberated from its bondage to decay and brought into the glorious freedom of the children of God. We know that the whole creation has been groaning as in the pains of childbirth right up to the present time. (Rom. 8:19–22; cf. Methodius, *From the Discourse on the Resurrection* II, *ANF* VI, pp. 370 ff.)

One gets the impression of the cosmos laboring for birth on a multibillion-year scale, hoping (in a way that only a universe could "hope") that God would fulfill the promise of cosmic redemption, and end the frustration caused by sin, even though this mysterious struggle in which we are now engaged remains penultimately ambiguous. Even though we may not here and now fully grasp God's will, in God's own time it will be known as reconciling all things (1 Cor. 13; 2 Cor. 5) so as to bring the whole cosmos within range of the redemptive purpose of Christ (Eph. 1). "A few drops of blood re-creates the whole world" (Gregory Nazianzen, *Second Or. on Easter*, or. 45, XXIX, *NPNF* 2 VII, p. 433).

Teaching of Creation Challenged and Refined by Alternative Views

As early as Theophilus (fl. 180), the sixth bishop of Antioch, the Christian teaching of creation had already taken explicit shape in relation to six different philosophical partners in dialogue:

Some of the philosophers of the Porch say that there is *no God* at all; or, if there is, they say that He *cares for none but Himself;* and these views the folly of Epicurus and Chrysippus has set forth at large. And others say that all things are produced without external agency, and that the *world is uncreated* and that nature is eternal; and have dared to give out that there is no providence of God at all, but maintain that *God is only each man's conscience.* And others again maintain that the *spirit which pervades all things is God.* But Plato and those of his school acknowledge indeed that God is uncreated and the Father and Maker of all things, but then they maintain that matter as well as God is uncreated, and aver that it is *coeval with God.* But if God is uncreated and matter uncreated, God is no longer, according to the Platonists, the Creator of all things, nor so far as their opinions hold, is the monarchy of God established. And further, as God, because He is uncreated, is also unalterable; so if matter, too, were uncreated, it also would be unalterable, and equal to God; for that which is created is mutable and alterable, but that which is uncreated is immutable and unalterable. And what great thing is it if God made the world out of existent materials? For even a human artist, when he gets material from someone, makes of it what he pleases. But the power of God is manifested in this, that out of things that are not, He makes whatever He pleases; just as the bestowal of life and motion is the prerogative of no other than God alone. For even man makes indeed an image, but reason and breath, or feeling, he cannot give to what he has made. But God has this property in excess of what man can do, in that He makes a work, endowed with reason, life, sensation. As therefore, in all these respects God is more powerful than man, so also in this; that out of things that are not He creates and has created all things that are, and whatever He pleases, as He pleases. (*To Autolycus* II.4, *ANF* II, p. 95, italics added)

In the compass of this brief passage, Theophilus implicitly dealt with major alternatives to the early Christian teaching of God's creation. These would be the dissenting voices that would continue to oppose the Christian understanding of creation for many centuries: (1) atheism, which denied any God who could have created; (2) cosmic narcissism such as that of Epicurus, who thought that if God exists at all God must be as egocentric and uncaring as human beings evidently are; (3) a reductive naturalism that viewed the entire physical cosmos as uncreated, and all causes are attributed to natural causes; (4) a moral reductionism combined with a metaphysical skepticism that reduced God to a subjective hypothesis or projection of consciousness; (5) pantheism, which identified the world with God; and (6) a soft Platonism, which although it rightly argued that God is uncreated, wrongly argued that matter also is uncreated and therefore as eternal as God. All these views were later to appear and grow into major challenges to the Christian teaching of creation and remain as modern challenges in the voices of (1) Nietzsche, (2) Freud, (3) Hume, (4) Kant, Schleiermacher, Feuerbach, (5) Wieman, and (6) Schelling (cf. Hartshorne and Reese, *PSG*, pp. 233 ff.).

The Apostles' Creed began with the confession: "I believe in God the Father Almighty, creator of heaven and earth" (*CC*, p. 24). It conspicuously affirmed and celebrated the Hebraic understanding of the One God, *'El Shaddaī*, almighty, *pater omnipotens, pantocratōr*, who holds all things in his hands, who makes all. Justin Martyr would write about A.D.165: "We worship the God of the Christians, whom we consider One from the beginning, the creator and maker of all creation, visible and invisible" (*Martyrdom of the Holy Martyrs* I, *ANF* I, p. 305). The Creed of Nicaea (325) declared: "We believe in one God, the Father All-Governing [*pantokratōra*], creator [*poieten*] of all things visible and invisible" (*CC*, p. 30).

The early Christian teaching of the unity of creation is intricately fused with the Christian teaching of the unity of the triune God. The Father creates through the Son and by the power of the Spirit (Basil, *On the Spirit* V, *NPNF* 2 VIII, pp. 5–8; Hilary, *On Trin.* II.5–12, *NPNF* 2 IX, pp. 53–56). Son and Spirit are not viewed as quiescent in creation. The triune God is present, three in one, from the beginning (Athanasius, *Defence of the Nicene Definition* III, *NPNF* 2 IV, pp. 153–58; *Four Discourses Ag. Arians* I.VI.17, *NPNF* 2 IV, pp. 316–19). The early Christians did not confess God the creator apart from God the redeemer and consummator.

The Goodness of Creatures

It is a primordially good world that God creates; only later is it to become distorted by the companionate wills that God permits. Doubtless the world has its dark corners and cruel characters. Ever present is the potential for destructiveness, loss, and distortion (Lactantius, *Div. Inst.* VII.4, *ANF* VII, pp. 198–99). It contains people like you and me. But if we could see it as a whole as God sees it, we would see the cosmos as an unimaginably good complexity. God pronounced it good at the outset (Archelaus, *Disputation with Manes* 21 ff., *ANF* VI, pp. 194 ff.). It was not Adam or Job or Judas who said of the whole: "It is good" (cf. Gen. 1:4, 13, 18). God did.

This is a watershed for all Jewish and Christian views of the world. Any world not created good is not God's world. Any bad world, irretrievably evil, is not the Jewish-Christian idea of God's world (Augustine, *Literal Interp. of Gen.* IX.15.26; Dionysius, *Div. Names* IV.1, pp. 86 ff.). Judaism and Christianity have had to fight steadily against alternative pantheistic or dualistic views of the world.

In view of the obvious troubles of human history, some have speculated that there must have been some devilishly evil controlling principle from the beginning in the world, against which the good must struggle ambiguously from beginning to end. Hebraic religion did not characteristically think of God as creating an intrinsically evil or unalterably alien world. To be sure, the world was in due course permitted to fall through the abuse of (primordially good) freedom into something worse than earlier permitted. But even in its worst moments, in its most tragically fallen state, its most wretched condition, something about the world is and remains good. An evil can only emerge out of some good. Goodness is God's diminishable but not wholly defeatable work and gift (Irenaeus, *Ag. Her.* V.16, *ANF* I, p. 544). Even those things that appear evil were created for some good (Lactantius, *Div. Inst.* VII.4, 5, *ANF* VII, pp. 198–200).

Humanity is given dominion and stewardship over the earth. The world, according to the Genesis account, is not given purposelessly, without awareness of potentially harmful contingencies, or without a redemptive plan in mind. The stewardship of creation was entrusted, according to Hebraic religion, to one particular part of it—humanity. "You shall have dominion" (cf. Gen. 1:26, 28) implies: "Take care of it. God entrusts the world to your care. In the guardianship of this fragile world, it shall be an arena, a stage, a context in which it is possible and morally required to respond fittingly to the One who gives and transcends all creaturely values" (cf. 1 Pet. 4:10; Epistle of Barnabas XIX–XXI, *ANF* I, pp. 148, 149; Tertullian, *Ag. Marcion* II.4–6, *ANF* III, pp. 299–302; Clementina, *Recognitions* VI.7, *ANF* VIII, p. 154). Men and women have been from the outset called to take initiative to order the world rightly under the permission and command of God, to make appropriate use of God-given rational capacities, strengths, imagination, and courage and to shape the world in a fitting response to God's unpurchasable gift—life. All this is implied in the notion of stewardly dominion over all that God gives in creation (Luke 16:1–12; cf. Origen, *Ag. Celsus* IV.73–88, *ANF* IV, pp. 530–36).

In the early Hebraic accounts of creation, the world is denied divine status, which it had inordinately enjoyed in animistic accounts of beginnings. Nature has a better purpose than idolatry (Athanasius, *Ag. Heathen* 19–27, *NPNF* 2 IV, pp. 14–18; cf. Calvin, *Inst.* 1.11.1, 2.1–5). Humanity has no need to bow down absolutely to the mysterious forces of nature or to make earth, air, fire, or water absolute. Rather, nature is purposefully given as the arena in which human freedom can engage in making human history. Nature is to be greatly respected, nurtured, and cared for, but not worshiped. The natural ordering of the cosmos is necessary for freedom to have reliable causal chains in which it can become responsible and can test out its capacity for responsiveness to the Creator (Basil, *Hex.* IX, *NPNF* 2 VIII, pp. 101–7; cf. Athenagoras, *Resurrection of the Dead* XVII–XXV, *ANF* II, pp. 158–62).

God's goodness and being are not diminished by the act of creating. It is "just as from one torch many fires are lighted, but the light of the first torch is not lessened by the kindling of many torches," wrote Tatian. "I myself, for instance, talk, and you hear; yet, certainly, I who converse do not become destitute of speech [*logos*] by the transmission of speech" (Tatian, *Address to Greeks* V, *ANF* II, p. 67). Accordingly, when God spoke to create, God did not lose a part of himself.

There is no hint of pantheism in Hebrew Scriptures, no motley overlapping or indistinct blurring or loss of the distinction between Creator and creature. God is utterly distinct from the creation, and far from being simply identical with the world itself (Athanasius, *Defence of the Nicene Definition* III.8, 9, *NPNF* 2 IV, pp. 155, 156; Augustine, *CG* XI.5, *NPNF* 1 II, pp. 208 ff.).

The Purpose of Creation: Divine Benevolence

Why did God create something rather than nothing? Something exists because God willed something rather than nothing. It is out of

God's will to create, which comes from God's goodness and wisdom, that the world is created.

But why *this* world with personal beings in it, and not another without them? Because God willed to communicate personally with companionate beings (John of Damascus, *OF* II.12–30, *NPNF* 2 IX, pp. 30–44; Calvin, *Inst.* 1.15.1–4). God determined to communicate the divine glory and goodness to creatures proportional to their capacity to receive (Tho. Aq., *ST* I Q47, I, pp. 246 ff.). "God Who is good and more than good, did not find satisfaction in self-contemplation, but in His exceeding goodness wished certain things to come into existence which would enjoy His benefits and share in His goodness. He brought all things out of nothing into being and created them, both what is invisible and what is visible. Yea, even man, who is a compound of the visible and the invisible" (John of Damascus, *OF* II.2, *NPNF* 2 IX, p. 18; cf. Gregory Nazianzen, or. XXXVIII.9, *NPNF* 2 VII, p. 347).

This is not to say that God has an inner, unresolved (perhaps neurotic) need to create. Rather, it is that God's goodness is so good that it would seem to be less good if it did not communicate itself to other beings. God's power is so powerful that it would be less powerful if it did not make itself known in tenderness as love. God's justice is so just that it would be less just if it never risked making a historical realm in which to allow divine justice to be played out, struggled for, recognized, and praised. God's joy is so joyful that it would be less joyful if it never had anyone else with which to share its depth of joy. So it could hardly be imaginable, assuming God's incomparable goodness, power, justice, and joy, that God would create nothing (Augustine, *Conf.* XI.1–10, *LCC* VII, pp. 244–52).

But is it, strictly speaking, necessary for God to create? That which is good wishes to communicate itself; it does not wish simply to withhold itself from communication—for an uncommunicated and unknown and unbeheld good is less good than one communicated, known, and beheld (Tho. Aq., *ST* I Q44, 45, I, pp. 229–39). Consequently, that which is unsurpassably good would most certainly will to communicate itself in some way to some world. Especially this is so if the unsurpassably good being is personal and desires to awaken in companion forms of self-determining personal being a corresponding awareness of the goodness of creation. This is a deductive argument from the premise of divine benevolence: it is precisely because God is personal and good that God is bound to find a way to communicate that goodness to other personal beings—creatures that have some intelligence, rational capacity, capacity to love, and some ability to respond. This is a greater creation than would exist if there were nothing but rocks, illimitable space, and inert matter that could not significantly respond. The actual Creator has allowed creatures who respond. This is a central fact of divine benevolence. The sole motive of creation is God's gracious willingness to share goodness with creatures (Salvian, *The Governance of God* IV.9–11, FC 3, pp. 106–10; cf. Clement of Alex., *Strom.* II.21 ff., ANF II, pp. 374 ff.).

If God is good, and if goodness wills to communicate itself, then creation is contingently necessary—contingent upon the premise that God is good. No particular world is necessary to God. Creation is the free act of God. There is no external compulsion or necessity upon God—nothing outside God prior to the beginning that says, "God, for some reason outside yourself, you must create a world" (cf. Clementina, *Recognitions* VIII.1–16, ANF VIII, pp. 165–69). "It is not therefore necessary for God to will that the world should always exist" (Tho. Aq., *ST* I Q48, I, p. 241). God could have refrained altogether from creating, had it not been that God's goodness irrepressibly takes joy in being shared. Hence there is no absolute necessity that any world exist, although there is a consequent necessity, that is, consequent to the purpose of God to love and be loved fittingly. If God is to pursue a relation with the world, then there obviously must be a world. As becoming known posits another knower, so becoming loved and enjoyed posits a companionate lover and enjoyer (Paulus Orosius, *Seven Books Ag. the Pagans* VII, FC 50, pp. 283 ff.; Raymond Lull, *The Book of the Lover*; Catherine of Genoa, *Spiritual Dialogue* I, CWS, pp. 109–14; Kierkegaard, *Works of Love*).

The purpose of creation is to show God's goodness through the history of covenant (Calvin, *Inst.* 2.9–11). Creation from the outset is intimately enmeshed in God's creating, covenanting, redemptive purpose. If there is to be a history of this relationship, the divine-human covenant, then there must be a place, a locus, a world in which it occurs. "For He brought things into being in order that His goodness might be communicated to creatures." "For goodness, which in God is simple and uniform, in creatures is manifold and divided; and hence the whole universe together participates in the divine goodness more perfectly, and represents it better than any single creature whatever" (Tho. Aq., *ST* I Q47, I, p. 246).

Is This Creation as Good as God Could Have Made It?

When Leibniz argued that God had created the best of possible worlds, he never implied that God is obliged to create what *we* might egocentrically imagine to be the best possible world. For our view of what is best, since distorted by self-assertive sin, is quite different from what God would view as best. God could create any world, this world or any other world, but this is the one God created, not those supposedly "better" ones our minds proudly imagine we could have invented. God's purpose is in fact being fulfilled precisely through the struggle and destiny of this world, not those fantasized others (Gregory of Nyssa, *Great Catech.* VI, *NPNF* 2 V, pp. 480, 481).

The Christian community takes a middle course between the radical optimism of utopians, who neglect the power of evil, and the radical pessimism of Marcion, the Gnostics, the Manichaeans, Schopenhauer, and many voices within Hinduism and Buddhism, which considers the world as *maya* or illusion, something to be escaped from as much as possible. Both modern naturalistic-evolutionary liberal optimisms and modern historical pessimisms are resisted by the central Christian tradition, which affirms a relative optimism, based upon the goodness of God in creation, combined with a realistic awareness of human fallenness. That fallenness is not just attributable to fate, but resides precisely in human willing, corporate and personal (Cyril of Jerusalem, *Catech. Lect.* IV.18–21, *NPNF* 2 VII, pp. 23, 24; R. Niebuhr, *NDM* I).

Although this fallen world is not the best abstractly conceivable world, nonetheless, even under these conditions it remains a remarkably good world, uniting in astonishing harmony and variety many levels of creaturely goodness. Thomas Aquinas celebrated the tremendous variety in God's design, the profusion of things in the world: "God makes creatures many and diverse, that what is wanting in one is supplied by another. Goodness in God is simple and consistent. Among creatures it is scattered and uneven. Contrast and oddness come not from chance, not from flaws in the material, not from interference with the divine plan, but from God's purpose. He wills to impart his perfection to creatures as they can stand it" (*ST* I Q47, I, p. 246). With our inadequate capacity—mental, emotive, physical—to receive God's goodness, God is imparting as much goodness as we can take. "The Church affirms and teaches that the one true God, Father, Son and Spirit is the creator of all things visible and invisible. These creatures are good because they were made by the supreme good, but they are changeable because they were made from derivative goods. The church asserts that there is no such thing as a nature of evil, because every nature insofar as it is a nature, is good" (Council of Florence, *COC* II). A further discussion of the problem of evil will follow the subsequent section on providence.

Created Good Though Prone to Fall

God does not make things badly. God is intent upon creating and sustaining a creation that is proportionally as good as sluggish matter can be and a freedom that is proportionally as good as distortable freedom can be. Yet all created goods remain derivative and consequent goods. Some creatures, especially human beings with intelligence and self-determination, are ingeniously capable of twisting and knotting the created goodness of the world (Ambrose, *Of the Chr. Faith*, III.20, NPNF 2 V, p. 245; cf. Wesley, *The New Birth*).

Repeatedly the Christian tradition has had to fight the notion that the created order is created fundamentally in a defective or evil way— that it is sinful simply by existing (Tertullian, *Ag. Marcion* I.2–23, ANF III, pp. 272–89; Athanasius, *Incarnation of the Word* XLIII, NPNF 2 IV, p. 59). Sin is not caused by God, it is caused by skewed freedom. Sin is of our making, not God's. Creation is good. Sin is a product of abused freedom (Athanasius, *Ag. the Heathen* II, NPNF 2 IV, pp. 4 ff.; Clementina, *Recognitions* IV.23–25, ANF VIII, pp. 139, 140). Freedom is created good, even if prone to fall (Cyril of Jerusalem, *Catech. Lect.* II.1, NPNF 2 VII, p. 8; Augustine, *Nature of the Good; Ag. Manichaeans* 36, 37, NPNF 1 IV, p. 359).

Against World-Hating

In the first two centuries, Christian teachers had to face Docetists, Gnostics, Manichaeans, and other novel theorists who detested the Jewish-Christian understanding of a good creation. They thought this was a dreadful world. They could not imagine that God could have been so ill advised as to create this sordid place. Essentially antimaterialists, they thought finitude was demeaning and matter intrinsically alienating. They concluded that such a bad world could not have been created by a good God. From its beginnings Christianity has had to deal with these world-haters and world-despairers.

The early Christian pastors responded to Gnostic competitors in a traditional Hebraic way: even though things are distorted and fallen, still it is God who made the world and wishes to restore it. Augustine did battle against Manichaeans who were saying that matter is so bad that we must remove God from the embarrassment of having created this regrettable world. Augustine had to show that God creates a good world by wisdom and grace, and through the abuse of freedom it becomes distorted (Augustine, *Writings Ag. Manichaeans*, NPNF 1 IV, pp. 41–365).

This Gnostic/Manichaean view has political significance, for if the world is evil, it can be treated negligently. Christianity attested the value of this world to God by celebrating God's own determination to become flesh and share in human history. Christianity is the most materialistic of all religions, argued William Temple, because of the incarnation (*Nature, Man, and God*).

Early Christian baptismal creeds confessed that God is the creator of this world, including matter (against Manichaean dualism), and also of the heavenly hosts, the spiritual world (against naturalistic materialists). God created not only the sun, earth, water, air, and living creatures, but also the angels, principalities, and powers. Humankind is created as a unique microcosmic tension embracing those two creaturely worlds, "a sort of connecting link between the visible and invisible natures" (John of Damascus, *OF* I.12, *NPNF* 2 IX, p. 30).

Summing up: Dualism is rejected; creation is *ex nihilo*; creation is good; the three persons of the Trinity act as one through creation.

The Happiness of God in Creating

Creaturely life is given in order that we might "glorify God, and enjoy Him forever" (Westminster Catechism I). The glory (*kabod, doxa*) of God attested by Isaiah (40:4, 5) and Ezekiel (1:29), which was manifested in salvation history and is destined to "fill the earth" (Num. 14:21, 22), was beheld by the shepherds at Christ's birth (Luke 2:9), in his entire life (John 1:14), and especially at the transfiguration (Mark 9:2–8; cf. John of Damascus, *OF* II.2, *NPNF* 2 IX, p. 18).

God is glorified in an extraordinary way by the creation of intelligent beings capable of praising and thereby of reflecting God's own glory in temporal, historical, physical, and moral acts (Ambrose, *On the Decease of Satyrus* I.45, 46, *NPNF* 2 X, p. 168). That God's glory is manifested in creation does not diminish God's goodness, but enhances it (Cyril of Jerusalem, *Catech. Lect.* IX, *NPNF* 2 VII, pp. 51–55).

The end of creation is indeed the glory of God, but this does not diminish the value of human life. God did not create humanity for human pride or merely to make us hedonistically or egocentrically happy about ourselves in an autonomous sense. That, for most of the biblical writers, is a form of pride, despair, and hence unhappiness (Arnobius, *Ag. the Heathen* 22–25, *ANF* VI, pp. 469–71; Luther, *Sermons on the Catech.*, *ML*, pp. 224–25). When we pursue happiness on an egocentric basis, asserted only for ourselves, we forfeit a deeper, wiser happiness (Wesley, *WJW* VI, pp. 431 ff., 443 ff., VII, pp. 267 ff.).

Rather, God creates us for an ordinate happiness, ordered in relation to the proportional variety of goods available to creatures and ordained in relationship to the purposes of God (*Epistle to Diognetus* VIII–XI, *ANF* I, pp. 28–29). Indeed, the purpose of creation is to make us happy in that sense, to make all creaturely life blessed, and to permit happiness to abound in creation, as seen in relation to the source and ground of happiness (Catherine of Siena, *Prayers* 13, pp. 108–14; cf. Bonaventure, *Life of St. Francis* VIII, *CWS*, pp. 250–61).

The One who in the fullest sense is happy is the eternally happy One—God. Human happiness is seen in relation to the truly happy, the infinitely blessed One. All creatures are in some way capable of sharing in God's happiness (Tho. Aq., *ST* I Q26, I, pp. 142 ff.). Thus the glory of the Creator and the happiness of creatures are inseparable, conjoint purposes of risk-laden creation and are best not treated abstractly. Human happiness is not an incidental part of the original purpose of God in creation (Gregory of Nyssa, *On the Making of Man NPNF* 2 V, pp. 387 ff.).

The possibility of the praise of God by creation is increased greatly when beings are created who are capable of speech, memory, will, and understanding. God is glorified in an extraordinary way by creating intelligent beings capable of reflecting God's own glory in a palpable, historical world (Lactantius, *Div. Inst.* II.10–16, *ANF* VII, pp. 56–64). If something is to be happy, it must first be alive (Basil, *Hex.* VII, VIII, *NPNF* 2 VIII, pp. 89–101). Without creation no creature could ever be alive; hence no creature could be happy. Creation enables space and time for life. Creation begins with the beginning of time and space. God not only produces matter and the space to hold created beings and enable life, but time's duration to sustain and enable them (Pss. 27:1; 36:9; Jer. 17:13).

Consequent Issues of Creation Teaching

Among major problems associated with the Christian teaching of creation are the relation of creation and time, the rejection of the eternality of matter, the inequalities among created beings, the hypothesis of natural evolution, and the speculation about other worlds than those now known.

Time

Repeatedly, Christian teaching has sought carefully to clarify the relation of the eternal and time. The key to the clarification is the assumption that the origin of time coincides with the origin of the universe. The creation of the world resulted in the beginning of time.

With the world, time was created. Before time existed, nothing was but God (Augustine, *CG* XI.6, *NPNF* 1 II, p. 208). "There was never a time when there was no time. There was no time, therefore, when thou hadst not made anything, because thou hadst made time itself" (Augustine, *Conf.* XI.13, 14, *LCC* VII, p. 254).

Time and space were coordinately created together. Both are part of the created order—not uncreated, hence not God. That time is created is opposed to the idea that God inserted the world into a time that was already proceeding, or into a preexistent framework, and to the notion that the world and time are coeternal with God (Augustine, *CG* XI.1–13, *NPNF* 1 II, pp. 205–13). It is more correct to say that the world was created *with* time (*cum tempore*) than *in* time. That means that in the very act of creating the world, God also at the same eternal nonmoment created time. "Eternity is neither time nor part of time" (Gregory Nazianzen, *Second Or. on Easter*, or. 45, IV, *NPNF* 2 VII, p. 424). Time was not proceeding before the creation of the world (Augustine, *Conf.* XI.13 ff., *LCC* VII, pp. 253 ff.). The work of God is done in history, yet God eternally transcends history. Time is finite, measurable, divisible in parts. Eternity is infinite, unmeasurable, not divisible in parts (Augustine, *Conf.* XI.15 ff., *LCC* VII, pp. 255 ff.).

While affirming the distinction between eternity and time, it is still possible to affirm that the universe is from the temporal point of view "everlasting," in the particular sense that before it no time was and at its end there will be no time. Thus creation is rightly said to be as old as time itself, yet eternity enshrouds all times. It is better to think of eternity not as chronologically "antecedent" to time, however, but, rather, logically presupposed in time. For there was no time "before" creation—the "before" implies a time, and a "time" before time is evidently self-contradictory (Augustine, *Conf.* XIII.48–53, *LCC* VII, pp. 330–33).

Jesus as remembered in John's Gospel prayed: "Now, Father, glorify me in thy own presence with the glory which I had with thee before the world began" (John 17:5). This does not imply that a time existed before time, but that time itself is encompassed by eternity and the Word made known in Jesus is eternal. In arguing that God has always had creatures over which to exercise lordship, Augustine clarified that "always" meant "in all time," yet time itself is created (Augustine, *CG* XII.15, *NPNF* 1 II, pp. 235 ff.; cf. *On Trin.* I.1.3). For the eternal did not begin only when the world began. To say that eternity encompasses time does not mean that eternity is a further temporal extension prior to the creation, but rather the ground and possibility of time itself (John of Damascus, *OF* II.1, *NPNF* 2 IX, p. 18). The eternal is simultaneously present to every moment of time, including past and future time. In the light of the incarnation, the now is rightly viewed as eternity currently manifesting itself as time (Kierkegaard, *Phil. Frag.* I, pp. 11–27).

It is hardly reasonable to suppose that the created order had no beginning. Some date, no matter how remote, must be hypothesized for the beginning of creation. That we cannot compute or estimate that date does not imply that we need not hypothesize it. Within time, the eternal is always acting, never sleeping; the divine activity is never done (Ps. 121; cf. Tertullian, *Apol.* XXVI ff., *ANF* III, pp. 40 ff.). Christianity teaches of an eternal One, eternally acting, whose activity is known through temporal effects (Clementina, *Recognitions* VIII.34, *ANF* VIII, p. 174). Datable events are grounded in an undatable source of events. The very idea of creation implies this paradoxical conjunction: as divine activity, creation is eternally occurring, transcending all specific times and places; as temporal effect, creation has a beginning and an end, however remote (Augustine, *Conf.* XI.10–13; Tho. Aq., *ST* I Q45, I, pp. 232 ff.).

The notion of created time is mystery enough, but various writers have speculated about what God might have been doing just before, or ages before, the creation of the world. Not lacking in humor, Augustine showed that the question itself was self-contradictory, since it asked about a time before time. "How, then, shall I respond to him who asks, 'What was God doing *before* he made heaven and earth?' I do not answer, as a certain one is reported to have done facetiously (shrugging off the force of the question). 'He was preparing hell,' he said, 'for those who pry too deep'" (Augustine, *Conf.* XI.12, p. 253). Although the question must not be laughed away, neither can it be directly answered (pp. 253 ff.). One may at least "give the same account of God's resting in the infinite times before the world as they give of His resting in the infinite spaces outside of it" (Augustine, *CG* XI.5, *NPNF* 1 II, p. 208).

The Creator provides time, the Redeemer restores time, the Spirit sanctifies time, yet God remains the one source and end of time. God is not bound to time in the same way that creatures are. "For He is the Maker of time, and is not subject to time" (Gregory Nazianzen, *Or. on the Holy Lights* XII, *NPNF* 2 VII, p. 356). "In Christ he chose us before the world was founded, to be dedicated, to be without blemish in his sight, to be full of love" (Eph. 1:4; cf. Ambrose, *Of the Chr. Faith* I.9–12, *NPNF* 2 V, pp. 210–13). One might say that something "occurred" in the mind of God before creation—namely, God chose to love the world and decreed that a world should be. God had eternity

in which many different creations could have been conceived. There is
no reason why God could not have created many creations or other
entire "times" prior to or simultaneously with this cosmic time. Any
world that God creates, however, must have a beginning (Augustine,
Hom. on John, tractate I, *NPNF* 1 VII, pp. 7–12).

Athanasius reasoned that if any change in any world occurs, this
must posit an unchanging One. This became the pivot of an argument
developed by Thomas Aquinas, who defined time as

nothing but the numbering of movement by *before* and *after*. . . . Now in a
thing bereft of movement, which is always the same, there is no before and
after. As therefore the idea of time consists in the numbering of before and
after in movement; so likewise in the apprehension of the uniformity of what
is outside of movement, consists the idea of eternity. Further, those things are
said to be measured by time which have a beginning and an end in time,
because in everything which is moved there is a beginning, and there is an
end. But as whatever is wholly immutable can have no succession, so it has
no beginning, and no end . . . being simultaneously whole. (*ST* I Q10, I, p.
40)

Everything in time is temporally measurable because it must have a
beginning and an end; only God is without beginning and without
end.

The tradition of Platonism developed the notion that the world
itself is eternal. This notion seems to be attracting less attention among
physicists today, although not long ago it held sway in the steady state
theory, which assumes the eternality of the world. Irenaeus, Athanasius, and Gregory of Nyssa thought the notion of the eternality of the
world was rationally deficient since it is impossible to have a creature
without a beginning (Irenaeus, *Ag. Her.* II.28, *ANF* I, p. 401; cf.
Athanasius, *Four Discourses Ag. Arians* I.29, *NPNF* 2 IV, p. 323; Gregory of Nyssa, *Ag. Eunomius* VIII.5, *NPNF* 2 V, pp. 206–11). One who
posits a creature must posit a beginning. Why? Because change involves succession of events, and that is the essence of the temporal.
Time means precisely that: changing in a succession of events (Basil,
Hex. homily I.5, *NPNF* 2 VIII, pp. 54, 55). To posit an "unchangeable
creature" is a contradiction in terms, because changeability has to
exist within finite limits. If any creature exists at all, it must exist in
time, must change, and cannot be timeless. All things created exist in
a succession of events. It is the key premise of all created things that
they exist in time (Ambrose, *Of the Chr. Faith* I.12.74, *NPNF* 2 X, p.
213). That is how one distinguishes between the uncreated Creator
and any creature (Athanasius, *Four Discourses Ag. Arians* I.8–10, *NPNF*
2 IV, pp. 322 ff.; Augustine, *Conf.* XI.11 ff., *LCC* VII, pp. 252 ff.).

On Inequalities of Creaturely Beings

Early in its history, Christianity was charged with a view of an unjust God who blessed inequalities. It was not Marx or Engels who first invented the criticism that Christian faith is like an opiate for those who suffer class oppression. As early as its second century, Christianity had to answer charges on a cosmic scale made by Marcion, Valentinus, Basilides, and others that "it cannot consist with the justice of God in creating the world to assign to some of His creatures an abode in the heavens, and . . . to favor others with the grant of principalities; to bestow powers upon some, dominion upon others" (Origen, *De Princip.* II.9.5, *ANF* IV, p. 291).

Furthermore, it was asked, how could it be fair if God made some celestial beings "of higher rank" and "others of lower rank"; and among human beings how is it that some are privileged to be born into happier circumstances than others? Some are born Hebrews and have the advantage of law, others Greeks and have the advantage of learning, but some were born "amongst the Scythians, with whom parricide is an act sanctioned by law; or amongst the people of Taurus, where strangers are offered in sacrifice. . . . If there be this great diversity of circumstances, and this diverse and varying condition by birth, in which the faculty of free-will has no scope (for no one chooses for himself either where, or with whom, or in what condition he is born), then . . . what other conclusion remains than that these things must be supposed to be regulated by accident and chance?" (Origen, quoting his opponents, in *De Princip.* II.9, *ANF* IV, p. 291). Origen considered these arguments to constitute a "strong objection" (p. 291) to Christian teaching of God as Creator. The problem of inequalities in a good created order has faced Christian teaching from the earliest to contemporary times.

Origen was among the first Christian teachers who sought to answer these devastating charges by arguing that the causes of diversity in the world harked back to the fallenness of heavenly beings, for all rational beings, he thought, were created equal. Yet some angelic beings, he said, abused the good gift of free will and opposed the Creator, and this is the "cause of the diversity among rational creatures, deriving its origin not from the will or judgment of the Creator, but from the freedom of the individual will" of the spiritual powers, who have corrupted the good gift of human freedom through temptation (Origen, *De Princip.* II.9, *ANF* IV, p. 292).

Augustine actively opposed Origen's view, and other views attributed to the followers of Origen, that seeming inequalities in creaturely beings (as between spiritual and corporeal creatures, and between various principalities and powers) were due to divine punishment, and that the world was provided as a punitive prison house for celestial sins, thus explaining creaturely inequalities. For in proportion to their various sins, according to certain Origenists, various creatures merited different degrees of debasement, and thus in the created order we see there are inequalities. Augustine answered that everything God created was approved by God as good, and everything seen together was "very good" (Gen. 1:31).

The apparent inequalities of creatures cannot be fully understood by human reason, for reason sees only from a limited, self-assertive, egocentric, and temporal view, but God sees the whole as good and beautiful: "For as the beauty of a picture is increased by well-managed shadows, so, to the eye that has skill to discern it, the universe is beautified even by sinners, though, considered by themselves, their deformity is a sad blemish" (Augustine, CG XI.23, NPNF 1 II, p. 218). Later, Thomas Aquinas would argue that the wisdom of God made distinctions in created beings, as shown in Genesis 1, between sun, moon, fish, birds, and so forth, and therefore the seeming inequality of these differences is a part of the unfathomable goodness of God. "For the universe would not be perfect if only one grade of goodness were found in things" (Tho. Aq., ST I Q47, I, pp. 246, 247).

The better creator, it would seem, is One who can elicit the best created goodness considered in its entirety, not merely in a single part. Consequently God does not make "every part of the whole the best absolutely, but in proportion to the whole. . . . God also made the universe to be best as a whole" (p. 247), so that all together are pronounced "very good" (Gen. 1:31). It would be a very boring universe if God created everything exactly the same. Creation is like a work of art with many distinct differentia, or like a house where the roof differs from the foundation, so that seen in perspective, seeming "inequality comes from the perfection of the whole" (p. 247). Thus "each and every creature exists for the perfection of the entire universe" (Tho. Aq., ST I Q65, I, p. 326).

Suppose a different world had been created in which all things were the same in value, precisely equal—all creatures (plants, animals, humanity, and inorganic beings) had exactly the same gifts and capacities, and no one could express competencies unique to him- or herself in the interest of sustaining the precise quanta of equality. Would such a world be a better world? Few would answer yes. The premise is implausible, however, because there could be no animal world without a plant world, and no plant world without a geologic base upon which to grow. So the inequalities of capacity for awareness seen in the differences of plants, animals, and humans appear necessary for a better world than that hypothesized.

Suppose another predetermined world in which every human creature were given an absolute *choice* before being born as to what level of education he or she would have, what his or her income would be, and what he or she would produce, enjoy, or attain. Would not there be an insufferable number of rich yuppies shouting "I'm number one"? The premise is implausible, because if all chose, none could attain the "superiority" they would seek. It is a better world where freedom is allowed to struggle against odds, where virtue can be nurtured amid that struggle, and where uncertainties remain to challenge freedom.

Evolution

Classical Christian doctrines of creation do not necessarily deny an evolution, or the possibility of a natural evolutionary development of nature and history. Matter is created *ex nihilo* in a primary sense, radically given by God, but, as emergently developing through secondary causes, that is, through the processes of natural causality, it can undergo its own development (Tho. Aq., *ST* I Q103–6, I, pp. 505–24; cf. Irenaeus, *Ag. Her.* IV.37 ff., ANF I, pp. 518 ff.; Origen, *De Princip.* III.5.4 ff., *ANF* IV, pp. 342 ff.). Everything is created out of nothing, but once something is created out of nothing, then something else can be in due time created out of the prevailing and developing conditions. God continues to create something out of all kinds of somethings. One can posit a gradual evolutionary process that is not a denial of creation (cf. Tertullian, *Ag. Hermogenes* XXIX, *The Gradual Development of Cosmical Order*, ANF III, pp. 493, 494).

Creation is not given without a reliable system of causality, secondary causes in nature, and natural order (Calvin, *Inst.* 1.16.7). All that occurs in creation depends on the Creator, but secondarily it depends upon natural causes permitted and sustained by the Creator. This is why there is a uni-verse instead of a hydra-headed world of many multi-verses: all causality is held in mutual interdependence by the Creator (John Chrysostom, *Concerning the Statues*, hom. X.9–12, *NPNF* 1 IX, pp. 410–12). This subject will be more deliberately pursued in the discussion of providence.

God is not under an external requirement to continue re-creating every moment. This is not necessary, because by God's providence through secondary orders of causes, the universe works according to reliable, God-given laws of nature. These secondary causes are God's own good creation, and enabled through grace by means of the Word in whom "all things are held together" (Col. 1:17) and who "sustains the universe by his word of power" (Heb. 1:3). Natural laws, such as those governing thermodynamics, are reliably given in order that we can have space, a human history, and a cosmological context through ' which God can make his grace and mercy known to us.

In the nineteenth century, evolutionary pantheisms challenged classical Christian teaching of creation. Many argued that the Creator needs the world, must have the world, that the world is as necessary to God as God is to the world. One who accepts this pantheism must take many steps backward to revise classical affirmations of God's almighty power and freedom. It was not until the nineteenth century, when the notion of universal evolution captured the popular imagination, that this idea began to be widely postulated—that a historical process, autonomously conceived, is absolute (Hegel, *Reason in History*; cf. Wesley, *WJW* XIII, pp. 448–55). The rudiments of process thought reside in Hegel, who argued that in the world-historical evolutionary process, God is postulated as related to the process as mind is related to body (cf. Hartshorne, *God as Social Process*; yet Hartshorne systematically neglects Hegel; cf. Hartshorne and Reese, *PSG*). A finite person cannot have mind without a body. The analogy sees the world as necessary to God—not necessarily this world, but some world.

Classical Christian exegetes, on the contrary, have insisted that the world is only consequentially necessary, not absolutely necessary, to God, that is, as a consequence of the divine will to become self-revealed. There could be no freedom in God if God is in fact a necessary part or appendage of the universe. Creation is a free decision, a free gift of God, not coerced by any external necessity (Gregory of Nyssa, *Ag. Eunomius* VIII.5, *NPNF* 2 V, pp. 205–10). God is at liberty to create either this world or some other world—or no world. Christian teaching has continued to reject both emanationism, the notion that the physical world emanates from the being of God, and an evolutionary idealism that holds that creation is proceeding progressively on its own apart from God as Creator.

Christian teaching of creation has sometimes distinguished between God's immediate creation and mediated creation, that is, between the immediate or primordial origin of creaturely being, followed by and distinguished from its ordering and growth. Such a distinction is implied in Genesis 1, in that God called into being light and then subsequently ordered it; God called the waters and earth into being and only then ordered them with "plants bearing seed, fruit-trees bearing fruit" (Gen. 1:1–11). Such development may be viewed as implicitly analogous to evolutionary development, which lends itself to reliable laws of evolutionary development so that scientific inquiry can proceed into various steps of the history of nature. "Science ensures right judgement about creatures. Their drawback is that they are occasions for our turning away from God. Consequently the gift of science corresponds to the third beatitude: 'Blessed are they that weep, for they shall be comforted' " (Matt. 5:5; Tho. Aq., *ST* IIa–IIae Q9.4, *TAPT,* pp. 128, 129).

Evolution of this sort presupposes an *in*volution wherein God permits creatures to have native capacities, natural potentialities, or resident powers through which natural and historical development can occur. There is no sound teaching on the power of God that wishes to reserve all possible causes directly to God alone so as to eliminate all natural causes. Such would be omnicausality instead of omnipotence. The freedom of God to allow companionate beings is greater in power than the hypothesis of a diminished divine freedom that would be unable to make such an allowance, and therefore be forced to do everything directly without the aid of other powers. If divine causality permits, enables, and provides natural causality, then natural causality can be subject to scientific study. What we can see objectively of this development, however, is hardly the whole of it. Our perspective is extremely limited, time-trapped, and culture-bound. The self-disclosure of God in history enables faith to grasp that the development of natural history is far greater than we can imagine, and that it does not proceed without God's own nurturing surveillance, guidance, and rule of the whole (cf. Gregory of Nyssa, *On the Soul and the Resurrection, NPNF* 2 V, pp. 458, 459).

Other Worlds

It may be objected that the cosmos, with its infinite number of galaxies and infinite possibilities for intelligent life, cannot be there only for human beings who are here on earth only perhaps a few million years and who quite possibly could blow themselves up. Suppose there are many other "histories" of free, personal, intelligent life out there in the galaxies. Even if we grant the hypothesis that there are many big bangs and thus many creations, that would not require any amendment in the fundamental Hebraic affirmation that whatever is or ever has been or will be is derived from God. One could entertain such hypotheses and still affirm that cosmic and natural history (whenever and wherever it occurs) exists purposefully as a context and arena for the responsible outplaying of the divine-human dialogue (Origen, *De Princip.* II.1–3, *ANF* IV, pp. 268–75; Wesley, *WJW* XIII, pp. 482–88).

Even if human events end cataclysmically, that need not obliterate the purpose of God, unless one conceives of God as interested only in a single planet and its history. Humanity is not big enough to destroy the divine purpose. Human strength, even in frightening nuclear dimensions, cannot compete with God's power. If the earth is as remote a place in the galaxies as many think it is, then the obliteration of human life would not affect other worlds, other histories; nor would it be an irredeemable loss for God, who has power to start anew with a new world and to do so an infinite number of times (cf. Tertullian, *The Resurrection of the Dead, ANF* III, pp. 551 ff.).

Creation nonetheless is given to humanity, even if not to humanity alone. Lactantius argued that the purpose of the cosmos was closely related to human destiny. He thought that the world was made as an arena for human happiness and responsibility, and humanity for the joy of God:

> Who but man looks up to the heaven? Who views with admiration the sun, who the stars, who all the works of God? Who inhabits the earth? Who receives the fruit from it? Who has in his power the fishes, who the winged creatures, who the quadrupeds, except man? Therefore God made all things on account of man, because all things have turned out for the use of man. . . . For it was befitting, and pious, and necessary, that since He contrived such great works for the sake of man, when He gave him so much honour, and so much power, that he should bear rule in the world, man should . . . acknowledge God the author of such great benefits. (Lactantius, *Div. Inst.* LXVIII ff., *ANF* VII, p. 252)

Christian teaching does not presuppose that our universe is the absolute center of God's creation, even though the only revelation of God that we know is on this particular earth through its history. Everything we know is known only from the vantage point of creaturely existence. Everything we can imagine being created is understandably judged by what we see of our own creation.

If one takes seriously the physics of black holes and the expected disappearance of time and space—and the potential re-creation of time and space—one might hypothesize many different creations. These speculations need not be viewed as a fundamental challenge to

Hebraic-Christian faith in God as Creator. Some physicists present probability evidence that there could be a great many created orders besides the one that we know. But one could reasonably speculate that whatever creation God created, it is likely that God would become known to that world. Suppose there is another world, entirely unknown to and unknowable by us. Why would it not be reasonable to hypothesize, on the basis of our own salvation-history memory, that the same God who has become self-revealed as loving Parent in this world would also become revealed as loving Parent in that world? If so, that Word of revelation would not be of a different God than the one that is made known in this world. And would not the same Spirit we have known be the enabler of the reconciling Word? (cf. Origen, *De Princip.* II.3.5, *ANF* IV, p. 273; Wesley, *WJW* XIII, pp. 482–88).

CHAPTER 7

God's Care for the World

John of Damascus defined providence as "the care that God takes over existing things. And again: Providence is the will of God through which all existing things receive their fitting issue" (*OF* II.29, *NPNF* 2 IX, p. 41).

Providence is God's own act by which God orders all events in creation, nature, and history, so that the ends for which God created them will be in due time realized. The final end is that all creatures will, in God's own time, manifest God's glory and reflect as they are capable the divine happiness.

The Meaning of Providence

Providence is the expression of the divine will, power, and goodness through which the Creator preserves creatures, cooperates with what is coming to pass through their actions, and guides creatures in their long-range purposes (cf. Calvin, *Inst.* 1.16; Heidelberg Catech., Q27, *COC*, p. 316; Belgic Conf. XIII, *COC*, III, pp. 396, 397). Hence classical Christian exegetes have thought of providence in three interrelated dimensions:

• The unceasing activity of the Creator by which in overflowing bounty and good will (Ps. 143:9; Matt. 5:45 ff.) God *upholds* creatures in time and space in an ordered existence (Acts 17:28; Col. 1:17; Heb. 1:3);

• God *cooperates* with natural and secondary causes to employ fit means to good ends through orderly and intelligible processes of natural causes (Prov. 8:29–31; Westminster Conf. V.2, CC, p. 200); and

· God *guides* and governs all events and circumstances, even free, self-determining agents, overruling the regrettable consequences of freedom and directing everything toward its appropriate end for the glory of God (Eph. 1:9–12).

The Christian teaching of providence holds up before us the caring of God for all creatures and the ordering of the whole course of things for good beyond our knowing. The principal actor in the drama of providence is the triune God who, in wisdom, orders events toward those ends most appropriate to the gifts and competencies of each discrete creature. The secondary actors and supporting cast include free human beings, who play against the backdrop of nature's vicissitudes and history's developing hazards (Augustine, *CG* III, *NPNF* 1 II, pp. 43 ff.). Boethius defined providence as that divine reason which "disposes all things" (*Consolation of Phil.* IV.6).

Divine providence is at one level analogous to the human moral virtue of prudence, which acts circumspectly, in harmony with sound reasoning, to avoid extremes and seeks appropriate means for intended ends. God's providing may be understood by analogy to motherly or fatherly caring for the young, through foresighted choices of fitting means to reach good ends (Tho. Aq., *SCG* III.16–19, pp. 70–76; *ST* I Q22, I, p. 121). Such caring requires not only formulating a plan but also acting patiently to carry out the plan over a long course of time.

The root meaning of the term *providence* is to foresee, or to provide (Greek, *pronoia*, Latin, *pro-videre*, to see ahead, to be able to anticipate). The question of providence concerns how God *thinks ahead* to care for all creatures, fitting them for contingencies, for the challenges of history, and for potential self-actualization to the glory of God. God's providing looks ahead for needs as yet unrecognized by creatures. But more than simply foresight, providence has to do with the active, daily caring of God for the world in its hazards.

The Relevance of the Question

The teaching of providence is much closer to the daily life of the believer than at first might be supposed. It is interwoven with the power and courage to live the Christian life day by day, to persevere through trying difficulties, to celebrate divine guidance present in hostile environments. It is faith in providence that enables Christians to pray that God will carry them through hazards, care for them, and be present to them amid ordinary and extraordinary human struggles. Without God's providing, the act of praying would be absurd (Augustine, *Of the Work of Monks* 31–37, *NPNF* 1 III, pp. 518–21). The Belgic Confession of 1561 stated: "This doctrine affords us unspeakable consolation, since we are taught thereby that nothing can befall us by chance, but by the direction of our most gracious and heavenly Father, who watches over us with a paternal care, keeping all creatures so under his power that not a hair of our head (for they are all numbered), nor a sparrow, can fall to the ground, without the will of our Father, in whom we do entirely trust" (*COC* III, p. 397).

Although providence has been among the most familiar and recurrent principal teachings of Catholic, Protestant, and Orthodox Christian belief, it is often misunderstood. No part of Christian teaching is more pertinent to pastoral care than the classical view of providence that one can find abundantly in the writings of Irenaeus, Lactantius, Augustine, and Thomas Aquinas, as well as major Protestant thinkers—Luther, Calvin, Edwards, and Wesley.

Many practical questions of care of souls amid sickness, personal crisis, poverty, and death hinge on how well one understands this pivotal issue of providence. From a right understanding of providence follows a more realistic assessment of human existence, sin, and the meaning of suffering in relation to the goodness of God. One had best not speak prematurely of Christian theodicy without first studying carefully the scriptural teaching on providence.

From the days of Cyril of Jerusalem to John of Damascus a time-tested sequence of reasoning has been devised and established. It moves from God to creation to providence to anthropology to salvation to ecclesiology and sanctification. We follow that sequence, grateful to those who first thought through and defined it. For one cannot adequately address questions of human existence until they are placed in the context of God's providential care of creation. One is not prepared to undertake the question of providence without first treating of creation, which is the first of all the works of God; and we could not speak wisely about the work of God until first having thought through the character and being of God, and the reality of God. Each step along the way depends upon the foundations previously laid, and opens up unfinished questions for subsequent stages.

Three affirmations summarize the Christian teaching of providence: God is preserving the creation in being. God is cooperating to enable creatures to act. God is guiding all creatures, inorganic and organic, animal and rational creation, toward a purposeful end that exceeds the understanding of those being provided for.

The Divine Economy

Since God cannot be seen in his essence, but his purpose can be discerned through his works (Tatian, *Address to the Greeks* IV, *ANF* II, p. 66; Theophilus, *To Autolycus* I.5, *ANF* II, p. 90; Basil, *Epis.* 234.1, *NPNF* 2 VIII), it became increasingly important to the earliest Christian teachers to consider the range, means, and ends of God's providential ordering or, as it was earlier called, God's *oikonomia* (economy).

The verb *oikonomeō* means "to administer or oversee" a complex process or community (Athenagoras, *Ag. the Heathen* 43, *NPNF* 2 IV, p. 27). The treasurer of an organization is one who exercises *oikonomia*, as did Judas among the disciples, and as did God in allowing Judas to do so (John Chrysostom, *Hom. on John*, hom. LXV.2, *NPNF* 1 XIV, p. 242). To economize means to dispense alms and supply the necessities of life (*Apost. Const.* II.25.2). It implies administration through a design or plan. *Oikonomia* implies the proper regulation and control of a complex process, as when the body economizes the functions of animal life, as when a mother's milk is "economized" in relation to giving birth (Clement of Alex., *Instr.* I.6, *ANF* II, pp. 215–22). The notion of *oikonomia* entered into trinitarian language when it was said that God had economized with himself together with his Son and Spirit to accomplish what was prepared from the beginning (*Letter to Diognetus* IX.1, *ANF* I, p. 28). To economize is to arrange and dispose fittingly.

In the light of God's eternal wisdom, God is said to manage and "economize" not only the affairs of history but also the processes of nature, the earthly seasons, and the heavenly cycle of changes (Origen, *Ag. Celsus* I.66–69, *ANF* IV, pp. 426–28). Eusebius argued that the Septuagint was a translation that had emerged out of the divine economy (*Preparation for the Gospel* VIII.1). God ordered revelation economically by revealing himself in two covenants (Origen, *Ag. Celsus* V.50, *ANF* IV, p. 565). Justin ascribed to the divine economy the varied dispensations of grace (*Dialogue* XVII, *ANF* I, p. 203). Paul's conversion was viewed as a part of the divine economy (John Chrysostom, *Comm. on Ephesians* 6.12). Many wonderful events of early church history were understood to have occurred "by the economy of God" (Eusebius, *CH* II.1.13; V.1.32; VII.11.2, *NPNF* 2 I). Suffering was also viewed in relation to the divine economy (Gregory Nazianzen, *On His Father's Silence*, or. XIV.19, *NPNF* 2 VII, p. 254). The angelic powers were viewed as an extensive part of the divine economy (Justin, *Dialogue*

LXXXV, *ANF* I, p. 241; Origen *Ag. Celsus* V.45, *ANF* IV, p. 563; Chrysostom, *Hom. on I Timothy*, XV, *NPNF* 1 XIII, pp. 459 ff.).

The greatest evidence of the divine economy is seen in the incarnation (John of Damascus, *OF* III, *FC* 37, pp. 267 ff.). Wherever the Spirit is at work, whether in the remission of sins, prophecy, or revelation, or the oversight and protection of Scripture, there the divine economy is evidencing itself (Origen, *Comm. on Jeremiah* 16.5; Justin, *Dialogue* LXXXIV, *ANF* I, p. 241; Irenaeus, *Ag. Her.* IV.31.1, *ANF* I, pp. 504, 505). Some wonder why the doctrine of providence has taken on such a wide application. Part of the answer hinges on the exceptionally variable way that it was used by early Christian exegetes.

It was this flexible word, so widely adaptable to so many applications, that the early church teachers chose to express a major segment of Christian doctrine, later called the doctrine of providence. Basil the Great and Gregory of Nyssa both discussed the incarnation in connection with the theme of the divine economy (Basil, *Letter* 136, *NPNF* 2 VIII, p. 276; Gregory of Nyssa, *Great Catech.* VIII–XXIV, *NPNF* 2 V, pp. 484–94).

The divine economy was a major part of Christian teaching by the time of John of Damascus, and in his summary he considered, under the divine economy, not only God's care for the world in providence, prescience, and predestination, but also the incarnation (John of Damascus, *OF* II.29, *FC* 37, pp. 260 ff.). John concluded that "if providence is God's will, then, according to right reason, everything that has come about through providence has quite necessarily come about in the best manner and that most befitting God, so that it could not have happened in a better way" (p. 260).

Since God is wise, the faithful can assume that his providing is wise. Since God is good, this providing, even when we fail to recognize it, is in some hidden way good. When others accuse God of injustice, the faithful are called to bear patiently with them, for "It is because of the fact that God's providence is beyond knowledge and beyond comprehension, and because to Him alone are our thoughts and actions and the events of the future known. However, when I say 'all,' I am referring to those things which do not depend upon us, because those which do depend upon us do not belong to providence, but to our own free will" (John of Damascus, *OF* II.29, *FC* 37, p. 261).

Rational Arguments on Providence

Classical exegetes thought that rational arguments concerning providence were secondary and limited, hinging largely upon how adequately scriptural arguments had been established, especially those concerning God's necessary existence, the divine attributes of wisdom, power, and justice, and the radically derived nature of creaturely existence. If God is as described in the classical discussion of divine attributes, then such a being could not exist without exercising providential care over a world wisely created.

This is a deductive argument that begins with the divine attributes and asks about their consistent application to the ordering of the world (Augustine, *Divine Prov. and the Problem of Evil* II.1–5, FC 1, pp. 273–93). For what sort of *wisdom* would it be that could possibly create a universe and leave it totally ungoverned? It is unthinkable to suppose that God would purposefully bring this vast cosmos into being and then not provide for its preservation and maintenance and the fulfillment of its original purpose. It is inconsistent with the divine *omnipotence* to limit God's influence to the beginning of creation and not to its sustenance and development. It would be equally inconsistent with divine *justice* that God would create beings with moral sensitivities and conscience, only to make a travesty of such moral awareness by abandoning human development to fate, chance, or unguided self-determination. It is inconsistent with God's *holiness* that God would allow evil to triumph in history without being finally corrected by active, redemptive divine love. By virtue of God's *omnipresence*, God determines not to be absent from any part of the universe. Thus the divine attributes that are necessary and intrinsic to God's nature logically require and imply God's free and gracious preservation and governance of the world. Such attributes and actions are necessary to that being worthy of the name of God (Cyril of Jerusalem, *Catech. Lect.* V.4, NPNF 2 VII, p. 20).

All characteristics of the divine life that we have previously discussed work together in the providential ordering of creation: The *will* of God determines the end for which providential means are fashioned. God's *all-wise knowing* understands, foresees, and grasps the appropriate relation of means to ends in the right ordering of creation. God's incomparable *goodness* wills the good of creatures consonant with each creature's ability to receive and participate in the good. God's incomparable *power* ensures the execution of the intent of the divine will.

The intelligibility and constancy of nature requires some hypothesis about the ground of this intelligibility and constancy. Each part functions in remarkable order and harmony with all other parts. Since the natural order is a system, no part is finally separable from the whole system. The extraordinary complexity of nature remains in principle intelligible, even if we inaccurately grasp it. The natural order is unfailingly reliable: The sun never forgets to rise. The seasons continue in their regularity. Plants and animals manage to continue over aeons to adapt and to propagate themselves, even when endangered by catastrophes or extinction. This immense system of natural ordering, so reliable in its movement, so varied and beautiful, proceeding from age to age without interruption, elicits in the beholding human mind the awesome and compelling conclusion that everything exists under the continuing governance of an almighty mind (Gregory of Nyssa, *Great Catech.* X ff., *NPNF* 2 V, pp. 485 ff.).

If it is objected that the order of which we speak may be accounted for by laws of nature without any hypothesis of God, a careful examination of the objection will reveal that it, too, reinforces the argument. For what is meant by laws of nature other than some rule or order established by some legitimate authority? That implies a combination of intelligence and power or a designing, governing mind, which is what providence essentially asserts. Inert, inanimate matter cannot spontaneously organize itself or even initiate or voluntarily stop any motion, for that requires mind. The hypothesis of natural law itself suggests and requires the intelligible order and governance implied in providence (Tho. Aq., *Compend.* 130, pp. 138, 139).

Furthermore, each of the arguments for the *existence* of God have their counterpart in arguments for the *providence* of God. That the presence in the world of design implies a designer need not apply only to the notion of an original or primordial designer, but also to the responsive Provident One who is enmeshed in each new phase of natural or historical development, redesigning in relation to emergent contingencies so as to work out in due course the purpose of God from the beginning. Similarly, the argument from the dependent nature of creatures that hypothesizes that something must necessarily exist, applies not only to the original dependency of the creation upon the creator, but in a continuing way to the ongoing dependency of all creatures on the provider and guide of creation (Tho. Aq., *SCG* III.89 ff., II, pp. 35 ff.).

The course of universal history itself, when properly and thoroughly studied, yields an inexorable impression that human frailty is being guided and human societies protected from their own follies (Augustine, *CG* V.10–26, *NPNF* 1 II, pp. 93–107). The preservation of the church through massive hazards and historical crises has often been held to be the supreme evidence of God's providence (Eusebius, *CH* VIII, *NPNF* 2 I, pp. 323–41).

Early Christian exegetes had available to them two fundamentally different philosophical opinions concerning providence, Epicurean and Stoic. These two views were often weighed against scriptural attestations of providence. The Epicureans explicitly denied providence, holding that, if we fear the gods, we exist in bondage and servitude to them, and that those who wish to live in serenity should ignore the gods because the gods ignore them. The Stoics, who were to exercise an important influence upon early Christianity, emphasized the unity of the whole of life and spoke of a providence at work universally, but not personally—rather, quite impersonally in all things—as the expression of an intelligible *logos* diffusely manifesting itself in human events. They urged the wise to adopt an attitude of *apatheia*, a weaning oneself away from passions in order that one might become more rightly oriented toward the universal principle of reasoning in all things.

Views Opposing Providence

The historic Christian understanding of providence must be distinguished from a whole series of imbalanced and undesirable views with which Christian faith has struggled. The classical understanding of God's providence has in fact gradually become more clearly defined through a history of debate with corrupted or inadequate views. Eight views in particular have challenged the ancient ecumenical tradition, which has gradually become defined in these ways:

• Providence is not a *pantheism*, which confuses God and the world by absorbing God into the world.

• The providing God is quite different from the God of *deism*, which cuts God off from the world by making God the Creator of the world that God then abruptly leaves, as a watchmaker might leave a watch behind, implying a complete separation between God and the world.

• Providence is not a *dualism*, which views the world as divided into two parts under a good power and a bad power who compete for control, neither of which could be final, and therefore neither of which could be God.

• Providence is distinguished from an *indeterminism*, which holds that the world is not under any intelligible control at all.

• Providence is not a strict or unqualified *determinism*, which posits a control so absolute that it destroys human responsibility, freedom, and accountability, viewing all events only in terms of their natural causal determination.

· Providence is also sharply different from a view of God's *omnicausality* that holds that God so does everything that all other agents do nothing.

· Providence distinguishes itself from a doctrine of *chance*, which denies that the controlling power can be intelligible or personal or rational.

· Finally, providence differs from a doctrine of *fate*, which denies that the ultimate power is benevolent.

In each of these cases, there is a well-meaning distortion that denies something important about God, about some attribute intrinsic to the being of God. We know from the *majesty* of God that God is different from the world, so we must distinguish pantheism from the Christian doctrine of providence. We know from God's *omnipresence and omnipotence* that God is intimately involved in every aspect of the world, so God's providence cannot be identified with the absentee God of deism. We know from God's *unity* that providence must differ from that view which asserts two absolute powers or competitive deities in history. Since Christian teaching affirms the *intelligibility* of the divine knower, it cannot affirm a fundamental lack of intelligibility in the world God creates, or deny order in nature. Since Christian teaching affirms the *goodness and wisdom* of God in enabling and empowering human freedom, it cannot be satisfied with a determinism that denies human freedom or asserts God's *almighty power or influence* in such a way as to eliminate all other influences; or a view of chance that denies divine *purposefulness*; or a view of fate that denies divine *benevolence*.

It is no easy task for Christian teaching to keep all these affirmations in a proper balance. The community of faith implicitly has them already in practical balance. It is the teaching pastor's task to try to explain how they can be in balance. Anything short of this steady balance is a fragile solution, a way of solving the problem prematurely. A more finely woven and satisfying solution will try to hold on to all these necessary affirmations simultaneously and in good balance: the sovereignty of God, the goodness of God, the intelligence of God, the involvement of God in the world, human freedom, the intelligibility of the natural order.

The Christian teaching of God's providence has had to do battle most often with pantheistic views that do not grasp the fundamental distinction between God and the world. One kind of pantheism tends idealistically to absorb the world and time into God (as in Hegel); others tend materialistically to absorb God into the world and time (as Wieman). Both amount to the same thing, because they erase the difference between God and the temporal world.

It has required of Christian teaching a long struggle to develop a view of providence that is both adequate to scriptural teaching and consistent with reason and experience and that avoids all these pitfalls. From its earliest decades Christian thinking about providence has had to distinguish itself against notions that the world is governed by chance or fate, and against various astrological determinisms which remain options in modern consciousness (Hippolytus, *Refutation of All Her.* IV, *ANF* V, pp. 24–46).

Divine Preservation and Cooperation with Natural Causality

The Modes and Scope of God's Caring

The basic modes of the economy of divine care are enormously varied, but have been conveniently distinguished by classical Christian teachers into upholding, allowing, and guiding providence (or preservation, concurrence, and governance). These three categories encompass the range of the care that God extends over all creatures and their development. By God's sustaining or conserving providential activity *(conservatio)* God preserves all things in being; by God's cooperative providential activity *(cooperatio)* God concurs and cooperates with secondary causes in the created order, and with human free, self-determined wills, to permit and enable the events of creaturely life; and by God's governing providential activity *(gubernatio)* God guides all things through fitting means toward ends appropriate to God's larger purpose in creation (Augustine, *CG* XII.13–15, *NPNF* 1 II, pp. 234–36, XV ff., pp. 284 ff.; John of Damascus, *OF* II.44, *NPNF* 2 IX, p. 42; Heppe, *RD*, pp. 251 ff.).

Preservation

Preservation refers first to the effective action of God by which all creatures are kept in being. Preservation is the providential means by which God maintains, upholds in being, and perpetuates what has been created. What God creates, God preserves in being (Ps. 138:7; cf. Tho. Aq., *SCG* III.65.9, II, p. 217). God "sustains the universe by his word of power" (Heb. 3:1).

Divine preservation encompasses history and nature: "O Lord, you preserve both man and beast" (Ps. 36:6, NIV). But the biblical focus is more often upon the fervent, personal awareness that one's own being is being daily preserved and the earnest petition for life's continuance: "For your name's sake, O Lord, preserve my life" (Ps. 143:11, NIV).

If God should withdraw this preserving activity from creaturely being, there would simply be no being there. For no creature can sustain itself in being without this divine preserving activity. "When you hide your face, they are terrified; when you take away their breath, they die and return to the dust. When you send your Spirit they are created" (Ps. 104:29, 30, NIV). In this One "we live and move and have our being" (Acts 17:28). "He exists before everything, and all things are *held together* in him" (Col. 1:17, italics added). It is as though the wisdom of God is the continuing ontological mucilage of creation, holding the creation together (Chemnitz, *LT*, I, p. 125; Wesley, *Letters, To Thomas Church* II, pp. 256 ff.).

Just as "the preservation of light in the air is by the continual influence of the sun" (Tho. Aq., *ST* I Q104, I, p. 512), so are all things continually dependent upon God for their perpetuation. The divine preservation of the cosmos is a free act of God. As God was free to create or not to create all things, so is God free to continue or not continue all things in being. Yet God continues by grace to uphold all things by the word of his power (Heb. 1:3; John Chrysostom, *Hom. on Hebrews* II, *NPNF* 1 XIV, pp. 372, 373).

One principle is evident throughout it all: God accommodates the divine majesty and power to the limited capacities of creatures. God allows creaturely goods to be received and achieved through creatures in a way that, taken as a whole, magnifies and manifests the divine glory (Pss. 8:1–5; 72:19; 139:5; cf. Calovius, *SLT* III.1194).

Although this preserving activity is indeed a mystery transcending our categories of understanding, God has made known the divine good will to preserve creatures in being in order that creaturely goods may be actualized. Through revelation in history, Scripture, and by responsive faith and prayer in the community of faith, believers are instructed in the ways by which God sustains every living creature (Ambrose, *Expos. of Chr. Faith* I.2–5, *NPNF* 2 X, pp. 203–7, *On the Decease of Satyrus, NPNF* 2 X, pp. 161 ff.). God maintains each creaturely being in its own unique way, with its own distinctive capacities for actualizing creaturely goods, in ways that reflect the divine wisdom even in insensate being (Calvin, *Inst.* 15.14; 1.16).

Suppose all of history could be put in brackets, as if in a parenthesis within a sentence spoken eternally. This metaphor permits us to make a distinction between the activity of God in history and the primordial being of God that preconditions history. In the order of causality, God is said to be the first or primal cause preconditioning all subsequent secondary causes. In this created order myriads of billions of secondary causes are every moment occurring, all sustained "by his word of power" (Heb. 1:3). The One who preserves in being through secondary causes is none other than the One who gives being originally. Hence the summary: the Creator is the Preserver (John of Damascus, *OF* II.29, *FC* 37, p. 260; Tho. Aq., *ST* Q103 ff., I, pp. 505 ff.; Quenstedt, *TDP*, I, p. 531; Gerhard, *LT*, IV, p. 83).

Divine providence does not exclude free human agency but enables and sustains it. There are indeed limits on human freedom, but God's providence, in fact, grants and permits freedom. Though God does not give aid to human distortions and sin, God nonetheless by grace sustains the human nature that falls into sin. God permits sin in an otherwise good and intelligible order, yet limits and finally overrules whatever distortions human freedom can create (Augustine, *CG* V.9–11, *NPNF* 1 II, pp. 90–93).

Thomas Aquinas argued that God preserves creatures both mediately (through secondary causes) and immediately (or directly), as "when what is preserved depends on the preserver in such a way that it cannot exist without it. In this way the being of every creature depends on God, so that not for a moment could one subsist, but would fall into nothingness, were it not kept in being by the operation of the Divine power" (Tho. Aq., *ST* I Q104, I, p. 512; cf. Augustine, *Literal Interp. of Gen.* IV.12; Gregory, *Magna Moralia XVI, LF*). Based on the biblical promise that "whatever God does lasts forever" (Eccles. 3:11), Thomas argued that finally nothing God has created will be annihilated, although its form of composition may change. "If God were to annihilate anything, this would not imply an *action* on God's part," he mused, "but a mere *cessation* of His action" (Tho. Aq., *ST* I Q104, p. 514, italics added; cf. Hollaz, *ETA*, pp. 421 ff., 442).

The Cooperation of God with Secondary Causes

Providential concurrence, or divine cooperation with secondary causes, is the second basic mode of God's caring activity discerned by classical exegetes. In both ancient and modern times, this part of Christian teaching has been crucial to the nurture of healthy dialogue between Christian faith and the natural sciences.

God's concurring activity refers to that cooperation of divine power with subordinate powers and secondary causes that sustains, empowers, and enables those myriads of billions of natural causes. Nature is an immense complex of multilayered causality. Christian teaching has pursued various means of relating God's providence to natural law and causality. How is God cooperatively or co-workingly present and empowering in those causes? Classical exegetes hypothesized the ever-recurring cooperation of divine power with all subordinate powers and secondary causes, according to the reliable laws of their operation, whether those laws are established in the natural, rational, or moral sphere (Lactantius, *Div. Inst.* III.25–30, *ANF* VII, pp. 95–100; Tho. Aq., *ST* I Q90 ff., I, pp. 993 ff.; Quenstedt, *TDP* I, pp. 431 ff.). These laws and powers do not work miscellaneously or autonomously, as if engendered by themselves. Natural and moral law are viewed by classical exegetes as being radically dependent upon the constant cooperation of God. This simply means that God concurs (*concursus*, runs alongside) with secondary causality (Tho. Aq. *St* I Q22, I, pp. 120–25; *SCG* III.94, pt. II, pp. 50 ff.). "God's providence does not remove but posits second causes" (Wollebius, *CTC* 30, in Heppe, *RD*, p. 258).

The scriptural references upon which classical exegesis based these conclusions held divine and natural causality together without denying either: "In truth all our works are thy doing, O Lord our God" (Isa. 26:12). "You must work out your own salvation in fear and trembling; for it is God who works in you, inspiring both the will and the deed, for his own chosen purpose" (Phil. 2:13; Origen, *De Princip.* III.1, *ANF* IV, pp. 302–8, 323 f.). Accordingly, God's concurrence does not do away with the efficacy of natural causes—on the contrary, it empowers and enables secondary causes.

This concurrence is occurring everywhere that anything is occurring. If something moves, it moves by divine concurrence. Anywhere any secondary cause is at work, God is at work, not absolutely or unilaterally determining that secondary cause, but cooperating so that it can work. It works, not as if autonomously on its own, but through the laws appropriate to its level of participation in being, that is, through one of many levels of natural and moral law (Tho. Aq., *SCG* LXVI, pp. 218 ff.; Hollaz, *ETA*, pp. 440 ff.).

Thomas saw clear evidence for providence in the observable fact that natural bodies are moved toward ends, even though they do not understand their end (Tho. Aq., *SCG* III.64, III, p. 210). "It is impossible for things that do not know their end to work for that end, and to reach that end in an orderly way, unless they are moved by someone possessing knowledge of the end" (p. 211), so wherever there is purposeful movement toward an end, the cause must lead back either mediately or immediately to God.

Even more persuasive is the fact that things of contrary natures merge harmoniously together in a single order. If one hears in the distance a lyre of many diverse strings playing in concord, one would easily perceive "that this lyre was not playing itself" (Athanasius, *Ag. Heathen* 38, *NPNF* 2 IV, p. 24). In naturalistic reductionism there is no adequate explanation for the intricate symphony of nature (Tho. Aq., *SCG* III, p. 211). God is the "cause of the whole" (p. 212). Hence Scripture ascribes to God the concurrent governance of all things (Ps. 46:8–11).

Concurrence and Freedom

This implies respect for human freedom and responsibility, for God does not simply *operate* our wills or directly will for us instead of allowing us to will. That would hardly be consistent with the stress in Scripture on God-given responsible freedom. If God were omnicausally and absolutely determining every event at this moment (i.e., if everything every creature is doing at this moment were being unilaterally and absolutely determined by God without any secondary causes), freedom would not be real, and therefore any assumption that persons are responsible for themselves would not be true. The biblical affirmation that in God we "live and move and have our being" (Acts 27:28) implies neither that God's being is constricted to finite being nor that human self-actualization is displaced or annihilated by the being of God. These are misconstructions of providence found in both pantheistic and fatalistic distortions of Christian teaching (Hippolytus, *Refutation* VI, *ANF* V, pp. 74–99; Pope, *Compend.* I, p. 447; Bavinck, *DG*, I; cf. Wieman, and Brightman in *PSG*).

Hence it is said that God's cooperative action does not unilaterally operate our wills, but cooperates with our wills so as to be present in and with our every activity. In this way the activity of God is supportive of variably determined freedoms. By this means God funds and resources our free wills. These effects are not produced by God apart from natural means, or by an individually abstracted human will as if a single willing agent could be separated from its social, natural, historical context. God is the primordial causal agent that cooperates with multiple secondary causes. Within and through the whole complex, evolving matrix of natural causality there emerges human free will, created good but permitted to go awry, able to stand, liable to fall (Clement of Alex., *Strom.* II.14, 15, *ANF* II, pp. 361–63; Wesley, *The New Birth*, pp. 97–111).

The abuse of freedom ends in self-alienation and wretchedness. God has permitted that freedom which is capable of falling. A fine distinction must be noted here: God cooperates so as to allow the *effects* of our freedom but to not applaud its *defects*. God allows freedom to be penultimately *effective*, even permitting freedom to distort an otherwise good creation, but that does not mean that God affirms or enjoys or permanently abides the *defective* side of freedom (Augustine, *Ag. Two Letters of the Pelagians* I, *NPNF* 1 III, pp. 377–90; Calvin, *Inst.* 3.22–24; Heppe, *RD* IX, pp. 220 ff.; Schmid, *DT* II).

At this point Christian exegetes have worked cautiously to preserve the teaching of the holiness of God from the charge that God directly causes evil. The *freewill defense* has become a standard response to the charge that God is the author of sin. Accordingly, it is not God that causes sin, but rather it is human freedom, which is a good but distortable creation of God, that elicits sin. We do the sinning ourselves; God does not do it. It is not sin with which God cooperates, but human freedom. God cooperates by empowering free will to act and by providing the secondary arena of natural causality in which our freedom is able to stand, though liable to fall (John of Damascus, *OF* II.24, 25, *NPNF* 2 IX, pp. 38–40). Hence the memorable formula: God concurs with the effect but not with the defect of our actions (Tho. Aq., *SCG* III.77, I, pp. 258 ff.).

This useful formulation helps protect Christian teaching against the notion of absolute divine omnicausal determination, such as that found in Islamic piety, which asserts a consistent determination of all things by God and nothing else. Such an argument has not, on the whole, been a characteristic of Christian doctrines of providence, even in traditions that have strongly stressed predestination. Christian doctrines of providence have sought earnestly to preserve the dimension of the free, responsible will that falls and becomes radically self-alienated through sin (Augustine, *Spirit and Letter*, chaps. 52–58, *NPNF* 1 V, pp. 106–9; Wesley, *WJW* VI, pp. 311 ff.). The notion that God is the sole agent of all creaturely actions eliminates the notion of cooperation with other wills, because no other wills could exist under those circumstances. That notion has created mischief on hospital wards and in mental institutions and has rationalized holy wars, crusades, and racism. Both the view that God absolutely determines human effects without any cooperation of human freedom and the view that human freedom occurs without divine concurrence equally lack grounding in the classical Christian understanding of providential concurrence. The concise scriptural affirmation balances these points: "Apart from me you can do nothing" (John 15:5); that is, without the cooperative grounding of our freedom in divine providence, we could not even have in the first place the freedom that is prone to go awry.

One cannot even sin without providence. God cooperates with freedom, not sin, but sin can come into being only in an order in which its preconditions are permitted by God. God cooperates by allowing moral freedom and natural causality to function, out of which freedom becomes fallen and self-alienated. That God permits us freedom to fall does not imply that God directly causes the fall, or that God delights to see freedom falling, or that God creates freedom already as fallen. God, rather, permits freedom to work its own blessedness or self-condemnation, to spell itself out in glory or disaster (Clement of Alex., *Strom.* II.14, 15, *ANF* II, pp. 361–63; John of Damascus, *OF* II.25–29; III.13, *NPNF* 2 IX, pp. 39–42, 58, 59).

In the midst of all this, however, God is constantly resisting, constraining, limiting, and working to prevent the consequences of sin from inordinately undermining God's larger purposes. God would never allow sin finally to frustrate or overcome God's good purpose in creation. Eventually it is faith's hope that, both within and beyond history, God will overrule whatever distortions, injustices, and alienations human freedom is able to create (Athenagoras, *Plea*, *LCC* I, pp. 309–11, 339 ff.).

The freedom of God is presupposed in any talk of divine cooperation with natural causality or human self-determination. God is not under any *absolute necessity* to proceed in a particular way. God freely chooses to order life in such a way that human freedom may be a companion to God's freedom without a denial of God's almighty power or goodness. These divine attributes must be held firmly together in appropriate balance, a difficult thing to do when there are so many cheap solutions at hand to oversimplify or reduce that tension. But though the concurrence of God in both natural causality and human freedom is not limited by any necessity external to God, such concurrence may be said to be a *proximate or consequent necessity*, consequent to God's will to create and to ennoble created beings with purposes that require history for their fulfillment (John of Damascus, *OF* II.29, *FC* 37, p. 263). There is no need to derogate secondary causes, for it is through these natural causes that God intends to convey to humanity the blessings of providence (cf. Calvin, *Inst.* 1.17, 18; Heidelberg Catech. 104; K. Barth, *CD* III/3, pp. 96 ff.; Tho. Aq., *ST* I Q105, I, pp. 515–17; J. Cocceius, *Summa Theologiae* XXVIII.25).

Commenting on Isaiah 26:12, "in truth all our works are thy doing," Thomas Aquinas argued against the view that understands "God to work in every agent in such a way that no created power has any effect in things, but that God alone is the immediate cause of everything wrought; for instance, that it is not fire that gives heat, but God in the fire, and so forth. But this is impossible" (*ST* I Q105, I, p. 518). For this would imply lack of power in the Creator, that is, the lack of power to invest any other agent with power. Furthermore, all things would seem purposeless if they lacked an operation proper to them. It is objectionable if the divine causality makes natural or human causality superfluous, for "if God produces the entire natural effect, then nothing is left of the effect for the natural agent to produce" (*SCG* III.70, II, p. 235). Thomas argued that causality is not partly accomplished by God and partly by the natural agent, but rather "the natural thing does not produce it except by divine power" (pp. 235, 236). "Every power in any agent is from God," Thomas concluded. "Every agent acts by the divine power" (Tho. Aq., *SCG* III.67, I, pp. 221, 222). Yet "we do not take away their proper actions from created things, though we attribute all the effects of created things to God, as an agent working in all things" (p. 235). Hence "God works in every worker" (*ST* I Q105, I, p. 518).

Divine Governance of the World

When Abraham's faith was tested with Isaac, "Abraham named that place Jehovah-jireh; and to this day the saying is: 'In the mountain of the Lord it was provided'" (Gen. 22:14). In the name Jehovah-jireh, which means "the Lord will see and provide," the central insight of God's governing providence is contained. Later the Fourth Gospel would report the remarkable saying of Jesus, "Your father Abraham was overjoyed to see my day" (John 8:56). The implication is that Abraham trusted that God's promise would be fulfilled, even if it required a long and arduous history to accomplish. The end was clear, and it was trusted that providence would find a means. Although God's ways are past our finding out (Rom. 11:33), the trusting community nonetheless beholds clues in nature, traces in history, and luminous disclosures in Scripture of the ways God uses evil for good and turns human wrath into his praising (Ps. 70:10).

God the Spirit is at work to guide all creaturely processes providentially toward greater purposes largely unknown to rational creatures. A particular moment of the disclosure of some divine providence may be compared to an archaeological find of a small pattern of a huge ancient mosaic. Even though the community may not see the whole of the mosaic, they grasp enough to reasonably imagine the larger pattern. Even if we see only one little corner of history, we may discern enough to trust that if we were able to see the whole of history, we would understand and enjoy the beauty of God's glory manifesting itself in all of history as in Christ (Origen, *Ag. Celsus* II.51, *ANF* IV, pp. 4551 f.; cf. Pannenberg, *Jesus, God and Man*).

Throughout this whole historical process is God's own guiding, directing activity. Each of billions of events has its own *telos*, or "purpose," at any given moment. Seen in the light of the scriptural revelation of God's providential activity, all of this is moving toward a plausible, trustable end: the fulfillment of God's purpose in creation (Tho. Aq., *ST* I Q103, I, pp. 505–11).

This is why the community of faith has always found comfort in the teaching of God's providence. God is working in complex ways to allow the glorious and wretched story of abused freedom to play itself out, so that the divine goodness may be manifested through and beyond our free activity and the struggles and lives of other creatures. God's providential governance is especially pertinent to the guidance of fallible human intelligence and moral freedom and political imagination. God's supervision functions without coercing or eliminating the priceless dimension of human self-determination (John of Damascus, *OF* II.29, *FC* 37, pp. 261–63).

God's governance cannot be separated finally from a consideration of the way God deals with sin and redemption. *Providence* is the term we use to speak of that entire history stretching between creation and consummation that has its central focus in the teaching of redemption. Redemption is the provision God makes to deal with a foreseen, permitted, restrained, condemned, and vanquished evil (Calvin, *Inst.* 3.14; Pope, *Compend.* I, p. 453). The ways in which God foresees, permits, restrains, condemns, and conquers evil are the subject of a larger set of questions concerning salvation, to be fully discussed later. At this point it is needful to note only that sin has a long career, and that the divine governance of currently ambiguous moral history must be seen finally in the light of Christ. In this way, the teaching of providence is the central bridge between creation and redemption.

Objects of Divine Governance

What is the extent of the embrace of the divine Care-giver? No creature is so great as to be beyond the need of God's care (Ps. 103). "Thy might dost fix the mountains in their place" (Ps. 65:6). No creature is so small as to be overlooked by God's care: ravens (Ps. 147:9), sparrows (Matt. 10:29), lilies and grass (Matt. 6:28, 30), and the hairs of our heads (Matt. 10:30). God's providential sustenance embraces the physical world (Job 37:5), animal creation (Ps. 104:21), the affairs of nations (Isa. 40 ff.), justice in societies (Job 12; Amos 5). God is responsive to prayer (Matt. 7:7). Nothing is beyond God's providence, even the superpersonal intelligences *(aggelos)* that have elicited so much speculation. Our lives are begun, continued, and ended through divine providence (Ps. 145:15). Everything is encompassed by this sustaining, preserving, cooperating, guiding power of God.

The scope of providence may be envisioned as the center of four widening concentric circles, encompassing all four classes of creaturely beings and sustaining each of them in correlated yet distinguishable ways. In an ascending scale they are

- lifeless matter (inanimate creaturely being)
- living plants (living, but immobile, vegetable beings)
- animals (living mobile beings lacking human rationality)
- humans (living, rational, accountable, self-determining moral agents)

Each sphere presupposes the sustenance of the previous spheres. In this way divine governance becomes an important meeting point for the encounter of Christian truth with four spheres of scientific and humanistic study in the university: physics, botany, zoology, and anthropology.

God's governing activity is adapted to the four spheres in which it operates—physical, biological, animal, and moral. One would not organize and design a garden in the same way one would guide a child, for the garden is in an order of life quite different from the human sphere, however analogous. Plants and children are in some ways alike, but in many more ways different. One would not take care of the family cat in the same way that one would take care of the family piano, because animal creation requires a very different kind of care than does a physical object. God's governing and guiding activity operates simultaneously on all four of these levels, human, animal, vegetable, and mineral, adapted at each level to the particular capacities of that level (*ST* I Q69–72, I, pp. 342–52).

Each of these distinct spheres of creaturely being has a nature peculiar to itself. God provides and sustains each sphere of creaturely being in accordance with its own particular conditions, needs, requirements, and nature. Here emerges an important providential principle: God's care over each of these creaturely spheres must be different, adapted to the nature of the things to be cared for (Calvin, *Inst.* 1.14–17; 3:20). For what is care if it is not individuated and responsive to and correlated with the particular needs of the one cared for? To imagine that God would employ the same mode of care in reference to creaturely beings so different as a rock, a tree, a bird, and a child would be to mistakenly estimate God's understanding of the variety of needs, natures, and requirements of each of these creaturely spheres. Given the differences in these four spheres, God works through ordinary channels of natural law, secondary causes, adaptive instincts, and contingent self-determinations, to enable creatures to reflect the divine glory by actualizing creaturely goods.

Providence in Material Creation

Since physical matter is lifeless and can be moved only as it is moved by something else, it is reasonable to expect that physical creation will be governed by physical force, not by ideas or persuasion. Lifeless matter can be governed only by physical laws. It is a valuable gift of the Provider that these physical forces, the study of which is called physics, are reliable, intelligible, and do not vary. We are made more thankful for this by imagining a universe in which the natural order is unreliable, or reliable only on certain Tuesdays. Only an invariable order is appropriate to inanimate material reality, which, without spirit, life, or mind, can only move when moved. It is by such laws of motion and causation that the physical world works, the stars turn in their orbits, the seasons change in their orderly way, and time moves relentlessly on (Ps. 33:6; Jer. 31:35; 33:22; Clementina, *Recogni tions* VIII.40–50, *ANF* VIII, pp. 176–79).

One cannot give a stone a moral command and expect it to be obeyed, because a stone does not have rational or moral awareness. These are competencies presupposed in the moral order.

Classical Christian exegesis has interpreted the laws of nature, causation, motion, and physical order as God's own method of working in the governance of nature (Prov. 8:22–31; Tertullian, *Ag. Hermogenes* XX–XXXII, *ANF* III, pp. 488–96). They are not independent of God. To assert that lifeless matter is governed by natural law, but without any influence of any ordering mind or source of intelligibility, is tantamount to asserting that there is no law or governance at all in nature, that nature is adrift as a spontaneous interaction of material substances without purpose or intelligible order. The appearance of order in any form must posit some ordering agent as sufficient cause (Ps. 65:9–13).

It is in this spirit that the psalmist poetically attributed to God the ordering of all physical causes: "He brings up the mist from the ends of the earth, he opens rifts for the rain, and brings the wind out of his storehouses " (Ps. 135:6, 7; cf. Theophilus, *To Autolycus* I.5, 6, *ANF* II, pp. 90, 91).

Providence in Vegetative Creation

Plant life is also under the divine governance, but in a different way than lifeless matter, which only moves by the coercive laws of motion, which are invariable. Material laws remain operative in plant life, but something is added: the laws of vegetation, reproduction, photosynthesis, the ability to take sun and water and minerals and make out of this inert matter *life*. The enormous difference between lifeless matter and vegetative matter is (unfathomably) life (Tertullian, *Treatise on the Soul* II ff., *ANF* III, pp. 182 ff.; John of Damascus, *OF* II.12, *FC* 37, p. 237). God governs life in a very different way than nonlife.

God's ruling care extends throughout the entire range of aeons of emergent life and endless fecundity and adaptivity of vegetable creation (Gen. 1:11, 12). Each sphere is dependent upon the sphere "beneath" it. The plants could not exist without the earth. In terms of sheer mass, most of the universe is taken up with lifeless matter. Life is a precious rare event on the outer crust of the earth, even more rare when viewed in relation to the whole cosmic order. Few planets can support life, even when viewed speculatively, but thus far we know of only one planet in the universe where plant life exists (Wesley, *WJW* II, pp. 515 ff.). This underscores the fact that when plant life occurs, it is extraordinarily precious and not to be discounted or treated as superabundant or worthless. This view has decisive political implications in both industrialized and developing nations.

Plants are highly capable of adaptation to changing atmospheric, natural, and interspecies circumstances through mutation and the genetic varieties that mutation devises. This whole process of bio-genetic selectivity has remarkable evocative power for the religious imagination, the awareness of God's providential care for plant life (Deut. 32:1, 2). Plants "learn" (by adaptation) how to gather resources from soil and energy from the sun in different climates, how to attract insects for fertilization, and so on (Tho. Aq., *ST* I–IIae Q17.8, I, p. 661). All this occurs by providential permission through natural adaptation to the created order. When faith beholds God's caring work in the varied spheres of vegetative life, its joy echoes in the psalm: "He veils the sky in clouds and prepares rain for the earth; he clothes the hills with grass and green plants for the use of man. He gives the cattle their food and the young ravens all that they gather" (Ps. 147:8, 9).

Note that the evolving process has higher purposes than the plant itself can conceive. The purpose of plant life is to sustain animal life, and ultimately human life and historical development, through which the divine-human companionship can emerge. God's plan does not come about without plants.

There is extreme variability in the way plants are ordered according to their special requirements, aptitudes, needs, and vulnerabilities. Scripture attests that God's way of caring for plants is intimately connected with and attentive to these special needs (1 Kings 4:25; Ps. 80:8; Isa. 5:2). Unlike rock and sand, plants respond to caring and wither when uncared for. God provides for plant life with more diverse competencies and more complex needs than mineral life (Jer. 2:22). God's purposes in caring for plants are closely integrated with God's purposes in caring for human beings: "Thou makest grass grow for the cattle and green things for those who toil for man, bringing bread out of the earth and wine to gladden men's hearts, oil to make their faces shine and bread to sustain their strength. The trees of the Lord are green and leafy, the cedars of Lebanon which he planted" (Ps. 104:14–16; Origen, *Ag. Celsus* VIII.67, *ANF* IV, p. 665).

Providence in Animal Creation

Scripture attests to the extent of God's care over animal creation: "With open and bountiful hand thou givest what they desire to every living creature" (Ps. 145:16). As the laws of physics are not sufficient for botany, so are the observations of botany not sufficient for zoology. Animals differ from plants in that they are capable of self-movement, but also in that they have a capacity for sensation and emotion. Animals can agonize in misery and experience pleasure and satisfaction far more complexly and consciously than can plants. God cares for animals through providing them with instincts that enable them to adapt in astonishingly varied ways to changing atmospheric conditions, physical and vegetative environments that enable self-preservation and preservation of the species. "Praise the Lord from the earth, you great sea creatures and all ocean depths" (Ps. 148:1), the psalmist exclaimed, "wild animals and all cattle, small creatures and flying birds" (v. 10). God takes joy in animal creation, even with the greatest of species, the leviathan, of whom it is said: "thou has made thy plaything" (Ps. 104:26).

In all animal creatures, preservation of the species is a more critical priority than preservation of the individual animal. Without reproductivity, a species would last only one generation. Animal sexuality is viewed as an important part of providential ordering of animal species, to ensure the continuity of the species (Tho. Aq., *ST* I Q72, I, p. 351). Not only the species, but also each individual animal is given powerful instincts for survival (Isa. 18:5, 6; Ezek. 19:2, 3).

The complex design and ordering of animal life is such that rational creatures have much to learn from it. "Go to the ant, you sluggard, watch her ways and get wisdom. She has no overseer, no governor or ruler; but in summer she prepares her store of food and lays in her supplies at harvest" (Prov. 6:6–8). "Four things there are which are smallest on earth yet wise beyond the wisest; ants, a people with no strength, yet they prepare their store of food in the summer; rock-badgers, a feeble folk, yet they make their home among the rocks; locusts, which have no king, yet they all sally forth in detachments; the lizard, which can be grasped in the hand, yet is found in the palaces of kings" (Prov. 30:24–28). Jesus took from animal life the most influential of all metaphors for the Christian teaching of providence: "Look at the birds of the air; they do not sow and reap and store in barns, yet your heavenly Father feeds them" (Matt. 6:26).

Providence in Human Life and History

Finally, Scripture attests to God's care over all human creation. Human creation is radically dependent, not only upon God, but also upon the health and conservation of plant and animal creation, which themselves are dependent upon the earth, the soil, and upon inanimate, lifeless, physical matter (Ps. 104:1–35). Yet while being dependent on mineral, vegetable, and animal orders, human creation is clearly superior to them in language, memory, imagination, and in musical, mathematical, and construction skills. The Lord "gave men tongue and eyes and ears, the power of choice and a mind for thinking. He filled them with discernment and showed them good and evil. He kept watch over their hearts, to display to them the majesty of his works. He gave them knowledge as well as endowed them with the life-giving law. He established a perpetual covenant with them and revealed to them his decrees. Their eyes saw his glorious majesty, and their ears heard the glory of his voice" (Ecclus. 17:6–13).

God's care embraces all human history and the course of all national and cultural destinies. "God reigns over the nations" (Ps. 47:7). "His sovereignty is never-ending and his rule endures through all generations" (Dan. 4:34). Under the conditions of recalcitrant sin, divine care may take the form of judgment: "He takes away their wisdom from the rulers of the nations and leaves them wandering in a pathless wilderness" (Job 12:24). But its intent is healing and corrective: "The Lord disciplines those whom he loves" (Heb. 12:6).

God's care embraces not only collectivities, but each individual person uniquely. "In God's hand are the souls of all that live, the spirits of all humankind" (Job 12:10). God's care is over both good and bad. The heavenly Father "makes his sun rise on good and bad alike, and sends the rain on the honest and the dishonest" (Matt. 5:45). God's care extends to every minute aspect of human life, "even the hairs of your head" (Matt. 10:30). It is a comfort to believers to remember God's care. "For thou, O Lord, wilt bless the righteous; thou wilt hedge him round with favour as with a shield" (Ps. 5:12). Divine care never ends or diminishes: "The guardian of Israel never slumbers, never sleeps" (Ps. 121:4).

From birth to death God's care extends. "Thou knowest me through and through: my body is no mystery to thee, how I was secretly kneaded into shape and patterned in the depths of the earth. Thou didst see my limbs unformed in the womb, and in thy book they are all recorded; day by day they were fashioned, not one of them was late in growing" (Ps. 139:14–16; cf. Job 10:8). God foreknows all human events yet without intrusion on the efficacy of human freedom (Job 14:5). God's care embraces all of life's circumstances. Nothing is governed finally by fate or absolutely by chance. Human free will has room to play in history, but it cannot overrule God's purposes: "A man's heart may be full of schemes, but the Lord's purpose will prevail" (Prov. 19:22). "My times are in thy hand" (Ps. 31:15, KJV).

God's care of humanity is made known through answering prayers. When Manasseh "in his distress" prayed to the Lord, "God accepted his petition and heard his supplication" (2 Chron. 33:13). Jesus urged his disciples, "Ask, and you will receive" (Matt. 7:7).

In a sense both good and evil proceed from God, the good as an abundant gift freely given, and evil as the consequence of sin—permitted, yet not allowed to rule, and overruled by grace in due time. It is in this dual sense that it is written: "Do not both good and the bad proceed from the mouth of the Most High?" (Lam. 3:39). Yet whatever evil results from freedom abused, God can overrule. Joseph not only became a provider for his estranged brothers, but reflected God's own providence when he said to his pleading brothers: "You meant to do me harm; but God meant to bring good out of it by preserving the lives of many people, as we see today. Do not be afraid. I will provide for you and your dependents" (Gen. 50:20).

Problems of Providence: Fate, Sin, and Evil

A series of difficult issues has arisen out of this teaching of providence: Does providence exclude fortuitous events or chance? Does it exclude contingency and choice? Fate? Does it exclude evil?

Does Providence Exclude Fortune, Fate, or Freedom?

DOES PROVIDENCE EXCLUDE FORTUITOUS EVENTS OR CHANCE?

Thomas Aquinas wisely observed that "an occurrence may be accidental or fortuitous with respect to a lower cause when an effect not intended is brought about, and yet not be accidental or fortuitous with respect to a higher cause" (Tho. Aq., Compend. 137, p. 146). This he illustrated by saying that an employer may send two employees to the same place; from their point of view they meet accidentally, but from the employer's view their meeting, though not intended by him, nonetheless is duly caused by him and understandable as orderly in relation to him. Many such events occur in human life, events regarded as fortuitous and for which human beings do not have the perspective to see their causal connection, yet God foresees them and knows their connection, but not in such a way as to preempt secondary causes.

For several reasons Thomas argued that, rightly understood, divine providence does not wholly exclude fortune or chance: (a) It would be contrary to the essential character of providence if all things occurred by absolute necessity. It would be "against the perfection of the universe if no corruptible thing existed, and no power could fail" (SCG III.74, I, p. 247). (b) Since a large number and variety of causes stem from the order of divine providence, "granted this variety of causes, one of them must at times run into another cause and be impeded, or assisted, by it in the production of its effect. Now, from the concurrence of two or more causes it is possible for some chance event to occur, and thus an unintended end comes about due to this causal concurrence," as when a gravedigger finds buried treasure (p. 247). (c) Accidental beings are necessary for the perfection of things, otherwise everything would be necessary, nothing contingent, and hence there could be no self-determining aspects of the world.

DOES PROVIDENCE EXCLUDE FATE?

Boethius defined fate as "a disposition inherent in changeable things, whereby providence connects each thing with His orders" (*Consolation of Phil.* IV.6; cf. Tho. Aq., *SCG* III.93, I, p. 50). "Nothing hinders certain things happening by luck or by chance, if compared to their proximate causes; but not if compared to Divine Providence, whereby 'nothing happens at random in the world'" (Tho. Aq., *ST* I Q116, I, p. 567, quoting Augustine, *CG* V.1). The divine economy can produce effects through secondary, mediate causes. Viewed as divinely caused, the ordering of all causes is called providence; viewed from mediate causes the effects may appear to have the nature of fate. Yet, "the name fate is not to be used by the faithful lest we appear to agree with those who have held a wrong opinion about fate, by subjecting all things to the necessitation of the stars" (Tho. Aq., *SCG* III.93, I, p. 50). This is why Augustine wisely concluded that "if anyone attributes their existence to fate, because he called the will or the power of God itself by the name of fate, let him keep his opinion, but correct his language" (Augustine, *CG* V.1, *NPNF* 1 II, p. 86).

DOES PROVIDENCE EXCLUDE FREE CHOICE?

No, for providence enables free choice. When it is said that God cooperates with the human will so as to enable the will to move, that does not deny that the human will also moves itself, for moving itself is precisely what the divine economy provides. The divine enabling of free choice is not opposed to choice, "just as God's activity in natural things is not contrary to their nature," for "God moves things in a way that is consonant with their nature" (Tho. Aq., *Compend.* 129, p. 137). Similarly, "While God knows all things beforehand, yet He does not predetermine all things. For He knows beforehand those things that are in our power, but He does not predetermine them. For it is not His will that there should be wickedness nor does He choose to compel virtue" (John of Damascus, *OF* II.30, *NPNF* 2 IX, p. 42).

Commenting on Deuteronomy 30:15, "Today I offer you the choice of life and good, or death and evil," Thomas Aquinas wrote: "These words are brought forward to show that man is possessed of free choice, not that his choices are placed outside divine providence" (*SCG* III.90, II, p. 39; cf. Ecclus. 15:14, 18). For if freedom were taken away, many other goods of creation would be taken with it. There could be no virtue, no justice, no reasoned deliberation, without freedom. Hence "it would be against the very character of providence if liberty of will were removed" (*SCG* II.90, p. 246).

Does Providence Exclude Evil?

Classical views of providence have consistently argued that God's permission of evil is not inconsistent with divine goodness. Thomas Aquinas tightly summarized the elaborate reasoning of classical Christian teaching in showing that providence does not altogether exclude evil:

• An unfree world where all evil is excluded would not be as good as the actual world in which freedom is permitted to fall into evil, called to struggle against evil, and offered redemption from evil. "If evil were completely excluded from things, much good would be rendered impossible. Consequently it is the concern of divine providence, not to safeguard all beings from evil, but to see to it that the evil which arises is ordained to some good" (Tho. Aq., *Compend.* 142, p. 151).

• There can be no evil unless it resides in something good (Augustine, *Enchiridion* XI ff., *NPNF* 1 III, pp. 240 ff.). "Accordingly, although God is the universal cause of all things, He is not the cause of evil as evil. But whatever good is bound up with the evil, has God as its cause" (Tho. Aq., *Compend.* 141, p. 151). The freewill defense holds that evil comes from distorted freedom, not from God, whereas the will that wills good is quietly shaped already by God's goodness.

• Evil is not an effect caused by God, but a *de*fect of secondary causes that are permitted by God. "Without prejudice to divine providence, evil can arise in the world because of defects in secondary causes" (Tho. Aq., *Compend.* 141, p. 150). It is possible to have a defect in the secondary agent (human will) "without there being a defect in the primary agent" (divine will) (Tho. Aq., *SCG* III.71, II, p. 237).

• Many creaturely goods are enabled in this world that could not occur unless there were evils against which to struggle, such as patience (which could not be nurtured in a perfect world). Thomas's example: There could not be the generation of a species unless there were also death in that species (*SCG* III.71, I, p. 239).

• The perfection of the universe requires some beings that are subject to defects. "If evil were completely eliminated from things, they would not be governed by divine providence in accord with their nature; and this would be a greater defect than the particular defects eradicated" (Tho. Aq., *Compend.* 142, p. 151). "For example, if the inclination to generate its like were taken away from fire (from which inclination there results this particular evil which is the burning up of combustible things), there would also be taken away this particular good which is the generation of fire" (Tho. Aq., *SCG* III.71, I, p. 239). That fire is potentially destructive does not mean that it is of itself evil. A world without fire is doubtless a less good world than a world with the risks that fire brings.

• We complain to God about that part of the good creation that we experience as opposed to our immediate interest. In our egocentricity we often fail to note how much we would miss what we complain about if it were taken away (such as heat and rain, for example). "The good of the whole takes precedence over the good of a part. It is proper for a governor with foresight to neglect some lack of goodness in a part, so that there may be an increase of goodness in the whole. Thus, an artisan hides the foundations beneath earth, so that the whole house may have stability. But, if evil were removed from some parts of the universe, much perfection would perish from the universe, whose beauty arises from an ordered unification of evil and good things" (p. 240).

• If all evils were removed, the good could not be known, because "the good is better known from its comparison with evil," just as "good health is best known by the sick" (p. 240).

• Finally, "if complete equality were present in things, there would be but one created good, which clearly disparages the perfection of the creature" (p. 238). It is a better ordered world when some things are better than others than if there were no grades of goodness whatever. "It does not pertain to divine goodness, entirely to exclude from things the power of falling from the good" (p. 238). At this point Thomas stated an early version of Murphy's Law: "What is able to fall does fall" (p. 238). But that does not imply evil in the Originator of distortable freedom.

For all these reasons, providence does not exclude evil. Hence to the question, "If God exists, whence comes evil?" Thomas surprisingly replied: "If evil exists, God exists. For, there would be no evil if the order of good were taken away, since its privation is evil. But this order would not exist if there were no God" (*SCG* III.71, II, p. 241).

Sin and Evil in Patristic Views of Providence

Much of the energy of patristic reflections upon providence focused on how to relate the claims of providence to the harsh presence of evil and suffering in this world that God has ordered. The crucial question as it presented itself to the church fathers was, How can evil and suffering be compatible with the caring providence of an incomparably powerful and good God? Several kinds of solutions were presented in the very early period of the church's struggle for self-understanding, from the second through the seventh centuries:

• Although sin occurs through the divine permission, it is inexact to suggest that sin is ordained by the will of God. Sin is attributable to providence only as a secondary result of a larger, better divine purpose that includes freedom (Origen, *De Princip.* III.1 ff., *ANF* IV, pp. 302 ff.; John of Damascus, *OF* IV.21, *NPNF* 2 IX, p. 94).

• Sin is due to the abuse, not the use, of free will. Accordingly, when we rightly *use* our free will, we do not sin, but are responsive to God. But the *abuse* of free will is our own self-assertive placement of our egocentric interests above the common interest so that the original intention, for which the will was created and toward which it is intended, becomes distorted (Augustine, *Spirit and Letter*, *NPNF* 1 II, pp. 106–9).

• Although the abuse of free will was foreseen by God, it could have been prevented by God only at the price of depriving human existence of its most noble attribute, namely, free will (Tertullian, *Ag. Marcion* II.5–7, *ANF* III, pp. 300–3; Cyril of Alex., *Contra Julian* IX.13, 10 ff., *MPG* LXXIV, pp. 120 ff.; Theodoret, *De prov.*, or. IX.6).

• We learn by experience, by moving through stages of growth, and by struggling toward good through evil. It is often only when we are forced to face adversity that we learn and grow strong by overcoming obstacles. So faith learns gradually to affirm that what at one point appears to be unmitigated evil and suffering may at a different point appear to serve our well-being or improvement, increasing patience and compassion (Lactantius, *On Anger of God* XIII, *ANF* VII, pp. 269–71; cf. Augustine, *Divine Prov. and the Problem of Evil* I.6, *FC* 1, pp. 253–55).

• One reason God permits the gift of freedom to result in sin is in order that we can arrive at a consciousness of our own finitude and our own inability to attain righteousness on our own. Hence Luther viewed temptation, sin, and suffering as closely related to providence. A major function of the law (the divine requirement codified in Mosaic law) is to train us to not rely upon our own righteousness. Thus providence works, even through the law, to teach us that we cannot achieve righteousness on our own, apart from God's sustaining help and grace. The germ of that idea was already present in the patristic writers (cf. *Letter to Diognetus*, *ANF* I, pp. 27, 28; Gregory the Great, *Magna Moralia* III.42, *LF*).

• According to Augustine, God would not permit evil at all unless He could draw good out of it (*Enchiridion* X–XVII, *NPNF* 1 III, pp. 240–43). Since we experience life egocentrically in a temporal flow, aren't we prone to evaluate one or more discrete parts as evil, artificially viewing these parts as separable from the whole? This is understandable, because of our finitude, but a broadened perception of the antecedents and consequents of our acts of human freedom often yields the insight that some good has emerged out of evil that could not have otherwise occurred. If the enlargement of our human perception yields this insight, surely God's infinitely larger perception of human moral experience will behold much as ultimately good that we under harsh and limiting circumstances have felt to be evil. Hence an important aspect of the struggle to understand evil has to do with gaining a wider perspective, a vantage point larger than personal needs or immediate desires. We are prone to judge the problem of evil purely on the egocentristic basis of what hurts me, what is painful to me, what is an obstacle to me. The larger our perspective, the more we are able to see these individual dislocations and disruptions in the light of the cosmic universal-historical purpose and to be consoled by that dimension of meaning, even though we may still suffer and not fully grasp that purpose (Origen, *Ag. Celsus* IV.99, *ANF* IX, p. 541; Augustine, *Divine Prov. and the Problem of Evil*, *FC* 1, pp. 239 ff.).

• In the last judgment the problem of evil will be solved; yet on the road that leads to the last judgment the workings of providence doubtless will remain something of a mystery to us. Our finite minds are simply unable to conceive the wisdom of this infinite process in which we live and move. Faith in divine providence calls the believer to walk without seeing, based on what is known from God's disclosure in Christ (John Chrysostom, *Concerning the Statues* IX.9, *NPNF* 1 IX, p. 404; *Letters to Olympias*, pp. 289–93).

In the next volume we will develop a fuller reflection on the problems of sin and evil. These observations do not ignore the fact that through sufferings, poverty, and disruptions we are deprived of much that we want. Yet such deprivations may help to wean us away from reliance upon fleeting temporal goods and toward faith in God. "Were you not raised to life with Christ? Then aspire to the realm above, where Christ is, seated at the right hand of God, and let your thoughts dwell on that higher realm, not on this earthly life. I repeat, you died; and now your life lies hidden with Christ in God. When Christ, who is our life, is manifested, then you too will be manifested with him in glory" (Col. 3:1–4).

Protestant developments of the doctrine of providence followed closely upon these reflections of the earlier pastoral writers. Luther and Calvin struggled against medieval Scholastic views of Scripture, tradition, Christology, and the sacraments, but not patristic views of providence.

Permission, Hindrance, Overruling, and Limiting

Classical exegetes have found it useful to distinguish four levels or aspects of God's way of parenting his creatures: through permission, restraint, overruling, and putting limits upon threats to the good. The governance of God functions situationally in ways that bear striking resemblance to the ways good human parenting functions: by *permitting* freedom to discover its competencies and interests; by *hindering* freedom from getting itself into too much difficulty; by *overruling* free self-actualization when it seriously mistakes its own best good, harms others inordinately, or seems to jeopardize the divine purpose; and by *limiting* other forces in freedom's way to prevent them from triumphing cheaply or tempting inordinately. The question asked on all these levels is, How does God guide? That question is related to the deeper question of what kind of parent God is.

• God guides and parents by *permitting* our freedom to play itself out, even if we play it out in the direction of our own suffering and others' suffering. Freedom could have no meaning if it did not risk going astray. To posit a freedom that cannot possibly fail is certainly not to posit human freedom. God graciously allows human freedom the room both to stand and to fall.

To affirm that God's parenting permits freedom does not imply that the divine parent enjoys watching freedom fall or good intentions stumble. Divine permission does not imply *carte blanche* to sin, but rather that God, in order to allow the larger good of enabling freedom, does not exert constant or absolute power to prevent sin. God permits the freedom that distortedly leads to sin, but God does not approve of sin. For classical exegetes, this was epitomized in Jesus' cryptic permission to Judas: "Do quickly what you have to do" (John 13:27; cf. Augustine, *On Psalms*, Ps. 3, *NPNF* 1 VIII, p. 4; cf. *Harmony of the Gospels* II.79, 80, *NPNF* 1 VI, pp. 173–76).

Scripture frequently attests to the willingness of God to allow freedom even when it results in stubborn self-assertiveness that becomes alienated and counterproductive: "My people did not listen to my words and Israel would have none of me; so I sent them off, stubborn as they were, to follow their own devices" (Ps. 81:12; cf.

Prov. 1:31; Jer. 18:12; cf. Origen, *De Princip.* III.1, *ANF* V, pp. 302 ff.). When freedom is abused, its consequences must be lived with: "Israel has run wild, wild as a heifer; and will the Lord now feed this people like lambs in a broad meadow?" (Hos. 4:7). Moral wisdom is not enhanced by rewarding irresponsibility. Paul and Barnabas at Lystra stated that divine providence has permitted "all nations to go their own way; and yet he has not left you without some clue to his nature, in the kindness he shows" (Acts 14:16, 17). God permits human self-determination even when what is permitted is not what God wants (Gen. 2 ff.; Irenaeus, *Ag. Her.* III.9, 10, *ANF* I, pp. 433, 434, IV.37, pp. 518, 519).

• God parents us by *hindering*, and at times directly resisting, our ill-motivated actions. God guides not by coercing freedom directly but by putting obstacles in the way of our hurting ourselves, like the parent who builds a fence so the child will not go into the street. The child still may find a way to get into the street, but not without confronting the serious effort of the parent at placing an obstacle in harm's way. "It was I," the Lord revealed to Abraham, "who held you back from committing a sin against me" (Gen. 20:6). Satan's complaint to God in the prologue of Job asked: "Have you not hedged him round on every side with your protection?" (Job 1:10; cf. 3:23). Israel's lamentation in captivity was that God's ways had so hedged escape that only one thing was required—repentance (Lam. 3:7). The psalmist prayed for constraint on his own freedom to harm himself: "Hold back thy servant also from sins of self-will, lest they get the better of me" (Ps. 19:13; Augustine, *Expos. on Psalms*, Ps. 71, *NPNF* 1 VIII, pp. 315–17).

• God parents us by *overruling* us when we are completely out of line. By such active direction or guidance, egocentric sinners are saved from harm and guided toward ends beyond their competence to know (Ezek. 20:33; Mic. 4:7). "Blessed is the man whom God corrects" (Job 5:17, NIV; cf. Clement of Rome, *First Corinthians*, XVI, *ANF* I, p. 20). "He who refuses correction is his own worst enemy, but he who listens to reproof learns sense. The fear of the Lord is a training in wisdom" (Prov. 15:32, 33). Jeremiah in frustration declared: "This is the nation that did not obey the Lord its God nor accept correction; truth has perished" (Jer. 7:28).

When the sons of Jacob had sold Joseph into slavery and then, as governor of Egypt, he became the means of the redemption of the whole family, Joseph observed that his brothers had meant their action for evil against him, but God meant it for good (Gen. 50:20). Scripture attests that God is forever working through such circuitous routes. Thinking about providence gradually increases faith's awareness of those circuits through which even our distortions of God's good creation become transmuted through grace. Wheel turns within wheel (Ezek. 1:16), and God turns our misdeeds into potentially redeemed relationships (Calvin, *Inst.* 3.2.26; Wesley, *WJW* VII, pp. 409 ff.).

• Finally, God parents wisely by *preventing* other forces in freedom's way from triumphing cheaply or tempting inordinately. The care of God attested by Scripture places fitting limits upon challenges to our faith and boundaries upon what the opponents of our good can do to us. This view of providence is epitomized by Paul's consolation for the faithful enduring severe trials and afflictions: "God keeps faith, and he will not allow you to be tested above your powers, but when the test comes he will at the same time provide a way out, by enabling you to sustain it" (1 Cor. 10:13; cf. Job 1:12; 2:6).

When faith perceives itself as being guided in these ways, it affirms its confidence that "in everything, as we know, he cooperates for good with those who love God and are called according to his purpose" (Rom. 8:28). Faith in providence places its active reliance upon the permitting, restraining, overruling, and preventing power of God's infinitely good parenting.

Biblical Paradigms of Divine Care for the World

From Hebrew Scriptures, classical Christian exegetes have constantly mined key texts that inform the Christian teaching of providence. If Scripture is taken seriously, providence must be taken seriously. The whole counsel of God cannot be taught without teaching faith in providence (Augustine, *CG* XV, *NPNF* 1 II, pp. 284–308). The theme is intimately interwoven with essential Judeo-Christian affirmations of the divine majesty, omnipresence, and care.

Abraham's faith that "God will provide" (Gen. 22:8), manifested through testing, became the key paradigm of faith in providence for classical Jewish and Christian teaching (Heb. 11:17; Irenaeus, *Ag. Her.* IV.21, *ANF* I, pp. 492 f.; Methodius, *Banquet of the Ten Virgins* V.2, *ANF* VI, p. 325; Calvin, *Inst.* 1.16.4).

The psalmist's thanksgiving for food became a liturgical model for table grace, and a doctrinal model for faith in providence: "The eyes of all are lifted to thee in hope, and thou givest them their food when it is due; with open and bountiful hand thou givest what they desire to every living creature" (Ps. 145:15, 16; cf. Ps. 136:25). The imagery associated with providence also powerfully shows how feminine metaphors were used to speak of God and Israel's faith in the care of God: "As a mother comforts her son, so will I myself comfort you," wrote Isaiah (66:13).

The One who creates the world does not then just leave it alone, or gaze passively upon it, but continues to nurture and care for it, and is constantly active on behalf of creatures (Ps. 104; John of Damascus, OF II.29, FC 37, p. 260). God's caring encompasses both individuals and societies, both nature and history. As God is architect of the world and initiator of the cosmic process, so God continues to be engaged as the guide and architect of the historical process, since it encompasses free agents who are prone to go awry (Wesley, WJW VI, pp. 318 ff.).

Jeremiah remarked that the people are in God's hands as clay in the hands of a potter (Jer. 18:4–6), yet the stuff of human history is woven with endless strands of rebellion. For men and women are not automatons but endowed with free will. This has been the case from the very first biblical picture of human existence, off on the wrong foot with Adam and Eve stumbling. After the fall it is an alienated will with which God has to deal, but a will that is nonetheless still given the possibility of joyful response to the grace of God.

The story of the biblical witness is not an idyllic account of perfect harmony between creature and Creator, but of an ongoing struggle involving seduction, revolt, rebellion, and tragic alienation. Eden is disrupted. The revolt continues with Cain, the generation of the flood, and the tower of Babel. There is a rhythm of rebellion and judgment, of oppression and exodus, of creation and redemption, of grace and repentance, of merit and reward (Augustine, CG XVI, NPNF 1 II, pp. 309–36). All these rhythms move in an interactive way through the Yahwist and Deuteronomic histories and continue generally throughout the whole biblical account.

Israel was the first people to write a history of providence. It is a history of God's caring for all creatures, God's dealing with humanity, God's unremitting involvement with the world. History is viewed in terms of its purpose, moving in a linear way from an original covenant with God toward the fulfillment of that covenant in a complex historical struggle that required moral accountability at each stage by the people of Israel to God, who gave them breath and life, who offered them a national identity and existence (Justin Martyr, Dialogue with Trypho, ANF I, pp. 194 ff.).

A pattern of understanding gradually emerged in Hebraic consciousness: God is leading people through a curious path that they do not always understand, yet whose end is *shālōm*—peace, blessedness, and universal human fulfillment. The ultimate expectation of the historical process is that through it God is accomplishing a slowly unfolding redemptive design. Human enmities, acquisitiveness, and pride are seen as petty episodes within the larger context of that ultimate hope. Faith in divine providence is the trust that God is somehow working out the divine purpose in the historical process, even when we cannot fully recognize it, and that whatever the distortions and disruptions of history, God's purpose will be accomplished in the long run (Augustine, *CG* XXII, *FC* 24, pp. 415 ff.).

Isaiah was able to grasp that, even amid the awesome dissolution of long-standing historical structures, God was working out a longer-ranged plan, and that through this plan the caring governance of God was unfolding (Isa. 40:1–11). Even when God allows emperors like Cyrus to hold for a time unparalleled power, God is only temporarily using Cyrus as an instrument of instruction for the people of Israel, and through them universal history (Isa. 44:28; 45:1; Arnobius, *Ag. Heathen*, *ANF* VI, pp. 413 ff.).

Similarly in Ezekiel, even the powers seemingly at enmity with God can finally do nothing other than serve God's plan (Ezek. 38). At the court of Nebuchadnezzar, Daniel grasped the astonishing vision that the hidden purpose of God was being worked out precisely through the captivity of the people (Dan. 2 ff.; cf. Isa. 8:10).

God's Plantings

God works to implant in the nature of things the potentiality of their future development. The scriptural witness to providence knows that God plants seeds that grow only slowly in history. It is as if a DNA imprint goes into the structure of each element of creaturely life, so that each creature is given some limited, creaturely potential for the fulfillment of the will of the One who is the ground, artificer, and designer of those imprints through evolutionary secondary causes. God undergirds the natural processes, which inconspicuously and unawarely cooperate with God (Isa. 49:19; 60:20; Matt. 13:1–38; 1 Cor. 3:1–9).

God is hiddenly at work throughout the whole sphere of natural causality, and is the mysterious, decisive ground of it all. The providential care of God is already in the nature of things, in the generation of things, in the transmission of things, and in their awesome movement through history. God is present in seedtime and harvest, cold and heat, summer and winter, the clouds and the rain, the fruits of the earth—all are the gifts of the caring God (Gen. 8:22; Calvin, *Inst.* 2.11–12).

So it is with human life, human labor, and human choice, which are all given their ground and possibility by God's own freedom. It is indeed necessary for each one to gain and grasp freedom on his or her own. Freedom is offered by God for responsible use, not abuse (John 8:32–36; 1 Cor. 9:19; Gal. 5:1). Even when human freedom asserts itself in a tainted or skewed direction, that can never constitute a permanent denial or undoing of divine providence. Our worst distortions of human freedom are best viewed in a larger providential frame of reference in which God continues to care for fallen, broken freedom, having mercy upon the sinner and silently governing all things (Ps. 67:4; Isa. 9:6, 7; Heb. 11:40).

Everything that occurs is, in a subtle sense, guided by the divine justice and goodness, even though the purpose be obscured or confused in the mind of the beholder (Isa. 14:24–32; Ps. 67:4). Biblical teaching does not view divine providence as dependent upon our recognition of it. God remains the unconscious "desire of all nations" (Hag. 2:7) in a hidden way by implanting in all human consciousness the restless hunger for God, so that God is quietly the desire of all humanity, not just the people of Israel or the church, although it is through them that this hope in time becomes universally manifested (Augustine, *CG* XVIII.45–47, *NPNF* 1 II, pp. 388–90).

Why Do the Righteous Suffer?

Both the reality of good and the possibility of the diminution of the good proceed from God, but in different ways, for the good proceeds as freely bestowed gift to which creatures may respond, whereas evil most often emerges as a consequence of sin, in which human beings fail to respond to the created good and to the Creator. Meanwhile all goods and absences of good exist only under the aegis of God's power and by the permission of God (Lam. 3:38).

"I will strengthen you though you have not known me, so that men from the rising and the setting sun may know that there is none but I: I am the Lord, there is no other; I make the light, I create darkness, author alike of prosperity and trouble. I, the Lord, do all these things" (Isa. 45:4–7). This does not imply that Yahweh directly creates misery, but that Yahweh sustains a healing, redemptive purpose in allowing misery to follow after ill-willed deeds (Heb. 12:3–13; Origen, *De Princip.* III.12, *ANF* IV, pp. 312, 313; *Ag. Celsus* IV.64–70, pp. 526–28).

The history of Israel is shaped powerfully by this trust that, even when the purpose of God appears unclear, somehow it is working itself out beyond Israel's capacity to see it. At times doubts and exceptions appear so intractable that it would seem that this idea of God's governance is a mistake, or that God has forgotten his people (as in the captivity or the holocaust). Yet even there, there is still in the heart of Israel's faith the latent hope that, nonetheless, somehow God will demonstrate his care in some new, unprecedented way so as to reveal the meaning of these obscure portions of the historical process, and in some way unknown to us, it will all be made clear in the course of history, and finally at the end there will be resurrection. Where it appears that God has permitted not just a small mistake but a great tragedy (as in the case of Job or Jesus), and when it appears that irremediable errors and injustices have occurred, there ensues a weighty struggle between faith and doubt in which faith in providence is sorely tested (Job 3:1–26; Lam. 1:1–22; Mark 15:35).

This recurring wrenching struggle has given rise to a series of standing biblical riddles concerning providence: Why do the wicked prosper? Why do the righteous suffer? Why are the sins of grandmothers apparently visited upon granddaughters? All these themes were dealt with by Jeremiah, Isaiah, Ezekiel, and, above all, Job. Job's most fundamental response to his pathos-laden struggle was that he did not know the answer because God's ways were beyond his ways, God's wisdom beyond his own wisdom (Job 40:3–5; 42:1–6). But, nevertheless, even for Job, faith somehow remained sustained and unshakable, even though plagued with penultimate confusion and doubt. These remain riddles, not because of the weakness of faith, but precisely because of the tenacity of faith in providence, inasmuch as they affirm the mysterious purpose of God even amid the wretched byways and curious meanderings and sufferings and inconveniences of actual lived history.

Given the inveterate tendency of human freedom to fall, God continues to come up with merciful alternatives. If Eden is Plan A, and Eden does not work out, due to the self-determining volatility, frailty, and fallibility of human freedom, then God has a Plan B and a Plan C. All contingencies, however, are known by eternal divine wisdom from the beginning. The Word, the Son, has from the beginning been made ready for revelation in the fullness of time (John 1:1–14; Eph. 1:4–10). God is willing to relate responsively to the intrinsically unpredictable development of human freedom. This story finally comes to a crossroads in Jesus Christ. Jesus constitutes a *krisis* for the world in the sense that he confronts the world with that crossroad—whether to trust God's coming governance or not.

Since the fall, God has been overseeing a plan for the redemption of fallen freedom. The plan pivots around Christ's coming and is to be consummated in Christ's final return. The goal is the regeneration of the disordered world (Rom. 8:19 ff.). Nothing can finally thwart this divine purpose (Isa. 11:1 ff.; Dan. 7:13 ff.).

The Care of the Father as Known Through the Son

God's purpose in history became fully disclosed in the history of Jesus (Eph. 3:1–13). The story of Jesus' last days echoes and transmutes the frequent theme of the prophets, that even when we oppose God we can only in the long run serve his purposes. For in the story of Jesus' death on the cross, even the injustices, apostasy, and crimes done against Jesus become precisely the means by which God brings deliverance to humanity (Col. 2:14; Heb. 12:2; cf. Ps. 76:10). What God wills for humanity is brought about even when humanity does not will the good that God wills. Nothing that we can will can put a final obstacle in the way of the accomplishment of the divine purpose.

In this spirit the New Testament faith remarkably grasped and transformed Old Testament faith in providence. The prophetic teaching was substantially reappropriated and profoundly reaffirmed. But a new note was sounded: the teaching of providence became intensely personalized in relation to the history of Jesus. The Sermon on the Mount strikes the key note of this personalization. We hear not only about the governor of nature and nations but "Our Father in heaven" (Matt. 6:9). The same fatherly one who "makes his sun rise on good and bad alike, and sends the rain on the honest and the dishonest" (Matt. 5:45) is personally present in Jesus.

Therefore I bid you put away anxious thought about food and drink to keep you alive, and clothes to cover your body. Surely life is more than food, the body more than clothes. Look at the birds of the air; they do not sow and reap and store in barns, yet your heavenly Father feeds them. You are worth more than the birds! Is there a man of you who by anxious thought can add a foot to his height? And why be anxious about clothes? Consider how the lilies grow in the fields; they do not work, they do not spin; and yet, I tell you, even Solomon in all his splendour was not attired like one of these. But if that is how God clothes the grass in the fields, which is there today, and tomorrow is thrown on the stove, will he not all the more clothe you? How little faith you have! (Matt. 6:25–31)

The good parenting of God as father (*Abba*) became the central feature of Jesus' highly personal conception of God's preservation and guidance of creatures. Jesus called his hearers to trust the Father as one who cares about "the least of these" (Matt. 25), who notices the tiniest sparrow (cf. Luke 21:18). The emphasis on God's parental care was so characteristic of the teaching of Jesus that it is often noted as its distinguishing mark (Cyril of Jerusalem, *Catechesis* VII.5–15, *FC* 61, pp. 172–79).

In the end time it is hoped that whatever doubts one may have had about the curious meanderings of God's providence in history will somehow be resolved. It is hoped that question marks will be erased when the conclusion of the process is known. Since we are now *in* the process, it is difficult for us to know or grasp its conclusion, except as it is reflected "through a glass darkly" (1 Cor. 13). But even with limited vision each hearer is invited to "Cast all your cares on him, for you are his charge" (1 Pet. 5:7).

The Epistles of Peter dealt with the problems of suffering and discipline amid persecution. They expressed the vital hope that in the end time the purpose of God made known in Jesus will be fully revealed for all to behold. Theodicy in the New Testament has a strong eschatological element. God's purpose is being worked out and will in due time be fully revealed, but for now the providential purpose of God is sufficiently clear in the ministry of Jesus and above all in Jesus' resurrection (Acts 17:18 ff.; Rom. 6:1–5; Phil. 3:10, 11).

Early in his letter to Rome, Paul had conceived of God's caring and providing activity manifesting itself through law, conscience, and nature, so that everyone has reason enough already to know and recognize the providence of God, so much so that our repeated failures to recognize it are inexcusable (Rom. 1:20). The turning point is set forth in Romans 3:21: "But now, quite independently of law, God's justice has been brought to light. The Law and the prophets both bear witness to it: it is God's way of righting wrong, effective through faith in Christ for all who have such faith—all, without distinction" (Rom. 3:21). In this light, all things are seen to work together for those who love God. The Christian belief in God's providence is thus brought into its most distinctive Pauline formulation in this summary phrase: "In everything, as we know, he co-operates for good with those who love God and are called according to his purpose" (Rom. 8:28). Those who realize this are "those who love God" in response to God's love in Christ. They realize that there is "nothing in all creation that can separate us from the love of God in Christ Jesus our Lord" (Rom. 8:39). Yet in this knowledge they also know that they do not have advantage over anyone else, because this divine care is a radical gift, unmerited grace, completely apart from any human qualifications (Eph. 2:1–8; Titus 3:7).

Few themes are more widely dispersed throughout the Scriptures than that of the caring of God for creation. It appears in the Pentateuch, the Prophets, the wisdom literature, the synoptic writers, Paul, John, and the general Epistles. The biblical story concludes with an account of how those who oppose God's providence will be overthrown (Rev. 19) and the purpose of God finally, despite fierce opposition, will be consummated.

General and Special Providence

Special providence means that God acts through particular events in special ways, as in the answering of prayer, and not by general providence alone. Rationalistic deism resisted the notion of special providence on the grounds that since God has created a good and intelligible system of natural order, God would not arbitrarily break that order on the whim of special or egocentric supplications. Some argued on the strength of general providence that God is powerless to intervene within the context of natural causality, and that it would be inconsistent with the divine majesty if God became enmeshed in special or petty occurrences of human history (John Toland, *Christianity Not Mysterious*; Matthew Tindal, *Christianity as Old as Creation*).

Indeed, it must be admitted that special providence may be easily trivialized. Yet classical exegetes have generally argued both for general providence and for the special competence of God to become intimately involved at any particular point in human history while still respecting the intelligible natural order (Tho. Aq., *SCG* II, I, pp. 209 ff.). Without general providence the scope of divine care is not universal. Without special providence the act of praying is made absurd (Tertullian, *On Prayer*, ANF III, pp. 681–91).

God's *general* providence works through regular and uniform natural law, not by arbitrary incursions into the natural order (Dionysius, *Extant Fragments, From the Books on Nature*, ANF VI, pp. 84–91). General providence in human affairs is not exerted as if on utterly plastic, inert, material substance, as if without freedom or will or self-determination. For divine guidance occurs in whatever way is most fitting in the caring for free, self-determining human agency, the wills of morally accountable persons, just as parental care looks for the most fitting situational mode of guidance (Prov. 4:11; Isa. 58:11; John 16:13; Wesley, *WJW* VII, pp. 171 ff., 240 ff.).

It is a misjudgment to view God's providence toward humanity as routinely coercing free wills. God did not create human freedom to destroy it. Rather God's own infinite Spirit groans with our spirits to draw our freedom toward the good—not to coerce but to persuade and enable our wills to do the good we can envision (Rom. 8:14–39).

The notion of general providence needs to be held carefully in close tension and proximity to two other scriptural teachings that we will discuss further in treating of human existence: First is the *solidarity* of human, social existence—for we live our lives out together as families, as nations, in larger social constructs than simple individuality. Were God's providence limited to private interiority and abstracted individuality, the divine influence would be less than that declared by Jesus and the prophets.

Secondly, the call and need for sacrificial *self-denial* or self-surrender is often closely intertwined with the unfolding of providence. For there may be important moments in which the good of the commonweal can only be served when a particular individual's good is diminished, or when one may be required to suffer for others. The Christian life is characterized by denying oneself, bearing the cross, and following Jesus (Mark 8:34). A right understanding of providence must leave room for the ironies of solidarity and self-denial, which are so boldly contrasted with the excessive individualism and narcissism so commonly assumed as normative in modern consciousness (Baxter, *PW* XI, pp. 60 ff.).

God not only works through the general structure of natural law and historical development to promote the well-being of the whole, but also in *special* contexts and with particular persons who trust God, who fervently pray, who are responsive to the specific promptings of grace, and who through experience learn the sense in which all things work together for good. All things work together for good for *those who love God* (Rom. 8:28) in a sense that is not and cannot be perceived by those who are not responsive to divine grace in history, who have neither sought nor received any special insight into the meaning of history (Clement of Alex., *Strom.* IV.6–8, *ANF* II, pp. 412–21; Wesley, *WJW* VI, pp. 225 ff., 315 ff.). Among those who know little of the grace of God, the implication is not that divine providence is absent, but that it is present with less awareness. For God's providence is not dependent upon human awareness of it (Baxter, *PW* XII, pp. 183–85).

God's caring is not just in impersonal forms of natural law or through social aggregates; God's care is also intimately and personally present to the needy, to the contrite, and to true supplicants. "You gave me life and showed me kindness, and in your providence watched over my spirit" (Job 10:12, NIV; Tho. Aq., *Compend.*, pp. 141 ff., 151 ff.).

General and special providence are not considered contrary or anti-
thetical, but complementary (Tho. Aq., *Compend.*, pp. 127 ff.). Although one cannot empirically prove providence, one can trust it,
according to the witness of apostles and martyrs whose lives have
become hid in Christ. They attest that the divine providence evidences
itself through events as trustable. This governance is once-and-for-all
clarified in the ministry of Jesus. Its demonstration continues day by
day for the faithful (Rom. 5:1–8; 8:12–17).

There is no natural equality of moments in the history of providence. There are many times at which it is deeply puzzling what God
could be doing with us. Our attentiveness is intensified at other times
and places in which God's will to communicate seems greatly increased (cf. Jonah 1–4). In certain events the care and purposes of
God appear to be more clearly revealed and visible to us; through
them faith is awakened to be sustained through adversity. Through a
history of such events, the providing of God becomes gradually clarified as trustable.

The Hidden Purpose Made Known

Providence becomes further illuminated when viewed by analogy
to any human activity that shows a firmly conceived human purpose
worked out over a very long period of time—earlier hidden, later
revealed. An example would be a vocational decision that is clearly
grasped inwardly by the decider but not understood outwardly by
passersby (I am indebted to Gordon D. Kaufman, *Syst. Theol., A
Historicist Perspective*, pp. 299 ff., for much insight in the analogy that
follows).

Imagine a young woman who at an early age has made a firm
decision to become a teacher. Many successive steps may be required
to reach this long-range goal. She must first come to a reasonably
clear decision inwardly about her vocational direction, perhaps struggling through deep ambivalence in order to gain clarity about herself.
That done, she must then study to achieve diverse competences and
must nurture various habits of mind and heart.

Suppose she has chosen a university, decided upon courses, and
organized her time carefully for accomplishing her objective. She also
finds, along the way, that she wishes to develop skills and interests
that are only indirectly related to her vocational choice, such as music
and dance. She also must work hard to find adequate financial resources. A serious examination of the steps along this way will reveal
their great complexity. Not only is the overall plan complex, but she

must be ready to meet unexpected contingencies. Yet suppose that at all points in the process there is, and has been from the beginning, a firmly conceived purpose: to become a teacher.

Now let us suppose that there are significant obstacles. Each is met in relation to the overall goal. Sometimes the path may be meandering. Suppose she survives a broken love affair, an accident causing a painful broken bone, and the loss of a good friend. Later, as a result of her hospitalization, she decides to serve as a hospital orderly. At one point she is called to appear before the district judge to testify on behalf of a friend in trouble.

While these detours are taking place, it may be impossible for someone glancing in from the outside to see the hidden, overarching internal purpose in this varied behavior. From outside the frame of reference of the vocational commitment, an unsympathetic observer might view her as a troublemaker (in court) or a malingerer (in the hospital) and fail to grasp any larger meaning in her actions on particular occasions. Yet through all these contingent events there remains within her self-understanding a firm long-range goal, a decision about herself that shapes everything else.

Suppose at some point she is forced to drop out of school and must take a job as a waitress. Acquaintances see her working at the local diner. They greet her, wondering vaguely what she is up to, but do not really understand what is happening.

An extended, complex set of actions arising out of a firm previous decision may force one to endure circuitous detours and long delays. The young woman's long-range purpose remains completely obscure when viewed from the outside. Yet inwardly she knows she has a plan that makes sense of the whole process. Let us suppose, however, that the ultimate objective of this varied trajectory is unknown to anyone except herself. Suppose she has not yet revealed her long-felt vocational decision to anyone else. Others who meet her at various places along this road will not discern any hint of her overall purpose. Suppose, however, one day she chooses to communicate her purpose to a few special friends. They would then instantly recognize the meaningfulness of activities that otherwise might seem unexplainable, even bizarre.

Suppose she becomes passionately interested in blue grass music, feels that it is not only a meaningful part of her self-expression, but also connected with her vocation as a teacher. Suppose she takes mandolin lessons, joins a group, writes songs, and views all this as an intrinsic part of her long-range trajectory. Others may fail completely to understand the way in which she views this as a part of her intentional vocational plan, but inwardly it is crystal clear to her. Externally its purpose remains undiscernible. This is the crucial part of the analogy: Someone simply looking from the outside at particular moments during the twists and turns of this motley, meandering, varied sequence of developments, could not deduce with certainty that any clear purpose is being realized—until the end of the process.

At the *end* of the process, when she finally becomes a teacher, others may belatedly realize that the person who was waiting on tables and playing the mandolin had an unrecognized intent all along. Various aspects of her earlier purpose may now be pieced together and made understandable.

Much human purposeful activity has this long-range character. We bind our time to long-range objectives that shape our decision making in the present (cf. G. Kaufman, *Syst. Theol., A Historicist Perspective*, pp. 301 ff.). We limit our freedom in behalf of a larger and more disciplined search for self-actualization. But in the midst of this lengthy development, others who are not privy to the original decision may fail to grasp crucial aspects of it.

This analogy is really about God's providence. It is as if God has made far-reaching decisions or decrees about human history that we do not yet fully perceive but meet only at some particular point along the way of their fulfillment. We glimpse only some tiny part of God's larger historical purpose. God knows what is occurring through the process. We may or may not recognize the deeper intention of God. Faith in providence is trust that whatever is occurring has some meaning within God's larger purpose, even if not fully understood by egocentric human subjects.

Resurrection

This analogy provides us with a beginning point for grasping the way in which the primitive Christian community viewed the resurrection. The cross and the resurrection of Jesus was for the primitive Christian community the primary clue to the end of history, and therefore to the meaning of the human story. According to Paul, if there had been no resurrection of Jesus, there would be no Christian theology, because there would have been no Christian faith, no Christian community, no Christian memory. "If there be no resurrection, then Christ was not raised; and if Christ was not raised, then our gospel is null and void, and so is your faith" (1 Cor. 15:13–15). The resurrection of Jesus is, together with the cross with which it is inextricably bound, the climax of the originative event of the Christian community (Rom. 6:1 ff.; 1 Pet. 1:3; Clement of Rome, *First Epis. to*

Corinth XXIV, *ANF* I, pp. 11, 12). It is constantly referred to in the New Testament as that which formed the community (Acts 4:33; 17:18).

Why was the resurrection so important? The idea of a general resurrection was widely understood in the first century as meaning the *end* of the historical process (Matt. 22:23 ff.; John 11:24). Resurrection is by definition at the end of all things. It is defined as the end event. One cannot understand the meaning of history until history is over. Similarly one cannot understand the meaning of an individual's life until that life is over, for otherwise its meaning would still be subject to change. This brings us back to the analogy we developed. Many did not grasp the young woman's purpose until the end of the process became clear. One may not know the purpose of another's long-range commitment until the goal of that commitment is reached. That is why the apocalyptic writers focused so intently on the question of what happens at the *end* of the historical process: only then would history's meaning finally be clear (Heb. 6:8 ff.; 1 Pet. 4:7; Rev. 21:6; 22:13).

At the general resurrection it was expected that history would end, and there would be the time of final judgment and decision (John 11:24). This view was not merely taught by the disciples or by Jesus but prevailed many decades before Jesus was born.

But Jesus, to everyone's surprise, appeared after his crucifixion. The resurrected Lord appearing after his death to the disciples signaled to them that the end had come; the final scene of history had anticipatively been revealed. They knew where history was headed, because its *end* was already being revealed.

The Gospel focused essentially upon the resurrection: "You are looking for Jesus the Nazarene, who was crucified. He has risen! He is not here. See the place where they laid him. But go, tell his disciples and Peter, 'He is going ahead of you into Galilee. There you will see him, just as he told you'" (Mark 16:6, 7). According to John's Gospel, Jesus himself had already intimated that this would happen when he said to Martha: "I am the resurrection and I am life. If a man has faith in me, even though he die, he shall come to life" (John 11:25, 26).

The resurrection of Jesus constituted a powerful reversal of historical expectations. Those who met the living Lord experienced a radical reversal of consciousness. It was an event without precedent—to be met by the resurrected Lord. It meant that even though history continues apace, those who live out of the resurrection are already sharing in the last days. By receiving and believing in the resurrected Lord, they were in effect already participating in the end, and therefore the meaning, of the entire world-historical process (Acts 26:23; 1 Thess. 4:16).

After his resurrection, Jesus was repeatedly experienced as a living presence, a newly alive person, by the faithful in the breaking of bread, in the fellowship of the remembering community, and walking back home (John 20:24–28). In this way the meaning of history was anticipatively disclosed before the actual ending of the historical process. Resurrection is an intractably historical way of understanding, a very Jewish way of reasoning, about how God lets us know his purposes—namely, through history. The courage of the early church to face death and persecution was directly based upon their continuing experience of the presence of the resurrected Lord.

As in our previous analogy, the purpose of a long-range commitment (either in a person or in history as a whole) could not be discerned merely by looking at one particular point of the story from the outside. There are many twists and turns in human history, yet at the end of the process the purpose is made known. Christianity proclaims that the purpose of the otherwise obscure process of history, which involves fallen freedom, sin, evil, and frustration, is revealed in Jesus' resurrection. That is precisely the reason one can, in the New Testament sense, trust in God's providence: because the resurrected Lord remains ever present in the community through Word and Sacrament, and because we have been met already by the end of the process. No theme of Christian teaching of God's care is more crucial than resurrection (cf. Wolfhart Pannenberg, *Jesus, God and Man*, who has astutely clarified what the resurrection meant to the people who beheld and responded to it, and remembered it).

Those who are grasped by the resurrection of Jesus are already anticipating, already living within the end of the process. That is the basis upon which trust is possible. Fuller probing of these themes will be found in the sequel volume to this one.

No one is pretending that Christian trust in God's providence, as made known through the resurrection, is going to give believers foreknowledge in specific detail of future events. Such claims are prone to fanatical distortion. Rather, the resurrection teaches us that even though outcomes are not objectively known, the Guide of outcomes is trustable. It is through the resurrection that the disciples gained the capacity for that trust. Through the resurrection the faithful have foretasted the end (1 Pet. 2:3). It is as though they have gained a tiny glimpse of the vision that reveals the will of God for the whole. They "have had a taste of the heavenly gift and a share in the Holy Spirit, when they have experienced the goodness of God's word and the spiritual energies of the age to come" (Heb. 6:4, 5).

Part IV

THE STUDY OF GOD

Modern study of theology typically begins by asking whether or how theology can be studied, and only then, after deliberately (often at sober length) accounting for method, begins to speak (often with great tentativeness) of God. The classical Christian exegetes did not characteristically or formally begin with detailed discussions of theological method, although they often appear to have been keenly aware of how they were proceeding. They were more likely to plunge into the substantive clarification of the being and activity of God, and only subsequently consider and examine their method.

Following these ancient ecumenical teachers, we began our study with the substantive questions of *who* God is, *whether* God is, and whether God is *triune Creator* and *Provider*. Although we have reserved questions of method to this more modest and ancillary position in the sequence of topics of the study of God, we do not imply that they are unimportant. But the classical sequence does signal several implications: that the living God is prior to and more crucial than our methods of inquiry; that the attributes and reality of God precede our inquiry into them; that methodological reflection best occurs as a retrospection upon the actual practice of the study of God rather than an arbitrary limitation upon practice before study has begun. The implication is that theological epistemology (the study of the knowledge of God) is best derived from the practice of the Christian life rather than vice versa.

Among early Christian teachers who tended to subordinate *method* to *the Subject* of the study are Ignatius of Antioch, Novatian, Hilary, John Chrysostom, Basil, and Ambrose. None set out first with an account of method. It was not until Gregory of Nyssa, Augustine, and Vincent of Lerins in the late fourth and early fifth centuries that the operative method of the ecumenical theologians became increasingly clear. By the time of Gregory the Great and John of Damascus, the methods articulated by Gregory of Nyssa, Augustine, and Vincent were thoroughly integrated into exegesis, preaching, and theological debate, but often referred to only obliquely.

Our purpose in this concluding part of this volume is to ask whether God can be studied, and if so by what means or methods, utilizing what resources, and according to what rationale. In Chapter 8 we will ask: whether the deliberate study of God is possible or necessary to faith; whether the revelation of God requires Scripture, tradition, experience, and/or reason to enable its reception; whether church tradition is an authoritative source of theology; whether the study of God is a science; whether the right study of God requires a particular temperament; and whether the study of God can be viewed as an academic discipline that corresponds with other disciplines. Then in the last chapter we will ask about the relation of reason and revelation, or the reasoning of revelation.

CHAPTER 8

Whether God Can Be Studied

Whether the Deliberate Study of God Is Possible or Necessary to Faith

The Limits of Human Language About God

Insofar as we speak any words at all about God's coming into our presence, we speak in fragile language about that knowledge we as creatures have, however fragmentary, of the infinite divine reality (Dionysius, *Div. Names* I). The study of God can only be an inquiry that fallible, finite sinners undertake. God does not study theology, for God already knows his own mind with full adequacy, and without needing our technical words or expert phrases about him (John of Damascus, *OF* I.1.2, *FC* 37, pp. 165–68; Wesley, "Imperfections of Human Knowledge," *WJW* VI, pp. 338 ff.).

Hence all "theo-talk" occurs within the limits of finitude and of a historical community that in time passes through many languages, national histories, and cultural memories. No human knower sees as God sees. We must employ human speech if we are to speak at all of this One about whom any speech is always inadequate, yet about whom fitting speech is so important (Augustine, *On Chr. Doctrine* I.6–13, *NPNF* 1 II, pp. 524–26; Luther, *Bondage of the Will* XII).

Hence there is an element of comedy about all theo-talk, which the recipient of grace can delight in and stands quick to confess (Kierke-gaard, *Concl. Unsci. Post.*, pp. 250–70, 431 ff.). For we are striving with all our might in frail language to talk about that which is finally quite indescribable—indeed, ineffable! (Dionysius, *Div. Names* I.1 ff.; John of Damascus, *OF* I.1, *NPNF* 2 IX, pp. 1 ff.). Nonetheless, we keep on trying to say a little better, or as well as we can, whatever we can about this incomparable reality that we meet in our own hearts, in the history of Jesus, in our own social experiences, and in universal history. If often seems as if it would be far more conscionable to give up speaking at all.

Christian Theology Emerges out of Christian Community

The intellectual enterprise that we call Christian theology is an activity that occurs within the sphere of church. That is precisely what distinguishes it from psychology of religion and philosophy of religion—legitimate disciplines that differ in method and subject matter from theology. Just as Islamic theology begins within the framework of Islamic prayer, law, and community life, and just as Jewish theology begins within a community of remembrance and expectation, so does Christian theology emerge precisely within a community whose "life lies hidden with Christ in God" (Col. 3:3). When we inquire seriously into Christian teaching, we normally do so as baptized members of the body of Christ—thus as communicants, worshipers, and recipients of the gospel—or as inquirers who wish to know what the church teaches (Augustine, *First Catech. Instr.* 1, 2, *ACW* 2, pp. 13–18).

The church long ago grasped that God has committed his revelation, as set forth with full adequacy in Scripture, to the keeping of the church under the guidance of the Spirit (Simplicius, *The Necessity of Guarding the Faith, Epis. to Acacius, SCD* 159, p. 64). The Bible is the church's book, lodged within the church for safekeeping and to provide continuing inspiration and instruction (Irenaeus, *Ag. Her.* III.4, *ANF* I, pp. 416, 417). It is the church (not the university) that has for centuries kept it, translated it, studied it, meditated upon it, and repeatedly looked to it for guidance.

The Holy Writ given to the church has spawned a lively history of religious ideas, theories, concepts, and symbols (Eusebius, *CH* VI, *NPNF* 2 I, pp. 249–93). Doctrinal formations arising from Scripture have employed many different conceptualities, thought-structures, languages, and symbol systems. The disciplines that study these forms are called historical theology, church history, and confessional theology.

This development of Christian theology is to some degree governed by the law of adaptation, in the sense that the truth of Scripture must be adapted to various historical circumstances and languages in which the ancient truth may again come alive and be knowable. The idea of an evolution of Christian language is hardly inimical to Christian orthodoxy, but precisely in line with the intention of orthodoxy, which prays that God's Spirit will spawn ever-new communities in each new historical context, language, and symbol system, each faithful to the earliest Christian teaching (Augustine, *On Chr. Doctrine*, prologue I.1 ff., *LLA*, pp. 3 ff.). The achievement of orthodoxy was never in making all believers look exactly alike, but in serving the hope that the one

Christ might be rightly known in many different contexts (Vincent of Lerins, *Comm.* XXIII, *NPNF* 2 XI, pp. 147–50; cf. Newman, *Development of Chr. Doctrine*).

Since the modern reader understandably may gasp at the term *orthodoxy*—that least of all modern words, which itself is largely a product of the classical Christian tradition—this term requires some unpacking. *Orthodox* means "right opinion" (*orthos* + *doxa*), or "sound doctrine," especially religious teaching, and more particularly that teaching which holds closely to the Christian faith as formulated by the classical Christian tradition. An opinion is orthodox if it is congruent with the apostolic faith. If social processes are to achieve multigenerational continuity, they require careful legitimation and tradition maintenance. Among modern orthodoxies are Freudian, Marxian, behaviorist, as well as Christian. Among modern religious communities who readily embrace the term *orthodoxy* the most evident are the Eastern Orthodox communions, the Roman Catholic church, and Orthodox Judaism, as well as various Protestant denominations.

For reasons spelled out in *Agenda for Theology*, I prefer to use the more explicit term *postmodern orthodoxy* in order to point to the type of theological reflection most needed today. That orthodoxy is postmodern which has seriously passed through and dealt with the possibilities and limits of modernity on its pilgrimage, a pilgrimage that has brought rediscovery of the early Christian tradition. Christianity views modernity from the point of view of its historical dissolution. We have already witnessed in the third quarter of the twentieth century the precipitous deterioration of social processes under the tutelage of autonomous individualism, narcissistic hedonism, and naturalistic reductionism, all of which have been key features of modern consciousness. Postmodern consciousness is characterized by the hunger for means of social stabilization, continuity, parenting, intergenerational tradition maintenance, and freedom from the repressions of modernity. Postmodern orthodoxy is Christian teaching that, having passed through a deep engagement in the assumptions of modernity, has rediscovered the vitality of the ancient ecumenical Christian tradition.

The Limits of the Church's Mandate to Teach

In spite of all limitations, we simply *must* study God, because God has touched our lives and has become our very life. There is no period of Christian history in which the attempt to study God has been completely disregarded or has entirely ceased.

Christianity has long assumed an inward moral requirement that it should learn to think and teach *consistently* about God, and that it should teach only that which has been revealed or is directly derivative from revelation. Out of this imperative has come the development of systems of Christian teaching, intended both to teach converts and to defend against error. Systematic or basic theology is a slowly developing expansion of what Luke called "the apostles' teaching" (Acts 2:24, NIV). Its more primitive forms were baptismal creeds, catechetical teaching, preaching, letters, and expository and pastoral theology aimed at edification.

As challenges to faith occurred from novel, experimental, and often distorted views of Scripture, it became necessary to defend Christian teaching. The faith had to be defended from challenges both within and without (Hippolytus, *Refutation of All Her.* X, *ANF* V, pp. 140–53). The defense of the faith to those outside the community was called apologetics (cf. 2 Tim. 2:24–26; 1 Pet. 3:15; Justin Martyr, *First Apol.* XIII, *ANF* I, pp. 166, 167).

Attempts to bring Christian teaching into a consistent, balanced formulation, as in John of Damascus' *On the Orthodox Faith*, were early forms of dogmatic theology (which only in the modern period has come to be called systematic theology). They were seeking to bring into ordered unity and cohesion all the doctrines of Christian teaching according to the consensual affirmations of the early ecumenical councils of Christian leaders and teachers (*OF* I.1, *NPNF* 2 IX, pp. 1 ff., cf. Cyril of Jerusalem, *Procatechesis, FC* 61, pp. 69 ff.; Rufinus, *On the Creed, NPNF* 2 III, pp. 541–63; Peter Lombard, *Four Books of Sentences*).

Even in the New Testament there appear several accounts of the meaning of Jesus' ministry, life, and death—those of John, Paul, Peter, James, Luke, Mark, and others—each stamped with distinct characteristics of its author. Despite differences of language, syntax, and cultural situation, all understood themselves to be proclaiming the same Lord, united in the same faith. All assumed that there was a "unity inherent in our faith" (Eph. 4:13) that undergirded all differences of perspectives and gifts. The earliest Christian teachers did not think that these teachings were their own personal innovations, but revelations given by God, as Paul specifically stated: "I must make it clear to you, my friends, that the gospel you heard me preach is no human invention. I did not take it over from any man; no man taught it to me; I received it through a revelation of Jesus Christ" (Gal. 1:11, 12).

Although Paul introduced many profound and influential ideas into the stream of Christian teaching, he was the one who gave most resistance to those who would assert that the New Testament faith can be divided into opposing types or parties. To those who asserted the body of Christ could be divided, Paul countered: "Surely Christ has not been divided among you! Was it Paul who was crucified for you? Was it in the name of Paul that you were baptized?" (1 Cor. 1:13; Tertullian, *On Baptism* XV, *ANF* III, pp. 676, 677). During the first five centuries the unity of the church was remarkably well preserved by the Spirit even amid and through political tyranny, persecution, harassment, and many challenges of heterodox claims to revelation.

The classic Christian consensus was expressed by the ecumenical councils and defined by the three creeds still most widely affirmed in ecumenical Christianity: the Apostles' Creed, which expanded the baptismal formula; the Nicene Creed, which defined the triune teaching; and the Athanasian Creed, which more precisely set forth the sonship of Christ (*COC* II, pp. 45–72). These consensual affirmations did not arise out of speculation or out of pedantic fixation upon hairsplitting distinctions. Rather, they emerged out of a long period of dialogue and controversy in which the apostolic teachings were repeatedly challenged by alternative teachings.

These controversies virtually exhausted the possibilities of alternative views of the relation of the Father, Son, and Spirit, so that for the next millennium the church's mission could proceed on the basis of ecumenically established definitions considered definitive for all Christian teaching. The creeds were not catholic because a majority of bishops decided they were, but because those representatives were guided by the Spirit to express the common conviction of all Christian believers (Vincent of Lerins, *Comm.* XXVII.38, *LCC* IX, pp. 78, 79). Had this self-defense not been undertaken, the church would later have been faced with having to struggle further against defective understandings of God. These would eventually have made great differences in the practical life, organization, ethics, and teaching of the church. The church had to protect itself from becoming captivated by various philosophical, political, and religious schools (Hippolytus, *Refutation of All Her.* X.2 ff., *ANF* V, pp. 140 ff.).

Theology today remains indebted to the work of the teachers who with great skill formed the ancient ecumenical consensus. Even though the ancient consensus eventually split up into Eastern (Constantinople) and Western (Rome) factions, both East and West were nurtured by the ecumenical councils and creeds. They in turn have informed Protestant faith in God, and they remain even today the basis for the latent promise of the unity of the church, affirmed by Catholic, Orthodox, and Protestant alike.

The Christian community has always been a learning and teaching community, concerned with the unity, coherence, and internal consistency of its reflection upon God's self-disclosure. It is constantly learning from the living presence of Christ and the Spirit in ever-new contemporary situations.

Jesus himself was a remarkable teacher, and the pastoral office that has patterned itself after him remains intrinsically a teaching ministry. It is impossible to conceive the history of Christianity without its teaching function and without the pastoral duty to teach Christian faith (Matt. 28:19, 20; John 21:15–17).

The concise account of apostolic activity in Acts 2:42 presents a pattern that must have been quite familiar to early Christian communities: "They met constantly to hear the apostles teach, and to share the common life, to break bread, and to pray." This remains a rough sketch of the spheres of activity of the early Christian community: first, teaching, then the nurturing of community, sacramental life, and prayer. If the church's teaching is deficient, then its fellowship, sacrament, and worship are likely to feel that deficiency.

The primary mandate of the church is not to teach miscellaneous opinions about psychology, politics, or sociology that are not derived from revelation. The church has received authorization to teach that which has been delivered to the church from God. Beyond that the mandate to teach is best viewed modestly. On the one hand, theology does not serve well by attempting to feed as a parasite on all the other disciplines of the university, as if it had nothing of its own to say. On the other hand, theology does even worse when it seeks to imperialize the various disciplines, imagining that it knows more about biology than biologists and more about medicine than physicians.

The Roots of Theo-Talk

The study of God, *theologia*, has been actively pursued for at least twenty-five hundred years. Homer, Hesiod, and Orpheus were called *theologoi* by the Greeks because their poetry concerned the gods. Plato spoke of *theologia* as the attempt to reason about the gods (*Republic* 379A). For Aristotle, *theologia* was that part of philosophy that reflects upon the cosmos as being grounded in a first cause or unmoved Mover (*Metaphy.* 1026A).

The same term, *theologia*, later became appropriated by the early Christian tradition through teachers like Origen and Athanasius to refer to an orderly, consistent, reliable understanding of God (Origen, *De Princip.*, preface I.1, *ANF* IV, pp. 239–45; cf. Athanasius, *Four Discourses Ag. Arians* I.18, *NPNF* 2 IV, p. 317). In this way *theologia* became distinguishable from faith itself as an attempt rightly to declare and apprehend faith and to bring some level of credible, cohesive, internally consistent understanding out of faith (Origen, *Ag. Celsus* I.9–11, *ANF* IV, pp. 399–401).

Both Tertullian and Augustine referred to the Stoic threefold division of theology into physical, mythic, and civic theology (Tertullian, *Ad Nationes* II.1–4, *ANF* III, pp. 129–33; Augustine, *CG* VI.5, *NPNF* 1 II, pp. 112, 113). Aware that preaching and public ministry required the study of sacred doctrine (*sacra doctrina*), Augustine sought to set forth a thoroughgoing systematic reflection on various scriptural teachings, especially under conditions in which the delivered ecumenical consensus was being challenged. Theophilus of Antioch, Hilary, Cyril of Jerusalem, and John of Damascus more than others influenced the sequence of theological subjects as they appear in classical theology.

It was not until the birth of the university, with Abelard and Peter Lombard in the twelfth century, that *theologia* came to be viewed as a disciplined academic study within the university, which would gradually distinguish itself from philosophy and other sciences by inquiring into the revealed God (Abelard, *Sic et non*; Peter Lombard, *Sentences*). The university itself may be said to be in large part a legacy of the study of theology. Thomas Aquinas, in the thirteenth century, crafted the medieval period's most systematic statement of theology as a disciplined field of academic learning that inquires into the whole arena of Christian learning and teaching, as distinguished from philosophy, which is necessarily related and complementary to it. Thomas's *Summa* was an elaborately ordered science of revealed truth, correlated with reasoning about God that integrated scriptural truth, philosophical reflection, and the church's hard-won historical wisdom (Tho. Aq., *ST* I Q1; *SCG* I.1–5).

Not only from Thomas but from many others who preceded and followed him do we have models of how to nurture, draw together, and articulate a cohesive statement of Christian faith. Since the time of Thomas, theology has come to mean the systematic elaboration of key questions concerning the truth of divine revelation. It proceeds by rational examination, enlightened by faith. It is in this sense that theology for almost a thousand years has been called a *science*—in the sense of an orderly way of knowing that has its own method, its own disciplined way of reasoning, and its own academic integrity as a reasoned exposition of the evidences of the attributes and existence of God, of God's saving history, and of the meaning of God's revelation.

Theology remains among the many areas of study in the university, although indeed some universities provide less freedom for this study than others (cf. Newman, *The Idea of a University*; Russell Kirk, *The Roots of American Order*, pp. 432 ff.). As psychology is reasoned reflection upon the *psychē* (the animating, emotive, energetic, motivating center of human existence), theology is a reasoned reflection concerning *theos*, and must from time to time provide some account to the other disciplines for its own method of studying its distinctive subject matter: God as known by a community of faith (Tho. Aq., *ST* I Q1, I, pp. 2–4; Calvin, *Inst.* 1.13; Wesley, *WJW* VII, pp. 453–60; Schleiermacher, *The Christian Faith*; Watson, *TI* I, pp. 5 ff.; Heppe, *RD*, pp. 1–12). The study of God, therefore, has a history (cf. H. R. Niebuhr, D. D. Williams, J. Gustafson, *The Purpose of the Church and Ministry*; E. Farley, *Theologia*). The subject area that inquires into that history has since the nineteenth century been called historical theology (or ecclesiastical history; cf. Eusebius, *CH*, *NPNF* 2 I).

What Makes the Study of God Systematic?

The discipline of *systematic theology* (or basic theology or Christian doctrine) seeks to formulate Christian teaching in an orderly, sequential, plausible way that is accountable to Scripture and tradition and meaningful to contemporary experience. The closely related term *Christian teaching* (like the German *Glaubenslehre*, or the teaching of faith) is generally interchangeable with *Christian doctrine*, referring to the settled convictions of the Christian community that have become established through investigation of Scripture and tradition and ordered into a logical and internally consistent sequence of argument. This study is called systematic not because the other terms (*basic theology* or *Christian doctrine*) are inappropriate but because its primary aim is the systematic presentation of the truth of the Christian faith. That is systematic which seeks to bring disparate parts of something into an organized whole (from *synistanai*, to place together). To systematize is to arrange, coordinate, organize discrete aspects of a system into a meaningful or working arrangement. An investigation is systematic if carried out deliberately, thoroughly, and with consistent design. It is in this sense that this present effort seeks to be systematic.

This intent corresponds with that of Athenagoras, who spoke in the second century of "the Christian doctrine of God," based on "witnesses of the things we apprehend and believe, prophets, men who have pronounced concerning God and the things of God, guided by the Spirit of God" (*A Plea for the Christians*, VII, *ANF* II, p. 132). It is precisely these convictions that we seek to bring together into a coherent system that is clearly stated and reasonably defended. Augustine stated the rules for removing ambiguities in the interpretation of Scripture so as to render Christian doctrine plausible and meaningful (Augustine, *On Chr. Doctrine*, preface II.27–42, *NPNF* 1 II, pp. 519–22, 549–55). Systematic theology attempts to formulate, order, clarify, and defend these convictions in a way that is both accessible to contemporary communities of faith and accountable to the apostolic witness (Justin Martyr, *First Apol.* LXI, *ANF* I, pp. 183; Watson, *TI* I pp. 5 ff.; Bultmann, *EPT* I; Tillich, *Systematic Theology* I).

It should be evident that I am not using the term *systematic theology* with the anti-Catholic assumptions that have been applied by some Protestant writers (A. H. Strong; H. Bavinck), or in the deliberately existentialist way of Paul Tillich. If Charles Hodge may be considered as a prototype of *premodern* Reformed systematic theology, and Tillich as a prototype of *modern* accommodationist systematic theology, I am striving for neither premodern nor modern but a deliberately *postmodern orthodox* systematic theology (in the sense in which that term has been defined in *Agenda for Theology*). This study stands closer to von Balthasar than Barth, to Pannenberg than Bultmann, to Geoffrey Wainwright, Albert Outler, and Clark Pinnock than Hans Küng or Leonardo Boff, to Letty Russell than to Mary Daly, to the traditions of Hooker and Baxter more than Christian Wolff or John Toland, to John Pearson and Thomas Watson than Francis Turretin, to Newman than Hegel, to William Burt Pope and Edwin Lewis than John Miley or E. S. Brightman. My interest in theo-comedy comes directly from Kierkegaard, who spoofed the unrelenting seriousness of the Hegelians.

The term *dogmatics* remains a vital concept in Reformed, Catholic, and Orthodox traditions with reference to Christian teaching. The term harks back to the Greek *dokei moi*, which meant not only "it seems to me" but also "it has been clearly determined as an authoritative fact." New Testament usage designated firm enactments, regulations, or decrees as *dogmata* (Luke 2:1; Acts 16:4; Col. 2:14; 1:15; cf. Josephus, *Apion* I.8). Ignatius urged his readers to "Study, therefore, to be established in the doctrines [*dogmata*] of the Lord and the apostles" (*To Magnesians* XIII, *ANF* I, p. 64). *Dogma* has come to refer to consensually received and established Christian truth as distinguished from individual opinion, wish, projection, or private view (Schmid, *DT* I; Barth, *CD* 1/1).

Christian teaching is not primarily focused upon an analysis of human feelings. However important our emotional responses may be to us, they are not essentially or finally the subject matter of Christian theology, which is a *logos,* a series of reasonings not about one's private feelings but about nothing less than *theos* as known in the faith of the Christian community (Gregory of Nyssa, *Great Catech.*, prologue, *NPNF* 2 V, pp. 472–74). Understandably, our dialogue with this incomparable One powerfully affects our feelings (Augustine, *The Happy Life, FC* 1, pp. 43–86; cf. Jonathan Edwards, *Religious Affections*), but Christian teaching is less focused on the aftereffects than on the One who elicits and grounds these effects (Calvin, *Inst.* 1.13; 3.20). The empirical inquiry into religious feelings and the emotive life that proceeds from religious experience is a quite different subject area called psychology of religion (an important study, but it is not theology), the study of affective experience that emerges when persons are psychologically and interpersonally impacted by God or by religious symbols and communities (William James, *Varieties of Religious Experience*).

Whether Revelation Requires Scripture, Tradition, Experience, and Reason

Sources for the Christian Study of God

By what authority or on what ground does Christian teaching rest? How does the worshiping community know what it seems to know? The study of God relies constantly upon an interdependent quadrilateral of sources on the basis of which the confessing community can articulate, make consistent, and integrate the witness to revelation. These four are *scripture, tradition, experience,* and *reason,* all of which depend upon and exist as a response to their necessary premise: revelation. All are functionally operative, although often implicitly, in the most representative of classical Christian teachers: Irenaeus, John Chrysostom, Ambrose, Augustine, and John of Damascus.

Revelation—the Primary Premise of the Christian Study of God

Each phase of the fourfold approach to the study of God hinges on the central premise that God has made himself known (Irenaeus, *Ag. Her.* III, *ANF* I, pp. 414–60). God has not concealed but revealed the divine will, love, and mercy through a historical process, so anyone who carefully examines history may discern that revelation (Pss. 33:9; 40:5; 105:5; 126:2, 3; Augustine, *CG* XVIII, *NPNF* 1 II, pp. 361 ff.). Jewish and Christian reasoning about God characteristically looks at history, the history of God's activity. This history tells a unique story that forms the people's memory of themselves. It tells of creation, of the fall, of a flood, a covenant, an exodus, a captivity, and a crucifixion and resurrection, a Spirit-bestowed church and an expected judgment. By looking intently upon that history, we can see that the whole fabric of events reveals the presence, reality, power, and character of God (Tertullian, *Ag. Marcion* III, *ANF* III, pp. 321 ff.; Augustine, *On Psalms* XC, *NPNF* 1 VIII, pp. 441–46).

Christian Scripture, Christian tradition, Christian reasoning, and Christian experience all exist in response to God's historical revelation in Israel and Jesus Christ, which may be pictured as follows:

CHRIST	SCRIPTURE	TRADITION	EXPERIENCE	REASON
The Revealed Word	Written Word	Remembered Word	Personally Experienced Word	Word Made Intelligible
Sources of the Study of God	Primary	Secondary	Secondary	Secondary

The sources of the study of God are in this way seen in a temporal sequence that moves from originative event (Christ the Revealer of God the Father) as proclaimed by the community, to the record of the earliest proclamation (written word), to the traditioning of that word intergenerationally through time (tradition), which elicits personal and social awareness and experience of the salvation event (experience), which then becomes the basis of the reflection required to think consistently about the meaning of the salvation event (reason)—each layer depending on the previous one (Hooker, *Laws of Eccl. Polity* III.8; cf. Clement of Alex., *Strom.* VI.10 ff., *ANF* II, pp. 496 ff.; Tho. Aq., *SCG* I.9; Calvin, *Inst.* 1.6, 7; 3.20).

The giver of this story is the Source and End of history. This is symbolized by pulling all history into a parenthesis, suggesting that history is radically finite, with an end and a beginning. The giver of history is known through history. The ground of history is revealed in history (Augustine, *CG* XVI, *NPNF* 1 II, pp. 309–36).

Three caveats before proceeding further: First, it is well to remember that the oral tradition of apostolic preaching preceded the written tradition of New Testament Scripture, so in that sense it is readily conceded that tradition stands chronologically and logically prior to Scripture. Subsequent to the ecumenical consensus on the canonization of Scripture, however, the church views the transmission of tradition from the postcanonical vantage point that assumes Scripture as already having been written and ever thereafter funding and enabling new embodiments of tradition. In sum, precanonically tradition is prior to Scripture; postcanonically Scripture is prior to tradition. It seems a picky point, but this remains a major sticking point between Catholic/Orthodox versus Protestant theological methods (Conf. of Dositheus, *CC*, pp. 485–516; Heidelberg Catech. *COC* III, pp. 307–55; cf. Tavard, *Holy Church, Holy Writ*).

Secondly, the method we are developing here we allege to be implicitly employed by ancient ecumenical teachers, but we do not find an adequate, explicit clarification of the relation of experience and reason to Scripture and tradition until the Reformation and modern periods. The medieval synthesis had held together revelation and reason as mediated by the conciliar tradition's interpretations of Scripture. The Reformation again asserted the written word as primary source of theology, yet affirmed the ancient ecumenical consensus where it could be shown to be consistent with Scripture. The Enlightenment challenged both the Protestant and Tridentine Reformations to rethink the relation of reason and revelation. It was not until the development of eighteenth-century pietism that experience again received the attention that had been paid to it in fourth-century theology (the Cappadocians, Ambrose, and Augustine) and early monasticism (Basil, Benedict, John Cassian, Gregory). For a functional view of this method, one sees it best operating in the central Anglican formularies, the *Homilies*, the *Book of Common Prayer*, the Thirty-nine Articles of Religion, the works of Cranmer, Jewel, Hooker, Gibson, Thorndike, Jackson, Taylor, and Wesley, as well as in Scholastic Lutherans like Gerhard, and in some measure in Calvinists like A. J. Niemeyer, as well as in many post-Tridentine Catholics.

Third, the term *quadrilateral* comes from the image of the four "fortress cities" of Lombardy, suggesting that if Christian teaching is constructed within such a fourfold fortress, the church can stand secure. The document most commonly associated with the term is the Lambeth Quadrilateral of 1888, which stated four essentials for a reunited church from the Anglican point of view: *Scripture* contains "all things necessary to salvation," as the "rule and ultimate standard of faith"; the ancient ecumenical *creeds* (Nicene and Apostles') as the sufficient rule of faith; the two *sacraments* ordained by Christ himself, as the means of grace; "The *Historic Episcopate*, locally adapted in the methods of its administration to the varying needs of the nations and peoples called of God into the Unity of His Church" (*ODCC*, p. 795; the 1930 Lambeth Conference spoke of *Historic Episcopate* as "Episcopate as it emerged in history without any speculation as to the mode of historic origin and without any specific constitutional form"; cf. W. R. Huntington, *The Church-Idea*; G. K. A. Bell, ed., *Documents on Chr. Unity*). The notion of quadrilateral became later adapted in 1972 to the United Methodist Discipline (Doctrinal Guidelines, par. 70), which affirmed "free inquiry within the boundaries defined by four main sources and guidelines for Christian theology: Scripture, tradition, experience, reason" (p. 75). Using this schema, we may further ask how revelation both empowers and requires a written word (Scripture), a remembering community (tradition), an appropriation process (experience), and internal consistency (reason).

What Is Revelation?

It happens sometimes in personal life that a particular occurrence bestows meaning upon all the other events of one's life. It is as if one were reading a book, somewhat confused, plowing through heavy ground, when suddenly a single sentence jumps out, and from that moment on one understands the book, what had gone before and what comes later. Such was the way the people of Israel experienced deliverance from Egypt, the prophets experienced the Babylonian captivity and return, and the apostles experienced the risen Christ (cf. Ambrose, *On the Belief in the Resurrection*, NPNF 2 X, pp. 174–79).

Something like revelation occurs in personal experience when I see through a single experience the rest of my experience. When I caught on to the difference between a C and a G chord, the guitar became understandable to me. When I learned to keep my eye on the ball, baseball became my game. When I fell in love, every aspect of my experience was impacted. When I left my hometown, its meaning to me became much clearer. Such occurrences in personal history are analogous to revelation in human history. Revelation is any act by which God makes himself known in human history—through particular events of nameable people—in order that humanity writ large may become more responsive to the disclosure of divine goodness, power, and love (Tho. Aq., *Compend. of Theol.* II.8, pp. 325–29; Kierkegaard, *Training in Christianity*; H. R. Niebuhr, *RMWC*).

Although revelation in a general sense is present in all the history of religions, God's special revelation to humanity is more particularly made clear, according to Jewish and Christian understandings of revelation, by looking at a particular history, at events through which the divine intent is disclosed. The study of God is essentially a study of revelation and therefore a study of history—of the people of Israel, the history of Jesus, and of the early Christian community (Gregory of Nyssa, *On the Baptism of Christ*, NPNF 2 V, pp. 521–24).

The study of God relies upon and assumes those disciplines that establish the most accurate versions of the *texts* of Scripture and tradition, and those that study the historical *contexts* in which Scripture and tradition emerged, in order to discern more clearly the meanings of those events (Eusebius, *CH* I.1, *NPNF* 2 I, pp. 81, 82; Jerome, *Lives of Illustrious Men, NPNF* 2 III, pp. 361 ff.). God continues to reveal himself in ever-emergent human history, but in ways that are finally illuminated only by looking at how God has become known in Israel and Christ (Julian of Norwich, *Showings, Long Text* 52–58, *CWS*, pp. 279–90). There is a complementarity and tension between the past self-disclosure of God in history and the ways in which God becomes revealed in the present, so that the present complements, extends, and develops, but does not negate, past disclosures (Heb. 1:1 ff.; Pastor of Hermas II.10–12, *ANF* II, pp. 26–30).

Even the nonbeliever may pose the hypothesis, in order to seek an understanding of Christianity, that God is known through a history of revelation (Justin Martyr, *Dialogue with Trypho, ANF* II, pp. 194 ff.). However opaque this Source and End of history may appear, it may be hypothesized that through the Christ event this reality has become known amid this historical process in such a way that a single person (Jesus) and event (cross/resurrection) clarifies the meaning of the whole historical process (Eph. 1:3–23). In fact, risk-taking Christian faith rests on this hypothesis, which remains open to inquiry by anyone (Lactantius, *Div. Inst.* IV.26, *ANF* VII, pp. 127–29).

As new events occur in ever-emergent history, their meanings are illumined, in this community, by reflection out of that primary revelatory event and its Revealer, Jesus as the Christ. In this way a worshiping community has developed that is constantly reflecting upon each new phase or moment of history in relation to that original event of revelation. This mode of reasoning was familiar to the Hebraic community prior to Jesus, wherein past revelatory events such as exodus and captivity became the matrix of understanding out of which new events were interpreted (cf. G. von Rad, *OT Theol.;* Pannenberg, *Essays* I). That is a distinctively Hebraic mode of thinking: "When your son asks you in time to come, 'What is the meaning of the precepts, statutes, and laws which the Lord our God gave you?' you shall say to him, 'We were Pharaoh's slaves in Egypt, and the Lord brought us out of Egypt with his strong hand,' " etc. (Deut. 6:20–22; cf. Rom. 3:21–31; cf. Irenaeus, *Ag. Her.* IV.21, *ANF* I, pp. 492, 493).

This is the central hypothesis of the Christian way of studying God: that through Christ the Revealer of God, we see into the meaning of other events from beginning to end. Jesus Christ is that moment in the historical process in which the part reveals the whole—through this particular lens, we come to know the One who is unsurpassably good, the One who is the ground of our being, who gives life, in whom all things cohere (Col. 1:3–20; cf. Tertullian, *Ag. Marcion* V.19, *ANF* III, pp. 470–72). It is out of participation in that event that Christian community continues to come alive, proclaim God's word, celebrate life together, and partake of the sacramental life that brings the community again in communion with that Word (Ignatius, *Ephesians* VI ff., *ANF* I, pp. 51 ff.).

Scripture: The Written Word

We will reserve until a later volume a full discussion of the sense in which divinely inspired Scripture is the utterly reliable source and norm of Christian theology. At this point we will show in a preliminary way how Scripture is presupposed in the study of God.

After the resurrection and before the writing down of the New Testament documents, many in the primitive Christian community expected the historical process to be concluded quickly (Mark 13:32–37). They assumed that an end time was eminent. But as history surprisingly continued, this community slowly began to realize that it needed to write down its message as historical experience continued to be extended for an indefinite (though limited) duration. If new generations were to be addressed, this would require writing down the history of Jesus the Revealer, and of early witnesses to him (Luke 1:1–4; Acts 1:1–5; John 21:23–25).

The New Testament contains these writings that survived—documents that ultimately went through a complex process of being transmitted, read in public worship, studied avidly, interpreted through preaching, analyzed, and finally in due time authorized as being credible witnesses to this revealing Word. After a long process of transcribing these documents, and reviewing and certifying them as of apostolic authorship, the New Testament became formally canonized as Holy Writ. It included letters, instructional documents, and accounts of Jesus' ministry, written in the last half of the first century, in which the attempt was made to state accurately the preaching of the apostles. The prime criterion for authorization was authenticity of apostolic authorship. The New Testament documents were regarded as credible apostolic witnesses, which signaled that all could trust them. This canonization process was accomplished by a living, growing, human historical community, by the consenting church in ecumenical consensus, utilizing the best historical information available to it (Tertullian, *Prescript. Ag. Her.* XV–XLIV, *ANF* III, pp. 250–65; *Apost. Const.*, "Eccl. Canons," 85, *ANF* VII, p. 505).

It took several centuries for this process of consensual formation to develop into a universally recognizable canon of apostolic tradition. By the fourth century all dioceses of Christian believers had basically agreed upon those documents that were universally accepted as apostolic tradition (Synod of Laodicea, canon LIX, *NPNF* 2 XIV, pp. 158, 159).

Catholic, Protestant, and Orthodox traditions have all agreed on the central premise that Scripture is the primary source and guideline for Christian teaching, although disagreement remains on the status of the Apocrypha ("hidden" writings). The Apocrypha includes fourteen books of the Vulgate Old Testament that were taken from the Septuagint but are not found in Hebrew. They were usually included in the canonical lists of the Roman tradition; included in the Eastern tradition until 1672 (when four were affirmed as canonical); to be read "for example of life and instruction of manners" (*CC*, p. 268), but not doctrine in the Anglican tradition; and excluded in most Protestant lists.

Although some differences on the status as canon of these fourteen exist, there has been virtually no dissent to affirming the other sixty-six books of the Old and New Testament as canonical. The Bible, composed of two sets of testimonies or covenants (Old and New), is the deposit of the sufficient and adequate witness to God's self-disclosure. Other valued sources of the study of God—tradition, reasoning, and experience—remain essentially dependent upon and responsive to Scripture, since they must appeal to Scripture for the very events, interpretations, and data they are remembering, upon which they reflect, and out of which their experience becomes transformed. Scripture remains the central preconditioning source of the memories, symbol systems, hopes, teachings, metaphors, and paradigms by which the community originally came into being and has continually refreshed and renewed itself (cf. Muratorian Canon, *ANF* V, p. 603; African Code, canon 24, *NPNF* 2 XIV, pp. 453, 454).

Each Scripture text is to be understood, received, and interpreted in the light of its relation to the Bible as a whole. All texts are open to be illuminated by both scholarly historical inquiry and by reverential personal insight. The meaning of each text is best understood when its intention and significance have been grasped in the light of the revelation known through other texts. Each believer has his or her own distinctive meeting with Scripture. Scripture does not speak in a monotonous voice or in a flat, uniform, rigid sense to every believer alike, without recognition that a distinctive dialogue emerges between the Spirit and each believer whenever and wherever one reads Scripture.

Scripture is the only written access that tradition has to the Christ event. Tradition is simply the history of the exegesis of Scripture. The traditionary process must occur ever again in each new historical circumstance (Quinisext Synod, canon XIX, *NPNF* 2 XIV, pp. 374, 375).

Scripture Funds Tradition, Reason, and Experience

A balanced quadrilateral of interdependent resources is recurrently needed in order to receive and reflect upon revelation: Scripture, tradition, experience, and reason—all of which are grounded in, responsive to, and thinking out of revelation. Revelation remains the precondition of all four basic sources of the study of God. Revelation is that from which the whole subject matter proceeds. There could be no Christian study of God without God's own initiative to become reliably known (Gen. 35:7; Ps. 98:2; Isa. 65:1; Rom. 1:18; 16:25, 26; Rev 1:1, Origen, *Ag. Celsus* III.61, *ANF* IV, p. 488; cf. Dionysius, *Fragments, From the Two Books on the Promises* I, *ANF* VI, pp. 81–84).

The Spirit's witness does not completely cease with the canonization of Scripture. New events emerge in the ongoing historical process that are to be understood in the light of the word of Scripture (Julian of Norwich, *Showings* I, *CWS*, p. 175). Yet no fundamentally new or different knowledge is required for the saving knowledge of God than that which is revealed in Scripture (Council of Rome, *SCD* 84, pp. 33, 34; Westminster Conf. I.1–10, *COC*, pp. 600–6).

Christianity differs from Judaism primarily in that it is not still looking for that fundamental messianic event to disclose the meaning of history. It remembers that event as having occurred in the ministry of Jesus, whose living presence is received and experienced in Holy Communion and the preached Word (Justin Martyr, *Dialogue with Trypho, ANF* I, pp. 194–270; R. Niebuhr, *NDM* I.1).

Tradition: The Word Remembered

Christian interpretations of God's self-disclosure have a complex history of their own. In each new developing historical situation, believers have come to discover, reformulate, and restate in their own language the revealed Word. These ever-new formulations of each new period of the tradition's reflection about itself have been refractions of the matrix of Scripture, yet each one is new, since historical experience is ever new (Gelasius, *Decretal, SCD* 164–66, pp. 68–70). There was a time when Athanasius and Thomas Aquinas and Calvin were new, even if they seem old to those who follow after them.

The uncritical use of the term *tradition* may leave the unwanted implication that Christian teaching is essentially an archaic or dogmatic traditionalism that is determined simply by rigid formulas and in-group prejudices. Rather, "tradition," as Jews and Christians live it, is a vital social reality that receives and transmits the history of revelation. Tradition wants to be danced, sung, feasted upon, and celebrated. Tradition is shared in a social process through seasonal celebrations and the recollection of mighty events (Quinisext Synod LXVI, *NPNF* 2 XIV, p. 395; *BCP,* passim). More will be said about tradition shortly.

The Word Experienced

Scripture awakens and allows the passing on and reexperiencing of a vast range of experiences, metaphors, symbols, and recollections of a historical community. The individual is invited to correlate personal experience with the social and historical continuum of the faithful by interacting with the social process and embracing the memory of a caring community (Deut. 6:20–25).

It is misleading to pit tradition against experience, for tradition is simply the memory of this vast arena of social and historical experiencing. There is a profound affinity and synchronicity between corporate tradition and personal experience: one is historical-social-ecclesial and the other is personal-individuated-unique, yet both are necessary embodiments of the body of Christ. What was once someone else's experience can become a part of my own experience. Christian teaching seeks to enable this corporate experiencing to become personally validated and authenticated as "one's own" (Wesley, *WJW* I, pp. 470 ff.; V, pp. 128 ff.; VIII, pp. 1 ff.; IX, pp. 8 ff.; cf. Buber, *The Hasidic Masters;* Herberg, *Faith Enacted in History*).

If a corporately remembered experience is to become personally appropriated, it must be or become congruent with one's own concrete experience—with what one is feeling (Rogers, *OBP*). The integration of the tradition into one's own feeling process most powerfully occurs in worship. This is what corporate celebration is about. Christian teaching does not simply reflect on corporate memory as an abstract or distant datum, but, rather, seeks to integrate social memory congruently within one's own feelings (Basil, *On the Spirit* XXVIII, *NPNF* 2 VIII, p. 44).

Hence, experience is to the individual as tradition is to the historical church. Both are enlivened by the Spirit. Experience seeks to
enable the personal appropriation of God's mercy in actual, interpersonal relationships. Faith becomes personal trust appropriated in a
disciplined and responsive way of life, sharing the love and mercy of
God with whomever possible (Clement of Alex., *Strom.* II.2, *ANF* II,
pp. 348–49).

The most convincing source of truth is that which corresponds
with the rest of one's experience, and which validates the meaningfulness of one's personal history. Any truth that is arrived at by circum-
venting personal experience is likely to remain somewhat implausible
to the individual, no matter how important it may be to others. This
is as true of psychological or moral truths as it is of the truth of
revelation made known in history. A truth that has not become a *truth
for me* (Kierkegaard, *Concl. Unsci. Post.*) is not likely to bear weight in
sustaining other conclusions in the study of God. The experiential side
of theology is working well, however, when our daily life provides
experiential evidences of the reliability of faith's witness to revelation.
This does not imply, however, that personal experience may unilaterally judge and dismiss Scripture and tradition. Scripture and tradition
are received, understood, and validated through personal experience,
but not judged or arbitrated or censored by it. Rather Scripture and
tradition amid the living, worshiping community are the means by
which and context in which one's personal experiences are evaluated
as "of God's family" (1 John 4:4; cf. 1 Cor. 4:3, 4; James 3:1; Tertullian,
Prescript. Ag. Her. XXXIII, *ANF* III, pp. 258, 259).

Reason: The Word Made Intelligible

The fourth wall of the quadrilateral fortress, reason, requires critical analysis of all that has been asserted in order to avoid self-contra-
diction, to take appropriate account of scientific and historical
knowledge, to credit appropriately new information and empirical
data, and to try to see the truth as a whole and not as disparate parts
or incongruently separable insights (Ambrose, *Duties* I.24–28, *NPNF*
2 X, pp. 18–23). The study of God is a cohesive, rational task of
thinking out of revelation, yet in thinking it does not cease being
active faith. One need not disavow the gifts of intellect in giving
thought to their Giver (John Cassian, *Conferences*, First and Second
Conferences of Abbot Moses, *NPNF* 2 XI, pp. 295–318).

Right use of reason in Catholic, Orthodox, and Protestant traditions resists the overextension of the claim of reason, that it could be

omnicompetent or the final source or judge of all truth. The Christian tradition does not characteristically view reason as autonomous, as if completely separable from other relational, historical, and social modes of knowing the truth. Reason, rather, seeks to provide for these insights some appropriate tests of cogency and internal consistency (Theophilus, *To Autolycus* I.3–II.4, *ANF* II, pp. 89–95; cf. Athenagoras, *Plea for Christians* XII–XVIII, XXXII, *ANF* II, pp. 134–37, 148).

The Christian study of God is, as Anselm taught, a faith that is seeking to understand itself (*fides quaerens intellectum*), a faith that is in search of its own intrinsic intelligibility, yet that respects mystery and knows of its own limits. Christian teaching lives out of a community of faith that does not hesitate to ask serious questions about itself (Anselm, *Proslog.* I, *BW*, p. 1). The study of God is precisely that dimension of faith which is willing to ask searching, penetrating questions about itself. In this sense our conversation with and about God presupposes a community that is already living out of that faith, searching for a proper understanding of itself (Bonaventure, *Breviloquium*, prologue I, p. 7).

The study of God proceeds with the limited tools of human language, socially shaped intellect, and moral awareness. How can such limitations pretend to penetrate the mystery of the infinite One? We are finite beings. We see everything from a highly constricted range of vision—our own. The knowledge we have of God is always a knowledge subject to potential distortions of our own self-assertiveness and sin—distortions of our own thinking, evasions, and constricted vision. We have limited competency to see even ourselves honestly, much less the whole of history. Nevertheless, the study of God proceeds with the sufficient resources of Scripture enlivened by the power of the Spirit, with candid admission of the recalcitrant egocentricity of the student (Clement of Alex., *Strom.* II.10–19, *ANF* II, pp. 358–68). The study of God continues to make the modest effort to reason from and about faith.

Christian teaching is not a knowledge that is magically induced or piped into consciousness through a heavenly channel. Human intelligence must work to attain it. The study of God requires intellectual effort, historical imagination, empathic energy, and participation in a vital community of prayer (Augustine, *Answer to Skeptics*, *FC* 1, pp. 103 ff.).

Catholic teaching stresses two fonts of revelation: First is the canonical books of both Testaments, received by the church as sacred writing (Council of Rome, *SCD* 84), as depositum of faith, inspired by

God the Spirit (Leo XIII, *Providentissimus Deus, SCD* 1951 f.), to be guarded and handed down by the church and interpreted in the light of the consensus of the ancient ecumenical teachers (Council of Trent, session IV, *SCD* 786) and the sense of the church, according to sound principles (Pius X, *Lamentabili, SCD* 2001 ff.). Second is ecclesiastical tradition, that is, the leading ancient exegetes of Scripture that have repeatedly been received by the church as providing the sense of Scripture on questions of faith and morals (Council of Nicaea II, action VII, *SCD* 302, 303; Council of Trent, session IV, *SCD* 783). Reason explains, guards, and defends revealed truth (Pius IX, *Qui pluribus, SCD* 1635), and faith should not be thought of as contrary to right reason (Pius IX, *Syllabus of Errors, SCD* 1706). Although faith is not merely subjective or private inspiration, yet there is required a reception of revelation in personal experience (Gregory XVI, *Faith and Reason, SCD* 1622 ff.; Pius IX, *Qui pluribus, SCD* 1634 ff.).

These four sources—Scripture, tradition, experience, and reason—must be always held in creative tension. All are responsive to the revealed word. When the word becomes written, we appropriate it amid changing cultural experiences, reflect upon it by reason, and personally rediscover it in our own experience. The study of God best proceeds with the fitting equilibrium of these four sources, one primary and three secondary. The best minds of the historical Christian tradition, such as Athanasius, Augustine, Anselm, Catherine of Siena, and Calvin, all utilized this quadrilateral of sources in a functional, interdependent equilibrium. The overstress on any one of the four ends in imbalance, like that of a chair with uneven legs. To study God with only one source is as precarious as the balancing act of a pole-sitter.

This approach to the study of God assumes that one will add one's own creativity and imagination to the interpretive process, within the bounds of the checks and balances of the four criteria. The study of God encourages individual expression, since divine mercy is individually addressed. Scripture aims for each reader to appropriate it individually (Kierkegaard, *Edifying Discourses*) yet always within the context of a community of celebration (*Divine Liturgy of James, ANF* VII, pp. 537–50).

Distinguishing the Sources of Theology

Two distinctions (between objective/subjective and authoritative/supplementary) will assist in sorting out the competing claims made concerning various sources of theology.

Since faith is an inward act, and since reasoning about faith occurs within the sphere of the subject self, we may distinguish *objective* sources of understanding or data for theology (Scripture and tradition) from the *subjective* faculties by which these data are appropriated, interpreted, and cohesively understood—especially two faculties, experienced faith and reason.

Scripture and written tradition may be seen in texts, and read in books, with a palpable sense that they are not merely internalized authorities. Not so with faith and reason, whose realm is the inward and hidden sphere of the subject-self. Faith and reason are major subjective means, processes, and sources by which the objective texts of Scripture and tradition are appropriated and reflected upon for cohesion and consistent meaning.

The objective/subjective equilibrium of a well-grounded theological method may be lost by undue stress upon either objectivity or subjectivity. Each needs the other to complete itself. The periods of rationalism, empiricism, skepticism, and pietism have been prone too readily to discredit the objective data of revelation. Some forms of orthodoxy and Scholasticism have been prone to undervalue or discredit the subjective reception of revelation by experiential faith and/or reason.

In speaking of "sources for theology" we imply a range broader than the specific idea of two fonts of revelation (canonical Scripture and ecclesiastical tradition; Council of Trent, *SCD* 783). We mean more generally those varied channels, means, or conveyances by which the divine address comes to humanity and an understanding of God is thus possible. As we have seen, these sources include creation, providence, reason, conscience, beauty, and personal experience, as well as Scripture and tradition. Broadly speaking, the sources of theology include any means (whether natural, rational, moral, textual, liturgical, spiritual, or divinely revealed) by which the divine goodness is conveyed to humanity. These sources are too simply distinguished when the terms *reason* and *revelation* are used to summarize them.

A clearer distinction between these sources, however, is that between authoritative and supplementary sources. The study of God in the Christian community proceeds out of (1) authoritative sources, such as Scripture, ecumenical councils, and consensus-bearing early ecumenical theologians, as distinguished from (2) unauthoritative or supplementary sources, which include nonconsensual theologians, scientific and moral inquiries, historical-critical studies, individual experience, speculation, meditation, philosophy, and psychology. To say these are unauthoritative does not imply that they are not useful, only that they do not carry the force of consensually legitimated authority for Christian thinking about God. Inputs or insights may be utilized from any or all of these quarters, but they do not present themselves to theology as authoritative for faith. Rather, they are to be used as needed (Clement of Alex., *Exhort. to the Heathen* V–VII, *ANF* II, pp. 190–93).

Scripture records the events of divine disclosure that form the basis of authoritative church teaching. Since Scriptures provide a divinely inspired record of the unfolding historical development of divine revelation, it is not necessary for the individual Christian to proceed as though revelation had to be found for the first time. Many experiences of previous Christian communities are awaiting assimilation by the contemporary believing community. Contemporary believers start, not at the beginning of history, but amid it, and not without a community, but with a community of prayer that has stored a mass of data about the lively experiences of an actual risk-taking historical community (*Apost. Const., Eccl. Canons, ANF* VII, pp. 500, 501). Only the wildest individualism would imagine that every believer must begin from nothing, as if no others had ever had any experience of God.

The authority of Scripture will be dealt with in more detail in a later volume, but at this point we must put that authority in the context of other claims to authority. The ends for which Scriptures are intended are many. Some portions of Scripture are more pertinent to particular articles of faith than are other portions. That does not imply that the others are only partly inspired or less valid, but that the Spirit meets us in Scripture, quite flexibly, in different ways. This is why it remains unwise to collect bits and pieces of Scripture for self-standing proof-texts without seeking also in Scripture the whole counsel of God, viewing each particular passage in relation to the whole of Scripture.

As no one ancient Christian teacher should be regarded as singularly adequate to represent all aspects of the church's mature wisdom, so also should no major theologian be altogether ignored. The message of the church seems to be expressed with greater fullness, health, and clarity in some centuries than in others. Some important witnesses may have to await "their century" for a hearing. Classic writers have one distinct advantage over modern sources: they have been thoroughly tested, questioned, interpreted, probed, analyzed, reinterpreted, preached, taught, and utilized in different historical situations. Modern interpretation does well to build upon that extensive examination.

Theology builds progressively upon previous generations of the study of God, using both the old and the new (Matt. 13:52). New or lately rediscovered insights into Scripture and tradition keep coming to the attention of the church at unexpected times. Each age has the possibility of contributing something to the storehouse for subsequent ages that will study God, yet that fact does not imply that the received faith itself is being substantively changed from generation to generation (Simplicius, *The Unchangeableness of Chr. Doctrine*, SCD 160).

Whether Church Tradition Is an Authoritative Source for the Study of God

The Rule of Faith

The task of Christian teaching is to clarify, illuminate, cohesively interpret, and defend the convictions distinctive to Christianity that empower and enable the Christian life. Perennially, it seeks to distinguish that which is essential, vital, and lasting as divine address in Christian faith from that which is accidental, culturally determined, human knowledge (Mark 7:4–9; Col. 2:8).

The rule of faith (*regula fidei*) is that which governs or determines what is to be believed for salvation. It is not necessary to decide between Scripture and what the church historically teaches in order to define the rule of faith. For what the church, at its best, teaches is precisely what the Scriptures teach. The Bible contains all that is necessary to be believed, and the church is commissioned to teach nothing less than that faith revealed in Scripture (Second Helvetic Conf., CC, pp. 132 ff.; cf. Tavard, *Holy Writ and Holy Church*). It is never fitting or possible for the church to dispense with the study of Scripture. The creeds of the church are derived wholly from Scripture and have no authority if they are not expressive of apostolic teaching (Luther, *Brief Explanation*, WML II).

An article of faith has three conditions: it must be based upon revelation, stated in Scripture, and ecclesiastically defined with ecumenical consent (Gallican Conf., COC III, pp. 357 ff.; cf. Vincent of Lerins, *Comm.* II, XX–XXIV, LCC, VII, pp. 37–39, 65–74; F. Hall, DTh, I). Teachings that lack any of these conditions are matters of opinion left open for continued debate and speculation.

The room for private opinion among Christians is vast, provided those opinions are not repugnant to articles of faith.

Nothing is required of any believer other than that which is revealed by God himself through Scripture as necessary to salvation, as propounded consensually by the Christian community as an article of faith reliably received by common ecumenical consent.

The Teaching Office

The teaching office given to the church requires transmission of the history of the events of God's self-disclosure to subsequent generations without distortion, and in its original vitality and integrity. This effort at transmission in all its oral and written forms is called *tradition*.

It is difficult to distinguish between Scripture and tradition since Scripture itself is a product of oral tradition, taken, like a still photo of a moving picture, and frozen at one crucial point, so that the heretofore oral witness could be transmitted to subsequent generations. The unwritten oral tradition was a preached word, a teaching of the living church prior to the writing down of New Testament Scripture. As such it is surely not less valid than the written word, although it remains less accessible to us precisely because it is not written down.

Paul in one of the earliest letters of the New Testament wrote: "Stand firm, then brothers, and hold fast to the traditions which you have learned from us by word or by letter" (2 Thess. 2:15). This assumes that in the earliest church there were two sources for the maintenance of the apostolic teaching: oral and written tradition. The revelation of God is therefore being preserved by the Spirit in the church through both oral and written tradition.

The oral tradition is more ancient, for until Mark, Paul, John, and others began to write their Gospels and letters, there existed much lively preaching and oral tradition, but as yet only minimal written tradition. The written tradition emerged only when the oral tradition was in danger of losing some of its immediacy and authority through the impending deaths of the eyewitnesses. The written tradition made the revelation more exact and transmissible to subsequent generations through a continuous succession of ministries of preaching and teaching.

There are strong injunctions in the New Testament itself to carefully transmit the apostolic teaching. Jesus taught the disciples that the Spirit would be given to "guide you into all the truth" (John 16:13). Paul faithfully passed on the tradition he had received, which he regarded as unalterable data: "I handed on to you the facts which had been imparted to me; that Christ died for our sins, in accordance with the scriptures" (1 Cor. 15:3). Paul regarded those in public ministry "as stewards of the secrets of God" who are "expected to show themselves trustworthy" in passing along the tradition (1 Cor. 4:1, 2).

Timothy was implored to "keep safe that which has been entrusted to you. Turn a deaf ear to empty and worldly chatter, and the contradictions of the so-called 'knowledge,' for many who lay claim to it have shot far wide of the faith" (1 Tim. 6:20, 21). Along with objective accuracy, there remains a personal element in the transmission of tradition: "Stand by the truths you have learned and are assured of. Remember from whom you learned them; remember that from early childhood you have been familiar with the sacred writings which have power to make you wise and lead you to salvation through faith in Christ Jesus" (2 Tim. 3:14, 15; Gal. 1:8, 9; cf. Clement of Alex., *Exhort. to the Heathen* IX, *ANF* II, pp. 196, 197; *Strom.* II.11, 12, *ANF* II, pp. 358–60).

Humanly devised traditions that deceptively claimed to be divine revelation (among New Testament examples are detailed food or Sabbath prohibitions) were resisted and not confused with the divinely revealed tradition received from the apostles. "Do not let your minds be captured by hollow and delusive speculations, based on traditions of man-made teaching and centered on the elemental spirits of the universe and not on Christ" (Col. 2:8; cf. 1 Tim. 1:4). The gospel means "freedom from the empty folly of your traditional ways" (1 Pet. 1:18), in the sense of man-made traditions that spuriously claim divine origin. Jesus rebuked the Pharisees because they neglected the commandment of God "in order to maintain the tradition of men" (Mark 7:8; cf. Tertullian, *On the Soul* I, II, *ANF* III, pp. 181–83; *On Prescript. Ag. Her.* VII, *ANF* III, p. 246). But the godly tradition concerning the memory of Jesus Christ must be maintained accurately and faithfully, since it is the living memory of God's own coming.

Patristic writers stressed the importance of maintaining accurately the tradition of teaching concerning Jesus. The Didache enjoined readers to keep what had been received without adding or subtraction (IV, *LCC* I, p. 173). Irenaeus (*Ag. Her.* III.4.3, *ANF* I, p. 417) and Tertullian (*On Prescript. Ag. Her.* 29–35, *ANF* III, pp. 256–60) thought that all heresies would be largely recognizable by their interest in making innovations upon the received tradition, mixing it up with more recent ideas unlike the original apostolic tradition. Clement of Alexandria argued that tradition was prior to heresy (*Strom.* VII.17, *ANF* II, pp. 554, 555). Origen accepted as Christian teaching only that which had been taught by the apostles and mediated through accurate memory of tradition (*De Princip.*, preface, *ANF* IV, pp. 239–41). Cyprian called Christ the fount of tradition (*Epis.* LXXIII, LXXIV, *ANF* V, pp. 386–97). Antiquity of teaching, meaning the ancient teaching of the apostles, was one of the criteria of the Vincentian rule of faith (Lerins, *Comm.* II, III, *LCC* IX, pp. 37–39). "The Holy Spirit was not promised to the successors of Peter, that by His revelation they might make known new doctrine, but that by His assistance they might inviolably keep and faithfully expound the revelation or deposit of faith delivered through the apostles" (Vatican Council I, Constitution I.4).

In the broader sense, the Scriptures themselves are sacred tradition. By searching the Scriptures any believer can compare later proposals for Christian understanding with the apostolic witness. The concept of tradition has been used in a more specific sense, however, to refer to the oral and written transmission of the faith from one generation to another, both before and after the writing of Scripture. An early example of the importance of oral tradition is found in a letter from Irenaeus to Florinus (in Eusebius, *CH* V.20, *NPNF* 2 I, pp. 238 f.) in which Irenaeus remembered clearly that he had conversed personally with Polycarp, who himself had talked with the apostle John of Jesus' miracles and teachings. Through only two intermediaries, Irenaeus understood himself to be accurately and faithfully in touch with the original events of Christian revelation.

During the time in which Rome was the capital of the Roman world, it is not surprising that when local traditions were compared with one another and found to be somewhat different, localities would appeal to the Roman church to help them identify the truest form of the tradition. After all, people from all over the known world were meeting in Rome. Where better would there be a place to establish consensually the most authentic and best forms of traditioned memory? Thus Roman traditions came to have a widely respected value, though not to the exclusion of those of other metropolitan areas and sees. In time the bishop of Rome came to have a widely acknowledged role as primary guardian of the apostolic tradition (Irenaeus, *Ag. Her.* III.3, *ANF* I, pp. 415, 416; Tertullian, *On Prescript. Ag. Her.* 21, 32–36, *ANF* III, pp. 252, 258–61). More important than that Rome was chosen (for that was a practical decision relating to the accessibility to consensual views) was the fact that the churches spread across the Roman Empire felt the need both to maintain tradition accurately and to seek to find those traditions that most accurately presented the apostolic tradition. Even the heretics appealed to the apostolic tradition for their support, only to find their views in due time rejected by the church itself on behalf of the apostolic tradition.

The practical position of Rome as capital of the empire made it the logical center for Christian thinking. This factor changed in the early

fourth century when the capital was moved to Constantinople. During
the Byzantine era, a long struggle continued between Rome and Constantinople over primacy, eventually bringing about the division into
Eastern and Western Christianity. The causes of the final split were
less doctrinal, however, than political.

No single classical Christian writer is rightly claimed to carry the
consent of the whole church in all things. Rather, the authority of any
writer gains weight only to the degree that he or she accurately represented the mind of the whole church. However great Augustine may
have been, his views of predestination were never widely received and
often modified, so those particular views can hardly be regarded as
having received the consent necessary for being viewed as ancient
ecumenical consensual tradition. Vincent of Lerins argued that even
the church's greatest theologians may err, but these errors are in time
corrected by the lack of consent (*Comm.* 10–11, 17 ff., 28, *LCC* IX, pp.
49–52, 60 ff., 79–82).

The strongest and surest medium of tradition is probably not teaching at all but liturgy and church practice. The practices of baptism,
Eucharist, Lord's Day services, and many elements of the Christian
year are powerful safeguards for the retention of the teachings of the
apostles (cf. *Early Liturgies, ANF* VII, pp. 537 ff.). Even when preachers
are heretics, as long as they celebrate Holy Communion in due order,
the liturgy is not invalidated, and the rite itself performs the ironic
task of contradicting what has been badly taught (Augustine, *The
Letters of Petilian, the Donatist* 45 ff., 82ff., *NPNF* 1 IV, pp. 540 ff., 551
ff.).

By this means it is made clear that the Holy Spirit again and again
turns human pride and distortion to the praise of God. The church
has been guided by God's Spirit through many historical crises. New
languages, concepts, and symbol systems have arisen repeatedly in
the history of Christian teaching. For a time a disproportionate emphasis may have been given to one or another concept, but eventually
all these concepts must stand the test of time and either be confirmed
or rejected by the living ecumenical church under the guidance of the
Spirit. The result is that by Scripture, creeds, institutions, liturgy, and
Christian teaching the Spirit continues to illuminate the mind of the
church and to make the apostolic teaching recognizable. By the Spirit's
guidance certain teachings, such as those of slavery and the place of
women in the church, have been to some degree corrected, or are
being corrected, through a process of historical ecumenical consent
(Wesley, *WJW* XI, pp. 59–79, XII, p. 507; Phoebe Palmer, *The Promise
of the Father*; Elizabeth Schlüssler-Fiorenza, *In Memory of Her*).

Critical historical inquiry into Scripture and tradition is not anti-thetical to faith. Sound, probing criticism is constantly needed in order to discern the meaning of Scripture's address. The Holy Spirit uses this too, to burn away the dross, to blow away the chaff. We are called by the Spirit to test all things without losing sight of inspiration: "Do not stifle inspiration, and do not despise prophetic utterance, but bring them all to the test and then keep what is good in them and avoid the bad of whatever kind" (1 Thess. 5:21; cf. Dionysius of Alex., *Extant Fragments, Epistle VII, To Philemon,* ANF VI, pp. 102, 103).

The Councils

It is in the light of this long-term sifting and discerning process that the general councils of the church must be seen and understood. The *episkopoi* can speak officially for the church, yet they are not independent of the church or church consent or apostolic tradition. Their views will not be received if they are not rooted in the ancient faith or if they are contrary to the mind of the historic church as a whole. The general councils of the church are providential, extraordi-nary expedients, not of the dominical appointment, but under the guidance of the Spirit, that seek to define questions under dispute in the light of scriptural teaching (cf. *Seven Ecumenical Councils,* NPNF 2 XIV, passim). General councils are not infallible in themselves, but the Spirit that guides the church is fully trustable. Sometimes the general councils have failed to gain consent, as in the case of the Arian Council of Ariminum (A.D. 359) or the Council of Ephesus (449) that tempo-rarily approved the Eutychian heresy, only later to be rejected by the church consensus (at Chalcedon, 451). That consent is what lets the councils know the mind of the church, and thus whether the council's decision was Spirit-led. A council's decrees must be ratified or con-firmed by ecumenical consent if they are to be regarded as established. When that consent over a long period of time is given, the council becomes received as an ecumenical council and is viewed by the whole church as rightly defining the church's teaching (Second Council of Nicaea, canon I, *NPNF* 2 XIV, p. 555). Conciliar decisions may remain unsettled for a very long time. Even while some questions are under suspended judgment, the church lives by Scripture, by its formularies and sacramental life, and by preaching.

Seven councils of the historic church are recognized as ecumenical councils, having the consent of the whole church: Nicaea, A.D. 325, defining the triune God in a way that rejected Arian claims; Constan-tinople, A.D. 381, affirming Jesus' humanity against Appollinarianism and the Spirit's divinity against Macedonianism; Ephesus, A.D. 431, affirming the unity of Christ's Person, and Mary as *theotokos*, against the Nestorians; Chalcedon, A.D. 451, affirming the two natures of Christ against Eutychianism; the Second Council of Constantinople, A.D. 553, against Nestorianism; the Third Council of Constantinople (680–681) against Monothelitism; and the Second Council of Nicaea (787) against Iconoclasm (Second Council of Nicaea, *NPNF* 2 XIV, pp. 555, 556; cf. Gregory the Great, *Pastoral Care, ACW* II; *Epis.* IX.105, X.13, *NPNF* 2 XIII, pp. 23, 53).

The Living Tradition

The events of the history of Israel and Jesus Christ are viewed by the church as the revelation of the will of God. This revelation is made palpable and concrete by the giving of a sacred deposit, Holy Writ, to be kept intact, neither added to nor taken away from. Paul repeatedly stressed: "If anyone, if we ourselves or an angel from heaven, should preach a gospel at variance with the gospel we preached to you, he shall be held outcast" (Gal. 1:8, 9). Jude thought it had become "urgently necessary to write at once and appeal to you to join the struggle in defence of the faith, the faith which God entrusted to his people once and for all. It is in danger from certain persons who have wormed their way in" (Jude 3, 4). From these passages it is evident that the effort at consensual definition and defense of the heart of faith began very early in Christian experience and did not await the second or third century.

This tradition was to be handed down from generation to generation. "Guard the treasure put into our charge, with the help of the Holy Spirit dwelling within us" (2 Tim. 1:14). "You heard my teaching in the presence of many witnesses; put that teaching into the charge of men you can trust, such men as will be competent to teach others" (2 Tim. 2:2). At this time there were no systematic theologies, but only highly valued texts circulating from congregation to congregation, from city to city, containing accounts of the life of Jesus, a short outline of the beginning of church history immediately after the crucifixion, and a series of letters and visions written by or on behalf of primary apostolic eyewitnesses (Tertullian, *On Prescript. Ag. Her.* XXXVI–XLIV, *ANF* III, pp. 260–65).

Once the Scriptures were canonized, the church has continued to live out of them, but the church also lives out of the Holy Spirit who called forth the Scriptures. Among the most fundamental consensual decisions of the church, however, is the affirmation that the Spirit will not lead the church in any direction that is contrary to the delivered written word (Pius IV, *SCD* 930; J. Meyendorff, *Living Tradition*). If such an erroneous leading is felt, it does not come from God's own Spirit. Furthermore, the church has decided that if one expounds one Scripture in such a way that it is repugnant to another Scripture, such interpretation is not of the Spirit's leading (Thirty-nine Articles XX, CC, p. 273). Scriptural arguments for theological conclusions must be arrived at by a fair and careful comparison of all relevant texts of Scripture. In this way the Bible is received as containing everything that one is required to believe as an article of faith. The church keeps the book, learns from the book, and seeks to assess varied interpretations of the book in terms of the totality of the book itself.

Whether the Study of God Is a Science

The Scientific Character of Christian Inquiry

A science is a branch of study concerned with the observation and classification of facts (especially with the establishment of verifiable general laws) chiefly through induction and hypothesis. A procedure such as science, so widely regarded as useful, can hardly be completely inapplicable (even if inadequate) to Christian inquiry.

Insofar as it seeks to make accurate observations, test evidence, provide fit hypotheses, arrange facts in due order, and make reliable generalizations, the study of God may be called a science. It employs both inductive and deductive argument. It relies upon the same primary laws of thought and the same categories of reason upon which all scientific inquiry depends.

The methods of inquiry into Christianity are held by many classical Christian writers to be a "science," according to the classical definition of *scientia* as an orderly knowing or knowledge, or a *disciplina*, as instruction or teaching or body of knowledge (Bonaventure, *Breviloquium*, prologue, pp. 6–23; cf. Tho. Aq., *Compend.* 2, 22, 35, 36, 42, pp. 5, 24, 33–35, 37). But the facts into which Christian teaching inquires are brought from an arena of data that is thought by some to be blocked out from scientific investigation: religious consciousness, moral awareness, the life of the spirit, and the history of revelation (Hume, *Dialogues*; Kant, *Critique of Pure Reason*).

No scientific inquiry proceeds without axioms and postulates that do not admit of empirical demonstration. Geometric inquiry, for instance, depends upon the postulate of parallels, but that postulate is far from being finally demonstrable. The view that scientific inquiry is independent of all authority is itself quite distorted. Theology is that sort of science that proceeds with a specific postulate: historical revelation.

Theology has a definite object to investigate, namely, the understanding of God as known in the Christian community. There is no doubt that such an understanding exists, and that it is capable of being inquired into. It is a historical fact that the modern university since the thirteenth century has been spawned in large part by the inductive and deductive methods developed by Jewish, Muslim, and Christian inquiry concerning God. There is no reason one cannot take as a subject of scientific investigation the modes of awareness of God that recur in Christian communities: the belief in God, that God exists, that God is triune, and that God pardons sin (cf. Schleiermacher, *The Chr. Faith*; Aulen, *The Faith of the Chr. Church*).

No botanist claims to provide the basic order by which plant life lives. Rather, the botanist ascertains an order that is already present in the nature of the facts themselves. Similarly the theologian is not the master of the facts, but their servant. The theologian cannot construct a system of Christian teaching to suit his or her fancy, any more than the geologist can rearrange the strata of rocks according to aesthetic whim or personal desire. Christian theology simply wishes to set forth that understanding of God that is known in the Christian community in a way that is fitting to its own proper order, harmonizing that wide body of facts and data so as to preserve their intrinsic relation to one another (Rufinus, *On the Creed*, NPNF 2 III, pp. 541–63; Nicolas of Cusa, *Concerning Wisdom*, U&R, pp. 101–27).

The Presentation of Evidence in the Study of God

Science is characterized by a method and a spirit. Its method is an orderly presentation of facts, showing their causes and their relationship to general truths or laws. The spirit of scientific inquiry is open-minded and unprejudiced; it does not omit relevant facts and is receptive to new evidence. This is the fundamental attitude or spirit that provides common ground for all the various sciences. Within this common spirit there are wide differences between the methods used in various sciences. For example, insofar as psychology is a science, it gathers empirical evidence on the basis of controlled studies, but psychology has found it difficult to rule out intuitive insight and holistic reasoning. Insofar as history is a science, it bases its conclusions on historical evidence and documentary witnesses, and has the same problems with establishing textual authenticity that theology does.

The forms of evidence differ for physical, historical, and spiritual truth (1 Cor. 2:10–16; Clement of Alex., *Strom*. I.6–20, *ANF* II, pp. 307–24). Truth in the physical realm must be established by empirical data gathering and experiment, and truth in the historical realm by testimony, documentation, and correlation of evidence. Truth in the spiritual realm must be tested in a more complex way, by examination of oneself, of history, of conscience, of one's sense of rational cohesion, and of claims of divine self-disclosure. Each sphere of inquiry must submit evidence appropriate to its subject. Psychological and humanistic inquiries have tried at times to employ the same evidentiary process appropriate for physics or mathematics. In doing so, one kind of evidence (empirical) has been applied to or transposed into a sphere that transcends it or that exceeds empirical competence (cf. Irenaeus, *Ag. Her.* IV.31–33, *ANF* I, pp. 504–11).

The forms of evidence that are presented in Christian teaching are highly diverse. They include scientific inquiry and demonstration, but they also include the kinds of evidence found in legal science, namely, the presentation of cases, circumstantial evidence, and testimony of eyewitnesses (2 Cor. 13:1; Acts 22:18). As legal inquiry proceeds from texts, testimony, and precedents, so the study of God deals with consensual precedents, with texts and testimonies of eyewitnesses to God's self-disclosure, and with consensual precedents that interpret these events (Luke 1:2; 2 Pet. 1:16). Christian teaching characteristically appeals to many different levels of evidence—historical testimony, moral awareness, life experience, the social history of a people, and the history of revelation—in order to establish a convergence of plausibility along different and complementary lines (1 Thess. 1:10; Titus 1:13; 1 John 5:9; 3 John 12).

As logical reasoning begins from concepts and ideas and proceeds to conclusions, so does much theological reasoning proceed from idea to idea inquiring into how those ideas are related logically. Well-developed and rightly presented evidence tends to elicit in the mind a sense of conviction of truth that resembles what Christianity calls belief or faith. Judgment moves with evidence (John 5:31–36; 1 Tim. 2:6).

Even though Christian teaching had been called a science for over a millennium before modern science preempted the term—claiming that it excludes nonempirical evidence—and even though Christian teaching has been responsible for nurturing many of the deepest values of modern science, there remains one principal reason why it is probably better not to call Christian teaching a "science": Today an unacceptable odor accompanies this term, especially as it is used by some who are seeking prematurely (and desperately) to preserve theology by forcing a cheap accommodation with empiricist science and reductive naturalism. Christian teaching can do without the name science, especially since science means to so many the ruling out of all forms of evidence that do not submit to naturalistic observation, quantification, and measurement. This sort of science is a restriction of the freedom to learn. To this diminution of science the Christian inquirer can say with Paul: "A man who is unspiritual refuses what belongs to the Spirit of God; it is folly to him; he cannot grasp it, because it needs to be judged in the light of Spirit" (1 Cor. 2:14). The Christian faith is finally built "not upon human wisdom but upon the power of God" (1 Cor. 2:4; Ambrose, *Of the Holy Spirit* II.11, 12, *NPNF* 2 X, pp. 129–33; John of Damascus, *OF* IV.9, *NPNF* 2 IX, pp. 79–81).

The reason we demand higher certainty for religious assertions than historical assertions is a telling one: They are more important. They have more behavioral consequences if we accept them. When the same level of evidence exists for Caesar and Christ, the testimony concerning Caesar remains largely uncontested, whereas that of Christ is hotly contested. The reason is that inquirers know all too well that they have a stake in the result of the inquiry. It makes little difference to us now what Caesar said or did, but much difference whether God has come and spoken.

At first it may seem to be a decided disadvantage to Christian teaching that it cannot establish its facts with the same objective or controlled certainty that physics and chemistry usually can. But there may be a hidden advantage to this seeming limitation. For if religious truth were capable of absolute objective certainty, then faith would become as compulsory for acceptance as the mathematical conclusion that two plus two equals four, or the scientific conclusion that water is constituted by hydrogen and oxygen. If religious conclusions had this compulsory character (because of the absolutely overwhelming character of objective evidence) then would there not be less place for the risk of faith? God would no longer be the incomprehensible, majestic One worthy of our worship and obedience, but merely a rationalized object of empirical data. No longer would "the just live by faith" (Hab. 2:4; Rom. 1:17; Heb. 10:38), with all the character building this involves. Christian faith would cease to be a choice altogether; God would no longer have sons and daughters who voluntarily and with risk choose to love and serve him (Kierkegaard, *Either/Or* II; *Fear and Trembling; Concl. Unsci. Post.* pp. 198 ff., 226 ff.).

Whether the Study of God Requires a Special Temperament

Temperament in the Study of God

Just as a wise judge requires a judicial temperament, or a teacher a pedagogical temperament, so does a good theologian require something called "theological temperament." The classic Christian pastors referred frequently to certain tempers, dispositions, or habits of mind that tend to engender responsible study of God. However much modern skepticism may disparage these qualities, they remain important ideals, if not imperatives. Among these qualities are:

HUMILITY IN THE FACE OF TRUTH

The lowered level of egocentricity and the humbled self-awareness that accompany sound Christian teaching arise out of a realistic consciousness of one's actual ignorance, the limitations of one's knowledge, one's tendency to be deceived and one's egoistic interpretation of the facts (Clement of Rome to the Corinthians, I.13, ANF I, p. 8; Gregory Nazianzen, First Theol. Or., NPNF 2 VII, pp. 285–88). It is to the humble that God teaches "his ways" (Ps. 25:9). "For the Lord, high as he is, cares for the lowly, and from afar he humbles the proud" (Ps. 138:6). "Do you see that man who thinks himself so wise? There is more hope for a fool than for him" (Prov. 26:12). "Thus Scripture says, 'God opposes the arrogant and gives grace to the humble' " (James 4:6). Jesus said: "Let a man humble himself till he is like this child, and he will be the greatest in the kingdom of Heaven" (Matt. 18:4, Rufinus, On the Creed I, NPNF 2 III, p. 542; Sulpitius Severus, Life of St. Martin, preface, NPNF 2 XI, p. 3).

REVERENCE

That sense of awe in the presence of God is viewed as "the beginning of wisdom" (Simeon, Hymns of Divine Love 20, pp. 89–94; Maximus the Confessor, Four Centuries on Charity IV.1, 2, ACW 21, p. 192). Those who live out of this reverence are far more likely to "grow in understanding" (Ps. 111:10; Cyprian, treatise XII.20, ANF V, pp. 539, 540). "The fear of the Lord is the beginning of knowledge, but fools scorn wisdom and discipline" (Prov. 1:7). When Moses beheld that the bush was on fire but not being burned up, and he asked why, Yahweh answered: "Come no nearer; take off your sandals; the place where you are standing is holy ground" (Exod. 3:5). Not everyone stands ready to come into God's presence: "Who may go up to the mountain of the Lord? And who may stand in his holy place? He who has clean hands and a pure heart, who has not set his mind on falsehood, and has not committed perjury. He shall receive a blessing from the Lord" (Ps. 24:3–5). Undertaken apart from the company of God's own Spirit, the study of God may either become a cold stone or a deadly poison (Kierkegaard, *Self-Examination;* cf. Strong, *Syst. Theol.* I, p. 40).

PATIENCE

Considered the habitual disposition to bear with trials and frustrations without complaint, to exercise forbearance under difficulties, to be undisturbed by obstacles, delays, and failures, and to persevere with diligence until an issue is further resolved or rightly grasped (Tertullian, *On Patience, ANF* III, pp. 707–17). Those who would think with haste about God are apt to pass God by. Only through patience does one "acquire one's soul" (cf. Luke 21:19; Kierkegaard, *Edifying Discourses* II.2, pp. 67 ff.; III.1, pp. 7 ff.). The study of God is best pursued by one for whom "the law of the Lord is his delight, the law his meditation night and day. He is like a tree planted beside a watercourse, which yields its fruit in season" (Ps. 1:2, 3).

PRAYER FOR DIVINE ILLUMINATION AND INSTRUCTION

A crucial premise of the study of God. It begins with an attitude of openness and receptivity to God, inviting God's presence and inspiration to enable one's thoughts to be, so far as possible, fitting to the divine reality (Origen, *Letter to Gregory* 3, *ANF* V, p. 296). It continues with the supplication: "Take the veil from my eyes, that I may see the marvels that spring from thy law. I am but a stranger here on earth, do not hide thy commandments from me" (Ps. 119:18, 19; cf. Origen, *Ag. Celsus* IV.50, *ANF* IV, p. 520). James urged petition for wisdom: "If any of you falls short in wisdom, he should ask God for it and it will be given him, for God is a generous giver who neither refuses nor reproaches anyone. But he must ask in faith, without a doubt in his mind" (James 1:5, 6). Paul interceded for the illumination of those who seek God, that God might "give you the spiritual powers of wisdom and vision, by which there comes the knowledge of him" (Eph. 1:17; Augustine, *On Chr. Doctrine* IV.30, *NPNF* 1 II, p. 597).

THE OBEDIENCE OF FAITH

If the study of God remains unaccompanied by "the obedience of faith" (Rom. 1:26), it is likely to become undisciplined self-expression.

No temperament is more important to responsible theology than obedience, or radical responsiveness *(hypakoē)*, to the divine address in Scripture and tradition. Obedience implies not merely hearing the truth, but acting upon it so as to embody it in one's life (Simeon, *Hymns of Divine Love* 45, p. 234; cf. T. Oden, *Radical Obedience*, pp. 9–11).

Jesus said: "What of the man who hears these words of mine and does not act upon them? He is like a man who was foolish enough to build his house on sand" (Matt. 7:26). "Why do you keep calling me 'Lord, Lord'—and never do what I tell you? Everyone who comes to me and hears what I say, and acts upon it—I will show you what he is like. He is like a man who, in building his house, dug deep and laid the foundations on rock" (Luke 6:46–48). "Happy are those who hear the word of God and keep it" (Luke 11:28). The writer of Hebrews noted: "For indeed we have heard the good news, as they did. But in them the message they heard did no good, because it met with no faith in those who heard it" (Heb. 4:2).

James employed a comic analogy of forgetfulness: "Only be sure that you act on the message and do not merely listen; for that would be to mislead yourselves. A man who listens to the message but never acts upon it is like one who looks in a mirror at the face nature gave him. He glances at himself and goes away, and at once forgets what he looked like" (James 1:22–24). Paul commended "the obedience that comes from faith" (Rom. 1:5, NIV), which through Christ's obedience leads to righteousness (Rom. 5:19; 6:16; cf. Heb. 5:8), which in turn calls for our active responsiveness that it may become complete (2 Cor. 10:6; cf. Clementina, *Recognitions* III.62–66, ANF VIII, pp. 249, 250; cf. Oden, *Radical Obedience*).

INTEGRITY

Classical pastoral writers viewed integrity of thought and speech as a mark of responsible Christian teaching (1 cor. 5:8; 2 Cor. 8:8). "In your teaching, you must show integrity and high principle, and use wholesome speech to which none can take exception" (Titus 2:7, 8). Jesus distinguished teaching out of one's egocentricity from teaching God's truth: "Anyone whose teaching is merely his own, aims at honour for himself. But if a man aims at the honour of him who sent him he is sincere, and there is nothing false in him" (John 7:17, 18; John Chrysostom, *Hom. on John* XLIX, NPNF 1 XIV, p. 171).

Aptness to teach was thought to include one's ability when serving in public ministry to confine oneself in public teaching strictly to the

exposition of the truth of Scripture and its implications, suppressing
to a large degree private opinion, supposed private revelations, subjective feelings, unnecessary matters of controversy, and matters upon
which one has no authority to speak (Quinisext Council, canon XIX,
NPNF 2 XIV, pp. 374, 375; cf. Baxter, PW V, pp. 428 ff.). Such a temper
was associated with the notion of theological integrity.

Another dimension of theological integrity is the determination to
study and teach integrally the whole Word of God in fitting balance,
without omission of central truths, after the pattern of Paul, who
wrote: "I have kept back nothing; I have disclosed to you the whole
purpose of God" (Acts 20:27). Christian teaching does not proceed
selectively but by attending to the whole counsel of God, without
private prejudice or idiosyncratic distortion (Tertullian, On Prescript.
Ag. Her. XXV, XXVI, ANF III, pp. 254, 255; Wesley, WJW VIII, pp. 283
ff., 317 ff.).

WILLINGNESS TO SUFFER FOR THE TRUTH

No Christian teacher or exponent is worth listening to who is not
willing to suffer if need be for the truth of what is taught (1 Pet.
4:13–5:9; cf. The Martyrdom of Polycarp, ANF I, pp. 37–44). The readiness to suffer for the sake of Christ is an intrinsic part of the whole
fabric of Christian living, and hence teaching, and thus not an optional
part of the equipping of the public teacher of Christianity (Phil. 3:10;
Cyprian, On the Lapsed, ANF V, pp. 437–47; cf. Kierkegaard, Attack on
"Christendom").

Paul stated the principle clearly to Timothy in his letter of instruction: "Take your share of hardship, like a good soldier of Christ Jesus.
A soldier on active service will not let himself be involved in civilian
affairs" (2 Tim. 2:3, 4). Paul's teaching was personally validated by
his willingness to be "exposed to hardship, even to the point of being
shut up like a common criminal; but the word of God is not shut up"
(2 Tim. 2:9). Those who teach faithfully of the one who was "nailed
to the cross" know that some hearers will find in the truth a "stum-
bling-block" and "folly" (1 Cor. 1:23; cf. Rom. 8:17, 18). Jesus did not
hesitate to make it clear that his disciples must be prepared to "be
handed over for punishment and execution; and men of all nations
will hate you for your allegiance to me" (Matt. 24:9; Irenaeus, Ag. Her.
IV.33.9, ANF I, p. 508).

The "right method for studying theology" was in Luther's view
concisely set forth in Psalm 119 in three rules: prayer, meditation, and
affliction (oratio, meditatio, tentatio). He wrote: "This is the touchstone;

this teaches you not merely to know and understand, but also to experience how right, how true, how sweet, how lovely, how mighty, how consoling, God's Word is, wisdom above all wisdom. That is why you observe how David in the 119th Psalm so often complains about all sorts of enemies, about nefarious princes and tyrants, about false prophets and factions, whom he must endure because he meditates, that is, as stated, is occupied with, God's Word in every way." Poignantly, Luther acknowledged how much he owed to his enemies, for "through the raging of the devil they have so buffetted, distressed, and terrified me that they have made me a fairly good theologian, which I would not have become without them" (Luther, *WLS* III, pp. 1358–60; cf. preface to Wittenberg ed., *LW* 34, pp. 283–88).

Intellectual and Moral Requisites for the Study of God

Christian reflection calls for many of the same intellectual abilities that are expected of the philosopher, logician, historian, and linguist (Augustine, *On Chr. Doctrine* II.1–12, *LLA*, pp. 32–44). It requires clear reasoning, right discernment of the relations between seemingly distant and varied teachings, multilayered powers of intuitive insight, sound movement from premises to conclusions, capacity for critical analysis, and the power of internally consistent reflection (Justin Martyr, *Dialogue with Trypho* I, II, *ANF* I, pp. 194, 195; Augustine, *Soliloquies*, *FC* I, pp. 343 ff.).

One is ill prepared who has not learned how to spot leaps in logic and spurious arguments. So varied are the questions under consideration, and so complex the evidence, that serious misjudgment at one point is likely to elicit a wave of distortions at subsequent points. A disciplined mind is ready to listen wisely, collect facts, hold many facts together in creative tension, and draw conclusions upon which the faithful can rely (Minucius Felix, *Octavius* XIII–XX, *ACW*, pp. 71–86; Augustine, *First Catech. Lect.* I.1–3, *ACW* 2, pp. 13–20).

Certain ethical values are also requisite to the right study of God: fairness of judgment, impartiality in weighing evidence, and respect for others (Augustine, *On the Profit of Believing* 14–22, *LF*, pp. 592–600; Tho. Aq., *ST* I Q16, I, pp. 89–95). Without self-acquaintance, Baxter argued, all studies would be irrational and misguided (*PW* XVI, pp. 97–101).

Since the pastoral study of God rests upon exegetical and historical disciplines, it requires qualities necessary to those disciplines: the search for an accurate text, empathic willingness to listen to ancient sources whose assumptions differ from one's own culture, ability to work with Hebrew and Greek, and an intellectual balance that brings complex materials into meaningful focus (Clement of Alex., *Strom.* VIII, *ANF* II, pp. 558 ff.). The laity hope that the language, reasoning, insights, and concepts of Scripture and tradition will be thoroughly digested and assimilated in the minds of their spiritual mentors (Clement of Alex., *Instr.* I.1 ff., *ANF* II, pp. 209 ff.). One who has not yet read the Bible carefully is hardly ready to study Christian doctrine, much less teach it (Athanasius, *Incarnation of the Word* 56, *NPNF* 2 IV, pp. 66, 67; Calvin, *Inst.* 1.2 ff.).

The laity pray for the gift of discernment in their leaders (Prov. 14:6; Phil. 1:10; 1 Cor. 2:14). Discernment seeks to grasp first principles and fundamental convictions that are not approached or approachable by logical demonstrations but lie prior to all argument and precondition reasoning. The realm of inspired truth into which the student of Scripture enters is not just an account book or a machine or a math problem or a political campaign or an advertising strategy (cf. Baxter, *PW* II, pp. 238 ff.). That realm requires special modes of listening—to the Spirit witnessing inwardly within oneself, to the witness of others, and to the Source and End of all things, whose mighty deeds in history call forth the inquiry (cf. Clement of Alex., *Exhort. to the Heathen* IX, *ANF* II, pp. 195–97). "You shall know his power today if you will listen to his voice" (Ps. 95:7).

This is why the study of God is said to depend through grace upon certain intellectual and moral virtues for its proper accomplishment: patience, love of truth, courage to follow one's convictions, humility in the face of the facts, loyalty to the truth, and a profound sense of awe in the presence of the truth (Tho. Aq., *ST* Ia–IIae Q59–66, I, pp. 837–70). These intellectual and moral virtues are also required in other sciences, but in the study of God their absence is keenly felt as harmful. The student of theology cannot claim exemption from these requisites on the grounds of fervent piety (Calvin, *Inst.* 2.8; Baxter, *PW* V, pp. 575–84).

Christian teaching about God is not merely a systematic presentation of ideas but also intends to have an impact on daily life, since Christianity is a way of life. Anyone who seeks to understand the living God celebrated in Christian worship must be willing to enter into the sphere in which praise, intercession, and supplication are taken seriously. One cannot merely stand outside the vestibule and expect to know what is happening inside from reading about it. If the Christian life can only be known from within, then the study of God is a subject that requires entry, engagement, and concrete participation in the worshiping community (Gregory Nazianzen, or. 2, *NPNF* 2 VII, pp. 204 ff.). Just as there could be no good sociology of bedouin life without ever visiting bedouins, and no study of Verdi without ever hearing Verdi, so there can be no good theology without actively and sympathetically entering into the community whose understanding one is seeking to explicate (Basil, *Concerning Baptism*, *FC* 9, pp. 339 ff.; Ambrose, *On the Mysteries*, *NPNF* 2 X, pp. 315–26).

A Habit of Mind

Thomas Aquinas described theology as a habit of mind that seeks to combine theoretical wisdom and analytical ability with practical and social wisdom. As a habit of mind, theology is comparable to a well-disciplined mathematical or musical habit of mind (Tho. Aq., *ST* I Q1, I, p. 2). Christian teaching seeks to develop and reinforce mental habits that embrace both contemplative and practical virtues.

If the spiritual guide does not have a contemplative capacity for imagination, wonder, and reflection, and is not able intuitively to seek a comprehensive view of things, the effort fails by omission of important insight (Bonaventure, *The Mind's Ascent into God*). Mentors are deficient if they lack prudence, contextual wisdom, and the capacity to enter the world of moral action and social process.

It is only with practice that the pastor-teacher gradually grows to have a well-furnished theological habit of mind, disposed to look carefully at language about God and to use language responsibly in the light of Scripture, tradition, and good moral sense (Tho. Aq., *ST* Ia–IIae Q49 ff., I, pp. 793 ff.; cf. II, pp. 1169 ff., 1663–76; Baxter, *PW* XXI, pp. 162 ff.). It is a habit that is willing to ask tough questions about our thoughts of God and to view those questions in the light of the best resources of Scripture and tradition, correlated with whatever else one knows about life through personal and social experience and through scientific, historical, psychological, and other inquiries (Augustine, *On Chr. Doctrine* IV, *NPNF* 1 II, pp. 574 ff.; Calvin, *Inst.* 2.15, 16; Wesley, *WJW* VI, pp. 351 ff.).

Learning to study God is like learning to dance; it cannot be done merely by reading books. One cannot dance without practice, without allowing the muscles to move and the neural synapses to respond. To learn to dance one must dance, even if badly. Good theology is more than a tome or a string of good sentences. It is a way of dancing, an embodied activity of the human spirit in a community embodying life in Christ.

As in sport one learns to play according to the rules—one does not invent new rules as the game proceeds—similarly, the study of God requires learning to think according to well-established, standardized, well-tested, proper rules. The inquiry into method in the study of God seeks to review these elementary rules (for early models, cf. Cyril of Jerusalem, *Procatechesis*, NPNF 2 VII, pp. 1–5; Augustine, *On Chr. Doctrine*).

The goal of the study of God is the delight of knowing God better with our minds, the pleasure of making sense, the joy of understanding and knowing the blessedness of divinity—an incomparably intriguing subject (Tho. Aq., *ST* Ia–IIae Q31–34, I, pp. 721–39; Calvin, *Inst.* 3.25.10). What other subject touches everything else in touching its own distinctive subject matter? Viewed merely as intriguing or fascinating, however, the study of God may remain merely an object of aesthetic interest, so that as one becomes tired of hearing of the infinite, the subject of God would soon become boring (cf. Kierkegaard, *Either/Or* I, "The Rotation Method"). Hence rigorous study is rightly viewed as a duty for those who serve in the public office of ministry, not merely a matter of inclination (Ambrose, *Duties* III.2, 3, NPNF 2 X, pp. 68–71).

Conserving and Progressing

Two opposite ideological predispositions are visibly at work in almost any of Christianity's eighty generations; either may affect or distort Christian teaching in any period: an excessive conservatism and an excessive progressivism.

The *conserving mind* rightly prizes the past, values achievements hard won from the long history of morality, reflection, political struggle, and cultural formation. The *progressive mind* rightly prizes the future of truth, and especially values the potential new insights that promise to correct long-held errors and obsessions.

Each struggles against a different temptation to become excessive: The conserving view may *over*value established views, making an idol out of past achievements and misjudging the capacity of dated forms to sustain themselves amid the emerging challenges of history. The progressing view may *under*value the inheritance of the past and too avidly imagine that the future holds unparalleled truth and values of which the past is thought to be totally ignorant (Gregory the Great, *Pastoral Rule* I.8–III.2, NPNF 2 XII, pp. 5–25).

The excess of either the conserving or progressing tendency may end in rigidity, self-righteousness, and dogmatism either of the right or the left. Between these two extremes, the balanced study of God welcomes truth both old and new, and seeks to be at the same time accountable to the apostolic witness and to the promptings of the Spirit to fresh unfoldings of ancient truth. Jesus said: "When, therefore, a teacher of the law has become a learner in the kingdom of Heaven, he is like a householder who can produce from his store both the new and the old" (Matt. 13:52; cf. Irenaeus, *Ag. Her.* IV.9, *ANF* I, p. 472; Clementina, *Recognitions* IV.5, *ANF* VIII, pp. 135, 136).

One who studies God, finally, must study his or her own era, and the spirit of his or her own times, yet not assume that one particular time, society, or era in itself absolutely reveals the truth (Augustine, *CG* III, IV, *NPNF* 1 II, pp. 43–83; Wesley, *A Caution Ag. Bigotry, WJW* V, pp. 479–92). Though not *of* the world in which I live, as a student of God I must be thoroughly *in* it, able to share empathically with its hurts and aspirations, able to hear the cry of my own generation, as well as empathize with the generations of my grandparents and grandchildren. The Christian teacher is assigned the task of communicating the Christian message to her or his own contemporary culture, not to a past or future one. One cannot wisely remain ignorant of that culture's politics, sciences, and arts (Clement of Alex., *Strom.* I.6, *ANF* II, p. 307).

The Benefits and Hazards of Theological Study

One who sets out to study God does well to ask: What is the proper motivation of such a study? What do I intend to do with this study? What is my aim in occupying my mind with thoughts of God and with systematic reflection upon "the things of God"? (1 Cor. 2:11).

The very greatness of the subject matter tends to intoxicate. Those who come under its influence may wrongly imagine that they are thereby morally above other Christians. When certain Corinthians thought they had become extraordinarily well informed, Paul wrote: "This 'knowledge' of yours is utter disaster to the weak, the brother for whom Christ died" (1 Cor. 8:11). Again: "This 'knowledge' breeds conceit; it is love that builds. If anyone fancies that he knows, he knows nothing yet, in the true sense of knowing. But if a man loves, he is acknowledged by God" (1 Cor. 8:1–3; Irenaeus, *Ag. Her.* IV.12.2, *ANF* I, p. 476; IV.33.8, *ANF* I, p. 508).

The study of God indeed enlarges our minds, provides the intellect with the loftiest themes on which the human mind can dwell, addresses moral conscience with the claim of God, and seeks to enliven the deepest religious impulses in human life. Yet it can elicit pride. At best, it brings "good tidings of great joy" (Luke 2:10), addressing every hearer, however bored, anxious, or guilty, with the blessing of God's pardon and peace. It invites people to a new life of responsible love and accountability to God for their neighbor. Yet it, like everything else, can become egocentrically distorted.

The right study of the living God should bear in mind the injunction of Moses to the people of the law: "For you they are no empty words; they are your very life, and by them you shall live long in the land which you are to occupy after crossing the Jordan" (Deut. 32:47). Such is the intention of the Christian study of God: to engender life, to enable the history of God's revelation to become one's own history, to reshape the lives of individuals and societies. The student of God needs to "know how to speak a word in season" (Isa. 50:4). To learn what is seasonable is the practical and pastoral side of the task of theology.

Whether the Study of God Is an Academic Discipline

Relation of the Study of God to General and Ordained Ministry

The study of God is a habit of mind that seeks to call upon God's name appropriately, pray and praise fittingly, proclaim God's action meaningfully, and set forth courageously the ethical responsibility flowing from the gospel. As a rigorous, unified discipline of study, theology in turn is supported by and correlated with companion university disciplines that seek truth in various spheres. This raises the question of how theology is at once specially related to ordained ministry yet also crucially related to the general ministry of the laity.

Not only the ordained, but laypersons in general, are called to be theologians, since Scripture and Christian teaching are rightly studied by all believers, learned as well as unlearned. Everyone who teaches and professes Christian faith fittingly is properly called a theologian, according to Luther (Luther, *Comm. on Rom. 12:7*, SL XII, p. 335; cf. Chemnitz, *MWS*, pp. 14 ff.; Gerhard, *De Natura Theologiae*, sec. 4).

Yet it has long been the custom to use the term *theology* to speak of that knowledge necessary for the administration of public ministry. In this sense theology is particularly related to a vocational practice that presupposes a particular pattern of education (*paideia*) based on aptitude (*hikanotēs*, in Latin *habitus*) and certain gifts (*charismata*) engendered by the Holy Spirit (1 Cor. 12; Eph. 4:7–16). Leaders who perform pastoral service must know how to teach the faith, "rightly dividing the Word of truth" (2 Tim. 2:15) made known in Scripture, and thus to lead sinners from idolatry, through doubt, to faith, hope, and love in Christ (1 Cor. 13). To do this they must become pastoral theologians, those who think thoroughly about the pastoral gifts and tasks as part of their responsibility for the care of others in the Christian community (John Chrysostom, *On the Priesthood* II–VI, *NPNF* 1 IX, pp. 39–83).

Lay theology is that knowledge which all believers are expected to have grasped, at least in an elementary fashion. Confirmation centers upon the question of developing in young people and inquirers a rudimentary awareness of the truth of the Christian faith and of the baptism in which one is baptized. The content or subject matter of lay and systematic theology is precisely the same. But systematic theology in preparation for ordained ministry pursues more deliberately, intentionally, critically and intensely the ground, roots, consequences, and practical effects of that same faith, in order vocationally to prepare the student to serve in the office of public ministry (Synod of Laodicea, canon XLVI, *NPNF* 2 XIV, p. 154; Second Council of Nicaea, *NPNF* 2 XIV, pp. 555–60; Theophilus of Alex., *Prosphonesus*, canon VI, *NPNF* 2 XIV, p. 614).

The thorough and systematic study of God is requisite to ordained ministry. Those who follow the call to sacred ministry must be prepared for an intensive inquiry into the living God, the Word of life, and life in the Spirit at a depth that laypersons do not ordinarily assume to be necessary for themselves (Tho. Aq., *ST Suppl.* Q34–40, III, pp. 2679–2707; Chemnitz, *MWS*, pp. 14 ff.).

All the various disciplines of the theological curriculum contribute to the church's general ministry. The whole church is engaged in acts of ministry; it is not something only ordained ministers do, since all laypersons share in Christ's general ministry to the world (Eph. 4:11–13). Theology is taught also by laypersons in Christian schools, studied in Christian education, and pursued in lay theological education (Cyril of Jerusalem, *Lenten Lectures, Catecheses* III, IV, *FC* 61, pp. 108–38).

Some laypersons attain high proficiency in the study of God (cf. Descartes, *Meditations*; Milton, *Areopagitica*; Kierkegaard, *Concl. Unsci. Post.*). There remains, however, a missional distinction, though not a difference in faith, between general ministry and ordained ministry. For the ordained minister is duly authorized and appointed to perform a representative ministry on behalf of the whole community of the baptized (Ambrose, *On the Duties of the Clergy* I.1 ff., *NPNF* 2 X, pp. 1 ff.; Leo the Great, *Letters* VI, *To Anastasius*, *NPNF* 2 XII, pp. 5, 6; Gregory the Great, *Pastoral Rule* I, *NPNF* 2 XII, pp. 1–9). The whole body needs leadership in order rightly to hear the preached Word, receive the sacraments, and receive pastoral care (Thirty-nine Articles of Religion XXIII–XXX, CC, pp. 274–77).

Timothy was instructed: "Keep before you an outline of the sound teaching which you heard from me, living by the faith and love which are ours in Christ Jesus. Guard the treasure put into our charge, with the help of the Holy Spirit dwelling within us" (2 Tim. 1:13, 14). The first task of the Christian teacher is to "hold fast" (*eche*) the sound teaching (*hygiainontōn*) passed on from the apostles. Timothy was not at liberty to teach his own private opinions or prejudices. Paul provided a living model (*hypotypōsis*) for the Christian leader to follow (Tertullian, *On Prescript. Ag. Her.* XXV ff., *ANF* III, pp. 254 ff.).

Disciplines Within the Study of Theology

The study of God seeks to develop a disciplined reflection on its own clearly defined subject matter: the reality, presence, mercy, and love of God as understood by the worshiping Christian community. It is an orderly exposition of evidences of divine revelation on the basis of Scripture, tradition, and historical and experiential reasoning, so as to speak accurately and clearly of the being and activity of God.

Theology requires a sequential order of presentation, a deliberate arrangement of themes, not merely a miscellaneous conglomerate of biblical or traditional statements (Cyril of Jerusalem, *Procatechesis, FC* 37, pp. 166, 167). One cannot say everything at the same time or in a single sentence, no matter how desirable this might seem.

There are four primary divisions of the study of God into which all other forms of theological reflection have tended to fall: biblical, historical, systematic, and pastoral theology. Systematic theology (*Glaubenslehre, sacra doctrina*) assumes and requires basic familiarity with all branches of the study of God. Consequently, most theological curricula have included at least these four divisions: biblical, historical, and systematic theology (sometimes questions of ethics and of church and society are included here, sometimes considered separately), and the practice of ministry.

Biblical Theology

Biblical (or exegetical) theology confines itself primarily to the Scriptures for its textual materials. It includes the study of the texts and sources of Scripture; the principles, conventions, and laws governing interpretation (hermeneutics); and the historical and literary criticism of Scripture, utilizing archaeological, geographical, and historical science. Systematic theology at every point is closely intertwined with biblical theology, since biblical teaching has always formed the core of classical Christian doctrinal reflection (Basil, *Concerning Baptism* I.3, *FC*, pp. 396–403; Tho. Aq., *ST* I Q1, I, pp. 6, 7; *ST* I Q68, I, p. 338).

The purpose of biblical study is to read the Scriptures wisely, interpret them fittingly, and stand prudently under their address (Augustine, *On Chr. Doctrine*; Calvin, *Inst.* 1.13; Kierkegaard, *For Self-examination*). In the modern period, Scripture study has often been subdivided into exegetical theology, which pays primary attention to the interpretation of specific texts, and biblical theology, which seeks to relate and combine the teaching of various Scriptures and bring them into cohesive doctrinal formulation. One may study the theology of Paul, or the theology of Amos, or even a subcategory of one of these, such as the Pauline teaching on grace, or Amos' view of justice.

Historical Theology

Historical theology studies the development of reflection upon biblical teachings from the time of the apostles to the present, embracing not only the thought of the Christian community but also its institutions, ethos, social life, ethics, law, and liturgies in their development, as well as the development of Christian teaching through controversies and through challenging historical conditions (Eusebius, *CH*, I.1, *NPNF* 2 I, pp. 81, 82; Theodoret, *EH*, *NPNF* 2 III, pp. 33–159). Historical theology lays the groundwork for systematic theology by inquiring critically into how various writers treated various topics, for example: How did Origen's view compare with Augustine's on the creation of the soul? How did Pelagius and John of Damascus view the relation of grace and free will? How did Anselm and Thomas Aquinas view the relation of faith and reason? How did Luther and Calvin redefine scriptural authority? Historical theology feeds constantly into systematic theology. Historical theology remains essentially a multigenerational commentary and debate on texts of Scripture (Jerome, *Ag. Rufinus* XXII, *FC* 53, pp. 87–91; Calvin, *Inst.* 1.7; 4.1.1).

Systematic Theology

Systematic theology uses the resources of exegetical and historical theology in seeking to build a consistent view of God, utilizing both general human knowledge and the witness to revelation (Clement of Alex., *Strom.*; Tho. Aq., *ST*, passim; Wesley, *WJW* VIII, pp. 1–247). It includes both the systematic study of Christian teaching and the study of the Christian life (i.e., both Christian theology and Christian ethics; cf. Luther, *Treatise on Good Works*; *On Chr. Liberty*, *WML* II).

The quality of theology depends upon a sensitive correlation of all these disciplines. Christian study of God cannot do its work without Scripture, or without the dialogue with tradition, or without rational criticism, or without cross-cultural dialogue, or without considering its social and political consequences. The study of God does not exist merely for itself but also intends to have some constructive effect upon individuals and upon society (Calvin, *Draft Eccl. Ordinances*, *JCSW*, pp. 229–44). It wishes to feed and nurture the practice of ministry (Ambrose, *Duties of the Clergy*, *NPNF* 2 X, pp. 1 ff.; *On the Chr. Faith*, pp. 99 ff.).

Constructive theology is sometimes viewed as a near synonym for systematic theology. It puts the focus on the ever-new human need for creative reflection in each varied sociocultural-historical situation. *Apologetic theology* is that theology which wishes to speak especially to those standing outside the Christian community, to provide clarification to nonfaith concerning how faith reasons about itself amid particular historical challenges. Apologetics seeks to build a bridge between the community of faith and its intellectual, moral, and ideological alternatives (Athenagoras, *A Plea for the Chr.*, *ANF* II, pp. 129 ff.; Augustine, *Answer to Skeptics*, *FC* 1, pp. 103 ff.). It differs in subject matter from *polemical theology*, which seeks to defend Christian faith against attack from within and to provide a corrective for misunderstandings and abuses (Irenaeus, *Ag. Her.* I.preface, *ANF* I, pp. 315, 316; cf. Hippolytus, *Refutation of All Her.* I.prologue, *ANF* V, pp. 9–11), and *comparative theology*, which sets forth the points of agreement and difference between important systems of religious belief (cf. Lactantius, *Div. Inst.* IV.28, 29, *ANF* VII, pp. 131–33; Calvin, *Inst.* 1.12.1; Heppe, *RD*; Watson, *TI* I, pp. 21 ff.).

Symbolic theology (or symbolics) is the study of the consensual documents, the creeds and symbolic statements of the Christian tradition (Seven Ecumenical Councils, *NPNF* 2 XIV, passim; cf. *CC*, pp. 1–11). Symbolic or confessional theology studies and weighs the Roman Catholic and Eastern Orthodox confessional statements and compares them with key Lutheran, Reformed, Baptist, and other statements of faith that are accepted consensually within their particular tradition (cf. *CC*, *COC*, *HPC* passim). Symbolic theology tends to be either denominationally oriented toward a particular confession, or ecumenically oriented toward a comparison of confessions. Symbolic theology antedates the modern ecumenical movement with its *ecumenical theology*, which is a modern reappropriation of symbolic theology that wants to bring all these symbols or creeds or confessions into a provisionally operational, shared, consensual theological and practical unity. *Irenic theology* is that theology that seeks to mediate differences and to bring different confessions into a feasible harmony so that their hidden affinities may be made visible (Augsburg Conf., CC, pp. 63–107; Wesley, *The Catholic Spirit, WJW* V, pp. 499 ff.).

Moral theology, or *theological ethics,* is theological reflection that is more particularly focused on how one moves from faith to action, from credo to decision. It asks how we get from the Christian understanding of life to and through concrete moral choices, habits, and modes of character formation, and ethical decision making within social structures. *Christian social ethics* is another mode of theological reflection that is particularly focused upon economic life, political change, domestic and family life, and social policy formation (Tho. Aq., *ST* Ia–IIae Q49 ff., I, pp. 793 ff.; Luther, *The Babylonian Captivity of the Church; On Christian Liberty, WML* II; Calvin, *Inst.* 3.6–10, 4.1 ff.).

In all of these subdivisions, the working theologian is called to be widely receptive to insights and contributions from varied quarters— biblical theology, historical theology, and the study of comparative religion—yet the discipline of systematic theology does not merely repeat the statements of these others. Rather, it is primarily concerned with the vital, contemporary clarification of that which is enduring and consistently present in the understanding of God as celebrated in the historical Christian community. Systematic theology receives contributions from exegetical and historical theology and, having transmuted them through consistent reflection, passes them on to pastoral and practical theology and ethics (Ambrose, *Duties* III–XII, *NPNF* 2 X, pp. 69–80; Gregory the Great, *Pastoral Rule* II, *NPNF* 2 XII, pp. 9–24).

Pastoral Theology

Pastoral theology builds upon exegetical, historical, and systematic theology to provide an understanding of the practice of ministry and of the practical application of the fruits of theology to the work of ministry. It includes *homiletics* (which studies the task of preaching of the Word, the sources of homily, and the composition and delivery of sermons), *catechetical theology* (or Christian education, which teaches all the people of God, especially young Christians and inquirers and those seeking baptism, the understanding of faith that is assumed in Christian baptism), *liturgics* (the study of worship, sacramental life, prayer, the Christian year, and rites of the church), *pastoral theology and pastoral care* (the study of the care of souls), and *administry,* or church administration (the equipping of the laity for ministry in the world).

The seminary curriculum is often spoken of simply as a course in *theology*, in the sense that it covers all of these subjects. It is called a seminary (from *semen,* seed) because it seeks to seed the learner in all of these areas so as to bring forth wholesome fruit.

Christian teaching has embraced different languages, symbol systems, and forms in different historical periods, showing astonishing flexibility; yet there remains a profound unity within that vast diversity, a remarkable continuity that sustains and feeds its inveterate, creative pluralism. The story of the diversity of Christian cultural history is a marvelously varied, multicolored, multiphased story, but there is a center to the wide circumference of that circle (Irenaeus, *Ag. Her.* III.3, 4, *ANF* I, pp. 415–17; Tertullian, *Prescript. Ag. Her.* 36, *ANF* III, pp. 260, 261).

The center is the Subject of this study: God in Christ by the power of the Spirit, nothing more, nothing less—not psychology, not our feelings, not philosophy, not historical science, not political ideology—but God the Father revealed in the Son through the Spirit. The cohesion of all these disciplines is the special interest of systematic theology.

The Study of Religion and the Study of God

Since God has never left himself without witness (Acts 14:17), humanity has never been without religion in some form. The hunger for God does not fully disappear even in an atheistic society in which religion is coercively disavowed. God is nearer to human life than we can know even while we are groping after God (Acts 17:24–28) or running from God (Jonah 1, 2).

According to Cicero (*De Natura Deorum* 2.28), religion is an instinctive aspiration of the human mind, an inbuilt inclination to ponder or recurrently go over again one's absolute duty (*religere*), as if an absolute duty were owed to someone. The classical Christian writer, Lactantius, had a different definition, based on a different etymology: religion is that which binds (*religare*) humanity to an awareness of the divine through rites, institutions, customs, and morality, in which the religious sentiment finds expression in worship, duty, and fellowship (*Div. Inst.* IV.28, 29, *ANF* VIII, pp. 131, 132).

These two views may be combined in the view that human nature tends instinctively to turn to God in prayer so persistently that this eventually becomes bound, by custom and established practice, into a religion. Religion has to do with *religio*, a reverent, dutiful turning of the spirit toward God manifested in conduct and in communities of worship (John Chrysostom, *Concerning the Statues* IV.6–12, *NPNF* 1

IX, pp. 367–70, cf. pp. 373, 384). Religion refers to the means by which one's life before God becomes sustained and expressed in terms of community, ritual, institutional life, and moral responsibility (Acts 25:19; 26:5; 1 Tim. 5:4; Augustine, *CG* X.1, *NPNF* 1 II, p. 181; Calvin, *Inst.* 1.12.1).

Religion is a much broader term than Judaism and Christianity. Religion is a universal human phenomenon. Religion usually implies an institutional context, priesthood, ritual, and worship, all of which are extremely varied in human history. No doubt Christianity is a religion, but a religion in the special sense of that which completes and fulfills the idea of religion. A religion may be said to be "true" insofar as it leads people to the true God (not to a false God) and to life in communion with the true God (1 John 5:20; cf. James 1:26, 27). Christianity does not claim that no truth exists in other religions, only that the true God has become human in Jesus Christ.

Religion addresses the interior life, the inward life of the soul, in giving thanks, confession, and commitment. But religion also exists in an exterior sense. Religion is a comprehensive ethos inasmuch as it involves both interior life and exterior manifestation of that spirit in community. Religion affects behavior in the most diffuse and fundamental ways. Religion was counted among the virtues in medieval Christianity, but even then it was clear that religion could also be turned into a vice in the forms of idolatry, superstition, and sacrilege (Tho. Aq., *SCG* III.II.120, pp. 133–41; *Compend. Theol.* 248, *TATT*, pp. 242, 243). All religions contain some truth concerning God, for God has not left himself without witness. Yet Christian teaching does not neglect Jesus' statement: "No one comes to the Father except by me" (John 14:6).

If so, what then is the relation of Christian study of God to general religious consciousness? The heart of Christian study of God concerns that knowledge of God the Father that is revealed in the Son through the Spirit (Lactantius, *Div. Inst.* IV.29, *ANF* VII, pp. 132, 133). Such a study is less oriented in general toward the study of religion than toward that form of the religious life that most truly fulfills and perfects the ethos and possibility of religious consciousness. Jesus is the supreme teacher both of theology and religion, and the two are united in him. Natural religion exists everywhere humanity exists, prior to and concomitant with the revelation in Jesus. But Christian Scripture and tradition view the religions in this sense as preparatory for the revelation of God the Father through the Son, the Revealer, Jesus Christ (Lactantius, *Div. Inst.* VI.10, *ANF* VII, pp. 172–74).

If religion in general has to do with the way human beings worship and respond to God, then Christian theology certainly concerns itself with religion. Classical Christian teachers have often thought of Christianity under the concept of "true religion," arguing that it is the appropriate and most fitting turn of humanity toward God, namely in response to God's own turning toward humanity (Augustine, *On the Profit of Believing* 28 ff., *NPNF* 1 III, pp. 361 ff.). This is not to say that other modes of religious consciousness have no validity.

Christianity is termed *true religion* by the classical exegetes because it has all the requisites of true religion. If religion in its proper sense is the fitting worship of God and the disposition of the soul toward God in a manner agreeable to God, and if religion manifests itself in love for the neighbor and the embodiment of the virtuous life, then Christianity is true religion, whose object of worship is not a false god but the One who makes himself truly known as God (Augustine, *CG* XIX.25, *NPNF* 1 II, pp. 418, 419; *On the Profit of Believing* 14 ff., *NPNF* 1 III, pp. 354, 355).

In arguing that Christianity is true religion, the classical teachers have not meant to imply that any given statement of Christianity holds absolute knowledge of God (such as God has of himself) or holds that fuller knowledge of God that the faithful are promised to have at the end time. Paul candidly said of himself: "My knowledge now is partial; then it will be whole, like God's knowledge of me" (1 Cor. 13:12). Rather, the assertion of true religion means that Christianity is viewed as conveying God's saving work with full adequacy, so that humanity needs no further disclosure of subsequent divine revelation. But why is Christianity's truth such that others' truth is viewed in terms of it? Because Christianity does not seek the divine-human reconciliation through human works or virtues, but through faith in God's own perfect and unsurpassable reconciling act in Christ (2 Cor. 5:18, 19).

Christianity is not true religion because its moral code is adequate to reflect God's righteousness, but because God's forgiveness of our moral lapses is sufficient. One hid in Christ is declared righteous before God (Rom. 3:28; 1 Cor. 2:4, 5), which means that the believer by grace is assuredly accepted in God's sight: "In him you have been brought to completion" (Col. 2:10). The "perfect" (*teleioi*) spoken of by Paul in 1 Corinthians 2:6 are not simply the more experienced or older or more mature Christians with higher forms of knowledge, but rather those who fully believe the gospel hidden to this world. The "perfect" to whom Paul refers are those who have unremitting faith in Jesus Christ. We do not need to look for some better religion or some future disclosure of truth that will improve upon God's own taking of responsibility for humanity in Jesus Christ. The sole source of true religion is not any human moral or intellectual achievement, but God's own justifying grace (Rom. 5:1–3; 6:14–18; 11:5, 6; Eph. 2:8, 9).

Christianity did not gradually attain this character of true religion by a process of historical development, but was from the outset, from the incarnation, true religion. There is a certain resistance in classical Christian teaching to speaking of Christianity as one among many religions, or as the result of a natural historical development that, by the laws of adaptation and evolution, would make it a greater or lesser religion. For such a premise forgets the once-and-for-all incarnation, which (if its claim is fully credited) makes Christianity distinctive in the sphere of the history of religions (Lactantius, *Div. Inst.* IV.5–12, *ANF* VII, pp. 104–13; Augustine, *CG* X.1, *NPNF* 1 II, p. 181). Admittedly, other religions have distinctive features too, but only in Christianity is promise of God to Israel fulfilled by God's own coming in the flesh.

The classical Christian teachers pointed to two essential differences between Christianity and other religions—the differences in their source and in their effect. Christianity's *source* is God making himself known personally and for all time—to be sure, within a process of historical development, but not explainable primarily as a natural or predictable result of that historical development. Secondly, Christianity's *effect* is true salvation from sin, deliverance from guilt, despair, and death, based upon God's own coming in Christ. Christianity differs from the religions of the world in that its understanding of God comes, not from human striving, intellect, and will, but from God's own self-disclosure in human history, through the people of Israel, which culminates and clarifies itself finally only in Jesus Christ. After Jesus, religion can never be the same (Arnobius, *Ag. Heathen* II.70–78, *ANF* VI, pp. 460–63). Christian theology can therefore be viewed as an orderly and systematic treatment of true religion and of the evidences of true religion in Scripture and tradition (Augustine, *CG* X, *NPNF* 1 II, pp. 180–204; Calvin, *Inst.* 1.12.1).

The questions raised in universal religious consciousness are also raised in Christianity: Who am I? How did the world come to be? What is good or evil, right or wrong? To whom am I finally accountable? Will I live after death? How can I know the eternal One who transcends all temporal realities? Why do I suffer? These are questions that are familiar to Islam, Buddhism, Hinduism, and other world religions. Christian theology is not entering an arena of questioning that has never been entered by other religions. But the overall interpretation of the meaning of universal history that it provides comes, not from human insight or ingenuity or moral struggle or intellect, but from God's own coming in Jesus Christ. The best Christian teaching is not contemptuous of other religions, but views each history of religious struggle as a statement of the presence of the Holy Spirit in all human history. Christians can learn from these histories of religions powerful insights that bestow greater light upon the biblical understanding of God (Tho. Aq., *SCG* I.20, I.60 f., pp. 112 ff., 204 ff.; Wesley, *WJW* VI, pp. 508 ff.; VIII, pp. 203 ff., 244 ff., 471 ff.).

CHAPTER 9

The Reasoning of Revelation

Does revelation elicit and require its own kind of reasoning? To what extent can the study of God expect to be reasonable? Does faith risk something essential to itself when it tries to be reasonable in the world's terms?

No study of God is complete without dealing with the limits and resources of human reasoning in God's presence. Four issues in particular need to be investigated: (1) At what points can or must the inquiry into God appeal to reason? (2) What is meant by reason, and why is radical skepticism finally untenable? (3) Could any disclosure of God occur without reason altogether? (4) Does faith reason in its own unique way?

Must the Study of God Appeal to Reason?

Reason (*dialegomai, ratio*), as classical Christianity understood it, includes all the capacities of the soul to behold and receive truth (Augustine, *Letters* CXXXVII, *NPNF* 1 I, pp. 473–80; cf. *Letters* 120.1, *FC*). These include intellectual, emotive, and volitional (thinking, feeling, and willing) aspects of the self, insofar as all these faculties enter into the discernment and interpretation of the truth (Augustine, *Conf.* IV.1 ff., *NPNF* 1 I, pp. 89 ff.).

The Participative Premise: Reasoning out of a Community

Christian study of God requires a risk-taking effort to enter into and explore that context in which the relevant data are found. The data of the religious communities cannot be effectively evaluated or even heard if we do not enter into the sphere of that community's life, its prayer, its confessional memory, and its acts of self-giving love. Those who elect to stand aloof from that worshiping community will have lost the chance to understand it from within. As one cannot undergo psychoanalysis merely by reading books, but only through analysis—so too, theology.

The study of God is not well grasped as an individualistic inquiry apart from a community that seeks to embody and celebrate it. In studying any discipline, one must enter into its language, artifacts, instruments, data bases, symbols, graphs, and diagrams—whatever that particular discipline requires—and live with those resources for a while, taking them seriously. Likewise, a participative element is required in Christian theology (Pss. 95:2; 34:8; Matt. 19:15–22; Acts 11:5; Teresa of Avila, *Life* I, pp. 17–20; cf. Calvin, *Inst.* 1.1–3; Bucer, *De Regno Christi* III, LCC XIX, pp. 200–207; Wesley, *WJW* V, pp. 185–201; XI, pp. 237–59).

Christian reflection well expounded should be reasonably intelligible to an educated person who is not a Christian (Justin Martyr, *Dialogue with Trypho*, ANF I, pp. 194 ff.; Athenagoras, *A Plea for the Chr.*, ANF II, pp. 123–49). But its evidences may not be completely plausible, persuasive, or even meaningful to one who has not made any participative effort, or to one who has not at the very least attentively listened to someone else who has made that integrative effort and lived it out in his or her own daily behavior (Clare of Assisi, *Rule*, CWS, pp. 209–25; Calvin, *Inst.* 4.15). It is a psychological axiom that our behavior authenticates our belief system so radically that we trust people's behavior far more than what they say they believe (James 1:23, 24; Clement, *First Epis.* IX ff., ANF I, pp. 7 ff.).

Theological reasoning involves at least a tentative sympathy with the data to be understood. That does not suggest an uncritical, naive, gullible acceptance, but rather an attitude of receptive, imaginative open-mindedness that examines facts without hardened, preconceived cynicism. Though Christian teaching does not expect a prior radical commitment to everything the church tradition has said, it does require some capacity for at least tentative openness to Holy Writ and holy tradition, in order to give it a chance to speak its own word, to declare its distinctive self-understanding (Augustine, *The Catechising of the Uninstructed*, chaps. 5–9, NPNF 1 III, pp. 288–92). Within this framework, the hearer is challenged to approach Christian teaching with a kind of risk-taking willingness, to be dissatisfied with cheap solutions, and to probe the deeper dimensions of internal consistency in the community that lives out of mystery, while seeking to reason as well as possible out of the mystery revealed (Augustine, *The Usefulness of Belief*, X.23–XVIII.36, *LCC* VI, pp. 310–18).

Christian teaching seeks to correlate a wide range of data, and therefore overlaps with companion disciplines (Augustine, *The Teacher*, *LCC* VI, pp. 69 ff.). It is something like sociology in that it requires complex data gathering and the interpreting of socially shared symbols and experiences. Sociology has methods, insights, and problems that overlap with those of anthropology, history, economics, and political thought (C. Wright Mills, *The Sociological Imagination*; cf. Tho. Aq., *The Division and Methods of the Sciences*, Q5, pp. 3–50). One cannot bracket out a small area of data and say: *This* is the absolute matter, subject, or text of sociology into which no other discipline can enter. The study of God is like this. It searches for proper balance in an extremely wide range of historical, psychological, moral, and religious input (Clement of Alex., *Strom.* II, *ANF* II, pp. 347–79). It is a broad-ranging intellectual exercise, yet a specific discipline with a single center—God's address through Jesus Christ and through Israel, as that word is made relevant to the whole range of other modes of human knowing, feeling, and acting.

Theology is a joyful intellectual task because the source of its task is the source of profoundest joy (Tho. Aq., *ST* I–II Q2–5). At the moment at which one feels one's theological endeavors becoming tedious and heavy, one may have forgotten that the center of the effort is the joy of God's presence—the ground of true happiness, the end of human despair. The God-inquiry furnishes the mind with its most radical challenge: God. It offers an unparalleled opportunity to think consistently, constructively, and fittingly about the One who gives life: this extraordinary, unduplicable being, God, who ultimately enjoys the penultimate goodness of creatures (Gen. 1:18–31).

Empathic Listening for Consistency

How may we weave our way through the fine distinctions that affirm reason as useful gift, yet with appropriate self-limits in the presence of the holiness and power of God?

Systematic theology is a critical discipline devoted to discovering, clarifying, understanding, defending, and extending the truth that is implied in the experience of the Christian community, the truth of God's self-disclosure as remembered in Scripture and tradition. Responsible discourse about God addresses the thoughtful, self-critical mind as it seeks clarity in understanding God. This inquiry wants to avoid obscurantism or evasion under the guise of piety, yet take seriously the energies of piety's own modes of reasoning (Anselm, *Concerning Truth, TFE*, pp. 91 ff.; cf. *Proslog.*, preface, pp. 103–5).

Christian theology necessarily requires the rational exercise of thinking, because it is by definition reasoned discourse about God, modestly framed in terms of the immeasurability of its Subject (Gregory Nazianzen, *Orat. XXVII, First Theol. Or., NPNF* 2 VII, pp. 285–88). Seen from the viewpoint of the university or the encyclopedia, theology is a discipline. As such it requires self-critical reasoning about the word of God delivered through Scripture, liturgy, proclamation, and counsel.

Theology has long been suspected of being slightly too simple and far too difficult, a reputation well-earned on both counts. It is only part of the modern quandary concerning theology that much of the language of Christian confession is delivered through premodern cosmologies, prescientific views of the world (Bultmann, *Jesus Christ and Mythology*, pp. 5 ff.). The conflict of cosmologies is not as deep as the conflict between faith and unfaith in the hearer. Even when clothed in the latest language and symbols of modernity, Christianity with its "Word made flesh" cannot remain completely nonoffensive (Kierkegaard, *Training in Christianity*, pp. 79 ff.). Since classical Christianity is a *tradition* of exegesis, it has from the second and third centuries faced the awkwardness of having had its eternal Word spoken and echoed through various views of the world—dated understandings and misunderstandings of nature, psychology, and society that in turn differ widely from current conceptions of causality, physics, and reality. Christianity's problem with what we call modernity is one that Christianity has faced many times before with many other "modernities." Bultmann wrongly imagined that the gulf between modern and premodern consciousness was larger than other gulfs the traditions of exegesis have managed to bridge (*EPT* I, II, passim). Our contemporary problems of cross-cultural communication do not pile higher than those faced by Athanasius, Augustine, John of Damascus, Thomas Aquinas, or Luther. Each had to struggle with making archaic language and symbol systems accessible to their own "modern" hearers of the fourth, seventh, thirteenth, or sixteenth centuries (cf. Athanasius, whose *Festal Letters* were mostly written amid massive persecution; Augustine, whose *City of God* was written amid the collapse of Rome; Gregory the Great, whose *Pastoral Care* was written amid continuing attacks upon Rome from both the north and the east; John of Damascus, whose *Orthodox Faith* was written in the then-new Muslim world, etc.).

A major obstacle to the modern hearing of classical Christian reasoning is an inveterate *modern chauvinism* that assumes that modern consciousness is intrinsically superior to all premodern modes of thinking; conversely, all premodern thinking is assumed to be intrinsically *inferior* to modern consciousness. That premise is deeply ingrained in the pride of modernity. In order to begin to hear the distinctive reasoning of the classical Christian consensus, that recalcitrant cultural egocentricity must be circumvented. How? The student of God must learn how to enter with historical empathy into archaic, seemingly outmoded, premodern frames of reference, accurately trying to hear what a text or a person is trying to shout as from a distant hill. The fact of distance does not mean that the message is in error.

It remains a problem of reason and will (being willing to reason, and reasonably willing) to learn how to employ *empathic imagination* to get into another frame of reference, to understand somebody else who thinks with different categories and out of different language frames—chiefly Hebrew, Greek, and Latin but also at various periods Aramaic, Coptic, Arabic, German, French. Classical Christian writers have preached and taught in all these symbol systems and more. They have often transcended their own thought world and embraced other symbol systems in the service of the truth (among the best exemplars: Paul, Irenaeus, Justin Martyr, Clement of Alexandria, Augustine, Thomas Aquinas, and Raymond Lull).

In listening for the internal consistency of the deep nuances of classical Christian reasoning, we face complex problems of cross-cultural translation of meanings readily available in one period but almost inaccessible to another. An intellectual effort is required by the serious student of God's revelation who must take in a wide range of data, listen to strange voices, place text in context, and pray for the guidance of the Spirit (Augustine, *On Chr. Doctrine* III, *NPNF* 1 II, pp. 556–73). The task requires rigorous understanding not only of Scripture but also of the tradition that remembers Scripture; in addition it requires the gift of putting all into a personally meaningful, internally cohesive formulation that corresponds to one's own experiencing process (Augustine, *Conf.* VI, *NPNF* 1 I, pp. 89–101; Gregory the Great, *Pastoral Care*, *ACW*, passim). All of that requires thinking; Christian faith cannot simply appeal to mystery or refer itself uncritically back to immeasurable divine wisdom.

Scriptural Teaching Concerning Reason

The biblical writers welcomed reason that is open to the evidences of faith. Isaiah appealed to his hearers: "Come now, let us reason together" (1:18, KJV). Prophets such as Amos denounced idolatry and greed for its unreasonable stupidity (Amos 3:14–4:3). It is the fool, not the wise one, who says in his heart, "There is no God" (Ps. 14:1; cf. Pss. 53:1; 92:6).

Paul spoke to his Corinthian audience as persons "of good sense" (1 Cor. 10:15, "of discernment," TCNT). He protested against the opponents of faith as those who were "unreasonable" or "wrong-headed" (2 Thess. 3:2, KJV, NEB). The writer of the letter to Colossians prayed that they might receive from God "all wisdom and spiritual understanding for full insight into his will" (Col. 1:9, 10). Jesus himself reasoned by analogy through parables, and often reasoned from pragmatic evidence.

Biblical faith has been poorly described as contrary to reason or inaccessible to any kind of rational analysis or critical judgment. This has encouraged obscurantism to parade as faith, and fidism to refuse to give or seek any reasons for faith. This stands contrary to the apostolic counsel that believers be prepared at the proper moment to give reasons for the hope that is in them. "Be always ready with your defence whenever you are called to account for the hope that is in you, but make that defence with modesty and respect" (1 Peter 3:15).

The early Christian writers followed the biblical assumption that reason was to be utilized positively within appropriate bounds in the discussion of revelation. Athenagoras declared that "natural reason is chiefly and primarily adapted . . . to delight unceasingly in the contemplation of *Him who is*" (*Resurrection of the Dead* XXV, *ANF* II, p. 162). Clement of Alexandria (*Strom.* VI.12, *ANF* II, p. 503a) and Origen (*Ag. Celsus* I.13, *ANF* IV, p. 402) argued for the inner affinity of faith and reason. Augustine formulated the relation with precision and wide influence: "If thou hast not understood, said I, believe. For understanding is the reward of faith. Therefore do not seek to understand in order to believe, but believe that thou mayest understand; since 'except ye believe, ye shall not understand'" (Augustine, *On Gospel of John*, tractate XXIX, *NPNF* 1 VII, p. 184, quoting Isa. 7:9; cf. Hooker, *Laws of Eccl. Polity* III.8).

Classical Christian exegetes sought to communicate both the importance and the limits of reason. They tried to avoid the rationalist exaggeration that reason is omnicompetent, thereby leaving no role for revelation (Tertullian, *Apol.* XLVI, XLVII, *ANF* III, pp. 50–52). They also resisted the opposite exaggeration, that reason is completely undone and incompetent in the presence of the mysteries of religion (Justin Martyr, *Dialogue with Trypho* II, *ANF* I, p. 195). A balanced, discriminating statement of the proper function of reason in theology requires firm grounding in Scripture and tradition (Clement of Alex., *Strom.* V.12–14, *ANF* II, pp. 462–76).

Feelings, passions, and emotive flow cannot substitute for analysis, observation, logical consistency, and historical awareness. Uncritical emotion may mislead, as Amos recognized in the irony of those who without reason *"feel* secure on the mountains of Samaria" (Amos 6:1, italics added). Modern psychological consciousness often finds it easier to talk about inner feelings than to provide a reasonable analysis of the motives of emotive life. One need not deny the importance of the emotive life in order to affirm the need for reason (Catherine of Genoa, *Spiritual Dialogue*, *CWS*, pp. 91 ff.; J. Edwards, *On Religious Affections*).

The plague of personalistic pietism has been the unconstrained notion that what is really important about God is only "what I feel about it right now." As a result, what one must finally trust comes down to little more than "gut feelings" and changeable, often self-assertive, emotive states—not the manifestation of God, not Scripture, not the historical experience of a community. Feeling disclosure is a primary objective in the intensive group experience. However useful, that in itself is incomplete; one's feelings may emerge out of cruelty, deception, or inordinate anxiety, for example. Classical Christian teaching asked for more than feeling-disclosure. It asked for rigorous, critical reflection, within the bounds of humble contrition, concerning the self-disclosure of God and its relevance for everything human.

Classical Christian teaching sought to nurture and assist this capacity for careful analytical reflection to avoid Christians becoming "slaves to passions and pleasures" (Titus 3:3; John Chrysostom, *Hom. on Titus* V, *NPNF* 1 XIII, pp. 535–40). Without the constraint of sound moral reasoning, the passions are prone to become "licentious" (2 Pet. 2:18), "ungodly" (Jude 18), "worldly" (Titus 2:12), or "dishonorable" (Rom. 1:26). Even the law, which is good, is prone to awaken "sinful passions," as Paul knew: "While we lived on the level of our lower nature, the sinful passions evoked by the law worked in our bodies, to bear fruit for death" (Rom. 7:5; cf. Maximus the Confessor, *Four Centuries of Charity* III.50–64, *ACW* 21, pp. 182–85).

Those who have been emotively grasped by the power of the Spirit to recognize the love of the Father through the Son do not merely feel without thinking. They owe it to themselves to seek whatever clarity is possible concerning the consequences of that experience (Tho. Aq., *ST* I Q78 ff., I, pp. 404 ff.). They may or may not reflect critically upon what inward religious experiences mean and require in such a way as to "conduct themselves wisely toward outsiders" (Col. 4:5, RSV), but those who do engage in such reflection tend to extend and deepen the meaning of the experience itself (Augustine, *Conf.* XIII, *NPNF* 1 I, pp. 192 ff.), even though reason seems always prone to overextend itself (III.6, *NPNF* 1 I, p. 63).

Reason and Certitude

Doubt and the Hunger for Certainty

It is understandable that a finite human being, troubled with the vicissitudes of life, should hunger for certainty in knowledge, or at least for high reliability, to whatever degree is possible. But how does one *know*? How is it possible to be sure that we know what we think we know? These are perennial questions of epistemology, but in certain crucial times, especially amid sorrow, illness, and death, our usual rational explanations become stretched to their limit. As every pastor knows, these are the very times when theological questions are profoundly asked. These crucial moments make it exceptionally difficult to answer the question, How do we know what we seem to know, or what we seem to know in part? Life constantly undoes our theories of knowing (Luther, *Letters of Spiritual Counsel* I, II, *LCC* XVIII, pp. 26–82; for much of what follows, I am indebted to Søren Kierkegaard, *Concl. Unsci. Post.*, Reinhold Niebuhr, *NDM*, and L. Harold DeWolfe, *TLC*).

The act of pardon in the Christian service of worship announces, "You are forgiven." But how does one know one is forgiven? Is there any relative certainty? Classical Christian teaching speaks of a circle of knowing: through the inner assurance of the Holy Spirit and the reliability of Scripture, the divine self-disclosure is knowable. But to what degree is certainty capable of being achieved in such statements? And if so, is it an empirical, or moral, certainty?

Multiple Levels of Reasoning

Christian teaching has long been aware of the difficulty of attaining rational certainty of any sort. All human reason, not theological reason alone, functions under the stubborn limitations of finitude and potential self-deception.

Reason may be defined in a preliminary way as the capacity for internal consistency of argument based on evidence. Both deductive and inductive processes are combined in this definition. Reason can too narrowly be defined in either an abstract, rationalistic, nonexperiential way or an excessively empirical, experiential way.

Rationalistic Method: Deductive Reasoning

Some rationalistic methods define reason in excessively nonexperiential, nonsensory, and abstract ways. Descartes wanted to reason by cutting off all sense experiencing, by locking himself up in a stove, blocking all sensory input, so that exclusively on the basis of his own internal reason he could see if he could come to any reliable knowledge (Descartes, *Meditations*; W. Temple, *Nature, Man, and God*). Descartes is a prototype of one who wanted to block out the experiential and sensory side of the dialectic of knowing. When he realized that he was doubting, he reasoned: If he could doubt, then he must be thinking, and if he was thinking, then he surely must *be*. Therefore he came to what he regarded as reliable knowledge (that he existed) on a purely nonsensory basis. In time, that tradition of rationalism (as represented by Descartes, Spinoza, Wolff, and others) easily became overextended, and its claims unqualified and overweening.

Classical Christian reasoning, by contrast, has not characteristically proceeded by discarding sense experience. It wants to use its deductive rational capacity, but only while utilizing to the fullest extent possible the inputs of sense experience, though admittedly there are finite limits to sense experience also. Reason depends, as Thomas Aquinas knew, upon sense perception, even though the senses may err. Thomas's arguments for the existence of God all began with sense experience, by looking around at the orderly processes of nature, causality, contingency, and language.

No one is consistently able to exact the rigorous tests of sense perception in order to gain knowledge that is familiar to much ordinary daily experiencing. Suppose we are considering the notion of the number 1000 squared. We can in our minds instantly calculate a million in order to find that exact number accurately. But we do not have to stop to count those one million units. If we did we would take the demands for sensory validation too far. We take for granted a reliable structure of interpretation, a (rational) mathematical formula, 1000 x 1000, and trust the reasoning by which we square a number.

Thus in a sense we take it on the authority of those who have worked with mathematics for a long time (and perhaps have even counted those numbers), even though counting may seem absurd if we already know the formula. We often work confidently on the basis of such nonsensory rational ideas without feeling any need to "count" (to validate our reasoning empirically).

Scientific Method: Inductive Reasoning

The *experimental method* that we find in modern natural and behavioral sciences is based upon careful observation of change under controlled conditions on the basis of sense experience. Vast scientific and historical accomplishments have resulted from this experimental method. Yet this method has been alleged by some modern advocates (e.g., B. F. Skinner, Ivan Pavlov, Karl Popper, A. J. Ayer) to be the only way to know anything. There is little doubt that Christianity can make admirable use of empirical data gathering and scientific experimentation, but they are of limited value when we are talking about the central concerns of Christian teaching: the meaning of history, sin, grace, atonement, and sacramental life. The experimental method is useful when quantifiable objects are measured and changes observed, but God is not a quantifiable object. Christian teaching does not dismiss or deride experimental psychology, sociology, biology, or physics. It has learned much and can learn more from the data of the experimental sciences, natural and behavioral, and does not object to those methodologies per se, where quantifiable objects are being investigated.

These sciences ordinarily seek to isolate a single variable and try to account through some kind of quantifiable data-gathering process for a demonstrable change in that single variable that is repeatable and that can be experimentally reproduced and validated in a laboratory. But can one utilize that method effectively when attempting to speak significantly to the question of the meaning of suffering, the forgiveness of sin, or the overarching purpose of the historical process? The empirical method has limited usefulness in approaching poetry, literary analysis, religious experience, or love, all of which are grasped intuitively by a *Gestalt* or pattern of looking at personal knowledge that is seldom subject to exhaustive empirical analysis. Christian teaching in particular is looking for a pattern at work in all human history, to grasp the meaning of history (Augustine, CG XVIII, NPNF 1 II, pp. 361 ff.), so empirical method can take one only incompletely toward this understanding.

Hence both these methods that are available to us have positive but

limited value: a rationalistic method and an empirical method. Both
are needed; both are insufficient to the subject matter of the study of
God.

Pragmatic Reasoning

There is another type of reasoning, prevalent primarily in the
American tradition, sometimes called pragmatic reasoning, which essentially judges the truth of a thing in terms of its results, practical
application, or impact (William James, *Pragmatism; Essays on Faith and
Morals*; C. S. Peirce, *Collected Papers*, vol. VI, par. 465 ff.). This method
of reasoning also has been useful to a certain degree in Christian
teaching about God, salvation, and community. For Christian truth
hopes also to "work," to turn into practical acts, to be applied. But
what pragmatism tends to neglect is the level of the truth question
that lies prior to its practical application. Pragmatism is not so much
interested in asking whether a proposition or affirmation is true or
false as in asking only whether it has a practical or useful effect of
some kind (J. B. Pratt, *What Is Pragmatism?*). That is not as deep as
Christian teaching seeks to go.

Convergence of Plausibility

The method of *comprehensive coherence* is yet another, more complex,
type of classical pastoral reasoning. The search for comprehensive
coherence is the attempt to grasp or see as most probably true that
proposed solution to a problem which is on the whole supported by
the greatest net weight of evidence from all quarters—deductive and
inductive reasoning, logic and scientific method, historical reasoning,
Scripture, and tradition. It is a centered intuitive act of drawing together of insights or data from widely varied resources and searching
for their interrelated implicit meaning or convergence of plausibility
(Clementina, *Hom.* II, *ANF* VIII, pp. 229, 230).

The knowing of God is at times something like a detective story,
but one in which the answer is crying out to be revealed, the clues
lying about everywhere. Some of the evidence is circumstantial, some
requires careful data gathering; other steps need clear reasoning, faithfulness to credible sources, or sharp intuition. Comprehensive coherence is that kind of reasoning which says that the most adequate
explanation of something is the one that brings into focus the most
widely varied inputs into a single, cohesive, tentatively meaningful
frame of reference. Intuitive reasoning based on facts seeks to ascertain whether the overall evidence is reasonable or not. It differs from
strict laboratory or experimental conditions in its breadth, variety, and

imaginativeness. Scientific experimentation tries to bracket out these broader intuitions and insights and focus upon a single, manipulatable, objective variable (cf. Anatolius, *Fragments from the Books on Arithmetic*, ANF VI, pp. 152, 153; Reinhold Niebuhr, *NDM* I, pp. 18–24, 104 ff.). But the single-variable approach can box the inquirer into a vision that is highly constricted.

The study of God, ironically, is distinguished from empirical science in that it seeks to account for the greatest possible number of variables, rather than a single variable. For this unique study asks about the meaning of history. This is one way of describing the central task of theology: to give a credible account for the meaning of history, creation to consummation, viewed as God's story (Luke 1:3; cf. 1 Chron. 11:11; 2 Chron. 13:22; Ps. 81:10). To deny a hearing to any kind of data by a prior and arbitrary limitation of method risks losing that part of the truth. Historically, theology has been relatively more willing to investigate speculative hypotheses, eschatology, psychological intuition, paranormal phenomena, and moral conscience than have the behavioral sciences, which have often ruled out such hypotheses.

In pleading for an attitude of openness to evidence, Augustine remarked that "every good and true Christian should understand that wherever he may find truth, it is his Lord's" (*On Chr. Doctrine* II.18, *LLA*, p. 54). If God is the deepest truth (even though not fully fathomed), wherever the truth appears, there is some evidence of God's presence (Clement of Alex., *Strom.* I.13, ANF II, p. 313). Truth has self-evidencing power (Clementina, *Hom.* III.36, ANF VIII, p. 123). So theology can look for evidence anywhere.

However open to any truth one may be, any evidence may be distorted by human egocentricity and finitude, for all our perceptions are finite. We see the world from a very limited perspective. We ourselves have not lived for more than a few decades, yet human beings have lived in cities for at least twelve thousand years. *Homo erectus* is said to date back three or four million years, and the earth's history perhaps four and a half billion years. Our sufferings for one another are placed by the historical reasoning of the New Testament in the context of the "purpose of God hidden for ages" (Eph. 3:9; cf. vv. 10–13; Col. 1:26).

The most perplexing problems of epistemology are rooted more fundamentally in the basic dilemma of human existence—human finitude, with freedom to imagine. The fundamental paradox of being a human being is the fact that we live in nature, and are restricted by nature, yet we are capable of self-transcendence, of life in the spirit. We are not explainable to ourselves merely in terms of naturalistic reductionisms, yet we are not transnatural or superpersonal angels or unembodied intelligences. Human existence is by definition a combination of the natural and transnatural, rooted in nature and the causal order, yet with capacity for self-determination and self-transcendence.

This is symbolized in the Christian community by shorthand language: body and soul, or *sōma* and *psychē*. There is no body/soul dualism, because in Scripture the psycho-somatic interface is kept so taut—the *psychē* is constantly affected by the body, and the body is nothing (except a corpse) without its living reality, the *psychē*. The soul is never in history unembodied (not even in the Resurrection!), and the body that lacks soul lacks life. The person (psycho-somatically, paradoxically conceived) is wrapped in causal chains, yet exists as free—finite, yet capable of transcending finitude. Human life is "a sort of connecting link between the visible and invisible natures" (John of Damascus, *OF* II.12, *NPNF* 2 IX, pp. 30, 31).

This boundary location of the perceiver makes perception all the more difficult to fathom. Even though one knows one is perceiving something, one does not always know the depths or limits of the perception. Every human being has the task of holding both sides of that composite together in a meaningful way (Kierkegaard, *Sickness unto Death*, I.1, pp. 146 ff.).

Epistemology is that troubled inquiry that seeks to understand how we can possibly know anything. It reflects the tension of the larger human problem: finite freedom. Empiricism has inordinately focused upon data gathered by sensory experience. Rationalism has inordinately focused upon the reason that transcends the natural, that which gives order to this natural vitality. The history of philosophy reveals both tendencies in various combinations in various periods (Reinhold Niebuhr, *NDM* I, pp. 1 ff.). Empiricism may become exaggerated, in the form of a radical skepticism, so as to overemphasize the competency of sense experience. Exaggeration of the power of reasoning may lead into a soft, fuzzy trap of abstract idealism, such as in Hegel. Regardless of which side comes to the fore, the problems of epistemology remain rooted in the fundamental dilemma of being a human being.

Problems and Limits of Radical Skepticism

Dependence of Reason on Experience

This brings us full circle, surprisingly, back to the limits of radical skepticism. Our data are not infallible. This is true even in the natural sphere—for example, when you put a stick in the water and it appears to bend. To account for this, you have to discount the bent appearance of the stick. Our sensory apparatus is always having to make these kinds of adjustments and to apply checks to itself. We are the victims of optical illusions, mirages in the desert, delusions, and dreams. Even when our sensory powers are working under the most favorable conditions, we still see the world from quite a limited perspective.

From critics like Hume we hear doubt cast upon causality itself. We had assumed that we could always rely on the fact that effects are produced by causes, but Hume argued that this is merely a habit of mind—assuming that certain causes are going to elicit certain effects—but that one cannot necessarily infer thereby that what now appear to be ironbound causal laws might not later be viewed with different eyes. Although overstated by Hume, this critique bids us be humble about the competency both of our capacity to reason and our capacity to rely upon sensory input (Hume, *Dialogues Concerning Natural Religion, Phil. Works* II, pp. 411 ff.).

Moreover, if all claims to have received a revelation from God were to be automatically accepted, fanaticism would be welcomed, and the easy credit would lead to constant bankruptcy. Reason functions to sort out the legitimacy of claims of alleged revelation in the light of whatever one has already learned about God through comprehensive coherence (1 Thess. 5:21; cf. 2 Cor. 11:1–21).

Data received must often be corrected on the basis of subsequent experiences, and those experiences in turn await being corrected by later experiences, only to find that later experiences then have to be again corrected by earlier experiences, and so on (Jer. 5:3). The dilemma deepens: How can we be assured that there are not yet-to-be-discovered important data that will challenge or contradict our currently assumed reliable and constructive knowledge?

The Dependence of Reason on Unproved Postulates

We not only have practical difficulties with establishing sensory evidence in every discrete case, but our reasoning also depends upon assumptions and postulates to which no data-gathering process can appeal, and that no data-gathering process can establish and that no reasoning process can prove without assuming these postulates precisely while the proofs are being attempted (Origen, *De Princip.*, preface, *ANF* IV, pp. 239–41). Two examples are the intelligibility of nature and the principle of consistency.

One example is the elementary principle of the intelligibility of nature: Any attempt to communicate through language involves the assumption that we are living in an intelligible order. Yet how can one prove that assumption? It remains an axiom, an assumption that lies quietly behind our reasoning (Augustine, *Soliloquies* II, *LCC* VI, pp. 41–63).

Another assumption is the principle of consistency: If genuinely contradictory ideas can be true at the same time, then no argument for or against any conclusion has any force. Yet there is no way to establish that principle empirically, and no way to demonstrate it rationally without first depending on it (Anselm, *Concerning Truth* IX ff., *TFE*, pp. 107 ff.).

The Impossibility of Radical Skepticism

This takes us to the hypothesis of complete skepticism about knowing anything. The ancient skeptic Carneades asserted that it is impossible to know anything at all. He thought that we must base any truth on premises that we already hold, and that if we attempt to prove the premises, we can only move back toward other premises upon which we base our proof (N. MacColl, *The Greek Skeptics*, cf. Augustine, *On the Profit of Believing*, NPNF 1 III, pp. 347 ff.). Thus we are pressed toward a total skepticism.

This is really the humorous conclusion of this chapter's trajectory thus far: The reason no philosophy has been able to teach or embrace a complete skepticism is that it is impossible to do it. *To believe that nothing can be known is to believe that even the meaning of that belief cannot be known.* If you believe that you can know nothing, you have to be skeptical also of that belief (Tho. Aq., *ST* II–II Q60, I, pp. 1448, 1449). So even the most radical skepticism stumbles back with an internal contradiction. Even if you should try to teach the notion that nothing can be known, you are involved in an absurdity, because to teach it would be to assert that you know something. Skepticism is the yielding of the mind to a conviction of the impossibility of certainty, accompanied by a complacency about such a condition. Since skepticism *believes* that there is no truth, it must itself be classified as a *faith* in the reliability of ignorance (Pope, *Compend.* I, p. 48; DeWolfe, *TLC*, I). This insight helps theology to move through and beyond the morass of skepticism.

Though absolute certainty is not deductively or inductively attainable, complete skepticism is even more logically absurd, and cannot be maintained in practice. It is unreasonable to lay a radical demand upon ourselves, as we proceed theologically, to prove everything empirically, as some scientific and philosophical critics of religion expect. But that is no excuse for not taking as seriously as possible the evidentiary process so as to try to bring into our consciousness as many factors as we possibly can that will appeal to a comprehensively cohesive form of reasoning.

Historical Reasoning

This is why the predominant form of reasoning in Christian theology has been a somewhat different form of reasoning, namely, historical reasoning. The Old Testament view of reasoning about God is historical in scope and method. Yahweh repeatedly refers to himself in distinctively historical terms: "I am the God of Abraham, Isaac, and Jacob" (Exod. 3:15, 16; Mark 12:26) and often rehearses to the Israelites the mighty deed he has done in history (Joshua 24:2–13; Ps. 136).

God meets us not just in our inner thoughts but in history, demonstrating the divine presence and power through events (Deut. 11:1–4; cf. 1 Cor. 2:4). "The Lord is righteous in his acts; he brings justice to all who have been wronged. He taught Moses to know his way and showed the Israelites what he could do. The Lord is compassionate and gracious, long-suffering and forever constant" (Ps. 103:6–8). That the Lord is compassionate and gracious is known by recollecting God's historical activity (Irenaeus, *Ag. Her.* V.21, 22, *ANF* I, pp. 548–51; Cyril of Jerusalem, *Catech. Lect.* VI, *NPNF* 2 VII, pp. 33–43).

One who wishes to get in touch with God's demonstration of his justice and mercy in history must look candidly at universal history and learn to reason about all of history from the vantage point of a special history—Israel's. To know Yahweh at all one must look particularly toward the distinctive ways in which Yahweh has become self-revealed in history. The Hebraic way of reasoning is to tell a story. History telling or narrative is the distinctively Hebraic way of reasoning—a highly complex mode of theo-historical reasoning (Ezra 1:1–4; Neh. 1:1–4; Amos 1:1–5).

Hegel employed a different kind of historical reasoning. He theorized that reason is manifesting itself in historical processes, so that what is going on in history he called Absolute Reason unfolding itself. This historical reason, he argued, displays a recognizable logic that can be seen in every discrete historical unfolding. His effort centered upon seeking to understand the logic of history. The pattern he recognized recurrently was that of a force followed by a counterforce, and then a synthesis made possible by the conflict of those two energies. The same form of reasoning is found in Hegel's psychology and political thought, epistemology and metaphysics. Everywhere Hegel looked he saw this kind of reasoning in history working itself out in thesis, antithesis, and synthesis. Scripture does not argue for this sort of predictable logic, yet Hegel's fundamental idea (however unbiblically rationalized) is derived from Hebraic historical consciousness. It is a unique type of reasoning—*reasoning derived from history*, especially the history of God's mighty deeds (Eusebius, *Preparation for the Gospel* VII, I, pp. 321 ff.; Augustine, *CG* XVI, *NPNF* 1 II, pp. 309 ff.; cf. Hegel, *Reason in History*; Kierkegaard, *Concl. Unsci. Post.*).

Ordinarily the final meaning of a person's or nation's history is only knowable at the end of the story. One cannot write a definitive biography of Gandhi until his life is over. A living person or nation could always take a new turn, and make subsequent choices that would bear upon the meaning of the whole. Suppose the meaning of human history is to become knowable only at its end, as virtually all late-Judaic apocalyptic writers assumed (the Books of Enoch, the Apocalypse of Baruch, and War of the Sons of Light against the Sons of Darkness), for *apokalypsis* refers to the final uncovering of meaning that had been hidden.

Jesus was born into a community saturated with expectations that the end of a grossly distorted history would eventually reveal its meaning, however disastrous the present may be (cf. Daniel, 2 Esdrus, and the Assumption of Moses). Suppose, however, that an event occurs in history that *reveals the meaning of the end before the end*. This is what happened in Jesus Christ—his incarnation, crucifixion, and resurrection, the one mighty deed of God that bestows significance upon all human deeds (Lactantius, *Div. Inst.* IV.25–30, *ANF* VII, pp. 126–34).

Supposing that such a revealing event had occurred in history, would it not be necessary that it be followed by a remembering community, one that sought to preserve the meaning of the whole historical process revealed in that event? Would it not be understandable if a community of celebration followed that event that remembered it, shared in it, and proclaimed its meaning to all who would hear? (Methodius, *Three Fragments, Hom. on the Cross and Passion of Christ, ANF* VI, pp. 399–401).

Such a community has emerged in Christian history, reasoning out of this event, seeking to make it understandable in each new cultural-historical context. Through a gradual process of canonization, the documents witnessing to this event became received as Holy Writ, attested by the Spirit as a reliable point of contact with the originative event through which the meaning of history—God's Word to humanity—became clarified. Something like this process occurred in the historical Christian community. Each phase of history has required astute historical reasoning (e.g., Justin Martyr, *Dialogue with Trypho* LXXXII–CXLII, *ANF* I, pp. 240–70). Each new situation of the church has demanded a modestly revised form of historical reasoning—the recollection of revelatory events amid *these* particular new historical conditions. Hence, theological reasoning is historical reasoning.

What Purpose Does Reason Serve in the Study of God?

There are five classical explanations of why reason is required in any revelation: Reason is needed to receive the truth, distinguish truth from falsehood, reveal reason's own limitations by pointing beyond itself, interpret the truth, and transmit it to new generations.

TO RECEIVE REVELATION

A revelation can be made only to a potentially rational being. Stones do not receive revelation. Without reason even the most obvious revelation could not be apprehended or grasped. If God wished to reveal the truth to a stone, it would first be necessary to create in a stone some capacity to understand, or the capacity to reason, in order for it to receive the revelation (Tho. Aq., *ST* II–II Q2, II, pp. 1179–88; Gamertsfelder, *Syst. Theol.*, p. 126). One must assume in any revelation both the capacity to apprehend truth and the active openness of the mind to the truth offered. Reason helps faith to understand the content of what is to be believed (Augustine, *WAS*, p. 59).

TO DECIDE WHETHER OR WHEN REVELATION HAS OCCURRED

All alleged revelations cannot be taken seriously. Some are patently spurious, fraudulent, or manipulative claims (Hippolytus, *Refutation of all Heresies*, VII, *ANF* V, pp. 100 ff.; Kierkegaard, *Authority and Revelation: The Book on Adler*). The community has to sort out which self-proclaimed revelations are true and which are not. When a murderer claims that he acted by divine revelation, faith must utilize its rational-analytical capacity to sort out what is alleged to be true through divine revelation, though falsely, as distinguished radically from that which, by a larger process of comprehensive coherence, can be consensually received and understood as truly God's own revelation (Tho. Aq., *SCG* I.3, I, pp. 63 ff.).

Reason is required in order to judge the evidences of religious claims to revelation (Clement of Alex., *Strom.* VI.7–11, *ANF* II, pp. 492–502; Wesley, *WJW* VI, pp. 350–61; Hodge, *Syst. Theol.* I.3, pp. 58,

59). The evidence must be fitting to the truth purported. Truth conveyed through history requires historical evidence plausibly set forth. Truths of nature require natural, empirical, scientific evidence. Truths of the moral sphere require moral evidence. The "things of the Spirit" (Rom. 8:5) require the self-evidencing assurance of the Spirit (The Pastor of Hermas, II, comm. 10, 11, *ANF* II, pp. 26–28). In this way sound reasoning and faith's response to revelation do not contradict but complement each other.

TO SHOW THE REASONABLENESS OF THAT WHICH REASON ITSELF CANNOT ATTAIN

Augustine wrote:

God forbid that He should hate in us that faculty by which He made us superior to all other living beings. Therefore, we must refuse to believe as not to receive or seek a reason for our belief, since we could not believe at all if we did not have rational souls. So, then, in some points that bear on the doctrine of salvation, which we are not yet able to grasp by reason—but we shall be able to sometimes—let faith precede reason, and let the heart be cleansed by faith so as to receive and bear the great light of reason; this is indeed reasonable. (*Letters* 120:1, FC)

It is through reason that we may see that reason points beyond itself. It is reasonable that right reason know its own limits. Reason serves faith by pointing both beyond itself and to its own limits (Augustine, *Sermons on New Testament Lessons* LXXVI, *NPNF* 1 VI, pp. 481 f.; cf. LXVII, p. 465).

TO INTERPRET AND APPLY REVEALED TRUTH

Even if a community had received divinely revealed truth, and recognized it as such, it must still use reason to discover the implications of this truth amid its historical context, expressed in its own language. Even after we have learned that God is revealed as just and requires justice, we still must ask what that justice means for us and how it is to apply to our particular situation. This requires reason (Tho. Aq., *SCG* III. 121–22, pp. 141–47; Wakefield, *CSCT*, pp. 20–22; Gamertsfelder, *Syst. Theol.*, p. 128; DeWolfe, *Theol. of a Living Church*). It is by reason that the believer learns to utilize analogies in the service of the truth, to make observations from nature and history, and to remove doubts by setting forth reasonable arguments. The teachings of faith are exhibited, clarified, and made rhetorically persuasive by good reasoning (Augustine, *Conf.* XI.25–31, *NPNF* 1 II, pp. 172–75).

Reason helps remove objections to belief (Augustine, *Letters* CII.38, *NPNF* 1 I, p. 425).

TO TRANSMIT THE MEANING OF REVELATION

To transmit truth to another, one must employ reasoning. To communicate from one rational mind to another, one must presuppose the rational capacity of both speaker and hearer. Reason is needed if one seeks either to understand or to make understandable the truth of Christian faith. No preaching, teaching, or apologetics can occur without some rational capacity. By reason, faith's wisdom is correlated with the insights of philosophy, history, political ethics, psychology, and other sciences (Clement of Alex., *Strom.* IV.18, *ANF* II, pp. 518–20).

Hence, reason is needed to receive revelation, to distinguish between true and false revelation, to help us to believe what we cannot see, to interpret the truth of revelation in the present, and to transmit revelation to emergent historical situations.

Authorized Prerogatives of Reason

No one can be required to believe absurdities. The mind is God-given and has a responsibility to reject falsity. If a claim of religion requires that which negates or contradicts a previous, duly authenticated revelation of God, it is to be rejected as false religion, and inconsistent with faith's reasoning. Paul went to great lengths with the Galatians to urge consistency of teaching with the original apostolic teaching: "But if anyone, if we ourselves or an angel from heaven, should preach a gospel at variance with the gospel we preached to you, he shall be held outcast" (Gal. 1:8).

God would be inconsistent as just and good if, holding human freedom *responsible* for its moral conduct, God provided neither sufficient means for human beings to *recognize* the moral good nor any evidence of the divine will. If human beings are to be held responsible for themselves, they must have some capacity to know the good, and to recognize their own failure to do good. "How could they invoke one in whom they had no faith?" asked Paul. "And how could they have faith in one they had never heard of?" (Rom. 10:14). Yet unbelief does not arise out of ignorance alone. It arises willfully because "men preferred darkness to light because their deeds were evil" (John 3:19).

The earliest Christians were warned against naiveté: "Do not trust any and every spirit, my friends; test the spirits, to see whether they are from God, for among those who have gone out into the world there are many prophets falsely inspired" (1 John 4:1). Furthermore, a standard of judgment is given: "This is how we may recognize the

Spirit of God: every spirit which acknowledges that Jesus Christ has come in the flesh is from God" (1 John 4:2).

Christian faith concedes to reason what is rightfully its due. God does not reveal himself to irrational, but rational, creatures, capable of distinguishing between true and false evidence. Revelation does not imply faith in the absurd or impossible, or faith based on ignorance. Christian faith opposes anti-intellectual obscurantism as much as it does extreme skepticism. Faith resists a blind fidism that believes without examining the evidence; and a defensive skepticism that believes only its doubt of the credibility of all evidence (Tho. Aq., SCG I.4–7, pp. 66–75; Wesley, WJW VI, 350 ff.; Hodge, I.3, pp. 54, 55).

The Tendency of Reason Toward Egocentric Distortion

Although reason is intended to be put to good use, it is prone to distortion. The intended uses of reason have been divided into three categories: First, reason functions as an *organic* part of faith's reflection upon itself, as in the right use of logic, grammar, rhetoric, induction, and deduction. It is necessary to use reason, for example, to translate Scripture into various languages (Augustine, *On Chr. Doctrine*; Justin Martyr, *First Apol.*, ANF I, pp. 159–87). Second, reason has crucial *apologetic* functions, assisting faith in stating reasons for its conclusions where doubts about it have arisen (Justin Martyr, *Hortatory Address to the Greeks*, ANF I, pp. 273–90). And third, reason has a *polemical* use in the correction of error by argument (Hippolytus, *Refutation of All Her.*, ANF V; cf. Gerhard, *Loci* I, p. 76; cf. *DT*, pp. 36, 37). None of these functions would be possible without the use and application of rational criticism.

Yet reason since the fall has been blind, proud, vain, wrapped in error and self-deceit (Rom. 1:21; 1 Cor. 3:1; Gal. 4:8; Eph. 4:17, 18). Fallen reason is not able, without grace, to lift itself up to a recognition of the divine mysteries (Matt. 11:27; 1 Cor. 2:14–16). Hence reason may become harnessed for evil as well as good. Reason may be utilized by egocentricity to more profoundly oppose revelation, faith, hope, and love (Rom. 8:6; 1 Cor. 2:11 ff.; 3:18–20; cf. R. Niebuhr, *Moral Man and Immoral Society*). Fallen reason stands in need of repentance, cleansing, and conversion, so that it too might become captive to the obedience of Christ (2 Cor. 10:4, 5). Hence, because of its self-deceptions, natural reason unaided by grace is not to be viewed as an adequate rule for judging faith or revelation (Gerhard, *Loci* II, pp. 362 ff.; cf. *DT*, p. 34).

The rational capacity of Adam and Eve (symbolic of all humanity) is twisted by pride, anxiety, guilt, and self-assertion. Thus our remarkable rational capacity has become, to some degree, an instrument of sin, guilt, and death. We use reason to promote wrongdoing and to do evil. The biblical notion of distorted, alienated, self-assertive reason has increased the realism of the Christian understanding of humanity. Nonetheless, the right use of reason is thought by most classical exegetes to be useful and necessary—not as a rule of faith, and never as absolute judge of faith, but as an aid to faith's reflection upon its source and ground. "Theology does not condemn the use of Reason, but its abuse and its affectation of directorship, or its magisterial use, as normative and decisive in divine things" (Quenstedt, *TDP* I, p. 43, in *DT*, p. 35).

Whether Faith Has Reasons That Reason Does Not Know

Faith

The term *faith* (*pistis*) is utilized in the New Testament with several levels of meaning. Faith is

- the recognition through the active life of the Spirit of, "the evidence of things not seen" (Heb. 11:1 KJV)
- an active trust or confidence, as when one asks "in faith, nothing doubting" (*en pistei, mēden diakrinomenos*, James 1:6)
- a belief, trust, and assurance in God's righteousness in Christ that is active by love and yields the fruit of good works
- the act of believing; for example, when one says, "I believe" (Apostles' Creed) one is saying "I have faith that . . . "
- a body of truth confessed as necessary for salvation, as in "the faith once delivered to the saints" (Jude 3, KJV), or the Christian religion for which the believer contends (1 Tim. 6:12)
- reliability, or constancy in fulfilling one's promises, as when Paul speaks of the "faithfulness of God" (Rom. 3:3)
- trust in the intelligibility of the cosmos that premises scientific inquiry (Ps. 89:1–8)
- obedience, or the obedience of faith, which stands ready to be guided by duly constituted authority (Rom. 16:26)

All these varied shades of meaning cohere, interflow, and coalesce in Christian teaching concerning faith (cf. Ambrose, *Of the Chr. Faith*, prologue, I.4; II.Intro.; II.11, 15, *NPNF* 2 X, pp. 201, 206, 225, 236, 240; Augustine, *On Psalms* LI, *NPNF* 1 VIII, p. 195; Luther, *Freedom of a Chr.*, *ML*, pp. 56–61; *TDNT*; *TDOT*). Faith includes the capacity to discern by grace the things of the Spirit, and to trust in the reliability of the divine Word (Cyril of Jerusalem, *Catech. Lect.* V, *NPNF* 2 VII, pp. 29–32). Faith embraces the complementary meanings of the trusting frame of mind that has confidence in Another and the trustworthiness that can be relied upon (Tho. Aq., *ST* I–II Q1–13, I, pp. 1169–1233; Calvin, *Inst.* 3.2).

Faith does not occur without grace: "Yes, it was grace [*chariti*] that saved you, with faith [*pisteōs*] for its instrument" (Eph. 2:8, Knox). When grace enlivens reason, reason is not subverted but empowered. Human reasoning, by grace, appropriates divine truth without ceasing to be human reasoning. When reason discerns the truth God speaks, it does not do so without God's grace. God cannot be comprehensively grasped by any human reason, but some aspect of God can be grasped by faith's reasoning which leads not to a false God or an illusion of God, but truly to God insofar as God becomes accessible to human knowing (Basil, *Letters, To Amphilochius*, CCXXXV, CCXXXVI, *NPNF* 2 VIII, pp. 274–79).

Since faith is the discernment of spiritual truth, faith is not separable from reasoning, rightly understood. Rather, faith is a way of reasoning out of God's self-disclosure, assisted by grace. In faith the reasoning is directed to the things of the spirit, rather than to empirical data. Hence it is impossible to have faith without reasoning, or belief without any form of thinking, although our thinking is always inadequate to its infinite Subject. Since faith enlarges human vision, the logic of faith is an enlarged, not a diminished, logic (Tho. Aq., *SCG* I.1–9, I, pp. 59–78).

The struggle of Christian teaching against various exaggerated rationalisms is not a struggle against reason but against the misapplication of reason—such as when reason is made the sole judge of revelation, or when reason completely refuses to credit true revelation. There can also be an overdependence upon speculative reasoning, or a distorted technical reason that functions without moral constraints. Hence excessive rationalisms pervert the function of reason and thereby undermine the appropriate service of reason to the study of God. Rationalism can turn into a tight and uncritical dogmatism just as religion can.

Classical Christian writers have sought to show that faith does not conflict with right reason, that there is harmony between revelation's historical way of reasoning and reason's respect for all the evidence, and that human reasoning is made more plausible and whole when the premise of historical revelation is received. But Christian reasoning cannot proceed without the assistance of grace and the premise of revelation.

The Data Base of Faith's Reasoning

If authority of Scripture and tradition are objective criteria of theology, then faith and reason must be considered as subjective criteria, but in different ways. For as Scripture is definitive for tradition, so does faith set the context and bounds in which faith's historical reasoning operates.

Unless we cling to the absurdity of rejecting the benefit of any experience of any others, our reasoning must depend upon some external authority. This is true of scientific reasoning, which is dependent upon the consensually shared authority of induction, observation, hypothecation, and deduction.

In theology, the inductive data base of experiences and observations is mediated to us from many others—countless examples of faith, suffering, martyrdom, and witness stretching over many centuries, relayed to us through unwritten and written sources. It is the language of this community's experience with which theology has primarily to deal. Among the written sources are those consensually designated by the community as canonical Scripture, as authoritative witness to the revelation of God. The Holy Spirit guides the preservation and guarantees the trustworthiness of scriptural witness. Scripture rightly interpreted remains the reliable guide to revelation upon which faith is based. Reason cannot proceed without the testimony of Scripture. Reason has its data base in Scripture as tested through tradition and experience.

However great may be the differences between philosophy and theology, as different as are reason and revelation, these two spheres are not locked in endless antagonism. One thinks in the light of natural intellect, the other in the light of God's self-disclosure in history. Both think either toward or from the truth.

It is from a surprising quarter, seventeenth-century Lutheran Scholasticism, that the faith/reason relationship is most beautifully stated: "Anyone who would deny those things which are visible in a greater light because he had not seen them in the smaller, would fail to appreciate the design and benefit of the smaller, so also he who denies or impugns the mysteries of faith revealed in the light of grace, on the ground that they are incongruous with Reason and the light of nature, fails, at the same time, to make a proper use of the office and benefits of Reason and the light of nature" (Johann Gerhard, *Loci* II, p. 372, in *DT*, p. 33).

Faith's Presentation of Evidences to Reason

The revelation given by God is addressed primarily to faith, and only in a secondary sense to reason. Faith receives the self-evidencing divine disclosure in the special certitude constituted by trust and by assurance through the Spirit. However, this same faith is then charged with the task of gaining the assent of unbelieving hearers in the world (Athenagoras, *A Plea for the Chr.*, ANF II, pp. 123–48; Tatian, *Address to the Greeks*, ANF II, pp. 59–84). As faith receives revelation, so faith then seeks to pass on the evidences of revelation to others, utilizing reason where appropriate to state, clarify, and present these evidences (Augustine, *Ag. the Epis. of Manichaeus* I–V, *NPNF* 1 IV, pp. 129–31).

In addressing faith primarily, revelation addresses a human faculty seated in the human constitution, the faculty of believing. This faculty is at work, accepting the truth on sufficient evidence, wherever human knowing occurs, and especially spiritual knowing (1 Cor. 2:11–16; Heb. 7:14–25; 11:1 ff.).

Believing is that faculty that "makes us certain of realities we do not see" (Heb. 11:1). It enables the heart to recognize "the truth as it is in Jesus" (Eph. 4:21). No other human faculty is sufficiently competent to recognize this truth. For faith is to the unseen world what the senses are to the visible world (Maximus, *Four Centuries on Charity* III.92–99, ACW 21, pp. 190–92). Faith is the eye that sees what the senses cannot see, the ear that hears what the senses do not hear. One who lacks this eye and ear "refuses what belongs to the Spirit of God; it is folly to him; he cannot grasp it, because it needs to be judged in the light of the Spirit" (1 Cor. 2:14; Gregory Nazianzen, *Or.* XXVIII, *NPNF* 2 VII, pp. 290–91).

Faith in God is not alien to the human condition, because "the Spirit of God himself is in man, and the breath of the Almighty gives him understanding" (Job 32:8). This Spirit already at work within us discerns the truth, receives its evidence, and celebrates its veracity (Augustine, *On Trin.* IV.22–32, *NPNF* 1 III, pp. 85, 95). The coming of Jesus is like the coming of a light that is offered to "enlighten every one," even though some prefer darkness (John 1:9–12). The Revealer "knew men so well, all of them, that he needed not evidence from others about a man, for he himself could tell what was in a man" (John 2:25). Since God empathized with our limitations, he radically adapted the evidence of revelation to the human condition, so that even amid our self-assertive deceptions we might be able to recognize the truth incarnate and the Spirit of truth (John 1:14; 16:13).

One who prejudicially resists this evidence has "a distorted mind and stands self-condemned" (Titus 3:11). Such persons "defy the truth; they have lost the power to reason, and they cannot pass the tests of faith" (2 Tim. 3:8).

Faith Is a Way of Reasoning

In this way the Scriptures viewed faith as sound reason. Hence faith and reason are deeply bound and melded together in inextricable spiritual kinship. The same Spirit who has called forth faith also awakens reason to receive "the mystery that has been kept hidden for ages and generations, but is now disclosed to the saints" (Col. 1:26), a mystery reason of itself cannot fathom. The evidences of God's self-disclosure that faith recognizes, faith now calls upon reason to recognize and credit. In this way the judgment of the mind is given the honor of examining the evidences of faith. While faith is raised up to receive and embrace revelation, reason is bowed low to behold its self-giving love. Faith does not despise reason, but presents those evidences for revelation in history that are understandable to reason (Wesley, WJW VI, pp. 351 ff.).

But what are these evidences that faith presents to reason? They are Scripture's recollections of the divine self-disclosure in history. Through the presentation of these evidences, the believer is taught to "be always ready with your defence [pros apologian, ready to provide reasons] whenever you are called to account for the hope that is in you" (1 Pet. 3:15). Luke wrote his Gospel as "a connected narrative" (diēgēsin) for Theophilus, "so as to give you authentic knowledge" (epignōs, Luke 1:4) of the coming of the Saviour (Luke 2:11). So every believer, and especially everyone in public ministry, needs to be supplied with such "authentic knowledge" to provide credible reasons concerning the reliability (asphaleian, certainty) of that in which they have been instructed (Luke 1:4). It was just such "an outline of the sound teaching which you heard from me" (2 Tim. 1:13) that Timothy was instructed to keep before him, so that the reasons for faith might be readily available to him.

The Clementine Recognitions (mid fourth century) commended the process of asking hard questions of faith, requiring faith to reason about itself:

Do not think that we say that these things are only to be received by faith, but also that they are to be asserted by reason. It is not safe to commit these things to bare faith without reason, since assuredly truth cannot be without reason. And therefore he who has received these things fortified by reason can never lose them; whereas he who receives them without demonstrations, by an assent to a simple statement of them, can neither keep them safely, nor is certain if they are true. . . . And therefore, according as any one is more anxious in demanding a reason, by so much will he be the firmer in preserving his faith. (*Recognitions* II.69, *ANF* VIII, p. 116)

The Trustworthiness to Which Trust Responds

Faith is not merely intellectual assent to propositions about God. Faith (*pistis, fiducia*) is an entrusting of oneself to someone or something that is regarded as trustable (John of Damascus, *OF* IV.10, *NPNF* 2 IX, p. 79). One can think of this by analogy by asking oneself: Who do I trust and why? To answer that question autobiographically is to reflect profoundly upon one's relationships with others.

We learn to trust certain people because they make themselves known as trustworthy. I may live through a history together with another in which I know that whatever that person tells me will be dependable. I would never know that, hence never trust that person, unless there were a concrete history (including names, dates, and pivotal events) of trustworthiness that revealed that person's reliability.

So it is in the Christian community, that one's trust in time is placed in that Source and End of all things—God—as that eternal One who has become known through a historical process as unfailingly trustworthy. That is the story the Bible tells. The events are remembered as revealing the trustworthiness of God to Israel. The Bible witnesses to that history, to elicit that kind of trust (Ps. 40:1–4; Augustine, *On the Psalms* XL, *NPNF* 1 VIII, pp. 119–28). Such trust is not based upon abstract propositions, nor is it based upon psychological feelings about ourselves.

Christian faith is not a faith in faith. The central predicament of introverted pietism is faith based on faith itself, moving, like a dog chasing its tail, in a frustrating circle. Sound faith is based upon that which calls forth faith—a history of trustworthy relationships through which the other (human partner) or Other (divine partner) becomes somehow known as trustable. Words in themselves cannot engender that trust. It takes a history. Such a faith is not based upon projections of need or rhetoric or conceptualities, however good, but upon a history in which God has made himself known as caring partner and has shared his existence with us faithfully (Athanasius, *Ag. the Arians*

II.14.6–11, *NPNF* 2 IV, pp. 351–54; John Cassian, *Conferences* XIII.7–12, *NPNF* 2 XI, pp. 425–30).

Reasonable Acceptance of Legitimate Authority

The classical ecumenical writers argued that the acceptance of legitimate and reasonable authority is itself an eminently reasonable act, for both scientific and religious knowledge. When the believer trusts the church's authority to discern and canonize Scripture, distill from it the creed, and propose a rule of faith as a guide to scriptural truth, that is viewed as a reasonable act. "It behooves us to flee to the Church, and be brought up in her bosom, and be nourished with the Lord's Scriptures" (Irenaeus, *Ag. Her.* V.20.2, *ANF* I, p. 548).

Amid the horrors of persecution, Cyprian observed that whoever is able to call God Father, must first call the church Mother (*Epistles* LXXIII.7, *ANF* V, p. 388). If reasons appear that make it clear that the church's judgment has become untrustworthy, or its consensual judgment misguided, then the believer has a duty to question that authority. Such a predisposition toward ecclesial trust does not imply an abandonment of reason; rather, it assumes that the community is merely providing the believer with evidence for consideration, reflection, and testing against other forms of knowing. This predisposition to ecclesial trust is the very thing most lacking in the Protestant psyche; the whole basis for the Reformation being a "hermeneutic of suspicion" toward the Roman church (cf. Ricoeur, *Freud and Philosophy*, pp. 20 ff.).

Children conditionally accept the word of their parents and teachers who are seeking to present them with evidence that they then can duly examine, test, and draw their own conclusions about. Educators do not normally regard that act of conditional acceptance as irrational but rather as a reasonable openness to evidence under competent guidance. It is far less reasonable to suppose that the child must begin with a consistent attitude of radical distrust, as in a "hermeneutic of suspicion," toward those who are seeking to permit the child to examine evidence.

Similarly, the knowledge received through Scripture and church tradition remains subject to further exploration, experiential confirmation, and amendment by subsequent evidence. To depend upon Holy Writ and holy church for supplying the very evidence with which faith deals does not imply sacrifice of intellect, however, but a reasonable act of openness to evidence.

The Possibility of Faith

How is faith possible? We do not attain faith by simply saying we ought to have it; we do not logically derive it from deductive premises. Rather, faith comes by trusting in God by the power of the Spirit (Ps. 26:1). It is by faith that Abel's sacrifice was greater than Cain's, that Enoch was carried to another life, that Noah built the ark, that Abraham left Ur to go where he had never been, that Sarah conceived, that Isaac received the promises, that Moses left Egypt (Heb. 11). Faith walks by trusting and not always by seeing (cf. 2 Cor. 5:7). "Commit your life to the Lord; trust in him and he will act" (Ps. 37:5). As we learn to trust others by taking risks, so we learn to trust God, step-by-step, by risking trust. Those who will not risk small steps of trust will find the larger vision of God's trustability implausible (Luther, *Freedom of a Chr., ML*, pp. 56–61).

Faith is not simply poured down our throats without any choice of our own. It is at times a risk-laden choice amid hunger, fire, war, and death. But we do not get very far reasoning about God until we somehow enter into that sphere in which faith in God's historical revelation is taken seriously—hence the world of Scripture, of the celebrating community, of preaching and sacrament. There again and again we meet others who have taken risks in relation to that trustworthy One, and again and again, according to their witness, God makes himself known as trustable (Cyprian, *Treatises* III, *On the Lapsed, ANF* V, pp. 437 ff.).

All this remains subject to critical reflection. A broad historical data base, imagination, and critical reason all have been richly employed by historical Christianity. As we test out the trustability of God, trust is given a chance to grow. Such is the testimony of Jewish and Christian communities. It is only in the process of risking trust that God's trustworthiness becomes credible.

Faith is indeed *possible*, because we know that in this community God has been trusted. Nonetheless, since faith remains a risk-laden decision, no one can do it for any one else. Just as nobody can die for anybody else, nobody can believe for another (Luther, *Eight Sermons, WML* II, p. 391; cf. *Freedom of a Chr., ML*, pp. 66, 67).

In any event, life demonstrates that faith of some kind is *necessary* (Theophilus, *To Autolycus* I.8, *ANF* II, p. 91). We in fact do not live as free self-determining persons without trusting something, without casting our reliance upon something that renders our existence worthwhile, plausible, and meaningful (H. R. Niebuhr, *RMWC*, pp. 124 ff.).

For we cannot be human beings without making choices. The very essence of choosing involves risk, and where risk is, there is some form of trust, even if misguided (Kierkegaard, *Either/Or* II; *Judge for Yourselves!*).

People admittedly can have faith in what is unreliable, or untrue, or incompletely true, or untrustworthy. It is reasonable that our faith be attached to that which is more rather than less trustworthy, that is based upon a larger rather than a smaller range of comprehensive coherence. Such a rational duty would apply to every person who has the capacity to reason. For God did not give us the capacity for reason in order that reason be abused, but used (Clement of Alex., *Strom.*, VII.6 ff., *ANF* II, pp. 531 ff.).

Postlude: On Theo-Comic Perception

Finally we note the fundamental comedic contradiction that inheres in the study of God. It is the same contradiction that clings to human existence generally. For theology displays comedy since the seriousness of being human invites comedy.

God offers to humanity, along with other well-made gifts, the spirit of comic perception. It was not formally listed among the gifts of the Spirit because it is not formal and does not belong on a list. But the gifted in faith are seldom without it. It sees through sobriety to the unexpected reversal of human pride. It glimpses God's own delight in creation, and joy for humanity. It not only lightens the burden of human existence, which is especially desirable around decaying piles of theo-talk, it makes of the burden itself a certain delight.

We students of God, look at us: God's own image scratching our eczema; irritated by hemorrhoids, yet capable of the refracting divine goodness; biped animals who dream of eternity; playing God yet being bums, clowns, and louts—yet bums who can say from the heart, "God bless"; clowns who mime the posture of Superman; louts who can conceive of the idea of perfect being. We are curious about divine judgment, but a little less so than about the brakes on our car; recipients of rationality who cannot balance our bank accounts; living souls puzzled by death. Such a creature it is who takes up pen and ink and scribbles vague sentences about God; who breathes polluted air and speaks of Spirit; who uses the name of God mostly to intensify cursing, yet who calls God the Adorner of creation.

It is because humanity is a paradox that the human study of God is and remains a paradox, strewn with blood and flowers, with passing wind and singing hymns.

The manuscript of this book came to its last page, fittingly, on the feast day of Saint Lawrence, a deacon of the church of Rome martyred during the Valerian persecution of A.D. 258. The oral tradition holds that Lawrence was martyred by gridiron, and that after he had been "cooked" on one side, he said to his tormentors: "That side is done now, you can turn me over." The tradition that can laugh, not unsympathetically, at martyrdom, is surely healthier than one that can only bemoan inhumanities. Today is a fitting day to end this work, Saint Lawrence Day, August 10. I conclude with this respectful caveat in honor of Saint Lawrence:

One who leaves no room for the utter unseriousness of theology will not be taken seriously in speaking of God. Theology and comedy remain in closest proximity. For comedy views objectively the seriousness of theology (Kierkegaard, *Concl. Unsci. Post.*, pp. 46–55, 412 ff., 457 ff.). Comedy sees tragedy from the viewpoint of its resolution; hence comedy transcends tragic consciousness. This is why Kierkegaard knew that humor was, of all stages of consciousness, the nearest to religious consciousness.

Without a sharp eye for theo-comedy, the grandeur and misery of the human story are mistaken; the joy and pain of God are missed. Only with the capacity for comedy does a greater capacity for tolerance grow. For egocentric temptations are always seeking to inflate the fantasy that one's own time-bound, parochial way of reasoning toward or from God is the only way. The healthier the study of God, the more candid it remains about its own finitude, the stubborn limits of its own knowing, its own charades, Band-Aids, closets, masks, and broken windows.

That is why the study of God is best understood from within a caring community that laughs a little at its own somber efforts. Those whose faith offers corrective love empathically to others give a great gift. The gift is best wrapped in the brightly colored tissue of hope, in an atmosphere where theo-comic lightness about the pretended gravity of our words abounds.

Abbreviations

ACW *Ancient Christian Writers: The Works of the Fathers in Translation.* Edited by J. Quasten, J. C. Plumpe, and W. Burghardt. 44 vols. New York: Paulist Press, 1946–1985.

AF *The Apostolic Fathers.* Edited by J. N. Sparks. New York: Thomas Nelson, 1978.

AFT *Agenda for Theology.* Thomas C. Oden. San Francisco: Harper & Row, 1979.

Ag. Against

Alex. Alexandria

ANF *Ante-Nicene Fathers.* Edited by A. Roberts and J. Donaldson. 10 vols. 1885–1896. Reprinted ed., Grand Rapids, MI: Eerdmans, 1979. Book (in Roman numerals) and chapter or section number (usually in Arabic numerals), followed by volume and page number.

Angl. *Anglicanism, The Thought and Practice of the Church of England, Illustrated from the Religious Literature of the Seventeenth Century.* Edited by P. E. More and F. L. Cross. London: S.P.C.K., 1935.

Apol. Apology

Apost. Const. *Apostolic Constitutions.* Or Constitutions of the Holy Apostles. *ANF,* vol. 7.

Arndt *A Greek-English Lexicon of the New Testament and Other Early Christian Literature.* W. F. Arndt and F. W. Gingrich. (Translation of W. Bauer, 1953.) Chicago: University of Chicago Press, 1957.

BC *The Book of Concord,* (1580). Edited by T. G. Tappert. Philadelphia: Muhlenberg Press, 1959.

BCP *Book of Common Prayer* (1662). Royal Breviar's edition. London: S.P.C.K., n.d.

BPR *Book of Pastoral Rule.* Gregory the Great. *NPNF* 2 X.

BQT *Basic Questions in Theology.* 3 vols. W. Pannenberg. Philadelphia: Westminster Press, 1970–1973.

Brief Expl. *Brief Explanation of the Ten Commandments, Creed, and Lord's Prayer.* Martin Luther,, in *WML,* vol. 2, pp. 351–286.

BW *St. Anselm: Basic Writings.* Translated by S. N. Deane. LaSalle, IL: Open Court, 1966.

BWA *Basic Works of Aristotle.* Edited by R. McKeon. New York: Random House, 1941.

Catech. Catechism or Catechetical

Catech. Lect. Catechetical Lectures. Cyril of Jerusalem. *NPNF* 2 VII. Or *FC* 61, 64.

CC *Creeds of the Churches.* Edited by John Leith. Richmond, VA: John Knox Press, 1979.

CCC *Creeds, Councils, and Controversies.* Edited by J. Stevenson. London: S.P.C.K., 1966.

CD *Church Dogmatics.* Karl Barth. Edited by G. W. Bromiley, T. F. Torrance, et al. 4 vols. Edinburgh: T. & T. Clark, 1936–1969.

CDG *The Christian Doctrine of God.* William Newton Clarke. Edinburgh: T. & T. Clark, 1912.

CFS *Cistercian Fathers Series.* 44 vols. to date. Kalamazoo, MI: Cistercian Publications, 1968–.

CG *City of God.* Augustine. *NPNF* 1 II.

CH *Church History.* Eusebius of Caesarea. *NPNF* 2 I. See also *EH.*

Chr. Christian, Christians

CLRC *Courtenay Library of Reformation Classics.* 5 vols. Appleford, Abingdon, Berkshire, England: Sutton Courtenay Press, n.d.

COC *Creeds of Christendom.* Edited by P. Schaff. 3 vols. New York: Harper & Bros., 1919.

Comm. Commentary. Or Commonitory. Vincent of Lerins. *NPNF* 2 XI.

Compend. Compendium. Or Compendium of Theology. Thomas Aquinas. New York: Herder, 1947. Or Compendium of Christian Theology. William Burt Pope. 3 vols. New York: Phillips and Hunt, n.d.

Concl. Unsci. Post. Concluding Unscientific Postscript. Søren Kierkegaard. Princeton: Princeton University Press, 1944.

Conf. Confession. Or Confessions. Augustine. *LCC* VII. *NPNF* 1 I. *FC* 21.

CPWSF *Standard Edition of the Complete Psychological Works of Sigmund Freud.* 24 vols. to date. London: Hogarth Press, 1953–.

Crit. Pract. Reason Critique of Practical Reason. Immanuel Kant. *LLA.*

CSCT *A Complete System of Christian Theology.* Samuel Wakefield. New York: Carlton and Porter, 1862.

CSK *The Cell of Self-Knowledge. Seven Early English Mystical Treatises (including Divers Doctrines, Katherine of Seenes, and Treatise of Contemplation, Margery Kempe).* Edited by E. G. Gardner. New York: Duffield, 1910.

CSS *Cistercian Studies Series.* 68 vols. to date. Kalamazoo, MI: Cistercian Publications, 1968–.

CTC *Christianae Theologiae Compendium.* Johnannes Wollebius. Edited by Ernst Bizer. Neukirchen: 1935. English translation by John Beardslee, in *Reformed Dogmatics.* Grand Rapids, MI: Baker, 1977.

CUP *Concluding Unscientific Postscript.* Søren Kierkegaard. Princeton, NJ: Princeton University Press, 1941.

CWMS *Complete Writings of Menno Simons.* Edited by John C. Wenger. Scottdale, PA: Herald Press, 1956.

CWS *Classics of Western Spirituality.* Edited by Richard J. Payne et al. 30 vols. to date. Mahwah, NJ: Paulist Press, 1978–.

CWST *Complete Works of St. Teresa.* Teresa of Avila. Edited by E. Allison Peers. 3 vols. London: Sheed and Ward, 1946.

DCC Documents of the Christian Church. Edited by H. Bettenson. New York: Oxford, 1956.

DG The Doctrine of God. Herman Bavinck. Carlisle, PA: Banner of Truth, 1977.

Div. Inst. Divine Institutes. Lactantius. *ANF* VII.

Div. Names Divine Names. Dionysius (Pseudo-Dionysius). Translated by C. E. Rolt. London: S.P.C.K., 1975.

Dogm. Dogmatic

DT Doctrinal Theology of the Evangelical Lutheran Church. Heinrich Schmid. 3d ed. Minneapolis, MN: Augsburg, 1899.

DTh Dogmatic Theology. Francis Hall. New York: Longmans, Green, and Co., 1907–1922.

Eccl. Ecclesiastical

ECF Early Christian Fathers. Edited by H. Bettenson. London: Oxford University Press, 1969.

ECW Early Christian Writers: The Apostolic Fathers. Translated by Maxwell Staniforth. London: Penguin Books, 1968.

EH Ecclesiastical History. Eusebius of Caesarea. *FC* 19, 29.

EL Everyman's Library. New York: E. P. Dutton, 1910–

Epis. Epistle

Elem. Theol. Dog. Elements theologiae dogmaticae. Francois Xavier Schouppe. Brussels: H. Goemaere, 1863.

EPT Essays Philosophical and Theological. Rudolf Bultmann. New York: Macmillan, 1955.

ESS Exercitationes sacrae in symbolum. Sacred Dissertations. Hermann Witsius. Translated by D. Fraser. Utrecht: 1694. Edinburgh: A. Fullerton, 1823.

ETA Examen Theologicum Acroamaticum (1707). David Hollaz (or Hollatz). Leipzig: B. C. Brietkopf, 1763.

Exhort. Exhortation

Expos. Exposition

FC The Fathers of the Church: A New Translation. Edited by R. J. Deferrari. 69 vols. to date. Washington, DC: Catholic University Press, 1947–.

FEF The Faith of the Early Fathers. 3 vols. to date. Edited by William A. Jurgens. Collegeville, MN: Liturgical Press, 1970–.

FER The Fathers for English Readers. 15 vols. London: S.P.C.K., 1878–1890.

FGG From Glory to Glory, Texts from Gregory of Nyssa's Mystical Writings. Translated by H. Musurillo. New York: Scribner's, 1961.

Mystical Writings. Translated by H. Musurillo. New York: Scribner's, 1961.

GC Of God and His Creatures. Thomas Aquinas (abbreviated translation of Summa Contra Gentiles). Translated by Joseph Ricaby. Westminster, MD: Carroll Press, 1950.

Her. Heresies

Hex. Hexaemeron

Hist. History

Hom. Homilies or Homily

HPC A Harmony of Protestant Confessions. Edited by Peter Hall. London: J. F. Shaw, 1842.

Inst. Institutes of the Christian Religion. John Calvin. *LCC,* vols. 20, 21. References by book and chapter number.

Inst. Instruction, or *The Instructor.* Clement of Alexandria. *ANF* II.

IW The Inspired Word. Luis Alanso Schoekel. New York: Herder and Herder, 1965.

JJW Journal of John Wesley. Edited by N. Curnock. 8 vols. London: Epworth, 1938.

KC Kerygma and Counseling. Thomas C. Oden. San Francisco: Harper & Row, 1978.

KJV King James Version, 1611

LACT Library of Anglo-Catholic Theology. 99 vols. Oxford: Oxford University Press, 1841–1863.

LCC The Library of Christian Classics. Edited by J. Baillie, J. T. McNiell, and H. P. Van Dusen. 26 vols. Philadelphia: Westminster, 1953–1961.

LCF The Later Christian Fathers. Edited by H. Bettenson. Oxford: Oxford University Press, 1970.

LF A Library of Fathers of the Holy Catholic Church. Edited by E. B. Pusey, J. Kebel, J. H. Newman, and C. Marriott. 46 vols. Oxford: J. Parker, 1838–1875.

Literal Interp. of Gen. Literal Interpretation of Genesis. Augustine. *CWS.*

LLA Library of Liberal Arts. Edited by Oskar Piest. Indianapolis, IN: Bobbs-Merrill, 1951–.

Loeb Loeb Classical Library. Edited by T. E. Page, et al. Cambridge, MA: Harvard University Press, 1912–.

LPT Library of Protestant Thought. Edited by John Dillenberger. 13 vols. New York: Oxford University Press, 1964–1972.

LT Loci Theologicorum. Martin Chemnitz (1591). 3 vols. Frankfurt: N. Hoffmann, 1606.

LW Luther's Works. Edited by J. Pelikan and H. T. Lehmann. 54 vols. to date. St. Louis, MO: Concordia, 1953–.

LXX Septuagint (Greek Old Testament)

Metaphy. Metaphysics

ML Martin Luther: Selections From His Writings. Edited by John Dillenberger. New York: Doubleday, 1961.

MPG Patrologia Graeca. Edited by J. B. Migne. 162 vols. Paris: Migne, 1857–1876.

MPL Patrologia Latina. Edited by J. B. Migne. 221 vols. Paris: Migne, 1841–1865. General Index, Paris, 1912.

MTEC Mystical Theology of the Eastern Church. Vladimir Losskii. London: J. Clarke, 1957.

MWS Ministry of Word and Sacrament: An Enchiridion. Martin Chemnitz (1595). St. Louis, MO: Concordia, 1981.

Myst. Mystical, or mystery

NBD The New Bible Dictionary. Edited by J. D. Douglas et al. London: Intervarsity, 1962.

NDM Nature and Destiny of Man. Reinhold Niebuhr. 2 vols. New York: Scribner's, 1941, 1943.

NE A New Eusebius: Documents Illustrative of the History of the Church to A.D.

337. Edited by J. Stevenson, (based on B. J. Kidd). London: S.P.C.K., 1957.

NEB New English Bible

NIV New International Version

NPNF A Select Library of the Nicene and Post-Nicene Fathers of the Christian Church. 1st Series, 14 vols. 2nd series, 14 vols. Edited by H. Wace and P. Schaff. References by title and book or chapter, and subsection, and *NPNF* series no., volume and page number. New York: Christian, 1887–1900.

OBP On Becoming a Person. Carl R. Rogers. Boston: Houghton and Mifflin, 1961.

ODCC The Oxford Dictionary of the Christian Church. Edited by F. L. Cross. Revised by F. L. Cross and E. A. Livingstone. Oxford: Oxford University Press, 1974.

OUED Oxford Universal English Dictionary. 10 vols. Edited by C. T. Onions. Oxford: Oxford University Press, 1937.

OF On the Orthodox Faith. John of Damascus. *NPNF* 2 IX. FC 37.

Or. or Orat. Oration or orations

Phi. J. B. Phillips. The New Testament in Modern English.

Phil. Philosophy

Phil. Frag. Philosophical Fragments. Søren Kierkegaard. Princeton, NJ: Princeton University Press, 1962.

Prescript. Prescription.

Princip. De Principiis. Origen. *ANF* IV, pp. 239–384.

Proslog. Proslogium. Anselm. Translated by S. N. Deane. In *BW*.

Prov. Providence

PSG Philosophers Speak of God. Edited by Charles Hartshorne and William L. Reese. Chicago: University of Chicago Press, 1953.

PW Practical Works. Richard Baxter. 23 vols. London: James Duncan, 1830.

RD Reformed Dogmatics. Heinrich Heppe. Translated by G. T. Thomson. London: George Allen and Unwin, 1950.

Ref. Dogm. Reformed Dogmatics. Edited by J. W. Beardslee. Grand Rapids, MI: Baker, 1965.

Relig. Religion

RMWC Radical Monotheism and Western Culture. H. Richard Niebuhr. New York: Harper & Bros., 1960.

RPR Readings in the Philosophy of Religion. Edited by John Mourant. New York: Thomas Y. Crowell, 1954.

RSV Revised Standard Version

Sacr. Sacrament

SCD Sources of Christian Dogma (Enchridion Symbolorum. Edited by Henry Denzinger). Translated by Roy Deferrari. New York: Herder, 1954.

SCG On the Truth of the Catholic Faith, Summa contra Gentiles. Thomas Aquinas. 4 vols. (with sub-volumes). Referenced by book, chapter, and page number. New York: Doubleday, 1955–1957.

SDF The Sayings of the Desert Fathers. Translated by Benedicta Ward. London: A. R. Mowbray and Co., 1975.

SGL A Shewing of God's Love. Julian of Norwich. Edited by Anna Maria Rey-
        nolds. London: Sheed and Ward, 1974.

SL St. Louis edition of *Luthers Werke—Luthers Bibliothek*. 30 vols. in 15. St.
        Louis: American Lutheran Union, Missouri Synod, 1859–1876.

SLT Systema Locorum Theologicorum. 12 vols. in 4. Abraham Calovius. Witten-
        berg: Johann Roehner, 1655–1677.

SSM The Spirit of Spanish Mystics. Edited by Kathleen Pond. New York: P. J.
        Kennedy, 1958.

ST Summa Theologica. Thomas Aquinas. Edited by English Dominican Fathers.
        3 vols. New York: Benziger, 1947. References include part, sub-part,
        question number, volume and page number of Benziger edition. See
        STae for the Blackfriars edition.

STae Summa Theologiae: Latin Text and English Translation. Thomas Aquinas.
        Edited by T. Gilby and T. C. O'Brien. Blackfriars edition. 60 vols.
        New York: McGraw-Hill, 1964–1976.

STC Syntagma Theologiae Christianae. Amandus Polanus von Polansdorf. Han-
        nover: C. Marnium, 1610.

Strom. Stromata, or Miscellanies. Clement of Alexandria. *ANF* II.

SW John Calvin, Selections from His Writings. Edited by John Dillenberger.
        Missoula, MT: Scholars' Press, 1975.

SWML Selected Writings of Martin Luther. Edited by T. Tappert. 4 vols. Phila-
        delphia: Fortress, 1967.

Syst. Systematic

TAG The Transactional Awareness Game. Thomas C. Oden. San Francisco: Har-
        per & Row, 1977.

TAPT St. Thomas Aquinas Philosophical Texts. Edited by Thomas Gilby. London:
        Oxford University Press, 1951.

TATT St. Thomas Aquinas Theological Texts. Edited by Thomas Gilby. London:
        Oxford University Press, 1955.

TCL Translations of Christian Literature. Edited by S. Simpson and L. Clarke.
        London: S.P.C.K., 1917–.

TCNT The Twentieth Century New Testament.

TDNT Theological Dictionary of the New Testament. Edited by G. Kittel. Trans-
        lated by G. W. Bromiley. 9 vols. Grand Rapids, MI: Eerdmans,
        1964–1974.

TDOT Theological Dictionary of the Old Testament. Edited by G. J. Botterweck
        and H. Ringgren. 5 vols. Grand Rapids, MI: Eerdmans, 1975.

TDP Theologia Didactico-Polemica. 4 parts in 1 vol. Friedrich Quenstedt. Witten-
        berg: J. L. Quensted, 1691.

TFE Truth, Freedom and Evil. Anselm of Canterbury. Translated by Jasper
        Hopkins and Herbert Richardson. New York: Harper & Row, 1967.

TGS Theology of God—Sources. Edited by K. Kehoe. New York: Bruce, 1971.

Theol. Theology, theological

Tho. Aq. Thomas Aquinas

TI Theological Institutes. Richard Watson. 2 vols. Edited by John M'Clintock.
        New York: Carlton & Porter, 1850.

TIR Trinity, Incarnation, and Redemption. Anselm of Canterbury. Translated by

Jasper Hopkins and Herbert Richardson. New York: Harper & Row, 1969.

TLC *Theology of the Living Church*. L. Harold DeWolfe. New York: Harper & Bros., 1953.

TNT *Theology of the New Testament*. Rudolf Bultmann. New York: Scribner's, 1952.

TPW *Taylor's Practical Works*. Jeremy Taylor. 2 vols. London: L. G. Bohn, 1854.

Trent *Canons and Decrees of the Council of Trent (1545–1563)*. Edited by H. J. Schroeder. London: B. Herder, 1955. See also *COC*.

Trin. Trinity

U&R *Unity and Reform: Selected Writings of Nicholas de Cusa*. Edited by John P. Dolan. Notre Dame: University of Notre Dame Press, 1962.

UEMA *The Universities of Europe in the Middle Ages*. Hastings Rashdall. 3 vols. Oxford: Clarendon Press, 1895.

WA *Weimarer Ausgabe, Dr. Martin Luthers Werke, Kritische Gesamtausgabe*. Wiemar: Hermann Böhlau, 1883–.

WAS *What Augustine Says*. Edited by Norman L. Geisler. Grand Rapids, MI: Baker, 1982.

WCB *World Christian Books*. Edited by John Goodwin. London: Lutterworth, 1954–.

WJW *Works of the Rev. John Wesley*. Edited by Thomas Jackson. 14 vols. London: Wesleyan Conference Office, 1872.

WJWB The Works of John Wesley. Edited by Frank Baker. Bicentennial Edition. 8 vols. to date. Nashville, TN: Abingdon, 1975–. (formerly published by Oxford University Press).

WLS *What Luther Says*. Edited by E. Plass. 3 vols. St. Louis, MO: Concordia, 1959.

WML *Works of Martin Luther: An Anthology*. Philadelphia edition. 6 vols. Philadelphia: Muhlenberg Press, 1943.

Name Index

Subject Index

Absolute, 86
Abstraction, 86
Absurdity, 174
Abuse, 298
Academy, academic,
 364–66. *See also* University, Disciplines
Accident, 294
Act, actions, 36, 66,
 100–3, 108, 195–201,
 228, 281, 286
Adam and Eve, 395. *See also* Humanity
Adaptivity, 290
Administry, administration, 108, 112, 273, 369
Adonai, 2, 32–35; Adon,
 32
Adorning of creation,
 234–39
Adversity, 311. *See also* Suffering, Affliction
Advocate, 200. *See also* Holy Spirit
Aesthetics, 116, 130,
 168–71
Affliction, 299–304, 358
African Code, 336
African theology, ix, 9
Agape, 119–21
Agent, 286, 296
Agnosticism, 87
Almighty, 34, 251, 278.
 See also Majesty,
 Omnipotence
Alpha and Omega, 62,
 248
Analogy, 42, 185, 222,
 311, 380, 393
Analogy of faith, 190
Angels, 85, 191, 240, 241,
 258, 288
Anger of God, 109, 124,
 129
Anglican Catechism, 181,
 229

Animal, animate, 43, 48,
 98, 145, 224, 230, 233,
 236, 276, 288, 291, 292.
 See also Life
Annihilation, 281
Antecedence, 260
Antecedent will of God,
 93–95
Anthropology, 151. *See also* Humanity
Antioch, Council of, 212
Antiquity, 8, 9, 239
Anxiety, 307
Apatheia, 277–79
Apocalypse, apocalyptic,
 206, 248, 314, 391
Apocrypha, 336
Apollinarianism, 349
Apologetic theology, 41,
 324, 395
Apophatic theology, 28
A posteriori argument,
 156–61
Apostle, apostolicity, xi,
 363
Apostles' Creed, 11, 14,
 76, 251, 325, 332
Apostolic Constitutions.
 See Constitutions of the
 Holy Apostles
A priori argument, 35,
 156
Aptness to teach, 357,
 358
Arguments, theistic,
 133–80, 359, 360, 383
Arianism, 111, 187
Ariminum, (Arian)
 Council of, 349
Arts, 363. *See also* Dance,
 Music
Aseity, 55
Assurance, 24
Astrology, 279
Athanasian Creed, 11,
 325

Atheism, 41, 87, 154, 251
Atonement, 123
Attributes, of God,
 28–34, 83–130,
 195–201, 275
Augsburg Confession,
 28, 210, 369
Authority, 6, 188,
 335–404
Availability, 68
Awe, 355, 360

Balance, 285, 358–61. *See also* Proportionality
Balyzeh Papyrus, 12
Baptism, 11–14, 181,
 202–4, 216, 365
Barnabas, Epistle of, 249
Batak Confession, 29, 187
Beatitude, 128
Beauty, 38, 107, 129,
 168–71, 237, 287
Being, being of God,
 48–52, 133–80
Begetting, Begotten, 214,
 236. *See also* Generation
Beginning, 261
Belgic Confession, 188,
 270, 272
Belief, 396. *See also* Faith
Benediction, 203
Benevolence, divine,
 116–18, 253, 278
Bible, biblical theology,
 xiii, 5, 40, 302–4, 360,
 366. *See also* Scripture
 Index
"Big Bang" theory of creation, 231, 267, 268
Biology, 288. *See also* Life
Birth, 152, 249
Black theology, ix, 9
Blessedness, 56, 110,
 128–30, 258, 259, 267,
 304, 362
Body, 240, 266, 387

Scripture Index